The Penal System

The Penal System

An Introduction

Michael Cavadino, James Dignan and George Mair

Fifth edition

Los Angeles | London | New Delhi
Singapore | Washington DC

Los Angeles | London | New Delhi
Singapore | Washington DC

SAGE Publications Ltd
1 Oliver's Yard
55 City Road
London EC1Y 1SP

SAGE Publications Inc.
2455 Teller Road
Thousand Oaks, California 91320

SAGE Publications India Pvt Ltd
B 1/I 1 Mohan Cooperative Industrial Area
Mathura Road
New Delhi 110 044

SAGE Publications Asia-Pacific Pte Ltd
3 Church Street
#10-04 Samsung Hub
Singapore 049483

Editor: Natalie Aguilera
Editorial assistant: James Piper
Production editor: Sarah Cooke
Copyeditor: Gemma Marren
Proofreader: Audrey Scriven
Indexer: James Dignan
Marketing manager: Sally Ransom
Cover design: Francis Kenney
Typeset by: C&M Digitals (P) Ltd, Chennai, India
Printed in Great Britain by MPG Printgroup, UK

Library of Congress Control Number: 2012953220

British Library Cataloguing in Publication data

A catalogue record for this book is available from the British Library

ISBN 978-1-44620-724-6
ISBN 978-1-44620-725-3 (pbk)

Brief Contents

Contents

Preface to the Fifth Edition

by Michael Cavadino

Now under (partial) new management ... When Jim Dignan decided to leave academia (good for him, bad for academia) I was in despair as to whether there could ever be a fifth edition of this 'essential text ... indispensable resource' (as the reviewers say). Where, I asked my old friend and esteemed colleague George Mair, could I ever find someone else who was as knowledgeable and dependable as Jim and knew how to write properly? To my surprise and delight, George agreed to do it himself (not that I had been hinting). There could not have been anyone more suitable to take up Jim's mantle (or gauntlet?)

This edition brings the story of the English penal system as up to date as possible with accounts of how a new Coalition government promised briefly to try to turn the tide of more or less constantly intensifying punishment that we have witnessed since the 1990s, raising and ultimately dashing the hopes of penal reformers in a manner to which they have become all too used over the years. Sadly, it looks as though Kenneth Clarke will go down as the King Canute of Coalition penal policy. We incorporate this gloomy tale into this edition, along with the relevant provisions of the Legal Aid, Sentencing and Punishment of Offenders Act 2012. (The rumoured detail that the phrase 'punishment of offenders' was inserted into the Act's title specifically to please David Cameron says a lot.) We may be bidding goodbye to IPPs and ASBOs (at least under that name), and some other New Labour totems of law and order, but the overall result seems certain to be no more humane or rational than before. Meet the new boss ... We still hope one day to write an edition of the book which talks about the **penal crisis** in the past tense, but that day seems no closer than it did.

This edition comes along with a new and improved *companion website*, which not only brings the reader up to date with all the latest developments since the book went to press, but also contains an unrivalled (we think) collection of summaries of recent legislation and the most important government policy documents. Plus a regularly updated (it needs to be, doesn't it?) list of useful websites and their web addresses, and teaching materials specially reserved for lecturers who have the wisdom and taste to recommend this book on their courses.

The book also contains an incredibly useful **glossary of key terms** (p. 327 onwards). Terms that are explained in the glossary are in **bold type** when they first appear in the main text of the book.

Our thanks are due to all those colleagues in the criminological community, who are either too numerous or too embarrassingly few to mention individually (you guess which). We again have to thank the team at Sage, who have been as helpful as ever. Thanks and the utmost appreciation also, as always, to Lucille Cavadino and Carmel Mair for their understanding, tolerance, patience and loving support during the writing of this book.

Companion Website

The Penal System: An Introduction (Fifth Edition) is accompanied by a full companion website, which you can access at www.sagepub.co.uk/cavadino5. Containing resources for both lecturers and students, the website intends to complement and build on the material here presented and includes the following material:

For students:
- Links to relevant websites
- Further reading lists, with links to relevant full-text SAGE journal articles
- Summaries of key legislation, White Papers, consultation documents and other official reports
- Updates on recent developments

For lecturers:
- A seminar programme with questions for discussion
- PowerPoint presentations

Introduction

This book is about the penal system – the system that delivers official **punishment** to those who have broken the law.[1] (See section I.3 below to find out exactly what we mean by 'punishment'.) More precisely, we are centrally concerned with the 'English' penal system, by which we mean the system in **England** and Wales. (Scotland and Northern Ireland have separate systems.) However, much of what we say (especially about penal philosophy and penal sociology in Chapters 2 and 3) is of relevance to more than one country; and at times we will be referring to other penal systems to help illuminate the English (and Welsh) experience. While we have tried to be factually correct, to outline differing viewpoints and to be as comprehensive as is possible in a book of this size, we have not felt any need to be shy about expressing our own opinions. In a nutshell, these are that the English penal system is unjustly and irrationally harsh, and that our penal practices and attitudes towards punishment require radical revision.

The Criminal Justice System

I.1 The penal system, which exists to punish those found guilty of crimes, is part of a larger entity known as the **criminal justice system**, a term covering all those institutions which respond officially to the commission of offences, notably the police, prosecution authorities and courts. It is often misleading or unsatisfactory to examine the penal system in isolation from the larger criminal justice system. Consequently at times in this book – for example in Chapter 9 – we deal with the criminal justice system as a whole.

There now follows a very brief and basic guide to the criminal justice system as a whole, to assist readers who may not be familiar with the system or its terminology. Figure I.1 is a simplified diagram of the criminal justice system up to the point where an offender is sentenced by a court, which is the moment when the offender enters the **penal system**.

---

[1]There is one very important exception to this. The prison system – part of the penal system – houses many remand prisoners, who currently account for 13 per cent of the total prison population. Most of these have not (at least yet) been found guilty of an offence, but are being kept in custody while awaiting trial. A minority of remand prisoners have already been convicted and are awaiting sentence (see further Chapter 4, section 4.1). Prison population figures also now include several hundred detainees in Immigration Removal Centres.

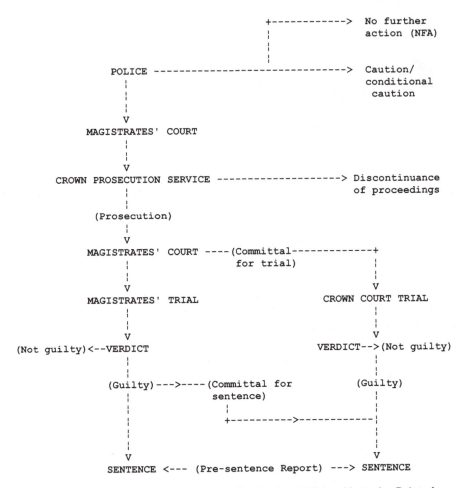

```
                                           +----------->  No further
                                           !              action (NFA)
                                           !
                                           !
               POLICE  ----------------------------->  Caution/
                 !                                         conditional
                 !                                         caution
                 !
                 V
          MAGISTRATES' COURT
                 !
                 !
                 V
     CROWN PROSECUTION SERVICE  ------------------->  Discontinuance
                 !                                        of proceedings
                 !
             (Prosecution)
                 !
                 V
          MAGISTRATES' COURT ---- (Committal------------+
                 !                   for trial)         !
                 !                                      !
                 V                                      V
          MAGISTRATES' TRIAL                     CROWN COURT TRIAL
                 !                                      !
                 !                                      !
                 V                                      V
    (Not guilty)<--VERDICT                     VERDICT-->(Not guilty)
                 !                                      !
                 !                                      !
            (Guilty) --->---- (Committal for       (Guilty)
                 !              sentence)               !
                 !                  !                   !
                 !         +---------->-----------!     !
                 !                                !     !
                 !                                !     !
                 V                                      V
         SENTENCE <--- (Pre-sentence Report) ---> SENTENCE
```

FIGURE I.1   The Criminal Justice System in England and Wales, Up to the Point of
Sentence

In many cases when a crime is committed – indeed, in most cases – the agencies of criminal justice never respond at all. For the criminal justice process normally starts to operate only when a crime is reported to the police, and fewer than half of all crimes are reported. In 2010/11 only 38 per cent of all the crimes uncovered by the official British Crime Survey were reported to the police (Chaplin et al., 2011: 37), and the police fail to officially record about a quarter of those crimes that are reported (Nicholas et al., 2005: 36). If an alleged offence is reported, or otherwise comes to the attention of the police, the police may then investigate it. The police have a wide range of powers (notably those contained in the Police and Criminal Evidence Act 1984) to carry out searches and to arrest and question suspects in pursuit of their investigations. If there appears to be sufficient evidence to put a suspect on trial, the police may **charge** an arrested suspect with the offence. This is the first stage in the **prosecution** process, and it is now the **Crown Prosecution Service (CPS)** – a state agency independent of the police – who instruct the police as to whether suspects should be charged in most cases of any seriousness. The police then normally take the suspect before the local magistrates' court, where the prosecution is conducted by the CPS.

An alternative procedure has historically been known as the *summons*. Under this procedure the police apply to a magistrate for a summons, which is an order to attend court, but the suspect remains at liberty for the time being. (Under provisions of the Criminal Justice Act 2003 which are being phased in, the existing 'charge' and 'summons' are replaced by a single procedure known as a 'written charge' which can be made by either the police or the CPS. This procedure still allows a suspect who has been released from arrest or never arrested to be prosecuted, but removes the necessity to apply to a magistrate.) Another possible alternative is to dispense with prosecution entirely and for the police instead to administer an official warning known as a **caution**. A caution should not be given unless the offender admits guilt. No formal punishment ensues, but the caution will form part of the offender's official criminal record. A variant is a **conditional caution**, where the caution is accompanied by specific conditions which the offender must comply with. (In recent years **young offenders** under 18 have received not cautions but **reprimands** and **warnings**, also known as **final warnings**. The Legal Aid, Sentencing and Punishment of Offenders Act 2012 replaces these with **youth cautions** and **youth conditional cautions** (YCCs): see further Chapter 8.) In 2009, 33 per cent of known indictable offenders were 'diverted from court' by being cautioned, reprimanded or warned rather than prosecuted. The police can also issue a 'cannabis warning' (which does not amount to an official caution) for first offenders found in possession of this drug. Yet another possibility is a **fixed penalty notice** (or spot fine), which can be imposed by police officers and certain other specified officials for a wide variety of minor offences.

When the alleged offender reaches the magistrates' court (and becomes a defendant), the court may have to decide whether to grant the defendant **bail** (conditional release prior to the actual trial) or whether the defendant should be remanded in **custody** for the time being (see further Chapter 4, section 4.1). Custodial **remands** are usually to prison or to a **remand centre** (a type of prison reserved for remandees).

Criminal offences fall into three categories: **indictable** only, **summary** only and **triable either way**.[2] This categorization determines at which court – **magistrates' court** or **Crown Court** – the trial will be held. The most serious offences are indictable only (for example murder, rape and robbery): these must be tried at the Crown Court before a judge, with a jury of 12 randomly selected lay people to decide on the verdict if the defendant pleads not guilty. In these cases the magistrates' court sends the case to the Crown Court for trial 'on indictment'. Offences which are summary only (for example, common assault, minor criminal damage and most motoring offences) must be tried 'summarily' at the magistrates' court before at least two and normally three lay justices of the peace or a

---

[2]Many statistics in this book refer to indictable offences, a category which includes both indictable only and triable either way offences.

single district judge (a professional judge, formerly known as a 'stipendiary magistrate'). Offences that are triable either way include theft, arson and most burglaries. If a defendant charged with one of these offences pleads not guilty, the magistrates then decide whether to commit the defendant to be tried in a Crown Court trial or whether the case may be tried in the magistrates' court; if the latter, the decision then lies with the defendant, who has the right to insist on a Crown Court trial for a triable **either way offence**. However in practice the great majority of triable either way offences are tried in the magistrates' court, either because the magistrates offer a summary trial which is accepted by the defendant or because the defendant pleads guilty. Magistrates can nevertheless still decide to commit a triable either way defendant to the Crown Court for sentence (see below).

If the defendant pleads guilty or is found guilty (in other words, is *convicted* of the offence), the magistrates or judge then pass **sentence**. The sentence is the punishment (or other order of the court) which is imposed upon the defendant as a consequence of committing the crime. A few offences have mandatory or semi-mandatory penalties attached, as explained in Chapter 4. Most offences, however, have a statutory maximum **penalty** – for example, seven years' imprisonment for theft – but no statutory minimum. The magistrates' court also has statutory limits on its sentencing powers: it cannot sentence an offender to more than six months in prison for a single offence or to more than 12 months in total. (These maxima will be increased to 12 months and 65 weeks if and when sections 154–155 of the Criminal Justice Act 2003 are brought into force.) However, a magistrates' court can commit an offender it has convicted to the Crown Court to be sentenced there if it feels that its sentencing powers are inadequate. As long as the statutory maxima are not exceeded, the court usually has a wide range of sentences to choose from. These include the *custodial* sentences of imprisonment (for adults), detention in a **young offender institution** (YOI) (for offenders aged 18 to 20) and **detention and training orders** (DTOs) (for young offenders under 18). **Non-custodial penalties** (to which we devote Chapter 5) include suspended prison sentences, **fines**, **community orders** (including what used to be known as probation and community service orders), and absolute and conditional discharges. The court may be assisted in its choice of sentence by a pre-sentence report, usually prepared by a probation officer (or, in the case of juvenile offenders, by a member of the **youth offending team** (YOT), see Chapter 8). Pre-sentence reports provide the sentencer with information about the offender's behaviour and social and family background, and normally include a proposal for what the sentence should be.

Convicted defendants may appeal to a higher court either against their conviction or against the sentence that has been passed, or both. Defendants convicted and sentenced in the magistrates' court normally appeal to the Crown Court; appeals from the Crown Court go to the Court of Appeal (Criminal Division). The **Attorney General** (a government law officer who is both a member of the government and its chief legal adviser) has the power to refer certain Crown Court cases to the Court of Appeal on the grounds that the acquittal was legally wrong or the sentence is too lenient.

A sentence of imprisonment (see Chapter 6) does not usually mean that the offender will serve the full term of the sentence pronounced by the court. For example, offenders sentenced to two years' imprisonment will normally be released after one year subject to a **licence** requiring them to be supervised in the community for the rest of the sentence, and at the discretion of the prison authorities they may be released earlier still under a **home detention curfew** (HDC) enforced by **electronic monitoring** (or **tagging**). (The system of **early release** from prison sentences is explained and discussed in Chapter 7.)

Non-custodial sentences (see Chapter 5) usually require the offender to carry out some action, such as pay a fine or compensation or perform **community service**. Alternatively, the offender may be required to refrain from acting in certain ways, in particular to avoid reoffending within a given time limit (for example, if the sentence is a conditional discharge or a **suspended sentence**). Offenders who **breach** the terms of their sentences either by disobeying their requirements or by reoffending can be brought back to court as a result, and the court then has a range of sanctions available. These sanctions often include the power to pass custodial sentences, which may be additional (or consecutive) to any custodial sentence imposed for a fresh offence.

Punishment in both prison and in the community is administered by the **National Offender Management Service** (NOMS). NOMS, which combines the Prison and Probation Services, was created in 2004 in response to a recommendation in the Carter Report (2003) (see further Chapter 5). The Chief Executive of NOMS is answerable to the **Secretary of State for Justice**. The latter is the senior government minister – also known as the **Justice Secretary**, and also bearing the title **Lord Chancellor** – who is in charge of the **Ministry of Justice**. The Ministry of Justice is the government department which since May 2007 has responsibility for the courts, prisons, probation and **youth justice**. (Previously the **Home Office** and **Home Secretary** were responsible for prisons, probation, sentencing and criminal justice policy; they retain responsibility for the police service.)

The whole of the criminal justice system is subject to the provisions of the **Human Rights Act 1998**, which incorporated the European Convention on Human Rights into English law. Under the 1998 Act, all public bodies – including criminal justice agencies such as the police and NOMS – are under a legal duty to act in accordance with the Convention. Furthermore, English courts are bound *where possible* to interpret English Acts of Parliament so that they are compatible with the Convention. If the court decides that English law is unequivocally incompatible with the Convention it must make a formal declaration to this effect; the government can then use special procedures to change the law to remove the incompatibility. As well as using the English courts, citizens can also take their cases to the European Court of Human Rights at Strasbourg when they have exhausted all domestic avenues of redress. Human rights law has had some important effects on English penal law, requiring for example significant alterations in arrangements for early release (see Chapter 7).

The Penal Crisis and Strategies for Criminal Justice _____

1.2 This book is largely concerned with the crisis in the English penal system and the policies that governments have developed in response to this crisis. Chapter 1 introduces the penal crisis, and we then go on to discuss facets of this crisis and the responses to it throughout this book. Chapters 2 and 3 are heavily theoretical, but unashamedly so, for they are also intimately connected to the crisis theme. The exploration of penal sociology in Chapter 3 underpins our analysis of how the crisis should be explained, while our investigation of the philosophy of punishment in Chapter 2 should contribute to an understanding of why the penal system suffers from its crucial **crisis of legitimacy**. Chapters 4 to 9 deal with various aspects of the system and its crisis. Chapter 4 identifies the sentencing decisions of courts as the crux of the crisis. Chapter 6 investigates the troubled prison system, while Chapters 5 and 7 deal with two developments which have so far had less than total success in relieving the pressure on the system: the proliferation of non-custodial penalties and the mechanisms for early release of prisoners. Chapter 8 examines the parallel system of youth justice, equally prone to its own parallel crises, and for similar reasons. Chapter 9 investigates the burning issue of bias within the criminal justice system. Finally, in Chapter 10 we discuss whether the crisis is likely to be solved and put forward our own agenda for change.

In analysing and discussing criminal justice policies we find it helpful to use a general, three-fold categorization of criminal justice policies which we call 'Strategies A, B and C' (based on Rutherford, 1993; see Cavadino et al., 1999). **Strategy A** is a highly **punitive** approach embodying what we call **law and order ideology** (see Chapter 1) and the **new punitiveness** (see Chapter 3, section 3.6): the attitude that offenders should be dealt with as severely as possible. A governmental strategy based on this attitude would involve making criminal justice harsher and more punitive at every stage and in every respect. Strategy A embodies an **exclusionary approach** to offenders, tending to reject them as members of the community (see Cavadino et al., 1999: 48–50). **Strategy B** (associated with the **new penology** which we discuss in Chapter 3, section 3.6) is a **managerialist approach** that seeks to apply administrative and bureaucratic mechanisms to criminal justice in an attempt to make the system as smooth-running and cost-effective as possible. **Strategy C** seeks to protect and uphold the **human rights** of offenders, **victims** and potential victims of crime. It seeks to minimize punishment and to ensure fairness and humane treatment within the criminal justice system, and is an **inclusive approach**, seeking to maintain offenders within the community and reintegrate them as law-abiding citizens. Proponents of Strategy C are not all of one mind: some favour measures to rehabilitate and reform offenders (see section 2.2 of Chapter 2), while others advocate **restorative justice** measures which seek to ensure that offenders perform **reparation** to their victims and to the community (see Chapters 2 (section 2.4), 5 and 8). Others again, while still being motivated by humanitarianism and a wish to lessen the harshness of punishment in general, propound the view that offenders should be punished in proportion to the seriousness of their offences, according to their **just deserts** (see Chapter 2, sections 2.3 and 2.5).

Chapter 10 provides a history of the strategies adopted by national governments up to the present day, but a brief summary is appropriate here to set the scene. In the early 1980s, the Conservative government of Margaret Thatcher injected a heavy dose of Strategy A into penal policy, deliberately making punishment harsher in many respects. However, from around 1987 onwards – a period we refer to as the **Hurd era**, after Home Secretary Douglas Hurd (1985–89) – the Thatcher government's penal policy became less dogmatic and more pragmatic. The centrepiece of this new strategy was the Criminal Justice Act 1991, which among other objectives sought to reduce the prison population and make it more easily manageable (a Strategy B aim) while also for the most part making punishments fairer and more proportionate (Strategy C). The idea was that more offenders than hitherto should undergo **punishment in the community** rather than being sent to prison; additionally, most offenders were to receive punishments which were in proportion to the seriousness of the crime (just deserts). However, within months of the Act's implementation in 1992 the Conservative government abandoned this strategy. From 1993 to 1997, in a development we call the **law and order counter-reformation**, John Major's Conservative government – especially in the person of Michael Howard, Home Secretary from 1993 to 1997 – pursued ever harsher Strategy A policies, marked by Mr Howard's famous declaration to the Conservative Party Conference in October 1993 that 'prison works'. Thus did we enter a phase which has been termed 'the New Punitiveness' (Pratt et al., 2005; see also Chapter 3, section 3.6). The **New Labour** government of Tony Blair (1997–2007; succeeded by Gordon Brown from 2007–10) sought to implement its famous campaign promise to be '**tough on crime and tough on the causes of crime**' by pursuing a mixture of policies with elements of all three of Strategies A, B and C. Although in ideological terms New Labour was less unremittingly Strategy A than its predecessor, nevertheless the prison population rose to unprecedented heights during this period. This rise has continued under the Conservative–Liberal Democrat coalition government which came to power in 2010, despite vain attempts by the Justice Secretary Kenneth Clarke to move penal policy in a less punitive direction.

Notes on Terminology: 'Punishment' 'and 'System'

'Punishment'

1.3 Terminological quibbles start here. Some people prefer not to use the word punishment for measures that are intended to help the offender, such as **probation** (or to help the victim, such as **compensation**) rather than to hurt or harm the offender. However, in this book we use the word to refer to any measure which is imposed on an offender in response to an offence.

Just to complicate matters however – and for want of a better word – we are more or less forced to use the word 'punitive' as an adjective referring to measures whose primary purpose is to take away the liberty of offenders or otherwise make them suffer, for purposes such as retribution or deterrence (terms explained in Chapter 2). Thus, in our terminology there are 'punitive punishments' such as imprisonment and 'non-punitive punishments' which have aims such as the reformation of the offender or providing reparation to victims.

We also occasionally use the term **penality**, which encompasses ideas about punishment as well as concrete penal practices.

'System'

Perhaps the title of this book is misleading. Arguably, one of the salient features of the English penal and criminal justice systems – at least until fairly recently – has been their highly *unsystematic* nature. For many years a number of disparate, relatively autonomous agencies have worked in relative isolation from each other, exercising wide and unaccountable discretionary powers, and subject to no overall co-ordination or strategic control (or 'joined-up thinking', to use a phrase recently popular with politicians). Some writers have even described criminal justice as a 'non-system'. Whether that description is still an accurate one is an issue to be considered in the light of developments in recent years (see in particular Chapters 4, 5 and 8). In any event, we do have penal and criminal justice systems in the sense that they are composed of different agencies which are *interdependent*: their activities intimately affect each other and they need to be studied within this context of interdependency. We see this kind of systems analysis as an important tool in understanding the penal system and attempting to bring about positive modifications.

1

Crisis? What Crisis?

Is there a Crisis?

1.1 The penal system is in a state of crisis.

This might not seem a controversial claim. Nor would most people in this country imagine that this penal crisis is either new or sudden. For many years, media reports have acquainted everyone with the notion that rocketing prison populations, overcrowding, unrest among staff and inmates, escapes and riots and disorder in prisons add up to a severe and deepening penal crisis. The term 'crisis' has been common currency in both media and academic accounts of the penal system for over 30 years now; the word recurs in newspaper headlines and in the titles of academic books and articles (for example, Bottoms and Preston, 1980). Evidence for the existence of a crisis seems to be constantly in the news. Recent years have seen – to mention just a few out of many possible illustrations – the prison system twice finding itself without a single spare cell space; a Home Secretary (Charles Clarke in 2006) being sacked because foreign prisoners were being released rather than deported; prison officers taking industrial action; other prison officers being jailed for planned and sustained attacks on inmates; the horrifying racist murder of Zahid Mubarek by a fellow inmate in Feltham Young Offender Institution in 2000; recurring riots and disorder in prisons; and the commission of disturbing crimes by offenders released early from prison or under probation supervision (Cavadino and Dignan, 2007: 304). All this comes against the background of a prison population scaling ever higher, all-time record levels and a continuing deep malaise running through the penal system as a whole.

Yet is it really a crisis? Perhaps few would dispute that the penal system has serious problems – but is it really in a state of *crisis*? Then again, how long can a crisis last while remaining a crisis rather than business as usual? Surely there is something paradoxical in claims that the crisis has lasted for decades, or even (as was once said) that the system has been 'in a perpetual state of crisis since the Gladstone Committee report of 1895' (Fitzgerald and Sim, 1982: 3).

If to be in crisis means that the whole system is on the brink of total collapse or explosion, then we probably do not have a crisis. (Although it should not be forgotten that when systems do collapse or explode – like the communist system in Eastern Europe in the late twentieth century, or the system of order within Strangeways Prison immediately before the historic riot of April 1990 – they can do so very suddenly.) But it can be validly claimed that there is a crisis in at least two senses, identified by Terence Morris (1989: 125). First, we have 'a state of affairs that is so acute as to constitute a danger' – and, we would add, a moral challenge of a scale which makes it one of the most pressing social issues of the day. Second, we may be at a critical juncture, much as a seriously ill person may reach a 'turning point at which the patient either begins to improve or sinks into a fatal decline'. In other words, either the present situation could be used as an opportunity to reform the system into something more rational and humane, or else it will deteriorate into something much worse even than the present. In this book we will be using the 'C word' in these senses to refer to the present penal situation in England and Wales, albeit with slight embarrassment and the worry that it has been used so often and for so long that there is a danger that it may be losing its dramatic impact.

Whether or not we choose to use the word 'crisis', what are the causes of the state the penal system is in, and how do its different problems relate to each other?

The Orthodox Account of the Crisis

1.2 The **orthodox account** of the penal crisis is probably still the kind of common-sensical analysis underlying most mass media reports of problems in the penal system. At least until Lord Justice Woolf's 1991 report into the Strangeways riot (Woolf and Tumim, 1991) versions of it were also regularly found in official reports purporting to explain phenomena such as prison disturbances. It is well summarized by the following extract from an old newspaper article entitled 'Why the Prisons Could Explode' (Humphry and May, 1977):

> Explosive problems remain in many of Britain's prisons – a higher number of lifers ... who have nothing left to lose; overcrowding which forces men to sleep three to a cell and understaffing which weakens security. Prisons, too, are forced to handle men with profound psychiatric problems in conditions which are totally unsuitable.

This passage gives us almost all the components of the orthodox account of the penal crisis. The crisis is seen as being located very specifically within the *prison* system – it is not seen as a crisis of the whole *penal* system, or of the criminal justice system, let alone as a crisis of society as a whole. The immediate cause of the crisis is seen as the combination of different types of difficult prisoners – what has been called a '**toxic mix**' of prisoners – in physically poor and insecure conditions which could give rise to an 'explosion'.

The orthodox account points to the following factors as implicated in the crisis:

1 the high prison population (or **numbers crisis**);

2 overcrowding;

3 bad conditions within prison (for both inmates and prison officers);

4 understaffing;

5 unrest among the staff;

6 poor security;

7 the 'toxic mix' of long-term and life sentence prisoners and mentally disturbed inmates;

8 riots and other breakdowns of control over prisoners.

These factors are seen as linked, with number 8 – riots and disorder – being the end product that epitomizes the state of crisis. Figure 1.1 shows how the different factors interact according to the orthodox account. The high prison population is held responsible for overcrowding and understaffing in prisons, both of which exacerbate the bad physical conditions within prison. The combination of poor

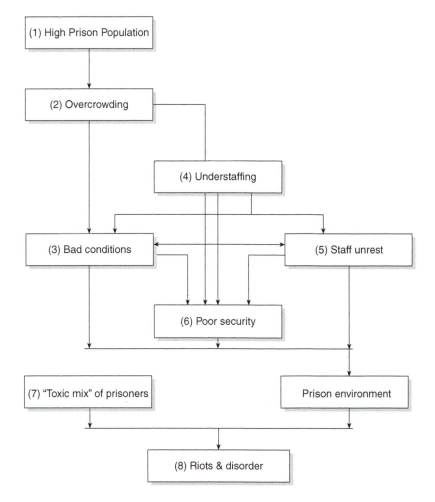

FIGURE 1.1 The Orthodox Account of the Penal Crisis

conditions and inadequate staffing have an adverse effect on staff morale, causing unrest which (through industrial action, for example) serves to worsen conditions still further. The four factors of bad conditions, overcrowding, understaffing and staff unrest are blamed for poor security, which is another factor contributing to the unstable prison environment. Finally, the combination of the 'toxic mix' of prisoners with these deteriorating conditions within which they are contained is thought to trigger off the periodic riots and disturbances to which the prison system is prone.

We do not believe that the orthodox account provides a satisfactory explanation of the crisis, for reasons we shall be giving shortly. But most of the factors identified by this account are real and important, as we shall now detail.

The High Prison Population (the Numbers Crisis)

It is widely agreed – although perhaps not by all politicians – that the number of prisoners in England and Wales is alarmingly high. It is also rapidly rising. Table 1.1 shows how (despite occasional dips), the prison population has more than doubled to 86,000 from under 40,000 since 1975 (a time when prison numbers were already causing serious concern) and have almost doubled since 1993. The prison population reached its highest ever peak so far of over 88,000 in December 2011. But only so far: official Home Office projections estimate that by 2017 the prison population could be up to 94,800 if current trends continue (Ministry of Justice, 2011d).

There are several factors involved in this increase in prison numbers in recent years. In Chapter 4 we discuss the relationship between some of these factors, and conclude that the most crucial is the pattern of decisions by the courts. The most important of these is the sentencing decision – whether convicted offenders should be sent to custody and, if so, for how long – which we call 'the crux of the crisis'. These court decisions can in their turn be greatly influenced by government policies, actions and rhetoric. As we stated briefly in the Introduction (section I.2) and detail further in Chapter 10 (section 10.2), for a long time both Conservative and Labour governments generally attempted to keep the size of the prison population under control by a mixture of legislation, executive action and exhortations to courts. However, from 1993 onwards John Major's Conservative administration reversed this stand and pursued policies whose explicit aim was to increase the numbers of people in prison, with Home Secretary Michael Howard famously declaring in 1993 that 'prison works' to control crime. The New Labour administrations of Tony Blair and Gordon Brown (1997–2010) may have dropped the slogan 'prison works', but showed little interest in trying to reduce custodial sentences; indeed, Labour Home Secretaries repeatedly called for tougher sentences for a wide range of offenders. Not surprisingly, therefore, the prison population rose to even greater heights under New Labour and the same trend has continued under the Conservative–Liberal Democrat coalition government despite attempts by the Justice Secretary Kenneth

Clarke to turn the tide. The rate of increase in prison numbers did slow in 2010–2011, but the situation altered rapidly and drastically in August 2011 as the courts began dealing with defendants charged with offences connected with the urban riots of that month. With the explicit encouragement of Prime Minister David Cameron, sentencers imposed harsh and widely criticized sentences on rioters and looters, and magistrates remanded large numbers in custody to await trial at the Crown Court, thereby pushing prison numbers to their new peak of 88,179 in December 2011.

TABLE 1.1   Prison Population of England and Wales 1975–2012, selected years

1975	39,820
1980	42,264
1985	46,233
1988	48,872
1993	44,552
1998	65,298
1999	64,771
2000	64,602
2001	66,301
2002	70,778
2003	73,038
2004	74,657
2005	75,979
2006	78,127
2007	80,216
2008	82,572
2009	83,559
2010	84,725
2011 (June)	85,266
2011 (December)	88,179
2012 (June)	86,352

Source: Ministry of Justice, *Offender Management Caseload Statistics 2010* Tables and *Prison Population Monthly Bulletins* (1975–2010 figures are average populations[1]).

---

[1]Average prison populations are figures for all prisons averaged across the calendar year. (Figures include inmates in remand centres and institutions for young offenders plus any prisoners held in police cells, and now also include several hundred detainees in Immigration Removal Centres.) The prison population fluctuates seasonally, and at times in the year the average population is significantly exceeded.

TABLE 1.2   Prison Populations in Western Europe

Country	Total prison population	No. of prisoners per 100,000 pop.
ENGLAND AND WALES	86,456	154
Scotland	8,121	154
Spain	70,840	153
Portugal	13,427	126
Luxembourg	645	124
Cyprus	900	112
Greece	12,586	111
Italy	66,310	109
Austria	8,694	104
France	67,073	101
Belgium	10,968	100
Northern Ireland	1,802	99
Ireland	4,401	98
The Netherlands	14,488	87
Germany	68,099	83
Switzerland	6,065	76
Sweden	6,669	70
Denmark	4,091	74
Norway	3,602	73
Finland	3,189	59
Iceland	149	47

Source: International Centre for Prison Studies, *World Prison Brief* website (accessed August 2012).

As Table 1.2 shows, England and Wales (along with Scotland) currently have the largest prison population in Western Europe in proportion to the total number of people in the country as a whole.[2] It is true that proportionate prison populations are even higher in some countries outside Western Europe: indeed, the United States has around five times as many prisoners relative to its population as do England and Wales.[3] Nevertheless, within the Western European frame of reference Great Britain does seem to be strikingly punitive, having maintained a high position in the prison population league table for many years now. This relatively high prison population does not seem to be because the UK has more crime, or

---

[2] In our opinion this measure of a country's 'imprisonment rate' is a useful, if crude, yardstick of the relative punitiveness of different countries. See further Cavadino and Dignan (2006: 4–5).

[3] The United States' two million prisoners give it the highest proportionate prison population in the world, with 730 people in prison out of every 100,000 people in the general population. The US, which contains 5 per cent of the planet's population, now accounts for a quarter of the world's prison inmates.

more serious crime, than comparable countries.[4] Rather, it is because more offenders are sent to custody, and for longer periods, in the UK than elsewhere in Western Europe (see, for example, Barclay and Tavares, 2000; NACRO, 1998; Pease, 1992).

There should be little doubt, then, that the present and predicted future size of the prison population is a major problem. If drastic steps are not taken to reduce prison numbers – and there is currently no sign of any such steps being taken – they seem likely to grow even more alarmingly in the coming years.

Overcrowding

At the end of June 2012 English and Welsh prisons officially had adequate space for 79,450 inmates, but actually contained 86,532, making the system as a whole overcrowded by a factor of 9 per cent. By adequate space we mean the official figure for the 'in use certified normal accommodation' (or 'uncrowded capacity'[5]) of all prisons in total. The Prison Service also identifies a higher figure, the 'operational capacity', defined as 'the total number of prisoners that an establishment can hold taking into account control, security and the proper operation of the planned regime'. Adding the operational capacity of all prisons together and deducting a safety margin of 2,000 yields a total 'useable operational capacity' – informally known as the **bust limit** – for the system as a whole. This bust limit was actually exceeded in April 2004 and again in February 2008. In recent years the prison population has spent many months hovering perilously close to the bust limit, often with just a few hundred places to spare.

Even these overall figures do not do justice to the overcrowding problem because prisoners are not spread evenly throughout the system. **High security prisons** (see Chapter 6, section 6.3) are frequently not filled to capacity, while overcrowding is concentrated in **local prisons** (which predominantly house remand prisoners and those on short-term sentences). At the end of April 2012, 83 out of 134 prisons were overcrowded, with many of them containing more than half as many prisoners again as they should (Shrewsbury Prison had nearly twice as many, see Prison Reform Trust, 2012: 17). As a result of overcrowding, currently over 20,000 prisoners (nearly a quarter of all inmates) are sleeping two to a cell designed for a single inmate, or otherwise housed in overcrowded cells (Prison Reform Trust, 2012: 17). Indeed, between 2006 and 2008 prisoners overflowed

---

[4]It is sometimes claimed that these figures can be explained by taking into account different countries' crime rates (for example, Barclay et al., 1995: 54; see also Pease, 1994). It is true that some recent international surveys of victims of crime (e.g. van Kesteren et al., 2001) do show the English rate for certain crimes to be higher than those of several other countries. However, the relatively high English prison population dates back to times when similar surveys (for example, Mayhew, 1994) found the level of crime in Britain to be similar to the European average for most offences.

[5]For these various measures of prison capacity, see Chapter 6, section 6.5.

into cells in police stations and courthouses. Independent monitors of prison conditions have expressed concerns that such overcrowding is likely to threaten safety and have multiple other serious adverse effects on prison conditions and regimes (Prison Reform Trust, 2006a: 7–8; see also Chapter 6, section 6.5).

Bad Conditions

Overcrowding, of course, contributes to bad physical conditions in prisons. But there are other causes of bad conditions as well as overcrowding: many prisons are old and decaying, and newer prisons have often turned out to be so badly designed that they are not a noticeable improvement.

The particular issue of inadequate sanitary facilities in prison is something of a cliché. The fact that many prisoners routinely had to spend long periods in their cells without access to a toilet, having to use chamber pots and queue up to 'slop out', was for a long time a potent symbol of the squalor of British prisons. Since 1996 all prisoners are supposed to have 24-hour access to toilet facilities, although it seems clear that this is still not always the case (see Chapter 6 section 6.5 for details).

In any event, the problem of prison conditions was never limited to **slopping out**. As we shall see in Chapter 6, other elements of prison life are equally important, such as the amount of time prisoners are kept cooped up in cells and the lack of opportunities for activities of all kinds. In these respects, there has been a general and continuing decline in prison conditions over a long period of time (King and McDermott, 1989). According to a report by the **Chief Inspector of Prisons** published in 2008 (HM Inspectorate of Prisons, 2008: 11), half of prisoners were then spending less than six hours per day out of their cells, and 20 per cent less than two hours. Things then got worse. From April 2008 all Friday afternoon activities in public sector prisons were cancelled to help meet targets for efficiency savings, meaning that most prisoners now have very little time out of their cells between Friday lunchtime and Monday morning.

The poor conditions in prisons affect staff as well as inmates, contributing to low staff morale and unrest.

Understaffing

It is a constant complaint on the part of prison staff that they are overstretched, especially with the ever-rising prison population. Currently, cuts in funding, which can hardly fail to affect staffing levels, are affecting prisons as well as other public services. The Coalition government's deficit-reduction strategy led to the Ministry of Justice being asked in 2010 to find cuts of 23 per cent to its overall annual budget over a three-year period. Cuts to the prisons budget were substantially less than this (2.72 per cent in 2010–11), but of course this reduced amount has to go around a fast-rising number of prisoners. Budgetary pressures mean that there is constant pressure on prisons to keep staff numbers to a minimum. Moreover, state-run prisons increasingly have to justify their spending levels in comparison with privately-run prisons, which limit their own running costs by economizing on staff (see Chapter 6, section 6.3).

If prisons are understaffed (or if those running the prison believe they are understaffed) this affects conditions and regimes. Prisoners are left locked in their cells for longer, because there is not the staff to supervise out-of-cell activities or to escort them from place to place. Visits to prisoners may be restricted or cancelled. And prison staff may become restless.

Staff Unrest

For many years the relationship between prison staff and the government has rarely been better than one of simmering discontent. Local and national industrial action by prison officers has been a recurrent event. The most alarming disruption ever took place in 1986, as protest action including a national overtime ban by prison officers over staffing levels sparked off the worst sequence of riots by inmates that had occurred up until that date. Industrial action over staffing arrangements continued (most notably at Wandsworth Prison in 1989, when police officers were drafted in to replace prison officers). Conservative government legislation placed severe legal restrictions on the ability of prison officers to undertake industrial action, although this did not put an end to protest actions of varying degrees of legality and illegality. Under New Labour the relationship between the government and the **Prison Officers' Association** (POA) seemed to improve for a while, and the statutory restrictions on industrial action were lifted in 2005 and replaced by a no-strike agreement. But in August 2007 prison officers held a snap two-hour national walk-out over pay. The government's response was to obtain a court injunction to enforce the no-strike agreement and to reintroduce the law forbidding industrial action by prison officers. In 2009 a POA ballot overwhelmingly rejected government proposals for a 'workforce modernisation programme' which would create a new lower (and lower paid) grade of prison officer, and also threatened strike action in response to government proposals for the 'market testing' (i.e. possible **privatization**, see Chapter 6) of existing public sector prisons. In November 2009 unofficial action was taken by officers at several prisons in the north west over allegations of bullying and harassment by management at Liverpool prison. In early 2011 staff at Birmingham Prison walked out following the announcement that it was to be privatized, while the government implemented plans to train soldiers in the running of prisons in the event of further industrial action.

Staff unrest never seems far away from the prison system and is likely to be exacerbated by increasing workloads due to rising numbers of prisoners, or other threatening developments such as prison privatization (see Chapter 6, sections 6.3 and 6.5).

Security

Security lapses always seem to have the potential to create more public uproar than almost any other event surrounding the penal system. A good example occurred in the mid-1990s when breakouts occurred from two high security prisons, Whitemoor and Parkhurst, leading to two official reports (Woodcock, 1994 and Learmont, 1995), a major security crackdown across the prison system, the sacking of the Director General of the prison service and furious political rows (Cavadino and Dignan, 2002: 184–6). Yet despite the air of moral panic which surrounds such incidents, it remains the case that since the 1960s the English penal system has not had a bad record overall for security, in the sense of managing to keep prisoners inside prison. Escapes are currently neither common nor increasing: indeed, they have decreased in recent years (see further Chapter 6, section 6.5). Breakouts from high security prisons had been extremely rare prior to the escapes in the mid-90s, and have not recurred since.

The word 'security' is often used in a different sense, to mean the adequate exercise of *control* over inmates inside prison – for example, preventing them from assaulting the staff or each other (see Chapter 6, section 6.5). Prison staff often complain that understaffing (combined sometimes with other deficiencies in material resources) reduces security in prisons, making assaults, breakdowns in control and even escapes more likely. It is often 'security considerations' – *fears* about security and control – which exacerbate the physical conditions of prisoners; for example, they may be kept locked in their cells almost all day because they are not trusted to be let out without a high degree of staff-intensive supervision. In the wake of the official inquiries into the mid-1990s escapes there was a noticeable and damaging shift of emphasis towards security (see Chapter 6, sections 6.4 and 6.5). Such shifts have the natural tendency of diverting resources towards ensuring security and changing staff practices in ways that adversely affect prison conditions and regimes still further.

'Toxic Mix' of Prisoners

We can agree with the orthodox account on many details concerning the component factors of the crisis. But the notion of a 'toxic mix' of prisoners is an issue on which we definitely part company. We do not deny that some characteristics of prison inmates may make them more or less likely to cause problems: if the prisons predominantly housed old people or nuns rather than young men with a record of anti-social behaviour they would doubtless experience fewer riots. But there are several difficulties with 'toxic mix' theory.

It is often said that one important constituent of the so-called 'toxic mix' is *lifers* – prisoners serving sentences of **life imprisonment**. Such prisoners are often said to have 'nothing left to lose' (for example, Humphry and May, 1977). Yet although there are more lifers and other indeterminate sentence prisoners than there used to be (see Chapter 7, section 7.3) most of them have a great deal to lose. A life sentence does not usually mean that the prisoner is kept in prison until he or she dies (although it may: about a dozen lifers die in prison each year), but lifers are only released at the discretion of the **Parole Board** (see Chapter 7). Few things jeopardize a prisoner's **parole** chances more than misbehaviour within prison, and especially participation in riots and protests. (Similar logic applies to other prisoners who are serving long **fixed-term sentences** but are eligible for early release.) Yet ironically, some recent policy developments have threatened to create a situation whereby some lifers and other long-term prisoners do have relatively little to lose. For example, there are now some lifers with 'whole life tariff' sentences who can never receive parole (see Chapter 7, section 7.3). If the provision for early release becomes less generous, it becomes all the more likely that prisoners serving long sentences will feel that they have rather less to lose.

There is widespread agreement that there are many mentally disturbed people in prison who would be better off in hospital. Various surveys over the years have estimated that up to 90 per cent of prisoners could be categorized as having some form of mental disorder (see, for example, Gunn et al., 1991; Singleton et al., 1998). The surveys which find the highest incidence of mental disorder among prisoners tend to include not only mental illness but also diagnoses over which some scepticism is arguably warranted, such as 'personality disorder' and alcohol and drug misuse. Even discounting such categories, however, it is clear that many prisoners suffer a disproportionate amount of mental distress and disturbance. And it is equally clear that the quality of psychiatric services for mentally ill prisoners is woefully inadequate (Reed and Lyne, 2000; Prison Reform Trust, 2006a: 27–8). As human beings we are suitably horrified by this state of affairs; but as penologists we wonder cynically how great a contribution this factor really makes to the penal crisis. Despite popular stereotypes, much mental illness makes the sufferers if anything more amenable to control rather than less, and mentally ill prisoners have not been prominent in organizing riots.

One interesting feature of Lord Justice Woolf's historic report into the Strangeways and other riots of 1990 (Woolf and Tumim, 1991) was its implicit rejection of the 'toxic mix' theory. We believe Woolf was right on this point. Apart from the difficulties we have already noted with the theory, we shall see shortly that the 'toxic mix' cannot always be implicated in causing riots, for it is often simply not present in prisons which experience disorder.

Riots and Disorder

To the general public, one of the most noticeable symptoms of the penal crisis – along with the occasional spectacular escape – is the prison riot. Apart from a riot at Parkhurst in 1969, disturbances were comparatively infrequent in British prisons until the year of 1972, which saw a major wave of rooftop demonstrations in many prisons. Subsequently – just to select some of the outstanding incidents – there were major riots at Hull in 1976, Gartree in 1978 and Albany in 1983. In 1986, as we have seen, a national overtime ban by prison officers sparked off riots in 18 prisons. April 1990 saw the worst ever series of prison riots, including a 25-day riot and siege at Strangeways Prison, Manchester. More riots have occurred in the years since Strangeways, including recent incidents at Ashwell Prison (2009), Moorland (2010), Cookham Wood Young Offender Institution (2010), Ford open prison (2011) and a young offender unit at Littlehey Prison (2011). Like staff unrest, inmate disorder shows no sign of disappearing from the scene.

Criticisms of the Orthodox Account

Generally speaking, then, most of the factors emphasized by the orthodox account are genuine enough (with the notable exception, in our opinion, of the 'toxic mix' idea). Where we believe the orthodox account to be seriously misleading is in the *causal relationships* it postulates between the different factors, and especially its explanation of prison riots.

One problem with the orthodox account is that it simply does not square with the facts about prison riots – and in particular, about where in the prison system they occur. If riots are caused by overcrowding, understaffing, bad physical conditions and poor security, one would expect them to occur exclusively in the local prisons and remand centres, which are the most overcrowded and understaffed, where conditions are worse and security less tight than in many longer-stay establishments. Yet prior to 1986, major disorder was almost entirely confined to high security prisons which house prisoners on long sentences, which are not overcrowded or understaffed, where conditions are relatively good and where security is by definition at a maximum. After 1986 the pattern was largely reversed, with most major disorders occurring in local prisons (such as Strangeways in 1990), remand centres and lower-security establishments. But these riots are not satisfactorily explained by the orthodox account either, for such institutions lack the particular 'toxic mix' of prisoners which is supposed to be an important causative factor in inmate disorder. In a nutshell, the worst conditions and the supposedly most 'toxic mixes' simply do not coexist in the same prisons. Then again, the prisons which experienced riots in 1986, 1990 and subsequently were not all overcrowded (for example Northeye in 1986 and Dartmoor in 1990) or the worst in terms of physical conditions (Wymott and Wayland in 1986).

The very phrase 'toxic mix', with its pseudo-scientific ring, indicates a more fundamental deficiency in the orthodox account. As we have portrayed it in Figure 1.1, the whole process of the crisis on this account seems very mechanistic (or *positivistic*, a term explained in Chapter 2, section 2.5). One thing leads automatically to another: prisoners and prison staff both seem to react to conditions in a mindless manner. The prisoners in particular seem to behave like molecules in a test tube: place such a combination in such a physical environment, agitate, increase the pressure, and an explosion is the automatic result.[6] We do not believe that

---

[6]Hennessy (1987: para. 9.06) – in an official report into widespread prison disturbances in 1986 – said almost exactly this in a passage which reads as not entirely metaphorical: 'It can perhaps be explained in terms of a chemical reaction. When a number of elements are brought together and a suitable catalyst is added, an explosion may result.'

people are like that. Rioting is not mindless behaviour; it is meaningful human action. Lord Scarman said in his famous report on inner city riots that 'public disorder usually arises *out of a sense of injustice*' (Scarman, 1986: xiii; our italics), and as the Woolf Report rightly recognized, this is as true in prisons as it is in the inner city. And this crucial sense of injustice is not a mindless automatic reaction, but an active interpretation of a situation. So for an adequate description and explanation of the penal crisis, we need to explore why there is this perception of injustice, and even to ask whether this perception is correct. In our opinion this is the main flaw in the orthodox account, and one we hope to go some way towards rectifying.

Improving on the Orthodox Account

1.3 We think a more adequate account of the penal crisis can be developed by taking on board and integrating into our explanation the insights of a variety of penal commentators. In what follows we draw in particular upon the Woolf Report (Woolf and Tumim, 1991); the radical account furnished by Mike Fitzgerald and Joe Sim in their book *British Prisons* (1982); the contributions of Tony Bottoms (1980, 1983 and 1995a; Bottoms and Stevenson, 1992); and Stuart Hall's work on the politics of law and order (1979 and 1980; Hall et al., 1978). To begin with, we shall highlight certain aspects of the crisis which the orthodox account either ignores or fails to address adequately.

The Crisis of Penological Resources

It is implicit in the orthodox account that there is a problem of limited resources such as space within prisons and numbers of prison officers. But the problem is wider and deeper than that. Tony Bottoms (1980) identified a general crisis of penological resources, affecting not only prisons (to which the orthodox account is limited) but also extending to the entire penal system. This includes the probation service, which provides and runs non-custodial penalties for a much increased number of clients (see Chapter 5) and post-custodial provision such as parole supervision (see Chapter 7). This twofold **crisis of resources** generates an imperative to limit the numbers in prison and to deal with more offenders outside the prison 'in the community', but without overloading the probation service. Another aspect of this crisis presumably is the lack of resources to keep prison officers sufficiently materially satisfied to defuse industrial relations problems within prisons, and to provide prison inmates with constructive and fulfilling ways of occupying their time.

This *material* aspect of the crisis – the ever-present issue of scarce material resources such as buildings, staff, equipment and money – is one which always needs to be borne in mind when seeking to understand the state of the penal system. As we shall see, however, this is only one side of the picture.

The Crisis of Visibility

Perhaps the **crisis of visibility** (so named by Fitzgerald and Sim, 1982: 6–11) does not deserve its own heading, but it is an interesting example of an aspect of the crisis which the orthodox account fails to encompass. It concerns the secrecy that has for many years shrouded prisons and what goes on inside them. Developments in recent years have meant that 'slowly, but surely, the secrecy behind the prison walls is being breached, as alternative sources of information about the prisons are more securely established' (Fitzgerald and Sim, 1982: 11; see further Chapter 6, section 6.5).

Fitzgerald and Sim seem to see the *existence* of secrecy as a 'crisis' in itself. Morally speaking, we have no doubt that it has been; but again reverting to our cynical sociological standpoint, we suspect that on the contrary it is often the *dispelling* of secrecy that causes problems for the system and exacerbates the crisis. For if we assume that there is much in prisons that will not bear being exposed (and if not, why keep it secret?) then opening up the prison is likely to decrease the **legitimacy** of the system. If 'knowledge is power' then there is a danger that the system will lose much of its power if it loses control of information about itself. (It may also increase staff unrest by leading prison officers to feel that their authority is threatened.) On the other hand, however, it is noticeable that many incidents of prison disorder – especially the popular form of demonstrating on the prison rooftop – have been clearly motivated by the very desire to make prisoners' grievances and allegations *visible* in a way that would never normally happen. And if greater visibility should lead to prisoners being better treated (for fear of abuse being exposed) then visibility rather than secrecy could help to defuse the crisis. So, while we have no doubt that it is right that prison secrecy should be dispelled, it seems as if (paradoxically) both secrecy *and* openness can contribute to the crisis – as long as there are secrets to hide.

The problem with secrecy is that the secret information is often of a discreditable nature which, if it gets out, can damage legitimacy. This means that the crisis of visibility is only a part of what has justly been termed 'the final and most crucial aspect of the crisis in British prisons' (Fitzgerald and Sim, 1982: 23), and to which we now turn.

The Crisis of Legitimacy

Whereas the crisis of penological resources is a *material* crisis, the crisis of legitimacy is *ideological* in nature: it exists in the minds of human beings. Sociologists use the term 'legitimacy' to mean *power which is perceived as morally justified*. The penal system wields power over its subjects, but its moral right to do so can be contested. Fitzgerald and Sim, who gave the crisis of legitimacy its name, related it to 'calls for the abolition of imprisonment' and to 'a more fundamental political crisis which transcends the prison walls' (1982: 23–4). There may have been an element of revolutionary wishful thinking here: if all the system had to worry about was the minority of people who seriously call for the abolition of prisons or the prospect of the imminent overthrow of capitalism there might not be much of a crisis. Nevertheless, even among non-abolitionists (and across much of the political spectrum) there has been grave disquiet about the state of the prisons. Even conservative commentators can regard the conditions within some prisons as morally intolerable to a civilized community. The squalor produced by prison overcrowding is perhaps the issue which most scandalizes the public conscience, but there are others. These include the high incidence of suicides among prisoners (see Chapter 6, section 6.5); the presence in prisons (as noted previously) of large numbers of people with mental health problems; the over-representation within prisons of members of ethnic minorities and the issue of racism in prisons (see Chapter 9, section 9.3).

Tony Bottoms (1980) also saw the penal system as suffering from a crisis of legitimacy (though he did not use the term), as well as from the crisis of resources discussed earlier. He identified as an important cause of the crisis of legitimacy the collapse of the **rehabilitative ideal**. Prior to the 1970s, the penal system could plausibly legitimate itself by claiming as its *raison d'être* the rehabilitation of offenders: the provision of training and treatment which would cure them of their criminality, benefiting both them and society as a whole. As we shall see in Chapter 2 (section 2.2), this claim subsequently became less plausible and less acceptable, with a general belief arising that '**nothing works**' in the treatment of offenders. This undermined the legitimacy of the penal system: not only of the prisons (whose claim to be providing effective rehabilitation was always shaky in many eyes) but equally for other components of the penal system. A notable example is the probation service, which has for many years now been demoralized and uncertain about what its proper rationale and direction should be (see Chapter 5). The system has found itself in dire need of new ways of legitimating itself, and this need has given rise to a variety of responses. We discuss these further in the following section; but they have included, most potently, the rise of what we shall be calling law and order ideology.

It is not only the system's legitimacy with outside observers and the general public which is important. The system will also suffer severe difficulties if it lacks legitimacy with its own employees, including prison staff and probation officers. Perhaps most important of all is *the legitimacy of the system with those who are its subjects* – in our opinion, the crucial factor in the genesis of prison riots and of many of the system's other problems. After all, a penal system can only run with the acquiescence of offenders. No prison could run for long if not for the fact that most prisoners most of the time are prepared simply to co-operate with the staff and 'do their bird'. This is not to say that they normally have no sense of injustice. They may bear grievances about the fact that they are locked up in prison, perhaps for longer than they feel they deserve or for longer than other offenders whom they regard as comparable. (We shall see in Chapters 2, 4 and 9 that they may well have good grounds for this belief.) They may have other grievances concerning the prison regime, early release, the behaviour of prison staff and the prison disciplinary system (see Chapters 6 and 7). Even so, prisoners do not normally riot unless this sense of injustice has been somehow inflamed beyond its normal simmering state.

Prisoners' sense of injustice was highlighted by the Woolf Report (Woolf and Tumim, 1991) on the prison riots of April 1990, which became established as a historic and classically liberal account of what is wrong with English prisons, what causes prison riots and what should be done to prevent them. Woolf's central finding was that:

> there are three requirements which must be met if the prison system is to be stable: they are *security, control and justice* . . . 'security' refers to the obligations of the Prison Service to prevent prisoners escaping. 'Control' deals with the obligation of the Prison Service to prevent prisoners being disruptive. 'Justice' refers to the obligation of the Prison Service to treat prisoners with humanity and fairness, and to prepare them for their return to the community in a way which makes it less likely that they will re-offend. (paras 9.19–9.20; our italics)

'Security' and 'control' are hardly novel concepts, figuring significantly in the orthodox account. Woolf also acknowledged as relevant factors such as overcrowding and insanitary physical conditions, but did not regard these as crucial. Their significance for Woolf was in contributing to *prisoners' sense of injustice*.

Woolf did not use the word 'legitimacy', but it is clearly the prison's lack of *legitimacy with inmates* which he saw as of central importance. He showed a keen awareness that, on the one hand, legitimacy is in the mind, but on the other hand what is in people's minds usually depends on the external reality: 'It is not possible for the Inquiry to form any judgment on whether the specific grievances of these prisoners were or were not well-founded. What is clear is that the Prison Service had failed to *persuade* these prisoners that it was treating them fairly' (para. 9.25). Despite not committing himself about specific grievances, Woolf believed that genuine injustice contributes to a lack of legitimacy, which in turn makes disorder more likely. A substantial number of prisoners participated in the riots 'at least in part, because of the conditions in which they were held and the way in which they were treated. If a proper level of justice is provided in prisons, then it is less likely that prisoners will behave in this way. Justice, therefore, contributes to the maintenance of security and control' (para. 1.151). Woolf's humanistic attention to the subjective *interpretation by prisoners of their situation* marks a distinct departure from the orthodox account.

While talking about the need to keep security, control and justice in 'balance', Woolf appeared to emphasize the importance of justice, and the imbalance he was most concerned about was the prospect of security and control measures exacerbating prisoners' sense of injustice. Although Woolf stated that 'there is no single cause of riots' (para. 9.23) it is perhaps not a great distortion to say that he saw the lack of legitimacy of the prison for its inmates as the key factor in explaining the disorders. For this reason he stressed in his recommendations not only measures to improve prison conditions but also reforms of grievance and disciplinary procedures (see Chapter 6) which might both improve the objective standard of justice within prisons and be seen as fairer by prisoners.

The penal system's legitimacy problems are – of course – by no means all related to feelings that the system is excessively harsh and inhumane. Rather more common among the general public is the perception (regularly encouraged by tabloid newspapers and many politicians) that the penal system is on the contrary over-lenient, lax and insecure. It is bound to be difficult for the system to achieve legitimacy with all its different audiences – public, press, politicians, penal practitioners and penal subjects – under these circumstances.

Responses to the Crisis

1.4 How have governments responded to the penal crisis? And not only governments, but other actors in the penal arena, such as practitioners, commentators, civil servants and opposition politicians? Their responses can be roughly split into two categories: *ideological* (or philosophical) responses to the crisis of legitimacy in particular; and *practical* responses to the management problems caused by the material crisis of resources.

On the *ideological* side, Tony Bottoms (1980) listed a number of varying responses to the collapse of the rehabilitative ideal and the consequent dire need for the penal system to find new ways of legitimating itself. These responses included the revival of the philosophy of 'just deserts' (see Chapter 2, sections 2.3 and 2.5) between the 1970s and 1990s. But the most prominent ideological response, amounting to a massive shift in penal ideology, has been the new punitiveness (see Chapter 3, section 3.6): the rise and rise of what we call law and order ideology – the appeal to a harsh, Strategy A programme of 'toughness' which is represented as being an effective remedy for crime. (See the Introduction, section I.2. for a further explanation of Strategies A, B and C.) In the sense in which we use the phrase, law and order ideology is more than just the unexceptionable beliefs that society should be governed by law and that crime should be effectively controlled. It is a complex if naive set of attitudes, including the beliefs that human beings have free will, that they must be strictly disciplined by restrictive rules, and that they should be harshly punished if they break the rules or fail to respect authority. Such an **ideology** naturally leads its adherents to favour a Strategy A approach to criminal justice policy. (The phrase **populist punitiveness**, coined by Bottoms (1995a), means much the same thing.)

The ideology of law and order was notably and provocatively analysed in the late 1970s and early 1980s by the Marxist theorist Stuart Hall (1979, 1980; Hall et al., 1978). Hall saw law and order ideology as an important component of what he called 'authoritarian populism', which in turn constituted an important strand in the political phenomenon of Thatcherism. However, not only did the 'drift into a law and order society' in Britain begin well before the accession to power of the Conservative Party under Mrs Thatcher in 1979 – although that was something of a defining moment – it also accelerated significantly under her Conservative successor John Major. It persisted to a great extent under the New Labour government (1997–2010) and has been at least as evident a force in shaping the policies of the current Coalition government (see Chapter 10, section 10.2). For Hall, law and order ideology forms part of a pro-ruling-class response to a wider crisis of social order whose roots lie partly in the problems of the British economy and of Britain's declining role in the world.

This is far from a full explanation, however. It does not account for similar developments in many other countries (most notably the USA) in recent decades (see generally Cavadino and Dignan, 2006), or for the reinvigoration of law and order ideology between early 1993 and 1997, at a time when Britain's role in the world may have continued to decline but its economy was not getting any worse. Other long-term social and political developments have led to a greater degree of **populism** in politics, in Britain and elsewhere, especially in respect of criminal justice policy. One likely partial explanation for this is that the decline of traditional communities has led to both an increase in crime and a general feeling of insecurity in the psyche of the modern individual. This in turn feeds into a fear of crime and a tendency to favour punitive fixes for the perceived threat it poses:[7] 'In such a context, a politician seeking popularity can reasonably easily tap into the electorate's insecurities by promising tough action on "villains"' (Bottoms, 1995a: 47). And modern politicians increasingly attune their policies according to the results of opinion polls and focus groups, which seek to identify policies that are (often very superficially) attractive to voters. It is largely along these lines – by reference to the quest of contemporary politicians for power – that we would explain the law and order counter-reformation under John Major from 1993 to 1997 and the persistence of a high dose of 'toughness' in criminal justice policy in the years since then. As Hall (1979: 15) says, law and order ideology is not an automatic 'reflection of the crisis: it is itself a *response* to the crisis'; in other words it is created by human beings operating in their own real environments, which for politicians is the world of politics.

This does not necessarily mean that pursuing Strategy A will be a genuine recipe for political success, let alone that it will solve the problems of crime and punishment. The fate of John Major's government – defeated by a landslide in the general election of 1997 – suggests that 'playing the law and order card' is by no means a sure ticket to electoral success. For one thing, although politicians currently tend to see law and order ideology as ruling public perceptions about criminal justice, and consequently calculate that it is to their own advantage to be perceived as being tough, research suggests that the public may be nowhere near as punitive-minded as is generally supposed (see Chapter 10: section 10.3). And even assuming they were, there would be no way of satisfying the constant media calls for ever tougher criminal justice policies. So – on the ideological side of things – Strategy A will not solve the crisis of legitimacy. Moreover, pursuing ever harsher policies and indulging in law and order rhetoric inevitably worsens the crisis of penological resources (on the material side of the equation). Recent history bears out what one would expect, that tough policies and rhetoric have had the natural result of increasing the harshness of punishment – and consequently

---

[7] Cf. Garland (2001). We would also highlight the shift towards neo-liberal economics as a factor in this process: see Chapter 3, section 3.6.

the size of the prison population and the scale of the penal crisis. Surges in the prison population (for example in the mid-1980s, from early 1993 onwards and following the urban riots of 2011) have also coincided with an increase in the intensity of law and order rhetoric emanating from government ministers (Travis, 1993; see also Hough et al., 2003).

For a long time – certainly until the law and order counter-reformation of 1993 – it could be said that the overall response of the British state to the penal crisis had been mostly directed towards the material crisis of resources rather than the ideological crisis of legitimacy. The response largely took the form of **penological pragmatism**: responding to developments and attempting to manage the resources crisis 'with no clear or coherent philosophical or other theoretical basis' (Bottoms, 1980: 4). This pragmatism – which is still a vital strand in policy even in these more ideological times – has not been completely shapeless. One strong theme, whose effect waxes and wanes repeatedly over time, was identified and christened by Tony Bottoms in a highly prescient paper back in 1977: the strategy of **bifurcation** (Bottoms, 1977, 1980). Bifurcation refers to a dual-edged (or **twin-track**) approach to punishment: differentiating between 'ordinary' or 'run of the mill' offenders with whom less severe measures can be taken on the one hand, and on the other hand 'exceptional', 'very serious' or 'dangerous' offenders who can be made subject to much tougher measures. In this way 'a bifurcated policy allows governments to get tough and soft simultaneously' (Pitts, 1988: 29). From the point of view of the resources crisis, bifurcation looks like a rational response: because there are so many more 'run of the mill' than 'serious' offenders, a bifurcated policy should save many more resources than it costs. In terms of legitimacy with the general public such a strategy could also be effective, since the public can be reassured that the really 'serious' offenders about whom they are most concerned will be kept locked up for long periods. Bifurcation can thus be seen as a pragmatic response to the combined crises of legitimacy and resources, conditioned by law and order ideology. But in terms of *legitimacy with prisoners* – and in terms of preventing disorder in prisons – bifurcation runs the risk of proving seriously counterproductive since it seems so unfair to those who are singled out as the 'very serious' cases in what they may see as an arbitrary manner.

As the politics of punishment have grown harsher, the other limb of bifurcation – being less harsh to less serious offenders – has come into conflict with law and order ideology. The Criminal Justice Act 1991 embodied what we have termed **punitive bifurcation**, a version in which even lesser offenders were to be treated with apparent toughness. For under that Act's policy of punishment in the community, although more offenders were to be kept out of prison they would be *punished* in the community; non-custodial penalties were to be more punitive and controlling than hitherto. But even this harsher version of bifurcation did not survive the law and order counter-reformation, and as Michael Howard declared that 'prison works' and that more rather than fewer offenders should go to prison, both pragmatism and bifurcation were sacrificed on the altar of ideology. Between 1997 and 2010 New Labour persisted with bifurcatory policies of varying kinds, but – probably because of the greater emphasis that was placed on the tough side of the coin – the results were further increases in the prison population and in the crisis of resources. The Coalition government temporarily toyed with punitive bifurcation but in the end the bifurcatory part went missing, leaving only punitiveness (see Chapter 10, section 10.2).

Another strand of the pragmatic approach to penal policy, one which seems to keep growing in strength over the long term, is the element known as **managerialism**. This is what we call the Strategy B approach to criminal justice (Cavadino et al., 1999: 41–5; Introduction, section I.2). (It is related to the new penology, which we discuss in Chapter 3, section 3.6.) This approach is based on the notion that modern managerial techniques can be successfully applied to the problems of crime and punishment, both to control crime and to deploy penal resources effectively and efficiently. The influence of managerialism (of different varieties) can be observed in such diverse developments as the **systems management** approach to dealing with young offenders (see Chapter 8, section 8.2), the creation of the National Offender Management Service (see Chapter 5), and the government interest in seeking and applying evidence of 'what works' to control crime and prevent criminals from reoffending (see Chapter 2, section 2.2). Above all it can be seen in successive governments' dogmatic attachment to the principle of private sector participation in the delivery of both custodial (see Chapter 6) and non-custodial (see Chapter 5) penal interventions. Managerialism – like penological pragmatism more generally – is primarily directed at the material crisis of resources rather than the crisis of legitimacy. Pragmatism and bureaucracy may have their place in the practical running of things but are hardly likely in themselves to inspire minds sufficiently to defuse the legitimacy problems of the penal system.

A particularly influential, right-wing version of managerialism (known as 'New Public Management' – see Hood, 1991; McLaughlin et al., 2001) sees private sector business techniques as the model for management and seeks to improve the public sector by introducing privatization, commercial competition and general 'marketization'. We shall have much more to say about the privatization and marketization of penal services in Chapters 5 and 6. Currently the Coalition government is pursuing the policy of privatization to greater lengths than ever before both in the realm of imprisonment and in non-custodial measures for dealing with offenders.

Eagle-eyed readers may have noticed that we have mentioned both Strategy A-type (harsh and punitive) and Strategy B-type (managerial) responses to the crisis, and wondered: have there been no Strategy C-type (humanitarian, human rights-based) responses? To be fair, there have – although in recent years they have tended to take a poor third place to the other two strategies. There has been a revival of interest in measures that can be taken to reform and rehabilitate offenders, which can be seen as a generally humanitarian approach as well as aiming at the efficient control of crime. And governments including the current Coalition government have shown increasing interest in the idea of restorative justice (see Chapters 2, 5, 8 and 10, sections 2.4, 5.3, 8.2 and 10.3), especially for young offenders. We will give more details about all these responses to the crisis throughout this book, and in Chapter 10 we return to these to provide a general

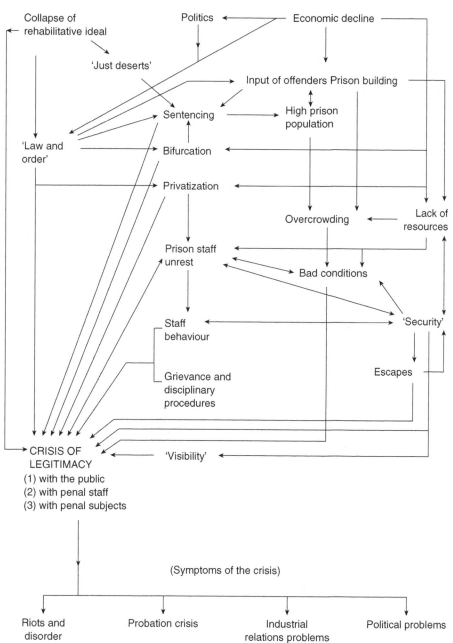

FIGURE 1.2 A radical pluralist account of the penal crisis

overview and give our own opinions, setting out the kind of responses we ourselves favour.

A Radical Pluralist Account of the Crisis

1.5 We said earlier that one problem with the orthodox account of the penal crisis is that it is *positivistic*: it sees the crisis in terms of mechanistic causes and effects and ignores the place of subjective human experience, perception, reflection and meaningful human action. It sees the crisis in overwhelmingly material terms – it recognizes the material crisis of resources but ignores the ideological crisis of legitimacy. In the previous two sections, by contrast, we have sought to emphasize that, although material circumstances are indeed of great importance in explaining the penal crisis, they are only one side of the story. The other side, equally crucial, is the realm of ideas and ideology. Material and ideological factors interact with each other in a manner that could be described (in unfashionable Marxian terminology) as 'dialectical'.

In seeking to explain and understand the penal crisis, we wish to go further than just widening the orthodox account and adding the ideological dimension to it. We think the crisis can be analysed within the context of a general theoretical framework which is both intellectually respectable and useful, a theory we call **radical pluralism** (Cavadino, 1992). The nature of this theory will be explained in greater detail in Chapter 3 (section 3.5), but it is a composite, compromise theory, which is capable of incorporating those elements of the crisis that the orthodox account rightly identifies while also drawing upon the insights of commentators such as Fitzgerald and Sim, Bottoms, Hall and Lord Woolf.

The word 'pluralism' in the title of this theory means that we recognize that a large number of varied elements (including a variety of interest groups with greater or lesser power) are involved in the penal system and its crisis, and that these elements interact in a highly complex manner. We see a need to analyse the crisis in the context of the relationships between politics and economics, ideology and material conditions. We do not believe that this kind of analysis can be politically or morally neutral – and nor should it, for our understanding of the situation is that the penal system is morally indefensible and is in dire need of a programme of radical reform which would inevitably be highly political. On the other hand, the penal crisis is not simply a by-product of a 'crisis of capitalism', and it could be largely solved without a complete political and social revolution.

Our account is represented in diagrammatic form in Figure 1.2. The most striking feature of the diagram is its complexity; and yet Figure 1.2 is vastly oversimplified. An arrow in the diagram means that one factor affects (often this means exacerbates) another in the direction shown. Some of the connections pictured have already been discussed or mentioned. For example, we have already indicated how economic decline, political developments and the collapse of the rehabilitative ideal helped to give rise to a resurgence of law and order ideology. Similarly, bifurcation can be seen as having been produced by a combination of law and order ideology and the practical need to do something about the high prison population in a situation of scarce penal resources and general economic stringency. Other factors and relationships will be dealt with in later chapters.

A few more points are worth stressing about this kind of account. First, it is crucial to emphasize again that the crisis is composed of both material and ideological elements, and we have consequently tried to organize Figure 1.2 accordingly. These two sides of the crisis interact in a complex fashion: indeed certain features of the system, for example bifurcation, cannot be neatly placed on one side or the other of the material/ideological divide since they are both ideologies and material practices at the same time.

The penal crisis is sometimes described as not one but several interlocking crises; indeed, we ourselves talk about, for example, the crisis of resources and the crisis of legitimacy as if they were separate things. But it may be best to think of the penal system as being essentially one highly complex system and the penal crisis as a single entity – albeit with multiplex causation and a variety of symptoms. For there is a single unifying factor of the penal crisis, into which all the exacerbating elements flow and from which most of the symptoms of the crisis proceed (as Figure 1.2 shows). This key factor is the *crisis of legitimacy*, which is ignored by the orthodox account, but which we see as crucial. Riots, staff unrest, the malaise in the probation service and the political problems caused by the penal system are not the *direct* results of a high prison population or a lack of money or of decent prison buildings (although these do contribute to the crisis). They result from what people believe and how they feel – from the *moral reactions* of people within and outside the penal system to the material situation. (In sociological jargon, the effects of the objective material conditions are 'mediated' through the subjective perceptions of human actors which are structured by ideology.)

The crisis of legitimacy, it is worth repeating, is at least threefold. The penal system needs to legitimate itself with different groups of people: with the public (including politicians, commentators, etc.), with penal staff (including prison staff and probation officers) and with penal subjects (prisoners, probationers and others who are subject to penal treatment). Failing to satisfy the sense of justice of these different audiences leads to the alarming visible symptoms of the crisis: political problems, industrial relations problems, malaise among prison and probation staff, and disorder among prisoners.

In saying that the crisis of legitimacy is central, we are saying that the penal crisis is in essence a *moral* crisis. By this we do not just mean that many people *believe* that the system is unjust. As we hope to make clear (especially in Chapter 2, but also throughout the whole of this book), the penal system is indeed in our opinion the source of very substantial injustice, and the crisis is unlikely to be solved unless this injustice is mitigated.

Finally, we are at pains to stress that, despite all the arrows in Figure 1.2, we do *not* believe that human actions and beliefs are mechanistically determined. For example, bifurcation was a policy which was *occasioned* and *encouraged* by the conjunction of overcrowding and a lack of resources in an ideological atmosphere of law and order and legitimacy crisis, but it was not inevitable: policy-makers could (and probably should) have decided to do something else instead. Nor were Michael Howard's law and order policies between 1993 and 1997 inexorably brought about by an economic decline and the collapse of the rehabilitative ideal; nor are the policies of the current government determined by iron laws of history. All of which means that the crisis was not inevitable and is not insoluble. But it cannot be solved unless we change people's ideas about punishment.

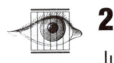

2

Justifying Punishment

Is Punishment Unjust?

2.1 In Chapter 1 we argued that the most crucial factor in the current malaise in the penal system is the crisis of legitimacy. A social institution is legitimate if it is *perceived as morally justified*; the problem with the penal system is that this perception is lacking, and many people inside and outside the system believe that it is morally indefensible, or at least defective. Are they right – is our system of punishment unjust? If they are wrong, and our penal system is morally defensible, then the obvious strategy would be to try to rectify their perceptions, by persuading people that the system is not unjust after all. But if the perceived injustices are real, then it is those injustices which should be rectified. This chapter accordingly deals with the moral philosophy of punishment and attempts to relate this philosophy to the reality of penal systems such as that of England and Wales today.

The basic moral question about punishment is an age-old one: 'What justifies the infliction of punishment on people?' Punishing people certainly needs a justification, since it is almost always something which is harmful, painful or unpleasant to the recipient. Imprisonment, for example, causes physical discomfort, psychological suffering, indignity and general unhappiness along with a variety of other disadvantages (such as impaired prospects for employment and social life). Also, and not to be overlooked, punishments such as imprisonment typically inflict additional suffering on others, such as the offender's family, who have not even been found guilty of a crime (Codd, 2008). Deliberately inflicting suffering on people is at least *prima facie* immoral, and needs some special justification. It is true that in some cases the recipient does not find the punishment painful, or even welcomes it – for example, some offenders might find prison a refuge against the intolerable pressures of the outside world. And sometimes when we punish we are not trying to cause suffering: for example, when the punishment is mainly aimed at reforming the offender or at ensuring that victims are benefited by reparation. But even in these cases punishment is still something *imposed*: it is an intrusion on the liberty of the person punished, which also needs to be justified.

If we ask what might be the aims and purposes of punishment, many answers have been given over the ages. Currently a number of these are recognized in English law (s. 142 of the Criminal Justice Act 2003: see section 4.3 in Chapter 4) as purposes which judges and magistrates may pursue in deciding on their sentences: these are '(a) the punishment of offenders [i.e. what we shall be calling **retribution** and **denunciation**]; (b) the reduction of crime (including its reduction by **deterrence**); (c) the reform and rehabilitation of offenders; (d) the protection of the public [**incapacitation**]; and (e) the making of reparation by offenders to persons affected by their offences'. We shall be dealing with all of these in this chapter and considering how plausible they might be as aims which might justify punishment.

As well as having a *general justification* for having a system of punishment, we will also require morally valid 'principles of distribution' for punishment, to determine how severe the punishment of individual offenders should be. This distinction (from Hart, 1968) will be of recurring importance in the following discussion.

The two most frequently cited general justifications for punishment are retribution, and what we call **reductivism** (following Walker, 1972). **Retributivism** justifies punishment on the ground that it is *deserved* by the offender; reductivism justifies punishment on the ground that it helps to *reduce the incidence of crime*. We begin with reductivism.

Reductivism

2.2 Reductivism is a *forward-looking* (or 'consequentialist') theory: it seeks to justify punishment by its alleged *future consequences*. Punishment is justified because, it is claimed, it helps to control crime. If punishment is inflicted, there will be less crime committed thereafter than there would be if no penalty were imposed. Reductivist arguments can be supported by the form of moral reasoning known as **utilitarianism**. This is the general moral theory first systematically expounded by Jeremy Bentham, an important figure in penal thought and history, of whom we shall have more to say later in section 2.5. Bentham's utilitarian theory says that moral actions are those which produce 'the greatest happiness of the greatest number' of people. If punishment does indeed reduce the future incidence of crime, then the pain and unhappiness caused to the offender may be outweighed by the unpleasantness to other people in the future which is prevented – thus making punishment morally right from a utilitarian point of view. But it is not necessary to be a utilitarian to be a reductivist. Indeed, at the end of this chapter we will be arguing an alternative position (based on human rights) which although non-utilitarian nevertheless takes account of the possible reductivist effects of punishment.

How is it claimed that punishment reduces crime? There are several alleged mechanisms of reduction, which we shall discuss in turn.

Deterrence

Essentially, deterrence is the simple idea that the incidence of crime is reduced because of people's fear or apprehension of the punishment they may receive if they offend – that, in the famous words of Conservative Home Secretary Michael Howard in a speech to the Conservative Party Conference in 1993, 'Prison works … it makes many who are tempted to commit crime think twice.' There are two kinds of deterrence, known as 'individual' and 'general' deterrence.

Individual deterrence occurs when someone commits a crime, is punished for it and finds the punishment so unpleasant or frightening that the offence is never repeated for fear of more of the same treatment, or worse. This sounds a plausible theory, but unfortunately it seems not to work too well in practice. If individual deterrence did work as the theory suggests, we would expect that if we introduced a new kind of harsh punishment designed to deter, the offenders who suffered the new punishment would be measurably less likely to reoffend than similar offenders who underwent a more lenient penalty. However – as was found with the **'short sharp shock' detention centre** regime for young offenders introduced in the early 1980s (see Chapter 8, section 8.2) – this simply does not seem to work. Indeed, there is some research which indicates – quite contrary to what the theory of individual deterrence suggests – that offenders who suffer more severe or punitive penalties (including penalties specifically aimed at deterrence) are *more* (and not less) likely to reoffend (Brody, 1976: 14–16; West, 1982: 109; Lipsey, 1992: 139; 1995: 74). And one particularly thorough research study on boys growing up in London seemed to find that if a boy offends, the best way to prevent him from offending repeatedly is *not to catch him* in the first place (West, 1982: 104–11)!

This research evidence seems contrary to common sense, but such findings are not as incomprehensible as they look at first sight. They do not show that punishment has no deterrent effect on offenders, or that no offender is ever deterred. But they do suggest that *overall*, punishment has other effects which may cancel out and even outweigh its deterrent effects. These anti-deterrent effects of punishment are known as 'labelling effects'. **Labelling theory** in criminology claims (and is supported by research studies such as those just mentioned) that catching and punishing offenders 'labels' them as criminals, stigmatizing them, and that this process can in various ways make it more difficult for them to conform to a law-abiding life in future. They may find respectable society and lawful opportunities closed to them while unlawful ones are opened up (custodial institutions are notoriously 'schools for crime' where offenders can meet each other, learn criminal techniques and enter into a criminal subculture), and their self-image may change from that of a law-abiding person to that of a **deviant**. Harsher penalties in particular could help to foster a tough, 'macho' criminal self-image in the young men who predominate in the criminal statistics. (For a fuller discussion of labelling theory, see Burke, 2009: ch. 9.)

So the notion of individual deterrence seems to be of little value in justifying our penal practices. But there is another, perhaps more promising category of deterrent effect: *general deterrence*. This is the idea that offenders are punished, not to deter the offenders themselves, but *pour encourager les autres* (to use Voltaire's famous phrase – 'to encourage the others'). General deterrence theory is often cited to justify punishments, including those imposed on particular offenders. One faintly ludicrous example is a 1983 case[1] where the Court of Appeal said that a particular sentence would 'indicate to other people who might be minded to set fire to armchairs in the middle of a domestic row that if they do, they were likely to go to prison for as long as two years'.

Now, there can be little doubt that the existence of a *system of punishment* has some general deterrent effect. When during the Second World War the German occupiers deported the entire Danish police force for several months, recorded rates of theft and robbery (though not of sexual offences) rose spectacularly (Christiansen, 1975). And if, for instance, on-the-spot execution were to be introduced for parking on a double yellow line, there might well be a significant reduction in the rate of illegal parking. But short of such extreme situations, it seems that *what punishments are actually inflicted* on offenders makes little difference to general deterrence. For example, in Birmingham in 1973 a young mugger was sentenced to a draconian 20 years' detention amid enormous publicity, and yet this sentence made no difference to the incidence of mugging offences in Birmingham or in other areas (Baxter and Nuttall, 1975). Similarly, studies have found little if any evidence that jurisdictions with harsh levels of sentencing benefit as a result from reduced crime rates (von Hirsch et al., 1999: ch. 6). (And incidentally, there is no good evidence that capital punishment is a more effective deterrent than alternative penalties for murder, and for all we know it could even be less effective: see, for example, Fagan, 2005.)

This does not mean that deterrence never works, but it does mean that its effects are limited and easy to overestimate. There are several reasons for this. First, most people most of the time obey the law out of moral considerations rather than for selfish instrumental reasons (Paternoster et al., 1983; Tyler, 1990). Second, people are more likely to be deterred by the likely moral reactions of those close to them than by the threat of formal punishment (Willcock and Stokes, 1968). Again, potential offenders may well be ignorant of the likely penalty, or believe they will never get caught. Research has found that bank robbers tend to be dismissive of their chances of being caught even when they already have been caught and sent to prison, and as a result most do not think twice about the kind of sentence they might get (Gill, 2000). Much the same seems to be true of burglars (Bennett and Wright, 1984: ch. 6). Or the offender may commit the crime while in a thoughtless, angry or drunken state. There is some good evidence (see Beyleveld, 1980: 147–9, 209–11; von Hirsch et al., 1999: 13, 45) that general deterrence can be improved if we can manage to increase potential offenders' *perceived likelihood of detection*, but little to suggest that more severe punishments deter any better than more lenient ones (see further Bottoms, 2004: 63–6).

These truths were officially recognized by a **White Paper** issued by a Conservative government in 1990, which wisely stated: 'There are doubtless some criminals who carefully calculate the possible gains and risks. But much crime is committed on impulse, given the opportunity presented by an open window or unlocked door,

---

[1] *R. v. Fairman* [1983] *Criminal Law Review* 197.

and it is committed by offenders who live from moment to moment; their crimes are as impulsive as the rest of their feckless, sad or pathetic lives. It is unrealistic to construct sentencing arrangements on the assumption that most offenders will weigh up the possibilities in advance and base their conduct on rational calculation. Often they do not' (Home Office, 1990a: para. 2.8).

All of this suggests that, while general deterrence might form the basis of a plausible general justification for having a system of punishment, it is more difficult to argue that the *amount of punishment imposed* by our system can be justified in this way. In terms of its deterrent effects, it seems almost certain that the English penal system is engaging in a massive amount of 'overkill'. As we saw in Chapter 1 (especially Table 1.2), England has more prisoners proportionate to its population than any other country in Western Europe. For example, contrast England with Finland, which currently has 59 prisoners per 100,000 population compared with England and Wales's 154. Unlike England, Finland from the mid-1970s onwards has as a deliberate matter of policy sought to reduce its prison population (Törnudd, 1993; Cavadino and Dignan, 2006: 160–7), and has succeeded in doing so without noticeably poor effects on its crime rate (which has gone up and down in much the same way as that of other European countries).

A utilitarian deterrence theorist ought to conclude from this that the English penal system is an immoral one. Jeremy Bentham (1970: 179) himself propounded the principle of 'frugality', more often referred to as **parsimony** in punishment, which states that penalties should be no more severe than they need to be to produce a utilitarian quantity of deterrence. 'Overkill' causes unnecessary suffering to the offender, and all suffering is bad unless it prevents a greater amount of suffering or brings about a greater quantity of pleasure. (Nor should the utilitarian overlook the economic cost of punishments such as imprisonment, estimated at around £40,000 per inmate per year.) So although for a utilitarian deterrence might justify having a penal system, it does not justify the one we actually have. We shall argue later that the same is true for our preferred approach based on human rights.

Incapacitation

'Prison works', according to Michael Howard in 1993, not only by deterrence, but also because 'it ensures that we are protected from murderers, muggers and rapists' – a reference to the reductivist mechanism known as 'incapacitation'. Incapacitation simply means that the offender is (usually physically) prevented from reoffending by the punishment imposed, either temporarily or permanently. The practice in some societies of chopping off the hands of thieves incapacitates in this way. Similarly, one of the few obviously valid arguments in favour of capital punishment is that executed offenders never reoffend afterwards. Lesser penalties can also have some incapacitatory effects. Disqualification from driving may do something to prevent motoring offenders from repeating their crimes. Attendance centres can be used to keep hooligans away from football matches. And imprisonment normally ensures that the offender is deprived of the opportunity to commit at least some kinds of offence for the duration.

Not all crimes, by any means: many thefts and assaults (on staff and other inmates) take place in prison, as do drug offences, while headlines such as 'Bootlegger ran £23m empire from prison' (*Guardian*, 2 December 1999) exemplify some of the other criminal opportunities still open to the incarcerated felon. But it is true that offences such as domestic burglary and car theft become rather more difficult when you are locked up in prison.

Life imprisonment is one sentence which is specifically used in many cases for the purposes of incapacitation. Most life imprisonment sentences would be more accurately described as *potentially* lifelong prison sentences, since most lifers are eventually released; but the life sentence means that they will not be released as long as it is believed that they pose an unacceptable risk of serious reoffending (see Chapter 8). Life sentences may be imposed, and lifers kept in prison, even though this exceeds what would be a normal length sentence proportionate to the seriousness of the offence. The sentence of **imprisonment for public protection** (IPP) created by the Criminal Justice Act 2003 (see Chapters 4 and 7, sections 4.4 and 7.3) was also aimed at incapacitating offenders.

Incapacitation could well be a justification (or partial justification) for non-custodial measures such as disqualification from driving and attendance centre orders. But how well can it serve to justify imprisonment? The key issue is the factual question of how effectively prison manages to reduce crime in this way. Although only rough estimates are possible, the best calculations suggest that the incapacitation effects of imprisonment are only very modest – as with deterrence, the effectiveness of punishment in this regard is much less than common sense would suggest. This is largely because most offenders' 'criminal careers' are relatively short, so that by the time they are locked away they may be about to give up crime or reduce their offending anyway. Moreover, supporters of incapacitation (for example, Green et al., 2005) tend to overlook the fact that offenders who are locked up are often replaced by a new generation of criminals. One authoritative estimate, by the former head of the Home Office Research and Planning Unit, Roger Tarling (1993: 154), is that 'a change in the use of custody of the order of 25 per cent would be needed to produce a 1 per cent change in the level of crime'. On the other hand, the prison population could be substantially *reduced* without creating a massive crime wave: if the numbers in prison were cut by 40 per cent, this could be expected to lead to an increase in criminal convictions of only 1.6 per cent (Brody and Tarling, 1980).

Nor is there much evidence that incapacitatory sentences can be targeted with any great success or efficiency on more selected groups of persistent offenders who are especially likely to reoffend (see, for example, Tarling; 1993: 154–60). It has been claimed that there are 100,000 offenders in the country who are responsible for half of all crime. Even if this is correct (and for doubts on this score see Garside, 2004) and we could identify and imprison them all, one in five of them would have dropped out of this Premier League of offending in the following year in any event. Nor can we accurately predict which offenders are likely to commit particularly serious crimes if they do reoffend (Ashworth, 2005: 206–7, 215–6): our powers of prediction are simply not up to the job, whether we use impressionistic guesswork, psychological testing, statistical prediction techniques or any other method. If we do try to pick out individuals in any of these ways and subject them to extra-long sentences on the basis of our predictions, we will be imprisoning a large number of people who would not in fact reoffend; typically at least twice as many as those who actually would offend again. And even if it was possible to target potential recidivists or those likely to commit grave crimes, this would run into the ethical objection that we were punishing people not for what they have done but for what they *might* do in the future – punishment for imaginary crimes in the future rather than real ones in the past – which might not be fundamentally wrong in principle to a utilitarian, but is a serious objection for most moral codes, including retributivism and **human rights theory**.

It seems unlikely, then, that incapacitation can provide a general justification for our present practice of imprisonment, let alone justify increasing our use of imprisonment, or introducing any new incapacitatory measures. Nevertheless, the current trend in both England and the United States is for governments to create new sentences explicitly aimed at achieving incapacitation even if the punishment inflicted is out of all proportion to the offence committed. Most US jurisdictions now have so-called '**three strikes and you're out**' laws, whereby repeat offenders are automatically jailed for life for a third offence.[2] Under these laws, people have literally been sent to prison for life for offences such as stealing a slice of pizza, which was the third offence of the unfortunate Jerry Williams in California in 1995 (*Guardian*, 13 October 1995). Since 1997 England has also adopted the 'three strikes and you're out' principle, with various mandatory prison sentences for burglars, drug dealers and those convicted of unlawful possession of firearms, as well as introducing extended and indefinite sentences (such as the now-abolished imprisonment for public protection) to protect the public from offenders who are thought to be dangerous (see Chapters 4 and 7, sections 4.4 and 7.3).

Reform

Reform (or **rehabilitation**: we shall be using these two words more or less interchangeably) is the idea that punishment can reduce the incidence of crime by taking a form which will improve the individual offender's character or behaviour and make him or her less likely to reoffend in future. Reform as the central aim of the penal system was a highly popular notion in the 1950s and 1960s, when penological thought was dominated by the rehabilitative ideal. Some proponents of

---

[2] 'Three strikes and you're out' sentences have also been defended on the grounds that they enhance deterrence; potential offenders are supposedly deterred by the knowledge that if caught and convicted they will receive an automatic prison sentence. Given what we have already said about deterrence, this seems unlikely. In any event, studies of 'three strikes' laws have demonstrated that, like so much else in criminal justice, they make no measurable difference to crime rates (Stolzenberg and D'Allessio, 1997; Zimring et al., 2001) whether by deterring or incapacitating.

reform (of a kind known as 'positivists': see section 2.5 below) have favoured a particularly strong version of this ideal called the **treatment model**. This viewed criminal behaviour not as freely willed action but (either metaphorically or literally) as a symptom of some kind of mental illness which should not be punished but treated like an illness.

For some advocates of rehabilitation, optimism about reforming offenders has extended to the sentence of imprisonment, with incarceration being seen not so much as a retributive or deterrent punishment but as an opportunity to provide effective reformative training and treatment. For most rehabilitationists, however, the conventional wisdom has long been that 'prison doesn't work' in reforming offenders, and so cannot be justified in these terms. Figures showing high rates of reoffending following release from custody are often quoted as bearing this out: currently, 48 per cent of adults released from prison are known to reoffend within a year (Ministry of Justice, 2012e), while an earlier study found that after seven years, 73 per cent of released prisoners have been convicted of another offence (Kershaw, 1999: 11). Statistics such as these once led a Conservative government to famously state (in the same 1990 White Paper we quoted previously) that imprisonment 'can be *an expensive way of making bad people worse*' (Home Office, 1990a: para. 2.7; our italics).

Although once dominant in penal discourse, the ideal of reform became discredited in the early 1970s, a development known as the '*collapse of the rehabilitative ideal*' (Bottoms, 1980). This was partly due to research results which suggested that penal measures intended to reform offenders were no more effective in preventing **recidivism** than were punitive measures. The received wisdom about reform came to be that 'nothing works', that 'whatever you do to offenders makes no difference', although this was always an exaggeration. It is true that in the 1970s extensive reviews of research in the United States (Lipton et al., 1975) and in Britain (Brody, 1976) found it to be *generally* the case that different penal measures had equally unimpressive outcomes in terms of reoffending. Similarly, many studies (for example, Kershaw et al., 1999) have found that, when account is taken of the differing characteristics of offenders sentenced to custody and various types of **community sentence**, the type of sentence they receive seems to make no discernible difference to whether they reoffend or not. However, studies from the 1970s onwards have also found examples of reformative programmes which seem to work to some extent with certain groups of offenders (see Palmer, 1975). The generalized conclusion (associated with the American Robert Martinson, 1974) that 'nothing works' became widely accepted – not so much because it had been shown to be true, more because the disappointment of the high hopes invested in reform led to an over-reaction against the rehabilitative ideal.

In recent years (since the early 1990s in Britain) there has been something of a revival of the reformative approach. The new attitude – sometimes associated with the managerialist Strategy B approach to criminal justice (see the Introduction) – has been that '*something* works', that systematic experimentation, research and monitoring can identify what works – effective methods of dealing with offenders – and is already doing so. However, the claims which are now made for the effectiveness of reformative measures are usually more modest than those which were put forward during the period of rehabilitative optimism. Few nowadays hold to the 'medical' or 'treatment' models of punishment, or claim that science can provide a cure for all criminality. Reform tends now to be seen not as treatment, which is imagined to work independently of the will of the offender, but as measures which enable or assist rather than force offenders to improve their behaviour – what has been called 'facilitated change' rather than 'coerced cure' (Morris, 1974: 13–20).

Many such measures have in recent years been based on the **cognitive behavioural** approach, which attempts to change how offenders think by improving their cognitive and reasoning skills. This often takes the form of confronting them with the consequences and social unacceptability of their offending in the hope that they will as a result decide to change their attitudes towards breaking the law. Cognitive behavioural training also seeks to teach offenders skills and techniques for altering and controlling their behaviour. (Anger management is one kind of training which is based on cognitive behavioural principles.) Claims have been made that programmes based on the cognitive behavioural approach can reduce reoffending by around 10–15 per cent, and by more if they are effectively targeted on those offenders who can best benefit from them, whereas punishments which are designed as deterrents tend to *increase* delinquency. (For example, Lipsey (1995), McGuire (1995 and 2002). For a more equivocal overview of the evidence see Debidin and Lovbakke, 2005.) The cognitive behavioural approach has won official backing, and accreditation processes have been set up both within the Prison Service and in the probation service to ensure that training programmes are in accordance with its principles (Debidin and Lovbakke, 2005: 32).

This kind of approach does not deny the offender's free will, rather it appeals to it, aiming to better enable offenders to do what they really want to do. It follows that reform depends at the end of the day on the offender's own choice, so it can never be guaranteed to work. But it may still be well worth trying, even though we retain a degree of scepticism about some of the more enthusiastic claims for the effectiveness of reformative programmes. The empirical evidence may have long ago destroyed the reformative aim as a plausible *general justification of the penal system*, but reform remains a reductivist aim which it is right to pursue *within* a system of punishment – including within prisons – provided we can find some other general justification.

A Rehabilitation Revolution?

A revival in official popularity of attempting to reform offenders was noticeable during the period of New Labour (1997–2010), and is currently being taken further by the Coalition government which came to power in May 2010 promising a '**rehabilitation revolution**', no less. This policy, which had been developed and announced by the Conservatives prior to the 2010 election (Conservative Party, 2008), combines enthusiasm for reforming offenders with Conservative belief in market mechanisms and the privatization of public services (discussed further in Chapters 5 and 6). It involves the introduction of 'payment by results' so that agencies with responsibility for offenders are paid more for producing lower reoffending rates. A pioneering payment by results scheme commenced in 2010 at Peterborough Prison: voluntary organizations are working to train and support inmates within prison and after release, and investors funding the project will only receive a return on their investment if reoffending rates are lower than would normally be expected. Then in 2011 it was announced that Doncaster Prison will henceforth be run by the private firm Serco on a similar payment by results basis, with Serco getting full payment only if its prisoners' reoffending rates are reduced.

The government believes that such schemes could lead to significant reductions in reoffending and thereby to considerable savings on reconvicting and re-imprisoning offenders. Without wishing to dampen the government's enthusiasm for rehabilitation, we fear that this may well be over-optimistic. For although as we have seen the notion that 'nothing works' to reform offenders is now discredited and it seems that *some* interventions can claim *modest* reductions in reoffending compared with other measures for *some* offenders, it is difficult to maintain significant relative success rates with any type of intervention (see Bottoms, 2004). The strategy also presupposes that penal agencies (especially in the private and voluntary sectors) will be adept at identifying and implementing effective rather than ineffective rehabilitation programmes. Given the still primitive nature of knowledge about how to reform offenders, such an assumption requires quite a leap of faith.

Just Deserts: Retributivism and Denunciation

Retributivism

2.3 The retributivist principle – that wrongdoers should be punished because they deserve it – is in some ways the complete antithesis of reductivism. Where reductivism is forward-looking, retributivism looks backwards in time, to the offence. It is the fact that the offender has committed a wrongful act which deserves punishment, not the future consequences of the punishment, which is important to the retributivist. Retributivism claims that it is in some way morally right to return evil for evil, that two wrongs can somehow make a right.

If people are to be punished because they deserve it, it is natural to say that they should also be punished as severely as they deserve – that they should get their just deserts. Retributivism thus advocates what is known as a **tariff**, a set of punishments of varying severity which are matched to crimes of differing seriousness: minor punishments for minor crimes, more severe punishments for more serious offences. The punishment should fit the crime in the sense of being in proportion to the moral culpability shown by the offender in committing the crime. The Old Testament *lex talionis* (an eye for an eye, a life for a life, etc.) is one example of such a tariff, but only one: a retributive tariff could be considerably more lenient than this, as long as the proportionate relationship between crimes and punishments is retained.

This is a point which needs stressing, because it is a common mistake – certainly among our own students – to assume that retributivists are those who advocate the harshest punishments, and to equate retributivism with a draconian, Strategy A approach to criminal justice. In fact, many retributivists (for example, those who follow the **justice model** of punishment discussed in section 2.5) actually favour relatively *lenient* punishment. On the other hand, some notable exponents of Strategy A – a still-iconic example being Michael Howard, Conservative Home Secretary from 1992 to 1997 – have attempted to justify their harsh penal policies by appeals to their supposed effectiveness in controlling crime by reductivist mechanisms such as deterrence and incapacitation. Confusing retributivism with penal severity is an understandable mistake, and there may be a certain psychological truth behind it. Maybe, whatever their proclaimed motives, many advocates of Strategy A are primarily motivated more by a hatred of criminals and a wish to see them 'get what they deserve' than by a desire to pursue rational steps to reduce crime. But retributivism is not inherently harsher than other philosophies, and indeed it has certain features which may be attractive to those of a humane disposition.

One of these attractive features is its consonance with what is generally acknowledged to be one fundamental principle of justice: that like cases should be treated alike. (For retributivists, 'like' means alike in the intuitively appealing sense of 'similarly deserving'.) Another attractive feature of retributivism is that there is a natural connection between the retributive approach and the idea that both offenders and victims have *rights*. Reductivist theory (at least in its utilitarian form) has always found it difficult to encompass the notion of rights, even when it comes to asserting that entirely innocent people have a right not to be punished. (Supposing we could achieve all the usual desired reductive consequences of punishment by framing an innocent person, why should a utilitarian logically object?) Retributivism has no such problem, since it follows automatically from the retributive principle that it must be wrong to punish non-offenders who obviously deserve no punishment. Nor may we punish criminals to a greater extent than their crimes are felt to deserve (for example, in the hope of reforming or incapacitating them or deterring others): under the retributivist principle offenders have a right to go free once they have paid their debt to society. Life imprisonment for stealing a pizza would be ruled out as disproportionate, for example. Retributivism thus fits in well with our common-sense intuitions which insist that it is indeed morally relevant whether the person we are punishing has behaved well, badly or very badly. Probably for this reason, it has proved a remarkably resilient idea. For many years retributivism was regarded (at least in academic circles) as outmoded and even atavistic, but it enjoyed a major revival from the early 1970s onwards, notably in the form of the justice model (see section 2.5 below) – though since the 1990s it has again been less fashionable.

However, retributivism is not without its own philosophical difficulties. One problem is how to justify the retributive principle itself. It may accord with some of our moral gut reactions, which seem to tell us that wrongdoers should be made to suffer. But maybe these reactions are merely irrational vindictive emotions (akin to vengeance) which, morally speaking, we ought to curb rather than indulge. A related objection is that it is not immediately clear how the retributivist principle relates to any general notion of what is right or wrong. At least utilitarian reductivism has the virtue that it can be derived from the general moral and political theory of utilitarianism.

Some theorists have attempted to counter these objections by reference to the 'social contract', a theory which provides a general account of political obligation (see especially Murphy, 1979). The idea is that all citizens are bound together in a sort of multilateral contract which defines our reciprocal rights and duties. The terms of this contract include the law of the land, which applies fairly and equally to all of us. The lawbreaker has disturbed this equilibrium of equality and gained an unfair advantage over those of us who have behaved well and abided by the rules. Retributive punishment restores the balance by cancelling out this advantage with a commensurate disadvantage. It thus ensures that wrongdoers do not profit from their wrongdoings, and is justified because if we failed to punish lawbreakers it would be unfair to the law-abiding.

This 'modern retributivism' was highly influential for a time, although it was always far from universally accepted and it eventually became discredited even in the eyes of some of its foremost former advocates (von Hirsch, 1986: ch. 5; Murphy, 1992: 24–5, 47–8; von Hirsch, 1993: ch. 2). But even if we assume that it is sound at an abstract philosophical level, it would be extremely dubious to assert that this theory can justify our present practices of punishment or anything like them. One serious difficulty is that the theory only applies if our society is a just one in which all citizens are genuinely equal; otherwise there is no equilibrium of equality for punishment to restore. If – as appears to be the case – detected offenders typically start from a position of social disadvantage (which means that the obligation to obey the law weighs more heavily upon them than on others) then punishment will tend to increase inequality rather than do the opposite. In fact, this was exactly the conclusion once reached by the modern retributivist Jeffrie Murphy (1979: 95), who stated that 'modern societies largely lack the moral right to punish'. Even if such a sweeping conclusion is not warranted, retributivists should be strongly critical of many aspects of our penal system. Not least among these are the lack of consistency in sentencing practices (see Chapter 4), and an increasing number of mandatory and incapacitatory sentences (see Chapters 4 and 7), which mean that offenders are to a great extent not dealt with in proportion to their just deserts. They should also disapprove strongly of provisions and practices which concentrate more punishment on persistent offenders rather than those whose current offences are the most serious. So despite its resilience and its various attractions, retributivism remains an implausible justification for our actual practices of punishment.

More promisingly, perhaps, retributivism is sometimes combined with reductivism to produce 'hybrid' or 'compromise' theories (Honderich, 1984: ch. 6). Often these compromise theories state, in effect, that punishment is only justified if it is both deserved *and* likely to have reductivist effects on crime (for example, von Hirsch, 1976: chs 5 and 6). One such compromise theory is 'limiting retributivism'. This theory states that punishment may be inflicted for forward-looking purposes such as the reduction of crime, but it is nevertheless wrong to punish anyone by *more* than they deserve. Thus the retributive principle *limits* the amount of punishment which may be imposed for reasons other than retribution. We shall return to this principle of limiting retributivism in section 2.7, and shall find reasons to approve of it – which are also, however, reasons to criticize many of the punishments which are actually inflicted within the penal system that we have.

Denunciation

Lord Denning classically explained the notion of denunciation as follows when giving evidence to the Royal Commission on Capital Punishment in the 1950s (Gowers, 1953: para. 53):

> The punishment for grave crimes should adequately reflect the revulsion felt by the great majority of citizens for them. It is a mistake to consider the objects of punishment as being deterrent or reformative or preventive and nothing else . . . The ultimate justification of punishment is not that it is a deterrent, but that it is the emphatic denunciation by the community of a crime.

The idea that punishment does and should demonstrate society's abhorrence of the offence, and that this somehow justifies punishment, is quite a popular one. For example, it was explicitly cited as a rationale for the sentence in the 1981 case of Marcus Sarjeant, an unemployed teenager who fired blanks at the Queen during the Trooping the Colour ceremony. Sentencing Sarjeant to five years' imprisonment, Lord Lane (the Lord Chief Justice) said: 'The public sense of outrage must be marked. You must be punished for the wicked thing you did' (*The Times*, 15 September 1981). Like retributivism, denunciation leads fairly naturally to the conclusion that punishments should be proportionate to the seriousness of the crime – just deserts – to ensure that the right amount of social condemnation of the crime is expressed.

Denunciation might be advocated for more than one reason. What we like to call *instrumental denunciation* is actually a form of reductivism (which we discuss at this stage for convenience). This is the idea that denunciation can help to reduce the incidence of crime – a notion which may at first seem somewhat obscure, but which has a distinguished intellectual pedigree. Émile Durkheim (1960: vol. 1, ch. 2; see below, Chapter 3, section 3.3) argued that one function of the criminal law and punishment was to reinforce the 'conscience collective' of society and thereby ensure that members of society continued to refrain from crime. Punishment, Durkheim thought, has an educative effect. It does not only teach people to obey the law out of fear and prudence (which is deterrence); it also sends a symbolic moral message that the offender's action is socially abhorred, and therefore wrong.

As with general deterrence, it is difficult on the evidence to make very strong claims about the effectiveness of denunciation in terms of crime control. Research suggests that members of the public are not influenced in their moral attitudes towards offences by the punishments which are imposed (or which they believe are imposed). People seem to have sufficient *respect for the law* to disapprove more strongly of an action when a law is passed against it, but they do not have sufficient *respect for the criminal justice system* to be influenced by the severity of the punishment inflicted (Walker and Marsh, 1984; cf. Tyler, 1990: 44–7). This suggests that instrumental denunciation cannot justify any particular level of severity of punishment; nor can the courts or penal system (as is sometimes fondly imagined) 'give a lead' to public opinion about the rights and wrongs of how people should behave.

A different version of denunciation theory (and the one we suspect Lords Denning and Lane subscribed to) is what we term *expressive denunciation*. This is the (non-forward-looking) notion that punishment is justified *simply* because it is the expression of society's abhorrence of crime. Sometimes this is explained in terms of the community showing its recognition of and commitment to its own values.

The claim is therefore that denunciatory punishment is justified *even if it has no good consequences* such as educating the public conscience and thereby reducing the amount of crime. When posed in such stark but accurate terms it becomes difficult to see why this is supposed to amount to a distinct moral justification for punishment. It looks suspiciously like knee-jerk retributivism, spuriously ennobled by reference to the 'community'. Perhaps it is right that the official institutions of a community should express moral judgements on behalf of its law-abiding members – but why should it have to take the form of *punishment*? Why – unless perhaps we are closet retributivists or reductivists – should not offenders simply be formally denounced with words and ceremony and then set free? Unless we care nothing for human freedom and are impervious to human suffering, denunciation seems an implausible *general justification* for a system which deliberately inflicts punishment on people.

Nevertheless, there may be something to be said for the notion of denunciation. The conviction and punishment of an offender carry a moral, condemnatory message and are seen as so doing. Perhaps, as we have seen, members of the public are currently not greatly influenced by such messages, but it is still wrong to make incorrect moral statements. It follows that it is wrong to convict and punish someone who has done nothing morally wrong. And if it makes sense to punish at all, there is some point in trying to punish offenders at least roughly in proportion to the moral gravity of their offences. Denunciation may not on its own provide a general justification for having a penal system, but it may help provide us with one acceptable *principle of distribution* for punishment, to be applied when we decide how severely individual offenders should be punished. But it is only one such acceptable principle, not the only one. Other relevant considerations, including the rehabilitation of the offender and the pursuit of restoration, can also legitimately enter the equation when deciding on punishments (see Cavadino and Dignan, 1997).

A theory which has something in common with denunciation is the 'communicative theory' of punishment put forward by Antony Duff (1986). Duff sees punishment as an attempt at a moral dialogue with offenders, censuring their actions and hoping to secure their contrition, with the result that they mend their ways. We doubt whether this theory can, on its own, provide an adequate justification for punishment, let alone for our current practices. But the idea that penal practices can and should be designed to foster this kind of moral dialogue is an attractive one.

It fits in well with the cognitive behavioural approach to reforming offenders (see above, section 2.2), and with the ideas and practices we discuss under the next heading.

Restorative Justice

2.4 The idea of restorative justice (see generally Dignan, 2005a) is an approach to dealing with crime which has come very much to the fore in recent years, including finding favour with both the New Labour government of 1997 to 2010 and the current Coalition government, although it has still made only limited inroads into criminal justice practice. Restorative justice (also sometimes known as reparative or relational justice) seeks to restore or repair the relations between the offender, the victim and the community, which have been damaged by the commission of the crime, and to reintegrate the offender back into the community. To put things right, the offender is encouraged to accept responsibility for having committed the crime, to acknowledge its wrongfulness and to make amends to those who have been hurt or harmed by the crime. Although, as we shall see, one possible benefit of responding to crime in this way is that it may encourage offenders to behave better in future and thereby reform them, the pursuit of restoration is very much an aim in its own right, not merely one way of achieving reformation.

Victims in particular are identified by advocates of restorative justice as being in numerous ways ignored, marginalized and mistreated by traditional criminal justice procedures which concentrate on the offender rather than the victim. (And indeed restorative justice schemes to date have a good record in terms of victim satisfaction, scoring significantly better in this respect than the ordinary criminal justice system (Dignan, 2005a: 163.)) Many proponents of restorative justice put it forward as a new 'paradigm' – a way of approaching crime and our responses to it which is completely different from our current system of criminal justice, and which should ideally replace it altogether. Others have more modest ambitions and intentions, merely seeking to incorporate elements of restorative justice into the existing system and provide increased opportunities to divert cases out of the traditional system into restorative schemes of various kinds. Most people accept that restorative justice has its limitations and is not appropriate for all crimes, all offenders and all victims (Dignan, 2005a: ch. 6); but it is more widely applicable than might initially be thought. For example, not all crimes have identifiable individual victims, but **mediation** can work very well when the victim is a corporate entity such as a business, even a large one (Dignan, 1991). Where there is no victim as such or the victim does not wish to participate in the process, the interests of victims and the wider community in general can nevertheless be represented in the restorative process, and amends can be made to the community or to victims generally in various ways (including community service work).

The objectives of restorative justice may be pursued by a variety of methods, which seek to provide an opportunity for those affected by the offence to deliberate together on the most appropriate way of responding to it. The three most important restorative justice processes which have been used in this country are *victim/offender mediation*, *conferencing* and *citizen panels*. Of these, only mediation actually requires the victim to participate, whether directly (involving a face-to-face dialogue between victim and offender in the presence of a neutral mediator) or indirectly (where the mediator acts as a go-between). People other than the direct victim – including the families of both victim and offender, and representatives of the local community – may also be 'stakeholders' with an interest in how the offence is resolved, and other restorative justice processes such as conferencing provide a forum within which they too may participate. 'Police-led conferencing', as the name suggests, is convened and facilitated by the police, whereas in 'family group conferencing' the facilitator is more likely to be a government official. Citizen panels provide an informal forum in which lay people may deliberate with offenders, family members and others (possibly including victims) about the offence and its impact with a view to negotiating a 'contract' with the offender who undertakes to make amends in agreed ways.

Restoration and reparation can take place within a variety of legal contexts. It can occur without any legal formality or compulsion being involved; it can happen in the context of offenders being cautioned by the police; or it can form part of a court sentence such as a compensation order, community order or young offender **referral order**. We discuss various measures which incorporate principles of restorative justice in later chapters, in particular Chapters 5 and 8 (sections 5.3 and 8.2), and shall have more to say about the general idea of restorative justice in Chapter 10 (section 10.3).

Both the previous New Labour government and the current ruling Coalition have shown support for restorative justice – not (needless to say) as a whole new paradigm to replace the entire criminal justice system, but as a principle and type of practice worthy of an enhanced place within and alongside the existing system. In 2003 the New Labour government published a strategy for restorative justice (Home Office, 2003b: 4), stating that 'restorative justice can have an important part to play at all stages of the criminal justice system'. The Criminal Justice Act of the same year established reparation as one statutory purpose of sentencing (in section 142, discussed later), while New Labour's previous Crime and Disorder Act of 1999 and other legislation contained a number of new provisions capable of being operated in a restorative manner (Dignan, 1999). The new Coalition government has also signalled its support for restorative justice. Junior Justice Minister Crispin Blunt said in July 2010 that he was looking to 'embed restorative justice measures across every phase of the criminal justice process' (*Guardian*, 21 July 2010), and similar sentiments were expressed in the 2010 **Green Paper** *Breaking the Cycle* and subsequent policy documents in 2011 and 2012, notably the consultation document *Getting it Right for Victims and Witnesses*, discussed further in Chapter 5 (section 5.3) (Ministry of Justice, 2010a; 2011a; 2012a).

Restorative justice's objective of communicating with the offender about the wrongfulness of the crime has clear affinities with Antony Duff's communicative theory discussed briefly under the previous heading. Two other objectives of restorative justice, which we now proceed to discuss, are reparation and **reintegrative shaming**.

Reparation is the notion that people who have offended should do something to 'repair' the wrong they have done. This can take the form of compensating the victim of the offence or doing something else to assist the victim. If there is no individual or identifiable victim (or if the victim is unwilling to accept it), reparation can be made to the community as a whole by performing community service or paying a fine into public funds. 'Symbolic reparation' can also occur, for example in the form of an apology for having committed the offence. Reparation is a sound and valid principle which we strongly favour (Dignan, 1994; Cavadino and Dignan, 1997). It can be seen as a desirable aim in its own right, or as a useful method for assisting the reintegration of offenders (as we discuss next), or as a valuable but secondary aim which may be pursued when imposing punishment that is justified on other grounds (such as reductivism). If punishment is to be inflicted, it is surely better that the punishment should take a form which directly benefits the victim or society rather than merely hurting the offenders or restricting their liberty.

Restorative justice has increasingly been linked to and underpinned by a general theory of crime and punishment propounded by John Braithwaite (1989). Braithwaite claims that successful societal responses to crime are those which bring about the reintegrative shaming of the offender. Offenders should be dealt with in a manner that shames them before other members of their community. But the shaming should not be of a 'stigmatizing' nature which will tend to exclude them from being accepted members of the community; this (as the labelling theory we mentioned in section 2.2 suggests) will be counter-productive, as it will make reoffending much more likely. Instead, the shaming should be of a kind which serves to reintegrate offenders, by getting them to accept that they have done wrong while encouraging others to readmit them to society. The measures and processes associated with restorative justice are particularly suitable for pursuing reintegrative shaming (Dignan, 1994), for the performance of reparation shames the offender symbolically while seeking to set matters right between the offender, the victim and the community. If this all works effectively, then restorative justice could be a valuable method of *reforming* offenders. Recent evidence on this score is encouraging. A study of three restorative justice schemes for adult offenders found that offenders who participated in these schemes committed significantly fewer offences in the following two years than similar offenders who were dealt with differently (Shapland et al., 2008).

Even if restorative justice were to prove no more effective in controlling crime than the traditional criminal justice system, it would still in our opinion be a preferable approach wherever it can feasibly be applied. (We shall return to this in Chapter 10.) It is obvious, however, that the principles and objectives of restorative justice cannot begin to justify the penal system that we have, since most punishments (and most notably imprisonment) contain little or no restorative element, and may even make it difficult or impossible for the offender to make amends. (It may be hard to do reparative work for the victim or community while you are locked up in prison, for example.) But if restoration were more consistently pursued, we should have a much more civilized and morally accept-able penal system than the present one.

Schools of Penal Thought

2.5 The various justifications for punishment we have outlined have waxed and waned in relative popularity over time. In this section we provide a brief history of the development of penal thought in the West to show how different combinations of penal justifications have found favour in different eras.

The Classical School: Deterrence and the Tariff

The year 1764 saw the publication of one of the most influential works of penal philosophy of all time – *Dei Delitti e delle Pene* [On Crimes and Punishments] by the Italian, Cesare Beccaria (Beccaria, 1963). This book, the seminal work of the 'classical' schools of criminal law and **penology**, provided a thoroughgoing critique of the criminal justice systems of eighteenth-century Europe along with a blue-print for reform along more rational and humane lines.

To understand the classicists it helps to have some understanding of what they were reacting against. Punishment under the *ancien régime* of eighteenth-century Europe was both arbitrary and harshly retributive, dominated by capital and cor-poral punishments. Moreover, **due process** in the form of effective legal safeguards against wrongful conviction was all but absent in the criminal justice system of the time, and even the laws defining which actions were criminal were vague and extremely wide. On the other hand, the existence of wide discretion in the hands of judges and of the sovereign (notably in the form of the royal pardon, which was extensively used) meant that the guilty were as likely to go unpunished as were the innocent to be wrongly convicted and harshly dealt with. The classicists claimed that such a system was not only inhumane and unfair, but also profoundly irrational and inefficient for the task of controlling crime.

Beccaria's blueprint called for clarity in the law and due process in criminal procedure combined with certainty and regularity of punishment. There should be a definite, fixed penalty for every offence, laid down in advance by the legislature in a strict tariff. These penalties should be proportionate to the gravity of the offence but as mild as possible, in contrast to the 'useless prodigality of torments' which characterized the existing system. Once an offender was found guilty, how-ever, the sentence should follow automatically; in the strict classicism of Beccaria there was no room for clemency by way of pardons, the reduction of sentences because of mitigating circumstances, or an early release from the punishment laid down. All people were to be treated as fully responsible for their own actions, including their own offences.

The intellectual influence of classicism, and of Beccaria in particular, was enor-mous. Its principles were praised by reforming monarchs such as Frederick II of

Prussia, Maria Theresa of Austria and Catherine the Great of Russia; the French Code introduced by the revolutionary regime in 1791 tried to directly implement his plan for a rigid tariff of punishments; and Beccaria also greatly influenced English jurists such as Romilly and Blackstone. His greatest impact was, however, on the framing of codes of criminal law rather than on penal systems. Beccaria's blueprint was never implemented in full.

Classicism grew out of the Enlightenment, the eighteenth-century philosophical movement which stressed the importance of human reason and which undertook the critical reappraisal of existing ideas and social institutions. Beccaria made particular use of the Enlightenment notion of the social contract as the source of legitimate political authority. He argued that rational people drawing up a just social contract would only be willing to grant governments the power to punish to the extent that was necessary to protect themselves from the crimes of others. It followed that punishments should be no harsher than was necessary to achieve reductivist ends by means of deterrence. From this he derived his proposal for a tariff of fixed, certain penalties, proportionate to the offence but relatively mild by the standards of his own day. (Thus, like retributivists he advocated a proportional tariff, although he was himself a reductivist.) Beccaria opposed capital punishment as being cruel and inefficient as a deterrent. Punishments should, he said, be public and of a kind appropriate to the type of offence: corporal punishments for crimes of violence, public humiliation for 'crimes founded on pride' and so on. This would, he thought, assist in deterrence because 'in crude, vulgar minds, the seductive picture of a particularly advantageous crime should immediately call up the associated idea of punishment' (Beccaria, 1963: 57).

In general, Beccaria's philosophy exhibits what could be regarded as a curious combination of concern with the rights of the individual under the social contract on the one hand, and utilitarian reductivism on the other – curious because **rights theory** and utilitarianism are often thought to be philosophically incompatible. Yet he explicitly appeals to both concepts. (Indeed, not only did Beccaria use the concept of utility, but Bentham himself acknowledged his intellectual debt to Beccaria in the most fulsome terms and is even believed to have first encountered the phrase 'the greatest happiness of the greatest number' in Beccaria's master work: see Beccaria, 1963: x–xi, 8.) This intriguingly attractive blend of rights theory with forward-looking reductivism is one of the features that make Beccaria a continually fascinating and influential penal thinker even today.

Bentham and Neo-Classicism: Deterrence and Reform

The Englishman Jeremy Bentham (1748–1832), the main founder of the utilitarian philosophy, was also a major penal thinker and reformer. His penal thinking was an application of his general philosophy that law and government should pursue 'the greatest happiness of the greatest number', which logically led him to espouse a purely reductivist approach to punishment, with no place for retributivism of any description. Despite the intellectual debt he acknowledged to Beccaria, his ideas differed from those of his Italian predecessor in several respects. At a philosophical level he had no time for notions of the social contract or human rights (he famously described the idea of natural rights as 'nonsense upon stilts'.) Like Beccaria he regarded clarity and due process in the criminal law as desirable, but from a purely utilitarian point of view. Similarly, he followed Beccaria in advocating a proportionate tariff of punishments for offences. Like Beccaria he said that punishment should be primarily justified because of its deterrent effects, but he also proclaimed that punishment of the right kind could serve a further reductivist aim: that of reform.

His model of utilitarian punishment was exemplified most famously in the **Panopticon** – a prison he designed and narrowly failed to persuade the British government to let him build. The Panopticon was designed in such a way that prisoners were under constant surveillance by inspectors in a central observation tower. Prisoners were to be made to perform productive work within the prison in a consistent and regular manner in order that they should acquire rational work habits which they would retain after release instead of returning to crime. Thus, whereas classicism's image of human nature portrayed all human beings as being fully responsible for their own actions, Bentham saw criminals as having limited rationality and responsibility, but thought that they could be made more rational by the correct application of reformative techniques in his 'mill for grinding rogues honest', as he called the Panopticon. His thinking also took account of limited human rationality on the question of responsibility for offences; unlike Beccaria he allowed for mitigating circumstances such as duress, infancy and insanity to reduce or even remove an individual's liability to punishment.

Beccaria's ideas had been fated to win great praise but achieve less by way of practical influence in the running of penal systems. Bentham's success was greater but far from total. Utilitarian reductivism became a prominent rationale for punishment but never displaced retributivism entirely. Criminal justice systems in the nineteenth century developed along *neo-classical* lines. This meant that criminal laws were clarified and in some countries codified, as both Beccaria and Bentham advocated, but leaving a greater degree of flexibility and judicial discretion than either would have found congenial. For example, the highly Beccarian French Code of 1791 was soon revised to reintroduce recognition of mitigating circumstances, judicial discretion in sentencing and the prerogative of mercy.

The Benthamite approach had its greatest impact in respect of one of its greatest points of difference from Beccarian classicism: the *form* that the punishment should take. Beccaria's scheme had no place for imprisonment as a punishment. (He only discussed imprisonment as the temporary incarceration of a suspect before trial, and while he did advocate penal servitude as a punishment for certain offences, this was not to be served in prison.) Bentham by contrast saw prison, in the shape of the Panopticon, as a useful method of dealing with offenders. Although the Panopticon was never built exactly as he had designed it (a modified version was constructed at Millbank on the Thames and opened, with extremely poor results, in 1817), imprisonment rapidly became the pre-eminent method of punishment. As Foucault (1977) famously observed, the end of the eighteenth century and the early nineteenth century saw a massive shift (which Foucault called the '**great transformation**') from *corporal* to *carceral* punishment (see further Chapter 5).

Moreover, this was a new form of imprisonment whose aims were not confined to containing offenders for a period and deterring the populace from crime. It also set out to retrain (or '**discipline**' to use Foucault's word) the inmates, along the kind of lines Bentham advocated. As Foucault (1977: 16) put it, punishment no longer addressed itself to the body of the criminal, but to the soul.

Positivism: The Rehabilitative Ideal

A century after Cesare Beccaria's *Dei Delitti e delle Pene* saw the light of day there came the publication of another work by an Italian called Cesare, equally seminal and revolutionary but in most respects diametrically opposed to Beccaria's way of thinking. This was Cesare Lombroso's *L'Uomo Delinquente* [The Criminal Man] (1876). Lombroso is best known for his theory, an extension of Charles Darwin's ideas, that criminals were atavistic throwbacks to an earlier stage of evolution. But more important than this particular theory (which he was later to modify substantially) was Lombroso's role as the founder of the *positive school of criminology*. The positivist view is that crime, along with all other natural and social phenomena, is *caused* by factors and processes which can be discovered by scientific investigation. These causes are not necessarily genetic, but may include environmental factors such as family upbringing, social conditioning and so on. Positivists believe in the doctrine of **determinism**: the belief that human beings, including criminals, do not act from their own free will but are impelled to act by forces beyond their control. Thus, where Beccaria's vision of human nature had been one of untrammelled free will and while Bentham had admitted that the responsibility of some humans was limited, **positivism** denies responsibility altogether.

It follows (for the positivist) that it is wrong to hold people responsible for their crimes and punish them in ways that imply that their crimes are their own fault. Criminality is no more the fault of the offender than illness is the fault of the invalid, and both require treatment not blame. So retributivism is clearly excluded as a justification for punishment. Positivists also tend to be sceptical about deterrence, on the grounds that empirical evidence scientifically assessed demonstrates that punishment is ineffective as a deterrent. The reductivist methods favoured by positivism are incapacitation, and especially reform. Criminological science should be able to predict which offenders are likely to commit further crimes – and perhaps even (as in the film *Minority Report*) identify people who have not yet committed crimes but will do so in the future. Such people should be diagnosed by experts and given appropriate treatment which will prevent them from offending. If necessary they should be detained to incapacitate them in the meantime and ensure that they are available to be treated.

Positivism in its purest form rejects two important doctrines common to both **classicism** and **neo-classicism**, namely due process and **proportionality**. Due process is not appropriate in the diagnosis and treatment of crime any more than it is in medicine, since the scientific investigative process does not and should not proceed along legalistic lines. Proportionality is similarly seen as a mistaken notion, since there is no reason why the treatment needed by the offender should be in proportion to the gravity of the offence. Instead of the punishment fitting the crime, the treatment should fit the individual criminal. (For this reason the positivistic approach is sometimes referred to as the *individualized treatment model*.) Positivism particularly favours the **indeterminate sentence**: it is premature to decide at the time of sentence how long the offender should be detained for, since this may depend on how quickly the treatment works. Ideally therefore the release decision should be left in the hands of treatment experts to take at a later date.

Positivism, and the rehabilitative ideal associated with it, gradually came to dominate criminological thinking and rhetoric, reaching its zenith in the 1950s and 1960s, especially in the United States. For example, indeterminate and semi-indeterminate sentences (such as 'one year to life') became more and more common in the USA, with release dates dependent not upon the sentence passed at the trial but upon the parole process. This was a time of 'rehabilitative optimism': there was a widespread belief that criminology and other behavioural sciences would progressively discover the causes of crime and the way to cure all offenders of their criminality. In the 1970s, however, the positivist approach was dealt a series of severe blows which led to the collapse of the rehabilitative ideal. One of these blows (mentioned under 'Reform' in section 2.2 above) was cruelly self-inflicted: positivistic criminological research, far from demonstrating the effectiveness of treatment measures, seemed instead to show that treatment did not work ('nothing works'). At much the same time, positivism came under a powerful and sustained political and theoretical critique associated with the justice model.

The Justice Model: Just Deserts and Due Process

The justice model (Bottomley, 1980; Hudson, 1987) first emerged in the US as a critique of the positivistic individualized treatment model. The first book-length statement of the justice model in the 1970s was the American Friends Service Committee's report, *Struggle for Justice*, published in 1971 (other important works include von Hirsch, 1976; 1986; 1993). The authors claimed that the treatment model was 'theoretically faulty, systematically discriminatory in administration, and inconsistent with some of our most basic concepts of justice' (American Friends Service Committee, 1971: 12). Theoretically faulty, because the individualized treatment model identified the cause of crime as a pathology within the individual, whereas the authors saw the true causes of crime as structural, resulting from the way in which society is organized. Systematically discriminatory, because the wide discretion which positivism vested in supposed experts within the criminal justice system operated in practice to disadvantage offenders from poorer sections of society. And inconsistent with justice, because the lack of due process and proportionality in the treatment model offends our moral intuitions about the rights of the individual and the unfairness of treating offences of similar gravity in possibly widely varying ways. It was also felt that the positivistic notion that offenders were not rational and responsible agents and that they should be reprogrammed until they conform to society, was a profound insult to human dignity.

The justice model asserts two central principles, both of which hark back to the classicism of Beccaria. The first is due process in procedure, and the general limitation of official discretion within the criminal justice system. The second is proportionality of punishments to the gravity of offences – or in other words, that offenders should receive their *just deserts* for the crime they have committed. Disproportionate sentences with the alleged purpose of reforming the offender are to be rejected. This is so whether the reformative sentence would be disproportionately long or disproportionately short, although most adherents of the justice model in the 1970s (who tended to be liberal or moderately radical in political persuasion) wanted a just deserts system which would punish less harshly overall – again like Beccaria two centuries previously. It is not only reform as an aim of punishment that the justice model eyes with suspicion. Justice model writers are also mostly sceptical of the effectiveness of deterrence and even more so of the validity of constructing a just tariff of punishment on the basis of deterrence theory (as Beccaria and Bentham claimed to do). The justice model's philosophy consequently relies heavily on either retribution or denunciation as at least a partial justification for punishment.

The justice model made its impact on both sides of the Atlantic and elsewhere. In the USA many states moved substantially away from indeterminate sentences and positivistic devices such as parole. The high water mark of the justice model's influence in Britain was the just deserts strategy which was pursued by the British Conservative government prior to 1993 and which centred around the Criminal Justice Act 1991 (see the Introduction and Chapter 10, sections I.2 and 10.2). Although by no means representing the justice model in a pure form, the 1991 Act sought to establish just deserts as the primary aim of sentencing (Home Office, 1990a: paras 2.1–2.4). But as we shall see in Chapters 4 and 10 (sections 4.4 and 10.2), both the 1991 Act and its just deserts principles were to come rapidly to grief.

From Just Deserts to the New Punitiveness – and Beyond?

It is sometimes said that the justice model, although originally proposed by liberals and radicals who wished to reduce the overall harshness of punishment, was co-opted from the late 1970s onwards by the political Right (for example, Bottoms, 1980: 11; Hudson, 1987: 72). Whether or not this is the best way of describing the situation, it is true that some important strategies and approaches to punishment in this period combined aspects of the justice model with a generous dash of the populist, punitive ideology of law and order, which we discussed in Chapter 1 and which gathered ever greater influence between the 1970s and the present day. In the United States for much of the late 1970s and 1980s, for example, a kind of right-wing just deserts approach was highly influential: this retained a retributivist approach and a preference for proportionate, just deserts punishments, but unlike the liberal justice model it advocated *more severe* fixed-term sentences. Reformative measures are disfavoured by this approach not because (as the liberal justice model feared) they might be disproportionately harsh, but because they may be too soft. This approach also differed from the liberal justice model markedly in its attitude to due process: if anything it *disapproved* of excessive procedural safeguards on the grounds that they are likely to act as an obstacle to ensuring offenders receive their just deserts.

From the vantage point of the present day, these more punitive versions of just deserts assume the appearance of temporary staging posts on a rapid journey heading towards a new punitiveness (see the Introduction and Chapter 3). In Britain, we have heard little about just deserts – certainly from either Conservative or Labour politicians – since the law and order counter-reformation of 1992–93. In terms of the philosophy of punishment, the Conservative government then abandoned just deserts in favour of the assertion that 'prison works' by incapacitation and deterrence – although this was perhaps not so much philosophy as a rationalization designed to legitimate a populist set of tough (Strategy A) penal policies. Arguably, the historical role of the justice model – entirely contrary to the intentions of its progenitors – was to pave the way for the transition to a more punitive penal system and a more authoritarian society. Much of this punitiveness lived on under the New Labour government of 1997–2010 which had little time for the philosophy of just deserts, justifying its policies not on the basis that they provided a fair amount of punishment for offenders, but because they claimed them to be effective in controlling crime – which is of course reductivism. Within that general punitive and reductivist orientation the New Labour approach amalgamated elements of law and order ideology, an avowed intention to do 'what works' to reform offenders and a nod towards restorative justice (within limited confines). The resulting mélange of policies and philosophies has been called **neo-correctionalism** (see below, Chapter 8, sections 8.3 and 8.4).

An as-yet unanswered question – in this country and internationally – is whether the new punitiveness might have reached or passed its peak. The advent of the Conservative–Liberal Democrat coalition government elected in 2010 triggered a struggle between penal philosophies as Justice Secretary Kenneth Clarke attempted and mostly failed to introduce measures designed to reduce the prison population and to introduce a 'rehabilitation revolution' (see further Chapter 10, section 10.2, and section 2.2 above). For the moment the penal system continues to be shaped by the legacy of an era in which the harshness of punishment has escalated and by the hybrid neo-correctionalism of the New Labour regime.

Philosophies, Strategies and Attitudes

2.6

It is not as simple as one might imagine to relate these philosophies and schools of thought to the broad Strategies (Strategies A, B and C) we detailed in the Introduction. (To recap briefly, Strategy A is harshly punitive, Strategy B is managerialist and Strategy C is humane and rights-based.) Newcomers to the subject tend to assume that retributivism (with its traditional overtones of 'an eye for an eye') is the harshest philosophy and the one underlying the punitive Strategy A. It is indeed possible to espouse Strategy A and call for maximum punishment on the basis of a harsh interpretation of retributivism. But, as we have seen, proponents of Strategy A often seek to justify their policies on reductivist grounds, claiming for example that 'prison works' to deter and incapacitate. On the other hand, the retributivist philosophy insists not only that punishment should be proportionate to the offence, but also that it *should not be disproportionately severe because this would be undeserved.* This is, indeed, a central message of the justice model, most of whose proponents we would place under the heading of Strategy C, because they were concerned to minimize the violation of human rights involved in the infliction of excessively severe punishments.

So Strategy A can be based – although not necessarily with any great intellectual coherence – on either retributivism or reductivism (or indeed on the theory of denunciation). Proponents of the lenient, human rights-based Strategy C can also draw on any of these philosophies and justifications for punishment. Those whose humanitarianism takes the form of advocating reformative measures invoke reductivism (and the belief that reformative treatment can help reduce future crime); while, as we have seen, proponents of the justice model can appeal to either retributivism or denunciation, typically combined with reductivism in a hybrid justification for punishment. Those who favour restorative justice could be reductivists (believing that this kind of justice is the most effective at controlling crime) or may appeal to the desirability of reparation as an independent aim in its own right.

There is therefore no simple equation between the *philosophies* of punishment and what we term *strategies*. Both reductivism and retributivism can be either harsh or humane. However, when it comes to considering Strategy B – the managerialist strategy – there is one general philosophy which fits it very neatly. This is the philosophy of *utilitarianism* – the notion that one should always act in the interests of the 'greatest number' of people. The emphasis that managerialism places on effectiveness and cost-efficiency has a decidedly utilitarian tinge. So does the way in which managerialism is not greatly concerned about the human rights of individual offenders or about ensuring that offenders get their just deserts (however much or little that is conceived to be). It follows that a proponent of Strategy B should, if consistent, espouse utilitarian reductivism as the basic aim of punishment. And indeed, the rise of managerialism in criminal justice has occurred in conjunction with an increasing interest in 'what works' to reduce crime (by both general crime prevention measures and penal sanctions aimed at reducing recidivism, including reformative treatments) – and, significantly, what works most efficiently and cost-effectively. This utilitarian (Strategy B) agenda was very prominent in New Labour's criminal justice policies, and can be seen as one element in the current Coalition's 'rehabilitation revolution' (section 2.2 above and Chapter 10, section 10.2 below).

Underlying much of the conflict between different penal philosophies and strategies we can perhaps discern a very general tension between what could be termed two fundamentally different *attitudes* towards offenders. This is the contrast between *exclusive* and *inclusive* attitudes. The exclusive attitude rejects offenders as members of the community and seeks to shut them out of mainstream society by measures such as imprisonment. This attitude is allied to notions of deterrence, incapacitation and an illiberal version of retributivism. The inclusive attitude, on the other hand, seeks to maintain offenders within the community and reintegrate them into mainstream society. It can be found embodied in notions and practices of reform, resocialization, restorative justice and more liberal versions of retributivism (such as the justice model) (see further Cavadino et al., 1999: 48–50). Strategy A is clearly aligned with the exclusive attitude, and Strategy C with the inclusive; Strategy B, however, is essentially indifferent to the inclusion/exclusion dimension, and would favour whichever approach happens to work best in practice. We can see this conflict between inclusion and exclusion of the offender being played out throughout this book, including the philosophical debates covered in this chapter.

Conclusions: Punishment and Human Rights

2.7 The philosophies we have been outlining exert a very real influence on the shaping of penal systems and penal practices in the real world, but none of the various schools of thought has ever been totally dominant, even at the height of its popularity. No penal system has ever been entirely retributivist, or entirely reductivist, or thoroughly Beccarian. This impurity of the real world can be seen in the existing English system, which as we have seen accepts as legally accepted justifications for punishment retribution, deterrence, incapacitation, denunciation, reform and reparation in a promiscuously eclectic mixture (Criminal Justice Act 2003, s. 142). Government policies have been similarly eclectic, as a variety of penal aims and philosophies have been cited (often simultaneously) to justify policies whether harsh or relatively lenient. Reductivism rather than retributivism is currently in the ascendancy as a general principle, but with deterrence, incapacitation, reform and reparation all finding favour to various degrees.

Given this confusing welter of competing and combining philosophies, can we reach any valid conclusions about the rightness or otherwise of punishment? We think we can, although any such conclusions will inevitably be inherently controversial.

Any verdict we pass on punishment must be soundly based on an acceptable general moral philosophy. This does not necessarily mean that a diversity of penal aims is ruled out, but each of the different aims must be justified by the same general philosophy if our position is to be coherent. Our preferred philosophical basis is human rights theory rather than utilitarianism. Along with theorists such as Ronald Dworkin (1978) and Alan Gewirth (1978) we hold that each individual human being has certain fundamental rights which they possess equally by virtue of being human. These fundamental rights are variously described and vindicated by a variety of philosophical arguments to which we cannot do justice here. Suffice it to say that we think that at least one important human right can be described as a right – belonging equally to each human individual – to maximum **positive freedom**, by which we mean the ability of people to make effective decisions about their lives (Cavadino, 1997a).

If there is a right to positive freedom, then punishment (which reduces the freedom of the person punished) is *prima facie* wrong and requires special moral justification. It is difficult to see how punishment could be justified on purely retributivist grounds consistently with the positive freedom principle, and the same goes for expressive denunciation as a general justification of the system. For if retribution and denunciation were all that punishment achieved, the criminal's freedom would be gratuitously diminished without this doing anything to increase anyone else's freedom. However, rights theory allows for one person's *prima facie* right to be overridden in the interests of other individuals' more important 'competing rights' (see Dworkin, 1978). The relevant competing rights here are those of the potential victims of crime in the future. The commission of crimes against them will have the effect of diminishing their positive freedom, to which they also have a right. For example, crimes of injurious violence reduce the victims' freedom to operate physically free from pain, while property offences will deprive them of resources and thereby remove their freedom to choose to act in ways which require the use of those resources.[3] *The general justification for having a system of punishment must therefore be forward-looking and primarily reductivist*: based on the claim that punishment does something to reduce the incidence of crime, and thereby prevents the diminution of some other people's positive freedom. The most plausible mechanism by which punishment may be thought to achieve this aim is general deterrence, although other reductivist effects such as instrumental denunciation and incapacitation may make a secondary contribution.

The reductivist aim must, however, be pursued in a manner consistent with the human rights of the offender. We think that retributivists and denunciationists are right to insist that there is no justification for punishing someone who has not deliberately and wrongfully broken a just law and thereby exercised a freedom to which they are not entitled (because to do so diminishes other people's freedom). Rights theory therefore provides a basis for a principled compromise between reductivism and retributivism. It also follows that, although offenders do forfeit some portion of the rights citizens should normally enjoy, they still retain the status of human beings and therefore retain important human rights (Richardson, 1985) – a point on which we are closer to some retributivist thinkers than to classical utilitarianism.

We further agree with retributivists, denunciationists and justice model theorists that one valid general principle for the *distribution* of punishment is that offenders should be punished at least roughly in proportion to the moral gravity of their offences. Our main reason for this is an argument we referred to when discussing denunciation: that to punish disproportionately is to convey incorrect moral messages about the relative gravity of offences. But this principle – known as 'retribution in distribution' – is only one valid principle among others (Cavadino and Dignan, 1997),

---

[3]Not all crimes have individual victims; but many crimes that do not, have indirect effects which threaten to reduce the positive freedom of (perhaps many) individuals. For example, tax evasion depletes the public purse, which may have the effect of reducing public provision and thereby removing freedoms of various kinds from members of the public.

and is hardly inviolate in every single instance. We would take some convincing that it can be right to depart from it by punishing more harshly than an offender deserves on a standard tariff, for example by sentencing an offender to an exceptionally long custodial sentence for purposes of reform or incapacitation.[4] But we see no reason why it should not be acceptable (and consistent with our human rights philosophy) for aims such as reform and reparation to be considered and pursued when it has to be decided what punishment (if any) should be allocated to individual offenders, as long as this does not have the result of making the punishment harsher. The operative principle should therefore be a limiting retributivism, or a 'retributive maximum' (as advocated by Norval Morris, 1974: 75). An offender may be punished up to the level indicated by the proportionate tariff, but no more harshly; and there is no obligation to exact punishment of this severity if other valid considerations indicate that a more lenient course will be more constructive or humane. As Morris says, 'deserved justice and a discriminating clemency are not irreconcilable'.

This human rights-based approach leads, naturally enough, to the inclusive attitude towards offenders and to a Strategy C-type approach to criminal justice: one, indeed, which incorporates the concerns of the different varieties of Strategy C which we have identified. There is a place in this approach for proportionality in punishment (just deserts) – as explained in the previous paragraph – and also for reformative and restorative measures where it is possible and appropriate to apply them (Cavadino, 1997b: chs 2 and 3; Cavadino and Dignan, 1997). We particularly favour the restorative justice approach, for a variety of reasons. One is that many reparation schemes afford both offender and victim a say in determining the nature of the offender's punishment. This increases the positive freedom of the victim as well as the offender, a consideration which should normally justify a downwards departure from the proportional tariff (Cavadino and Dignan, 1997).

Strategy A is, as one would expect, anathema to this human rights approach for at least two reasons. First, it leads to punishments – such as 'three strikes and you're out' sentences – which are unfair to individual offenders because they are disproportionate, exceeding the offender's just deserts for the crime committed. And second, the general levels of punishment called for by Strategy A are also grossly excessive because of the 'overkill' involved: the relatively small amount of crime which is prevented by such heavy penalties compared with a more lenient regime is outweighed by the suffering and loss of liberty caused (Cavadino et al., 1999: 37–41). There is, however, room in our approach for Strategy B-type managerial techniques, provided these are used in the pursuit of human rights-based aims (Cavadino et al., 1999: ch. 2). For example, there is nothing wrong with using techniques such as research and monitoring to discover and apply 'what works' to reform offenders or help secure reparation for victims, and indeed we strongly favour such an evidence-based approach.

If our rights-based theory is the correct moral framework for punishment, how should we judge our current penal practices? Our own judgement is a severely

---

[4] Adopting the rights-based reasoning of Bottoms and Brownsword (1983), we would rule out extra-long incapacitatory sentences for all but the most 'vividly dangerous' offenders.

negative one, and for one central reason: *we punish too much* – and in particular, we imprison far too much. For the **principle of parsimony** applies as much to our forward-looking human rights theory as it does to utilitarianism: offenders have a right not to have their freedom gratuitously diminished to a degree greater than is necessary to produce the desired reductivist results. We would go so far as to argue that a thoroughgoing application of the principle of parsimony means that imprisonment should be used very sparingly indeed. It should be reserved for offenders who represent a serious danger to others and need to be incapacitated, and perhaps also – for very brief periods only – for offenders who intransigently refuse to co-operate with non-custodial measures. Otherwise, there is no morally legitimate aim of punishment which cannot be achieved just as well and more humanely by the use of non-custodial punishment (Cavadino et al., 1999: 117–20). But it is not necessary to follow us as far as this to accept the evidence that – as we saw under the heading of deterrence in section 2.2 – the existing penal system is engaging in a massive 'overkill' operation. This amounts to a scandalous infringement of the human rights of those who are punished excessively. And as punishment levels increase, so does the immorality of our penal practices.

It is not necessary to subscribe to human rights philosophy to agree with this conclusion. Indeed, we find it impossible to imagine a plausible and consistent moral philosophy which could justify our present penal practices or anything like them. (We have already seen that utilitarians and retributivists should also condemn our existing system.) It is difficult to resist the implication that our penal system is morally unjustifiable – morally bankrupt might not be too strong a phrase. Of course, not everyone is well versed in moral philosophy. But this is hardly necessary in order to make valid observations about how the penal system treats people unfairly, causes unnecessary suffering, does little to reduce crime and fails to punish offenders in accordance with their moral deserts. So perhaps it is no wonder that we are not the only ones who perceive the system as unjust, and that it finds itself with a crisis of legitimacy on its hands.

3

Explaining Punishment

The Sociology of Punishment _____

3.1 Why do we have a penal system? Why does punishment take different forms in different societies and at different stages in history? Why, for example, have penal ideas and practices altered over time in the West in the ways described in the 'Schools of Penal Thought' section (2.5) of the previous chapter?

The *sociology of punishment* is the area of inquiry which seeks to answer questions such as these. The answers put forward are often controversial. Like many areas of sociology, the sociology of punishment lends itself to (often radically) differing approaches which provide rival explanations of penality. (We shall be using the word 'penality' to include *ideas* about punishment as well as concrete penal practices; cf. Garland, 1990a; Garland and Young, 1983a.) Also, other fields of sociology, these approaches can be conveniently located within competing traditions which each owe their orientation to one of the three great founding fathers of the discipline of sociology: Karl Marx, Émile Durkheim and Max Weber. It is equally convenient for us to divide this chapter accordingly.

The Marxist Tradition _____

3.2 Karl Marx (1818–83) was not only the founder of modern communism but also originated one of the most influential traditions in sociology. His message was that societies had to be understood in terms of their economic structures, and in particular their social relations of production and the conflicts between the different economic classes which exist as a result of those relations. He claimed that capitalist society was polarizing 'into two great hostile camps, into two great classes directly facing each other: Bourgeoisie and Proletariat' (Marx, 1977: 222). The bourgeoisie or capitalist class (the ruling class under capitalism) is the class of people who own the means of production (including factories, industrial machinery, etc. in an industrialized society), while the proletariat or working class comprises those who need to sell their 'labour power' (their ability to work) to the capitalists in order to live. The struggle between these two classes was for Marx the key to understanding modern society and its future, which he envisaged as the revolutionary overthrow of capitalism by the proletariat leading ultimately to a classless communist society.

In a key passage, Marx wrote (1977: 389):

> The sum total of these relations of production constitutes the economic structure of society, the real foundation, on which rises a legal and political superstructure and to which correspond definite forms of social consciousness. The mode of production of material life conditions the social, political, and intellectual life process in general. It is not the consciousness of men that determines their being, but, on the contrary, their social being that determines their consciousness.

This passage is the source for one of the most debated features of Marxist social theory, known as the *'base and superstructure* metaphor': the idea that the economic 'material base' of society determines developments in the 'superstructural' realms of law, of politics and of people's ideas generally. Marx described the consciousness of people in a situation of class conflict as *ideological,* meaning that although they might represent and believe their ideas to be objective and of universal validity, in reality these ideas express and serve class interests. In particular, Marx claimed that 'the ruling ideas of each age have ever been the ideas of its ruling class' (Marx, 1977: 236).

Marxist penology applies this method of analysis (known as 'historical materialism') to the study of penality. It relates punishment to the economic structure of the society in which it takes place and to the class interests furthered by penal practices and ideologies. A general point is that punishment is inflicted by the state for breaches of the law. Marxists see both state and law as operating in the interests of the ruling class rather than society as a whole. Punishing people for disobeying the existing laws – which maintain the status quo and the position of the ruling class – functions to reinforce the power and privilege of that class.

Historical materialism can also be used to explain the history of penal thought sketched in the previous chapter. For example, it has often been observed (by no means only by Marxists) that the ideas of Beccaria – and the Enlightenment generally – were linked to the interests of the bourgeois class who were gaining in economic and political power at the time but still needed legal protection against the old ruling class, the landowning aristocracy who retained a corrupt control of the levers of state power (Beccaria, 1963: xxi; Taylor et al., 1973: ch. 1). Similarly, Bentham's penology – and utilitarianism generally – were functional to the interests of the bourgeoisie at a slightly later historical stage (Ignatieff, 1978; Hogg, 1979). Positivism in turn can be seen as a set of ideas tending to reinforce the ideological domination (or hegemony) of the bourgeois class at a yet later stage when it had become the ruling class in Europe: if criminal actions can be described as the result of mindless pathology rather than rational choice this both absolves capitalism of any blame for crime and helps to delegitimize protests against the existing order (Taylor et al., 1973: ch. 2). Conventional histories of punishment tend to represent these developments in thought and practice as rational, progressive, scientific and humane; Marxists are sceptical of such claims and see the furtherance of class interests as of prime importance. When we come nearer the present with the rise of law and order ideology in recent decades, Marxists are likely to have little difficulty perceiving whose interests are being served by the notion that crime is entirely the fault of individual, predominantly working-class offenders who should be punished as severely as possible (Hall et al., 1978; Hall, 1979; 1980).

While much of the above would probably be unobjectionable to most Marxists, there are some important fissures within the Marxist tradition itself, especially in relation to the base and superstructure metaphor, which have an important bearing on the nature of the explanations of punishment offered by different kinds of Marxists. It will be instructive therefore to examine some of these different strands within Marxism.

Economic Determinism: Rusche and Kirchheimer

In the minds of many people, Marxism means simple **economic determinism**: the idea that economics determines everything, that the superstructure of law, politics and ideology merely reflects the state of the economic base. Few Marxists today believe this (and certainly Marx himself never believed anything so crude), but the misconception is understandable since this simplified version of Marx's message was communist orthodoxy for a long time. The economic determinist approach produced one classic, pioneering work of Marxist penology: Georg Rusche and Otto Kirchheimer's *Punishment and Social Structure* (1939).

Rusche and Kirchheimer attempted to demonstrate that penal practices in any society were directly connected to the mode of production: 'Every system of production tends to discover punishments which correspond to its productive relationships' (1939: 5). For example, 'it is self-evident that enslavement as a form of punishment is impossible without a slave economy; that prison labour is impossible without manufacture or industry, that monetary fines for all classes of society are impossible without a monetary economy'. Moreover, 'if a slave economy finds the supply of slaves meagre and the demand pressing' it will be likely to introduce penal slavery. But once society had advanced from a slave economy to feudalism, penal slavery was no longer an option. Nor were fines an option for punishing the majority of (thoroughly impoverished) offenders, so feudalism relied instead on capital and corporal punishments (1939: 6).

A similar economic explanation was offered for the rise of the 'house of correction' (the forerunner of the modern prison) from the end of the sixteenth century onwards. Early capitalism needed more labour power, so it became uneconomic to kill and mutilate offenders. It was better for capitalism that offenders should be incarcerated and set to productive work (whose profits would, naturally, be pocketed by the capitalist class in the usual manner). Punishment could therefore be used to 'fill out the gaps in the labour market' (Rusche and Kirchheimer, 1939: 7). Even where this was not the case, Rusche and Kirchheimer argued that the choice of methods of punishment is largely influenced by fiscal interests, such as how much a punishment costs to administer.

This analysis of punishment is inadequate for at least two reasons. First, it fails to explain the mechanisms linking an economic imperative with a penal practice. Capitalism needed the house of correction, and somehow it magically came into being as a result. Unless the capitalist class was engaged in a conspiracy which was simultaneously crudely self-interested, brilliantly well hidden and (remarkably) informed by economic analyses of a kind which had never been published at the time, it is hard to see how and why this occurred. It is also hard to see in this theory any picture of real human beings (capitalist or otherwise) operating with limited rationality and knowledge in a recognizably real world. Or to put it another way, the analysis lacks both humanism and a theory of ideology – a theory about why people have the ideas they have, and what effects they have.

A second problem is that the theory embarrassingly fails to fit the facts of history. Rusche and Kirchheimer themselves admit (1939: 102) that imprisonment became the standard method of punishment at a time when the demand for prison labour had *fallen* as a result of technological and other developments. Again, a theory of ideology seems necessary to explain this seeming disjuncture between base and superstructure (Garland and Young, 1983b: 25).

This is not to say that economic imperatives play no part in penal developments. For example, it seems very likely that pragmatic considerations including essentially economic ones (concerning stretched penal resources) have played their part in the expansion of the parole system (see Chapter 7). It has also been argued strongly, especially by Andrew Scull (1977), that the move towards creating 'alternatives to custody' in the 1960s and 1970s was primarily a product of fiscal calculation (see Chapter 5, section 5.5). And the current crisis of resources in the penal system is an economic reality which certainly has had its effects on penal policy. But economics do not determine penal practices in a simple and direct manner; if they did we should hardly have the extremely wasteful penal system which exists in this country today, with its needlessly and expensively high prison population. Economic considerations are mediated through the minds of human beings who live in a social world, which means that the impact of economics is crucially conditioned by ideology – a notion which has been explored and expanded by the Marxist theorists to whom we now turn.

Ideology and Hegemony: The Legacy of Gramsci

Antonio Gramsci (1891–1937) was not a penologist – but he was, famously, a prisoner. Imprisoned by the Italian fascists for his communist affiliation and activities from 1926 until his death, his contribution to Marxist theory was written inside prison (Gramsci, 1971).

Gramsci's writings marked a major shift away from the one-sided economic determinism of writers such as Rusche and Kirchheimer. For Gramsci, the superstructure of ideology, law and politics was of great significance in the revolutionary struggle in an advanced capitalist society. Central to his ideas was the notion of *hegemony* – the ideological domination exercised throughout society by a successful ruling class. Hegemony meant that one class has persuaded the other classes to accept its own moral, political and cultural values. This was important because the ruling class (and the state which was its instrument) did not merely rule by coercion – which for our purposes means in particular by punishing people for breaking its laws. Equally important was the ideological factor of *consent*: in a situation of hegemony, subordinate classes consent to the existing social relations because they are effectively represented as being universally beneficial. The production of this consent is one vital task for the state, and one necessary component of the continual reproduction of existing social relations.

Thus ideology and the superstructure are not merely reflections of the material economic base, but interact with it in a two-way relationship. The economics of the base could not explain everything that existed or occurred in the superstructure; as Marx's collaborator Engels had suggested, the economy was only the mainspring of history 'in the last analysis' (Gramsci, 1971: 162). And the superstructure could make a difference to the base. If consent were not successfully produced and reproduced, this could ultimately affect the condition and prospects of the economic base, not least by making a great deal of difference to the likely success of the revolutionary struggle.

Importantly, Gramsci did not believe that consent was produced as the result of a ruling-class conspiracy to hoax the workers; for him, ideologies arose out of the material realities within which human beings live and work. Or, as Marx said, people's consciousness was determined by their social being (albeit not entirely determined by their *economic* position). Nor was hegemony an inevitable or universal phenomenon, and conscious efforts to combat it at the ideological level were a necessary part of the socialist project. (These ideas of Gramsci's have been notably developed and applied to modern criminal justice policy by Stuart Hall (Hall et al., 1978; Hall, 1980), whose account of law and order ideology we touched on in Chapter 1, section 1.4.)

There is much more to Gramsci than this: for example, Marxist theory is indebted to his pioneering use of concepts such as 'praxis', 'civil society', 'class fractions' and the 'historical bloc', and his analysis of the nature, role and composition of the state in class societies. Perhaps above all, Gramsci injected a sense of humanism into Marxism: for him, history was made by human beings. He believed that socialism would not come about as the inevitable result of impersonal laws of economic development but would have to be built by active human beings working purposively and creatively. However, it is in his treatment of ideology that Gramsci's legacy has been most pervasive and where he is the unmistakable precursor of all the Marxist and **post-Marxist** theorists we now proceed to discuss.

Structuralist Marxism and Althusser

The French philosopher Louis Althusser (1918–90) created a sophisticated reinterpretation of Marxism often referred to as 'structuralist Marxism'. Although Althusser himself disclaimed the label 'structuralist' it is at least loosely apt to describe his ideas, since he regarded the structure of the social system (and in particular the relationships between its different 'levels' or 'instances') as central to the task of understanding society.[1] Among the important features of Althusser's **structuralism** is a rejection of humanism as a valid element in Marxism. He claimed to detect an 'epistemological break' in the writings of Marx in the year 1845, discarding Marx's (undoubtably humanist) early works as juvenilia and constructing a non-humanistic 'scientific' Marxism on the basis of his later works only (Althusser, 1969). History, according to Althusser, is not made by freely acting human beings but by 'structural causality'.

Society, according to Althusser, is a complex unity of different, unevenly related levels or instances. The economy is the ultimately determining instance, but the superstructural instances of ideology and politics are not mere reflections of it: they possess a 'relative autonomy' (Althusser, 1969: 111, 240; 1971: 135). Indeed, the different instances are mutually determining: there is a 'reciprocal action' of the superstructure on the base (Althusser, 1971: 135), and the ideological and political instances are part of the essential conditions of existence of the entire social formation. It is still the case that the economy is determining 'in the last instance', but the economy never functions in isolation from the other instances. As Althusser put it (1969: 113): 'the economic dialectic is never active *in the pure state*; in History, these instances, the superstructures, etc. – are never seen to step respectfully aside when their work is done … From the first moment to the last, the lonely hour of the "last instance" never comes.'

It is difficult to see how, on this account, the economy is supposed to retain its ultimately determining role. Since the political and ideological instances are just as necessary for the existence of a social formation, they seem to be equally determining, and the economic base no longer looks to be especially basic. Perhaps Althusser was unwilling to acknowledge this outright, because to do so would be to run the risk of departing from the fundamental Marxist doctrine which asserts the primacy of economics in social explanation. Consequently Althusser denied the logical conclusion of his own theory by continuing to invoke 'economic determination in the last instance' as a dogmatic but essentially metaphysical, almost religious assertion.

Be that as it may, it is clear that ideology was at least as important to Althusser as it was to Gramsci. All societies (not only class societies, according to Althusser) need ideology as part of their conditions of existence. And a society's ideology must be constantly reproduced if the society is to survive, just as (for example) an industrial society must continually renovate and update its machinery and ensure that the next generation of workers is produced, kept alive and prepared for productive labour. For production could not continue unless the proletariat were ideologically conditioned in each generation to submit to the rules of the established order within which production occurs.

---

[1]Althusser disclaimed the label 'structuralist' to distance himself from other theorists (notably the anthropologist Lévi-Strauss), for whom the structures of thought and language are determining. For Althusser, by contrast, it is the structure of the entire social formation, including the economic and political 'instances', which determines history.

Althusser stressed the role in this reproductive process of what he called 'Ideological State Apparatuses' (ISAs) (Althusser, 1971: 127–84). Among these he included the educational system and also many institutions that are not usually thought of as part of the state, such as the family, churches, the media, trade unions and political parties.[2] These ISAs were to be distinguished from the more instantly recognizable 'Repressive State Apparatus' (RSA), consisting of 'the Government, the Administration, the Army, the Police, the Courts, the Prisons, etc.'. As the names suggest, the RSA functions predominantly by overt coercion to ensure that the conditions of production are maintained, while ISAs function predominantly to reproduce existing ideology, which is the ideology of the ruling class.

For our purposes it is interesting that although Althusser locates the penal system logically enough within the Repressive State Apparatus, he also makes it clear that there is no such thing as a purely repressive apparatus, and that the RSA also functions (if only secondarily) by ideology. (Similarly, he identifies the law as both an ISA and part of the RSA since it functions both to coerce and to reproduce ruling-class values.) This provokes the consideration that the penal system may perform a dual function in the reproduction of the social formation. On the one hand, and most obviously, it comprises a set of repressive practices which among other things may help to preserve the conditions of production by deterring crime. But it may also function ideologically, by conveying conservative moral messages. For example, retributive punishment might help inculcate law-abiding ideology in the populace by telling them that breaking the law is wicked and deserves punishment. Reformative punishment could assure people that the existing state was effectively combating crime to the benefit of all, including even the offender – disguising the truth that the capitalist state in fact operates for the benefit of the ruling class. A Marxist approach which takes the role of ideology seriously needs to analyse punishment in terms such as these.

In the last analysis (as it were) we doubt whether Althusser's theory represents a significant advance on the work of Gramsci. In some important respects – particularly Althusser's dogmatism, determinism and anti-humanism – we think it represents a definite step in the wrong direction. But aspects of his work, especially his insistence on the importance of ideology, were a positive influence on modern Marxism and on some Marxist studies of crime and punishment. For example, Stuart Hall's analysis of law and order owed much to Althusser as well as to Gramsci. Fitzgerald and Sim's *British Prisons* (1982) was another example of radical analysis which paid at least as much attention to ideology as to economics. Whatever the overall balance sheet, Althusser's impact has been undeniable.

---

[2]Althusser's remarkably broad concept of the state relates to an important intra-Marxist debate which we cannot explore here. Many of the institutions which Althusser categorizes as part of the state would be viewed by Gramsci as part of 'civil society'. For what it is worth, we prefer the Gramscian approach.

Post-Structuralism, Discipline and
Power: Michel Foucault

Michel Foucault (1926–84), who studied under Althusser, took the step his teacher never did and distanced himself from Marxism while remaining politically radical. Perhaps even more than Althusser, Foucault represents a decisive move away from economic determinism. Like Althusser, Foucault was once called a structuralist, but although he showed great interest in structures (including the structures of thought and of discourse in different ages) he differed significantly from both Althusser and other structuralists, often being described consequently as 'post-structuralist' (and also as post-Marxist and **post-modernist**). He shared structuralism's anti-humanism, but had a much more dynamic conception of structures. The structuralist account portrayed structures as relatively unchanging and self-reproducing; the **post-structuralism** of Foucault discerned and investigated a continual flux and change in society and in structures themselves. As Alan Sheridan (1980: 90) says, 'there is a sense in which his work is profoundly anti-Structuralist. Far from wishing to "freeze" the movement of history in structures, his whole work has been an examination of the nature of historical change.'

For penology, Foucault's most important examination of historical change is his great work *Discipline and Punish: The Birth of the Prison* (1977). In this book Foucault investigated the massive shift or 'great transformation' (mentioned in Chapter 2, section 2.5) from *corporal* to *carceral* punishment between the late eighteenth and mid-nineteenth centuries (see also Chapter 5, section 5.5). His explanation for the coming of the prison at that time was that this was 'the moment when it became understood that it was more efficient and profitable in terms of the economy of power to place people under surveillance than to subject them to some exemplary penalty' (Foucault, 1980: 38). The new industrial social order required new techniques of power and new institutions to control the subordinate classes. The prison was one of these new institutions, along with the factory, asylum, school and workhouse, all of which shared certain common features with the prison.

Two central concepts here are *discipline* and *power*. Discipline was the new feature of the Benthamesque industrial-age prison, whereby the inmate was 'normalized' or schooled into conformity by constant surveillance and the imposition of a highly regulated physical routine including repetitive forced labour. Where the earlier forms of corporal punishment were directed at the body of the convict, disciplinary punishment aimed, via the body, at the 'soul' of the offender. Not that 'prison worked' in its intended goal of reforming criminals; on the contrary, its failure in this respect was almost immediately apparent. But the prison was (and is) paradoxically successful in a different way precisely because of this. It successfully *produces delinquents*, creating a criminal section of the population and thereby dividing the subordinate classes into mutually antagonistic fractions. The criminals created by prison could be used by the bourgeoisie for a variety of political purposes, for example as informers, *agents provocateurs* and strike breakers (Foucault, 1977: 264–92; 1980: 40–2) – essentially a 'divide and rule' strategy.

The concept of power for Foucault is intimately connected with that of knowledge, which in turn is not a matter of objective truth separable from power relations.

'Power and knowledge directly imply each other … there is no power relation without the correlative constitution of a field of knowledge, nor any knowledge that does not presuppose and constitute at the same time power relations' (Foucault, 1977: 27). Thus, the disciplinary surveillance of the prison created a new kind of knowledge of the convict's body which created a new kind of power. However, power for Foucault is not merely exercised in a simple manner by the state or by one class over others via punishment and other mechanisms, but is a ubiquitous and many-sided phenomenon; there exists a multiplicity of power relations in society which are the constant focus of negotiation and struggle. It follows that punishment – or indeed any social phenomenon – is an inevitably highly complex phenomenon which should require extremely subtle analysis. Ironically, however, one criticism of Foucault is that his penology is actually too crude and simple, reducing the complex phenomenon of penality to questions of power and little else, and postulating what looks suspiciously like an old-fashioned class conspiracy theory to explain the advent and historical persistence of the prison (Garland, 1990a: ch. 6; 1990b).

Foucault's cryptic style leaves the nature of his theory obscure in many respects. The traditional Marxist base and superstructure is conspicuous by its absence in Foucault, but it is less clear what he thought is the role of economics in social and penal change. As Stan Cohen (1985: 24) remarks, Foucault 'veers between a materialist connection between prison and emerging capitalism and an idealist obsession with the power of ideas'. Clearly though, he was more concerned with the ideological genesis and effects of punishment than with its relationship with economics.

Foucault has been much analysed, and criticized by some on both theoretical and historical grounds (Ignatieff, 1981; Garland, 1985; 1990a: ch. 7; 1990b) – although even his critics in the field of penal sociology have been profoundly influenced by Foucault. Foucauldian concepts such as **normalization** and discipline have become standard tools of analysis; for example, there is one major debate (discussed in Chapter 5, section 5.5) as to whether we have been witnessing a 'dispersal of discipline' emanating from the prison and spreading throughout society (Cohen, 1979; Bottoms, 1983). Foucault's contribution has certainly transformed the sociology of punishment.

Humanistic Materialism: The Case of E. P. Thompson

The English historian E. P. Thompson (1924–93) represents a humanistic current of Marxism far removed from either Althusser's structuralism or Foucault's post-structuralism. He contributed not only to general Marxist theory, but also directly to penology in *Whigs and Hunters* (1977), his painstaking historical study of the passing of the 'Black Act' of 1723, a penal **statute** of extraordinary scope and ferocity.

Thompson's *The Poverty of Theory* (1978) is an extended polemic against Althusser and his disciples. Above all, Thompson insisted that history is made, not by the inevitable operation of impersonal structures, but by the actions of real human beings. 'For all these "instances" and "levels" are in fact human activities, institutions, and ideas. We are talking about men and women, in their material life, in their determinate relationships, in their experience of these, and in their self-consciousness of this experience' (Thompson, 1978: 289).

He also accused Althusser of covert idealism in that his structuralism in effect denies the genuine role of the economy in constraining legal and ideological forms. Thompson claimed, for instance, that when he was researching *Whigs and Hunters*, 'on several occasions, while I was actually watching, the lonely hour of the last instance *actually came*' (Thompson, 1978: 288). A change in the mode of production from feudalism to agrarian capitalism required and forced the emergence of new forms of law and punishment appropriate to the new economy, such as Enclosure Acts and laws to penalize poor foresters who attempted to exercise their customary rights of grazing and timber-cutting in the forests.

Thompson had much to say about law. He accepted that law is 'relatively autonomous' of the economy, but he found little use for the base/superstructure metaphor, rejecting what he saw as Althusser's rigid division of social formations into different instances or levels. Law, he said, is to be found 'at *every* bloody level'.[3] Law can function ideologically, to legitimate the existing order and 'mystify' subordinate classes into acquiescence (what Gramsci called 'consent'). But 'people are not as stupid as some structuralist philosophers suppose them to be. They will not be mystified by the first man who puts on a wig … If the law is evidently partial and unjust, then it will mask nothing, legitimize nothing, contribute nothing to any class's hegemony' (Thompson, 1977: 262–3). So law was never the exclusive possession of the ruling class; rather it provided 'an arena for class struggle, within which alternative notions of law were fought out' (Thompson, 1978: 288). The foresters' view that customary law vindicated their rights to use the forest conflicted with an emerging capitalist version of law under which these customary rights were extinguished; thus a class battle was fought in the forum of legal debate.

Much of what Thompson said about law can also (we think usefully) be applied to punishment. Penality can also be found 'at every bloody level', although it can perhaps be roughly divided into (material) penal *practices* and (ideological) penal *rhetoric*. The relationship between the two is not necessarily straightforward; for example, penal rhetoric might be predominantly positivistic at a time when actual penal practice is predominantly classicistic and deterrent. (Arguably this was the case in the English penal system during the supposed reign of the rehabilitative ideal.) Yet such discrepancies are not caused by the logic of structures but by the messy and often far from inevitable ways in which people come to understand the world around them and their own practices. Again, like law, punishment and ideas about punishment can serve to mystify and legitimate oppression, but can also afford 'an arena for class struggle'; and as we suggested earlier in this chapter, the history of penal thought can be fruitfully viewed in these terms. Readers will doubtless have already gathered that, if forced to choose a version of Marxism, we should favour one similar to Thompson's.

---

[3]This may be unfair on Althusser, who as we have seen described law as both part of the Repressive State Apparatus and as an Ideological State Apparatus, and who said that the different instances never exist or function in a pure manner independent of each other.

The Durkheimian Tradition

3.3 Émile Durkheim (1858–1917) addressed himself directly to the question of punishment to a much greater extent than either Marx or Weber ever did. He did this especially in two works: *The Division of Labor in Society* (1960, first published 1893) and the article 'Two Laws of Penal Evolution' (1973, first published 1900).

The Division of Labor expounds Durkheim's theory about the development of specialized work in society. Durkheim distinguishes between simple, pre-industrial societies in which there is little division of labour (sometimes referred to as *Gemeinschaft* societies) and more advanced (*Gesellschaft*) societies in which people perform specialized jobs. The central question for Durkheim was *social solidarity*, or 'the bonds which unite men one with another' (cited in Lukes, 1975: 139). This solidarity took different forms in the two different kinds of society, but in each case Durkheim saw punishment as playing an important role in the creation and maintenance of the solidarity which was a necessary condition for social order and the continued existence of society.

Durkheim said that simple societies were held together by 'mechanical solidarity through likeness': people were united by the similarity in the labour and the general social roles they performed, which also gave rise to a homogeneous *conscience collective*. Conscience collective is variously translatable as 'collective conscience' or 'collective consciousness', and means 'the totality of beliefs and sentiments common to average members of the same society'. Crime, for Durkheim, could be defined in terms of the conscience collective: 'an act is criminal when it offends strong and defined states of the collective conscience' (Durkheim, 1960: 79–80). Criminal acts call forth a collective hostile response in the shape of punishment, and the punishment serves to restore and reinforce the outraged conscience collective. So punishment is not primarily deterrent or reformative; it is produced by collective *retributive* emotions and has a useful *denunciatory* effect: 'Its true function is to maintain social cohesion intact.' The conscience collective 'would necessarily lose its energy, if an emotional reaction of the community did not come to compensate its loss, and it would result in a breakdown of social solidarity' (Durkheim, 1960: 108).

In *The Division of Labor*, Durkheim claimed that the conscience collective played only a small part in maintaining social cohesion in more advanced, industrial societies. Differentiated labour meant that people now differed from each other to a much greater extent, including in their consciences. Social solidarity was now 'organic', deriving from the interdependence of people who were no longer largely self-sufficient as a result of their own labour alone. The conscience collective became weaker, vaguer, less religious and more humanistic in character. Punishment would consequently also dwindle in importance as the division of labour progresses, and punitive law would come to be replaced by 'restitutive law' which requires lawbreakers to make reparation to their victims rather than suffer retributive punishment.

By the time Durkheim came to write *Two Laws of Penal Evolution*, he had modified his theory about the decline in importance of the conscience collective (a phrase he ceased to use) and had come to believe that 'collective sentiments' were a crucial factor in any society. However, he still held that the nature of these collective sentiments differed at different stages of society's development, being of a predominantly religious character in simple societies but becoming much more secular, humanistic and individualistic in industrial societies.

His first 'law of penal evolution' was a two-pronged 'law of quantitative change': 'The intensity of punishment is the greater the more closely societies approximate to a less developed type – and the more the central power assumes an absolute character' (Durkheim, 1973: 285). The first part of this law he explains as follows. In simple societies, whose collective sentiments are based on religion, all crimes (even crimes such as murder) are essentially 'religious criminality': they are seen as offences against God or the gods. Consequently punishments tend to be severe because any sympathy for the offender is overwhelmed by the need to appease the God. But as collective sentiments change, it is 'human criminality', comprising only offences against other people, which shocks collective sentiments and attracts a punitive response. The shock value, however, is less: 'The offence of man against man cannot arouse the same indignation as an offence of man against God. At the same time, the sentiments of pity which he who suffers punishment evokes in us can no longer be so easily nor so completely extinguished by the sentiments he has offended and which react against him; for both are of the same nature' (Durkheim, 1973: 303). The same humanistic sympathy which causes crimes against people to be criminalized also serves to mitigate the punishment; so in general the severity of punishment should diminish as societies develop. But this progression will not continue indefinitely until punishment disappears; on the contrary, Durkheim predicted that the tendency would reverse, and less serious crimes against the person would come to be criminalized.

A second, independent factor affecting the severity of punishment is the degree of absolutism in government. Where government takes the form of absolute power 'the one who controls it appears to the people as a divinity … this religiosity cannot fail to have its usual effects on punishment' (Durkheim, 1973: 305), making punishment more severe than one would expect for a society of the same level of development but with a less absolute government. For Durkheim this explained the harshness of punishment in the seventeenth and eighteenth centuries, when absolute monarchy was at its height.

Durkheim's second law was: 'Deprivations of liberty, and of liberty alone, varying in time according to the seriousness of the crime, tend to become more and more the normal means of social control' (1973: 294). Durkheim saw the centrality of the prison as largely brought about by the operation of the first part of his first law: prison was a milder penalty than capital and corporal punishments and so became adopted as collective sentiments became more sympathetic to the criminal's suffering. (This account stands in marked contrast to Foucault's explanation of the same historical phenomenon, discussed previously. What Foucault saw as a self-interested, indeed cruel strategy for exercising power, Durkheim saw as motivated by sympathy for the criminal; see Garland, 1990b.)

Durkheim's social theory differs sharply from Marxism in several respects. One of these is the role of economics. Although Durkheim did not see economic developments as unimportant, for him they were in no way basic. The most important determining social force to Durkheim was collective sentiments, and especially religion – a factor which some would describe as 'cultural' and Marxists tend to characterize as 'ideological'. In this respect, the more recent Marxist theories which give greater explanatory weight to ideology have narrowed (but far from closed) the gap between Durkheim and Marxism.

Another difference from Marxism is the stress Durkheim places on the existence of consensus and the need for order in society (and for change to be of a peaceful and evolutionary nature), where Marxism stresses the centrality of class conflict and the necessity of revolution. To some extent this can be seen as a matter of political temperament determining which side of the coin one emphasizes. Even a Marxist such as Gramsci, who spoke of the 'consent' of the subordinate classes, saw consensus as false consciousness and hoped for revolutionary change. On the other hand Durkheim, a reformist socialist of sorts, was passionately opposed to violent revolution and agitation, and was concerned to identify and encourage the social consensus that made possible a peaceful social order for the benefit of everyone.

One of Durkheim's main legacies is the sociological tradition known as *functionalism*. Functionalism analyses social phenomena in terms of their functions – that is, their positive effects in helping the entire social system to continue operating. (The two most eminent functionalists to follow Durkheim were Robert Merton (1968) and the 'structural-functionalist' Talcott Parsons (1937; 1951).) Like Durkheim, functionalists assume that a certain degree of order is necessary for societies to survive, and see shared social values as vital in securing this order. They see society and human action as being structured by social rules and values, and portray social systems as reproducing themselves via socialization – the transmission of social values to new generations through the family, the educational system and so on. Another functionalist concept, present in Durkheim's work and elaborated by his successors, is **social control**, a term which encompasses all the methods whereby society keeps its members obedient to its rules.

Although functionalism has often been attacked as a conservative sociological tradition, some of its terminology and aspects of its mode of analysis have been appropriated by Marxist and radical theorists. Clearly, for example, Althusserian structuralism has at times a quite tangible functionalist flavour, especially in its account of the reproduction of capitalist relations of production. Most notably, the concept of social control has been taken over wholesale by radical criminologists with little apparent sense of embarrassment (see Cohen, 1985) – but for radicals social control is usually a term of abuse denoting capitalist repression.

The Durkheimian tradition remains a source of influence for non-Marxist penologists as well. Tony Bottoms (1977) used Durkheim's 'two laws of penal evolution' to offer an explanation of the trend towards bifurcation in British penal policy, whereby (at that time) policy makers attempted to combine less severe punishments for the majority of offenders with harsher measures for the minority of really serious offenders (see Chapter 1, section 1.4). The trend towards greater leniency for most offenders could be explained by the operation of the first part of Durkheim's first law, which postulates increasing leniency as collective sentiments become more secular. On the other hand, Bottoms saw the central power of the British state as having become more absolute in recent years, which part two of law one says should lead to harsher punishment. This duly transpires, but only for the more serious offenders. The concentration of punitive attention on more serious and violent offenders is an 'attempt to reassert an agreed *conscience collective*, or other kind of consensus, in a time of great social and moral doubt and confusion. Such a reassertion will, in the criminal field, result in the attempt to create consensus at any rate around the crimes which we almost all abhor, such as serious violence' (Bottoms, 1977: 90). Whether or not Bottoms's analysis was correct – and clearly it would need some modifying to explain later shifts away from this kind of bifurcation with the rise of law and order ideology – the Durkheimian concern with shared social values and sentiments as an explanatory factor remains highly relevant to sociology, and to the explanation of punishment in particular.

The Weberian Tradition

3.4 Despite being one of the major streams of modern sociological thought, the theoretical tradition founded by Max Weber (1864–1920) has produced relatively little explicitly Weberian penology.[4] But this probably reflects negatively on penology and penologists rather than on Weber and his thought. We shall concentrate briefly on those aspects of Weber's sociology which have the most obvious relevance to penology.

Weber's sociology is sometimes described as 'a debate with the ghost of Marx' (MacRae, 1974: 52). Weber recognized the importance of economics in shaping social reality, but was concerned to demonstrate that **culture** and religion influenced economic development just as much as economics influenced culture. He explored this theme most famously in *The Protestant Ethic and the Spirit of Capitalism* (1930) and related works, arguing that Calvinistic Protestantism's individualistic ethos and positive attitude to the accumulation of private wealth provided the key to understanding why capitalism first arose in the West rather than in Asia where the economic conditions for capitalist development existed to at least an equal extent. But he also accepted that economics in turn influenced culture; it was the version of Marxism which saw culture as a mere 'reflection' of the economic base that Weber was concerned to refute. The difference between Weber's position and the more sophisticated Marxisms which see culture as relatively autonomous and interacting with the economy in a reciprocal (or 'dialectical') relationship is perhaps not great.

Another important contribution of Weber's was his analysis of different kinds of power in society (Weber, 1968: chs 1 and 3). He distinguished between simple *power* (the ability to make one's will prevail against the resistance of others), *domination* (enduring power associated with a habit of obedience on the part of the subordinate person or group), and *legitimacy* (power which exists and endures because those subject to it believe it is morally right to obey). All governments and powerful

---

[4]However, Garland (1990a: ch. 8) argues convincingly that Weber has been a major influence on some significant penological work, including that of Foucault, often without receiving due acknowledgement.

groups seek to acquire legitimacy, for the very good reason that it is the most efficient and stable basis for exercising power. As we saw was true of Durkheim, much of this analysis and terminology of Weber's has been adopted by radical and Marxist theorists; thus we find radicals such as Fitzgerald and Sim (1982) identifying a crisis of legitimacy in the penal system (see Chapter 1, section 1.3).

Weber went on to distinguish three types of legitimate authority: traditional authority, charismatic authority and legal authority. He saw legal authority as characteristic of modern Western societies. A person who wields authority in such a society does not do so typically by virtue of traditional rules (about kingship or hereditary authority, for example) or because of that person's supposed special charismatic qualities, but as a result of an impersonal rule which has been consciously created by a rational legislative process, Weber says that the appropriate administrative form for a system of legal authority – because it is the most efficient form – is 'bureaucracy' (Weber, 1968: chs 3 and 11). Characteristics of bureaucracy include impersonality, the interchangeability of officials, routinization of procedure and a dependency on the existence of recorded information.

In Weberian vein, Kamenka and Tay (1975) suggest that advanced capitalist societies tend to develop 'bureaucratic-administrative law' which increasingly regulates human activities for impersonal collective purposes such as general economic efficiency. Tony Bottoms (1983) suggests that this analysis may explain some recent developments in penal systems, such as the rise in importance of relatively impersonal and standardized penalties such as the fine. Other penal developments can also be seen in this light. Obvious examples are the emergence of fixed penalties for certain motoring offences, the (highly bureaucratic) parole system (see Chapter 7), the move towards standardization in sentencing by means such as **sentencing guidelines** (see Chapter 4), and the general trend towards managerialism and Strategy B in criminal justice (see Introduction and Chapter 1, sections I.2 and 1.4). One manifestation may have been the 'blizzard of paper' which the Learmont Report of 1995 (para. 3.125) complained had been engulfing a Prison Service 'strangled by bureaucracy'.

Finally we should mention Weber's general importance in the development of humanism in sociology. For Weber, the sociologist needed to understand (*verstehen*) the subjective experience of 'ideal-typical' human individuals located within particular societies, classes and cultures – not, of course, denying that social forces shape and influence individuals, but insisting that individual human beings and the meanings they use to interpret their social world are of prime importance in understanding society. This must be as valid an insight in the penal field as in any other.

Pluralism and Radical Pluralism

3.5 In our opinion the most satisfactory framework for explaining penal phenomena is one which draws on several different sociological traditions. We call this a *radical pluralist* position, since it represents a compromise between Marxism and the pluralist tradition in sociology.

Pluralism (for example, Dahl, 1961) holds that, at least in modern Western democracies, power is not monopolized by a single ruling class but is distributed between a plurality of interest groups of different kinds, which are represented in the political arena by a variety of organizations including political parties. Politics is a process of competition, bargaining and compromise between the different interest groups in which the state plays an impartial and independent role as 'honest broker' between the various parties. This vision of society contrasts with that of Marxism, which sees power in capitalist society as concentrated in the hands of the (bourgeois) ruling class, and society as primarily divided into two great opposing classes rather than a motley of interacting interest groups. Similarly, the state for Marxists is by no means neutral and independent but is, in the words of Marx and Engels, 'but a committee for managing the common affairs of the whole bourgeoisie' (Marx, 1977: 223). Although the state might operate as an honest broker between different sections of the ruling class and may seek to give the appearance of neutrality to mystify its class nature and role, it will never be neutral as between the general interests of the bourgeoisie and the proletariat.

Neither traditional Marxism nor conventional pluralism seems adequate to us. Marxism's main flaw is its insistence on economics and the economic category of class as the one fundamental explanatory factor. This has meant, for example, that despite some valiant efforts Marxism has been ultimately unable to deal with other important social dimensions such as race and gender differences without reducing them to a mere aspect of class oppression and class struggle. We are not convinced that the penal realities concerning race and gender outlined in Chapter 9 can be satisfactorily explained in this manner.

Nor can all the groups involved in penal developments and penal conflicts and struggles be easily defined in terms of economic classes (although an attempt could perhaps be made to analyse them as representing 'alliances of class fractions'). The campaigning of non-state groups (such as Women in Prison) has often had noticeable effects in penal developments. Recently there has been an emergence of populist non-state groupings, such as the Victims of Crime Trust, which campaign noisily and in tandem with the popular media for harsher penal policies.

Again, as devotees of the classic 1980s BBC television comedy *Yes, Minister* may recall, the state bureaucracies and their members have their own organizational and personal interests to pursue which are often at variance with those of their supposed political masters, which in turn are not invariably identical with those of either the electorate or of any coalition of interest groups (see also Chapman, 1978; Kellner and Crowther-Hunt, 1980). This would appear to be true, for example, of the Home Office, which for many years (prior to the advent of Michael Howard as Home Secretary in 1993) was largely successful in getting its strategy of penological pragmatism implemented (see Chapters 1 and 10, sections 1.4 and 10.2; Bottoms, 1980; and Fitzgerald and Sim, 1980). Joanna Shapland (1988) has shrewdly likened both non-state groups and the state agencies involved in the criminal justice system (such as the police and the courts) to feudal '**fiefdoms**'. While of course we do not live in a feudal society, this analogy is in some ways highly apt: such fiefdoms represent partially autonomous concentrations of power and interest that are not readily reducible to class analysis.

Pluralism on the other hand is unembarrassed by the existence of a plurality of important social divisions. But conventional pluralism has its own defects, chiefly its 'honest broker' conception of the state. It seems clear, at least to us, that the state is by no means fully independent of, and impartial between, all groups and classes in society. ('Relative autonomy' is not perhaps a bad description.) For one thing, the personnel of the state are members of some of these interest groups themselves, and the more powerful state personnel will tend to be members of, or sympathetic to – or sharing the ideologies of – the more powerful and entrenched classes and groups. In the penal field, certain kinds of (more respectable) interest and pressure groups have at times been allowed a degree of influence on official policy, while others – especially those which challenge ruling ideologies – have had to struggle much harder to make an impact (Ryan, 1978). (In recent years, however, even the more respectable groups have struggled to combat the influence of populist punitiveness on the political realm.)

The chasm between the pluralist and Marxist views has narrowed encouragingly in recent times (McLennan, 1989). Marxists have discovered the state to be relatively autonomous and classes to be composed of 'class fractions' which seem to interact in a manner curiously reminiscent of the pluralist account. (They have also recognized the political virtues of pluralistic multi-party democracy, which pluralism appeared to celebrate while Marxists previously derided it as 'bourgeois democracy' which merely served to mystify the reality of class oppression.) The modified Marxism of E. P. Thompson approaches even closer to pluralism. For Thompson (1978: 298–9), classes are not the inevitable creation of economic relations, but 'arise because men and women, in determinate productive relations, identify their antagonistic interests, and come to struggle, to think, and to value in class ways'. Furthermore, law and the state afford 'an arena for class struggle' (Thompson, 1978: 288) in which victory for the ruling class is not necessarily assured. If this is true of classes, why should it not also be true of other interest groups, and what ultimately differentiates this from pluralism? Especially since there has been convergence from the pluralist side as well. Some pluralist writers have accepted that class division and class competition are pervasive factors in modern society, and that not all interest groups are equal in power or equally able to compete in the political arena (for example Dahl, 1985).

Radical pluralism can build on the common ground which has emerged between these two traditions. It can also incorporate some features of the Weberian and Durkheimian traditions – and perhaps not only the ones which, as we have seen, have already been purloined by Marxism – and can equally avail itself of the insights of other modes of sociological analysis. There are some who would object on philosophical grounds to this kind of synthesizing approach. Different theoretical traditions, it is sometimes claimed, belong to 'incommensurable paradigms' (Kuhn, 1962); one can work within only one of them at a time. But there is no good reason, philosophical or otherwise, why a synthesis of different theories should not be sought, as long as the assembled components do not actually contradict each other. (It would be incoherent, for example, to amalgamate wholesale the theories of E. P. Thompson and Michel Foucault since the humanism of the former is incompatible with the anti-humanism of the latter.)

We think that a coherent radical pluralism can be constructed on the basis of a humanism which accepts, as Marx put it, that human beings 'make their own history, but they do not make it just as they please; they do not make it under circumstances chosen by themselves' (Marx, 1977: 300). These constraining circumstances on human agency include the economic, political, cultural and ideological factors which shape our social world, but neither economics nor ideology is 'basic'. The economic situation may set limits on what is socially possible, but (as Weber for one insisted) this is equally true of the prevailing ideological situation. Economics and ideology are thus both determining in a weak sense, and they interact with each other, but neither makes a single future inevitable. Indeed, much of what happens in human affairs, including the realm of penality, depends on the 'swarming circumstances' (Garland, 1990a: 285) which hold sway at any particular moment, and on how the people subject to those circumstances make sense of them and respond to them.

As we said in Chapter 1 (section 1.5), we think that the current penal crisis should be seen in terms such as these. Material factors (such as the shortage of penal resources) interact with ideological developments (such as law and order ideology and the all-important crisis of legitimacy) in a complex and sometimes unpredictable manner. Much of this complexity and unpredictability is precisely because the intersection between the material and the ideological occurs in the practices of living human beings: offenders, sentencers, employees of the penal system, politicians, penal campaigners and members of the public. This vital human element makes the study of penality a complex and uncertain business. But it also means that people can, by their efforts, have a positive (or of course a negative) effect on the reality of punishment.

We now proceed to consider some of the ways in which punishment has varied – both over time and between different societies at the same time – to see how penal sociology might be applied to help explain these variations.

Applying Penal Sociology

The New Penology and the New Punitiveness

3.6 Punishment in many countries has changed significantly in recent decades, and a number of very noticeable penal trends have been categorized and variously named 'the new penology' (Feeley and Simon, 1992), 'the new punitiveness' (Pratt et al., 2005) and 'postmodern penality' (Pratt, 2000). The most notable international trend has been a new punitiveness: a general increase in the harshness of punishment. One measure of the severity of punishment is the **imprisonment rate**: the number of prisoners a country has per 100,000 of its general population. In recent years nearly three quarters of all the countries in the world have seen increased imprisonment rates (Walmsley, 2005). In many respects, this new harshness has been led by the United States, whose prison population and imprisonment rates are the highest in the world[5] and where numbers of prisoners have quintupled since the early 1970s. (The US has also in effect reintroduced and massively expanded its use of capital punishment since 1977, despite having carried out no executions between 1967 and 1977.) England, along with other nations, has followed this trend for a new punitiveness, if not to anything like the same extent, as we saw in Chapter 1. Associated with this punitiveness has been the law and order ideology (or populist punitiveness) we discussed in Chapter 1 (section 1.4), as the public and media discourse about crime has increasingly taken the form of urging tougher punishment as the appropriate response to crime. The new punitiveness is also very much bound up with what we term Strategy A (see the Introduction, section I.2). Populist policies and slogans, such as 'three strikes and you're out' or **zero tolerance**, are manifestations of the new punitiveness.

There have been other significant international trends as well as this increasing severity. The new *penology* is a very different concept from the new *punitiveness* – it relates to Strategy B rather than Strategy A. What has been called the new penology is 'managerial rather than transformative' (Feeley and Simon, 1992: 452): it is not concerned with reforming and treating the offender (or indeed – unlike the new punitiveness – with placing moral blame on the criminal). Instead 'it is concerned with techniques to identify, classify, and manage groupings sorted by dangerousness' (Feeley and Simon, 1992: 452). Such techniques include statistical methods of carrying out risk assessments of offenders, and applying new tools of offender management (for example, electronic surveillance and monitoring) based on the outcome of such assessments. This managerial new penology is one strong trend influencing the penal strategy of recent governments, which have combined elements of both the new punitiveness and the new penology.

Can the sociology of punishment – and our radical pluralist approach in particular – help to explain or elucidate developments such as these? We think that they can. First, the new penology. Of the sociological theories and traditions we have covered in this chapter, it is the Weberian tradition (assimilated into our radical pluralism) which would seem to provide the most appropriate tools to understand this phenomenon. The new penology is managerial, bureaucratic and impersonal, just as Weber theorized that administration in a developed and complex society would be. In other words, it is *modernizing*:[6] it represents an attempt to deal with crime and offenders in a rational and scientific manner untrammeled by traditional attitudes

---

[5]See Chapter 1, note 3.

[6]Consequently, like Garland (1995a) and unlike Pratt (2000) and Simon (1993), we do not see the new penology as being postmodern, but as being a development of late modernity. The rehabilitative approach was also an attempt to be rational and modern, but the more recent downplaying of rehabilitation is not postmodern but equally modernist in a different way. See further Cavadino and Dignan (2006: 7–9).

and practices, such as retributivism and a concentration on morally condemning offenders and making them suffer.

Although this Weberian analysis might explain the new penology, it can hardly account for the new punitiveness, which precisely *does* aim at making offenders suffer. To try to explain this paradox, we need to digress briefly into the fascinating realm of **comparative penology**.

Comparative Penology and the New Punitiveness

If we compare the practice of punishment across different countries (see Cavadino and Dignan, 2006), it is instantly noticeable that there are wide variations. Countries differ in the *methods* of punishment they employ: witness, for example, the use of capital punishment in the United States but not in Europe. They also differ in the general degree of *severity* with which they punish offenders. Again looking at imprisonment rates, these currently range from a high of 730 prisoners per 100,000 of population in the United States of America to a low of 19 in the Cental African Republic.[7] Even if we confine ourselves to developed Western countries, the US imprisonment rate far exceeds that of England and Wales (152) and even more so those of, for example, Germany (83) and Finland (59). What is it about different societies that makes for such different rates of punishment?

It is possible to relate some important characteristics of a country's *political economy* – and in particular its welfare system – to the severity of its penal practices. Modern Western countries can be categorized as either **neo-liberal**, **conservative corporatist** or **social democratic** nations (Lash and Urry, 1987; Esping-Andersen, 1990; Lash and Urry, 1994). Neo-liberalism refers to the (politically conservative) free-market capitalism exemplified by the United States, but also characterizing to a lesser extent countries such as Britain, Australia and New Zealand in recent decades. The general ethos – or the culture, or ideology – of neo-liberalism is one of individualism rather than communitarianism or collectivism. Under neo-liberalism the welfare state is minimalist, consisting mainly of means-tested welfare benefits, entitlement to which is often heavily stigmatized. The economic system creates much material inequality and this results in the social exclusion of many people who find themselves unable to participate to any great extent in civil, political and social life. Indeed, typically whole communities find themselves excluded in acutely deprived ghetto areas. In conservative corporatist countries (such as Germany and other nations in continental Western Europe), important national interest groups (notably organizations representing employers and workers) are integrated with the national state and are expected to act in accordance with a consensual national interest. In return, members of these groups enjoy welfare benefits that are more generous than those found in neo-liberal countries. The ideology and culture of conservative corporatism is a communitarian one which seeks to *include*

[7]Source: International Centre for Prison Studies, *World Prison Brief* website (accessed August 2012).

and integrate all citizens within the nation, via individuals' membership of interest groups. Conservative corporatist states offer their citizens greater protection against the vagaries of market forces and produce significantly less inequality than does neo-liberalism, but they are not strongly egalitarian. Their welfare states enshrine and perpetuate traditional class, status and economic divisions between different groups of citizens who are entitled to different levels of welfare benefits. A third arrangement (on the political left) is the social democratic version of corporatism – more egalitarian than the conservative version – whose prime example is Sweden and the other Nordic countries. These countries share the consensual, communitarian approach of conservative corporatism, but their welfare systems are more generous and more egalitarian, being based on universal benefits.

TABLE 3.1 Political Economy and Imprisonment Rates

	IMPRISONMENT RATE (per 100,00 population)
NEO-LIBERAL COUNTRIES	
USA	730
South Africa	310
New Zealand	190
England and Wales	154
Australia	129
CONSERVATIVE CORPORATIST COUNTRIES	
Italy	109
France	101
Netherlands	87
Germany	83
SOCIAL DEMOCRACIES	
Sweden	70
Finland	59

Source: International Centre for Prison Studies, *World Prison Brief* website (accessed August 2012).

Table 3.1 shows the imprisonment rates of a sample of eleven countries, divided into these three categories. It also shows that currently there are clear dividing lines between these different types of political economy as regards imprisonment rates in these countries. All the neo-liberal countries in this sample have higher rates than the conservative corporatist countries, while the Nordic social democracies[8] have the lowest imprisonment rates. But why should there be this relationship between political economy and rates of punishment?

---

[8]Denmark (74) and Norway (73) have similar imprisonment rates to that of Sweden.

One likely answer is that in these different kinds of political economy we find different *cultural attitudes* towards our deviant and marginalized fellow citizens. (This is perhaps more true among the political class of policy-makers than among the general public: see Cavadino and Dignan, 2010.) The neo-liberal society tends to *exclude* both those who fail in the economic marketplace and those who fail to abide by the law – in the latter case by means of imprisonment, or even more radically by execution. Both types of exclusion are associated with a highly individualistic social ethos – the attitude that, in Margaret Thatcher's famous words, 'there is no such thing as society'. Economic failure is seen as the fault of the individual, not the responsibility of society – hence the minimal, safety-net welfare state. Crime is likewise seen as entirely the responsibility of the offending individual. The social soil is fertile ground for a harsh law and order ideology. On the other hand, corporatist societies like that of Germany – and to an even greater extent, social democratic ones like Sweden's – have traditionally had a different culture and a different attitude towards the failing or deviant citizen. Corporatist and social democratic states offer their citizens a far greater degree of protection against the vicissitudes of market forces and seek to ensure that all citizens are looked after. Similarly there is a more communitarian, less individualistic attitude towards the offender, who is regarded not as an isolated culpable individual who must be rejected and excluded from law-abiding society, but as a social being who is still the responsibility of the community as a whole. A more developed welfare state goes along with a less punitive penal culture. The most developed welfare states of all – the Nordic social democracies – also have the lowest imprisonment rates among these Western nations (see further Cavadino and Dignan, 2006; 2010).

This association between types of political economy and levels of punitiveness may also go a long way towards explaining the rise of the new punitiveness of recent decades:[9] as neo-liberalism has advanced, so has law and order ideology. It is no coincidence that the United States has since the 1970s been leading the world in the direction both of neo-liberalism and of the new punitiveness, for the two go together. And this also helps to explain why so many other countries have gone down the punitive road, for so many of them have adopted neo-liberalism to a greater or lesser extent. Britain is very much a case in point, despite retaining a relatively well-developed welfare system compared with that of the US. The Conservative governments of 1979–97 moved Britain decisively towards neo-liberalism, a shift their New Labour successors accepted and indeed in most respects embraced, as have the current Coalition. And the new punitiveness towards offenders has come along with it. At the same time, however – in a parallel and sometimes conflicting trend – there has also been a long-term move towards the more managerial new penology we discussed under the previous heading.

The different sociological traditions covered in this chapter would view and explain this association between political economies and punitiveness in different

---

[9]There may well be other factors involved, such as an increase in sensationalist reporting about crime and punishment in the tabloid media and (associated with this) more penal populism on the part of politicians (see generally Cavadino and Dignan, 2006; 2010).

ways. The Durkheimian approach (see, for example, Greenberg, 1999) would emphasize the culture and 'collective sentiments' of different societies, and might seek to explain both a country's welfare system and its penality by saying that they were *both produced by* the society's culture. For example, the individualistic culture of the United States made the nation inclined to adopt both a minimalist welfare state and severe penal policies. Marxists, on the other hand, would see economics rather than culture as basic, and might assert that it is the economic facts of a society's welfare system which condition the ideology of its citizens in either an individualistic or communitarian (and in an egalitarian or inegalitarian) direction, leading to a harsh or lenient penality. More sophisticated Marxists would accept that it is not all one way and that ideologies can have a reciprocal action on the economic base, but (if they remain Marxists) they must assert the primacy of the latter. Again, we, and the radical pluralism which we favour, would take a view more akin to that of Weber: the realms of culture (or ideology) and of economics *interact* with each other, and although at times one might seem a more dominant determining factor, neither is basic. So it is true (as the Durkheimian approach suggests) that a society's cultural attitudes towards our deviant and marginalized fellow citizens affect both our penality and the economic system we adopt. But these attitudes are not only *embodied* in the economic system, they are also *embedded* in them, and the reality of living life in a society which is organized and runs on either individualistic lines or communitarian ones is likely to condition, reinforce and reproduce our attitudes towards others in society, thus (normally) helping to continue the existing system and culture, including the penal culture and the penal practices which that culture brings about.

These systems and cultures can of course change and evolve, in interaction with each other. And so it has been that in countries such as Britain, the welfare state, the economic system and the general culture have all altered markedly in recent decades, as has the 'penal *Zeitgeist*'.[10] For now at least, in an age of neo-liberalism, the new punitiveness predominates.

---

[10]For which apt phrase we thank Hanns von Hofer.

4

Sentencing: The Crux of the Crisis

The Crux of the Crisis

4.1 'Why', asked Justice Secretary Kenneth Clarke in June 2010, 'is the prison population twice what it was when I was the Home Secretary not so very long ago?' (1992–93) (*Guardian*, 14 June 2010).
In theory there could be several possible answers to this question. One obvious one might be that there are more people in prison because crime rates have gone up so there are more criminals to imprison. However, this is most certainly not the case if we compare the present day with the early-to mid-1990s. Indeed, crime (as recorded by the Crime Survey for England and Wales, formerly called the British Crime Survey) has *decreased* by a remarkable 50 per cent since 1995 (Office for National Statistics, 2012a). Nor has there been any increase in the number of offenders coming before the courts or any increase in the *seriousness* of their offences (Carter, 2003: 10; Hough et al., 2003: 10–1). But the sentences meted out for offences have become more severe. In 1991, 15 per cent of people who were found guilty of an indictable offence received a custodial sentence; in 2011 the corresponding figure was 25 per cent.[1] Moreover, the average *length* of custodial sentences has also risen substantially, at least in the Crown Court: from 20 months in 1993 to 25.5 in 2011. Overall, offenders who a decade and a half ago might have received a fine are now likely to receive a more onerous community penalty, whereas those who might have received community penalties are now more likely to be imprisoned, and those who are imprisoned face longer prison terms (see generally Hough et al., 2003: ch. 2; Morgan, 2003). The entire relationship between crime and punishment has been 'ratcheted up' (Morgan, 2003) a gear by more severe sentencing.

Sentencing is the crux of the penal crisis we outlined in Chapter 1. It is mainly judges and magistrates who determine the size of the prison numbers crisis when they decide which offenders to send to prison and how long those sentences should be. This in turn determines how great is the more general crisis of penal resources and the size of many other penal problems such as overcrowding and impoverished prison regimes and conditions. They are also

---

[1]From Carter (2003: 11) and statistics available online at www.justice.gov.uk/statistics/criminal-justice/criminal-justice-statistics (accessed 12 December 2012).

a potent source of perceived injustices which fuel the penal system's crisis of legitimacy.

This is not to say that sentencing is the only factor contributing to the crisis. Here are some of the others:

1   Decisions by the courts to *remand* defendants (and convicted offenders awaiting sentence) in custody rather than allow them their liberty in the interim by granting them bail (see Introduction and Cavadino and Dignan, 2007: 93–7). Remand prisoners currently account for 13 per cent of the prison population, making a significant contribution to the crises of numbers, resources and other associated problems. Remand decisions can also exacerbate the crisis of legitimacy if defendants are remanded in custody inappropriately or unjustly. The conditions of their custody are typically worse than those of many sentenced prisoners, since they are more likely to find themselves in overcrowded local prisons and remand centres, despite the fact that they are still supposed to be innocent in the eyes of the law, or (in the case of unsentenced convicts) have not yet been sentenced to imprisonment. Of particular concern is the enduring, chilling fact that remand prisoners are consistently and significantly more likely to take their own lives than are other prisoners (Scott and Codd, 2010: 96).

    It is not just that these large numbers of remand prisoners contribute to the practical problems of the penal system. Nor is it merely that they are technically 'innocent until proven guilty'. Some are actually innocent. Of defendants who have been denied bail before trial in either the magistrates' or Crown Court, a disturbingly high proportion – around one in five – are acquitted altogether or have the charges against them dropped. Many others are convicted, but receive a non-custodial sentence. This means that – remarkably – only 42 per cent of those who are remanded in custody while officially innocent end up being sentenced to immediate imprisonment (Prison Reform Trust, 2011: 23). In response to this situation, Schedule 11 of the Legal Aid, Sentencing and Punishment of Offenders Act 2012 was passed to restrict courts' powers to remand unconvicted defendants in custody if there is no real prospect that they will receive a custodial sentence if convicted.

2   **Mode of trial** decisions (Cavadino and Dignan, 2007: 97–101). As we saw in the Introduction, in triable either way cases either the defendant or the magistrates can insist that the trial takes place in the Crown Court rather than the magistrates' court. Waiting times are significantly longer for Crown Court trials, so the more cases are committed there with the defendant remanded in custody in the meantime, the more remand prisoners there will be at any one time. Moreover, offenders who are tried and sentenced in the Crown Court are in general likely to receive considerably more severe sentences than those sentenced in the magistrates' court (Hedderman and Moxon, 1992); thus the more cases tried in the Crown Court, the higher the prison population is likely to be.

3 The mechanisms for *early release* of prisoners (see Chapter 7) also affect how many prisoners there are at any one time, as will the number (which has risen significantly in recent years) of those released early who are recalled to prison.

4 The number of offenders serving *community sentences* (see Chapter 5) who are returned to court for breaching the terms of their orders and imprisoned as a result (which has also been rising) can also have a significant effect on the prison population.

Despite these other contributory factors, however, it is historically and statistically true that in England the sentencing practice of the courts (and especially of the Crown Court) has had by far the greatest effect on prison numbers. This has been particularly noticeable in the last decade and a half, when increasingly severe sentencing has been the main cause of the rocketing prison population (Halliday, 2001: 79–81; Carter, 2003: 9–12). Responsibility for the massive increase in the prison population in recent years thus rests largely in the hands of sentencers. Not to be overlooked, however, is the encouragement of severe sentencing by elements in the media – with some newspapers missing few opportunities to brand judges as 'soft' – and politicians who promulgate rhetoric, policies and legislation imbued with law and order ideology. Some legislation – such as that which introduced the mandatory and minimum sentences we shall discuss later – actually requires stiffer sentences. But even 'mere' rhetoric can have potent effects, as we noted in Chapter 1 (sections 1.2 and 1.4), and this is hardly surprising: sentencers feel a need to be responsive to (not 'out of touch' with) what they perceive as public opinion, which they take to be represented by media and political discourse.[2]

English courts seem to use custody to a greater extent than courts in many other comparable countries, even when dealing with similar offences. Studies which ask judges from different countries to indicate appropriate sentences for various offences (International Bar Association, 1990; NACRO, 1998) have found English sentences to be harsher than those of most other jurisdictions, and than almost any other European country involved in the studies. It is this more severe sentencing which seems to account for England's high imprisonment rate compared with other Western European states (as seen in Table 1.2 in Chapter 1).

Within England and Wales, some courts are much quicker than others to pass sentences of imprisonment (and longer ones) than others – which suggests that the more severe courts are being unnecessarily harsh. The Crown Court in particular uses imprisonment much more readily than the magistrates' court even in similar cases. Research we mentioned earlier (Hedderman and Moxon, 1992) found in a sample of comparable cases that the Crown Court passed sentences of immediate custody almost three times as often as magistrates' courts, and such sentences were on average two and a half times as long in the Crown Court. Another study – carried out when sentencing was significantly less harsh

---

[2]As we shall see in Chapter 10 (section 10.3), however, the evidence is that public opinion is by no means as punitive as is usually assumed.

than it currently is – found that where the Crown Court convicted a defendant of a minor property offence (involving property worth less than £200), as many as two fifths received unsuspended custody, despite much concern expressed at the time about the need to restrict custody to only the most serious property offenders (Moxon, 1988: 15).

There is also considerable *geographical* variation in sentencing within England and Wales. A succession of research studies over the years (commencing with Hood, 1962) has repeatedly demonstrated wide *disparities* in the sentencing practice of different magistrates' courts. In 1999 one court sentenced half of its domestic burglars to immediate custody while another did so for only 13 per cent. The percentage of custodial sentences for actual bodily harm ranged from 2 to 53 per cent (Halliday, 2001: 90). An earlier study (Tarling et al., 1985) showed that similar variations could not fully be explained by differences in either the kind of offences with which each court had to deal or the offenders coming before them; in other words the disparities were real. Similar disparities in the sentencing practices of different Crown Courts have also been demonstrated, with imprisonment rates for domestic burglars ranging from 56 per cent to 92 per cent, and average lengths of imprisonment from 12 months to 31 months (Halliday, 2001: 90–1). These figures again suggest that those courts which make relatively heavy use of imprisonment 'frequently have no reason to do so if the experience of other courts is any criterion' (Hood, 1962: 122). (In theory, the development of sentencing guidelines (see below) since these findings were made might be expected to have reduced these disparities, but evidence as to whether this has occurred is lacking.)

Such excessive and inconsistent sentencing does not merely fuel the crises of prison numbers and resources. It also diminishes the legitimacy of the penal system – as, for example, when courts were widely perceived to be passing unfairly draconian sentences on defendants who had participated in the riots of summer 2011 (while simultaneously pushing prison numbers up to a record level). This is not just a public relations problem. For those who are likely most keenly to perceive sentences as unjust are those who are on the receiving end of relatively harsh sentencing. Prisoners who owe their confinement to a sentence more severe than it needed to be might be excused for having a sense of injustice, especially if they rightly perceive that other similar offenders have been treated more leniently. Inconsistent sentencing violates the basic principle that like cases should be treated alike, and inevitably adds to the penal system's crucial crisis of legitimacy.

Who are the Sentencers?

4.2 Within the English criminal justice system the power to pass sentence is conferred on two completely different sets of sentencers who contrast not only in the powers at their disposal, but also in their social background, composition, mode of selection and training and much else besides. Around 95 per cent of all criminal cases are dealt with in the magistrates' courts. Offenders who are convicted here are normally sentenced by a bench of three lay (unpaid, and largely untrained) magistrates (also known as justices of the peace, or JPs). In larger urban areas these lay benches are supplemented by full-time professional magistrates known as district judges (magistrates' courts) – formerly known as stipendiary magistrates – who sit alone. Although magistrates are officially supposed to be broadly representative of the communities they serve, successive studies and surveys from the 1970s on have confirmed that this is far from the case: JPs are still overwhelmingly middle-aged and middle-class. For example, Dignan and Wynne (1997: 4–5) found over 80 per cent of their sample of magistrates to be aged 50 or more, with only 5 per cent being under 40 and just a quarter of male JPs being wage earners. Eight per cent of magistrates are of ethnic minority origin (Ministry of Justice, 2011c: 81) compared with around 14 per cent of the general population of England and Wales. However, women – formerly seriously under-represented on the bench – now account for 51 per cent of magistrates (Ministry of Justice, 2010b: 58). Magistrates tend to be conservative, and not only with a small 'c' (for example, Dignan and Wynne (1997: 8) found them to be significantly more likely to vote Conservative than the general population in their local area).

Magistrates are given a small amount of training, in which sentencing matters feature fairly prominently, and when sitting in court are assisted in the exercise of their powers by legal advisers (formerly known as court clerks). Advisers may bring relevant laws and sentencing guidelines to the magistrates' attention, but the sentencing decision belongs to the magistrates. Studies (Hood, 1962, 1972; Parker et al., 1989) have shown that the chief formative influence on sentencing practice in magistrates' courts is not the law, their training or the advice they receive from other professionals, nor even the way similar cases have been decided by that particular court in the past. Instead the principal influence is the 'sentencing culture' of a particular bench, into which new recruits are gradually socialized by watching their more experienced colleagues at work. Their perception of their role as magistrates is based on an ideology – a set of shared ideas – embedded in the bench culture. This ideology holds, first, that every individual case is unique. This means that consistency in sentencing is not recognized as a virtue. Instead, each case is seen as requiring a special judgment 'on its individual merits', a judgment that only the magistrate is deemed qualified to make. Because sentencing is viewed by magistrates as a craft or mystery, whose rites are known only to initiates (as opposed to a rational enterprise dedicated to the pursuit of defined goals), this renders it both impervious to criticism from outside, and highly resistant to attempts at external control. Thus, magistrates subscribe to a strong notion of 'magisterial independence', essentially identical to the inflated version of the doctrine of **judicial independence** which we discuss in the next section.

Judges sitting and sentencing in the Crown Court include High Court judges (in the most serious cases), circuit judges and part-time recorders. Crown Court judges differ from magistrates in a number of important respects (though it could be said that their ideologies are similar). One important difference between them is that judges are not only legally trained but have also invariably spent most of their working lives as practising barristers (or, less often, solicitors). They receive little training for their role *as judges*, in contrast to most West European countries which have a professional career structure for judges who are recruited immediately on graduating from law school. In England, training for Crown Court judges is provided by the Judicial Studies Board, and consists of short induction courses for new recruits and continuation courses for more experienced judges. Although judicial attitudes towards training are becoming less dismissive than they were in the past, it remains the case that the main method of 'perfecting the art' of sentencing is practising on actual offenders.

The fact that Crown Court judges are recruited almost exclusively from the ranks of successful practising barristers has also had the effect of narrowing considerably the background from which the judges are drawn, even in comparison with the far from representative magistracy. Judges who sit in the Crown Court tend to be slightly older than magistrates on average (around 60 for judges and 56 for lay justices). However, in contrast to magistrates, Crown Court judges are predominantly male: in 2009–10, only 16 per cent of recorders were women (Ministry of Justice, 2010b: 60). They are also more unrepresentative than magistrates in terms of race, with only around 5 per cent from ethnic minorities.

As for the social composition of the judiciary, many surveys have shown an overwhelming predominance of upper and upper middle-class backgrounds among judges (see, for example, Griffith, 1997: 18). Not only did around 80 per cent of the country's judges received a public school education, with over three quarters attending either Oxford or Cambridge universities, but also this social profile has remained virtually unaltered over the last half century. Thus, there exists an enormous social gulf between those who pass sentence in the Crown Court and those on the receiving end. Even more importantly, this social profile helps to explain the uniqueness of English judicial culture compared with that found in other countries. This judicial culture is founded on an ideology whose cornerstone is the doctrine of judicial independence, which we discuss in the next section.

Constraints on the Powers of Sentencers

Judical Independence and Traditional English Sentencing

4.3 For a long time in England and Wales there were few constraints on the powers of sentencers other than the system of maximum sentences we will outline shortly. The ideology (discussed in the previous section) that sentencers should be left to judge each individual case on its own unique merits led to the acceptance of a peculiarly broad version of the *doctrine of judicial independence*. The doctrine of judicial independence is not controversial in itself. It is generally accepted that the judiciary should be separate and independent from the legislature (Parliament) and the executive (the government of the day): this is part of the basic constitutional concept of the 'separation of powers'. Judicial independence is usually interpreted – in most countries and by most people – to mean, simply and uncontroversially, that governments must not be allowed to influence the decisions of the courts *in individual cases*. However, in England in the twentieth century this principle became distorted and inflated by the judiciary into the much more sweeping claim that the sentencing discretion of judges should be left untouched, and that it is improper for government or Parliament even to lay down broad sentencing policies (Ashworth, 2005: 50–4). This claim – which of course has the effect, attractive to judges, of maximizing their powers to sentence in any way they want – clearly has no basis in constitutional law and theory, not least because Parliament is entitled to legislate on sentencing as well as on anything else. Nevertheless, for a long time governments in practice accepted the extravagant version, largely doubtless for fear of provoking a confrontation with the judges. On the rare occasions that government and Parliament threatened to infringe the doctrine, the judiciary would typically protest loudly and end up getting its own way.

'Judicial independence' became a potent myth, which had the effect of perpetuating the largely untrammelled sentencing powers enjoyed by the courts in England, meaning that for many years sentencing was left not only out of control but also in a policy vacuum. More recently, governments and judges have both moved in the direction of accepting the legitimacy of legislative intervention and governmental strategy in sentencing, with the result that more recently sentencing has become subject to a developing framework of legal rules, guidelines and other constraints. Nevertheless, the extravagant version of the doctrine of judicial independence continues to cast a shadow, with the result that English sentencers normally retain a wide discretion to sentence offenders as they see fit and that this discretion remains jealously guarded in opposition to any proposals to limit it further.

One manifestation of this has been that sentencers have not only generally been left free (within certain defined limits) to decide which specific sentence to choose out of the wide range usually available for any individual offender, they have also been free to decide for themselves *what their sentencing is supposed to be trying to achieve*. We saw in Chapter 2 that punishment can be seen as having a wide variety of aims and purported justifications, not all of them obviously consistent with each other, including retribution, deterrence, reform, incapacitation, denunciation and reparation. Traditionally sentencers have been free to decide for themselves which of these aims is to be pursued in each individual case. This eclectic tradition lives on in section 142 of the Criminal Justice Act 2003, which sets out the purposes of sentencing as being: '(a) the punishment of offenders [i.e. retribution and denunciation]; (b) the reduction of crime (including its reduction by deterrence); (c) the reform and rehabilitation of offenders; (d) the protection of the public [i.e. incapacitation]; and (e) the making of reparation by offenders to persons affected by their offences'. Although the section states that sentencers must 'have regard' to all these purposes, the effect is to allow sentencers to pick and choose their penal aims and philosophies as much as ever.

The traditional English method of sentencing therefore is for the sentencer to decide, in a largely impressionistic manner, what penalty is most appropriate for this particular offence committed by this particular offender. Normally this is for the most part dictated by how serious the offence is perceived as being. The sentencer takes account of any aggravating and mitigating circumstances which make this particular offence more or less serious than it would otherwise be, or which makes it appropriate to punish this individual offender more or less severely. In particular, a sentence will typically be more severe if the offender has previous convictions: the worse the offender's record, the harsher the sentence. The sentencer may then also take into account any other factors that seem relevant, for example whether the offender is thought to need some particular reformative measure, and then decides on the sentence. Sentencers have a legal duty to give reasons for the sentences they pass, albeit only 'in general terms' (Criminal Justice Act 2003, s. 174).

This deliberative process is assisted (but of course not dictated) by information and advice contained in *reports* which may be supplied to the court. One such is the statement known as 'the antecedents' provided by the prosecution and containing brief details of the offender's previous convictions, sentences and cautions. In the case of offenders who appear to be mentally disordered, the court may receive a medical report from a psychiatrist. In some cases there may be 'victim personal statements' (first introduced in 2001: see Edwards, 2002) whereby victims of the crime (or bereaved relatives of homicide victims) can explain the effect it has had on them.

One particularly important source of information and advice consists of the **pre-sentence report** (or PSR), which is prepared for the court by probation officers, or in the case of young offenders by members of the local youth offending team (see Chapter 8). As well as providing factual information about offenders and their backgrounds and histories, PSRs can make proposals as to what the sentence should be (which the courts usually follow). Sentencers are normally required to consider a PSR before imposing either a custodial sentence or one of the more restrictive community sentences (see Chapter 5). However, there is a wide get-out clause: for adult offenders, sentencers may dispense with a PSR 'if, in the circumstances of the case, the court is of the opinion that it is unnecessary to obtain a pre-sentence report' (Criminal Justice Act 2003, s. 156). It has been found that around 15 per cent of adult offenders are given custodial sentences without the benefit of a PSR, but community sentences are rarely imposed in the absence of such a report (Charles et al., 1997). The proposals for sentences contained in PSRs have become more severe in recent years: between 1990 and 2000 explicit proposals for custody doubled from 2–3 per cent to 5–6 per cent, while proposals for fines and discharges halved. Thus probation officers – who have faced long-standing pressure to make more 'realistic' proposals – have responded accordingly, thereby playing their own part in the 'ratcheting up' of sentencing (Morgan, 2003: 15).

In many jurisdictions it is common for prosecutors to recommend particular sentences to the court and argue in favour of them. Traditionally in England and

Wales prosecutors have played little part in the sentencing process (one exception being the role of the Attorney General in appealing against allegedly lenient sentences, which we mention later). However, advice to courts on sentencing from prosecuting counsel, the Crown Prosecution Service and other prosecuting agencies could become more of a feature in future. Guidelines issued in 2009 (Attorney General, 2009) encouraged prosecution counsel to 'assist the court to reach its decision as to the appropriate sentence', including drawing the court's attention to information about the impact of the offence and to relevant sentencing legislation and guidelines, and making submissions as to the appropriate range of sentences for the individual case. This could potentially mark an important development in the sentencing system. But indications so far are that senior judges at least will be wary of being dictated to by prosecutors. In *R v. Dougall*[3] the Court of Appeal held that a prosecution recommendation for a **suspended sentence order** (SSO) was excessively specific advice for the judge, and stressed that the court should never be presented with 'an agreed package for the court's acquiescence'.

Unless mandatory penalties (discussed shortly) apply, there is no such thing as a legally correct sentence. However, for a long time there has existed a fairly vague and impressionistic notional scale of penalties familiarly known as the *tariff*, which is based on the normal range of sentences that have been passed by courts for similar offences in the past. This tariff essentially follows the principle that the severity of a sentence should be proportionate to the seriousness of the offence – in other words, that offenders should receive their just deserts (as discussed in Chapter 2). There is, however, one major caveat affecting the application of this 'offence-based tariff', which is that sentencers may take into account factors relating to individual *offenders* which do not necessarily bear on the seriousness of the *offence* for which they are being sentenced – most importantly the extent of the offender's *previous* criminal behaviour. The result is that in practice courts also operate an 'offender-based tariff' in awkward tandem with the offence-based version.

How sentencers juggle all this information and advice, conflicting considerations and the two tariffs is still very much up to them. Nevertheless, there are some limits and controls on sentencers' decision-making, taking various forms, and in recent years the tendency has been for these limits and controls to be increased and extended. Generally speaking the exercise of any power to make discretionary decisions (such as that enjoyed by judges and magistrates) can be controlled and influenced in various ways (Davis, 1969). Discretion can be *confined* by setting fixed limits on the decisions that can be made; it can be *checked* by allowing appeals and reviews after the decisions have been made: or the exercise of the discretion can be *structured*, by devices such as principles, guidelines and codes of

---

[3][2010] EWCA Crim 1048. This was a case of 'plea bargaining', where the prosecution and defence agreed on a particular sentence in return for the defendant's plea of guilty, which can be seen as usurping the role of the court.

practice. All of these types of control can now be seen encircling and constraining the sentencing decision in England and Wales.

Confining Discretion

Compared with some other jurisdictions, relatively little attempt has been made in England and Wales to confine the exercise of sentencers' discretion by rules which rigidly limit the extent of their powers. Magistrates, it is true, only have limited powers: they cannot impose a custodial sentence that is longer than six months in respect of a single offence. (This could change in the near future. Section 154 of the Criminal Justice Act 2003, which has not yet been implemented, provided for this limit to be raised to 12 months and the Coalition government currently favours introducing this change at some stage.)[4] Nevertheless, they enjoy a considerable degree of discretion up to these upper limits. Crown Court judges have much more extensive powers. Each particular offence carries a statutory *maximum* penalty, but many of these maxima were set so long ago, and in such different circumstances, as to render them largely irrelevant for the control of judicial sentencing today. Moreover, the tendency during the twentieth century was to create broadly defined criminal offences (such as theft), with a sufficiently generous maximum to cater for the worst contingency.

There are still relatively few *mandatory* or *minimum* sentences. For a long time the only major exception was the mandatory life imprisonment sentence for murder. Even this has long been unpopular with the judiciary as an infringement on their discretion to do justice in individual cases, and there have been repeated calls for its abolition (for example, Lane, 1993; Blom-Cooper and Morris, 2004). (As we shall see more fully in Chapter 7, the nature of this mandatory life sentence has changed over time and the sentencing judge now has much more say over how long a convicted murderer remains in prison.) There is also a long-standing 'semi-mandatory' sentence of disqualification from driving for the offence of driving with excess alcohol in the blood; 'semi-mandatory' meaning that the sentence is required unless the court finds that there are exceptional circumstances in the individual case.

A number of new semi-mandatory and minimum sentences have been introduced since 1997, some of them based on American 'three strikes and you're out' sentences which require automatic or minimum sentences for repeat offenders. Thus a minimum sentence of at least seven years' imprisonment is mandated for an offender convicted of a Class A drug trafficking offence for the third time ('three strikes and you're out'), unless the court considers this to be 'unjust in all the circumstances', and courts are similarly required to impose a minimum sentence of at least three years on an offender convicted of a third offence of domestic burglary

---

[4]Nor can magistrates at present normally impose a fine of more than £5,000, although this limit is to be removed by s. 85 of the Legal Aid, Sentencing and Punishment of Offenders Act 2012.

(Powers of Criminal Courts (Sentencing) Act 2000, ss. 110 and 111). A single offence suffices to attract a minimum sentence of five years' imprisonment for various offences involving the unlawful possession of firearms under section 287 of the Criminal Justice Act 2003, introduced in response to concern about rising levels of gun crime, unless the court finds that there are 'exceptional circumstances'.

The latest additions to this list of mandatory sentences are to be found in the Coalition government's Legal Aid, Sentencing and Punishment of Offenders Act 2012. Section 142 of this Act introduces a new minimum sentence of six months' imprisonment for making threats with a knife or other weapon, unless this would be 'unjust in all the circumstances'. Section 122 introduces a new mandatory 'two strikes and you're out' sentence of life imprisonment for certain adult offenders convicted of specified serious offences, again unless particular circumstances would make this sentence unjust.

Apart from these still limited inroads, little attempt has been made to *confine* the discretion of sentencers by statute. Even these sentences (apart from life for murder) are strictly speaking only semi-mandatory, all of these legislative provisions containing 'get-out clauses' which allow courts to avoid imposing them in cases where the sentence normally required would be 'unjust in all the circumstances' of the individual case (the exact statutory wording varies). Sentencers, who tend to resent mandatory sentences as an intrusion on their discretionary powers, can often if they so wish exploit these provisos to pass the sentences they want. Thus, there have not been nearly as many 'three-strike' sentences passed as one might have imagined, although the courts have been slower to find the 'exceptional circumstances' required to avoid the minimum sentence for unlawful firearm possession (Cavadino and Dignan, 2007: 116, 118).

Checking Discretion: Appeals

People who are convicted and sentenced by the courts can appeal against their convictions, against their sentences or both. Those tried at the magistrates' court normally appeal to the Crown Court; those tried in the Crown Court may take their case to the Court of Appeal. It is also possible for the prosecution (in the form of the Attorney General) to appeal to the Court of Appeal against the passing of a Crown Court sentence which is alleged to be unduly lenient, although this procedure is only available for a limited number of relatively serious offences and only happens in a few score cases each year.

As we have seen, although there is usually no single legally correct sentence, it is possible to distinguish a vague normal range of sentence for many offences in the form of the tariff. And as we shall see below, this traditional vague tariff has more recently been supplemented and to some extent superseded by officially framed sentencing guidelines which also provide normal ranges for offences of different kinds – guidelines that courts are bound to consider but not necessarily follow in all cases. If a court imposes a sentence that is clearly outside the normal range and there is no obvious reason for the departure (or the sentence is for some other reason thought to be contrary to principle), the sentence may be altered on appeal. However, appeal courts will often be slow to interfere with a lower court's decision unless it is clearly well out of line. Again, in theory a sentence could be quashed if the sentencer fails to give adequate reasons for it; but it seems unlikely in practice that this would ever occur. And of course, all of this depends on the offender (or Attorney General) taking the case to appeal in the first place. Consequently the retrospective checking of sentencing decisions via the appeal process provides only a limited amount of control over sentencers' discretion.

Another difficulty, certainly with the traditional tariff, is the fact that there are probably at least as many different tariffs in practice as there are levels of court (Court of Appeal, Crown Court and magistrates' court). As we noted earlier, when sentences for similar cases tried in the Crown Court and the magistrates' court are compared, it has been found that those sentenced in the Crown Court are almost three times as likely to receive a custodial sentence, and that the Crown Court's custodial sentences are on average two and a half times as long (Hedderman and Moxon, 1992). Similarly, it seems likely that the sentences imposed by the Court of Appeal are in general more severe than those typically passed by the Crown Court. For the Court of Appeal normally hears appeals by defendants against Crown Court sentences they consider too severe, and hence usually only comes to hear about relatively harsh Crown Court sentences (and never about sentences passed in the magistrates' court), shaping and distorting its perceptions about what the 'going rate' actually is in practice. One illustration of this was the 1980 case of *R. v. McCann*,[5] in which the Court of Appeal reduced the sentence for a relatively minor burglary from two years' imprisonment to nine months. Even this reduced sentence considerably exceeded the maximum penalty that could have been imposed in a magistrates' court (where the majority of burglars of this type would normally have been tried). And indeed in the magistrates' court in 1980 less than a third of such cases would have received a custodial penalty at all. Thus, it seems highly likely that a sentence which is genuinely much more severe than the general 'going rate' in the Crown Court (let alone the magistrates' court) may easily be wrongly perceived by the Court of Appeal as quite normal, and will be confirmed. It is possible that, now there are sentencing guidelines covering all courts (see under the next heading), this may have the effect of reducing some of these disparities between different courts and sentences, but it is too early to say.

Structuring Discretion: Principles and Guidelines

Discretion is *structured* by providing formal guidance in advance to decision-makers to assist their deliberations. Typically, structuring is more flexible than the confinement of discretion by rigid rules (such as mandatory sentences) and leaves it open to the decision-maker to depart from the guidance in individual cases where it seems appropriate.

---

[5](1980) 71 Cr App R 381: see Ashworth (1983: 41).

One type of structuring is the setting out of relatively *broad rules and principles* about the aims to be pursued in sentencing and the criteria which must be considered before deciding how severe the penalty should be and especially before imposing particular penalties (such as imprisonment). Such principles and criteria may be expressed in Acts of Parliament or in the pronouncements of senior judges, and can take a variety of forms. For example, there is a general principle which has found expression in differing ways in various statutory provisions (including the Criminal Justice Act 2003, s. 152(2)). This is the *principle of last resort*, the idea that imprisonment should only be used if no lesser sentence can be considered appropriate. Sentencers regularly claim to be following this principle in any event, as a matter of custom and conscience. And yet in 2002 the courts sent 3,000 people to prison for minor thefts (such as shoplifting and the theft of bicycles) despite having no previous convictions.[6] Clearly, some sentencers are relatively quick to convince themselves that they have reached the last resort. A related principle is one we mentioned in Chapter 2 in connection with Jeremy Bentham's utilitarianism: the *principle of parsimony*, that punishment (especially custodial punishment) should be used as sparingly as possible. Another general principle is that of *proportionality* or *just deserts*, the idea that the severity of the punishment should be in proportion to the seriousness of the offence. Yet another principle is one which competes and conflicts with proportionality: the *principle of progression* (or the 'principle of persistence'), according to which offenders should be punished more severely the more they reoffend.

It is principles such as these which underlie the notion of the traditional sentencing tariff, briefly explained previously, which does guide sentencing to a degree but (as we have seen) only to a limited degree, due to its inherent vagueness and other factors. One perennially controversial issue, arguably still unresolved, is to what extent sentences, and the tariff, should reflect the offender's past criminality. Should the tariff be – as the principle of proportionality and the theory of just deserts would suggest, and as we would prefer – primarily *offence-based*, with sentences in proportion to the current offences? Or should it follow the principle of progression and be more *offender-based*, so that – for example – petty persistent offenders can be imprisoned even though their latest offence taken in isolation would not warrant this?

Currently the most important method of structuring sentencing discretion is the **sentencing guideline**, published in advance for courts to follow when sentencing. Guidelines prescribe, with varying degrees of precision, the appropriate penalty for a whole range of combinations of offence and offender. These can take various forms.

One type of guideline is exemplified by the world-famous 'Minnesota Sentencing Guidelines Grid' (see Figure 4.1). The grid is a table made up of rows which specify the current offence and its level of seriousness, and columns specifying the offender's criminal history score (number of previous offences); these two factors

---

[6]Cited by Martin Narey, House of Commons Select Committee on Education and Skills Minutes of Evidence, 17 November 2004.

SEVERITY LEVEL OF CONVICTION OFFENSE	CRIMINAL HISTORY SCORE						
	0	1	2	3	4	5	6 or more
Assault, 1st Degree *Controlled Substance Crime, 1st Degree*	86 *74–103*	98 *84–117*	110 *94–132*	122 *104–146*	134 *114–160*	146 *125–175*	158 *135–189*
Aggravated Robbery, 1st Degree *Controlled Substance Crime, 2nd Degree*	48 *41–57*	58 *50–69*	68 *58–81*	78 *67–93*	88 *75–105*	98 *84–117*	108 *92–129*
Controlled Substance Crime, 3rd Degree	n/c	n/c	n/c	39 *34–46*	45 *39–54*	51 *44–61*	57 *49–68*
Residential Burglary *Simple Robbery*	n/c	n/c	n/c	33 *29–39*	38 *33–45*	43 *37–51*	48 *41–57*
Nonresidential Burglary	n/c	n/c	n/c	n/c	24 *21–28*	27 *23–32*	30 *26–36*
Theft Crimes (Over $5,000)	n/c	n/c	n/c	n/c	19 *17–22*	21 *18–25*	23 *20–27*
Theft Crimes ($5,000 or less) *Check Forgery ($251-$2,500)*	n/c	n/c	n/c	n/c	n/c	n/c	21 *18–25*

Non-italicized figures indicate presumptive sentence lengths in months of imprisonment.

Italicized figures indicate the range within which the judge may sentence without it being deemed a departure from the guidelines.

n/c (our editing) means that the presumptive sentence is non-custodial.

FIGURE 4.1   The Minnesota Sentencing Grid (edited extract)

Source: www.msgc.state.mn.us

in combination determine a fairly narrow range of prescribed sentences. Thus these guidelines operate like a road mileage chart, enabling the appropriate penalty to be simply read off from the appropriate box in the grid. The guidelines only provide a 'presumptive sentence' or starting point for the sentence, and sentencers are free to depart from this if they think it appropriate in an individual case, but they must give reasons for doing so, and departures from the prescribed normal range are likely to be overturned on appeal if no adequate justification is given.

This is just one form of guideline. Guidelines can also be much less mechanical than this, simply providing a range of standard sentences for different kinds of typical offence, along with guidance on roughly how much to adjust the standard sentence in the light of common aggravating and mitigating circumstances. This is the form that sentencing guidelines have taken in England and Wales.

Guidelines potentially allow a tighter and more consistent control of sentencing than could ever be achieved just by retrospectively checking individual sentencing decisions on appeal. In theory they could help attain greater consistency in sentencing, helping to avoid unjust and delegitimizing disparities, and could also be designed to pursue other aims such as a reduction in the general level of sentencing (and hence in the prison population). Moreover, sentencers seem to respond more willingly to the structuring of their discretion by guidelines than to having it confined by maximum, minimum and mandatory sentences. They resent the latter, which constrain their power to do justice as they see it in individual cases. But sentencers often welcome external guidance as to how they should make their (often difficult, sometimes agonizing) sentencing decisions, whether this comes from official guidelines or the informal sentencing culture of the bench or advice from more experienced colleagues.

In England, sentencing guidelines originally began to develop as an extension of the checking function of the Court of Appeal which, especially from the mid-1970s onwards, would take the opportunity when hearing appeals in individual cases to lay down general guidance for lower courts to apply in similar cases in the future. These guideline judgments spelt out, for example, the range of appropriate penalties for offences of varying degrees of seriousness within a given category. Thus, for instance, in *R. v. Billam*[7] the Court laid down a series of *starting points* for sentences for rape, with higher starting points for more serious types of case. This self-regulation of the judiciary by the Court of Appeal had a number of serious limitations as a control on sentencing practice. Guideline judgments tended to be vague, sometimes contradictory, and far from comprehensive. For a long time the Court of Appeal provided no real guidance at all in respect of many common offences such as theft and burglary. Nor could the Court of Appeal issue guidelines covering summary offences (which never came before the Court of Appeal) – although this gap was partially filled when in 1989 the Magistrates' Association began issuing its own sentencing guidelines for use in magistrates' courts.

The system for producing guidelines was to change drastically during the lifetime of the New Labour government of 1997 to 2010 – not once, but three times. First, the Court of Appeal's role in issuing guidelines was extended and made more proactive by the Crime and Disorder Act 1998. This Act gave the Court of Appeal a duty, when-ever hearing an appeal against sentence, to consider whether it should take the oppor-tunity to issue a new sentencing guideline. It also created a new body, the **Sentencing Advisory Panel** (SAP), chaired by a legal academic, with responsibility for advising and assisting the Court of Appeal on the issuing of sentencing guidelines. The Criminal Justice Act 2003 took the history of sentencing guidelines an important stage further, by removing the main responsibility for framing and issuing guidelines away from the Court of Appeal and bestowing it on a new body, the **Sentencing Guidelines Council** (SGC), chaired by the **Lord Chief Justice** (the senior judge who presides over the Court of Appeal), with the SAP remaining in being to advise the SGC. The idea was that the SGC would over time create comprehensive sentencing guidelines to cover all offences and governing both the Crown Court and magistrates' courts.

(The Criminal Justice Act 2003 also introduced a new set of statutory guidelines – contained in the Act itself (Schedule 21) – to cover one specialized area of sentencing, namely the setting of the 'tariff' element of the sentence for those convicted of murder.

---

[7](1986) 8 Cr App R (S) 48.

The tariff is the minimum period of the mandatory life sentence that must be served before the murderer can be released on parole, as will be discussed and explained in greater detail in Chapter 7, section 7.3.)

In 2007 the New Labour government commissioned their 'trouble-shooter' Lord Carter to investigate the use of custody, and in particular to look at how the balance could be improved between the supply of prison places and demand for them. Carter's (2007) report favoured the creation of a more 'structured sentencing framework' to improve the transparency, predictability and consistency of sentencing and the criminal justice system. Predictability was a key word: the English prison system has proved vulnerable to unpredicted surges in the prison population, so Carter favoured mechanisms to render sentencing and its effects more certain. Carter was impressed by the example of Minnesota, whose relatively rigid sentencing grid we have already mentioned. The Minnesota grid is framed and regularly revised by Minnesota's Sentencing Guidelines Commission, employing mathematical models to such effect that it is able to predict next year's state prison population to within 1 per cent and ensure by its periodic adjustments of the grid that prisons do not become overcrowded. (Minnesota has a low prison population by US standards, although that still leaves its imprisonment rate significantly higher than England's.) Carter envisaged a similar set-up in England, with a new-style Sentencing Commission issuing grid-style guidelines, so that (in line with his remit) the demand for prison places created by sentencing could be kept in line with the supply of such places within the prison system.

The government thereupon set up a working group to look into these ideas and canvass views. The idea of a Minnesota-style system of commission and grid met with widespread horror by judges, with the Council of Circuit Judges describing such a system as a 'nightmare' and others denouncing the advent of what they called 'tramline sentencing'. One problem perhaps not fully taken into account by Carter was that grids like that of Minnesota allow very little scope for aggravating and mitigating circumstances (other than the seriousness of the offence and the offender's past record) to play much part in the sentencing decision; but if the guidelines are framed more flexibly to give sentencers more leeway to take account of such factors – which can vary greatly from case to case – we are likely to lose that predictability in sentencing which was Carter's main aim. The working group's report (Sentencing Commission Working Group, 2008) recommended a watered down (more 'evolutionary') approach, which was fairly rapidly adopted by the Coroners and Justice Act 2009.

This entailed creating another new body, but not a Minnesota-style commission. The Coroners and Justice Act 2009 combined the Sentencing Guidelines Council and its Sentencing Advisory Panel into a single body, the **Sentencing Council**, which came into being in April 2010. It is made up of eight judges and six other members, chaired by Court of Appeal judge Lord Justice Leveson. Sentencing courts are now required to *follow* the guidelines unless satisfied 'that it would be contrary to the interests of justice to do so' (s. 125). (Previously courts were only required to 'have regard' to SGC guidelines.) Courts are also required to identify any guidelines they are following, and if they decide not to follow a relevant guideline they must give reasons explaining why to do so would be unjust (s. 174 of the Criminal Justice Act 2003, as amended).

When producing its guidelines, the Council must have regard to the cost of different sentences (s. 120(11)), and it must also accompany any new guidelines or draft guidelines with an assessment of their implications for prison places and other penal resources. However, there is no new requirement (as some had urged, along the lines of Carter's thinking) for the Council to *have regard to the available penal resources* when framing the guidelines. This represents a victory for those who contended that allowing the prison places available to dictate the sentences that are passed would be an unjust wagging of the dog by its tail over those who regard this as quite a sensible idea. The Council has statutory duties to monitor the effects of its guidelines (s. 128), to assess the effects of sentencing practice, policy and legislative proposals and other factors on penal resources (ss. 130–132), and to promote awareness of sentencing matters (s. 129), including giving courts information about their local sentencing patterns.

Guidelines are created as follows. The Sentencing Council produces and publishes a draft guideline. It then must consult the Justice Secretary and Parliament's Justice Select Committee, and may also consult anyone else it deems appropriate. In practice consultations are open, with any interested person or body able to feed their views on draft guidelines back to the Council. Finally, the Council issues a definitive guideline. When framing these, the Council must take into account (as we have seen) the costs of different sentences. It must also consider the relative effectiveness of different sentences in preventing reoffending; the sentences currently imposed by the courts; the need to promote consistency in sentencing; the impact of sentencing decisions on victims; the need to promote public confidence in the criminal justice system; and the results of the Council's monitoring of the effects of its guidelines.

Guidelines for particular offences normally now divide offences into levels of seriousness and specify both a range of sentences and a starting point for each level of seriousness. Thus, for example, the guideline for common assault divides the offence into three categories of seriousness. For offences in the most serious category ('greater harm and greater culpability') the starting point is a 'high level community order' and the normal range for sentences runs from a 'low level community order' to 216 weeks' custody. The guideline also identifies a number of common aggravating and mitigating factors (not an exhaustive list) which might induce the court to opt for a more or less severe sentence than that indicated by the starting point, or in an appropriate case may mean that the court passes a sentence completely outside the normal range. Once a definitive guideline is in force, sentencing courts are required to follow it unless satisfied 'that it would be contrary to the interests of justice to do so' (Coroners and Justice Act 2009, s. 125). Courts are required to identify any guidelines they are following, and if they decide not to follow a relevant guideline they must give reasons explaining why to do so would be unjust (Criminal Justice Act 2003, s. 174, as amended).

Some critics have expressed fears that, despite the watering down of Carter's suggestions, guidelines under the revised system will be akin to a sentencing grid which courts will have to apply almost mechanically (or 'tramline sentencing'). This has been denied by the Council's chair Lord Justice Leveson (*The Times*, 3 June 2010), and indeed on the contrary one eminent commentator has described the Act's provisions for influencing sentencing, as 'pitifully loose' (Ashworth, 2010.) Certainly, while the statutory duty of courts to follow guidelines is in theory stricter than it was, much discretion still, as ever, rests in the hands of individual sentencers.

The Current Legal Framework of Sentencing

The Criminal Justice Act 2003 (as amended), originally passed under the New Labour government of 1997–2010, currently provides the majority of the most important legislative provisions framing the current sentencing system for adults in England and Wales. Section 142 sets out the approved *purposes of sentencing*[8] as: '(a) punishment of offenders [i.e. retribution and denunciation]; (b) the reduction of crime (including via deterrence); (c) the reform and rehabilitation of offenders; (d) the protection of the public [i.e. 'incapacitation']; and (e) the making of reparation by offenders'. Sentences which may be passed in pursuance of these aims include all those mentioned in the Introduction, including fines, compensation orders, community orders, suspended sentence orders and imprisonment (including imprisonment for life). As explained in section 4.3 of this chapter, maximum sentences apply to all offences, while in some cases there are mandatory or minimum sentences. Within these statutory fixed points, courts are normally bound to follow guidelines laid down by the Sentencing Council (and by its predecessor the SGC), as explained under the previous heading.

Section 152(2) lays down a '*seriousness threshold*' for the use of custody: courts should not normally pass custodial sentences unless the current offences are '*so serious that neither a fine alone nor a community sentence can be justified for the offence*'.[9] Similarly, the length of any custodial sentence should be 'the shortest term … commensurate with the seriousness of the offence' (s. 153(2)). At first sight these provisions appear to conform to notions of retributivism and just deserts (see Chapter 2), for they seem to require an offence-based tariff whereby the severity of the sentence is proportionate to the gravity of the *current* offence, rather than an offender-based tariff, which punishes offenders according to their

---

[8]For adults: for young offenders the principal aim was stated as being 'to prevent offending by children and young persons' by section 37 of the Crime and Disorder Act 1998. Section 9 of the Criminal Justice and Immigration Act 2008 (not yet in force) supplements this by requiring courts also to have regard to the welfare of the offender, the punishment of offenders, reform and rehabilitation, the protection of the public and the making of reparation by offenders.

[9]Italics added. A custodial sentence may also be passed if the offender fails to agree to the terms of a proposed community sentence, or fails to comply with an order for a pre-sentence drug test (s. 152(3)).

record of *past* offences. However, the Act was deliberately framed to embody the principle of progression, which requires persistent offenders to be dealt with more harshly. This was achieved by means of section 143(2), which radically alters the meaning of the word 'serious'. It instructs courts to treat previous convictions as an aggravating factor increasing the seriousness of the offence – thus instituting a tariff in which the offender's past record is a highly significant factor. Thus courts have the power to send petty offenders to prison provided they are sufficiently persistent, and to lengthen sentences on the basis of the offender's past record.

Although these statutory provisions were intended to make successive sentences on repeat offenders highly 'progressive', their effect has (at least in theory) been moderated by a guideline on assessing seriousness issued by the SGC in 2004 (Sentencing Guidelines Council, 2004b). This states that 'the culpability of the offender ... should be the initial factor in determining the seriousness of the offence', thus (in line with 'just deserts' thinking) seeming to prioritizing the culpability or blameworthiness of the offender above the offender's previous criminal record. The guideline mentions previous record as an aggravating factor rendering an offence more serious, but only as one in a long list of such factors.

Another departure from the principles of just deserts in the 2003 Act takes the form of specially severe sentences intended to protect the public from violent or sexual offenders. Sections 227–228 provide for **extended sentences** of imprisonment which the court may impose if it considers this necessary to protect the public from serious harm. Imprisonment under these sentences comes with restricted eligibility for early release (see Chapter 7) and is followed by an extra-long period of supervision in the community. More drastically, section 225 of the 2003 Act also introduced a new indeterminate sentence of imprisonment for public protection, discussed in section 4.4 above and Chapter 7, section 7.3); however, this sentence has now been abolished by section 123 of the Legal Aid, Sentencing and Punishment of Offenders Act 2012.

This is the current state of play, but will surely not be the end of the story. The legal framework for sentencing is the result of a long and complex history of (typically hotly debated and contested) developments and amendments of policies and legislation over the years – including, often, the introduction of changes which then end up being jettisoned. We now turn to a relatively simplified account of that history so far.

A Brief, Tangled Recent History of Sentencing

1991: From the Strategy of Encouragement to Just Deserts

4.4 For many years following the Second World War, successive governments deferred to the judiciary and allowed them the 'judicial independence' in sentencing they desired. This virtual abdication of government responsibility for developing a coherent sentencing policy left the courts with wide discretion which was only marginally constrained by guidance from the Court of Appeal. Very few attempts were made by governments during this time to fill the policy-making vacuum, and even these were met by implacable and almost invariably successful opposition from the judiciary. The main response of successive governments to the growing prison numbers crisis from the 1960s to the 1980s was what we call the **strategy of encouragement**. Parliament provided a wider range of non-custodial penalties, such as community service and suspended sentences (see Chapter 5) and then, out of deference to the principle of judicial independence, the government relied on exhortation rather than legislative control in an attempt to encourage the courts to use these 'alternatives to imprisonment'. In the early 1980s Home Office ministers and the Lord Chief Justice worked together to press the case for restraint in the use of custody, but with only very temporary and limited effect. The prison population continued to rise in the 1980s, and record prison numbers helped to persuade the Conservative government of the day that something more than encouragement was needed.

The government's approach changed around 1987: it began to discuss punishment, and especially imprisonment, in a strikingly different way. A 1988 Green Paper (consultation document) (Home Office, 1988a: 1.8) stated bluntly that 'imprisonment is not the most effective punishment for most crime. Custody should be reserved for very serious offences, especially when the offender is violent and a continuing risk to the public'. A 1990 White Paper famously stated that imprisonment 'can be an expensive way of making bad people worse' (Home Office, 1990a: 2.7). The attitude towards judicial independence was also much changed. The government was now prepared to set out a logical framework for sentencing which would give much clearer instruction and guidance to sentencers with one aim being to reduce the prison population.

The keystone of the government's strategy was the Criminal Justice Act of 1991. This Act sought to establish just deserts – punishment in proportion to the seriousness of the crime – as 'the principal focus for sentencing decisions' (Home Office, 1990a: 2.2), and also to embody the principle that custody should only be used as a last resort. Offenders were only to receive custodial sentences if the current offence was 'so serious that only such a sentence can be justified for the offence' (s. 1(2)(a)); similarly more onerous community sentences, such as probation, community service orders and **curfew** orders, could only be passed if the current offence was 'serious enough to warrant such a sentence' (s. 6(1)). The Act also laid down that the lengths of custodial sentences and the restrictions on liberty represented by community sentences should in general be 'commensurate with the seriousness of the offence' (ss. 2(2)(a) and 6(2)(b)). Sentencing aims other than just deserts were still allowed a place: violent and sexual offences could attract particularly long prison sentences if the court deemed this necessary to protect the public. In general, however, just deserts was to be the guiding principle.

An important part of the Act's strategy was *punishment in the community*. This entailed the creation of yet more new alternatives to imprisonment including curfew orders (see Chapter 5), the emphasis being on punishment in the community along just deserts lines, of a severity in proportion to the seriousness of the offence (rather than, for example, reform of the offender, although the principle of reform was by no means abandoned). Penalties such as community service were toughened up by national guidance and took on a more punitive aura. The idea was that community sentences should no longer be seen as 'soft options' or 'let-offs', so that courts would be encouraged to use them in place of shorter prison sentences.

This statutory framework for sentencing contained in the 1991 Act was still not one which tightly constricted the judiciary; it provided only a loose statutory *structuring* of the courts' sentencing discretion. Nevertheless, the Act did at least initially achieve some of its aims, most notably in bringing about an immediate reduction in custodial sentences for minor offenders and a consequential fall in the prison population to a low of 40,600 in December 1992. But it was not to last.

1992–97: The Law and Order Counter-Reformation

The 1991 reform strategy all began to unravel in spectacular fashion from late 1992 onwards (see Chapter 10, section 10.2) as John Major's Conservative government performed the remarkable U-turn we term 'the law and order counter-reformation'. Some central provisions of the Criminal Justice Act 1991 were hastily repealed, but more important were the drastic changes in political rhetoric which accompanied them, the most notable instance being Home Secretary Michael Howard's famous 'prison works' speech to the 1993 Conservative Party Conference (see Chapters 2 and 10, sections 2.2 and 10.2). Imprisonment was no longer described as an expensive way of making bad people worse, but touted as an effective solution to crime. The result of this counter-reformation was a marked increase in both the proportionate use of custody and also the average lengths of prison sentences, and a long upward climb in prison numbers.

The law and order counter-reformation reached its climax in the Crime (Sentences) Act 1997, which introduced three new (semi-)mandatory and minimum sentences, based on the American 'three strikes and you're out' model. The 1997 Act (in a section since repealed) required the imposition of a life sentence when an offender was convicted of a second serious violent or sexual offence unless there were exceptional circumstances. It also (in provisions which live on) required minimum imprisonment sentences for Class A drug traffickers and domestic burglars convicted of a Class A drug trafficking offence for a third time. Although this Act was passed in the dying days of John Major's Conservative government, these provisions were implemented by their New Labour successors, to whom we now turn.

New Labour, Mixed Messages

When the 'New' Labour Party came to power in 1997 led by Tony Blair its penal policy slogan was 'tough on crime and tough on the causes of crime'. The overall strategy was always more pragmatic and managerial than the one pursued by their immediate Conservative predecessors – more Strategy B, less Strategy A. However,

New Labour was always concerned not to appear 'soft' on law and order issues, and in any event its leaders, Home Secretaries and Justice Secretaries often appeared to be more than sympathetic to populist calls for tougher sentencing. This Strategy A streak created a tension between the government's much-vaunted 'toughness' and its desire to keep the prison population and the penal crisis within manageable proportions. The message coming across from the New Labour government was always a mixed one. On the one hand New Labour called loudly for greater toughness with some offenders, including more serious ones but also importantly encompassing petty persistent offenders and people who were responsible for low-level anti-social and disorderly behaviour, for whom the **anti-social behaviour order** (or ASBO, discussed at greater length in Chapter 8) was introduced. On the other hand, ministers also (more *sotto voce*) urged that prison should only be used as a last resort for minor non-violent crime (Cavadino and Dignan, 2007: 117). Not surprisingly, perhaps, sentencing and prison population figures seemed to demonstrate that the former, harsher and more strident message had a greater impact (Travis, 2003).

Tougher sentences for more serious offencers included what was in effect a new kind of life imprisonment sentence known as imprisonment for public protection. When first introduced by the Criminal Justice Act 2003, this was a mandatory sentence for any adult offender convicted of one of a long list of specified serious offences provided the court was of the opinion that there was 'a significant risk to members of the public of serious harm' from the offender committing further crimes. This new mandatory penalty – introduced despite stern warnings from the judiciary – proved to be a disaster whose use by the courts far exceeded expectations, worsening the numbers crisis and threatening to add thousands to the prison population on a long-term basis. The government was forced to respond by introducing measures in the Criminal Justice and Immigration Act 2008, which made the sentence discretionary instead of mandatory and restricted its use to more serious cases. (The sentence was eventually abolished entirely by s. 123 of the Legal Aid, Sentencing and Punishment of Offenders Act 2012.)

As well as wanting punishment to be both tougher (for some) and less harsh (for others), New Labour also wanted it to be more consistent. This desire led, as we have seen, to not one but three successive changes in the system for producing sentencing guidelines during New Labour's 13-year rule: first, the Crime and Disorder Act 1998 which enhanced the Court of Appeal's role in issuing guidelines and created the Sentencing Advisory Panel; then the creation of the Sentencing Guidelines Council by the Criminal Justice Act 2003; and finally the introduction of the Sentencing Council by the Coroners and Justice Act 2009.

New Labour's legislative legacy also included a new legal framework for sentencing in the shape of the Criminal Justice Act 2003 (see section 4.3 above), which replaced the remnants of the Criminal Justice Act 1991 as amended and eviscerated in the latter years of John Major's government.

Following the 2003 Act the mixed (one could say contradictory) approach of New Labour continued during the rest of its term of office with no one clear direction of policy being pursued for long, not assisted by a fairly rapid succession of Home Secretaries and the creation of the Ministry of Justice which took over lead responsibility for sentencing policy from the Home Office in 2007. In 2003 a review of correctional services by government 'trouble-shooter' Lord Carter found that sentencing had become more severe to no good purpose and suggested methods (including tighter and more comprehensive sentencing guidelines to ensure better 'targeting' of sentences) whereby the rising prison population could be capped at 80,000. This goal was initially accepted by the government, but then abandoned in 2005 in the face of persistent Conservative criticism that this amounted to being 'soft on crime'. A second report by the same Lord Carter in 2007 recommended expanding prison capacity to 96,000; the government accepted this and ordered new prison building accordingly while at the same time (as we have seen) diluting Carter's renewed calls for a tighter guideline system. And then came the 2010 general election.

Coalition False Dawn

The Conservative–Liberal Democrat coalition government which came to power in 2010 led by David Cameron as Prime Minister had veteran Conservative and former Home Secretary Kenneth Clarke as Secretary of State for Justice. Conservative sentencing policy before the general election of May 2010 had been to increase the sentencing powers of magistrates (allowing them to pass custodial sentences of up to 12 months), and to introduce mandatory prison sentences for knife crime. (The overall harshness of this approach was, however, leavened by the simultaneous promise to bring about a 'rehabilitation revolution': see Chapter 2, section 2.2.) The Liberal Democrats, on the other hand, had proposed restrictions on short-term prison sentences. When forming the coalition the parties agreed to hold a 'full review of sentencing policy', which led to the Green Paper *Breaking the Cycle: Effective Punishment, Rehabilitation and Sentencing of Offenders* (Ministry of Justice, 2010a), followed in turn by the Legal Aid, Sentencing and Punishment of Offenders Act 2012.

Kenneth Clarke's early pronouncements indicated a strong desire to reduce the prison population by ensuring that more offenders received community sentences and fewer received prison sentences. But this proved to be a false dawn. Clarke's efforts to make sentencing less harsh encountered strong opposition from the right wing of the Conservative Party and sections of the media, tacit disapproval from the Prime Minister and no visible support from the Liberal Democrat Party. By the time the Legal Aid, Sentencing and Punishment of Offenders Bill was published in June 2011, proposals to restrict the passing of short prison sentences and to increase the maximum 'discount' on the sentences of defendants who plead guilty at the earliest opportunity from one third to 50 per cent had been dropped. The 2012 Act did contain restrictions on custodial remands for defendants unlikely to receive custodial sentences (see section 4.1 above), but also new minimum and mandatory sentences, one for threatening with a weapon and another in the form of a 'two strikes and you're out' mandatory life imprisonment sentence for serious offenders (see section 4.3 above), the latter replacing New Labour's ill-fated imprisonment for public protection sentence. Kenneth Clarke had favoured retaining the existing six-month limit on magistrates' sentencing powers, repealing unimplemented provisions in the Criminal Justice Act 2003 which would enable magistrates to pass prison sentences of up to 12 months for a single offence, but again this battle was lost, and the provisions remain on the statute book ready to be implemented.

This revised package of measures seemed almost certain to increase the prison population rather than reduce it. And this was before the urban riots of August 2011 and the Cameron government's hardline response to them which threatened to inject further doses of law and order ideology into government criminal justice policy. The government is currently proposing to 'strengthen community sentences' (Ministry of Justice, 2012a; see further Chapter 5) – in other words, a further dose of 'punishment in the community', no more likely than previous doses to encourage courts to use community sentences rather than imprisonment. Indeed, the government's consultation document is at pains to stress that these toughened community sentences are not even intended to act as an alternative to custodial options. In the meantime the prison population, which had reached new record levels under New Labour, has continued to set new records.

A Rational Approach?

4.5
What would a rational approach to sentencing look like?

The Carter Report of 2003 was right to say that sentencing has become much harsher, and this harshness achieves little. If the penal crisis is to be contained, let alone solved, then sentencing must be reined in somehow. We should start by recognizing that penal resources, and in particular places in prison, need to be treated as scarce resources, for reasons of economy, efficiency and humanity. We must also acknowledge that fairness and consistency in sentencing, although never perfectly realisable and perhaps not paramount, are both desirable in themselves and important for the legitimacy of the system. Thus what we need is a system which strongly embodies and enforces the principles of parsimony and last resort while also striving for consistency. Consistency and a perception of fairness will in general be best achieved by (for the most part) adhering to notions of just deserts, or at least to the limiting retributivism we outlined in Chapter 2 (section 2.7).

Leaving sentencers to their own devices does not and has never achieved such a system. Nor is it good enough for Parliament to provide a wide range of sentencing options while the government encourages sentencers to use non-custodial rather than custodial ones, especially if this strategy of encouragement also entails making the non-custodial measures ever more stringent ('punishment in the community'). We have seen the results of these strategies in the last decade and a half: custody has in fact been used more and more, while the toughened-up community penalties have instead replaced lesser penalties such as fines for many offenders. Thus we have had not a more parsimonious use of punishment but the 'ratcheting up' of the whole spectrum of punishment we pointed to at the start of this chapter.

Admittedly this ratcheting up has been assisted and encouraged by a fluctuating but ever-present level of law and order rhetoric from politicians throughout this period – most strident during the 'prison works' era of Michael Howard (when all the encouragement was in the direction of greater harshness), followed by New Labour's mixed messages and the more recent situation which saw some milder tones from Kenneth Clarke derailed by powerful political forces. But even if policies such as Clarke's were to prevail and government rhetoric were to swing firmly against custody, most historical evidence suggests that this would be unlikely to meet with much success. It seems easier for politicians to talk sentencing up than to talk it down.

This means that any strategy to make sentencing more parsimonious and humane must involve controls on the discretion of sentencers. As we have seen, these controls are in many respects far more extensive than they once were, with a number of mandatory, semi-mandatory and minimum sentences and a fast-developing system of guidelines. In earlier editions of this book we described English sentencing as a system out of control. Developments since then require us to modify that judgment. There is still a certain lack of control over the discretion enjoyed by the courts, and a tendency for this discretion to be exercised without regard for the impact that their decisions may have on other parts of the criminal justice system, such as the prison and probation services. But our overall judgment now is that English sentencing is *inappropriately* controlled. Sentencers are subject to more formal controls than they were. However, some of these (notably minimum and mandatory penalties) are the wrong kind of controls, while other controls (such as guidelines) are set at the wrong levels or are still ineffective to prevent sentencers using their discretion to pass inconsistent and excessively harsh sentences. This might not matter so much if judges and magistrates were not so inclined by their sentencing culture to impose such penalties – if the courts did not have a long-standing 'love affair with custody' (Travis, 2003) which has intensified in recent years, and if they were not constantly encouraged in this infatuation by external pressures such as 'law and order' rhetoric from politicians.

How then should the controls on sentencers be altered? One suggestion that has received significant support recently (including from the Prison Governors' Association, the National Association of Probation Officers, the Liberal Democrats and, briefly, Kenneth Clarke) is the idea of a new statutory restriction on the passing of short prison sentences (such as the presumption against passing prison sentences of three months or less in Scotland 'unless the court considers that no other method of dealing with the person is appropriate', introduced by section 17 of the Criminal Justice and Licensing (Scotland) Act 2010. Supporters of such reform point out that such sentences provide no opportunity for rehabilitative work, that there is no compulsory post-release supervision, and that (perhaps partly as a result) reoffending rates following release are particularly poor for such offenders (Ministry of

Justice, 2011b). The administration costs of allocating, admitting and discharging such prisoners are also seen as excessive for stays in prison which are on average less than two months. However, because by definition short-term prisoners only stay in prison for a short time, they only occupy a relatively small proportion of prison places at any one time. (Most custodial sentences passed are in fact less than six months, but short-sentence prisoners only account for about 8 per cent of the total prison population.) Hence, to engineer a more significant drop in the prison population it would be necessary to reduce the lengths of longer sentences.

Other questions can be raised about the proposal for a legal restriction on short sentences. It might take the form of a provision forbidding sentencers from passing a custodial sentence of less than a certain length (for example, six months), but with some kind of 'get-out clause' allowing such sentences where the court was satisfied that there were exceptional circumstances in the individual case, or (less strongly) that it was in the interests of justice in this case. In how many cases would courts in practice invoke such get-out clauses, and might the provision prove largely ineffective as a result? Another possibility is that courts might *increase* sentences from what they would have passed up to the legal minimum of six months (or whatever), leading to at least some offenders going to prison for longer.

So an attempt to *confine* sentencing discretion in this way might achieve little – although different attempts at confinement, such as reducing some maximum penalties and making some offences non-imprisonable, could perhaps be more effective.

A more promising general strategy might centre on further changes in the *structuring* of discretion by guidelines (see section 4.3 of this chapter). In the recent past and at present, however, the guidelines system has not been and is not being used to try to reduce the numbers in prison. Indeed, such evidence as there is suggests that the development of guidelines to date in this country has actually played a part in the 'ratcheting up' of sentencing, as there has been a distinct tendency for guidelines to become harsher over time (Carter, 2003: 12; see also Wasik, 2004a and 2004b). The Sentencing Council is legally required to consider the costs and effectiveness of different penalties when framing its guidelines, but unsurprisingly it has not as a result sought to produce guidelines which would engineer a significant shift away from (costly and ineffective) prison sentences. Instead (no doubt cognisant of its other duties to consider the sentences currently imposed by the courts and to promote public confidence in the system) it has tended to pitch its guidelines in such a way as to broadly maintain existing sentencing levels, while also trying to ensure consistency and proportionality.[10]

Were it not to do so there would doubtless be trouble. The system whereby the Sentencing Council must consult the Justice Secretary and Parliament before issuing final versions of guidelines seems almost designed to encourage populist politics to influence the content of guidelines by making them harsher in the course of this

---

[10]See, for example, the Sentencing Council's (2010) resource impact assessment on its draft guideline for assault sentencing, which predicted a small overall reduction in the need for prison places following the guideline's implementation.

process (as indeed occurred in 2004 over draft guidance for murderers who plead guilty), and certainly to inhibit the Council from suggesting anything which could be represented as over-lenient. Resistance could also, of course, be expected from the tabloid media and other quarters. Thus, for example, in 2005 the Sentencing Guidelines Council published draft guidelines for robbery cases, which made it clear that the starting point for sentencers should almost always be a custodial sentence; however, for young first time offenders who used minimal force or threat of force a community order might be appropriate. One tabloid responded with the headline 'RIDICULOUS: Muggers Must Not Be Sent to Prison Says the Lord Chief Justice' (Sentencing Guidelines Council and Sentencing Advisory Panel, 2006: 2). In 2006 a consultation paper suggested that ordinary shoplifting should not attract a custodial sentence (unless perhaps the offender was seriously persistent). Although broadly in line with current sentencing practice, this attracted a scathing attack from the British Retail Consortium, who said that it sent 'entirely the wrong message to would-be thieves' (*Guardian*, 25 August 2006).

Nevertheless, the potential is there in the guidelines system. There is much to approve of in the current framework for creating and enforcing such guidelines, the system created (admittedly in fits and starts) by the New Labour government and culminating in the introduction of the unified Sentencing Council with its remit to produce comprehensive guidelines which courts must then generally follow. Equally, it was wise not to opt for 'Minnesota grid-type' guidelines, which (because of their rigid inadequacy in failing to allow sufficient account to be taken of mitigating circumstances) might well have actually increased sentencing levels. English-style guidelines leave sentencers with much greater discretion; nevertheless, they have the potential to reduce inconsistency in sentencing, and – *if well framed and if followed by the sentencers* – could also reduce the prison population. This could all be achieved, not by removing or confining sentencers' powers, but by guiding and structuring their use. The government would have to be committed to engineering a reduction in imprisonment, and would have to give the Sentencing Council a clear remit to produce this. The ensuing guidelines would need to be skillfully calculated so that they were pitched at the right level to reduce rates of imprisonment. To do this they would need to embody principles of limiting retributivism, including a strongly *offence-based* tariff, drastically restricting the imprisonment of petty persistent offenders on the grounds of their persistence rather than the seriousness of the current offence.

But even if a strategy to reduce prison numbers via guidelines were to be assiduously and fearlessly implemented, there are a variety of ways in which it might fail to work. The Sentencing Council could fail to produce sufficiently clear or comprehensive guidelines. Or it could produce what turned out to be the wrong guidelines, which when followed had the effect of increasing the prison population rather than reducing it; indeed, this seems to have been the general effect of sentencing guidelines to date in this country. Another possibility is that the Council could set excellent guidelines, but that these were not adequately followed by the sentencers themselves, who are used to sentencing harshly and will not easily be guided out of their old ways. And a final danger is that, like the Criminal Justice

Act 1991 (Cavadino et al., 1999: 68–73), the strategy might *fail politically:* as a result of attacks from the media, judiciary and politicians, the system could be abandoned or heavily modified, with sentencers thereafter reverting to their old ways or worse.

Despite these dire possibilities, we remain of the view that a strategy based on sentencing guidelines represents the best prospect of achieving a degree of appropriate control over the discretion of sentencers and bringing about a reduction in punishment – but making it work would require an enormous amount of political wisdom, courage, skill and goodwill from politicians and the judiciary as well as the Sentencing Council. We would stress the need for the judiciary to play its part in this, and for the senior judiciary to seek to lead judges in the right direction. Ultimately we need to recognize that formal and legal controls on sentencing, however well designed, are fairly blunt instruments. Arguably more important than these formal controls is the sentencing culture of the judiciary. If sentencers resent the controls, they can undermine and avoid them in a whole variety of ways (as indeed history has often shown). Political leadership and rhetoric can play a part. But for would-be penal reformers the depressing pattern has often been that exhortations to sentencers to 'get tough' have been effective, while encouragement to use custody less has fallen on deaf ears. Like any culture, sentencing culture is not always easy to influence from the outside, hence the need for effective leadership from within the judiciary.

The immediate prospects for the emergence of a strategy such as the one we favour are undeniably poor. At one stage, following the 2003 Carter Report, it seemed as if the New Labour government would seek to use guidelines at least to restrain the rise in prison numbers (seeking to cap it at 80,000), but even this modest objective was swiftly abandoned under political pressure. Even when the current Coalition government was promising to seek a reduction in the numbers of people in prison, guidelines did not figure largely in its strategy: indeed there was talk by Kenneth Clarke of increasing the discretion of sentencers rather than further controlling it. Since then even the aspiration to control prison numbers seems to have evaporated. Despite the escalating prison numbers crisis, the government seems more than ever willing to follow the media's enthusiastic campaign for a tough approach, and there is little effective opposition to be found within the judicial and political realms. Ending the courts' 'love affair with custody' could never be an easy task, and it is all the more daunting when both the media and the government share their passion for imprisonment.

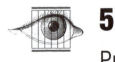

5

Punishment in the Community

Community Punishment in a Rapidly Changing Penal Landscape

5.1 The brief period since the turn of the millennium has witnessed an unprecedented transformation of the context within which community punishment is administered. As we will see in this chapter, there have been important changes in community punishments: not just in the various *types* of punishment (probation supervision, community service, the fine, etc.), but also in the *forms* that punishment takes (e.g. supervision, surveillance, the levying of penalties on the offender's money or time) and the *methods* by which it is delivered (e.g. by state agency or by the private or voluntary sectors). The two key agencies that have in the past been responsible for administering the delivery of punishment – probation and the prison service – have officially been merged to become the National Offender Management Service and the entire basis on which they each operate is in the process of radical restructuring. Indeed, at an even more fundamental conceptual level, the long-standing assumption of a mutually exclusive binary division *between* community punishment and custodial punishment has itself been undermined by the introduction of the suspended sentence order which combines elements of both. And even the traditional division of labour between judges and those responsible for delivering community punishment is showing distinct signs of unravelling.

Periods of seismic upheaval are often marked by confusion and uncertainty as familiar landmarks are overturned and new formations have yet to be mapped in detail. The same can also be said of the state of community punishment in England and Wales following the radical reforms of the past few years. In this chapter we will begin the mapping exercise by setting out the current legal framework that shows the various non-custodial (and semi-custodial) options that are available to the courts. This will pave the way for an overview of changes in community punishment in which we briefly trace and discuss the historical development of the main forms of non-custodial punishment and in the next section we identify the various strategies governments adopted to try to influence their use by the courts. Next, we turn to some important operational issues including the way community penalties are enforced, their effectiveness, the emerging concept of **sentence management** that appears to herald a significant change in the traditional role of the judiciary and **contestability** which threatens the very future of the probation service. In the penultimate section we will critically examine three rival theories that offer contrasting interpretations of the significance of some of these developments for the future of social control systems, before drawing our own conclusions.

Non-Custodial Punishment: The Current Sentencing Framework

5.2 The current sentencing framework for non-custodial punishment is set out in Figure 5.1, which locates the various penalties broadly in terms of ascending severity from the purely nominal absolute discharge at the bottom to custodial sentences at the top. This framework was established by the Criminal Justice Act 2003, replacing an earlier version introduced by the Criminal Justice Act 1991 (see Cavadino and Dignan, 2002: 124). In this section we provide an overview of this legal framework within which sentencers operate before examining the evolution of some of the main types of non-custodial punishment and the penal strategies that have helped to shape them.

Nominal and Warning Penalties

Where a court is satisfied that it would be 'inexpedient to inflict punishment', it may **discharge** the offender instead. This discharge can take one of two forms. The first is an *absolute discharge*, which is the most lenient response a court can make following a conviction since it requires nothing from an offender and entails no restrictions on future conduct. Absolute discharges are rarely used, and account for only around 1 per cent of court disposals. In part this may be because cases that are likely to be dealt with by means of a purely nominal penalty tend to be discontinued or dealt with by means of a caution instead of being prosecuted, so never reach court at all.

Most discharges are *conditional*, which means that the offender is required not to commit a further offence within a specified period of up to three years. If this condition is breached, the offender may be dealt with not only for the fresh offence but also in respect of the one for which the conditional discharge was originally imposed. In essence the conditional discharge represents a reprimand to the offender and a warning of punishment in the future if the offending is repeated, so the sentencing aims with which it is most closely associated are denunciation and (especially) deterrence (see Chapter 2).

Another warning measure that is also available to sentencers is the ancient common law power to **bind over** the offender. Its use is not restricted to convicted offenders: indeed, a Law Commission survey undertaken in 1987 indicated that nearly three-quarters of bind-overs were directed against non-offenders, including witnesses, complainants or anyone else involved in the proceedings. A bind-over is in effect a suspended fine since the offender stands to forfeit a specified sum of money unless he or she abides by an undertaking to be of good behaviour and keep

CUSTODIAL SENTENCES

Immediate imprisonment

Suspended sentence order

CUSTODY THRESHOLD

Criterion:
offence is 'so serious' that neither a fine alone nor a community sentence can be justified - s. 152(2) Criminal Justice Act 2003

COMMUNITY ORDERS

Community orders contain one or more of the following requirements:-

Exclusion requirement
Curfew requirement
Residence requirement
Mental health requirement
Drug rehabilitation requirement
Alcohol treatment requirement
Alcohol abstinence and monitoring requirement
Unpaid work requirement
Programme requirement
Activity requirement e.g. reparation
Prohibited activity requirement
Attendance centre requirement
Supervision requirement
Foreign travel prohibition requirement

COMMUNITY ORDER THRESHOLD

Criterion:
offence is 'serious enough' to warrant such a sentence – s. 148(1) CJA 2003
AND
the constituent requirements are in the opinion of the court the 'most suitable' for the offender and also 'commensurate with the seriousness of the offence' – s. 148(2) CJA 2003

FINANCIAL PENALTIES

Compensation Order   Fine

WARNING PENALTIES

Conditional discharge   Bind-over

NOMINAL PENALTY

Absolute discharge

FIGURE 5.1   The sentencing framework for adult offenders established by the Criminal Justice Act 2003

the peace. Although the Law Commission (1994) recommended the abolition of this increasingly anachronistic power, its flexibility and popularity with magistrates (over 20,000 individuals were bound over in 2001: Home Office, 2003d) may yet ensure its survival for a while longer.

Finally, a much more recent (and controversial) form of warning penalty is the quasi-criminal anti-social behaviour order that was introduced by the 1998 Crime and Disorder Act. ASBOs are disproportionately invoked in respect of younger offenders, and hence will be dealt with more fully in Chapter 8 (section 8.3), though they may also be imposed on adult offenders whose behaviour has caused or has threatened to cause 'harassment, alarm or distress' to others. ASBOs are flexible civil orders and may entail a variety of prohibitions that are felt to be necessary in order to protect people living in an area from further anti-social acts committed by the defendant. Failure to comply with these requirements is a criminal offence, and in the case of adults can result in a prison sentence of up to five years. The government has recently announced plans to replace ASBOs with a range of orders including a rather similar criminal behaviour order (Home Office, 2012, and see Chapter 8, section 8.3)

Financial Penalties

There are two main types of financial penalty: the fine and the compensation order (there is also the confiscation order introduced by the Proceeds of Crime Act 2002; and courts have a number of other sentencing options too – disqualification from driving and hospital orders, for example). The chief difference between the two is that the compensation order requires the offender to pay the victim a specified compensatory sum whereas a fine is paid to the state itself. Although the needs of victims were for many years seriously neglected by the criminal justice system, courts were given the power to award compensation for the first time in 1972 in cases involving injury, loss or damage (some victims of violent crime can receive compensation under the Criminal Injuries Compensation Scheme: see Dignan, 2005a). Initially it could only be ordered as an ancillary measure alongside some other form of punishment. Ten years later, however, courts were given the power to award compensation in its own right, and since the 1982 Criminal Justice Act they have been ordered to prioritize compensation at the expense of the fine in cases where the offender cannot afford to pay both. Courts are also obliged by law to consider compensation in every case where there has been loss or damage to personal property or personal injury and to give reasons for not making an order. And the Legal Aid, Sentencing and Punishment of Offenders Act 2012 now gives the courts an express duty to consider making a compensation order where a victim has suffered harm or loss.

Fines may be imposed in respect of almost all offences irrespective of the type of court, and there is no upper limit on the amount a Crown Court can impose (for the way in which fines are calculated, see below). Magistrates' courts had been restricted to a maximum of £5,000 in most cases, but the Legal Aid, Sentencing and Punishment of Offenders Act 2012 removes this limit. The general principle is that the level of a fine should reflect the seriousness of an offence (Criminal Justice Act 2003, s. 164). However, the court also has to take into account the financial circumstances of the offender (Criminal Justice Act 2003, s. 164(3)), and in order to do that it is required to investigate an offender's financial circumstances

(Criminal Justice Act 2003, s. 164(1)); offenders may be ordered to furnish the court with any information it requires for this purpose. The fluctuating fortunes of the fine and the problems associated with its use are discussed in the following section (5.3).

Community Penalties

Prior to the introduction of the sentencing framework contained in the Criminal Justice Act 2003, the range of non-custodial sentences available to English courts was probably unparalleled anywhere in the world and included no fewer than ten mid-range community orders as they were officially termed. These were replaced in 2003 by a single 'generic' sentence known as a community order with a maximum length of three years, which can be customized to suit each individual offender by selecting one or more requirements from a menu of possible options (originally 12 in total, but expanded to 14 by the Legal Aid, Sentencing and Punishment of Offenders Act 2012). These are set out in Figure 5.2.

- Unpaid work (40–300 hours to be completed within 12 months)

- Supervision (up to 36 months; 24 months maximum for SSO)

- Accredited programme (length to be expressed as the number of sessions; must be combined with a supervision requirement)

- Drug rehabilitation (up to 36 months; 24 months maximum for SSO; offender's consent is required)

- Alcohol treatment (up to 36 months; 24 months maximum for SSO; offender's consent is required)

- Mental health treatment (up to 36 months; 24 months maximum for SSO; offender's consent is required)

- Residence (up to 36 months; 24 months maximum for SSO)

- Specified activity (up to 60 days)

- Prohibited activity (up to 36 months; 24 months maximum for SSO)

- Exclusion (up to 24 months)

- Curfew (up to 12 months and for between 2–16 hours in any one day; if a stand-alone curfew order is made, there is no probation involvement)

- Attendance centre (12–36 hours with a maximum of 3 hours per attendance; only for those aged up to 25)

- Foreign travel prohibition requirement (up to 12 months)

- Alcohol abstinence and monitoring requirement (up to 120 days)

FIGURE 5.2 Requirements for the Community Order and the Suspended Sentence Order (SSO)

A community order can only be imposed if one of two sets of conditions is satisfied. The first and principal one is where a court takes the view that the offence is serious enough to warrant such a sentence, and also that the requirements it imposes are the most suitable for the offender and commensurate with the seriousness of the offence. The second, alternative condition for imposing a community order applies to those relatively minor offenders who have previously been dealt with solely by means of a fine in respect of three or more previous convictions and whose current offence would not normally satisfy the seriousness test. The court can nevertheless impose a community order in such cases where it considers that a community order is 'in the interests of justice' (Criminal Justice Act 2003, s. 151). Sentencing guidelines urge sentencers to exercise restraint when applying these conditions, stressing the need to avoid disproportionate responses to relatively minor offences (Sentencing Guidelines Council, 2004a), though it remains unclear what impact if any this guidance actually has on sentencing practice.

We now detail each of the requirements that may form part of a community order (or a suspended sentence order – see under the next subheading).

The *supervision requirement* is descended from the traditional probation order (or the **community rehabilitation order** as it was renamed in 2000). It can last for up to 36 months (24 in the case of the SSO) and is one of the most commonly used requirements, although there is some evidence that its use has been decreasing (Mair, 2011). Section 213 of the Criminal Justice Act 2003 explicitly states that the purpose of the requirement is to promote the offender's rehabilitation, and although the Coalition government agrees with this aim, it pointedly notes that 'it is not primarily punitive and, on its own, fails to send a clear message that offending behaviour will be dealt with' (Ministry of Justice, 2012c: 12)

The *attendance centre requirement* is available for offenders up to the age of 25, who are obliged to attend a local attendance centre (if available) for a period of between 12 and 36 hours for a maximum period of 3 hours per attendance.

The *prohibited activity requirement* can, for example, prohibit an offender from driving a car or mixing with named individuals for a period of up to 36 months (24 months in the case of the SSO). It tends to be used for more intensive orders. The prohibition can be used in a punitive manner, or it could be intended to keep the offender away from future trouble.

The *activity requirement* requires offenders to attend a specified place where they are obliged to participate in such activities as are directed for a period of up to 60 days. This may include reparative tasks (so this requirement could potentially be used to expand the use of the restorative justice approach), as well as those aimed at rehabilitating offenders.

A *programme requirement* also obliges offenders to participate in specific activities which, in this case, take the form of specially accredited programmes that are devised with the requirements of particular groups of offenders in mind. Examples include programmes for treating sex offenders, anger management and drink driving. The programme requirement lasts as long as the accredited programme and must be combined with a supervision requirement.

The *unpaid work requirement* is the old community service order (or the **community punishment order** as it was renamed in 2000) and requires the offender to carry out unpaid work for between 40–300 hours. The work has to be completed within 12 months. Unpaid work is the most commonly used requirement for community orders and for SSOs and this is likely to continue given the Coalition government's interest in having a punitive element in every community order (Ministry of Justice, 2012c).

The *alcohol treatment requirement*, as its name suggests, is aimed at offenders who are dependent on alcohol. Before imposing it, the court must be satisfied that the offender's dependency is susceptible to treatment, that such treatment is available and the offender consents. It can last for a maximum of 36 months (24 for the SSO). (See also the new *alcohol abstinence and monitoring* requirement, below.)

The *drug rehabilitation requirement* (which derives from the old drug treatment and testing order) is similar in terms of length and the need for consent, but it differs in two important respects. First, it requires an offender to submit to regular testing, as well as treatment; and second, it permits the court to review periodically the offender's progress during the course of the order in hearings that the offender may have to attend, and to modify the terms of the requirements accordingly. In this way, it allows for an approach similar to that of the 'drug courts' that originated in the USA (see below, section 5.4).

The *mental health treatment requirement* requires an offender to submit to treatment either as an in- or out-patient with a view to improving their medical condition. Like the previous two requirements it can last for up to 36 months (24 in the case of the SSO) and consent is necessary. (Treatment for a mental health condition was originally introduced as a requirement for a probation order in the 1948 Criminal Justice Act.)

The *residence requirement* is likewise a reformulation of a longstanding additional condition that could be attached to a probation order, whereby an offender can be required to reside at a specified place such as a probation hostel, at the offender's own home or with a relative for up to 36 months (24 for the SSO).

The *curfew requirement* reconstitutes the pre-existing curfew order. It originally obliged the offender to remain for specified periods of not less than two hours or more than 12 hours a day at a place designated in the order (usually the offender's home); the maximum duration was six months. The Legal Aid, Sentencing and Punishment of Offenders Act 2012 raises the daily limit to 16 hours and the maximum duration to 12 months. There is a presumption that any curfew requirement will be enforced by **electronic monitoring**. Curfews with electronic monitoring may also be imposed alongside most of the other requirements available. If a stand-alone curfew requirement is made, the probation service will not be involved: the monitoring is carried out by private companies.

An *exclusion requirement* prohibits an offender from entering (either totally or at particular times) a place that is designated in the order for a period of up to 24 months. As with curfews, there is a presumption that such a requirement will be monitored by electronic monitoring.

The Legal Aid, Sentencing and Punishment of Offenders Act 2012 added two new requirements. A *foreign travel prohibition requirement* (s. 72) prohibits an offender from travelling to any country outside the British Isles for a period of up to 12 months. An *alcohol abstinence and monitoring* requirement (s. 76) orders the offender not to drink alcohol for a period of up to 120 days during which time his/her alcohol level will be monitored. This requirement can only be used where alcohol is a contributing factor to the offence but where the offender is not *dependent* on alcohol (if this is the case, an alcohol treatment requirement is appropriate).

Semi-Custodial Penalties

The only semi-custodial penalty remaining in the English penal system is the suspended sentence order, which combines elements of community punishment with the imposition or threatened imposition of a term of imprisonment. In theory this is a fully custodial sentence, but since it consists of a period of imprisonment which may never have to be served and also involves requirements placed on the offender in the community, it is appropriate to deal with it in this chapter. However, being in theory custodial, the SSO is subject to the 'threshold' test for custody, and can only be imposed if the court is satisfied that the offence is so serious that neither a fine alone nor a community sentence would be justified (Criminal Justice Act 2003, s. 152(2)).

Suspended sentences have been available as a sentencing option in some form since 1967 but have changed over the years. The Criminal Justice Act 2003 introduced a new suspended sentence order that allowed a suspended prison sentence to be combined with one or more of the requirements that can form part of a community order (ss. 189–192, and for a history of the suspended sentence, see below, section 5.3). These requirements (see above) have to be completed within the operational period (which can be between six months and two years) during which the prison sentence is suspended. There are also provisions for the order to be reviewed periodically, giving the court a chance to monitor the offender's progress. If, during this operational period, the offender commits a further imprisonable offence, the court is obliged to send the offender to prison, unless it considers that it would be unjust to do so (Schedule 12). Under the 2003 Act's original provisions the suspended term of imprisonment could be between 28 and 51 weeks; but the Legal Aid, Sentencing and Punishment of Offenders Act 2012 now permits custodial sentences of between 14 days and two years to be suspended, and gives the courts discretion about whether or not to impose any requirements.

The 2003 Act also introduced two other semi-custodial sentences – **intermittent custody** (which was tried on an experimental basis but then abandoned) and **custody plus** (which was never implemented at all: see further below, section 5.3), but these provisions have been repealed by the Legal Aid, Sentencing and Punishment of Offenders Act 2012.

The Changing Shape of Non-Custodial Punishment

5.3 Non-custodial punishments may assume a variety of forms and over the years have been used in various ways and with varying levels of enthusiasm. In this section we provide a brief history and discussion of the main types of non-custodial punishment and the changing ways in which they have been used down the years. In discussing the impact of the various non-custodial options that are available to the courts, particularly their impact on the prison population, we shall be referring to Table 5.1, below, which indicates their changing pattern of usage (for indictable offences) over the last 60 years. As a result of the changes made in the 2003 Act, the 2011 column of Table 5.1 is not comparable to

TABLE 5.1 Adult Indictable Offences: Types of Sentences (%)*

Type of sentence	1938	1959	1975	1989	1994	1999	2004	2011
Custody	**33.3**	**29.1**	**13.4**	**17.5**	**18.2**	**26.0**	**28.6**	**27.2**
Supervisory penalties								
Probation	15.1	11.9	7.0	9.0	12.0	12.7	12.0	N/A
CSO	N/A	N/A	0.5	5.4	10.7	8.8	8.6	N/A
Combination order	N/A	N/A	N/A	N/A	2.4	3.4	2.3	N/A
Curfew	N/A	N/A	N/A	N/A	N/A	0.2	2.0	N/A
DTTO	N/A	N/A	N/A	N/A	N/A	N/A	3.2	N/A
Community sentences								24.5
Total	**15.1**	**11.9**	**7.5**	**14.4**	**25.1**	**25.1**	**28.1**	**24.5**
Suspended sentence/ SSO	N/A	N/A	11.2	10.5	1.1	1.1	0.9	**11.4**
Non-supervisory penalties								
Fine	27.2	44.8	55.3	41.4	34.9	29.5	22.7	18.7
Discharge/other	24.4	14.2	12.6	16.2	20.6	18.3	19.5	18.2
Total	**51.6**	**59.0**	**79.1**	**68.1**	**56.6**	**48.9**	**43.1**	**36.9**
Number	38,896	75,358	209,709	216,400	215,500	229,900	223,600	299,974

Source: Criminal Statistics.

*The format in which the Criminal Statistics are published has changed considerably since 2004: the 'community sentences' row is made up almost wholly of community orders plus a few of the supervisory penalties that existed prior to April 2005; in the 'Suspended sentence/SSO' row there is a handful of suspended sentences; the majority of the 'Discharge/other' row is made up of conditional and absolute discharges

TABLE 5.2   Adults Sentenced for All Offences by Type of Sentence (2005–2011)

Sentence	2005	2006	2007	2008	2009	2010	2011
Custody	6.9	6.8	6.8	7.4	7.2	7.6	8.0
SSO	0.7	2.5	3.1	3.3	3.4	3.7	3.9
Community order	4.0	9.0	9.7	10.1	10.5	11.0	10.7
Old-style community sentences*	6.4	0.8	0.3	0.2	0.1	0.1	0.1
Total community sentences	**10.4**	**9.8**	**10.0**	**10.3**	**10.6**	**11.1**	**10.8**
Fines	72.8	71.4	70.5	69.0	70.6	68.5	68.3
Discharge	6.8	6.6	7.1	6.8	6.3	6.9	6.8
Other	2.4	2.8	2.5	3.2	1.8	2.2	2.2
Total other	82.0	80.8	80.1	79.0	78.7	77.6	77.3
Number	1,377,072	1,319,134	1,309,401	1,265,562	1,316,734	1,283,734	1,229,792

*Includes community rehabilitation orders, community punishment orders, community punishment and rehabilitation orders, drug treatment and testing orders, curfew orders.

earlier years. Table 5.1 is however helpful in assessing the influence of the various penal strategies that have helped to shape the development of non-custodial and, more specifically, community punishment over the years. Table 5.2 sets out sentencing trends for adults for all offences between 2005 (the first year of operation of the sentencing framework introduced by the Criminal Justice Act 2003) and 2011.

Warning Penalties

The use of *warning penalties* such as the conditional discharge has fluctuated over time, and the way they are viewed by policy-makers has also wavered confusingly. As can be seen from Table 5.1, after experiencing a sharp decline after the war, the proportionate use of the conditional discharge for adult offenders increased steadily during the 1980s (perhaps influenced by the philosophy of **minimum intervention** which was popular at the time – see Chapter 8, section 8.2), began to fall back again in the mid-1990s but has recently increased. The sentencing aim of deterrence, with which it is most closely associated, sat awkwardly with the just deserts based philosophy that underpinned the 1991 Criminal Justice Act. The Halliday Report of 2001 (para. 6.19) was much more supportive, commenting favourably on its lower than predicted **reconviction rates**. However, the New Labour government was more hostile towards it, forbidding its use in respect of certain young offenders (see Chapter 8, sections 8.3 and 8.4) and also when dealing with those who breach anti-social behaviour orders, not deeming it sufficiently controlling in these cases. Somewhat surprisingly, as Mair (2004a: 139) points out, there has been virtually no research on this particular measure, in marked contrast to most of the other disposals available to the courts.

Financial Penalties

The performance of *financial penalties* such as the fine has been even more erratic over the decades. As can be seen from Table 5.1, the post-war years coincided with a dramatic expansion in its usage, culminating in a 'market share' of over half of all sentences imposed on adult indictable offenders by the mid-1970s. Thereafter its decline has been equally precipitous, falling steadily to just 19 per cent in 2011.

The sentencing philosophy on which the fine is based has been described as straightforwardly punitive (Ashworth, 2005: 303), thus fitting the aims of retribution, denunciation and deterrence. However, it can also be seen as reparative: the offender literally pays back something to the community to make amends for the offence. The fine is also flexible, non-intrusive, does not require the intervention of a penal agent and is relatively easy to adjust in accordance with an offender's just deserts or personal circumstances. Unusually, it is also one of the few penal measures to raise revenue as opposed to consuming scarce penal resources. Moreover, reconviction rates for the fine in general compare favourably with those for other penalties (Home Office, 1964; Softley, 1978; House of Commons, 1998). All of these attributes help to explain the post-war popularity of the fine – particularly for straightforward run-of-the-mill offenders who lacked any obvious social problems that might warrant the assistance of a probation officer – during an era of near full-employment. Moreover, unlike probation, the fine did not become tarnished by association with the discredited treatment model (see below).

During the 1980s and 1990s, however, the fine steadily lost much of its attraction for sentencers during a period of rising unemployment levels, growing competition from other sentencing disposals and an increasingly punitive penal climate. In particular, sentencers were constrained by both the law and conscience from imposing large fines on the unemployed people who constituted the majority of offenders because of the requirement to take account of their financial circumstances. But to fine them a small sum would seem derisory to magistrates, even though a small fine would have just as great an impact on a poor offender as a large sum would have on a well-off one.

Attempts were made to halt the decline of the fine, most notably by introducing a new system of **unit fines** into the magistrates' courts as part of the 'just deserts in sentencing' reform programme embodied in the Criminal Justice Act of 1991. Unit fines were derived from the 'day fine' principle that is employed in other countries (notably Germany and Sweden) as a way of ensuring equal impact on offenders by fining them so many days' pay rather than a fixed amount. The unit fine system was a similar attempt to relate fines to offenders' means systematically. Instead of imposing a fine of a set amount of money, the court imposed a fine expressed as a number of units related to the seriousness of the offence. The size of these units varied according to the assessed means of each offender – so offenders with different means committing crimes of equal seriousness would receive fines of different amounts, but the fine should in theory have the same impact on each offender. Not only does such a system promote greater fairness in fining, but it was also hoped that it would encourage sentencers to use fines for a wider range of offenders irrespective of their income levels. And indeed it worked, since the downward slide in magistrates' use of the fine was reversed when unit fines were brought in, and its use for unemployed offenders increased sharply (Home Office, 1994), However, despite being a relatively unusual penological success story, the unit fine also proved to be a political failure, and this led to its early demise. It failed politically mainly because it resulted in hitherto uncharacteristically high fines being imposed on relatively well-off middle-class motoring offenders (and on some people who refused to declare their means), whose cause was vigorously championed by sections of the media at a time when the government was deeply unpopular for other reasons. Although there were some teething problems associated with the unit fine system (see Cavadino and Dignan, 2002 and Ashworth, 2005 for details) these could almost certainly have been overcome without too much difficulty (Mair, 2004a: 143). However, a politically enfeebled government decided instead to peremptorily abolish it in the summer of 1993.

Following the demise of the unit fine, the use of fines resumed its downward trajectory and research found different magistrates' courts adopting different strategies for taking account of an offender's financial circumstances (Charman et al., 1996). Morgan (2003) has demonstrated that offenders who would previously have been fined are now being given community orders, with the result that they are given unnecessarily harsh and expensive penalties which add to the resources crisis by helping to overload probation caseloads. This upwards shift in harshness is part of the general 'ratcheting up' of sentencing that Morgan has identified.

The 2003 Carter Review of correctional services suggested that the fine could usefully be rejuvenated if a system similar to the short-lived unit fine – called the **day fine** – were to be introduced. Provision for such a system was indeed included in the Management of Offenders and Sentencing Bill 2004–5, which, however, failed to pass through Parliament due to the 2005 general election, and when John Reid replaced Charles Clarke as Home Secretary in 2006 the idea disappeared from government thinking. However, new sentencing guidelines for magistrates' courts introduced in 2008 (Sentencing Guidelines Council, 2008) represent an attempt at a similar approach. Magistrates' guidelines now state as a matter of principle that, 'The aim is for the fine to have an equal impact on offenders with different financial circumstances.' They suggest as starting points for each offence not particular sums of money but 'Bands' (A to E) which represent differing proportions of the offender's income (or rather, flexible ranges: for example, Band B is 75 to 125 per cent of weekly income). In terms of ensuring the equal impact of fines, this represents in theory a step in the right direction, but compared with the unit fine system it does less to ensure that the sentencer first decides (blindfold, as it were) on the proportion of income to be paid, which is then multiplied by the offender's means. Nor is the system likely to work well with offenders on benefits (whose relevant weekly income is currently deemed to be £110 for fining purposes); with those whose earnings are irregular; or with high income offenders, in whose case the court is (remarkably) encouraged to reduce the fine if it appears 'disproportionate' (Sentencing Guidelines Council, 2008: 150). Nor is there any sign that these guidelines have made magistrates any more inclined to use the fine as a sentence. The suspicion is that in meting out routinized summary justice, magistrates are not following either the letter or spirit of the guidelines as perhaps they might, but rather continuing to do the job in their accustomed manner.

As Tables 5.1 and 5.2 show, the long-term decline of the fine has continued in recent years. Despite the assertion of the new Coalition government in the Green Paper *Breaking the Cycle* (Ministry of Justice, 2010a: ch. 4) that they wished to encourage greater use of the fine and that they would 'work with the Sentencing Council to encourage greater use of financial penalties' (Ministry of Justice, 2011a: 5), there is little evidence of any significant initiative. Indeed, it is difficult to see how the fine can be successfully revitalized as a penalty for any but the pettiest offenders without a wholesale ratcheting down of the existing scale of penalties to reverse the remorseless escalation in severity that Morgan (2003) identified.

Currently many financial penalties are being levied not by the courts but by the *police*, under the fixed penalty notice scheme explained in the Introduction (section I.1). This scheme serves to widen the net of those subject to punishment without the trappings and safeguards of traditional due process. The development is also notable in that the scheme of fixed penalties is, of course, the very reverse of the equal impact, means-related approach to financial penalties embodied by the unit fine and day fine systems and the magistrates' sentencing guidelines. Recent research has noted a reduction in the use of fixed penalties since 2007 and suggests that there are considerable disparities in police use of them, and in 2011 almost half of all fixed penalty fines were never paid (Policy Exchange, 2012).

In future, *prosecutors* may also be allowed to impose financial penalties: section 17 of the Police and Justice Act 2006 provides that a conditional caution (see Introduction) may come with a condition that the offender pay a financial penalty of up to £250 for specified offences, but to date this has only been brought into force on a trial basis in a few police areas. Probation officers, too, in future may be permitted to fine an offender for failure to comply with an order; if the fine is not paid within a fixed period of time breach proceedings would proceed (Ministry of Justice, 2012c).

Compensatory Penalties

Ironically, in view of the fact that requiring offenders to make reparation to those affected by their offences was acknowledged as one of the official aims of sentencing by section 142 of the Criminal Justice Act 2003, the use of *compensation orders* by the courts has, like the fine, also declined sharply in recent years, at least for relatively serious offenders. Thus, the proportion of indictable offenders who were ordered to pay compensation in the Crown Court was just 5 per cent in 2011, compared with 21 per cent in 1990, while in the magistrates' courts the figure was 19 per cent compared with 29 per cent in 1990. One possible reason for the decline relates to the steady growth in the use of custody over the same period, since the Court of Appeal generally discourages combining a compensation order with a sentence of imprisonment. A Home Office study (Flood-Page and Mackie, 1998: 62 and 111) found that one reason sentencers themselves gave for not awarding compensation was that the offender lacked the means to pay, and some felt reluctant to award compensation if the amount that could be afforded would appear too derisory. (As with fines, courts are obliged to relate the amount of any compensation awarded to the offender's means.) Sentencers also complained that information about the value of the loss or harm caused is often lacking, and the Court of Appeal has advised sentencers against 'simply plucking a figure from the air' (*R. v. Oliver* (1989) 11 Cr App R (S) 10).

Victims who are awarded compensation from their offenders may have to wait up to two or three years for this to be paid (always assuming the offender pays up and does not default). This is an added source of frustration that could have been avoided had the government accepted a proposal that the court should immediately pay the victim the amount awarded in full and then recover it from the offender in the normal way (Home Office, 1988a: para. 3.10). As a matter of principle, however, even this proposal does not in our view go far enough. For it hardly seems fair that a victim's entitlement to court-ordered compensation should depend entirely on an offender's ability and willingness to pay while the state profits handsomely from fines that are imposed on offenders. We would therefore favour a scheme in which the revenue from fines is used to fund a reformed criminal compensation scheme that would not be subject to the vagaries of offenders' financial circumstances and willingness to pay up. Indeed, this could form an important part of a more radical reformulation of our existing system of punishments in which the elements of reparation for victims and the reintegration of offenders are given far greater prominence (see Chapter 10, section 10.3). A pale echo of such a scheme was introduced in 2007, with the 'victim surcharge' – an additional flat-rate £15 added to all court fines, the proceeds of which go towards funding a range of services for victims and witnesses, but not to compensate them financially.

Other urgent reforms are required to ensure that sentencers start to take more seriously their legal responsibilities to prioritize victims' entitlement to compensation, instead of relegating this to a subordinate consideration, as so often seems to happen. For example, compensation is commonly not awarded or reduced in amount, not because the offender lacks the means to pay, but simply because courts insist on imposing fines or awarding costs against offenders, despite clear legislative directions to give precedence to compensation in such circumstances (Flood-Page and Mackie, 1998: 127). It will be interesting to see if the number of compensation orders increases following the duty that has been laid on the courts to consider awarding compensation by the Legal Aid, Sentencing and Punishment of Offenders Act 2012, given that similar statutory duties have been routinely ignored in the past. Likewise, the statutory obligation to give reasons for not awarding compensation is ignored altogether in over 70 per cent of cases (Flood-Page and Mackie, 1998: 60–4). The solution probably does not lie in tinkering with the court's legal duties but rather in exploring administrative means of monitoring and enforcing these duties and ensuring that they are routinely brought to the attention of sentencing courts.

Even if the existing compensation system were to be reformed along the lines we have suggested, it would remain inherently limited in scope, however. For one thing, it only affords one limited form of redress for victims since it is restricted to financial compensation for material loss or damage, although this may change if the government's proposals in the consultation paper *Getting It Right for Victims and Witnesses* (Ministry of Justice, 2012a) are taken forward (see below). However welcome this may be (see Shapland et al., 1985 for victims' positive response to compensation), it may do little to repair any harm that may have been done to the victim's mental or psychological sense of well-being, or to restore the social or moral relationships that may have been damaged by an offence (Watson et al., 1989: 214). Moreover, neither victims nor offenders are likely to feel greatly empowered by an award of compensation since they are not directly involved in the decision-making process and have no control over its outcome. (For more on the needs of victims generally see Christie, 1978; Shapland, 1984; Shapland et al., 1985; Zehr, 1985; Blom-Cooper, 1988; Dignan, 2005a.)

Reparative Penalties and Restorative Justice Approaches

Reparation can in principle take a variety of other forms apart from financial compensation, however. For example, it can also include offenders apologizing to victims; making amends in other ways by doing things for or on behalf of victims; or combining an undertaking to change their behaviour with constructive steps to facilitate this. Where these reparative outcomes are negotiated by victims and offenders themselves in the course of a fair process that provides appropriate safeguards for all who participate, this is likely to be more empowering than a conventional court hearing. Conceivably it could also help them come to terms with what has happened and move beyond it. These are the basic premises on which a variety of restorative justice procedures have been developed in recent years, the three best-known of which involve some form of *mediation*, *conferencing* or *citizen panels* (see Chapter 2, section 2.4).

Conventional criminal justice systems tend to afford very limited scope for these more interactive restorative justice processes and the more flexible forms of reparation that they make possible. Where officials are allowed sufficient discretion, however, it is sometimes possible for them to be accommodated within existing procedures. During the 1980s, for example, a number of experimental 'victim offender mediation and reparation schemes' were established (see Marshall and Merry, 1990 for details). Some of these operated at the pre-court stage and aimed to divert offenders away from prosecution by referring them instead to a reparation/diversion bureau with a view to negotiating an appropriate form of reparation that might also involve a meeting with the victim. Most of such schemes were aimed at juvenile offenders and were criticized for neglecting the interests of victims in order to improve the chances of diverting offenders from prosecution (Davis et al., 1988; 1989). However, one scheme that was aimed at adult offenders (operated by the Kettering Adult Reparation Bureau) demonstrated that it was possible to pursue a philosophy of even-handed reparation. A three-year evaluation showed that it was possible to combine **diversion** for offenders with acceptable reparation for victims in a reasonably high proportion of cases to the satisfaction of both parties (Dignan, 1991; 1992). Schemes such as this helped pave the way for the introduction of conditional cautioning (see the Introduction).

Other schemes operated at the point of sentence or immediately prior to sentence when the court referred a case to the probation service for a pre-sentence report. The possibility of mediation leading to some form of reparation was then explored, and, if the parties agreed, a proposal might then be presented to the court as part of a package involving some form of non-custodial sentence instead of imprisonment. Many of these schemes were only concerned with less serious low-tariff offences, in which case their potential to divert offenders from custody was obviously limited (since few of these offenders would have been imprisoned in any event). A notable exception, however, was the very ambitious Leeds Mediation and Reparation Service, which deliberately targeted high-tariff offenders including adults with the aim of providing an alternative to custody (Wynne, 1996).

More recently, the Home Office has funded a number of pilot projects to test the scope for restorative justice approaches to be used in connection with more serious and relatively high-volume offences such as robberies, burglaries and grievous bodily harm, and also with adult offenders. Three separate sets of projects have been funded, each of which is quite distinct in terms of the type of restorative justice interventions on offer (though they include both mediation and conferencing processes) and also the stage in the criminal justice process at which they are available. The three schemes have been independently evaluated (Shapland et al., 2004; 2006; 2007; 2008) and the results have been positive in terms of both reconviction rates and victim and offender satisfaction. Restorative justice schemes of this kind potentially offer a way of combining diversion from prosecution with constructive reparation for victims. Indeed, experience elsewhere (notably in New Zealand and Australia; see, e.g. Morris et al., 1993; McElrea, 1994) gives ground for cautious optimism that this kind of approach might assist in the development of a more restorative system of criminal justice in general, with the potential to ameliorate many aspects of the current penal crisis (see also Dignan, 2002).

Although the development of restorative justice measures in England and Wales has been slow and cautious, some progress has nevertheless been made since the early experimental schemes in the 1980s. Some initiatives – for example the introduction of conditional cautioning for adult offenders and the recent Home Office pilot projects – we have mentioned already. And the **reparation order** – whereby the offender makes reparation either to the victim or to the community – is available for juvenile offenders aged between 10 and 17 (see Chapter 8, section 8.4). The Coalition government made its interest in restorative measures clear in the Green Paper *Breaking the Cycle* (Ministry of Justice, 2010a) six months after it came to power. As we have seen, a victim surcharge of £15 has been added to all fines since 2007 to help services for victims and witnesses. Similarly, the new government implemented provisions in the Prisoners' Earnings Act 1996 whereby deductions can be taken from the earnings of low-risk prisoners who are working while on pre-release licence, with the money to be used for victim support services. They plan to 'explore other ways to make deductions from prisoners' wages and consider how they should be used, including making reparation to victims and communities' (Ministry of Justice, 2010a: 16). In addition, three other ways of using restorative justice approaches were proposed: first, using restorative approaches as a 'better alternative' to the formal criminal justice system; second, restoration becoming part of a court sentence; and third, using restorative conferences carried out before sentence which could then be used to inform court decisions (Ministry of Justice, 2010a: 22). Following the consultation period for the Green Paper, this encouragement of greater use of restorative approaches was confirmed in the government's response to the consultation (Ministry of Justice, 2011a).

The government's commitment to develop and encourage restorative approaches has been taken forward in *Getting It Right for Victims and Witnesses* (Ministry of Justice, 2012a). The somewhat fragmented way in which restorative initiatives have developed up to now may – hopefully – be coming to an end: the Ministry of Justice and the Home Office plan to work together to 'develop a framework for restorative justice' and to consider how to 'better integrate restorative justice with sentencing and the criminal justice process as a whole' (Ministry of Justice, 2012a: 39, 40). This would certainly be a significant development, but one might still question how far there is a serious commitment to the ideals of restorative justice. It is relatively easy to see how this keenness for restorative justice might be driven not by these ideals but by a wish to save money and to make sentences even more demanding. Indeed, the saving money factor is evident in the proposals in *Getting It Right* for extending the £15 victim surcharge currently added to fines. In July 2012 the then Justice Secretary Kenneth Clarke announced that the surcharge would henceforth also be applied to conditional discharges, community sentences, penalty notices for disorder, suspended sentence orders and custodial sentences. (For details of the ways in which the surcharge will be applied to the various sentences see Ministry of Justice, 2012b). Victim and witness support services will thus be provided with extra resources, but not at the expense of the state. (Just how those with scant financial resources are meant to pay is an interesting question.)

Restorative approaches now play a key part in ways of dealing with young offenders as we will discuss in Chapter 8, but it is possible that their potential could also be realised with adult offenders. Recent developments have not yet moved restorative justice into mainstream criminal justice, but if they were to become commonly used as part of the requirements for community orders and SSOs, and if they begin to be used more often for serious offences, then a radical change will have taken place in how offenders are dealt with.

Supervisory Penalties and the Changing Role of the Probation Service

For many years the **probation order** provided the only major alternative to a custodial sentence apart from a fine or warning penalty, and for offenders with personal or social problems it was the only disposal offering any form of assistance or guidance. This helps to account for its early popularity with sentencers though, as Table 5.1 indicates, it suffered a sharp decline in popularity during the early post-war period followed by a modest revival during the last two decades of the twentieth century.

Until relatively recently, the history of penal supervision has been inextricably bound up with the often turbulent history of the probation service. This has experienced a number of profound transformations between its official inception in 1907 and concerns over its possible effective demise just under a century later when it was subsumed into the National Offender Management Service. This is not the place to set out a history of probation (for that see Vanstone, 2004; Whitehead and Statham, 2006; Nellis, 2007; Raynor and Vanstone, 2007; Mair and Burke, 2012), but essentially the service began in the late nineteenth century with what was missionary work carried out by workers from the Church of England Temperance Society. Following the Probation of Offenders Act 1907 (which provided the statutory basis for the probation order), probation slowly became more professional with a regular career structure and trained staff. Work with offenders developed from a philanthropic paternalism to a more scientifically based case-work approach, but still with the traditional duty to 'advise, assist and befriend' their 'clients'. By the middle of the 1970s the loss of much work with juveniles to social workers, the collapse of the rehabilitative ideal, the introduction of community service and the new objective of acting as an alternative to custody (rather than providing offenders with such help as they needed) had profoundly changed the probation service. And the election of a Conservative government in 1979 with a policy agenda of cutting spending, public services and crime did not augur well for probation. The probation service had always been subject to criticism as being soft on criminals and this was not something that the new government was likely to welcome.

The 1982 Criminal Justice Act introduced two new additional requirements that could be added to a probation order to toughen it up: to participate in specified activities and to attend a day centre. But the first manifestation of government wishing to take greater control of what was still very much a collection of independent probation services came with the Statement of National Objectives and Priorities (Home Office, 1984b). This urged local probation committees and chief officers to ensure that probation resources were managed 'efficiently and effectively' in pursuit of clear objectives with a view to delivering value for money to the taxpayer. Perhaps more significant was the use of the term 'National'. It was rapidly augmented by a barrage of initiatives such as performance indicators and National Standards. The Green Paper *Punishment, Custody and the Community* (Home Office, 1988a), the subsequent White Paper (Home Office, 1990a), and the Criminal Justice Act 1991 turned probation into 'punishment in the community' and the service into a criminal justice agency. The Act introduced two new orders – the **combination order** (which combined probation supervision and community service into a high-tariff sentence), and the curfew order with electronic monitoring (see below) – and made probation legally a sentence of the court for the first time; in practice a rather innocuous but hugely symbolic change.

In 1985, only 15 per cent of probation orders had been made with an additional requirement; by 1997 when the Conservatives lost power the figure had more than doubled to 33 per cent. Probation was becoming more rigorous and demanding and probation officers were being pushed into becoming penal control agents, which inevitably affected their relationships both with offenders and the courts. Increasingly, courts had been granted powers to augment the straightforward supervision that a probation order entails with a variety of additional requirements, such as requirements to attend probation day centres or engage in offender training programmes. (Many of these additional requirements, or equivalents, can now be incorporated in the new generic community order that was described in section 5.2 above.) These greatly increased the scope for the control and discipline of offenders as well as providing the basis for special programmes aimed at preventing or reducing reoffending. They also increased the demands which could be placed upon offenders who were given probation orders, thereby multiplying the risks of non-compliance. This in turn added to the responsibilities placed on probation officers, as they were expected to execute and enforce the increasingly detailed commands that were likely to be embodied in probation orders. As Table 5.1 shows, use of the probation order increased under the Conservative administrations.

By the time of the 1997 election the probation service was increasingly subject to government control: financing, training and styles of work were all being regulated. The probation order itself was more punitive due to the use of added requirements, and the need for offenders to consent to the making of an order had been removed by the Crime (Sentences) Act 1997. Probation was now in the business of public protection.

Under New Labour, there was some shift of emphasis back towards rehabilitation (notably in the shape of 'doing what works' to confront and change offenders' attitudes towards crime via the Effective Practice Initiative: see Mair, 2004b). However, the stress on 'protection of the public' via firm control of offenders remained. In 2000, the probation officer's historic statutory obligation to 'advise, assist and befriend' the offender (first enacted in the Probation of Offenders Act 1907) was finally abolished and replaced with a new set of aims in which protection of the public had pride of place, and which included 'the proper punishment of offenders'. A Joint Prison/Probation Accreditation Panel was set up in 1999 to regulate and plan the development of programmes. A government review encouraged closer working between the prison and probation services and recommended a unified, national probation service (Home Office, 1998b). In April 2001, the 54 separate and partly autonomous local probation services were replaced by a single National Probation Service (NPS) comprising 42 areas with a single national Director, directly accountable to the Home Secretary. The Criminal Justice and Court Services Act 2000 which set out the new structure also spelt out (in section 2) the aims of the new service: to protect the public, reduce offending and provide for the proper punishment of offending, as well as the rehabilitation of offenders. This was followed by the publication – by the new Director of the service – of a new integrated management strategy (National Probation Service, 2001).

Almost before the ink was dry on this document, and before the NPS had any chance to settle down, the government-commissioned Carter Report on the correctional services (2003) recommended that the delivery of custodial and non-custodial penalties be brought together under the auspices of a new organization to be known as the National Offender Management Service. The government unreservedly accepted Carter's proposal, and NOMS came into existence in June 2004, although even now almost a decade after its introduction, NOMS remains organisationally vague (McKnight, 2009). Probation's place in it is undefined. The government also accepted an approach suggested by Carter which, if implemented in full, would entail the effective demise of the probation service in anything like its current form. This involved the introduction of a 'purchaser-provider split' for the delivery of non-custodial services (similar to that introduced in the National Health Service in the 1980s), whereby NOMS (the purchaser) would identify the services needed in its different regions and would buy them from a range of different providers. This contestability would involve the probation service being required to compete with private commercial or voluntary sector rivals for contracts to deliver non-custodial services. These might include contracts to supervise particular groups of offenders within a given area, to deliver specified training programmes or to deliver any of the other requirements that might form part of a community order (for more on contestability see section 5.4 below).

The 2003 Criminal Justice Act scrapped the old probation-run community penalties (including the probation, community service and combination orders, which had been renamed in 2001) and replaced them with the single community order (see section 5.2) which became available to the courts in April 2005. The new order was planned to rationalize the existing large number of community penalties and requirements that had grown up in an unco-ordinated way since the mid-80s. It was also intended to offer a credible alternative to short custodial sentences. As Table 5.2 shows, the community order made up almost 11 per cent of all court sentences for adults in 2011, and for indictable offences the figure was 22 per cent. The popularity of the new order cannot be denied, but there is disturbing evidence that only around half of the available requirements are used to any extent, that there has been a shift towards more punitive requirements, that almost half of the community orders made by the courts are passed for summary offences, and therefore that they have made no impact as an alternative to custody (National Audit Office, 2008; Mair, 2011). Instead, it seems that the order has been predominantly replacing fines as part of a continuing 'ratcheting up' of sentences as identified by Morgan (2003).

The community order could potentially involve sentencers much more closely in specifying an offender's particular obligations, as opposed to simply selecting an off-the-peg penalty as in the past. So far, however, there is no evidence that sentencers have been taking up this possibility. The community order (and the SSO) also offer the possibility of sentencers regularly reviewing the progress of offenders and adjusting the terms of the sentence as necessary. Again, there is little evidence that this option has been taken up – indeed it seems to be relatively unknown (Mair et al., 2008). However, although it is not yet happening, one possible longer-term result of these developments could be to encourage a much closer partnership between sentencers and those responsible for delivering community orders since they are likely to require much more detailed feedback relating to the offender's performance while subject to the order. Probation officers would prepare brief reports for sentencers on offenders' performance for review meetings which might take place monthly for the first few months of an order.

The pressure to make community penalties more punitive and controlling continued with yet another intensive community supervision initiative. Intensive Alternatives to Custody (IAC) operated between 2008/9 and 2010/11 in seven probation areas in England and Wales. These were community orders combining intensive probation supervision with a mix of demanding requirements and interventions and each IAC had an average of 3.4 requirements and usually lasted for 12 months. The Ministry of Justice evaluation of the pilots contained little in the way of any empirical evidence that the IAC programme was acting as an alternative to custody as opposed to merely making community sentences more intrusive (see Hansbury, 2011). By 2008 a number of other developments significant for probation had occurred. The Offender Management Act 2007 provided for probation services to be delivered by public, private or voluntary providers, and for the replacement of probation boards by trusts which would be much more business-oriented than their predecessors. The banking crisis, which would lead to severe economic recession in the West – and would have serious implications for public spending – had begun. And two French students had been murdered by an offender who should have been recalled to prison. This last, which led to the resignation of the Chief Officer of the London Probation Area, was the culmination of a number of murder cases (John Monckton, Robert Symons, Mary-Ann Leneghan, Naomi Bryant) where the probation service was seen to be at fault. The morale and public image of probation by the time of the general election of 2010 was at a particularly low ebb. The culture of probation had changed: it was now a national service in the business of risk management (a development that had begun in the 1990s – see Robinson, 1999; 2002 and the discussion of the new penology in Chapter 3, section 3.6); resource limitations meant that most of the work carried out with offenders was now done by unqualified probation staff; old-style pre-sentence reports which had focused on detailed analysis of the offence and the offender had been largely replaced by fast delivery reports, many of which were oral reports made on the day of appearance in court. There has been a fragmentation of service delivery (Robinson and Dignan, 2004) within probation services, but also as a result of the increasing use of working in partnership with other bodies – a fragmentation that has been exacerbated by the community order with its various requirements.

In his first speech as Justice Secretary following the 2010 election, Kenneth Clarke spoke of a 'rehabilitation revolution' (see section 2.2 of Chapter 2) but noticeably failed to mention the probation service (Clarke, 2010). The Green Paper *Breaking the Cycle* (Ministry of Justice, 2010a), despite using the rhetoric of rehabilitation, made it clear that community sentences had to be 'more robust and rigorous punishments' and 'tougher and more intensive' (Ministry of Justice, 2010a: 9). One might ask just how much more robust, just how much more intensive community sentences can be? But the key proposal in the Green Paper was the idea of payment by results – agencies providing and managing punishments should be paid according to how effective they proved to be in reducing reoffending. In principle perhaps, a sensible way to proceed, but the issues raised by such an approach are many. For example, how is effectiveness defined, how is payment allocated to the various agencies who might have been involved in dealing with an offender, and when would payments be made (see Fox and Albertson, 2011)? National Standards are being relaxed but this can all too easily be seen as a way of encouraging private and voluntary sector agencies to bid for probation tasks without the need to adhere to rigorous standards.

A House of Commons Justice Committee Report (2011) pointed out that the arrangements were not yet in place for the commissioning of services, but agreed in principle with the aim of creating a mixed economy in the provision of probation services and with payment by results. It also noted with some astonishment that 'up to three-quarters of officers' time might be spent on work which does not involve direct engagement with offenders' (House of Commons Justice Committee, 2011: 106). This figure starkly symbolises the kind of changes that had taken place in probation work which had in the past been characterized by close, one-to-one work with offenders. In March 2012, two further consultation papers were published setting out in more detail the Coalition's plans for probation (Ministry of Justice, 2012c; 2012d). No longer were community penalties to be in the business of acting as alternatives to custody; and every community order was to have a 'clear punitive element' in it – a proposal taken further forward by Clarke's successor Chris Grayling in October 2012. In the words of Justice Secretary Kenneth Clarke in his foreword to one of these papers, 'we plan to go further, not in order to create an alternative to short prison sentences, but to address the fact that reoffending rates for sentences in the community are still far too high, and that they fail to command public confidence as an effective punishment' (Ministry of Justice, 2012c: 1). Thus, tough punishment in the community is no longer an attempt to encourage sentencers to use non-custodial penalties instead of prison, but amounts to a further deliberate 'ratcheting up' of punishment. Probation Trusts will retain responsibility for dealing with high-risk offenders, reports to the courts and enforcement while all other probation services will be opened up to competition. It is estimated that competed services amount to more than half of the budget for community offender services, which raises the possibility of what we have known as the probation service becoming a minority provider rather than the monopoly provider it always was. In future, the provision of probation services may become the responsibility of local authorities or the new Police and Crime Commissioners who will be elected in November 2012. Another proposal is to give offender managers (as well as courts) the power to fine offenders if they fail to comply with the requirements of their orders; failure to pay would mean that breach proceedings would go ahead with the offender being dealt with in court.

Yet another intensive order was proposed: an intensive **community punishment order** which would include **unpaid work (community payback**: see below), restrictions on liberty, a driving ban and a fine. The idea of supervising offenders (the old-style probation order and the supervision requirement of the community order) was condemned as ineffectual: 'it is not primarily punitive and, on its own in a sentence, fails to send a clear message that offending behaviour will be dealt with' (Ministry of Justice, 2012d: 12). Unless there are clear reasons for not doing so (for example, an offender might have mental health problems which preclude it), a punitive element will in future be included in all community orders. Use of the supervision requirement in the community order has been decreasing steadily (in the first quarter of 2009, 20,771 supervision requirements commenced while the figure for the last quarter of 2011 was 16,211, a drop of 22 per cent) and if the government's proposals are taken forward it is possible to envisage the withering away of the supervision of offenders, which has been the backbone of the probation service for more than 100 years – and even the withering away of the service itself.

Community Payback (Community Service or Unpaid Work)

Powers to impose an obligation to undertake unpaid work in the community date back to the introduction of the community service order (CSO) by the Criminal Justice Act 1972. The CSO was an independent court order, but the provision of community service was made the responsibility of the probation service. As can be seen from Table 5.1, the measure swiftly established itself and thereafter maintained a reasonably consistent level of popularity among sentencers. The type of work to be undertaken is decided by the probation service in consultation with relevant agencies, many of which operate in the voluntary sector, who offer work placements that are approved by the probation service as being suitable.

Part of the popularity of community service probably derives from its appeal to a range of different sentencing philosophies since it combines elements of reparation, rehabilitation and retribution. However, the *reparative* element in unpaid work penalties *requires* the offender to make amends (to the community as a whole rather than to the individual victim), and thus – contrary to the ethos of restorative justice – is often imposed on an offender who has no choice in the matter (originally, the offender's consent was necessary before a community service order could be made, but (like the probation order) this prerequisite was removed by the Crime (Sentences) Act 1997). However, in principle there is no reason why offenders should not agree to undertake unpaid work of a particular kind in the context of a restorative justice process such as mediation or conferencing. Anthony Duff (2001) has argued that community service fits well with his communicative theory of punishment (see Chapter 2, section 2.4). Others (for example, Walgrave, 1999; Dignan, 2002: 184) have also spoken of its potential if the criminal justice system were to be reformed in accordance with restorative justice precepts.

There is some evidence to support claims of community service's *rehabilitative* potential, since offenders in receipt of this sentence have been shown to have lower reconviction rates than would have been predicted (Lloyd et al., 1995; May, 1999). There is also evidence that the rehabilitative potential of community service might be enhanced by improving the quality of the work undertaken by offenders. McIvor (1998), for example, found that community service placements which were viewed by offenders as most rewarding were associated with reductions in recidivism, while Killias et al. (2000) found that offenders who perceived their sentence as fair had lower than expected reconviction rates.

However, it is also possible to conceptualize community service in an unambiguously punitive manner, as a 'fine on an offender's time', particularly where the offender is required to perform tasks that are pointless, demeaning or unrelated to the crime (Bottoms, 2000). In recent years there has been a tendency to prioritize this aspect of the penalty at the expense of the other two aims (one can see some of this in the change of name from 'community service' to 'community punishment' and then 'unpaid work'). Thus, the National Standards that were published in 2000 stressed that work placements should 'occupy offenders fully and be physically, emotionally or mentally demanding' (Home Office, Department of Health and Welsh Office, 2000: D16). In a similar vein, the maximum number of hours that can be imposed was increased from 240 to 300 by the Criminal Justice Act 2003 (s. 199). The evidence referred to above suggests that a government that was interested in penal effectiveness as opposed to penal posturing would do better to focus on the reintegrative and rehabilitative aspects of the penalty instead of being punitive for its own sake. In 2003 the National Probation Service launched 'enhanced community punishment' which added a rehabilitative element to the punitive and reparative elements. All those subject to the order were expected to address their employment-related skills and thinking skills in addition to the work element (see HM Inspectorate of Probation, 2006).

The Labour government sought to rebrand unpaid work with the label 'community payback' (a term suggestive of both retribution and reparation) arguing that it should be 'at the heart of community sentences', an aspiration that was central to the 'Five Year Strategy' published by Home Secretary Charles Clarke in February 2006 (Home Office, 2006b: 3.16). This strategy aimed to double the number of hours of unpaid work carried out from 5 million hours in 2005 to 10 million. In 2008, Louise Casey, who had been asked by the government to examine crime, justice and community involvement, reported on her findings (Cabinet Office, 2008); one of the ten key facts being that '90% of the public agree that community punishments for crime should involve some form of payback to the community' (Cabinet Office, 2008: 7). Casey was very keen on unpaid work, proposing that its name should be changed to community payback, that it should be made much more visible to the public and more demanding for offenders, that its organisation and operation should be contracted out from the probation service, and that probation officers should be given the power to add extra hours in cases of breach rather than taking offenders back to court. Intensive community payback of 300 hours was introduced in September 2008 for unemployed offenders convicted of knife crime. This involved working for a minimum of 18 hours a week rather than the current minimum of six hours. From December 2008 offenders performing unpaid work had to wear high-visibility orange jackets emblazoned with the words 'Community Payback'. The government's response to Casey's report envisaged giving the public more say on what kind of work should be done by offenders on community payback (introduced in April 2009) and extending intensive community payback to a wider range of offenders (Ministry of Justice, 2009a).

Since the introduction of the community order in April 2005, unpaid work has been the most frequently used requirement, comprising around one third of all community orders. However, there is little to suggest that members of the community are aware of the opportunity to nominate community payback work (Moore et al., 2010). The Coalition government made it clear that it intended to continue this trend of more intensive payback in *Breaking the Cycle* (Ministry of Justice, 2010a) and in their response to the consultation that followed: 'We will improve Community Payback so it is more intensive and demanding. Offenders will work a longer day and a longer working week' (Ministry of Justice, 2011a: 5), including unemployed offenders having to work a full working week. Again, one is entitled to wonder just how demanding and intensive it can be; and how can employed offenders work more hours per week?

Whether or not the introduction of community service in 1973 is the most significant cause of the current weakened state of the probation service as Mair and Burke (2012) suggest, community payback now lies at the heart of the community order and will provide the foundation of the proposed intensive community punishment (see above) as an unashamedly punitive requirement (Ministry of Justice, 2012c).

Surveillance and Restrictions on Movement: Curfews and Electronic Monitoring

They may sound similar, but the concepts of 'supervision' and 'surveillance' imply two fundamentally different techniques of social control that have radically different implications for offenders and, indeed, the penal system as a whole. Supervision is a more holistic and humanistic concept: it implies the existence of a personal relationship based on periodic contact between supervisor and supervisee and entails a degree of watchfulness combined with the possibility of guidance on the part of the supervisor, but ultimately depends on the supervisee acting in a trustworthy manner. Surveillance, on the other hand, implies the existence of a form of impersonal technology that offers the prospect (although not always the reality) of monitoring a person's whereabouts and movements. It gives the appearance of being backed by a more intensive and ostensibly more reliable enforcement regime that is less dependent on the trustworthiness of the offender. Even before the development of advanced technological monitoring systems, attempts were made to regulate the movement of offenders; for example, by imposing residence requirements, by means of more intensive reporting or tracking requirements linked with probation supervision, or by imposing curfews. But in the absence of a reliable enforcement mechanism these tended to lack credibility. The advent of a new form of electronic surveillance during the 1980s laid the foundations for a new and controversial form of social control (see Nellis, 2004).

Electronic monitoring (or tagging) was first used in England on an experimental basis, initially as a means of enforcing bail restrictions in 1989–90 and then as a means of enforcing a free-standing home curfew order (introduced by the Criminal Justice Act 1991). In 1999 curfew orders enforced by electronic monitoring were made available nationwide and the same technology was also used to release certain categories of prisoner early under home detention curfew (see Chapter 7). Electronic monitoring is also used on young offenders who are placed on **Intensive Supervision and Surveillance Programmes** (ISSPs; see Chapter 8). As we have seen, under the Criminal Justice Act 2003 (s. 177) a curfew enforced by electronic monitoring can now be included in a community order, either on its own or in combination with one or more of the other 13 possible components of such an order. Moreover, the court can now also order electronic monitoring to be used as a means of enforcing any other requirement of a community order. The Legal Aid, Sentencing and Punishment of Offenders Act 2012 extends the maximum length of a curfew requirement from 12 to 16 hours a day, for a maximum period of 12 months rather than six.

In its original (and still by far commonest) form, electronic monitoring takes the form of an electronic device attached to the offender's ankle or wrist, which is in radio contact with a device on the offender's domestic telephone. This can confirm or deny that the offender is abiding by a curfew. However, technological developments offer the prospect of developing more sophisticated methods of keeping offenders under surveillance. They include the use of voice verification technology that makes it possible to monitor an offender's presence at multiple locations, and satellite-based global positioning systems with which it is possible to track an offender's movements; thus, for example, it can be used to enforce **exclusion requirements** in a community order, which allows offenders to leave home but prohibits them from going to certain places or areas. Satellite tracking pilots took place in three area in England and Wales between 2004 and 2006. The technology was very accurate in pin-pointing the whereabouts of an individual, but still had blind spots if the unit was inside a building or there were tall buildings in the way. Overall, more than half of those tracked (58 per cent) were either recalled to prison or had their community penalty revoked (Shute, 2007). (This can be for non-compliance with the order's requirements, including by simply removing the tag.) One distinctive feature of this emergent social control technique, at least in England and Wales, is its reliance on *private* security firms rather than the probation service – which was initially ideologically strongly opposed to the new technology – in order to monitor compliance. Much of the research into tagging has noted failures to communicate effectively between these private firms and the probation services (Mair, 2005; Criminal Justice Joint Inspectorates, 2008).

The use of curfews as a punishment has risen sharply since their introduction. A curfew requirement is now the fourth most commonly used requirement for community orders and SSOs: 17,375 were used for the former in 2011 – an increase of 11 per cent since 2008 – and 8,851 were used in SSOs, an increase of 42 per cent since 2008. The fact that electronic monitoring is now available as a means of enforcing compliance with *any* community order, and not just a curfew, as well as the extension of the period for which a curfew can be made, is likely to consolidate still further England's position as world leader in the proportionate use of electronic monitoring (Nellis, 2003: 245). The Coalition government is committed to the further extension of tagging and we have already noted the proposal for intensive community punishment, which would be underpinned by an electronically monitored curfew. Tracking technology is seen as capable of monitoring exclusion requirements, residence requirements and the new foreign travel and alcohol abstinence requirements; and the possibility of using electronic monitoring to track offenders for the purpose of preventing reoffending (rather than to secure compliance with a community order or SSO requirement as at present) has recently been mooted (Ministry of Justice, 2012c).

Although the use of electronic monitoring has been credited with contributing to significant reductions in the use of imprisonment in Sweden (Carlsson, 2003; Olkiewicz, 2003), this does not appear to be the case in England and Wales. Research commissioned by the Home Office found that the curfew order was used as an alternative to imprisonment in only around 20 per cent of cases, whereas it replaced a fine or a discharge in nearly 45 per cent of cases and some other community penalty in just under 33 per cent of cases (Walters, 2002: 40). Nellis (2003: 253ff) has suggested, plausibly, that one possible explanation for this could have to do with people's acclimatization to a growing 'surveillance culture'. As the notion of personal surveillance and 'locatability' becomes more entrenched as a result of developments in closed circuit television (CCTV) technology and mobile phone ownership, the monitoring of offenders' whereabouts is seen as being qualitatively little different from people's everyday experience. Consequently, the fact that offenders' movements may theoretically be subjected even to constant monitoring is considered to be insufficiently punitive to count as a serious alternative to prison.

The penalty that could be most seriously threatened by the spread of electronic monitoring is the more traditional form of supervision conducted by the probation service. Its vulnerability was heightened by a growing sense of moral panic between 2005 and 2008 following a number of high-visibility failures (mentioned above) in which offenders who were supposedly under supervision in the community went on to commit other serious offences. One of the attractions of electronic monitoring stems from the fact that it *appears* to improve the enforceability of community penalties without having to rely on the trustworthiness of offenders and the limitations of their human supervisors. However, analogous concerns have been voiced by probation staff about the number of violations involving offenders who are subject to electronic monitoring before they are breached, and the fact that – unlike probation supervision – there is no routine monitoring of violations (National Association of Probation Officers, 2005). There has also been considerable debate about whether or not electronic monitoring is cost effective: the National Association of Probation Officers (2005) has claimed that it costs twice as much to tag offenders as it does for a probation officer to supervise them, but a 2006 study by the National Audit Office concluded that electronic monitoring provided value for money and was much cheaper than custody (National Audit Office, 2006).

Electronic monitoring does *not* of itself stop an individual from offending. It is always possible for an offender to break their curfew or exclusion requirement or simply remove the tag, although this should in theory be detected and sanctions can occur after the event. Indeed, as a means of effective control over offenders, tagging can have serious limitations. In one case a young tagged offender (released on home detention curfew: see Chapter 7, section 7.3) called Peter Williams was convicted of assisting in the murder of Nottingham jeweller Marian Bates in 2003. Williams had repeatedly breached his curfew order and removed his tag, but little was done to control him (*Guardian*, 19 September 2005).

Nevertheless it is difficult to deny that the image of automated enforcement, even if not matched in reality, has helped to shore up the political credibility of electronic monitoring at a time when confidence in more personalized forms of supervision appears to be rapidly waning (Nellis, 2004: 239). When these developments are set in the context of a decisive shift in the direction of greater private sector involvement in the administration of community punishment under the guise of contestability (see section 5.5, below), the prospects for more traditional forms of probation-linked supervision look even more insecure.

'Hybrid' Penalties

Historically, there was a sharp dichotomy between custodial and non-custodial forms of punishment that manifested itself conceptually, institutionally and also experientially for those convicted offenders who were sentenced to either one or the other, but never both at the same time. In recent years, however, the previously watertight boundaries between them have become increasingly permeable with the emergence of electronic monitoring of curfews and the introduction of the suspended sentence order.

The history of this new generation of 'hybrid' penalties in England and Wales dates back to the introduction of the suspended sentence in 1967, one of the first initiatives to be adopted in the post-war era as a means of restraining the rapidly expanding prison population (Bottoms, 1981). Sentences of imprisonment of up to two years could be suspended for an 'operational period' of from one to two years; if the offender committed a further imprisonable offence in this time, the suspended sentence would normally be activated by the court reconvicting the offender. In this original guise the suspended sentence of imprisonment imposed no constraints or obligations on an offender beyond the requirement not to reoffend during the operational period (courts could pass a suspended sentence **supervision order** which combined probation supervision with a suspended sentence, but this was rarely used). Despite its popularity with sentencers over many years (see Table 5.1), the suspended sentence was a penological failure inasmuch as it failed to reduce, or even curb, the increase in the prison population. This was largely because – although supposedly a direct alternative to custody – it was often seen and used by sentencers as an alternative to other non-custodial penalties rather than a substitute for imprisonment (the phenomenon known as **net-widening**). This in turn may have had an inflationary effect on prison numbers, as those who reoffended were far more likely to go to prison, and for longer periods, than if they had received an alternative sentence.

Courts were discouraged from using the suspended sentence by the Criminal Justice Act 1991, which restricted its availability to cases involving 'exceptional circumstances', and this caused a dramatic slump in its usage as can be seen from Table 5.1. This trend was, however, reversed by the Criminal Justice Act 2003 (ss. 189–194) which – following a proposal in the Halliday Report (2001) – replaced the old suspended sentence with a completely new version known as the suspended sentence order. This allowed the court to pass a sentence of imprisonment for a fixed term (between 28 and 51 weeks), which could be suspended for an operational period of between six months and two years. As we have noted, the Legal Aid, Sentencing and Punishment of Offenders Act 2012 amended the length of sentence that could be suspended to between 14 days and two years. The suspended sentence order introduced in 2003 differed from its predecessor in two important respects.

First, the court passing the suspended sentence order could additionally order the offender to comply with one or more of the 12 requirements (now 14) that were available as part of the new generic community sentence (see above). These requirements take effect during a specified supervision period (which cannot be longer than the operational period). This feature may be seen as a response to the oft-voiced criticism that the original suspended sentence consisted of a 'let-off' inasmuch as it entailed no serious consequences for an offender – provided, of course, there was no further offence. But the Legal Aid, Sentencing and Punishment of Offenders Act 2012 now permits the SSO to be made without any requirements, thereby reintroducing the old-style suspended sentence (and it will be interesting to see how often this option is used). Second, s. 191 of the Criminal Justice Act 2003 provided that the suspended sentence order should be reviewed periodically by the court, which allows it to amend the requirements at a later stage, either by strengthening them where an offender's compliance may be in doubt, or relaxing them if the offender is making satisfactory progress. This aspect of the sentence is another example of a potentially radical change in the role of the court, which is no longer confined to simply pronouncing a sentence, but increasingly can also entail a sentence management function (see below).

Both aspects of the new suspended sentence order give it added punitive bite and accentuate its position as a high-tariff measure. The suspended sentence order is subject to the custody threshold set out in s. 152(2) of the Criminal Justice Act 2003: the requirement that the offence is 'so serious that neither a fine alone nor a community sentence can be justified for the offence'. Moreover, sentencing guidelines (Sentencing Guidelines Council, 2004a: para. 2.2.11) reinforce this requirement. They also stipulate that courts should be careful not to make the community punishment requirements of the sentence too onerous (2004a: para. 2.2.14). It seems likely, however, that these measures are failing to avoid the malfunctions associated with the old-style suspended sentence. In Canada, the introduction of a similar provision known as the conditional sentence did contribute to a reduction in prison numbers without endangering public safety (Roberts, J., 2003; 2004). However, much depends on the willingness of the English courts to apply the custody threshold strictly and comply with the guidelines. Given the courts' track record in the past, this remains a cause for concern, and there is every reason to believe that the SSO has been largely used in place of community orders and only rarely used instead of immediate custody (Ministry of Justice, 2008a: 7; Mair and Mills, 2009). Moreover, offenders serving suspended sentence orders with additional requirements are liable to have them activated not only if they reoffend during the operational period, but also if they fail to comply with the community punishment requirements during the supervisory period. The Legal Aid, Sentencing and Punishment of Offenders Act 2012 introduced the possibility of a fine for breach of an SSO (and for breach of a community order) which may make it less likely that imprisonment will be the result of a failure to comply. So, although the suspended sentence order might have the *potential* to ease some of the pressure on the prison population if used properly, like its predecessor it is also vulnerable to misuse and malfunction which could have – and probably is having – the reverse effect.

The SSO has proved to be very successful – at least in terms of its usage by the courts. By July 2006, the number of SSOs commenced was twice that estimated by the Home Office (Mair et al., 2007) and there were claims that it was being over-used by magistrates (Mair et al., 2008). In 2011 a total of 47,798 SSOs were made by the courts, 55 per cent of which were passed by magistrates, of which almost half were made for summary offences. Bearing in mind that the SSO is – legally – a custodial sentence, this suggests that magistrates may well be over-using the sentence for relatively minor offences. Contrary to the sentencing guidelines mentioned above, since its introduction the SSO has had on average slightly more requirements than the community order, and in terms of the kind of requirements used for the SSO there is evidence that it is becoming more punitive with significant increases in the use of stand-alone unpaid work and curfew requirements (Ministry of Justice, 2012e). Despite its punitive nature, there is no evidence to suggest that the SSO is being used as an alternative to custody (Mair and Mills, 2009).

It is worth noting briefly two other 'hybrid' penalties. *Intermittent custody* was also introduced in the Criminal Justice Act 2003 (s. 183) and resembled the new suspended sentence order in terms of sentence length (28 and 51 weeks). It enabled a court to prescribe a number of days – between 14 and 90 – that had to be served in custody, though they could be served intermittently rather than as a continuous term. The new sentence was tried out in two prisons from April 2004. It always seemed improbable that intermittent custody could achieve much that was worthwhile – being at least as likely to widen the net and give to many offenders a taste of custody who might otherwise have been given a fully non-custodial sentence as to divert others from full-time imprisonment. Moreover, it was practically inevitable that it would waste scarce prison cells, and so it proved. A Prisons Inspectorate Report on Kirkham Prison in June 2005 found that a 39-place intermittent custody unit contained only one prisoner during the week, and had never had more than three (HM Chief Inspector of Prisons, 2005c: 8.80; *Guardian*, 3 June 2005.) In November 2006 intermittent custody was summarily ended, with the government pleading the need to prioritize protecting the public from more serious offenders (*BBC News*, 2 November 2006).

The 2003 Act's trio of new 'hybrid' semi-custodial penalties was meant to be completed by a penalty known as *custody plus* (ss. 181–182). This was intended as a replacement for all custodial sentences of less than 12 months by the Halliday Report (2001) which identified a number of serious shortcomings associated with existing short prison sentences. Custody plus was to combine a short period of custody with a period on licence during which offenders would be expected to comply with community punishment requirements. The proposed new sentence was prominent in Charles Clarke's 'Five Year Strategy' published in February 2006; at this stage the plan was to bring in custody plus in the autumn of 2006. However, in July 2006 its implementation was shelved by incoming Home Secretary John Reid in the wake of an increasingly vitriolic debate over sentencing levels following a number of high-profile incidents involving offences committed by offenders serving community penalties or while on licence, and the Legal Aid, Sentencing and Punishment of Offenders Act 2012 repealed the statutory provisions for both custody plus and intermittent custody.

Community Punishment: Strategic Issues

Changing Penal Strategies[1] and Their Impact on the Use of Imprisonment and Community Punishment

5.4 The quest for alternatives to imprisonment dates back over a century, with the introduction of probation and an expansion in the use of the fine. During the 1960s and 1970s, however, it became apparent that these traditional alternatives to custody were unable to contain the prison numbers crisis. It was in this context that suspended sentences of imprisonment and community service orders were introduced (in 1967 and 1972 respectively), steps were taken

---

[1]See Bottoms et al. (2004) for a fuller analysis of the shifts in penal strategy since the early twentieth century.

to encourage the use of compensation orders and new forms of probation were introduced (notably in 1982). However, the prevailing strategy was still heavily influenced by continuing deference on the part of governments towards the 'extravagant version' of the doctrine of judicial independence, resulting in a strategy of encouragement regarding the use of non-custodial penalties instead of custody (see Chapter 4, sections 4.3 and 4.4). This deferential approach was also reflected in a lack of clear guidance to sentencers as to how the new measures should be used. By 1991, it was obvious that the policy of widening the sentencers' repertoire of non-custodial sanctions had notably failed to alleviate the prison numbers crisis (except perhaps in the realm of **juvenile justice**: see Chapter 8, sections 8.2 and 8.5). The general tendency was for non-custodial alternatives to supplement, rather than supplant, existing custodial measures and to function as alternatives to one another as much as to custody. Indeed, empirical evidence suggested that even when touted as direct alternatives to custody, new non-custodial penalties such as the CSO or suspended sentence usually replaced other non-custodial penalties at least half the time (Bottoms, 1981; Pease, 1985). Moreover, the proportionate use of custody by the courts actually increased significantly during much of the period in which the various new alternatives were made available, and this was reflected in a continued expansion in the size of the prison population. The penal and custodial nets had widened to catch increasing numbers of offenders, not narrowed.

The failure of this *laissez faire* approach by government contributed to a radical shift in policy towards the use of non-custodial penalties during the late 1980s. As we saw in Chapter 4 (section 4.4), this culminated in the introduction of a new sentencing framework in the Criminal Justice Act 1991. The new approach was symbolized by an important change in terminology, in which the terms 'punishment in the community' and 'community penalties' were substituted for the more traditional phrase 'alternatives to imprisonment'. The switch was intended to emphasize the government's initial desire that non-custodial measures should be seen as demanding penalties in their own right, and therefore appropriate for all but the most serious of offences. Efforts were also made to give substance to this tougher image for community penalties by greatly intensifying the restrictions they imposed on the liberty of offenders, and also by tightening up on the way they were enforced (see below). This, too, was intended to make them more attractive to sentencers for the less serious offenders whom the government at that time wished to see being diverted from custody. We call this a policy of *punitive bifurcation* since it was based on a differentiation between serious and not-so-serious offenders (bifurcation), but also involved a more overtly punitive approach across the whole range of punishments. But the Act still relied heavily on the strategy of encouragement, since sentencers' discretion remained wide and was therefore capable of being exercised in widely varying ways. Indeed, the scope which the Act afforded sentencers was to prove capable of accommodating itself to further and more punitive shifts in the penal policy agenda.

The penal policy U-turn associated with the law and order counter-reformation of the early 1990s ushered in a far more punitive climate as the 1991 Act's emphasis on just deserts and punishment in the community gave way to a different set of concerns centred around the newly emergent priorities of public protection and risk reduction (as exemplified by the Multi-Agency Public Protection Arrangements introduced by the Criminal Justice and Court Services Act 2000). This mixture of the new punitiveness and the new penology (see Chapter 3, section 3.6) in turn helped to shape a new generation of community penalties that sought to harness a variety of strategies: managerialist techniques, technological controls, closer collaboration between agencies and attempts to relate restrictions on liberty to perceived risks of reoffending (rather than what the offender 'deserved'). The effect of this strategic shift can be seen in Table 5.1. This shows that the proportionate use of community penalties *which involve some form of supervision or surveillance* almost doubled for adult indictable offenders from 14.4 to 28.1 per cent between 1989 and 2004. This sharp increase was not gained at the expense of custody, which also increased its 'market share' over the same period (from 17.5 per cent to 28.6 per cent). The penalties that lost out most spectacularly were the least intrusive and punitive measures such as the fine and the (old-style) suspended sentence in particular. Rod Morgan (2003: 17) demonstrated that at the end of this period offenders who would previously have been fined were receiving community penalties such as probation and community service. Meanwhile those who might previously have been given lower-level community punishments were now receiving more intrusive penalties, or being sent to custody.

It is now almost a decade since the 2003 Criminal Justice Act introduced the community order and the SSO with their 12 (now 14) requirements, and these represent a further turn of the punitive screw. While there is no evidence of requirement overload with either order, there are signs that use of the more rehabilitative requirements (such as supervision and accredited programme requirements) is decreasing, while the more punitive requirements (community payback, curfew) are being used more often (Mair, 2011). As we have noted, Intensive Alternatives to Custody (ICAs) were introduced in 2008 but with – as usual – no effect upon prison numbers. Although the Coalition government initially made encouraging noises about a 'rehabilitation revolution' and restricting the use of short custodial sentences, Kenneth Clarke lost that battle. More intensive community orders have been proposed and all community orders are to have a punitive element. The government seems to have lost any interest in trying to use community sentences to divert offenders from custody or in justifying increasing their punitive bite in order to encourage their use as alternatives to custody. Community sentences are now punitive for their own sake – without any evidence whatsoever that this will be an effective approach and the consequences could be serious. More demanding orders could lead to stricter enforcement and increasing breach, which could in turn increase prison numbers; and this could be a vicious circle that proves difficult to escape.

Enforcement of Community Sentences: Sticks or Carrots?

If offenders breach the conditions of their community punishments, they can be returned to court (breached) as a result. The court can then impose one of a range of sanctions (see below), which can include imprisoning the offender. For many years decisions about enforcement of conditions were left to the discretion of local professionals (notably, individual probation officers). In recent years, however, enforcement policy has been more and more regulated by increasingly prescriptive National Standards (see, for example, Home Office, 2002) and legislative require- ments. Schedule 8 of the 2003 Criminal Justice Act requires a probation officer either to issue a warning or to initiate breach proceedings when dealing with a first breach of a community order requirement where there is no reasonable excuse. A second such breach *must* be dealt with by commencing breach proceedings and returning an offender to court. Sanctions that can be imposed by the court for breach include the power to amend the terms of a community order with a view to imposing 'more onerous requirements' or to revoke the order and deal with the offender for the original offence (paras 9 and 10 of Schedule 8). If the court con- siders that an offender has 'wilfully and persistently failed to comply with the requirements of an order', it may impose a prison sentence of up to 51 weeks, even in cases where the original offence may not have been imprisonable. However, the Sentencing Guidelines Council (2004a: para. 1.1.47) has issued guidelines instructing courts that their primary objective should be to ensure compliance with the requirements of the sentence, and to reserve custody as a last resort for cases of deliberate and repeated breach where all reasonable efforts to ensure compliance have failed.

The adoption of a much tougher enforcement strategy in recent years dramati- cally increased the number of offenders who are jailed for breaching their com- munity sentences from 5,364 in 1994 to 7,018 in 2004, only one quarter of whom faced a further charge (*Guardian*, 31 August 2006). The largest proportion of those recalled for breaching community punishment orders (30 per cent) were considered 'out of touch', 18 per cent were breached for problems with their behaviour, 8 per cent for non-compliance with residence requirements and 18 per cent for other reasons. Government proposals to introduce a new national enforce- ment service by 2007/2008 (Home Office, 2006c) were dropped.

The rationale for adopting such a rigorous approach with breach proceedings is to maintain the credibility of community sentences in the eyes of sentencers (Hough et al., 2003: MORI, 2003). Whether this is the most effective way of ensuring that offenders comply with their orders is open to doubt, however. There is some research evidence that adopting appropriate enforcement action (by issu- ing warnings or initiating breach proceedings) may result in lower reconviction rates than overlooking non-compliance (May and Wadwell, 2001). However, another study, which compared enforcement practice in areas with different enforcement strategies, found that there was virtually no difference in terms of reconviction rates for offenders against whom breach proceedings were initiated between tough and lenient areas (Hearnden and Millie, 2003). Hedderman and Hough (2004) have argued that (despite some methodological flaws), this study indicates that strictness of enforcement appears to have little impact on overall reconviction rates, and that offenders appear to be relatively immune to the deter- rent threats or practices of probation officers. Moreover, their contention that the 'big stick' is neither the only nor the best way of securing offenders' compliance has been supported by a number of other commentators.

Ellis et al. (1996), for example, have suggested that more might be done to sustain an offender's engagement with community orders by such means as issuing appointment cards or co-ordinating appointments with signing-on days for the unemployed. (Reminder phone calls and text messages might also be helpful.) Others have taken on board Bottoms's (2001) observation that the punitive techniques of constraint and deterrence, which currently underpin official enforcement strategies, afford only one means of securing compliance and may be less effective than alternative approaches based on recognition and reward (Underdown, 2001; Hedderman, 2003; Hedderman and Hough, 2004). For example, the restrictions and demands imposed on an offender by the order could be relaxed or reduced as a reward for satisfactory compliance. This has only rarely been done up until now: only around 10 per cent of community orders and SSOs were terminated early in response to good progress in 2011 (Ministry of Justice, 2012h: Table 4.11). With the introduction of the community order and the SSO, options for dealing with breach were reduced (for example, the possibility of taking no action, issuing a warning or imposing a fine was removed) which made the possibility of imprisonment more likely. In the first quarter of 2012 one third of both orders were terminated early for what could be termed negative reasons (failure to comply, conviction of an offence and other reasons; Ministry of Justice, 2012h: Table 4.11).

The Legal Aid, Sentencing and Punishment of Offenders Act 2012 provides for a fine of up to £2,500 in cases of breach of the new orders, which at least offers another option. The recent Consultation Paper on *Effective Community Sentences* (Ministry of Justice, 2012c) proposes fixed penalties for breach similar to fixed penalty notices (see Introduction, section I.1 and above, section 5.3). This would be for offender managers (such as supervising probation officers) to apply, not the courts; it would only be available once and if the fine was not paid within a fixed period the offender would be taken to court. If taken forward this may avoid the use of court for some breaches, but it would load offenders with a financial penalty that might prove difficult to pay.

'Sentence Management' and the Changing Role of the Judiciary

The traditional image of the sentencer was aptly summed up by Zimmerman's reference (cited in Rottman and Casey, 1999: 13) to the 'dispassionate, disinterested magistrate', whose responsibility for influencing the offender's behaviour began and ended with the pronouncement of the sentence itself. This left the various tasks entailed in administering the penalty, including monitoring and enforcing an offender's compliance, for the most part in the hands of other criminal justice practitioners.

In recent years, this 'culture of compartmentalism' has been in retreat, and provisions authorizing the courts to monitor and review the progress of offenders have been attached to a number of penalties including, as we saw above, the new-style suspended sentence of imprisonment (similar powers are available in referral orders for young offenders: see Chapter 8, section 8.4). Review hearings also form an integral part of many community orders with drug rehabilitation requirements, an arrangement which implies a much more collaborative partnership between those responsible for administering the order and the sentencing court, which is expected to actively monitor an offender's compliance with it. One prominent model for such a partnership is provided by American 'drug courts' (which have also been piloted in Scotland; see Eley et al., 2002). In these courts, sentencers are highly proactive, participate greatly in monitoring and reviewing sentences – and are noticeably more interested in securing compliance from offenders than in merely sanctioning them in the event of a breach. Judges in drug courts (who receive training in how to deal with substance abuse) often actively engage with offenders, with a view to motivating and encouraging them, and this may result in occasional lapses being overlooked provided the offender is making genuine attempts to comply with the order. This kind of enforcement strategy comes much closer to the more constructive approach favoured by many critics of the current punitive mentality and research suggests that is usually welcomed by offenders (McSweeney et al., 2008; McIvor, 2009).

Recent tentative steps to encourage English judges to adopt a more proactive sentence management function fall a long way short of emulating these drug courts. Nevertheless, they represent a step in that direction. A possible pointer to the future was contained in the Criminal Justice Act 2003 (s. 178), which empowered the Justice Secretary to direct all courts to make routine use of review hearings for the purpose of monitoring and reviewing the progress of offenders who are subject to community orders. If the traditional division of labour and responsibility between sentencers and those responsible for administering punishment was to be ultimately broken down, this would have major implications for the relationship between them, which would need to accommodate both their new responsibilities and also the need for new mechanisms of accountability. Such an approach has been tried in the North Liverpool Community Justice Centre, where the relationship between the judge and offenders plays a crucial part in the sentencing and review process (see Mair and Millings, 2011). But a study of sentencers' views of the community order and the SSO suggested that judges and magistrates tended to be unaware of the power to review and thought this was more a task for the probation service than for them (Mair et al., 2008). As David Faulkner (2005: 39) has aptly put it: 'The old rules may no longer apply, but the new rules have not yet been written.'

Effectiveness of Community Sentences

We take the view that community sentences should always be used in preference to custodial punishment unless the offender represents a serious risk to the safety of others, or (exceptionally and for brief periods only) where confinement is the only possible means of gaining the co-operation required to make the appropriate community sentence work. This opinion is founded on moral, rights-based considerations (see Chapter 2) rather than purely practical calculations. Nevertheless, whatever one's angle on the morality of punishment, we would also argue that community punishment is capable of serving almost all the purposes that are conventionally associated with imprisonment at least as effectively as custody itself, and in some cases more effectively (see further Cavadino et al., 1999: 117ff).

The relative effectiveness of penal sanctions (in terms of their success in reforming or individually deterring offenders) is conventionally measured by comparing reconviction rates, despite their well-known shortcomings as a measure of penal success (see, for example, Brody, 1976; Maltz, 1984; Lloyd et al., 1994). When the reconviction rates that are associated with custody and community penalties are compared – after allowing for factors that are known to influence the risk of reconviction (such as age at first offence, type of offence, criminal history and gender) – the differences between them are usually found to be negligible. However, this may be because community penalties have not been living up to their potential. It has been claimed that community sentences which conform to certain principles – for example, those focusing on social skills or utilizing cognitive behavioural methods – can have measurable positive effects on recidivism, whereas those with strong punitive effects can increase recidivism by some 25 per cent (McGuire and Priestley, 1995). Research in Scotland has shown that offenders whose experience of community service is rewarding and worthwhile tend to have lower reconviction rates than those who find it unrewarding (McIvor, 1992); and it is worth thinking about this finding in the context of the increasingly punitive nature of community payback we have noted. Research evidence also seems to show that comparable reformative programmes are more likely to be successful in community settings rather than in custody (see, for example, Andrews et al., 1990; Lipsey, 1992; Vennard et al., 1997; Goldblatt and Lewis, 1998; Andrews, 2001).

Moreover, there is no reason in principle why community penalties should not also serve denunciatory or retributive ends, just as custody is supposed to. (For example, community punishments of differing onerousness (or 'penal weight') can be prescribed for offences of differing seriousness.) Indeed, community-based restorative justice processes such as mediation and conferencing have the added advantage, if conducted properly, of denouncing an offender's conduct without at the same time denigrating and stigmatizing the offender as a person, in the way that conventional penalties (and particularly custodial ones) do. As for the pursuit of other purposes such as reparation and reintegrative shaming (see Chapter 2, section 2.4), it also seems highly probable that these are more likely to be successful where offenders are kept in the community, for fairly obvious reasons: it is hard to make amends to the community and become part of it again if you are locked away from it. This leaves, as the main apparent advantage that custody has over other penal measures, the public protection it appears to offer by incapacitating offenders from committing certain kinds of offences (see Chapter 2, section 2.2). We accept that there are some serious violent and sexual offenders who present such a clear and vivid threat to the safety and wellbeing of others that custodial incapacitation is both justifiable and right. However, for the great majority of less serious offenders who are routinely incarcerated it is highly doubtful whether the temporary gain in public protection that custody appears to offer can be justified in view of the economic, social and personal costs that such an extreme sanction inflicts. The fact that community penalties appear to be at least as effective as custody in preventing reoffending, while at the same time affording greater opportunities for the needs of victims to be addressed, should in our view be conclusive.

Contestability and Privatization

The same Carter Report (2003) which led to the organizational restructuring that created NOMS was also responsible for advocating an even more controversial – and arguably, potentially devastating – development in the shape of the principle of contestability. Although the precise meaning of the term remains unclear and, indeed, is itself hotly contested, it is all about promoting greater involvement by the private and not-for-profit sectors in the delivery of community interventions. (The contestability agenda is an example of the New Public Management approach to which we referred in Chapter 1, section 1.4.)

As Nellis (2006: 55) has pointed out, contestability could mean little more than an extension of the principle of 'market testing' (which had been applied in the case of prison privatization: see Chapter 6) to the sphere of community punishment as a mechanism for injecting better value-for-money and neutralizing opposition to modernizing reforms from hostile public sector trade unions. Or it could entail the deliberate introduction of a mixed economy model in which the probation service would lose its former status as the near-monopoly provider of community interventions and become merely one declining player among several service providers operating in an increasingly competitive and uncertain environment. Initially the New Labour government (Home Office, 2004c: 14) claimed to be 'not interested in using the private sector for its own sake'. By 2006, however, it was making no secret of its goal 'to harness the dynamism and talents of a much more diverse range of best-in-class public, private and not-for-profit providers, each with their own set of special skills and expertise' (Home Office, 2006b: 31). Not surprisingly, the Coalition government has been equally keen to involve the private sector in delivering penal sanctions, notably in the context of its 'rehabilitation revolution' (see Chapter 2, section 2.2).

This dogmatically driven strategy raises a number of major concerns. The first relates to an obvious tension between the desire to promote a more holistic and better integrated approach to the management of offenders and the government's apparent determination to engineer a massive proliferation in the number and range of players involved in the delivery of criminal justice interventions. This 'balkanization of the criminal justice system'[2] is likely to result in a further fragmentation. Indeed, if the experience of prison privatization is anything to go by (see Chapter 6), when the various service providers are operating in a competitive environment the

---

[2]A 'mot juste' that was coined by our former colleague, Joanna Shapland.

problems of communication, information-sharing and co-operating with one another are likely to grow rather than diminish.

A second problem concerns the unknown consequences that are likely to ensue when the value-base that underpins the machinery for delivering community interventions shifts from the relatively disinterested altruistic orientation of the traditional probation service to a more instrumental commercially minded focus. This is likely to have major implications for the individual relationships between practitioners and offenders and also for relationships between those agencies that are responsible for delivering criminal justice interventions, the courts they serve and the wider public. As Liebling (2006: 75) has argued, it is disturbing that such fundamental issues do not seem to have received any serious consideration from those promoting the reforms, who seem quite content to press ahead in an evidential vacuum. For example, will the range of services to be contracted out extend to the preparation of pre-sentence reports, in which case what safeguards will be put in place to ensure that the recommendations are not coloured by commercial considerations? And even if they are not, can a probation service that operates in a commercially competitive environment be expected to provide the same kind of disinterested advice to the courts that it gave in the past, or will it be motivated to make recommendations which provide itself with customers?

Other difficult questions relate to the need for accountability and the added tensions that are likely to ensue between a service provider's accountability towards the court, the probation trust and its shareholders, and the need for political accountability at both a local and national level (Hough, 2006: 5). And finally, what will be the effect on the morale and operational effectiveness of the probation service itself? Mike Nellis (2006: 62) has correctly pointed out that the NOMS and contestability reforms are an expression of visionary 'blue skies thinking' at the heart of government. The problem with blue skies thinking is that it is, almost by definition, insufficiently grounded in empirical realities. Nellis is also right to warn (Nellis, 2006: 64) that, when attempts are made to actualize blue skies thinking without regard to those realities, 'the distance between blue skies and scorched earth is often far narrower than many contemporary modernisers would have us believe'.

Notwithstanding such concerns, contestability has developed apace. Indeed, in 2005 the Probation Boards' Association Annual Lecture was delivered by Sir Digby Jones, Director General of the Confederation of British Industry, with the title 'Offender rehabilitation: business as a deliverer of criminal justice' (Jones, 2005). In July 2007 – the year in which probation celebrated its 100th birthday – the Offender Management Act introduced provisions for probation services which could be provided by public, private or voluntary providers. Probation boards were replaced by probation trusts (described as 'smaller, more business-focused bodies': Home Office, 2005f) whose members need not have any connection with the locality. Any part of probation work could be open to competition, although the Act stipulated that core offender management work would remain in the hands of the probation service until at least 2010. While it would be a simplification to claim that privatization was now underway, there is little doubt that the way was open for increased private sector involvement in working with offenders in the community. Indeed, the very structure of the community order and the SSO, with their 14 requirements, encourages partnership working, fragmentation and – ultimately – could lead to the marginalisation of the probation service.

Predictably, contestability has been pushed on by the Coalition government. By 2010, the 42 probation areas had become 35 probation trusts and the Green Paper *Breaking the Cycle* (Ministry of Justice, 2010a) discussed how the trusts could develop new business models and be permitted greater freedom. Probation staff, too, were to be granted more discretion (after two decades of removing it) and National Standards were to be relaxed. While probation officers might welcome such a development, it is all too obvious that the relaxation of standards is also intended to encourage outside providers to compete for probation work. The Green Paper made it clear that payment by results was to be a cornerstone of the new government's approach to working with offenders whether in prison or in the community. While there are many issues to be ironed out with this approach (Fox and Albertson, 2011), perhaps the most disturbing from a probation point of view is the question of just how prepared temperamentally, financially and organisationally probation services might be to compete in this brave new world. The government has emphasised that it wishes to use the market and payment by results 'to deliver more and tougher requirements' (Ministry of Justice, 2011a: 4).

All probation services are to be opened up to competition except for (at present) the initial assessment of risk, advice to the court, the supervision of high-risk offenders (however that may be defined) and dealing with recalls and breaches. In total, it is estimated that around 60 per cent of the £1 billion per year budget for community offenders' services will be competed for. Probation trusts themselves can compete for services and where this is the case, they will have to become separate entities (Ministry of Justice, 2012f). There has already been one farcical development where the governor of three prisons ordered all probation staff out of his prisons because the local probation trust had joined up with private security company G4S to bid to run the jails (*Guardian*, 1 March 2012). With large private companies likely to bid to run such services as community payback, and electronic monitoring already run by the private sector, the probation service could be left on the margins. Justice surely requires certain national standards, yet the fragmentation of probation services looks set to continue. Probation is in crisis and its future does not look healthy.

Shifting Patterns of Penality: Theoretical Reflections

5.5 In this section we turn to the question of whether it is possible to make sense of the various developments (including the changing fortunes of the main sentencing disposals as depicted in Table 5.1) we have been examining so far. We will also ask what light, if any, theories of penality can shed on such changes, and whether they have anything to tell us about the nature and future direction of social control mechanisms in general.

Although, as we shall see, there is considerable debate at present concerning the exact nature and significance of recent developments within the penal system, there is also much common ground between the various protagonists regarding the context within which these changes are said to be taking place. All are agreed that the starting point for the current debate lies in the so-called 'great transformation' of punishment which has been most notably chronicled by Foucault (1977) (see also Rothman, 1971 and Ignatieff, 1978). This original transformation was the major shift in the form of punishment from corporal to carceral punishment, which occurred around the end of the eighteenth and beginning of the nineteenth centuries (see Chapters 2 and 3, sections 2.5 and 3.2).

There is also a broad measure of agreement on the part of contemporary penal commentators that a number of significant changes affecting the penal system have occurred since then, and particularly since the mid-1960s. But opinions differ as to whether these amount to a 'second transformation', and, if so, what form it is taking or how exactly it should be characterized.

Scull's 'Decarceration' Thesis

The opening shot in the present debate was fired by Andrew Scull in 1977 with the publication of his book *Decarceration: Community Treatment and the Deviant – A Radical View*. Although he has subsequently revised some of his ideas (Scull, 1984), Scull originally argued that we are now experiencing a major shift in the ideology and apparatus of social control that amounts to at least a partial reversal of the original 'great transformation'. Scull used the word **decarceration** to refer to 'the state-sponsored policy of closing down asylums, prisons and reformatories' (Scull, 1984: 1).

The term thus encompasses two parallel tendencies. One is the so-called 'community corrections movement' whereby offenders are increasingly dealt with in the community instead of locking them up in custodial institutions. The other is the move towards 'community care', which extends the same principle to the treatment of people with mental disorders, and which results in the systematic closure of large-scale psychiatric institutions. Scull not only lumps together policies for dealing with the 'mad' and the 'bad' and uses the same term – decarceration – to cover both tendencies, he also illustrates his thesis with reference to both British and American developments, believing that the forces responsible for decarceration policies are at work throughout the contemporary capitalist system (see below).

According to Scull, the most potent of these forces are economic considerations, which now favour decarceration whereas at the time of the original transformation of the penal system a policy of incarceration made greater economic sense. In brief, by the turn of the nineteenth century the old poor law system was quite unable to cope with the growing number of desperately poor people, many of whom were economically unproductive for much of the time and unable to provide for their own subsistence. Moreover, traditional methods of social control (based mainly on a feudal pattern of social obligations between rich and poor) were losing their effectiveness at this time. Consequently, the most economically efficient way of dealing with the problem of poverty and its attendant risk of social disorder was to move to a system of large-scale institutions within which the unproductive and the deviant could be provided for and controlled.

However, by Scull's era (the late twentieth century), these economic and social considerations no longer applied. Instead, the cumulative effects of increased public expenditure over the years (on welfare, housing and industrial assistance programmes, among others) had plunged the state into a serious and worsening fiscal crisis, making it imperative for public expenditure to be drastically curbed. One way of doing this was by using welfare payments and social services to enable many of the so-called 'problem populations' (Scull, 1984: 135) who were previously incarcerated in institutions to be looked after and controlled in the community instead. From the state's point of view it now seemed much more expensive to keep people locked up in institutions than to subsidize others to look after them in the community. Scull was not convinced that community alternatives *are* necessarily cheaper to operate in practice than the institutions they displace – because of opposition from vested interests and the difficulty of achieving more than marginal cost-savings unless whole institutions can be closed down. But he did strongly maintain that decarceration has more to do with cost-saving imperatives than with the development of more effective forms of treatment, or any genuine commitment to humanitarian improvements in the lot of the incarcerated.

Indeed, far from being humane, he considered that decarceration is not in the interests either of all the deviants themselves, or of the community into which they are unceremoniously decanted. In the case of the elderly and the mentally ill, for example, he argued that such a policy results in many ex-inmates being herded into 'newly emerging "deviant ghettoes", sewers of human misery ... within which ... society's refuse may be repressively tolerated' (1977: 153). As far as offenders are concerned he spoke of 'burglars and muggers ... being left to walk the streets', and even 'the perpetrators of violent crime' as being 'turned loose under conditions which guarantee that they will receive little or no supervision'. As a result, he considered that decarceration 'forms yet one more burden heaped on the backs of those who are most obviously the victims of our society's inequities. And it places the deviant in those communities least able to care for or cope with him' (1977: 1–2).

Scull was surely right to insist that we should look behind the façade of official rhetoric when examining the reasons for major penological change. But his thesis is vulnerable to three main lines of attack. It is theoretically shaky since it is based on an over-simplistic form of economic determinism (see Chapter 3, section 3.2); it fails to fit the facts in a number of crucial respects; and Scull himself fails to probe sufficiently deeply behind the rhetoric of decarceration to expose the real consequences of the changes to which he refers. We will now deal briefly with each of these charges in turn.

One major difficulty with Scull's fiscal crisis argument is its rather simplistic assumption that because traditional methods of treating and controlling problem populations have become relatively more expensive to operate, the state is obliged to adopt decarceration rather than seeking savings elsewhere, for example through cuts in welfare programmes. In fact, as critics such as Matthews (1979: 106) have noted, this is precisely what the state has done. Cuts in public expenditure during the late twentieth century were very selectively distributed, with the result that spending on law and order actually increased substantially during this period at the expense of other public expenditure programmes, notably welfare spending: for example, during 1956–78 spending on the prison system in England increased two and a half times more than for public expenditure generally (Rutherford, 1986b: 90); and for 1980–90 spending on public order increased threefold compared to a two or two-and-a-half increase in other public services such as education, health and social services (Central Statistical Office, 1991: Table 9.4) What the fiscal crisis argument fails to take into account is that in any given period penal policy is a product of the complex interplay between political and ideological pressures, in addition to the economic forces with which Scull was almost exclusively concerned.

Another serious problem that results from Scull's economic determinism is a tendency to over-generalize from the available data in a way that is not supported by the facts. Many commentators (see, for example, Cohen, 1979; Matthews, 1979; Burton, 1983; Hudson, 1984) agree that his thesis applied quite well to developments in mental health policy in the late twentieth century. However, he is almost universally criticized for assuming that because the same economic pressures presumably apply to the treatment of offenders as well, it follows that developments in penal policy must necessarily be part of the same phenomenon. In fact, as we shall see, this contention is fatally undermined by empirical evidence drawing on geographical, historical and contemporary data relating to trends in the use of imprisonment.

Geographically, the fiscal crisis theory is seriously weakened by evidence relating to the Dutch experience following the Second World War. For although the Netherlands between the 1940s and mid-1970s provided almost a textbook example of decarceration in the penal sphere (Cavadino and Dignan, 2006: ch. 8), it spectacularly fails to conform to the fiscal crisis argument – in fact, quite the reverse. As Downes (1988: 58) has pointed out, the dramatic reduction in the Dutch prison population mostly occurred during a time of unprecedented prosperity which preceded the onset of the fiscal crisis to which Scull refers. Conversely, a significant expansion of Dutch prison numbers coincided with a period of heightened economic uncertainty. McMahon (1992) also provides a counter-example to Scull's thesis for the Canadian province of Ontario in the 1960s and early 1970s. Like Downes, she attributes the decarceration that occurred to the influence of a then-prevailing ideology of rehabilitation, in contrast to Scull's economistic explanation.

Scull's decarceration thesis is also undermined by historical evidence relating to the use of imprisonment. This quickly dispels the notion that decarceration is a uniquely distinctive feature of post-war penal policy as it seeks to respond to novel economic constraints. For example, there was a remarkably rapid decline in the prison population from 1908 to 1918 (see Ruggles-Brise, 1921: ch. 17; Fox, 1934: ch. 17; Rutherford, 1986b: 122–31; Bottoms, 1987: 178–9). During this period – and against a background of steadily rising conviction and recorded crime rates (Rutherford, 1986: 129) – the prison population more than halved from 22,029 to 9,196. By comparison, during the supposed post-war decarceration era that Scull refers to, his own figures show a near doubling of the prison and borstal population from 21,370 in 1951 to 38,382 in 1972.

It could be argued that such increases in the absolute number of people imprisoned are misleading unless account is taken of changes in the crime rate and, in particular, of the total number of convicted defendants (Bottoms, 1983: 183). When the *proportionate* use of imprisonment for all adult indictable offenders is examined (see Table 5.1), it can be seen that there was indeed a fall in the proportion of the sentenced population that was sent to prison from 29 per cent in 1959 to 13 per cent in 1975. But thereafter it rose again and the rate of imprisonment doubled from 13 per cent in 1975 to 26 per cent in 1999; in 2004 it was 29 per cent. So even on this weaker definition of decarceration, Scull's thesis was not borne out by events, at least at the level of penal practice. Barbara Hudson (1984) has suggested that decarceration during this period occurred only at the level of rhetoric,[3] in official discourse about the use of imprisonment, and that Scull failed to probe behind this rhetoric to see what was really happening.

Scull's original assessment of the *consequences* of decarceration has also been criticized (see, in particular, Cohen, 1979: 361) for taking at face value claims that decarceration would lead to non-intervention (and not to intrusive control over offenders in the community), and for complaining that this would lead to a weakening of sanctions against offenders. In later works (Scull, 1983; 1984), Scull acknowledged that the position was rather more complicated than this, and went on to claim that the community corrections movement had actually resulted in an undesirable *extension* of the state's social control apparatus. This he attributed to 'a strong conservative backlash against anything smacking of leniency towards crime and criminals' (Scull, 1984: 175), which he saw as the product of 'the accelerating volume of crime over the past quarter century' (Scull, 1984: 177).

Even with these revisions, however, Scull's decarceration thesis is still defective. For example, no attempt is made to explain how the ideological factors favouring stronger control measures came to outweigh the economic imperatives favouring decarceration. Nor does he give sufficient weight to the influence of humanistic, inclusive penal ideologies in bringing about limited decarceration in those times when it did occur. Another major issue which the thesis fails to address fully is the debate about 'alternatives to custody' and how they relate to the 'extension of social control' argument. For an attempt to confront these issues we turn now to a rival thesis which has been put forward by two very influential theorists of social control, Stanley Cohen and Thomas Mathiesen.

---

[3] A Marxist, or post-Marxist, might see this gap between the 'rhetoric' (or ideological message conveyed by the 'discourse' of the penal system) and its material reality as significant. See Chapter 3 (section 3.3) for a more detailed discussion of the idea that the penal system may form part of a state's Ideological State Apparatus.

Cohen and Mathiesen: The 'Dispersal of Discipline' Thesis

In a series of works, especially his 1979 article 'The Punitive City' and his 1985 book *Visions of Social Control*, Stanley Cohen painted a nightmarish vision of the city of the future as being increasingly subjected to a sophisticated social control network. Unlike Scull, who initially described the community corrections movement as a reversal of the original 'great transformation', Cohen always considered it to be simply a continuation of the same 'disciplinary' project, albeit on a much more ambitious scale. Whereas the first transformation had the effect of concentrating the social control energies of the state on highly selected populations of deviants *inside* specially designated institutions like the prison and the asylum, he pointed out that this was no longer the case. Instead, penal developments associated with the community corrections movement demonstrated that the state was now spreading its tentacles of control ever more deeply into the tissues of society by significantly widening the reach and scope of its social control apparatus. Cohen described the key features of this second transformation in a memorable series of metaphors (see McMahon, 1992: 32 for an incisive critique of the simplistic use of such metaphors). They include:

- *Widening the net*. This concept (which has already featured several times in this chapter) refers to the process whereby community programmes tend to 'capture' many who would not formerly have been subjected to the attentions of the criminal justice system. One example is when police cautioning is used not only as an alternative to prosecution but also for those who would otherwise have been informally dealt with. The end result is to 'increase rather than decrease the total *number* who get into the system in the first place' (Cohen, 1979: 347, italics in original).

- *Thinning the mesh*. Not only are more offenders brought into the system, those who are dealt with by means of newer more intensive community orders also experience a greater *degree of intervention* than would have been the case if a more traditional alternative to custody, such as a fine, traditional probation order or conditional discharge, had been used instead.

- *Blurring*. As a result of these and other developments – notably home curfews and electronic monitoring – there is a blurring of formerly rigid distinctions between institutional and non-institutional forms of control, or even between what is or is not regarded as punishment. Very presciently, Cohen foresaw a day when 'it will be impossible to determine who exactly is enmeshed in the social control system' (1979: 346).

- *Penetration*. The combined effect of these tendencies is that the whole (considerably enlarged) system of social control is now extending more and more deeply into the *informal* networks of society. Even more important, though, is the fact that these measures actually *augment* the existing prison system. They do not displace it; on the contrary, they enable the prison to reach out into the community. And so, as Downes has put it, '[w]e end up with the worst of both worlds: an unreconstructed *ancien régime pénal* and a new-style carceral society' (1988: 60).

Cohen saw the whole of the community corrections movement as 'merely an extension of the overall pattern established in the nineteenth century' (1979: 359), whereby the mode of control founded on *discipline* is dispersed out of the big institutions in which it originated, and into the rest of society. ('Discipline' is the concept developed by Foucault (1977) to characterize the attempt to transform the 'soul' of the offender – see Chapter 3, section 3.2). Cohen cited (1979: 347, 357) community service (unpaid work) as just one obvious example of a form of punishment that penetrates deeply into the informal social networks of civil society by requiring offenders to undertake socially useful work in the community. Moreover, the fact that community service is often used in place of less intrusive penalties such as the fine is seen as evidence of its mesh-thinning tendencies.

This 'dispersal of discipline' thesis was taken a stage further by the Norwegian criminologist, Thomas Mathiesen (1983). In a prediction which echoed the concerns voiced by Cohen he too foresaw that 'the control system as a totality may *expand rather than shrink*' (Mathieson, 1983: 140) as a result of proposals to strengthen society's social control mechanisms by, among other things, developing 'crime care in the community'. But whereas Cohen's main concern was with crime control strategies that are individualistic in the sense that they still aim at 'a disciplining of the law-breakers one by one' (1983: 132), Mathiesen discerned in certain other recent developments the emergence of a new and complementary strategy that could 'move fully away from individualism, and focus on *control of whole groups and categories*' (1983: 139) by means of general surveillance. Mathiesen gave the following examples of the kind of social control techniques he had in mind:

> TV cameras on subway stations and in supermarkets, the development of advanced computer techniques in intelligence and surveillance, a general strengthening of the police, a general strengthening of the large privately-run security companies, as well as a whole range of other types of surveillance of whole categories of people – all of this is something we have begun to get, and have begun to get used to. (1983: 139)

Mathiesen believed, presciently, that these new societal or collective forms of control would increasingly impinge on the everyday lives of groups and categories of people and that, as such, they represent a break with individualism as the archetypal form of social control.[4] Nevertheless, he still characterized them as disciplinary measures and so they too were seen as extensions of the original carceral project, in which more efficient disciplinary social control measures are dispersed into the wider society. The difference for Mathiesen was that the new

---

[4]Others have discerned in such developments the emergence of a 'new penology' (Feeley and Simon, 1992; see Chapter 3, section 3.6) in which the adoption of a 'managerialist' perspective is increasingly harnessed to the task of regulating levels of deviance by targeting categories and sub-populations rather than individual deviants. In recent years the groups that have been targeted in this way have included squatters, new age travellers, political protesters, participants in raves, hunt saboteurs, nuisance neighbours and others engaging in anti-social behaviour.

techniques he described involved 'a change *from open to hidden discipline* ... The new control out there in society is either completely outside the individual's range of vision, or at least quite a bit less visible than the control forms of pure individual liberalism' (1983: 139).

While CCTV cameras of the kind mentioned by Mathiesen undoubtedly extend the range of surveillance, their impact is still partial and limited: they normally either still depend on the capacity and attentiveness of operatives who monitor the screens to identify those incidents meriting a response, or are only used retrospectively after an incident has occurred in order to obtain evidence and help to identify an offender. As such, these relatively passive technologies at best represent a quantitative increase in the capacity of social control agencies to *detect* (and to some extent deter) law-breaking whether by individuals or groups of individuals rather than the exertion of constant control.

However, recent technological developments hold out the prospect of a further significant *qualitative* change in the nature of social control, which for some heralds the dawn of a new era of 'technocorrections' (Fabelo, 2000; see also Haggerty, 2004; Jewkes, 2004/5; Franko Aas, 2005). These developments include potential refinements in the capabilities of electronic monitoring as it switches from radio frequency to satellite tracking technology (already trialled and with plans for more widespread use: Ministry of Justice, 2012c), the planned introduction of biometric identity cards by the Labour government (now dropped) and associated applications together with prospective advances in the development and utilization of DNA databases and gene therapy for crime control purposes. The crime control potential of these various developments is admittedly fairly embryonic at present, though it would be rash to imagine that this will always be the case. One highly plausible scenario might involve the immense capacity of computerized databases – drawn from a variety of official and commercial sources (such as loyalty cards) – being harnessed with the ability to undertake algorithmic analysis of digitized CCTV footage.[5] The effect of this kind of technological convergence – which Haggerty and Ericson (2000) refer to as a 'surveillant assemblage' – would add depth and intensity to the somewhat superficial capability of current systems. An even more sobering prospect would be a further synergization between the kind of general surveillant measures described by Mathiesen and high-tech versions of personalized crime control measures – perhaps utilizing satellite tracking technology linked with smart microchip implants – aimed at individual law breakers. This would indeed conjure up a truly dystopian vision of a Panopticon society (see Chapter 2, section 2.5) in which the authorities are able to exert near-total control over the lives of large groups of people or even entire populations.

Although these somewhat gloomy assessments of recent developments in social control may be in keeping with the spirit of the times – and while their Orwellian

---

[5]Sophisticated computer software enables digitized video images to be converted into numerical data that can then be analysed by means of complex algorithms (Norris, 1995). This makes it possible to automatically read vehicle number plates or facial features which can then be checked against large databases; see also Norris (2003).

overtones fit the concerns of social control theorists speculating on the future – they are not without their critics. David Garland (1995b: 3), for example, has reminded us that, viewed sociologically, surveillance is and always has been an essential element of social control and, quite apart from being an inescapable adjunct of modernity, does have benevolent as well as repressive potential. Moreover, while technologies of the kind we have referred to above could be used to increase *detection* rates, there is no necessary connection between this and any increase (or indeed reduction) in the level of *penalties* for offenders once they are caught. Indeed, it can be argued that an increased probability of detection could enable punishments to be made more lenient, since deterrence is far more likely to be achieved by increasing the *perceived risk* of detection than by more severe penalties. (This is not to belittle the important issues concerning civil liberties and privacy which undoubtedly do exist regarding the access to and use of the information which is gathered by way of these new technologies.)

More generally, Tony Bottoms (1983) – while finding much to commend in Cohen's and Mathiesen's analysis of specific control mechanisms – questioned the way they analysed these developments in terms of the dispersal of discipline thesis. The central thrust of Bottoms's critique was that many of the new community control measures that are described by Cohen and Mathiesen are not in fact *disciplinary* measures; at least, not in the sense in which Foucault used the term. Bottoms argued persuasively (1983: 182) that Foucault's notion of discipline contained two key elements: one is *surveillance*, and the other involves the 'mechanics of a training' which aims to produce an obedient subject by repeatedly working on the offender's 'soul'. This, according to Foucault, was the fundamental objective of the original carceral project which emerged from the first 'great transformation' of punishment. But if this is the case then Mathiesen was mistaken to characterize the recent move towards a more collective form of social control as a dispersal of *discipline*. For the techniques he describes depend almost exclusively on the technique of surveillance alone, making use of advanced technological developments and improved methods of policing rather than any 'mechanics of a training'.

Of the more individualistic forms of control, community service was cited by both Cohen and Mathiesen as evidence of their contention that punishment was beginning to penetrate ever more deeply into the informal networks of society, and again this was depicted as an extension of *discipline*. Bottoms agreed that it appears to conform to some of the tendencies described by Cohen – mesh-thinning and community penetration in particular – but again he doubted whether this alone is sufficient to warrant the term discipline. For although work can be, and indeed has been, used for disciplinary purposes ever since the birth of the carceral system, other aspects of community service – such as the element of reparation that it can entail – make it less congruent with the dispersal of discipline thesis. Bottoms was, of course, writing before the introduction of uniform standards, the wearing of orange vests drawing attention to the offenders and the relentless attempts to toughen up community payback. He did, however, anticipate that the measure 'could yet be developed in a more disciplinary form' (Bottoms, 1983: 180), and might well have viewed the measure in a different light on the basis of these more recent developments. Much the same point could be made in respect of other recent surveillance and control measures including those based on electronic monitoring, which by themselves do little or nothing to train offenders in habits of obedience.

Another serious charge against the dispersal of discipline thesis in Bottoms's eyes was its neglect of certain other features of contemporary penal systems that are not at all consistent with the dispersal of discipline thesis and which therefore cast some doubt on its universal applicability. Chief among these neglected features of contemporary penal systems (at the time he developed his critique) was the dramatic post-war growth in the use of the fine, particularly in the period up to 1980 (but later reversed, as we have seen). This was crucial to his argument for two main reasons. First, because the fine is manifestly *not* a disciplinary penalty in Foucault's sense of the word; and, second, because (as can be seen in Table 5.1 above) the fine did more to displace the use of imprisonment – at least during the early post-war period – than any of the more disciplinary penalties (such as probation).

This is not at all what one would expect of an emerging carceral society. Rather, it chimes in with Bottoms's more general observation (1983: 169) that '*penalties not involving continuing supervision by a penal agent*' – that is, such non-disciplinary measures as the fine and the suspended sentence – were at that time flourishing at the expense of more disciplinary measures such as imprisonment and probation (see Table 5.1). Finally, Bottoms noted that the recent growth of concern for victims within the criminal justice system is another development that cannot be explained by the dispersal of discipline thesis.

For all these reasons Bottoms concluded that the dispersal of discipline thesis was not a particularly helpful way of characterizing contemporary penal developments. What was needed instead, he believed, was a thesis that could account for the relative *decline* in the significance of disciplinary punishments at that time within the total apparatus of social control. With this aim in mind he tentatively advanced a third thesis which we call the 'juridical revival' thesis.

Bottoms's 'Juridical Revival' Thesis

In developing his rival theory, Bottoms reminded us (1983: 176) that at the time of the original 'great transformation' there was a third model of punishment besides the traditional or *corporal* model (aimed at the body of the offender) and the *carceral* model (based on imprisonment) which displaced it. This third model, which Bottoms called the *juridical* system of punishment, was proposed by the classical reformers such as Beccaria (see Chapter 2) but ultimately exerted much less influence on forms of punishment at the time than did the disciplinary ideas of reformers such as Bentham. Bottoms suggested (1983: 195) that the reason for this was because the social control techniques that were available at that time were largely ineffective in maintaining order. However, circumstances change, and the essence of Bottoms's thesis was that we might now be heading towards a second 'great transformation' from a carceral to a juridical system of punishment. The effect of this could be seen not as the dispersal of discipline throughout society, as Cohen and Mathiesen argued, but as *diminishing* rather than increasing the role of punishment as a method of social control.

Unlike the carceral project which, as we have seen, was founded on reforming offenders through discipline, the juridical project aimed at 'requalifying individuals as subjects' (Bottoms, 1980: 21). This requalification was to be achieved through the application of a standard set of penalties that were intended to be fixed in duration and proportionate to the seriousness of the offence. Once the punishment was completed the offender would be re-admitted to society as a full member with undiminished rights of citizenship. Most importantly, the preventive message that the punishment was intended to represent was to be transmitted by the simple symbolic fact of punishment itself. Accordingly, there was no need for specific social control agencies designed to 'mould' offenders into obedient subjects (1983: 176).

In the light of this analysis Bottoms concluded that many of the penal developments to which he had drawn attention were more accurately characterized as embodying juridical rather than carceral tendencies. This was particularly true of the fine, which Bottoms correctly suggested is more of a 'classical' than a disciplinary punishment (1983: 178), but there were other pointers in the same direction. These included the general increase (at the time) in penalties not involving supervision by a penal agent, the increase in compensation payments by the courts, and also the recent growth of interest in the principle of reparation.

As for the reasons underlying these developments, Bottoms suggested (1983: 196) that the key to the debate lay in a more detailed appreciation of the nature of the transition from early to late capitalism than is to be found in any of the previous accounts. One strand in his proposed explanation was based on certain changes in the nature of law and social control that had occurred during this period (and in many ways have continued to develop since Bottoms wrote). These changes have been characterized by Kamenka and Tay (1975) in terms of a shift towards a bureaucratic-administrative social and legal order in advanced capitalist societies (see Chapter 3, section 3.4). A key feature of this development was a shift in the locus of social control from the formal punishment system to other bureaucratic agencies, both public and private (for example, government departments, local authorities, television licensing authority, private security firms). Another aspect is the increased reliance on non-disciplinary forms of social control, based on a variety of techniques such as increased surveillance, negotiation and formal warnings.

Some aspects of Bottoms's analysis do not fit the penal scene of the twenty-first century as well as they did the early 1980s when he was writing. Most notably – as Table 5.1 dramatically demonstrates – the proportion of punishments which involve supervision or surveillance of some kind, following the decline which Bottoms charted, thereafter experienced an even more marked rise which has continued with the introduction of the suspended sentence order containing community requirements. Conversely, the (non-supervisory) penalties of fines and straightforward suspended sentences followed their previous steep rise with a steeper decline, although it will be interesting to chart the use of the SSO with no requirements, an option introduced by the Legal Aid, Sentencing and Punishment of Offenders Act 2012. One interpretation of this is that when Bottoms wrote, disciplinary punishment was reaching a nadir but has since recovered to reach record proportions. Is the 'punitive city' indeed upon us?

Conclusion: The Future of Punishment?

5.6 So far the development of punishment in the community has done nothing to solve the penal crisis, and in some respects can be said to have made it worse. Community punishments were, as we have seen, developed and promoted as alternatives to custody in the hope that they would alleviate the crisis of prison resources, but the failure of the strategy of encouragement allied with the toughening of community sentences merely led to a general 'ratcheting up' of penalties. The prison numbers problem got worse, matched by crises of resources, morale and legitimacy within the probation service. Current government policy is to toughen community punishments further without even the aspiration that they might thereby be used as alternatives to custody (see, for example, *Guardian*, 5 October 2012 and the speech of new Justice Secretary Chris Grayling to the Conservative Party Conference on 9 October 2012). Could things be different in the future?

It might depend on who is right in the debate we examined in the previous section about the nature of our contemporary social control system. Even at the time he wrote there was little evidence to support Scull's decarceration thesis, except at the level of official rhetoric, and even that has now ended. However, the reforms of the Hurd era which centred around the 1991 Criminal Justice Act did offer some support for both of the other theories (dispersal of discipline and juridical revival), suggesting a possible emerging bifurcatory approach whereby discipline and juridical measures would be applied to different groups of offenders (see Cavadino and Dignan, 1992: 197). At the time it seemed possible that the introduction of unit fines might herald a reinvigoration of this juridical-style penalty, particularly for less serious but impoverished offenders who might previously have been imprisoned instead. Many developments in the treatment of younger offenders around that time were also more consistent with a juridical rather than a disciplinary approach, as was the attempt by the Criminal Justice Act 1991 to grade penalties according to just deserts criteria. However, other features of the just deserts package suggested a strengthening of the disciplinary and control elements associated with community penalties such as probation and community service.

This package of reforms came to grief soon after its launch. Since then, in the light of the punitive counter-reformation which took off in 1993 and continues to maintain a stranglehold in the minds of penal policy-makers, there has been little obvious prospect of an imminent resurgence in the use of juridical penalties. Indeed, Table 5.1 shows a continuing increase in the proportionate use of supervisory community sentences (due to the introduction of the SSO in 2005, which unlike previous suspended sentences normally contains some supervisory element), and also custodial sentences, at the expense of non-supervisory penalties. This tendency is consistent with the dispersal of discipline thesis. On the other hand, the new measures of conditional cautioning and fixed penalty notices for less serious offenders (see the Introduction, section I.1) look more juridical and could be seen as the first tentative signs of a juridical revival. Note, however, that they are also potentially net-widening (as are anti-social behaviour orders). Because formal penalties can now be imposed by the police in respect of increasingly trivial forms of misbehaviour with minimal legal safeguards or constraints, this also means that formal control mechanisms are penetrating ever deeper into society (as suggested by Cohen). Ever-increasing government enthusiasm for electronic monitoring and the advent and popularity of the SSO seem destined to blur still further the distinction between institutional and non-institutional forms of social control (also á la Cohen). On the other hand, the seemingly relentless upsurge in the use of custody since the early 1990s represents a dramatic shift in the direction of penal policy back towards custody and away from community punishments, at least for the time being. So, much of Cohen's vision has been vindicated to date. But if discipline is being dispersed into the community, this does not seem to mean the shrinking of the sphere of the prison proper. The social control exercised by the prison is supplemented, not supplanted, by control in the community.

Realistically, albeit reluctantly, we have to acknowledge that the recent track record strongly suggests that substantial decarceration is unlikely to occur in England and Wales at least in the foreseeable future. If it ever does occur it will almost certainly not be brought about either as a result of a mere strategy of encouragement, nor from a revival of the old rehabilitative ideal. Likewise, it seems improbable that pressures from advocates of just deserts will succeed where they failed before (even though such an approach has had occasional undoubted successes in some other countries: von Hirsch, 1993: 91–4). As for electronic monitoring, which has been credited with contributing to a reduction in the Swedish prison population (Cavadino and Dignan, 2006: 158), we agree with Nellis (2003: 256) that this is unlikely to happen in England and Wales where community orders with monitoring requirements are much more likely to be used to supplement or supplant other community penalties rather than be used as an alternative to imprisonment (for the home detention curfew, see Chapter 7). Moreover, we share Nellis's concerns (2005: 142) that growing government support for the measure signifies a disturbing shift from a predominantly humanistic low tech paradigm to a predominantly surveillant high tech paradigm in community supervision and punishment.

Any significant change in the direction of penal policy of the kind we are advocating is likely to require a drastic restructuring of sentencing discretion (see Chapter 4) and/or a vigorous and well-supported application of systems management techniques (see Chapter 8, section 8.2). But neither of these is likely to come about without a radical change in the penal ideologies of sentencers, the public, other criminal justice practitioners and policy-makers and (above all) government politicians. Above all, we need a 'replacement discourse' (see Ashworth, 1997; Cavadino et al., 1999: 31; Dignan, 2003) and a new ideology in which punishment in the community is seen as the paradigm of *normal punishment* and not as a let-off in which criminals scandalously walk free. Sentencers, politicians, media and public need to end their long-standing and passionate 'love affair with custody' (Travis, 2003). Could this happen?

Despite the gloomy short-term prognosis, we hope that the longer-term future of penality remains open. We do not believe that there is any irreversible tendency at work in the evolution of penal policy, whether in the direction of increased use of custody, net-widening or an intensification of social control via high tech gadgetry. In spite of the many recent policy failures that we have recounted we remain convinced that decarceration and diversion from custody are desirable and achievable goals. We are fortified in this conviction by the fact that genuine decarceration has occurred in other jurisdictions such as the Netherlands (Downes, 1988; Cavadino and Dignan, 2006: ch. 8), Ontario, Canada (McMahon, 1992) and Finland (Törnudd, 1993; Cavadino and Dignan, 2006: ch. 10) in the recent past. Indeed, it happened in England and Wales last century, when the prison population was halved between the years 1908 and 1923 (Rutherford, 1986: 123–31). A substantial decarceration also occurred with young offenders in England and Wales in the 1980s (as we shall recount in Chapter 8, section 8.2), and in the last few years there have also been reductions in the numbers of young and female prisoners (Chapters 8 and 9, sections 8.2 and 9.4).

Moreover, we are reasonably hopeful that strategies could be devised to ensure that decarceration can be attained without widening the criminal justice net – or thinning its mesh – to an unacceptable extent. Several pieces of research (see, for example, Bottoms, 1995b: 10–11) confirm that it is possible for relatively intensive non-custodial penalties to be accurately targeted so that they do not serve to thin the mesh or 'up-tariff' offenders (see Chapter 8, sections 8.2 and 8.5). McMahon (1992) also found that decarceration in Ontario in the 1960s and 1970s was not accompanied by any general net-widening, except in the near-inevitable sense that if a supervisory community sentence is used as a substitute for a short prison term then the offender is likely to stay within the net for longer. The experience of the Kettering Adult Reparation Board (Dignan, 1991) was that the introduction of a reparation scheme may have had some net-widening and mesh-thinning effects with a small proportion of offenders (although a higher proportion were diverted from prosecution altogether); however, we would regard these particular effects as acceptable, since one result was that victims were benefited by the reparation carried out as a result.

While it may be possible to envisage decarcerative strategies, and even to identify ones that have been successful either elsewhere or in the past, this is no guarantee that they are likely to happen in England and Wales in the near future. For example, some of the genuine decarceration documented by McMahon in Ontario happened because there was a strong prevailing belief in the rehabilitative ideal which is unlikely to return, at least in its previous form. Nevertheless, we think that it is not impossible that moves towards decarceration could occur in the not-too-distant future. The reasons for our cautious optimism are based on a reading of the penality debate that differs in several key respects from the three accounts we have been considering.

In the first place we are not convinced that the term 'carceral' is the best way of describing the original penal transformation that took place during the late eighteenth and early nineteenth centuries. For in reality the displacement of corporal and capital punishment during this period was accomplished by a variety of practices (including transportation for a time), in addition to the various non-custodial penalties that have subsequently been developed alongside the carceral system. In our view the change in the nature of penality that accompanied the original 'great transformation', and also those that have taken place thereafter, are more accurately characterized according to the functions they perform (or are intended to perform), as opposed to the precise institutional form they may take at any given time (see Chapter 6, section 6.2 for a somewhat similar analytical-explanatory framework devised by Thomas Mathiesen, 1974; 1990).

In the early days of imprisonment, one of the main functions it was intended to perform was to transform offenders into obedient subjects (as opposed to changing the way in which offenders are punished – or the system and institutions of punishment – which is a rather different kind of transformation) by subjecting them to the disciplinary techniques to which Foucault referred. Subsequently other, non-custodial penalties – notably probation – developed with similar transformatory objectives in mind. Although the collapse of the rehabilitative ideal cast doubt on their transformatory potential, existing penal measures such as imprisonment and probation were not abandoned, though they were displaced to some extent by the introduction and expansion of alternative penal measures such as the fine, suspended sentence, community service and others. Following the collapse of the rehabilitative ideal, the justification for all penal measures came to rest on rather different philosophical foundations (see Chapter 2) which, in turn, were founded on the rather different functions that punishment can perform.

We will examine the various aims and functions of imprisonment in Chapter 6 (section 6.2). Here, we wish to emphasize that the various non-custodial penalties that have been introduced alongside imprisonment itself are likewise intended to perform a range of different functions. One function involves the application of some form of unpleasantness or *deprivation* on offenders for purposes of retribution, denunciation or deterrence. The 'commodity' of which the offender is deprived may take a number of different forms: liberty in the case of imprisonment, time and effort in the case of community service and money in the case of fines. One of the most distinctive aspects of the 1991 reforms was their attempt to rank these different penal currencies in a comprehensive tariff covering the full range of offences from the most to the least serious. However, deprivation is not a feature of all penalties (the conditional discharge, for example). Finally, it is worth noting that some non-custodial penalties may also be intended to perform preventive or incapacitative functions. For example, disqualification is intended to stop motoring offenders from driving, exclusion requirements are used to keep offenders away from the locations where they are likely to offend, and curfew requirements backed by electronic monitoring can be used to prevent offenders being at large at times when they are thought most likely to offend.

Most contributors to the nature of penality debate have tended to gloss over these differences in the functions performed by different forms of punishment and the way in which the importance that is attached to them has waxed and waned over time. They have also overlooked one feature which is shared by virtually all the conventional forms of punishment (including more recent innovations such as electronic monitoring) we have been considering up till now. This is the fact that they rely almost exclusively on the application of *external* as opposed to *internal* *sanctions* and, as such, are directed primarily *against* an offender.[6]

During the last few years, however, a rather different set of penal responses has emerged which could, conceivably, contain the seeds of a distinctly different kind of penality. These responses seek to engage offenders in a variety of processes that require them to reflect on the harm they have caused to others and encourage them to try to make amends for what they have done. Some of these processes involve some form of dialogue between victims, offenders and members of the community affected by the crime (for example, mediation, family group or community conferencing or circle sentencing) and are associated with the restorative justice approach. Others involve the use of cognitive behavioural techniques (see Chapter 2, section 2.2) that do not necessarily require the participation of victims or community members. One feature that both sets of processes have in common is that they rely on evoking *internal sanctions* which operate on the basis of an offender's conscience rather than the application of external sanctions of the kind that characterize most conventional forms of punishment. (This fits in well with Antony Duff's communicative theory of punishment, discussed in Chapter 2, sections 2.3 and 2.4.) These approaches, along with a revival of interest in rehabilitation by way of studies of desistance from crime (see, for example, Farrall and Calverley, 2006; McNeill, 2006; Ward and Maruna, 2007), may hold out some promise.

We are inclined to believe that the best chance of ending our 'love affair with custody' and achieving significant decarceration in the future could rest on the development of restorative and reintegrative techniques of the kind we have just described. At the very least, a comprehensive strategy that aimed wherever possible to combine appropriate reparation for victims with the reintegration of offenders back into the community would offer a coherent and humane basis for moving away from the prevailing obsession with imprisonment as a response to crime. We are encouraged by the rapid growth of interest in such techniques on the part of penal policy-makers in very many penal jurisdictions around the world (including, not to be churlish, the interest shown by our own government). In our view they offer the best prospect for the development of a replacement penal

---

[6]There have been exceptions, such as probation (at least in its early 'police court missionary' phase), and also the 'silent' penitentiary system. What is distinctive about the responses we are about to describe is their reliance on a form of 'normative' or 'moralizing' discourse with an offender. As such, they fit well with Anthony Duff's communicative theory of punishment, which we mentioned in Chapter 2. This kind of approach can also be deployed within a custodial setting (see Chapter 6, section 6.5).

discourse that could challenge and change the basic assumptions that inform the current debate about punishment and the form it should take. On the other hand, and more cynically, the increasing pressure on prison numbers and their costs, along with the recession, may at some point do something to make the government incline more towards non-custodial sentences. We shall return to these issues and to our own vision for a just and humane (and predominantly non-custodial) penal system in our final chapter.

6

Prisons and the Penal Crisis

Overview

The degree of civilization in a society can be judged by entering its prisons. (Dostoevsky, 1852)

6.1 Imprisonment is both the most important and also the most problematic of all punishments in terms of its impact on the rest of the English penal system. While other punishments may be imposed with greater frequency, imprisonment retains a symbolic dominance by virtue of its status in the eyes of politicians and public alike as the gold standard measure of punishment. Nevertheless, as we shall see in this chapter, imprisonment spectacularly and persistently fails to achieve one of its primary avowed aims, which is to reduce the level of reoffending by those who have been punished in this way. Partly for this reason the very purpose and rationale of imprisonment is also a matter of persistent debate and contention.

In addition, the high cost of imprisonment contributes massively to the crisis of penological resources (see Chapter 1, section 1.3 and below, section 6.5). It not only fuels the seemingly inexhaustible demand for more prison capacity but also ties up resources that might otherwise be used to assist and support victims of crime or to develop alternative ways of dealing with offenders more constructively, effectively and humanely in the community. The average cost of a prison place in 2010–11 was £39,573, although this varied from a high of £62,566 for male high security prisons to a low of £28,647 for male **open prisons** (Ministry of Justice, 2011e). Between 1997 and 2005, 20,000 prison places were provided at an average cost of £99,839 per place.[1] The 2010–11 budget for the Ministry of Justice was £8.9 billion with more than one-quarter of this going to NOMS, most of it to prisons rather than probation and it has been required to make cuts of around 25 per cent over the following four years. It is a remarkably complex matter to compare prison costs with those for probation, but the planned actual budget for prisons in 2008–9 was £3.9 billion compared to £897 million for probation (see Mills et al., 2010). In this chapter we will examine the size and

---

[1] House of Commons Written Answers, 16 March 2005, col. 124WH and 30 June 2005, col. 1669W.

configuration of the prison estate as well as the social composition of the population it houses. In discussing the prison estate we will investigate the controversial issue of privately run prisons and consider whether privatization is a positive development which may help to alleviate the crisis within the penal system (and in particular the prison system's crisis of resources).

The prison system continues to be afflicted by a variety of seemingly intractable problems that help to perpetuate the image of a penal system that is forever teetering on the brink of a potentially devastating crisis. Serious policy failings by successive governments are responsible for many of these problems, so we will also provide a brief overview of some of the key developments in prison policy-making in recent years, with particular emphasis on the period since the 1990 Strangeways riot and associated prison disturbances.

We shall then focus on several distinct aspects of the ongoing prisons crisis, though most of them are closely inter-related. We will begin by examining the prison system's many-stranded *managerial* crisis. With regard to the crises of *containment* and *security*, it may appear as if the imminent threat of high-profile prison escapes has receded. As we shall see, however, the actions taken in response to this particular crisis continue to have serious ramifications for the rest of the prison system and in this sense the crisis is far from being resolved, quite apart from continuing concerns over the security and well-being of prison inmates. Next we will deal with the *prison numbers* crisis and the associated problems of prison overcrowding. In discussing the crisis of *conditions*, the main emphasis will be on the physical environment and facilities that are available to prisoners. Relationships between inmates and with prison staff are discussed in the context of the broader crises of *control* and *authority*, which also encompass the various formal and informal responses to indiscipline and other forms of collective disobedience by prison inmates. The handling of inmate grievances by prison authorities and the operation of the various monitoring mechanisms are examined as aspects of the crisis of *accountability*. Last, but by no means least, we will discuss the perennial crisis of *legitimacy*, with particular emphasis on the action that will be needed if it is to be effectively tackled.

The Aims and Functions of Imprisonment

Official Aims of Imprisonment

6.2 In the early nineteenth century, the chief official aims of imprisonment were the imposition of deterrent and retributive justice on offenders, while not ruling out the possibility of reform and a return to society. By the turn of the century, the twin imperatives of deterrence and reformation had been adopted as official policy, and the subsequent ascendancy of the treatment model was soon enshrined in the Prison Rules themselves. (These Rules have been repeatedly updated; the latest version was published in 2010 and is available on the HM Prison Service website.) In 1964 the following classic formulation was given pride of place as Prison Rule Number 1: 'The purpose of the training and treatment of convicted prisoners shall be to encourage and assist them to lead a good and useful life.' Following the collapse of the rehabilitative ideal in the 1970s (see Chapters 1 and 2, sections 1.3 and 2.2) various attempts were made to come up with an alternative formulation (see previous editions of this book for details). These attempts to fill the moral vacuum created by the demise of the treatment model proved insuperable, however, and the original formulation still appears in the latest edition of the Prison Rules, though it has now been relegated to Rule Number 3 (although it is the first substantive rule).

As part of its current statement of purpose, the Prison Service sets out three rather more prosaic objectives: to hold prisoners securely; to reduce the risk of reoffending; and to provide safe, well-ordered establishments in which prisoners are treated humanely, decently and lawfully. With regard to the second of these aims, the Prison Service's record in preventing reoffending is not at all inspiring and, perhaps in an effort to 'improve' the figures, the Ministry of Justice now publishes 12 month reconviction rates rather than 24 months (which would give a higher rate of reconviction). Latest figures show that 59.4 per cent of all prisoners sentenced to less than 12 months custody were reconvicted within 12 months, compared to 51.1 per cent of those given community orders (Ministry of Justice, 2011b: Table 1). This compares poorly with the situation almost 20 years ago: of inmates who were discharged from prison in 1994, 56 per cent of males and 45 per cent of females were reconvicted within two years (Home Office, 1999).

As for the third of the above aims, we will be assessing the Prison Service's record later in the chapter; but the underlying message is that there is a very long way to go before it could claim to be providing safe, well-ordered establishments in which prisoners are treated humanely, decently and lawfully.

Even with regard to the first aim – holding prisoners securely – the record is extremely uneven. As we will see, until relatively recently escapes from custody were periodically a source of acute embarrassment to both the Prison Service and government ministers. Although concerns over the level of absconding have subsided in recent years, this improvement has come at a cost that has to be measured not only in financial terms but also by the many adverse consequences that flow from the excessive preoccupation with external security matters. Again we will examine these issues in more detail later in the chapter. Holding prisoners securely should mean more than simply preventing them from escaping, however, since they also need to be kept safe and free from danger. When we come to examine the Prison Service's performance with regard to preventing suicides and keeping inmates safe from assaults and free from anxiety, it will become apparent that its performance is far less impressive and continues to give rise to serious concern.

One obvious question that is prompted by this rather dismal track record concerns the rationale for what appears to be a chronically failing institution. Another is how we can account for its longevity and apparent resilience despite its continuing inability to achieve its stated objectives. In order to answer both questions it is necessary to probe behind the official rhetoric and examine the hidden social functions that prisons may continue to perform in modern societies even though they seem incapable of achieving their more instrumental crime control objectives.

Social Functions of Imprisonment

Historically, the birth of the modern prison was part of a much broader movement – described by Foucault (1967: ch. 2) as the 'great confinement' – in which institutions of various kinds came to be adopted as the solution to a wide range of social problems. The start of this process can be traced back to the 1600s, though the replacement of physical suffering by imprisonment as the *dominant* form of punishment (a process that Foucault (1977: 15) termed the 'great transformation') did not occur until the end of the eighteenth and beginning of the nineteenth centuries. This coincided with the emergence of industrial capitalism as the dominant mode of production in all the large European countries.

In Chapters 3 and 5 we discussed some of the sociological explanations which have been put forward for the birth of the prison (see also Matthews, 1999). An interesting radical explanation for the *continued existence* of the prison has been put forward by Norwegian penologist Thomas Mathiesen (1974, 1990 and 2000). Mathiesen suggests that the reason why imprisonment remains the dominant mode of punishment has to do with the important social functions which it performs within advanced capitalist societies. (A not dissimilar account linking the recent expansion of incarceration with the rise of neo-liberal capitalism has recently been put forward by Loïc Wacquant, 2009.)

The first of these Mathiesen terms 'the expurgatory function'. Those who are both unproductive and disruptive of the normal processes of production are liable to find themselves being siphoned off and contained in prison where they can do least damage. When we come to examine the demographic profile of the prison population in the next section, it will become apparent that many of those in custody could, at least from a rather crude functionalist perspective, be described in this way. Or, as Pat Carlen (2006: 6) has put it, 'Today, the prison still fulfils its age-old function of catering for the homeless, the mentally ill, the stranger, the non-compliant poor, the abused and the excluded.'

The second he calls 'the power-draining function', which refers to the fact that those who are contained in this way are not only prevented from interfering with the normal processes of production but are also denied the opportunity to exercise responsibility. For the institution in which they are detained is designed to function on the basis of minimal practical contributions from the prisoners themselves. Once again this rings true with much of the literature on prison life, though quite how it helps inmates to lead a good and useful life on release is less easy to appreciate.

A third, 'symbolic function' refers to the stigmatizing effect of imprisonment, which enables those on the outside to distance themselves, in terms of their own moral self-perceptions, from those who have been publicly labelled in this way.

This is closely related to a fourth function, the 'diverting function' of imprisonment. Here Mathiesen draws attention to the fact that the commission of socially harmful acts is by no means the prerogative of one particular section of society. Rather, he suggests that 'socially dangerous acts are increasingly being committed by individuals and classes with power in society' even though they are most unlikely to be punished for their transgressions (1974: 78). This is because the ultimate sanction of imprisonment tends to be reserved for a highly selected group of offenders, drawn mainly from the lower working class who are most likely to commit a fairly narrow band of offences (for example, personal violence and relatively petty property offences). Consequently, concern in the media and in the population at large tends to focus almost exclusively on transgressions of this kind. Mathiesen suggests that this has the effect of diverting public attention away from much more serious forms of social harm: those resulting from the destruction of entire ecosystems, major acts of pollution, or deaths and injuries resulting from the deliberate compromise of safety standards in the pursuit of profit, for example. Those who are responsible for such harms are generally not seen as appropriate subjects for the ultimate sanction of imprisonment. This is partly because the harms themselves are committed by, or on behalf of, powerful corporations that have the legal power to act as a 'natural person', but are rarely subject to the same legal constraints and penalties. Moreover, those natural persons who take the decisions within such corporations are not only powerful individuals in their own right, but are themselves also actively engaged in the process of production at a high level.

Finally, Mathiesen identified (1990: 138) a fifth social function of imprisonment, which he called the 'action function'. Because prison has the highest profile of any sanction in common use in our kind of society, it plays an important part in reassuring people that something is being done about the problem of law and order, and the social threats which they are persuaded to take most seriously. This function has been all too evident in recent years starting with the Conservative government in 1993, followed by the Labour governments between 1997 and 2010, and currently the Coalition government.

Perhaps, however, imprisonment is not so functional to modern capitalism as Mathiesen suggests. For there is also a heavy price to be paid, not only in terms of resources and human suffering, but also in managing the increasing tensions that are associated with the steadily enduring penal crisis, as we shall see.

David Garland (1990a) has also highlighted the need to look beyond the prison's overt crime control functions, and to appreciate its more social and symbolic purposes, albeit in rather more Durkheimian terms than Mathiesen has used. Like Mathiesen, he sees the prison as a mechanism for enhancing solidarities and emphasizing divisions within communities (Garland, 1990a: 284), but he also sees it as a social institution that reflects a community's cultural values including the pursuit of 'justice, tolerance, decency, humanity and civility' (1990a: 292). Drawing attention to the more subtle symbolic functions of the modern prison can help us to *understand* the resilience of the modern prison despite its instrumental failings. However, it does not absolve us of the responsibility to put its rhetorical aspirations to the test and to *critically assess* its conformity with the moral values it professes. This is what we will be doing in the second half of this chapter.

The Prison System

The Prisons and the Prisoners

6.3 At the time of writing there were 131 prisons in England and Wales. Adult males are generally held separately from adult female inmates (except at Peterborough, which is the first purpose-built prison to house both men and women), and young offenders (see Chapter 8) are likewise held in separate institutions. The four main functional categories comprise high security prisons, closed training prisons, local prisons and open or semi-open prisons. High security prisons (formerly known as **dispersal prisons**; see section 6.5 below) are intended to hold those high-risk inmates whose escape would be dangerous. Closed training prisons are intended to offer education, training and work opportunities for medium risk inmates serving reasonably lengthy sentences. Local prisons, many of which are located in inner city areas, are generally very large and were originally designed for remand inmates, those newly sentenced and those serving short sentences.

At the end of June 2012, the prison population in England and Wales stood at 86,048 (excluding another 401 held in secure children's homes and **secure training centres** (STCs): see Chapter 8, section 8.4). Ninety-five per cent of these were men, though at 5 per cent, the proportion of female inmates had increased significantly since 1987 (3.6 per cent). While adults accounted for the vast majority of those in custody (89.8 per cent), those under the age of 18 (who are still technically children) made up 1.5 per cent of the total, the remaining 8.6 per cent consisting of young adults (aged 18 to 20).

The custodial population is not only heavily skewed in terms of gender and age but also in respect of its racial composition and social profile (see also Chapter 9, sections 9.2 and 9.3). One quarter of the prison population at the end of June 2012 was non-white in composition (13 per cent black, 7 per cent Asian, 4 per cent mixed and 1 per cent Chinese or other). The proportion of prisoners from ethnic minority backgrounds is nearly three times that of the general population.

In terms of its social composition, data compiled by the Social Exclusion Unit a decade ago (2002) paints a depressing picture of a prison population that is disproportionately drawn from marginalized and disadvantaged sectors of the community (and there is no reason to believe that this picture has changed much since then). Moreover, many prisoners lack even the basic life skills that are required in order to subsist and cope with the demands of everyday life (calling to mind Mathiesen's reference to the 'expurgatory role' of the prison; see above).

In terms of family background almost half of all prisoners ran away as a child (compared with 11 per cent of the general population) and over one quarter were taken into care (27 per cent compared with 2 per cent overall). Forty-three per cent came from a family one of whose members had been convicted of a criminal offence (compared with 16 per cent overall). In terms of their educational experience, nearly half of all male offenders and one third of female offenders had been excluded from school (compared with 2 per cent overall) and 30 per cent regularly truanted (ten times the national average). Just over half of all male offenders and 71 per cent of female offenders have no educational qualifications (compared with 15 per cent overall) and levels of innumeracy and illiteracy are also extremely high. Perhaps unsurprisingly, over two thirds of all prison inmates are unemployed at the time they enter custody; 72 per cent are in receipt of benefits (compared with 13.7 per cent of the working age population) and just under half have a history of debt. Levels of homelessness are also high (32 per cent compared with under 1 per cent of the general population).

Prisoners also suffer from much poorer mental and physical health than the general population. On one estimate, at least 70 per cent of sentenced inmates suffer from two or more mental disorders, while levels of hepatitis and HIV are also significantly higher among prison inmates than in the general population.

In short, prison inmates are disproportionately likely to be drawn from disadvantaged, indeed multiply disadvantaged, sections of the community. The most obvious question this prompts is whether prisons are the most appropriate institutions in which to deal with those whose serious and often acute personal and social handicaps are all too likely to have contributed to their offending behaviour. An equally pertinent question is what effect imprisonment itself is likely to have on such prisoners.

The literature on the effects of imprisonment (for an overview see Liebling and Maruna, 2005) highlights a range of damaging consequences that are highly likely to reduce rather than improve the prospects for a crime-free existence once they are released. Thus, imprisonment can itself impair the physical and mental health of inmates and can also induce post-traumatic stress. It is known to disrupt the very social ties that can help to reduce the likelihood of reoffending. For example, up to one third of prison inmates are deprived of their housing as a result of being imprisoned (Social Exclusion Unit, 2002), often as a result of the way the housing benefit scheme operates. Two thirds of those who were employed at the time of sentencing are known to lose their jobs. Family relationships are often difficult to maintain while a person is in prison and even where this is not the case the imprisonment of a family member often imposes additional hardships on the rest of the family (Codd, 2008). The well-known institutionalizing effects of imprisonment – whereby inmates become habituated to prison life and simultaneously less able to cope with life outside – are all too often liable to exacerbate rather than ameliorate an inmate's deficiencies in life skills.

Factors such as these help to explain the lamentable reconviction figures that we referred to earlier. Equally disturbing is the fact that more than 50 inmates commit suicide each year and over 50 ex-prisoners are known to commit suicide each year shortly after release (Howard League for Penal Reform, 2002; Scott and Codd, 2010: ch. 6). These 'pains of imprisonment' (Christie, 1981: 16) are the cause of real human suffering on a massive scale. If, as seems plausible, imprisonment increases the likelihood of further offending on release, the suffering of future victims represents an additional pain that is no less real for being impossible to quantify. In purely financial terms, however, the Social Exclusion Unit (2002: 5) has estimated that the cost of reoffending by ex-prisoners amounts to £11 billion per year.

One additional aspect of the profile of prison inmates needs to be mentioned. Of those in prison at the end of June 2012, 13 per cent were on remand. Most of these remand prisoners are not yet convicted and legally therefore should not be treated as offenders. Almost inevitably, however, they are exposed to many of the above 'pains of imprisonment'. Indeed, in some respects their predicament is even worse than that of sentenced prisoners. For they are not only liable to be detained in some of the worst prison establishments (see below) but may also find it more difficult to defend themselves against the charges they face, even when innocent, than if they were remanded on bail.

Of the sentenced prison population at the end of June 2012 (73,435), 28 per cent had been convicted of offences involving violence against the person (which includes murder but also encompasses a wide variety of less serious physical assaults and woundings). A further 14.3 per cent were sentenced for sexual offences. Robbery accounted for 12.6 per cent of the total and burglary for 10 per cent. Drug offences made up 14.5 per cent, theft 6 per cent and fraud and forgery a further 2 per cent of the total.

Privatization

Of the 131 prisons in England and Wales, a total of 13 are run by private-sector companies, and these private prisons account for 13.5 per cent of the prison population. Privatization has been one of the most significant issues for prisons in England and Wales for the last 25 years, and we need to provide a brief overview of its origins and development (for further details see Cavadino and Dignan, 2007: ch. 7). It is important to emphasize that privately run prisons are not just a recent phenomenon, however. From the Middle Ages to the nineteenth century, the running of English prisons was frequently entrusted to private jail keepers, who received no official payment but were expected to charge fees from their captive 'customers' for the services they provided (Pugh, 1968; McConville, 1981). Prisons were eventually 'nationalized' in 1877 when this private enterprise system was deemed to produce excessive inconsistency, squalor and corruption.

The antecedents of prison privatization (or re-privatization) in England and Wales in more recent times can be traced back to 1970 when the government entered into a contract with the private security firm, Securicor Ltd, to operate airport detention centres for suspected illegal immigrants (McDonald, 1994). The next tentative step was a response to growing alarm over the use of police cells as temporary accommodation for remand prisoners as a result of chronically overcrowded prisons. One temporary expedient which the Home Office resorted to in May 1988 involved the use of a military barracks. Although the prisoners were guarded by military police and troops, the catering service was contracted out to a small private company in what Shaw (1992b) described as 'virtually the first breach in the state monopoly of imprisonment since "nationalization" of the county gaols and recidivist prisons in the late 1870s'.

The Adam Smith Institute (a right-wing think-tank) advocated the contracting out of prisons themselves in 1984 but there was very little governmental interest at this time. In 1987 the House of Commons Home Affairs Committee published a report calling for private sector involvement in the construction and management of custodial institutions in order to alleviate overcrowding in the remand sector in particular. Privatization was also seen as a means of breaking the monopolistic provision of imprisonment by the state and also as a way of countering the influence of the Prison Officers' Association (both of which were dear to the hearts of many Conservative MPs: see Young, 1987). The first real signs of a change in the government's attitude towards privatization came with the publication of a Green Paper in the autumn of 1988 (Home Office, 1988b). This specifically proposed the contracting out of court and escort duties that had hitherto been carried out by police and prison officers, and also recommended an experiment to assess the scope for greater involvement by the private sector in the management of remand prisons. The latter had experienced a disproportionate increase in inmate numbers over the previous decade, and were felt to raise fewer operational difficulties or issues of principle than those holding sentenced prisoners.

When Home Office interest in including provision for privatization in the Criminal Justice Bill seemed to be lukewarm, the Prime Minister Margaret Thatcher personally stepped in, insisting that the move towards privatization should go ahead (Windlesham, 1993: 298). Before the first remand centre to be contracted out – Wolds Prison – had received its first inmates in April 1992, the Home Secretary Kenneth Baker announced the contracting out of Blakenhurst, which was to be another new prison catering for both remand and sentenced prisoners; this was soon followed by Buckley Hall, near Rochdale. The next three private prisons (at Fazakerley, Bridgend and Salford) were the first **DCMF** prisons – designed, constructed, managed and financed by the private sector – which is the model that has subsequently been followed for all new private prisons. By May 1997 the process of contracting out had been extended to include all prison–court escort services and a wide range of other ancillary services, such as education and some catering services. Of even greater long-term significance was the launch of the **private finance initiative** (PFI) in November 1992 (see further, section 6.5 below), a policy forbidding any new public expenditure from being agreed by the Treasury unless the use of private finance had first been considered and rejected. In May 1995 the Prison Service commissioned a report by a firm of management consultants, which concluded that there was considerable scope for the use of private finance projects to be extended. Among the examples cited were major refurbishment projects involving whole prisons, projects to replace or refurbish ancillary service functions (such as catering, prison industry workshops, health care, non-core administration and so on), and large-scale electronic projects such as the installation of CCTV, IT or communication systems.

For a brief period following the 1997 general election the future of prison privatization appeared to be in doubt, since the victorious Labour Party had pledged while in opposition to take private prisons back into public ownership. However, this principled opposition began to melt away within days of the election victory. One week later Jack Straw (who as Shadow Home Secretary had assured the POA annual conference in 1996 of the party's opposition to the policy of prison privatization), now the new Labour Home Secretary, announced that he would be prepared to sign contracts that were already in the pipeline if this proved to be the only way of providing new accommodation quickly. Just over a year later he confirmed that all new prisons in England and Wales would be privately built and run (Prison Reform Trust, 1998b).

By way of consolation for the public sector, the Prison Service was allowed to tender for private management contracts when these expired, or when existing state-run prisons were market-tested for possible privatization, and over the next four years it secured three such contracts in the face of competition from the private sector (Buckley Hall, Blakenhurst and Strangeways). These individual setbacks for the private sector did not, however, signal any weakening in the Labour government's new-found enthusiasm for the general policy of prison privatization. The policy of both New Labour and Coalition governments has been for a mixed economy of provision for both prisons and probation and the introduction of payment by results (see below). In 2011 Birmingham Prison became the first ever to pass from state to private control, and it was announced that the private sector would be permitted to compete to run a further nine prisons.

However, the effects of competition are not always beneficial. As we have already noted in Chapter 5, in 2012 policy turned to farce when the governor of three prisons in South Yorkshire ordered probation staff who worked in the prison to leave the premises as the local probation trust had gone into partnership with G4S (a private security company) to bid to run the prisons (*Guardian*, 1 March 2012). The role of the voluntary sector – much of which might have been expected to have ideological reservations about 'prisons for profit' – is also intriguing (see Silvestri, 2009). In 2008 the prison reform charity NACRO announced that it would be participating in a consortium along with private security firm G4S bidding to build and run two new prisons, Belmarsh West (London) and Maghull (Merseyside), with the intention of overseeing rehabilitation services in the prison, but not to be involved in security or the work of prison officers. Other charities followed suit, and in July 2010 the contract for Belmarsh West (a new prison in London) was awarded to a consortium including Serco but also the charities Turning Point and Catch 22 whose role will be to provide resettlement services (*Guardian*, 14 July 2010).

The Debate Around Prison Privatization

The main philosophical justification for prison privatization derives from the *laissez faire* free-market economic theories originally championed by right-wing governments in the 1980s and 1990s and since adopted with equal enthusiasm by governments and parties that claim to represent the centre-left (notably New Labour). Various economic nostrums were invoked by 'true believers' in order to champion the case for privatizing areas of public provision (see particularly, in relation to prison privatization, Young, 1987; Hutto 1990; and Logan, 1990). They included a reliance on free competition through the marketplace as the best spur to efficiency and quality of service, and also as the most effective scourge of restrictive practices and vested (trade union) interest. The case for privatization was also fuelled by a rhetorical belief in 'rolling back the frontiers of the state', at least to the extent of reducing its 'social rôle and responsibilities' (Kamerman and Kahn, 1989: 256). In order to achieve this it was necessary to engineer a split between the producers and purchasers of public services in order to establish an internal or quasi-market. To put it crudely, the seductive appeal of prison privatization is that it claims to offer more (prison capacity) and better (quality of service) for less. But perhaps the strongest selling point of privatization is the lamentable and all-too-obvious failings associated with the publicly run prison service, which we document below – surely private prisons would have to be an improvement? Moreover, competition between private and public prisons could serve to drive up standards and efficiency across the board. Before examining the specific claims advanced on behalf of prison privatization, we wish to comment on these more basic arguments underpinning the programme.

First, whatever the sentimental attachment some might feel towards a mythical bygone era in which a free and unregulated market supposedly delivered the best of all possible outcomes in response to the laws of supply and demand, today there is no such thing as free competition within an unregulated market. Moreover, such a model is singularly inappropriate with regard to the public sector in general and the sphere of penal policy in particular. For the size of the custodial market itself, the nature of the services to be supplied, and also the terms on which this is to happen, including even (to some extent) the identities of the players are all determined by the state. Indeed, the state is quite at liberty to forbid public sector institutions from submitting a bid should it choose to do so, which is precisely what happened with both the Wolds and Blakenhurst prison tenders. Not only that, the government also has it in its power to alter the balance of advantage between the public and private sectors. It can, if it chooses, simply starve publicly run prisons of the resources required to implement much-needed reforms, while investing lavishly in privately operated prisons in order to show the private sector off in the best light (something that has been claimed in respect of certain privately run correctional institutes in the US, see Shichor, 1995). So much for the notion of free competition in an unregulated marked place. One of those best qualified to pass judgement on the debate – Lord Browne, former chief executive of BP – has publicly derided attempts by government to create what he pointedly refers to as 'pseudo-markets' in the public sector (*Financial Times*, 28 January 2005). He sees them as damaging to the professional ethos within public sector institutions such as the prisons, universities and hospitals and potentially counter-productive by alienating people against business in general.

Governments are not the only ones who are capable of rigging the market, however. For, as Sutherland (1956: 90) pointed out, 'big business does not like competition, and makes careful arrangements to reduce it and eliminate it'. This is most easily done where there are relatively few powerful corporations, the entry price into the market is high, and opportunities for reallocating the contract are limited, all of which applies to the privatized prisons market. Despite an increase in the number of companies aspiring to join the 'corrections-commercial complex' (Lilly and Knepper, 1990; 1992), the market itself is dominated by a small handful of multinational corporations or conglomerates for whom various mechanisms are open to limit competition. One is price-fixing; another is the taking over of rivals. One danger is that once a government comes to depend on a small number of private companies, it may be held to ransom and have little choice but to pay the higher prices charged to increase profitability. The risk would appear to be even greater where private operators are licensed not only to operate a particular institution but also to build, own and run it, as is now the case with all tenders in England and Wales. As we will see below, there are ample opportunities for correctional corporations to engage in market rigging practices, and abundant evidence that they avail themselves of these opportunities to the full.

Although under the classical free market model the laws of supply and demand are supposed to ensure responsiveness by the producer to the needs of the purchaser, it is extremely difficult to see how this is supposed to apply in the context of prison privatization (Shichor, 1995: 71–3). For instead of the traditional two-party relationship linking vendor and purchaser (or provider and client), with prison privatization there are three parties in the relationship. In addition to the private contractors, who build and operate the prisons, and the prison inmates who are the recipients of the services they provide, there is also the state, which stipulates the type of facilities to be provided and pays the money. At the very least such an arrangement is likely to distort the normal operation of supply and demand mechanisms. Thus, the inmates who receive the contractor's services are self-evidently not free to shop around or 'take it or leave it' (Palumbo, 1986). Consequently, unlike typical recipients of services in a market, they have almost no power or leverage to affect the situation let alone dictate what contracts are made, particularly given their general political, economic and social impotence (Geis, 1987). Conversely, the service providers are much less dependent on the consumers of their services for their economic success than they are on their primary customer or paying client, the government. Consequently, inmates may have even less control over their fate in a privatized prison system than in one being provided directly by the state itself. In short, it is not the inmates (or direct consumers of prison services) whom the prison firms must satisfy, but the government as keeper of the purse.

As for the argument that private prisons must be better because public ones are so bad, the deplorable state of the publicly run prison system clearly has to be acknowledged. At the same time, it is worth remembering that the main reason the state assumed responsibility for prisons in the first place (in the nineteenth century) was because of excesses and shortcomings associated with an earlier era of private provision. At the very least this should warn us against accepting at face value simple dogmatic assertions that the private sector is inherently superior to the public sector in this sphere. Whether the private sector is in practice capable of delivering a superior performance for less money is in part an empirical question that we will address in passing in the next section. However, it is worth observing at the outset that the evidence base on this issue remains grossly inadequate. One of the main reasons for this is because governments and private contractors seem strangely reluctant to commission the kind of rigorous analysis that is insisted on for other penal policy initiatives (for example, restorative justice, where the government at one time refused to consider any further developments until the outcome of an extremely rigorous randomized control trial had been published) or even to publish the available data that would help to provide more definitive answers to the question. In our view, though, the crucial question raised by prison privatization is not whether it is capable of delivering more for less, as it claims, but whether it is likely to alleviate or aggravate the various pressing crises that continue to confront the English prison system. We see no sign that, overall, it is achieving the former.

Privatization and the Crisis of Resources

Although we would not see this as the overriding issue, a major selling point of prison privatization has certainly been the promise that it holds out of helping to alleviate the crisis of penological resources which we introduced in Chapter 1 (section 1.3). Privatization claims to be able to do achieve this in three main ways:

- by achieving efficiency gains that can significantly reduce operating costs in the running of prisons;

- by enabling new prison buildings and facilities to be procured more efficiently and economically; and

- by providing governments with a fiscally advantageous method of investing in this new infrastructural capacity.

With regard to *operating* costs, imprisoning people is highly labour-intensive and staff costs account for 80 per cent of total running costs (National Audit Office, 2003). Savings might in principle by sought by taking on fewer staff, paying staff less, reducing the fringe benefits to which they are entitled and withholding union recognition as a means of securing a more compliant workforce which is easier to pay and deploy efficiently. There is evidence that private prison operators have pursued most of these strategies as a means of reducing their operating costs, though other problems have often been encountered in doing so.

Thus, staffing levels are reported to be far lower at contracted-out prisons, which have 17 per cent fewer staff per prisoner than those in prisons operated by the public sector (Andrews, 2000). One way of reducing staff numbers is by investing instead in advanced technology, electronic surveillance and security and control systems. However, several privately operated prisons that have done this have encountered serious operational difficulties. Both Doncaster and Blakenhurst, for example, experienced serious disturbances and were subsequently authorized to appoint large numbers of additional staff (Nathan, 1995b: 15), which may be seen as a tacit admission that the original staffing levels had been set much too low; something that staff at both prisons had voiced concerns about (HM Chief Inspector of Prison, 1995; *Guardian*, 1 February 1995 and 8 September 1995). Most dramatically, a revolutionary new keyless prison (Parc, near Bridgend in Wales) opened in 1997 with a system relying on computers and smartcards instead of keys. Within months the prison suffered serious disorder and two suicides, while the computer system proved so slow that keys had to be reintroduced (*Guardian*, 30 May 1998). So the scope for savings from such sources may be rather smaller than envisaged.

Pay and staff conditions for basic grade prison officers at privately run prisons also compare very unfavourably with those in the public sector (although this is not the case for senior management; see DLA MCG Consulting, 2005: Table ES2). For example, the average starting salary in the public sector is 11 per cent higher than in the private sector, while the average basic pay rate is fully 41 per cent higher. The contracted working hours are longer in the private sector than in the public sector (41 and 39 hours respectively), pension provision is markedly inferior and both overtime and annual leave arrangements are much less favourable. Overall, private sector workers are estimated to spend 7 per cent more time at work than their public sector counterparts, which is one of the main reasons why contracted-out prisons can operate with fewer staff (Andrews, 2000). However, these differentials only apply to newly commissioned private prisons. For if an *existing* public sector prison is contracted out (as Birmingham Prison was in 2011), its employees' pay and conditions are protected under the European Union's Acquired Rights Directive. This could be one reason why the private sector has shown much less interest in tendering when such prisons have been market tested. As for union recognition, the main prison officers' union (the POA) has not been recognized for collective bargaining purposes in any of the privately managed prisons (private firm G4S recognises the GMB at its prisons), despite a number of applications to the Central Arbitration Committee (Bach, 2002).

Not surprisingly, the markedly inferior conditions of employment in private prisons are also reflected in very high levels of staff turnover compared with their public sector counterparts, which can give rise to serious problems. Staff turnover among private sector prison custody officers is 25 per cent, which is ten times greater than the 2.5 per cent turnover rate among public sector prison officers (DLA MCG Consulting, 2003; see also Sachdev, 2004: 23). Apart from the direct costs to the employers, high turnover rates make it difficult for private prison contractors to meet the staffing levels stipulated in their contract bids and can have adverse consequences for the quality of facilities and services such as education that are provided for inmates (National Audit Office, 2003: 32).

In view of these marked differentials in terms of pay and conditions, it might be expected that the private sector's claim to be able to deliver significant operational savings would be unequivocally supported by convincing evidence but, perhaps surprisingly, this is not at all the case. In part this is due to technical problems in ensuring that like is being compared with like across the two sectors.

One problem is that no new public sector prisons have been commissioned since Woodhill in 1992 and the vast majority are considerably older than that, with some such as Dartmoor dating back to the early nineteenth century. This is important because differences in age, design, composition of inmates and occupancy levels are all likely to have a significant bearing on operating costs. Another problem is that the expenditure figures quoted by private prison operators may frequently under-represent the true costs by omitting ancillary costs such as the market testing and contracting processes themselves; indeed a study of competitive tendering has concluded that the government has heavily subsidized the tendering process (Centre for Public Services, 2002: 26). Nor are they likely to acknowledge the costs of various hidden benefits that may continue to be provided by the public sector. These may include the cost of utilities, repair of vandalism, and also the public support services that might be required in the event of a major disturbance or other difficulties (Shichor, 1995: 140). There is also a risk that private contractors may be tempted to put in unrealistically low bids at the outset, to establish a presence in the market, after which they will seek to recoup lost profits once the government has come to depend (politically or economically) on their services. Confirmation from a somewhat unlikely source that such practices may have taken place is provided by the CBI (Confederation of British Industry, 2003: 42, also cited by Sachdev, 2004: 23), which states that some private contractors may have 'engaged in aggressive competition to build market share', only to falter subsequently.

Quite apart from these technical problems, attempts to compare public and private sector prison costs are bedevilled by a persistent refusal on the part of government and the private contractors themselves to disclose the necessary financial information on the grounds of 'commercial confidentiality'. For all these reasons, although various government-commissioned studies have claimed to find that the operating costs of privately operated prisons are between 11 to 15 per cent cheaper per prisoner per day (see, for example, Woodbridge, 1999; Andrews, 2000; Park, 2000), such findings should be viewed with considerable caution. In the absence of a rigorous independently conducted comparison of costs, or the production of sufficiently detailed and reliable data to support them, such claims are at best premature, if not positively misleading. Moreover they are contradicted by conclusions based on several authoritative studies including a number of published comparative evaluations in the US, which has a much longer experience with privatized prison institutions (see United States General Accounting Office, 1991; 1996; Shichor, 1995: chs 6 and 9; Abt Associates, 1998; Pratt and Maahs, 1999; Austin and Coventry, 2001, Raher, 2002).

Yet British governments have continued to invest heavily in prison privatization largely for dogmatic reasons, despite the lack of evidence of cost-effectiveness and the huge sums of public money that are involved. An equal cause for concern is that none of the bodies that are supposed to hold the government to account – Parliament and its Public Accounts and Home Affairs Committees, the National Audit Office and the Audit Commission – have challenged or criticized this state of affairs. We will return to this lack of accountability later in this section.

Turning briefly to some of the ancillary services that have been contracted out, here too the promise that has been held out by advocates of privatization has frequently not been matched by its performance. At Coldingley Prison at the time of privatization in 1997 the industrial facilities were losing around £250,000 per year; less than a year later the company concerned (Wackenhut UK Ltd) had incurred losses estimated at £474,200 (*Guardian*, 29 January 1999), despite paying inmates only £7 per day for their labour. In 1999 the scheme ignominiously became the first prison privatization project to revert to Prison Service control, when the five-year contract was rescinded and the staff once again became public sector employees. A scathing (but unpublished) internal audit report accused the management at Coldingley of showing 'a total disregard for many of the fundamental tenets of government accounting and Prison Service financial policy' (Prison Reform Trust, 1999). Nor was this an isolated example. The high cost of the private catering contract at the (public sector) Woodhill Prison, for example, was criticized by the Chief Inspector of Prisons for being 'far higher than that of employing prison officer caterers assisted by inmates' (Nathan, 1994: 15). Moreover, plans to contract out the prison escort service for the one remaining area in England and Wales received an embarrassing setback in December 1994 when all four private sector bids were found to be higher than the existing costs of providing the service (Nathan, 1995a: 16). Not that this stopped the privatization from ultimately going ahead.

A second major sphere in which it is claimed that private sector involvement can help to alleviate the crisis of resources is in respect of prison *construction* (as opposed to operating) costs. It is often simply assumed, even by those who are opposed to the privatization of operational and custodial functions (see, for example, Raher, 2002: 3), that it may well be cheaper to engage the private sector to undertake such major construction tasks. Once again, however, the evidence to support this contention is surprisingly thin and lacking in rigour. It is also difficult to disentangle this aspect from the debate over the method of financing such projects even though there is no necessary connection between them. In the early days of the prison privatization debate it was often claimed that the private sector could design, plan and build a prison inside a year, compared with around seven years for the public sector. The difference between the two sectors was, in reality, much more modest than this, however, largely because of the inevitable delays incurred by either sector at the planning stage. In any event, the National Audit Office reported in July 1994 that the average time taken to build a prison by conventional means had fallen from seven to just four years (Nathan, 1994: 18).

The third way in which it is claimed that privatization can alleviate the crisis of penological resources is in the *financing* of new prisons. Here, just as with the operational and construction costs, the comparative capabilities of the private and public sectors have never been systematically put to the test. Instead, the Treasury simply decided in 1992 that its preferred method of procurement for any major new public spending projects would be for them to be privately financed. In the case of prisons, this effectively meant that they would all in future be designed, constructed, financed and managed by the private sector. The main attraction of this PFI to the Treasury is that it removes the need to borrow large sums of money up front in order to defray the costs of building a prison several years before it is ready to take its first inmates. Instead, the government only starts to pay for the use of the facility – at a daily rate per prisoner – once the prison is ready to receive its first inmates. In technical parlance, the effect of the PFI is that major capital investments no longer count against the government's public sector borrowing requirement, which successive governments over the last quarter of a century have been at pains to reduce. Or, to put it another way, it has the effect of appearing to move major capital spending off the balance-sheet.

In reality, however, the benefit to the Treasury is just as illusory as the accountancy sleight of hand that seems to magically convert capital into revenue spending. For exactly the same effect could be achieved just as easily – and far more transparently – by simply altering the Treasury's own self-imposed accounting rules themselves. One way of doing this, which has been proposed by the Centre for Public Services (2002: 61), would be for the government to employ the General Government Financial Deficit as its measure for public sector current and capital expenditure accounting rather than the public sector borrowing requirement (or Public Sector Net Borrowing as it is now known). More importantly, it could enable public bodies to borrow money from the European Investment Bank and European Investment Fund for capital investment projects without this counting as government borrowing.

Two other justifications are frequently cited in support of the PFI approach: that it represents better value for money and that it enables the government to transfer the risk involved in any major long-term capital project to the private sector. Neither of these arguments is convincing, however. With regard to the value for money claim, governments (being the ultimate safe credit risk) can typically borrow money at significantly better rates than private sector concerns can. So while it is true that any state institution seeking capital investment for new projects is supposed to test the projected costs of PFI procurement approach against those procured by conventional state funding, the basis on which this is done has been called into question (see comments by the Deputy Head of the National Audit Office quoted in Kochan, 2002; also the Centre for Public Services, 2002: 21).

The claim that PFI projects represent better value for money is further undermined by the bidding process itself, which bears little resemblance to the classical free market competitive model enshrined in private enterprise rhetoric. Instead of an open competition between rival bidders who would each submit a fully costed tender document, a preferred bidder is identified quickly and it is at this point that the detailed negotiations begin between client and prospective contractor over the particular terms of the contract including the actual specifications, allocation of risk and eventual price. All these discussions take place behind closed doors on a non-competitive basis during a lengthy process (6–18 months) in which the balance of advantage lies decidedly with the prospective contractor. As Monbiot (2002) points out, their consultants and advisers are well placed to extract the best possible deal from the government effectively at public expense and with minimal risk to the contractor (see also the Centre for Public Services, 2002: 21–1). Perhaps not surprisingly, it is not unknown for the projected costs of a project to rise two or three times between the allocation of preferred bidder status and the final allocation of a PFI contract.

As for the transfer of risk argument, this is equally unconvincing. The theory is that the contractor bears all the risks of project failure including unanticipated cost over-runs. In reality, however, private sector contractors seek to protect themselves by effectively setting up specific companies (known as 'special purpose vehicles') that are backed by limited equity reserves to undertake the project (Kochan, 2002). This has the effect of restricting liability if something should go wrong with the latter rather than the parent corporation itself. From the government's point of view, however, the supposed advantage of a PFI deal is once again illusory as at the end of the day the state inevitably continues to bear both the political and financial risks of a project failure. Nor is this merely a hypothetical risk. The illusion that the private firm bears the risk was dramatically exploded in 2012 when security firm G4S – a major player in the private prisons market – admitted at the last minute that it was incapable of providing adequate security services for the London Olympic Games, with the result that troops had to be deployed instead. As regards prisons themselves, in 2002 insurance companies refused to provide cover for two new private prisons after rioting led to the destruction by fire of a privately run Yarl's Wood asylum and immigration centre, thereby pressurizing the government to either meet the cost itself or at least accept part of the risk. Conversely, however, when the consortium that secured the contract for HMP Altcourse secured windfall profits that were 81 per cent higher than anticipated following a lucrative refinancing arrangement they were under no obligation to share these gains with the Prison Service (the Centre for Public Services, 2002: 34).[2]

The attractions of the PFI procurement policy for the private sector are self-evident. However, whether it holds any advantage for the state and for the public is much more questionable. After all, the public purse still has to pay the full economic cost of the facilities and services, as well as needlessly inflated borrowing costs and the massive cost of the procurement process itself, plus whatever profit margin is necessary to attract private investment in the first place. The only apparent benefit is that capital-intensive projects can be funded on the basis of long-term revenue repayments that avoid the *appearance* (though not the reality) of contributing to government debt. Ordinary consumers are familiar with the advantages – and drawbacks – of

---

[2]A deal between the Prison Service and consortium was eventually negotiated and, in the wake of an investigation into the controversy by the National Audit Office, it was announced that future contracts would make provision for refinancing benefits to be shared with the Prison Service. However, the underlying issue of excess profit-taking by PFI contractors was not addressed in the NAO report (the Centre for Public Services, 2002: 34).

such hire purchase arrangements. But whereas companies providing hire purchase finance are obliged to spell out the full cost of the transaction including the annual rate of interest, neither the government nor the contractors are under any obligation to provide such information to the taxpayer who ultimately has to foot the bill. Far from alleviating the crisis of resources, private sector involvement in the penal system is all too likely to exacerbate it in the long run.

We shall also see in section 6.5 below that privatization shows little sign of being able to solve any of the other crises besetting the prison system.

Key Phases in Recent Prison Policy-Making

6.4 In this section we provide a brief descriptive overview of some of the key phases in the tortuous development of recent prison policy in order to set out the historical context in which these particular issues have come to prominence (see also Liebling and Arnold, 2004: ch. 1).

1995–1999: The Security and Control Agenda – Post-Woolf Backlash

Lord Woolf's 1991 report following the riot at Strangeways Prison, Manchester and other prison disturbances the previous year had – for a brief moment – suggested a new dawn for the prison service with its emphasis on the need to balance security, control and justice (Woolf and Tumim, 1991). However, the government response was feeble. The White Paper (Home Office, 1991) which purported to set out a strategy for delivering the Woolf reforms failed to specify an implementation plan, a timetable or any commitment to resourcing the changes.

Instead of delivering the promised panacea of a safe, stable and secure prison system, the post-Woolf era was rocked by a series of extremely embarrassing high-profile escapes from maximum security prisons and mounting concern over the level of disorderly conduct throughout the system. Both sets of incidents are described more fully in section 6.5 below. Here, it is sufficient to note that the first escape, in September 1994, involved six extremely high-risk inmates, including five IRA terrorists, who broke out of a supposedly escape-proof Special Security Unit at Whitemoor Prison. Although the men were swiftly recaptured, the government's embarrassment was heightened by the discovery of Semtex explosive and detonators at the prison, and also by allegations that prison staff undertook errands for inmates. Less than six months later three high security life sentence prisoners escaped from Parkhurst Prison on the Isle of Wight in January 1995, and remained at liberty for five days before being recaptured. Meanwhile, concerns were being voiced – although with little hard evidence – that the Prison Service's attempts to improve relationships between staff and inmates, far from encouraging compliance and defusing tensions, had resulted in lax regimes that were characterized by lethargy on the part of many inmates, and disturbingly high levels of bullying and drug-taking.

By this stage, Michael Howard had taken over as Home Secretary (in 1993), and the law and order counter-reformation was already in full swing (see Introduction, Figure 1.2 and Chapter 10, section 10.2). His immediate response to the security lapses was to commission two reports, one focusing on the Whitemoor incident (Woodcock, 1994) while the second was a more general inquiry into prison security that also took account of the Parkhurst episode (Learmont, 1995). The government unquestioningly accepted their conclusions that the fault lay with over-permissive regimes in which effective power and control lay with inmates rather than prison staff, and resolved to return power unequivocally to prison officers and management by adopting a 'decent but austere' regime. Policy changes included an increase in internal and perimeter security, restrictions on temporary release, the introduction of dedicated search teams, mandatory drug testing, restrictions on personal possessions,[3] and a new sticks and carrots regime of incentives and earned privileges (see section 6.5, below; Creighton and King, 2000: 136). The consequences for prisoners were immediate and profound since they emerged with fewer privileges, less personal property and were subject to far more frequent and thorough searches than before (Liebling, 2001). Practices were adopted that were widely perceived as dehumanizing if not barbaric, such as the shackling of pregnant female prisoners giving birth in civilian hospitals, and there was even an apparent resurgence of staff violence against prisoners. As early as 1996, the Chief Inspector of Prisons had expressed anxiety about the illegal use of force against inmates in the segregation unit at Wormwood Scrubs. Then, on 6 September 2000, three prison officers had the dubious distinction of becoming the first in modern English penal history to be imprisoned for acts of brutality against prisoners (HM Chief Inspector of Prisons, 1999c). Between 1 January and 30 June 1999, a total of 44 prison officers (including those at Wormwood Scrubs) were suspended in prisons in England and Wales for a variety of alleged assaults against prisoners.

1999–2002: The 'Decency Agenda' and 'Effectiveness Credo' – the Quest for a Balanced Approach

The preoccupation with security matters lasted until 1999, by which time there had been a change of government and yet another change in the Prison Service's senior management (see section 6.5 below). In the face of the escalating threat to the legitimacy of the Prison Service and its tactics, Martin Narey took over as Director General in 1999 and signalled a dramatic change of emphasis by invoking moral principles rather than security concerns when articulating the service's priorities (Narey, 1999). In a speech (Narey, 2001) whose bitter eloquence was born out of personal knowledge, he complained of a 'litany of failure and moral

---

[3]Achieved by a policy of 'volumetric control' which effectively restricted the number of possessions an inmate could keep in prison to what could be contained within a box of a standard size.

neglect', lamented the 'very immorality of our treatment of some prisoners and the degradation of some establishments', and admitted that for too long the Prison Service 'used to tolerate inhumanity'. With equal frankness, he also appeared to acknowledge the monumental scale of the task and strength of cultural resistance from within the service by threatening to leave his post unless he received the support he required in order to push through the radical changes he believed were needed. This new approach has come to be known as the 'decency agenda' (Liebling and Arnold, 2004: 33), which involves treating prisoners fairly and with dignity while nevertheless effectively challenging their offending behaviour.

As Narey's address also made clear, however, the quest for decency was to be pursued as part of a broader attempt to modernize the Prison Service in a bid to extirpate some of the shameful and unacceptable attitudes and practices of the past and improve its performance. Failing prisons would no longer be tolerated and all prisons would be expected to embrace a new working credo of effectiveness (Liebling and Arnold, 2004: 34ff) dedicated to the reduction of reoffending and protection of the public. The means by which these goals were to be pursued were overtly managerialist and included the promulgation of acceptable standards, the use of accreditation procedures to monitor prison programmes and regimes, improved links with other agencies and, underpinning all of these, an emphasis on 'best value'. Another important aspect of this 'effectiveness credo' was its implicit belief in the superiority of private sector methods and the value of competition as means for driving up standards, overcoming obstructionist attitudes and ensuring the efficient use of resources.

2002–2006: Keeping the Lid On – Pragmatism Reasserts Itself

Martin Narey relinquished responsibility for English prisons to become Chief Executive of the children's charity Barnado's in 2005. But outwardly at least, the Prison Service retained its commitment both to Narey's decency agenda and also to the effectiveness ethos as the surest way of pursuing it. The former was reflected in the Prison Service business plan for 2006–7 (HM Prison Service, 2006), which listed the decency agenda as second only to the reduction of reoffending among its list of main priorities or deliverables for 2006–7. Likewise, the effectiveness ethos was reflected in the various **key performance indicators** (KPIs) listed in Appendix 2 of the plan. Unfortunately, however, the rediscovery of the importance of moral principles as the lodestar for Prison Service reform coincided with a period of unprecedented growth in the size of the prison population that rendered many of its worthy aspirations unattainable (Liebling and Arnold, 2004: 40). An equally inevitable consequence of the relentless rise in the number of prison inmates was that prison staff would find it increasingly difficult to attain many of their targets, as the service itself admitted (HM Prison Service, 2006: 6). Those relating to the reduction of overcrowding, curbing the rate of self-inflicted deaths and providing constructive educational training or employment opportunities prior to release were likely to be particularly difficult to achieve in such circumstances. Consequently, the main priority for the Prison Service for the foreseeable future was the much more prosaic and pragmatic one of simply trying to accommodate the ever-growing number of inmates within a system that was almost literally creaking at the seams.

2006–2012: Where Do We Go From Here?

In February 2006, Home Secretary Charles Clarke published a *Five Year Strategy for Protecting the Public and Reducing Reoffending*. This reiterated that prison should be reserved for the most dangerous, violent and seriously persistent offenders (Home Office, 2006b: 22). It also reaffirmed the government's commitment to implementing the custody plus provisions that were intended to reduce the length of time that many less serious offenders served in custody (see Chapter 5, section 5.3). Second, it announced an ambitious plan to reconfigure the prison estate by developing a network of **community prisons** that would make it easier for less serious prisoners to be housed closer to where they lived. This in turn would enable them to maintain closer links with their families and communities to assist with the process of reintegration on release. Fifteen years earlier, the Woolf Report had also favoured the development of a network of community prisons by dividing up many of the larger inner city prisons into a series of smaller living units. Woolf had also proposed that within these units different kinds of specialist regimes could be made available for meeting the requirements of different categories of prisoners.

Just three months later, a new Home Secretary – John Reid – was in post, and plans had been announced for the construction of an additional 8,000 prison places, but the 'Vision for Community Prisons' that was due to have been published in spring 2006 had still not materialized, and never has since. The Carter Report of December 2007 addressed the question of how to match the demand for prison places with the increasing rise in prison numbers and recommended that an extra 6,500 additional places be provided by the end of 2012 (in addition to the 8,500 extra already planned by government). Three new 'Titan' prisons should be built, holding 2,500 prisoners each, and this would allow the closure of a number of older institutions. Ironically, just four years earlier Carter had advised on how to limit the prison population to 80,000, yet his new proposals would bring prison capacity to 96,000. Initially, his recommendation was accepted, but in April 2009 the government changed its mind, announcing that no 'Titans' would be built. Instead there would be five new prisons each holding 1,500 inmates; all of these would be built and run by the private sector and would bring the total capacity to 96,000 by 2014.

Despite Justice Secretary Kenneth Clarke's attempts to change the direction of penal policy (see Chapter 10, section 10.2), the Coalition government quickly made it clear that they were 'not aiming to cut the prison population' (Ministry of Justice, 2011a: 2). But their key policy plans for prisons – all part of their 'rehabilitation revolution' (see Chapters 2 and 10, sections 2.2 and 10.2) – were threefold: to make prisons places of hard work and industry; to pay by results; and to ensure that all rehabilitation services were open to private, voluntary or community sector competition. The Legal Aid, Sentencing and Punishment of Offenders Act 2012 provides for prisoners' pay to be deducted and to go towards victim and community support. In March 2011 it was announced that Doncaster Prison (run by the private company Serco) would be the first to run on a payment by results basis – the firm to be paid more the better its ex-inmates behave following release. It will be interesting to follow this initiative as even the government acknowledges (Ministry of Justice, 2010a: 41) that there are problems in organizing and operating a payment by results scheme (see also Fox and Albertson, 2011). As for the push to get more prisoners doing an honest day's work, there are likely to be problems there as well. Already there are claims that prisoners are being paid £3 a day to work at a call centre and that other workers have been fired as a result (*Guardian*, 8 August 2012). It is open to doubt how well this will all work – and indeed, given the historical volatility of penal policy, how long government will continue to pursue such rehabilitative initiatives with any real enthusiasm.

In the next section we examine the various crises to which the prison system appears to be congenitally prone.

The Prison System and Its Crises

6.5 The problems that beset the English prison system can be described in terms of a set of interlocking crises – over numbers and overcrowding, the way in which the system is organized and managed, security, conditions and regimes, the maintenance of order and control, and the lack of effective accountability mechanisms or grievance procedures. Many of these individual crises are related to a general *crisis of resources*, which has intensified as the prison population has continued to grow to ever-higher record levels. All the individual crises have contributed to a deep-seated *crisis of legitimacy* within prisons. In recent years there has been an air of almost permanent crisis-management throughout the Prison Service, but this is compounded by the fact that senior government policy-makers of whatever political party have lacked the vision and courage to take effective action to tackle the underlying causes of the crisis. We discussed the general crisis of resources in Chapter 1, and inspected the (in our opinion highly dubious) claim of privatization to be able to alleviate it in section 6.3 above. We will continue by examining various other crises which beset the prison system.

The Managerial Crisis

Successive Home Secretaries, Justice Secretaries and their junior ministers have failed to provide the Prison Service with appropriate strategic direction, whether in terms of defining the purposes of imprisonment or formulating sensible criteria to ensure that its use is not allowed to exceed the resources that the government chooses to make available. Instead, as a former Chief Inspector of Prisons has made clear in a trenchant critique, ministers have persistently failed to ameliorate the 'competing burdens of unrelieved overcrowding and remorseless resource constraints' that continue to bedevil the Prison Service and deflect it from pursuing its primary aims (Ramsbotham, 2005: 216).

In addition to these pivotal political failings, the Prison Service also suffers from acute organizational weaknesses. As Andrew Coyle (2005: 180) observes, the Prison Service is just about the only major organization that is totally under central government control, despite its enormous size and labyrinthine complexity. The organizational crisis within the Prison Service was cruelly exposed by the Strangeways riot of April 1990. At that time the Prison Service formed an integral part (the Prison Department) of the Home Office and was characterized by a top down structure with a very high level of central control (Prison Reform Trust, 1991). This caused particular problems for the Strangeways governor at the time of the riots, who was required throughout to consult his superiors within the Prison Department, many of whom had no experience of running prisons. The organizational problems confronting the Prison Service had long been recognized. The Woolf Report spoke scathingly of the gulf that existed between Home Office ministers, Prison Headquarters staff and those working in the service itself, and of the deep 'dissension, division and distrust' that existed at all levels of the service (Woolf and Tumim, 1991: paras 12.1–12.4). Woolf's primary concern was the need for 'clear and visible leadership' of the service by someone recruited internally. His call for a much less directive hands-off approach by ministers which would leave the Director General free to manage and be publicly answerable for the performance of the service was also echoed at around the same time by an independent review of Prison Service management (Lygo, 1991).

The Prison Service became an executive agency in April 1993. In theory, the aim of **agency status** is to allow the Prison Service to operate at arm's length from central government. Operational matters are the responsibility of the Director General, who works to a policy and resources framework set by the Secretary of State. Meanwhile, much responsibility and authority for implementing policy is supposed to be devolved from headquarters to individual governors. In practice, however, this management structure signally failed to give the Prison Service greater freedom from political interference in the day-to-day running of prisons. The clearest illustration of this failure came in the wake of the security débâcle that culminated in the embarrassing prison escapes at Whitemoor Prison in 1994 and Parkhurst Prison in 1995 (see section 6.4, above). The Director General, Derek Lewis, swiftly found himself embroiled in an unseemly and unprecedented fracas with a politically embattled Home Secretary – Michael Howard – over who was responsible for the escapes. The extraordinary struggle culminated first in the removal of the Parkhurst prison governor, amid allegations that he was being made a scapegoat for policy failings at a higher level. This was followed, shortly afterwards, by the very public sacking of the Director General himself, who subsequently succeeded in his legal action against the Home Office for wrongful dismissal (Jenkins, 1995; Lewis, 1997: ch. 13). The whole episode achieved lasting notoriety thanks to a famous 1997 appearance by Michael Howard on BBC2's *Newsnight*, when Howard failed 14 times to answer a particular question from Jeremy Paxman.

Since the general election of 1997 the Prison Service has experienced further organizational upheaval accompanied by several changes of personnel. Agency status was confirmed in 1999 (HM Prison Service, 1999) following a quinquennial review. A new area structure was adopted in April 2000, which was based on the same geographical and operational boundaries as other criminal justice agencies such as the police and probation. Subsequently, and much more fundamentally, the NOMS has been set up, as we saw in Chapter 5. The effect of this change was to incorporate the prison and probation services within a unified service under the direction of a single Chief Executive, the National Offender Manager, who is accountable to ministers for punishing offenders and reducing reoffending. In Chapter 5 we discussed this new system in terms of its implications for the non-custodial treatment of offenders. What does it mean for the running of the prison system?

At first glance the NOMS structure (which had been proposed by the 2003 Carter Report) appeared to address the concerns of those who had called for a statutory separation of the Prison Service from the Home Office whereby operational responsibility would be devolved from Whitehall control to a completely independent agency. Advocates of such an approach included official government reports on the management of the Prison Service (Laming, 2000), the former Director General of the Prison Service, Derek Lewis (1996), and the former Chief Inspector of Prisons, David Ramsbotham (2005). Likewise the appointment of ten Regional Offender Managers appears to meet the concerns of these and other critics who have complained of an over-centralized Prison Service that would benefit from the delegation of specific responsibilities to more manageable geographical areas.

On closer inspection, however, the way the changes were implemented is disappointing for those wishing for a systemic break with the past. One problem concerns the personnel and occupational background of those who were appointed to oversee the reforms. Following the sacking of Derek Lewis, who was the first external appointment to the post of Director General, Richard Tilt became the first former prison governor to occupy the post. In 1999 he was succeeded by Martin Narey, a former career civil servant from the Home Office, initially as Director General and subsequently as the first Chief Executive of the newly established NOMS. Alison Liebling has described this development as a clear break from the 'independent chief executive' model and a reversion to Whitehall control (Liebling and Arnold, 2004: 33). By this stage it had also become clear that, although the Carter Report was originally commissioned by the Prime Minister as well as the Home Secretary, responsibility for its implementation had been very firmly wrested back by the Home Office (Ramsbotham, 2005: 256ff). Instead of publishing the report and allowing adequate time for consultations before responding to the recommendations, the Home Office preferred instead to issue its own blueprint for change simultaneously with the Carter Report itself. Such precipitate haste, combined with a reluctance to involve others in the reform process, heightened suspicions that the Home Office was more concerned with fending off perceived threats to its fiefdom than engaging in a dispassionate review of the most appropriate way of organizing and administering the Prison Service.

At the heart of this saga is a still unresolved debate over the appropriate constitutional relationship between the politicians who are responsible for formulating the overall direction of prison policy and those officials who are charged with implementing that policy. At present the doctrine of ministerial responsibility perpetuates the constitutional fiction that the Secretary of State (now the Justice rather than the Home Secretary) is responsible for everything that goes on within the department. The sad reality, as Derek Lewis (1996: 10) found to his cost, is that ministers continue to wield authority without responsibility, while the Prison Service has responsibility without authority. In principle, it should be possible to reformulate the doctrine of ministerial responsibility so that prison officials are made directly accountable for clearly defined operational matters while ministers are held responsible for their policy decisions, which include the allocation of resources (Lodge and Rogers, 2006). In its present unreformed state, however, the doctrine of ministerial responsibility remains a deeply flawed mechanism for securing the accountability of those whose actions and policies contribute to or exacerbate the continuing crises within the prison system: there is still no adequate safeguard against ministerial meddling. But this is far from being the only source of the managerial crisis within the prison system.

A second important aspect of the managerial crisis relates to very general, indeed all-pervading changes in the conduct of prison management *within* the prison system during the post-war era. Ditchfield (1990: 147–52) has characterized this in terms of a shift in the source of authority from a highly personalized form of power to a 'bureaucratic-lawful' model (Barak-Galanz, 1981), in which authority is increasingly derived from a more bureaucratic system of general rules and regulations. Particularly since the late 1980s, this transition has come to be associated with the approach known as *managerialism*, whereby the management of organizations is conducted with reference to the need for strategic planning, performance targets, efficiency and value for money (McEvoy, 2001: 254–8). More specifically it has been closely linked with the New Public Management approach (see Chapter 1) which regards the private sector as the repository of all managerial wisdom and efficiency. The appointment of Derek Lewis – a private business executive with no experience of prisons – as Director General of the Prison Service in 1993 greatly accelerated the move towards a more managerialist style of prison governance. His tenure was associated with the introduction of the Prison Service's first corporate plan that set out its aims over a three-year period, together with a business plan that focused on the programme of activities planned over the next 12 months (Coyle, 2005: 48). Two of the most distinctive techniques associated with managerialism involve the setting of targets for an organization and regular monitoring of its performance as a means of prompting compliance. The Prison Service currently has 14 KPIs or targets with which it is expected to comply. These cover a variety of measures including reoffending, prison escapes, drug use, overcrowding, self-inflicted deaths, race equality measures, staff sickness rates and resettlement measures (see Ministry of Justice, 2012i for current performance as measured by these targets).

This rush to embrace these managerialist techniques has not been universally welcomed even though the substitution of written instructions and rules for personal supervision and leadership was evident long before the onset of managerialism. One of the fiercest criticisms in the Learmont Report (1995) on the escape from Parkhurst Prison was reserved for the avalanche of instructions and communications received daily from prison headquarters. Learmont estimated that, if extrapolated to all prisons for the length of the enquiry, they would amount to 47 tons of paper that would produce a pile almost a mile high or 800 feet higher than Ben Nevis.

Coyle (2005: 4) has pointed out that one of the distinguishing features of managerialism is its emphasis on process and the way things are done (outputs) rather than on outcomes and what is being achieved. This is often linked to the criticism that managerialism tends to concentrate somewhat arbitrarily on those measures that can easily be *counted* rather than those things that *ought to count* in strategic terms. Another problem with the use of targets is that those who are subject to them may become more adept at demonstrating that they have met the target than in improving the performance the target is intended to measure. This is an example of a phenomenon sometimes referred to as Goodhart's Law which states, in effect, that once a measure becomes a target, it ceases to be a useful measure. From a more theoretical perspective Sennett's (1998) telling critique argues that an emphasis on shallow, short-term flexible output measures may have a corrosive effect on deeper civic values such as trust, loyalty and commitment, to the detriment of individuals and, ultimately also, the organizations for which they work.

A third important aspect of the managerial crisis concerns the extremely poor industrial relations record of the prison system. Repeatedly, attempts by prison management to introduce changes that are perceived by the workforce to adversely affect their conditions of employment have been met by a willingness to resort to strikes and other forms of militant industrial action. Obduracy on the part of Prison Service managers may be partly responsible, but much of the blame for this state of affairs has also been ascribed to the POA, which is widely portrayed as one of the last bastions of 'unreconstructed Trades Unionism' (Ramsbotham, 2005: 232; see also Laming, 2000). In 1994, the Conservative government of the day sought to resolve the problem by withdrawing the right to take strike action (Criminal Justice and Public Order Act 1994, section 127), but this caused considerable resentment on the part of the POA and, if anything, worsened the already bleak industrial relations climate. In 2004, the Labour government lifted the strike ban[4] in return for a voluntary industrial relations protocol that amounted to a virtual 'no strike' agreement since it obliged the union to give 12 months' notice of a strike. However, in September 2006 the POA, having rejected a salary increase proposed

---

[4]By the Regulatory Reform (Prison Officers) (Industrial Action) Order 2005 (SI 2005/908).

by the Prison Service Pay Review Body, voted for strike action which was only averted at the last moment. Clearly there is still no obvious solution in sight to the continuing problem of prison staff unrest.

A fourth and final aspect of the managerial crisis within the prison system concerns the state of relations between prison officers and inmates. Since this forms part of a wider crisis of authority and control, however, we will return to this issue once we have dealt with the separate crises of security, prison numbers and conditions. What might be the impact of prison privatization on the managerial crisis? It encouraged another major structural reorganization of the correctional services (NOMS) partly designed to facilitate the extension of a mixed economy 'contract culture' to other parts of the system. This, however, has led to further fragmentation of the Prison Service. The presence of semi-autonomous private prisons can only make strategic planning more difficult. And the relationship between prison service management and public sector prison staff has been exacerbated as a result of the different pay and conditions between public sector and private prisons; public sector prison staff are anxious about their jobs and associated benefits, which has contributed to a loss of morale and increased industrial unrest. So it would be fair to conclude that the advent of prison privatization has had an adverse impact.

The Crises of Containment and Security

An important task of any prison system is to hold prisoners securely, and one important aspect of this is *containment* – preventing them from escaping. The record of the English prison system in this respect has been uneven, and is punctuated by periodic panics over prison security. The first major **crisis of containment** in the post-war English penal system occurred in the mid-1960s. Until then, security considerations had been low on the prison authorities' agenda. However, this was already beginning to change as a result of changes in the composition of the prison population, due mainly to an increased willingness on the part of judges to pass very long terms of imprisonment for some offences they regarded as particularly serious. Growing official concern over security was brought to a head by a succession of highly publicized escapes including two of the Great Train Robbers (Charlie Wilson in 1964, and Ronnie Biggs in 1965) and the spy George Blake in October 1966 – all of whom were serving unprecedentedly long sentences. But this was only the most visible tip of a steadily growing iceberg as the escape rate had been steadily increasing ever since the turn of the century (Thomas and Pooley, 1980: 32). With the appointment of Lord Mountbatten to inquire into prison security in 1966, the crisis of containment moved to the top of the political agenda. The responses adopted in the wake of Mountbatten's report did much to shape the prison system of today, with continuing repercussions for the contemporary penal crisis.

The Mountbatten Report (Home Office, 1966) identified a number of weaknesses, both in the physical security of prisons and in the way they were administered. One recommendation which was immediately adopted was to categorize convicted prisoners according to their security risk on reception into prison, and to use this categorization when determining the type of institution to which they are ultimately allocated. As a result of this change, all other aims (including those of training and treatment, preparation for release and the maintenance of internal control) were subordinated at a stroke to the requirements of security. Under Mountbatten's classification system – which with certain refinements remains with us today – there are four security categories:

Category A consists of 'those whose escape would be highly dangerous to the public or the police or to the security of the state'.[5] Such inmates are invariably housed in maximum security conditions.

In Category B are 'those prisoners for whom the very highest conditions of security are not necessary, but for whom escape must be made very difficult'. Such inmates are likely to be housed in closed but not necessarily maximum security conditions.

Category C comprises 'prisoners who cannot be trusted in open conditions, but who do not have the ability or resources to make a determined escape bid'.

In Category D inmates are 'those who can reasonably be entrusted to serve their sentences in open conditions' where there is little physical security. (All those held in open prisons have to be in Category D, although they account for less than 10 per cent of the total prison population.)

In terms of physical security, Mountbatten believed that existing prisons were sadly deficient, and so he proposed that one new, 'escape-proof' top-security prison should be built on the Isle of Wight to house *all* Category A prisoners in 'as liberal and constructive a régime as possible'. This 'concentration policy', as it was dubbed, would have allowed lower security conditions to prevail throughout the rest of the prison system. Ultimately Mountbatten's proposal was rejected, however, partly because of fears that *control* would be difficult in a 'fortress prison' populated by many of the country's most desperate and difficult inmates. It was also feared that the regime would inevitably become repressive, despite Mountbatten's hopes for a liberal approach. There were also concerns over the problems posed by other inmates who, while they may not pose a threat to security, are nevertheless highly disruptive and present a challenge to the maintenance of order in the wider prison system (Coyle, 2005: 141).

In the end a compromise policy was adopted, which is still in operation, suggested by the Advisory Council on the Penal System (1968). This sought to

---

[5]Category A status is the only one that can apply to all types of prisoners, whether male, female, juvenile, sentenced or remand. Following a helicopter escape from Gartree in 1988, Category A prisoners are now assigned to one of three further sub-categories: 'standard risk', 'high risk' or 'exceptional risk'. In addition, prisoners who either have escaped, or have attempted to, or who are believed to be planning to escape may be placed on a supplementary 'Escape' or 'E List', which will also affect the kind of prison in which they may be held (Fitzgerald and Sim, 1982: 46; Adams, 1994: 151; Creighton and King, 2000: 55).

dilute the anticipated control problem by spreading the high security risk prisoners among a small number of prisons and subjecting them to the same regime as the lower security (Category B) inmates with whom they would be housed. Although this strategy came to be known as the 'dispersal policy', this is something of a misnomer as it entails a considerable degree of concentration within a few establishments – formerly called 'dispersal prisons' but now known as high security prisons, of which there are officially eight: Belmarsh, Frankland, Full Sutton, Long Lartin, Manchester, Wakefield, Whitemoor and Woodhill. It also involved a drastic (and expensive) upgrading of the security arrangements in these prisons despite the fact that many of their inmates were designated Category B. However, its most pervasive and, in many respects, most detrimental impact was on the configuration of the overall prison estate, which became divided into several different types of penal establishments, each designated for a different category of inmate. This not only distorted the amount of money spent on the different types of prisons, but also rendered them much less flexible in the way they are used, particularly during periods of overcrowding (see under next heading).

Within the high security prisons themselves, the arrangements designed for a relatively small number of Category A prisoners (such as double security fences, geophonic alarms, high-mast floodlighting and dog patrols) result in a much more restrictive and custodial regime for the majority of prisoners who do not present a security risk. King and Morgan (1980: 74) have described how, following the introduction of dispersal prisons, security considerations permeated inwards from external defences to focus on internal buildings and even the regime itself. As a result, surveillance was increased by the installation of closed-circuit television, freedom of movement and time spent on association were drastically curtailed, and communal dining was phased out in favour of solitary meals provided in cells. Although the effects were experienced most intensely within the dispersal prisons themselves, the rest of the prison system was not immune from the growing security syndrome. Perimeter security was strengthened throughout the closed prison system even if the level of paranoia was not quite so acute. And all establishments were affected indirectly, first by the considerable diversion of resources required to upgrade security at the dispersal prisons; and second, as we shall see, by a policy of avoiding overcrowding and under-manning within the dispersal system, thus concentrating these problems in other prisons.

As we have seen, Lord Woolf spoke in his report of the need to maintain a proper balance between security, control and justice in the prisons. In particular he warned (Woolf and Tumim, 1991: para. 9.40) that excessive security and control would be counter-productive since they would foster genuine grievances and a sense of oppression. Unfortunately, these warnings went unheeded almost from the outset. The Woolf Report was published in February 1991; by the summer, security concerns were once again in the ascendancy following the escape of two IRA suspects from Brixton Prison.

In the ensuing White Paper, *Custody, Care and Justice* (Home Office, 1991) the government's sense of priorities was starkly reflected in the adoption (in effect) of a two-speed approach on implementing the Woolf proposals. In the fast lane was, most conspicuously, a package of measures to improve security and control including the introduction of annual security audits and the installation of X-ray machines and metal detectors in the entrances to maximum security prisons. These were to be given first claim on the Prison Service's budget and were accompanied by the introduction (in the Prison Security Act 1992) of a new offence of prison mutiny, and increased penalties for those convicted of assisting prison escapers. In the slow lane – to be implemented only over a timescale of 20 to 25 years, and then only out of existing resources – were many of the reforms to which Woolf had attached particular importance (to be discussed shortly).

Then, almost exactly 30 years after its emergence as a paramount policy concern, the crisis of containment returned to the top of the political agenda during the mid-1990s following the series of highly embarrassing security lapses that we described in section 6.4 above. The government's predictable response was to set up an inquiry, headed by Sir John Learmont (1995), who was asked to undertake a general review of prison security. Like his predecessor Lord Mountbatten, Learmont called for a new system of prisoners' classification, this time to be based on six separate security categories. The sense of penological *déjà vu* was heightened by a reopening of the 'concentration versus dispersal' policy debate (Penal Affairs Consortium, 1995b). Learmont doubted whether dispersal prisons could meet the requirements of the next century even after upgrading. He therefore proposed a single new high security prison (a so-called 'super-max' prison) for the estimated 200 or so prisoners who would be assigned to his proposed new categories 1 ('exceptional security risk' inmates) or 2 ('high security risk' inmates). The parallels with Mountbatten did not stop there, for Learmont also favoured a 'purposeful training régime', at least for the high security prison, offering a wide range of facilities.

In the end the government decided not to proceed with Learmont's proposal for a single 'super-max' high security prison. However, it did implement most of his other recommendations (118 out of 127), once again highlighting the continuing overwhelming influence of security on prison policy at the expense of justice and humanity. Inmates who are identified as constituting an 'exceptional escape risk' are currently held in two Special Security Units (SSUs) located in Belmarsh and Whitemoor Prisons, which are effectively prisons within a prison. Within the SSU they are held in small group isolation in conditions that were described as 'cramped' and 'claustrophobic' by a former Chief Medical Officer; and are denied many of the basic rights to which other prisoners are entitled including access to the library, gymnasium and chapel. They are also subjected to 'closed' visits in which the inmate sits behind a glass barrier and communicates via a telephone or grill and, despite such intensive security, are also subjected to strip-searches before and after every visit, supplemented by occasional even more intimate (and humiliating) 'squat' searches. Human rights organizations (for example, Amnesty International, 1997) have complained that such conditions constitute cruel, inhuman or degrading treatment, and the government's own inquiry, carried out in 1996, concluded that conditions in the SSUs could lead to mental illness (see Creighton and King, 2000: 44). Similar concerns were echoed more recently by the Council of Europe's Committee for the Prevention of Torture and Inhuman or Degrading Treatment (CPT, 2006) following an inspection of the treatment of terror suspects and detainees awaiting deportation in a number of prisons including Belmarsh, Full Sutton and Long Lartin. The unremitting emphasis on security at the expense of humanity in the Learmont Report was roundly condemned by the former Chief Inspector of Prisons Judge Stephen Tumim, who described it as 'the road to the concentration camp' (*Guardian*, 28 October 1995).

As for the crisis of containment itself, the Prison Service regularly claims to have successfully abated it; only two Category A prisoners have escaped since 1995 (in 2001 and 2012), and these were escapes from prison escorts rather than from inside prison itself. It has also met its performance target of ensuring that the overall escape rate is lower than 0.05 per cent of the average prison population (Ministry of Justice, 2012i); the overall escape rate is broadly comparable for both public and private prisons. However, this success has come at a considerable price, as we have seen, that has to be measured not only financially but also in terms of the impoverishment inflicted on prison regimes and consequent hardships experienced by prison inmates throughout the system. Moreover the escape statistics only provide part of a much bigger picture. For in addition to its responsibility to keep prison inmates locked up, the Prison Service also has a duty to keep them secure in the sense of keeping them *safe*; measured against this broader yardstick its performance is far less impressive and continues to give rise to serious concern.

One disturbing barometer of the Prison Service's continuing failure to keep prison inmates safe is the rate of self-inflicted deaths by prisoners, which doubled during the 1970s, and doubled again in the 1980s (Shaw, 1992a: 162; see also Scott and Codd, 2010: ch. 6). The trend continued during the 1990s and the 76 prison suicides recorded in 1998 were more than twice those recorded in 1982. Since then both the number of self-inflicted deaths among prison inmates and also the rate of suicides per 100,000 prisoners have fluctuated. In 2011 a total of 57 self-inflicted deaths were recorded (with another 20 still unclassified). The highest rate of prison suicides per 100,000 inmates was 140 in 1999. Compared with the general population, adult male prisoners are five times more likely to kill themselves, but boys aged 15–17 are 18 times more likely to do so than those living in the community (Fazel et al., 2005; cited in Prison Reform Trust, 2006b: 11). Even allowing for their generally adverse psychiatric profile (see section 6.3 above), this is unacceptably high.

Suicides are disproportionately high among remand inmates, who account for more than half the annual total even though they make up barely a fifth of the prison population (Howard League for Penal Reform, 2005). Not surprisingly local prisons, which house most remand prisoners, have the highest rate of prison suicides of any category in prison. Suicide rates are also disproportionately high among young prisoners, mentally disordered prisoners and those beginning very long sentences (Prison Reform Trust, 1997). Prison suicides are believed (see Liebling, 1992; Liebling and Krarup, 1993; Crighton and Towl, 1997; Liebling, 1997) to result from an interaction between a number of factors. They include a pre-custodial history of vulnerability, such as anxiety or depression; background stress factors, such as bullying; and situational triggers, such as changes of location or missed visits (see below). Compared with the general population, however, prison inmates who commit suicide are far *less* likely to have had a history of psychiatric illness or treatment (Liebling, 1997).

Alison Liebling has intriguingly sought to account for the fluctuating suicide statistics during the period 1995 and 2002 by postulating an inverse relationship between prison suicide rates and variables that purport to reflect levels of respect, humanity and the strength of staff–inmate relationships (Liebling and Arnold, 2004: 48). This period encompasses the era characterized by the security and control agenda (1995–99; see section 6.4, above), during which prison suicide rates rocketed to unprecedented levels (peaking at 140 per 100,000, as we have seen). It also embraces the era characterized by the decency agenda (1999–2002), during which suicide rates fell sharply back. She then hypothesizes that since 2002 the relentless pressure of prison numbers and consequent overcrowding has swamped the humanizing tendencies and thus helps to account for the resurgence in the prison suicide rate during 2003 and 2004. However, the sharp decline in the suicide rate during 2005 and its stability during 2010 and 2011 suggests that there may be other factors at work. One possibility is that, somewhat paradoxically, the doubling up of cell occupancy in response to worsening overcrowding may afford some protection for vulnerable inmates by ensuring closer levels of informal monitoring by cellmates.[6]

The problem of prison suicides has long been recognized (HM Chief Inspector of Prisons, 1990a), and a programme of suicide prevention measures was introduced in 1994. In 2004–5 the Prison Service set itself the target of reducing the suicide rate to below 112.8 per 100,000; in 2011–12 it was 70 per 100,000 – an improvement but still unacceptably high.

Another barometer of the Prison Service's continuing failure to keep prison inmates safe and secure relates to the level of violence that inmates experience at the hands of their fellow prisoners. It is very difficult to assess the scale of this particular problem since the statistics compiled by the Prison Service for official purposes (especially with regard to the rate of compliance with key performance indicators) are likely to under record the true incidence rate. In one survey covering two adult male prisons and two male young offender institutions in 1994–95 victimization of inmates was found to be pervasive (O'Donnell and Edgar, 1996 and 1998; see also Edgar et al., 2003). No fewer than 46 per cent of young offenders and 30 per cent of adult offenders reported that they had been either assaulted, robbed or threatened with violence in the preceding *month*, though most reported that they felt safe most of the time in spite of this very high level of victimization.

---

[6]However, there are also dangers with such a policy if care is not taken to assess the compatibility of inmates before forcing them to share the claustrophobic conditions of a single cell. They are graphically illustrated by the tragic deaths of Christopher Edwards at the hands of a mentally disturbed cell mate (see note 13 below), and of Zahid Mubarek at the hands of a violent racist cell mate (see Chapter 8, section 8.1).

There is a relatively high level of assaults in private prisons compared with their public sector counterparts. An early study conducted by the House of Commons Home Affairs Committee (1997) reported a significantly higher rate of assaults in all of the private prisons operating at the time compared with newly opened public sector prisons. Likewise, in 2001–2 no fewer than five out of seven PFI prisons had assault rates in the upper quartile for their category of prison (National Audit Office, 2003: Figure 14). In 2003–4 six out of nine private prisons failed to meet their targets on the number of serious assaults recorded against prisoners or staff expressed as a proportion of the prison population. Moreover, three of them – Dovegate, Parc and Wolds – were among the highest of any English prison (Prison Reform Trust, 2005: 9). Low staffing levels and inexperienced staff are likely to be two of the contributory factors giving rise to such a consistently poor performance.

One private prison that has given rise to particular concern recently is Rye Hill, which was inspected in July 2005. The report noted that 'the prison had deteriorated to the extent that we considered that it was at that time an unsafe and unstable environment, both for prisoners and staff' (HM Chief Inspector of Prisons, 2005a: 5). In this instance the problems were specifically attributed to low staffing levels and a 40 per cent turnover of staff. A few months earlier one inmate was stabbed to death by fellow inmates; and in a separate incident five staff members were suspended and one arrested on suspicion of supplying controlled drugs after another inmate was found dead in his cell (*Guardian*, 20 April 2005). A further report by the Chief Inspector of Prisons on Rye Hill, published in 2007, found it still to be 'fundamentally fragile' two years after the previous report and suggested sending in a team of experienced managers from the public sector for a temporary period.

The Prison Numbers Crisis and the Problem of Overcrowding

Compared with the crisis of security, the ongoing prison numbers crisis – and the related problem of overcrowding – may appear less dramatic. However, it is just as insidious in terms of its impact both on the development of prison policy and also on the lives of inmates. Prison overcrowding is predominantly a post-war phenomenon and follows a sustained period of surplus capacity between 1908 and 1938, during which period the average daily prison population was halved from 22,000 to 11,000 and some 25 prisons were closed (Rutherford, 1986b: 130–1). The period since the war has been one of almost relentless expansion, however (see Table 1.1 in Chapter 1), and even though periodic attempts have been made to expand the size of the prison estate, for most of the time these have been insufficient to stave off serious overcrowding in the system. As we mentioned previously, 20,000 additional prison places were created between 1997 and 2006, yet 2006 saw the prisons yet again bursting at the seams and this situation has continued.

Unable to keep pace with the relentless growth in the size of the prison population the Prison Service has been obliged to resort to overcrowding on a massive scale, though the official measures it uses mask the true extent of the problem. The most objective measure of overcrowding is with reference to the occupancy level for which prison cells were initially designed, which in the vast majority of cases is a single inmate. Measured in this way, over 20,000 prisoners – a quarter of the prison population – are currently being held in overcrowded conditions.

Traditionally, however, the Prison Service uses a looser definition of overcrowding based on the number of prisoners for whom government-appointed inspectors in consultation with prison authorities certify that each prison has adequate space, even though many prisoners may be sharing accommodation designed for a single inmate. This figure – the **certified normal accommodation (CNA)** – is potentially flexible since there is nothing to stop the CNA being revised upwards by determining that single occupancy cells are, in fact, capable of holding two inmates, as indeed happened during the 1990s when the pressure on prison accommodation became more acute (Coyle, 2005: 108). Thus, by a stroke of the pen a substantial degree of overcrowding was built in to the system. Additionally, a second official measure of overcrowding has been introduced, based on a higher figure than the CNA – the operational capacity of the system. The operational capacity is defined as the maximum number of inmates the prison system can hold after allowing for a safe level of overcrowding. Not all cell accommodation is useable, however. Some spare capacity is required to accommodate receptions and transfers, and also to allow for the fact that some cell accommodation may only be available for particular categories of inmates: determined by gender, age, security categorization, criminal justice status (convicted or remand) or geographical location. The Prison Service has determined that it requires an operating margin of 1,700 places in order to allow for this unavoidable inflexibility within the system. This figure is subtracted from the total number of spaces available to provide the useable operational capacity – or the bust limit as it is informally known – beyond which even the Prison Service accepts that it is operating beyond its safe capacity level. (The European Committee for the Prevention of Torture (CPT, 2005: para. 20) has criticized the Prison Service for the way it defined the system's useable operational capacity.) This bust limit was actually exceeded in April 2004.

On 22 September 2006 the useable operational capacity was 79,968 at a time when the total prison population stood at 79,285 (NOMS, 2006), prompting a frantic quest for emergency solutions to the problem. Measures considered included plans (seemingly vetoed by the Prime Minister – *Times Online*, 31 August 2006) to make emergency use of existing powers of administrative release for short sentence prisoners (*Guardian*, 6 July 2006), and to convert other accommodation including a disused army barracks near Dover (a plan abandoned in November 2006) and a wing of Ashworth secure hospital in Merseyside into prison cells (*Guardian*, 20 September, 2006). In October 2006 the government sought to commission new prison ships as temporary holding accommodation, a practice which had been discontinued since the decommissioning of HMS Weare in August 2005 (*Observer*, 22 October 2006), and implemented emergency measures to use police cells to house prisoners (*Guardian*, 21 October 2006). Nevertheless, the bust limit was again exceeded in February 2008. Since then, the need for desperate emergency measures has receded somewhat as new prisons have been built. However, in July 2012 the prisons were holding nearly 7,300 more inmates than they were designed for with almost 60 per cent of prisons overcrowded and almost one-quarter of inmates either doubling up in single cells or held three to a cell designed for two (*Guardian* 28 August 2012). Private prisons have not alleviated the overcrowding issue: according to the Prison Reform Trust private prisons have held a higher percentage of their inmates in overcrowded accommodation than public sector prisons every year for the 13 years to 2010/11; indeed at one private prison (Doncaster) two-person cells have been turned into three-person cells by making one prisoner sleep in the shared toilet (*Society Guardian*, 22 July 2008).

Faced with these difficulties, it now seems almost incredible that in 1991, during a brief period in which the prison population was steadily falling, Lord Woolf felt sufficiently confident to predict that prison overcrowding could soon become a 'thing of the past' (Woolf and Tumim, 1991: para. 1.189). Likewise, his call for each prison to be given a maximum occupancy level based on its CNA (para. 11.141) now seems fanciful. Instead, the drastic increase in the size of the prison population over the last few years has put paid to any prospect of an early end to the crisis of overcrowding – and the air of crisis management with which it is associated – at least for the foreseeable future.

The corrosive effects of prison overcrowding, and its impact on penal policy, continue to make themselves felt, however. It obviously has an adverse effect on living conditions (see next section), and results in restricted regimes since there is neither the space, facilities nor resources to provide inmates with a full range of training, work and educational opportunities when there are too many prisoners to cope with. Relations between staff and inmates can also be adversely affected in such circumstances. Moreover, overcrowding frequently results in the postponement of long-overdue and badly needed refurbishment programmes, thereby perpetuating squalor and dilapidation, even when it does not result in grossly inappropriate alternative accommodation being pressed into service, as has happened in the past and seems destined to happen again. Another consequence of overcrowding is the need to transfer prisoners around the system in the quest for available accommodation. This is not only highly disruptive to prisoners and their families but also contributes to the sense of bitterness and hostility which Woolf identified as a factor increasing the likelihood of reoffending on release (Woolf and Tumim, 1991: para. 10.27). Finally, the increase in tension and frustration caused by overcrowding is widely believed to aggravate the **crisis of control** (see below) by increasing the risk of disturbances, such as the riot at Strangeways in 1990.

The Crisis of Conditions

The present crisis of conditions comprises several elements that, individually and collectively, help to influence the quality of life of those living and working in the English prison system:

- first, the sheer wretchedness of the physical accommodation in which the great majority of prisoners are housed;

- second, the impoverished and repressive nature of the regimes to which most of them are routinely subjected; and

- third, the difficulties inmates experience in maintaining relationships with family and friends and sustaining links with the wider community to which they belong.

The accommodation in which prisoners are held is obviously a key element in the quality of life they experience. In recent decades the state of that accommodation in some parts of the prison system has become a byword for squalor, as reports by the Chief Inspector of Prisons have repeatedly testified; for example, in 2003 Wealstun Prison was condemned as unfit for human habitation (HM Chief Inspector of Prisons, 2003), as was a wing of Leeds Prison two years later (HM Chief Inspector of Prisons, 2005b). As Lord Woolf (1991: para. 10.19) observed, justice itself is compromised if prisoners are held in conditions that are 'inhumane or degrading, or are otherwise wholly inappropriate'. Perhaps the nadir for the Prison Service was a finding by the European Committee for the Prevention of Torture (CPT, 1991) that a number of features found in three English local prisons (Brixton, Wandsworth and Leeds) – including the overcrowding, lack of integral sanitation and inadequate regime activities – were inhuman and degrading.

For many years inmates' lack of access to integral toilet facilities symbolized the decrepit condition of much of the contemporary prison estate. Following its condemnation by the Woolf report, the government proudly proclaimed in April 1996 that the anachronistic practice of inmates 'slopping out' their overnight waste buckets was finally at an end, though even this belated announcement proved to be premature. Prison inspection reports confirmed in 2006 that female inmates at Bullwood Hall Prison in Essex were still routinely enduring the degrading practice. Meanwhile, the pressures of overcrowding are such that it is no longer possible for the Prison Service to guarantee continuous access to toilet facilities even in other parts of the English prison estate (HM Chief Inspector of Prisons, 2004). In Scotland the scale of the problem is even worse, and in 2004 a prisoner successfully sued the Scottish Ministers responsible for the Scottish Prison Service for breach of his human rights under Article 3 of the European Convention on Human Rights.

In any event, the introduction of integral sanitation has made only a limited improvement to prisoners' quality of life since it involved the installation of a toilet and wash basin in an already cramped cell measuring between six and eight square metres. As we have seen, this tiny space is frequently occupied by two inmates instead of the single occupant it was designed for. A lack of adequate screening round the toilet means that they not only lack privacy when using the cramped facilities but also have to eat their meals and sleep in the same unhygienic conditions (Shaw, 1992a: 169; HM Chief Inspector of Prisons, 2000a).

Basic guidelines for prison conditions and regimes are set out in the Council of Europe's European Prison Rules, first promulgated in 1973 and revised in

1987 and 2006. The European rules emphasize the importance of exercise and recreation and, in particular, recommend that prisoners should have the opportunity of at least one hour of exercise every day in the open air (Rule 27.1). However, these rules have no legal force in England. For many years English prisoners were indeed allowed out into the fresh air for an hour a day, although usually this just meant trudging around within the confines of a drab internal courtyard. But in 1998 even this minimum entitlement was withdrawn when a new order came into force which prescribed that prisoners should have daily exercise in the fresh air 'for such a period as may be reasonable in the circumstances' (Prison Service Order No. 4275, 1998). As a result it is now not unknown for outdoor exercise to be confined to just half an hour each day, a practice that drew sharp condemnation from the European Committee for the Prevention of Torture following its inspections in 2001 and 2003 (CPT, 2005).

As with so many other aspects of prison life, it is in the local prisons that the provision of facilities and constructive activities are particularly deplorable. They are the most overcrowded, holding on average 26 per cent more inmates than their certified normal accommodation (HM Chief Inspector of Prisons, 1999b). In July 2012 of the ten most overcrowded prisons in England and Wales – each with an occupancy rate of more than 150 per cent – seven were local (*Guardian*, 28 August 2012). Yet these same institutions house many prisoners on remand who are awaiting trial and who have not been found guilty of any offence. Logically, those still presumed innocent might expect better treatment than those proved guilty. But as the government's own Chief Inspector (HM Chief Inspector of Prisons, 2000a) has pointed out, the reality – despite all the evidence and repeated criticism – continues to defy this logic.

Deplorable as the physical conditions in most English prisons undoubtedly are, their effects on the inmates who have to endure them may be less damaging than the restrictive and repressive daily regimes to which many of them are routinely subjected.[7] Prison regimes are restrictive in many respects, but one of the most obvious of these is the serious lack of suitably constructive and purposive activities for inmates to engage in. European Prison Rule 25.1 states that '[t]he régime provided for all prisoners shall offer a balanced programme of activities'. In English prison parlance the term 'purposeful activity' is used to encompass time spent at work, in education, training or physical recreation or participating in programmes such as those designed to tackle offending behaviour. Time spent 'in association' – mixing with other inmates – is not included in the term. In general the performance of the Prison Service over many years with regard to providing inmates with a balanced and adequate programme of activities has been abysmal. In the current climate of gross and worsening overcrowding and cuts in budgets,

---

[7] As with prison conditions, it is impossible to generalize about English prison regimes since many operate constructive programmes that are delivered by committed and well-trained staff, while others are unrelentingly impoverished. Again, it tends to be the local prisons that suffer the worst forms of deprivation in terms of constructive activities, work or educational opportunities or even simply time spent out of the cell.

there is little or no realistic prospect of any improvement in this state of affairs at least for the foreseeable future.

Until 2004 the Prison Service did at least aim to provide a minimum level of purposeful activity even though the target it set itself was as woefully inadequate as it was purely aspirational. Until that date the key performance indicator for purposeful activity was an average of 24 hours per week, or just 3.4 hours per day, leaving the other 20.6 hours each day without any structured activity. Even this modest aspiration proved unattainable in seven out of the preceding eight years, however, whereupon the KPI itself was simply and summarily abandoned by the Prison Service in 2004, in a tacit admission of defeat. This episode also exposed the chronic limitations of a managerial culture that elevates the pursuit of whatever arbitrary, shifting and often meaningless targets it sets for itself over the need to identify, report and address the real challenges and impediments it faces.

With regard to work activities, Rule 26.2 of the European Prison Rules states that 'prison authorities shall strive to provide 'sufficient work of a useful nature'. Rule 26.7 states that 'the organisation and methods of work in the institutions shall resemble as closely as possible those of similar work in the community'. In reality, much of the work that has traditionally been provided in prison is dull, repetitive and demeaning, including as it does wing cleaning, maintenance and orderly work. Far from equipping prisoners with useful skills which might improve their prospects for employment on release, it seems only to reflect a narrow work ethic that approves of hard manual labour as an instrument of punishment in its own right. Some work is available in prison workshops that approximate more closely to the conditions experienced in workplaces in the community. However, they only employed around 10,000 prisoners (equating to 13 per cent of the total prison population) in 2003–4, each inmate working an average of 25 hours per week (House of Commons Home Affairs Committee, 2005: para. 143). Regrettably, the recent massive expansion in the size of the prison population has far outstripped the provision of workshop facilities. An internal review of prison industries concluded that it was 'indefensible that the Prison Service cannot find enough work or purposeful activity for prisoners' (Prison Industries Review Team, 2003). The low priority that both government and Prison Service have accorded to prison work schemes seems all the more remarkable in view of the importance that is attached to resettlement initiatives of various other kinds. The Coalition government aims to make prisons 'places of hard work and industry' (Ministry of Justice, 2010a: 14) where prisoners will be expected to work a full working week. But while the average number of prisoners working per month increased between 2010–11 and 2011–12 from 8,600 to 9,000 (Ministry of Justice, 2012g), a study by the Policy Exchange (2011) think-tank claimed that the average weekly hours worked per prisoner had dropped from 13.3 in 2005–6 to 11.8 in 2009–10. The desire to involve the private sector more in prison work may be laudable in principle, but the reports we mentioned previously that prisoners working in a call centre were being paid only £3 per day while other workers at the call centre had been fired do not inspire confidence. Given the level of budget cuts it is difficult to see how making prisons places of work can be achieved satisfactorily, given that at present only around 10 per cent of the prison population is engaged in purposeful work (even ignoring their abysmally low levels of pay).

On the subject of prison education, the European Prison Rules state that '[e]very prison shall seek to provide all prisoners with access to educational programmes which are as comprehensive as possible and which meet their individual needs while taking into account their aspirations' (Rule 28.1). Once again, however, the performance of the Prison Service in this respect has been decidedly mixed. In purely financial terms more money than ever before is now being spent on prison education, funding for which more than doubled from £47.5m in 1999–2000 to £122m in 2004–5 (House of Commons Education and Skills Committee, 2005). However, this major investment was preceded by more than a decade of chronic under-funding for prison education, and the average spending per prisoner on prison education of £1,185 in 2002–3 was less than half the amount spent on secondary school pupils per year (Braggins and Talbot, 2003). As for the content of prison education, considerable emphasis has been placed on the provision of basic skills such as literacy and numeracy. While it is true that very many inmates have extremely poor educational attainments (see section 6.3, above), this has skewed resources away from further and higher education programmes to the detriment of more able inmates (House of Commons Education and Skills Committee, 2005: para. 11). It also fails to take account of individual prisoners' needs and aspirations as enjoined by European Prison Rule 28.1.

A number of other fundamental failings in the prison education system have been highlighted in reports compiled by the Chief Inspector of Prisons (1999c) and the House of Commons Home Affairs Committee (2005). One persistent failing relates to the huge disparity in the level of investment in different categories of prisons and between individual prisons, which reflects a lack of unified prison education policy across the entire estate and results in disturbing variations in levels of access to education classes. A second shortcoming relates to the continual disruption of planned educational programmes, either as a result of inmates being moved to other establishments before completing a course, or because of alleged shortages of security staff for the purposes of supervision. A third problem relates to the narrowness of the core curriculum that is provided by the Prison Service.

Apart from the physical conditions and regimes within prisons, a third element that has an important bearing on the present crisis of conditions relates to the ease with which prisoners are able to sustain relationships with their families and communities. The European Prison Rules require prison authorities to assist prisoners in maintaining contact with the outside world and to provide them with the appropriate welfare support to do so (Rule 24.5). Inmates should be allowed to communicate as often as possible with families and others (Rule 24.1) and visits should be arranged in such a way as to allow prisoners to maintain family relationships in as normal a manner as possible (Rule 24.4). Unfortunately, the configuration and geographical location of the prison estate make it extremely difficult for family and community links to be sustained, while the relentless pressure of overcrowding causes further disruption and hardship for prison inmates and, more especially, their families.

At the end of February 2003, over 27,000 prisoners (more than one third of the prison population) were located over 50 miles from the town in which they were committed for trial, and 12,500 (more than one sixth) were held over 100 miles away (House of Commons Home Affairs Committee, 2005: para. 40). This inevitably causes major hardships for both inmates and their families, who are restricted to two-hourly visits in a general visiting room that is supervised by prison staff and monitored by high definition closed circuit television cameras. Unlike other countries, which allow private visits of longer duration in a manner that is more compatible with the right to family life enshrined in Article 8 of the European Convention on Human Rights, the British government has always resisted such arrangements (Coyle, 2005: 112). Moreover, the relentless pressure of prison numbers and associated problem of overcrowding has resulted in a massive increase in the number of prison transfers as prisoners are moved around the country in order to make full use of the limited space that is available. In 2003–4 there were over 100,000 prison transfers, compared with 60,000 in 2000–1 (House of Commons Home Affairs Committee, 2005: para. 40). This continual 'churn', as it is known, causes huge disruption not only for prison educational and rehabilitative programmes but also for the inmates and families whose lives are further disrupted.

One way of minimizing the inevitable dislocation of family and community ties would be to reconfigure the prison estate into a more flexible system of multi-functional community prisons, situated where possible close to the main centres of population. This would make it very much easier for most prisoners irrespective of their security classification to maintain close links with family and community, and thus assist in the process of reintegration on release. It would also have the advantage of reducing or even eliminating altogether the practice of regularly transferring inmates, often at short notice and frequently to distant parts of the country, thereby removing another major source of grievance for prison inmates. As we saw earlier (section 6.4), Lord Woolf advocated just such a system as a means of radically improving prison conditions. But although the idea was resurrected in early 2006, it would be impossible to achieve without a massive financial investment and, almost certainly, a significant reduction in the size of the prison population, neither of which seems likely at present.

Even if it proves impossible to overcome the geographical barriers thrown up by an inflexible prison estate there are other ways of enabling prisoners to maintain links with families by making it easier for them to communicate by telephone. Until recently most prisons allowed inmates to purchase phone cards for the purpose, but because this system was open to abuse (in the form of trafficking in phone cards) most prisons have now moved to a PIN number system. This allows inmates to call pre-specified numbers only by keying in their own unique PIN number, the cost of the calls being automatically deducted from money earned while working in prison. Although such facilities provide some compensation for the lack of social contact, this form of communication is not completely unfettered as prison officers are liable to listen in on some conversations, and some may be tape-recorded.

Interestingly, private prisons do seem to out-perform the public sector in regard to the crisis of conditions, but only slightly. Admittedly, most of the private prisons have been newly built so would be expected to provide better facilities and conditions than the older public sector prisons. In terms of the amount of time prisoners spend out of their cells and engaging in purposeful activity, private sector prisons have performed slightly better than their public sector counterparts. But there is evidence that over time, this slight edge diminishes, either because the private prisons' performance deteriorates or public sector performance improves.

In very general terms, the trend since the Woolf Report is that there have been some improvements in physical conditions, though the scope for further improvement is severely restricted by the continuing population pressure. There were some very significant deteriorations in prison regimes during the mid-1990s, as the Prison Service struggled to cope with a rapidly expanding prison population during a period of financial stringency and an officially endorsed policy of austerity towards inmates. Since 1997 there has been a significant investment in the development of more constructive prison regimes, with the aim of reducing the stubbornly high reconviction rates that are associated with the use of imprisonment. However, much of the emphasis has been on the introduction of specific high-profile treatment programmes in individual prisons rather than securing overall improvements in prison regimes as a whole. Some of the petty restrictions associated with the austerity regime of the mid-1990s, such as the blanket ban on televisions in cells, have also been relaxed. However, progress overall has been patchy to date, and it would be true to say that the crisis of conditions is still as intractable as ever. It is likely to remain so unless and until the fundamental problem of grossly excessive prison numbers is finally resolved. And yet the case for drastic improvement in prison conditions remains unanswerable not just on humanitarian grounds, but because it would also be likely to elicit a more positive attitude on the part of prisoners. It could even have a beneficial effect on the problem of control within the prisons, as we will argue in the next section.[8]

The Crises of Control and Authority

Prisons are coercive institutions, housing people who have little or no control over where they are allocated, how they spend their time, with whom they have to associate or the conditions in which they are kept. Many are resentful of their

---

[8]This appears to have been the case in France, for example, where a single improvement – the introduction of colour televisions in cells – has been credited with transforming both the attitudes of prisoners (by increasing their willingness to work, in order to pay for the hire of the sets) and also the problem of disorder (by helping to counter boredom and reduce the level of antagonism between inmates) (HM Chief Inspector of Prisons, 1990b). In England and Wales limited access to in-cell television is now available to certain prisoners as part of the Incentives and Earned Privileges Scheme (see below).

captive state, some have severe behavioural or personality problems and many feel aggrieved – often understandably and justifiably – about the way they are dealt with by basic grade officers and the prison authorities alike. Maintaining order and control in such an environment presents a massive challenge for everyone who is employed within the Prison Service and also for those who are responsible for prescribing the policies that will help to determine how this challenge is met. The scale of the challenge – devising firm and effective procedures that are also fair and humane – is daunting, and the persistent failure of the Prison Service over many years to rise to it has generated a pervasive and persistent crisis of control that is far from being resolved.

Prison riots are the most visible and spectacular symbols of a more deep-seated crisis of control within the prison system (although it should be acknowledged that despite overcrowding, poor conditions and transfers there have been relatively few prison riots in recent years). At a more mundane level the problem of disruptive behaviour poses a predictable – but equally intractable – problem for prison authorities. Having briefly examined prison riots and the competing explanations of their causes in Chapter 1, we are more concerned in this section with the issue of day-to-day control and the responses that have been developed for dealing with disruptive inmates. It is important to differentiate at the outset between the formal disciplinary system, which is used to deal with offences against prison discipline, and the informal control system, which affords a wide range of strategies for dealing with disruptive behaviour. As we shall see, both of these regulatory systems have all too often proved counter-productive in practice, and have diverted attention away from the need to improve the quality of the regimes themselves, the most important aspect of which is the state of relations between staff and inmates.

The formal prison disciplinary system

The disciplinary procedures to which prisoners are subject can substantially increase their period of captivity or worsen its conditions, and yet until recently they lacked many of the safeguards that are normally associated with judicial processes. Consequently, the prison disciplinary system was generally perceived by prisoners as operating in an arbitrary and unjust manner and has long been a focus for discontent on the part of inmates.

Before 1992 there was a two-tier system for adjudicating alleged disciplinary offences in which responsibility rested either with the prison governor or the prison Board of Visitors (the predecessors of Independent Monitoring Boards, see below), depending on the seriousness of the offence. Prison governors were responsible for carrying out a preliminary investigation into all cases, and also for dealing with the least serious of these (constituting the vast majority). More serious cases were adjudicated by the prison's Board of Visitors, but although these were nominally independent of the prison system, with many of their members being lay magistrates, they were generally viewed by prisoners as being not so much independent as part of the prison authority system. Both tiers exercised considerable disciplinary powers that were not matched by the kind of judicial safeguards available to those on trial for ordinary criminal offences, which heightened still further the suspicion felt by inmates (see Maguire et al., 1985; Prior, 1985: Appendix 11).

As part of its attempt to improve the standard of justice within prisons, the Woolf Report recommended that Boards of Visitors should no longer be involved in the adjudication of disciplinary proceedings, and that there should be a clear differentiation between disciplinary and criminal proceedings. These recommendations were implemented by the Prison (Amendment) Rules, 1992 (SI 1992/514). Under the reformed system, relatively minor disciplinary offences are dealt with by a governor or deputy governor, though their disciplinary powers were considerably enlarged. Currently (under the 2010 Prison Rules) the penalties they can impose include cautions, the forfeiture of privileges (for up to 42 days), exclusion from associated work or activities (21 days), stoppage of earnings (84 days), and cellular confinement (for up to 21 days). However, they are expected to refer to the police more serious forms of indiscipline (such as assault or possession of drugs) that constitute offences under the ordinary criminal law as opposed to more minor infractions of the prison disciplinary rules. The most severe punishment which may be imposed is the award of 'additional days', in other words delaying the prisoner's potential release date (explained further in Chapter 7, section 7.2). If the governor decides that the offence is so serious that additional days (up to a maximum of 42) may be imposed, then an independent adjudicator hears the case and the prisoner is entitled to legal representation.

In 2009 there were 104,745 offences against prison discipline, which yields a rate of 125 offences per 100 prisoners compared with 161 offences per 100 prisoners a decade earlier (Ministry of Justice, 2010c: Tables 8.3 and 8.1). The commonest offences were disobedience or disrespect, unauthorized transactions/possessions (drug offences and possession of unauthorized articles) and violence (fights and assaults) (Table 8.3). The most frequently imposed punishments were forfeiture of privileges (7 per cent of the total), stoppage or reduction of earnings (29 per cent), cellular confinement (13 per cent) and the imposition of additional days (6 per cent) (Table 8.3).

Another major complaint about the prison disciplinary system used to be that it lacked any appeal to an outside body. The only appeal procedure involved an application to Prison Service Headquarters for determination by an Area Manager, but the success rate for such actions was less than 10 per cent (Livingstone and Owen, 1993: 203). However, in 1994 a **Prisons Ombudsman** (see below under 'crisis of accountability') was appointed following a recommendation to that effect by Lord Woolf. The Prisons Ombudsman is available as a final avenue of appeal against disciplinary findings, but only after all internal appeal procedures have been exhausted. Moreover, the Ombudsman is heavily dependent on information provided by prison staff in reaching a decision. It is still hard to say how far the existence of the Prisons Ombudsman has managed to assuage inmates' concerns about the fairness of the prison disciplinary system.

The three principal informal methods of exerting control over inmates who are perceived to be disruptive involve the use of physical force or restraint, segregation and transfer. In the past, punishment or repression based on the use of physical force was the standard response for those who resisted good order and discipline in prisons. The official punishments of flogging and birching fell into disuse after 1962, and corporal punishment was formally abolished in 1967 (Thomas, 1972: 201). However, the tradition of exercising control by force lives on in a variety of other ways.

The use of force has frequently been authorized, albeit often clandestinely, as a means of coping with prison disorder. As long ago as 1931 a mutiny in Dartmoor Prison was suppressed by prison officers backed up by armed police (Coyle, 2005: 32 and 149). During the prison riots of the 1970s specially trained prison staff (known as the MUFTI – Minimum Use of Force Tactical Intervention – squad) served as in-house riot squads to quell disorder in a number of prisons including Gartree in 1978 and also at Hull, Styal and Wormwood Scrubs in 1979. It later emerged that no fewer than 54 prison inmates had sustained injuries at the hands of the squad during the incident at Wormwood Scrubs (Thomas and Pooley, 1980: 136; Adams, 1994: 180).

When the dispersal system was adopted, it was erroneously assumed that the problem of control was just another aspect of the security problem, and that the most disruptive prisoners would be the high security inmates and vice versa (King and Elliott, 1977; King and Morgan, 1980; King, 1985; Adams, 1994: 181).[9] Not only was this assumption soon to be disproved, but it also became apparent that the relatively relaxed regimes and undifferentiated interior space associated with the dispersal prisons posed enormous control problems within their high security perimeters. When, almost from the outset, the dispersal prisons began to experience serious control problems, prison authorities resorted to a combination of physical force, segregation and reallocation, none of which was conspicuously successful in averting or even quelling disorder.

Use of force is currently allowed under Rule 47 of the 2010 Prison Rules, which prescribe that it should not be used unnecessarily, and then only as much as is necessary. Where it is necessary, any means of restraint used 'shall be of a pattern authorised by the Secretary of State' (Rule 49(7)). Although the control and restraint manuals that have been issued by the Prison Service are classified, the techniques are said to be based on the martial art known as Aikido (Leech, 1995: 264; see also Coyle, 2005: 151 for a detailed account of the techniques used). Serious disturbances are likely to be dealt with by specially trained 'incident control teams' comprising negotiators and specialist control and restraint staff (Coyle, 2005: 152). Other less sophisticated forms of physical restraint have also been used routinely in the recent past, including bodybelts, ratchet handcuffs, staves and batons.

In addition to these approved methods of force and physical restraint, prison staff are frequently alleged (Boyle, 1977: 174; Scraton et al., 1991: 19ff), and

---

[9]Even Category C prisons experience control problems. See Marshall (1997) for a study of the methods used to deal with these.

sometimes proved, to resort unofficially to unapproved and unlawful methods, including deliberate assaults or the use of excessive force in restraining trouble-some inmates. For many years it was exceedingly rare for allegations of flagrant brutality on the part of prison officers to receive any official confirmation, so impenetrable was the shroud of secrecy surrounding the prison system. And even when this veil of concealment was occasionally pierced, those responsible were unlikely to be made fully accountable, or even identified. For example, following a disturbance at Hull Prison in 1976 several prison officers were ultimately con-victed of conspiring to assault and beat prisoners but escaped prison sentences. Then in 1992 an inquest jury returned a verdict of unlawful killing on Barry Prosser, an inmate at Winson Green Prison, who was kicked to death by the staff who were being paid to look after him (Coggan and Walker, 1982). So powerful was the conspiracy of silence, however, that no one was convicted for his death despite the jury's verdict (Scraton et al., 1991: 133).

More recently, however, allegations of continuing staff brutality have received incontrovertible confirmation from several authoritative official sources, although the problem of holding those responsible to account remains as intractable as ever. In 1996 the Chief Inspector of Prisons expressed his disquiet over allegations concerning the illegal use of force against inmates in the segregation unit at Wormwood Scrubs, a prison he memorably described as a 'flagship dead in the water' (Ramsbotham, 2005: 104). Just over two years later a second, even more damning, report was published (HM Chief Inspector of Prisons, 1999a), deploring the fact that no action had been taken in the meantime and that the treatment of inmates appeared to have deteriorated still further. Then in September 2000 three prison officers had the dubious distinction of becoming the first in modern English penal history to be imprisoned for acts of brutality against prisoners (*Independent*, 7 September 2000). Between 1 January and 30 June 1999, a total of 44 prison officers (including those at Wormwood Scrubs) were suspended in prisons in England and Wales for a variety of alleged assaults against prisoners. However, the convictions of those who had been imprisoned for assault were subsequently overturned on appeal (Ramsbotham, 2005: 106). Nor is this just an isolated example. In January 2006 staff bullying and intimidation of inmates was alleged at Leeds Prison, in which excessive and inappropriate use was made of the segregation unit, which in turn was described as being run 'in a militaristic fash-ion' (HM Chief Inspector of Prisons, 2006). An internal report leaked to the press in November 2006 spoke of a nine-year reign of terror involving over 160 prison officers at Wormwood Scrubs between 1992 and 2001. Abuses were said to include savage beatings, death threats and sexual assault on inmates, while some managers turned blind eyes to the situation (*Guardian*, 13 November 2006).

Apart from the use of physical force, one of the commonest options adopted by the authorities when confronted with disruptive prisoners is the physical segrega-tion of those responsible. Under Rule 45 of the 2010 Prison Rules, a prison gover-nor has the power to order the 'removal from association' of a prisoner where this appears desirable 'for the maintenance of good order or discipline'. (Prisoners can also be removed from association in their own interests: this provision is usually used for the protection of vulnerable inmates such as child or sex offenders). Prisoners removed from association may be held in a 'close supervision centre' for up to a month (simple removal from association is for up to 72 hours, although this can be extended by the authority of the Secretary of State) and this can be renewed 'from time to time for a like period'. The use of this measure can often make matters worse by fuelling discontent among prisoners. In spite of the severe deprivations it entails, removal from association is categorized as an administrative procedure rather than a disciplinary sanction, and although reasons have to be given for segregation, they may simply state that the inmate's behaviour posed a threat to the smooth running of the prison. Attempts to challenge the legality of the segregation procedure have proved unsuccessful in the past,[10] and it is by no means certain that a renewed challenge under Article 3 of the European Convention on Human Rights would succeed unless the conditions were wholly exceptional (see below).

Segregation was often combined in the past with another administrative process – the temporary transfer procedure – whereby difficult or disruptive prisoners were reallocated from their original prison to the segregation unit of a local prison. Although intended to provide a temporary (one month's) cooling off respite before returning to the original prison, the governor there could meanwhile apply to the Prison Service to have the inmate transferred to yet another establishment. At the time of the Strangeways riot a large number of inmates who were alleged to be especially disruptive were being shunted from one prison to another every few months. The procedure was known by a variety of nicknames including the 'magic roundabout' or 'merry-go-round'.

For a long time temporary transfers – sometimes as many as 100,000 each year – were authorized under Home Office Circular Instruction 10/74 (otherwise known as Rule Ten-Seventy-Four or, in prison jargon, the Ghost Train). Following recommendations contained in the Woolf Report a new procedure for managing persistently disruptive inmates known as the Continuous Assessment Scheme was introduced. This revised procedure still authorized the use of transfers in the interests of 'good order and discipline', but only as a last resort, and subject to a regime of safeguards. The current strategy is to house the great majority of disruptive inmates in special units known as 'close supervision centres' (CSCs), the first of which were set up in 1998. This has not by any means eliminated temporary transfers, which still occur on much the same scale as before, though now mostly for administrative reasons in order to utilize every available space in response to the prison numbers crisis.

The use of specially adapted segregation units for particularly disruptive prisoners who could not be controlled within the relatively liberal and constructive regime of the standard dispersal or high security prison has a long and not very honourable or successful history. It began in 1974 with the introduction of a special

---

[10]For example in R. v. Deputy Governor of Parkhurst Prison, ex p Hague (1992); Weldon v. Home Office [1992] 1 AC 58.

control unit at Wakefield Prison, following widespread prison disturbances in 1972 (the unit was modelled on austere segregation units at Peterhead and Inverness Prisons in Scotland; see Boyle, 1977). Within the control unit, both the physical conditions and the regime were intentionally spartan, and any amelioration of the conditions had to be earned by satisfactory behaviour over a prolonged period. Following the controversy surrounding its use, the operation of the control unit was suspended in 1975. Then in 1983 the government's own Control Review Committee accepted that this particular response to the problem of disorder within the prison system represented a blind alley (Home Office, 1984a: para. 52).

In its place, the Committee recommended the creation of a new system of small sized Special Units (see Bottomley and Hay, 1991) which offered a variety of different non-punitive regimes as a way of coping with seriously disruptive prisoners. Within these units, the need for tight security was counterbalanced by a liberal and humane regime in which the emphasis was on the resocialization of violently disruptive and aggressive prisoners who have often proved extremely difficult to handle in the normal prison environment. Three such Special Units were operational at any one time – at Parkhurst, Lincoln and Hull, with Woodhill replacing Lincoln in 1993 – between them holding around 22 inmates in 1996. However, the Special Units themselves fell victim to the more repressive penal climate that accompanied the security clamp-down of the mid-1990s, despite some evidence of success in coping with some of the most intractable prisoners in the prison system (Boag, 1988, 1989; Cooke, 1989; Bottomley, 1990; Martin, 1991).

In July 1995, the Prison Service established a project (see Liebling, 2001) to investigate the feasibility of introducing a new 'strict regime' unit, which in 1998 resulted in the creation of a radically different system of close supervision centres based at Woodhill and Durham Prisons, though the latter was subsequently closed. Their operating philosophy owed far more to the discredited and unsuccessful control unit initiative of the 1970s than the rather more enlightened (and penologically better informed) approach that had been pioneered in the Special Units they replaced. In a depressing illustration of the tendency for English penal history – and particularly its mistakes – to repeat itself, the CSCs were founded on the notion of a progressive or staged system that incorporated a crude and mechanistic stick and carrot approach to eliciting good behaviour. The stick consisted of a restricted regime offering no association, and basic or minimal privileges. The carrots on offer consisted of a graded series of earned privileges that were intended to operate as a reward for compliant behaviour. Thus, prisoners were expected to graduate initially to a so-called structured regime providing some opportunity for participating in association, constructive activities and behaviour programmes and thence to an intervention unit, in which privileges would reach the standard level on offer in the rest of the high security estate.

Unfortunately (but all too predictably) the early experience of the CSC system disclosed a number of extremely serious operational failings which exposed basic flaws in the assumptions on which it rested. A thorough evaluation of the system found that out of 51 prisoners housed during its first 28 months of operation, only 12 inmates 'progressed' from it and, of these, only four managed to settle 'on normal location' without any recurrence of their disruptive behaviour (Clare and Bottomley, 2001: 103). Although 30 prisoners were thought to show reduced levels of disruptive behaviour within the CSC compared with outside, six showed an increased level of assaultive behaviour. Moreover, a group of eight prisoners 'refused to co-operate with the system from the outset and embarked upon a persistent campaign of confrontation and challenge, involving dirty protests, violence and/or threats of violence against staff, as well as litigation against the system'. Noting that for several of these prisoners their behaviour had deteriorated dramatically following their transfer to the CSC, the report authors noted laconically that 'it would be unwise to claim that the overall effect of CSCs on these prisoners had been anything other than very negative'. Liebling (2001: 156) suggested that several of these inmates became more violent (and more disturbed) than they had been at any stage during their prison careers. Her interviews with this group of inmates revealed a sense of injustice with regard to every aspect of the system's operation which 'gave every excuse they needed to vent all the anger, frustration and hatred they could muster against its staff' (2001: 159).

A thematic review of the CSC system undertaken by HM Chief Inspector of Prisons (1999e) complained that the majority of prisoners who failed to progress were consigned to varying degrees of restriction, 'with a significant proportion experiencing open-ended, long-term segregation in conditions that equate with punishment'. He was even more outspokenly critical of both the regime itself and also the absence of any effective monitoring and oversight of the system in a subsequent account he wrote of his experiences as chief inspector (Ramsbotham, 2005: ch. 6, esp. p. 126).

A similar though less extreme sticks and carrots regime known as the Incentives and Earned Privileges (IEP) scheme was also introduced to the rest of the prison system in July 1995, as part of the post-Learmont security clamp-down. A Home Office funded evaluation of this scheme (Liebling et al., 1999) found that there had been no significant overall improvements to prisoner behaviour in the five establishments studied. Significantly, however, there were reductions (from relatively high levels) in favourable inmate perceptions of staff fairness, relations with staff, regime fairness, consistency of treatment and progress in prison. (Indeed, the introduction of the scheme sparked off a protest by inmates at Full Sutton Prison which was only quelled with the aid of a prison officer riot squad together with police and other emergency services.) Negative feelings such as these among inmates are known to be highly detrimental to the maintenance of order in prisons (see Sparks and Bottoms, 1995; and Sparks et al., 1996) even though, paradoxically, maintaining order was supposed to be the main aim of the IEP system itself. Thus, it appeared that perceptions of unfairness on the part of inmates offset and outweighed any beneficial effects of the new system. None of this should have come as any surprise in the wake of the Woolf Report. As it is, the entire episode serves to highlight the chronic inability of English penal policy-makers to learn from either the depressingly long litany of well-documented policy failures or the much shorter (and often unsung) paean of more constructive interventions.

As for Woolf himself, his main strategy for tackling the control problem (as we shall see below) was to attend to the genuine sense of grievance that he accepted was primarily to blame for most of the disturbances. However, he did also accept the need for some improvements in the security and control apparatus to deal with the much smaller number of disruptive and difficult prisoners who would undoubtedly remain; typically, there is little agreement about how many such prisoners there are, ranging from the Chief Inspector of Prisons estimate of 1,400 (HM Chief Inspector of Prisons, 1999e: 2) to Liebling's (2001) figure of no more than 40. In order to tackle this residual control problem, Woolf's proposed solution was heavily influenced by recent American thinking on the prison design. Instead of the large-scale, relatively inflexible, open access wings of conventional prison design, he favoured the use of a rather different model that is often referred to as a 'new generation prison', based on a collection of small, self-contained decentralized units (Ditchfield, 1990: 84–7). The first such prison in England – Woodhill, near Milton Keynes – was opened in July 1992. The theory is that within such a system, a variety of regimes may be offered to cater for the specific requirements of different groups of prisoners under the one roof. Being smaller, such designs are said to offer better standards of surveillance and control and also better interpersonal relations between staff and inmates. However, Andrew Rutherford (1985: 408), one of the few British observers to have examined the new generation prisons in operation in America, has cautioned that they should not be seen as a panacea for all the existing system's ills. While there are undoubtedly some very successful new generation prisons in operation, such as Oak Park Heights in Minnesota which was visited by the Woolf inquiry team, there are also some not-so-successful ones that can be just as repressive and brutal as those they were designed to replace (see also Scraton et al., 1991: 138ff). Rutherford's conclusion – that the key to success lies in the management approach that is adopted and the way prisoners are treated rather than in prison architecture – chimes in well with Woolf's general approach.

One sadly neglected response to the control problem in prisons is the need to develop an appropriate strategy to improve the generally very poor state of staff–inmate relations. Or, as the government's own Control Review Committee put it in 1984: 'relations between staff and prisoners are at the heart of the whole prison system and … control and security flow from getting that relationship right' (Home Office, 1984a: para. 16). Perhaps one reason for the continuing neglect of this issue (including by Woolf) is to do with a rather different crisis in which prison officers themselves are a central part of the problem. This is the long-standing *crisis of authority*, to which we now turn.

Part of the problem stems from a persistent ambivalence over the role of prison staff that is reflected in the way they are recruited, trained and managed, and also in the tasks they are expected to undertake. Until the middle of the twentieth century, the role of mainstream prison officers was unambiguous enough and could be exclusively described in terms of their 'turnkey' functions. Their job was simply to lock and unlock prisoners in their custody and make sure they were where they were supposed to be and doing what they were supposed to be doing (Coyle,

2005: 84). No formal skills or qualifications were expected of basic grade officers, many of whom were recruited from the armed forces, as were many of their superiors. Prison officers (and indeed governors) were not expected to show any initiative in the discharge of their duties, nor were they encouraged to fraternize with those in their charge, largely for fear of corruption. Even now the bulk of their training is devoted to the security aspects of their job. The Prison Service was, and still is, a hierarchical organization with a rigidly centralized command structure in which considerable emphasis is placed on the importance of obeying instructions. It is also characterized by mutual suspicion and hostility between all levels within the hierarchy, but particularly between basic grade officers and senior management.

From the middle of the twentieth century, however, many of these traditional verities were undermined as the Prison Service began recruiting growing numbers of professionally trained specialist welfare staff – probation officers, educational workers and prison psychologists – to undertake the treatment and training functions associated with the ethic of rehabilitation. Their responsibilities not only required a much higher level of interaction with inmates than had previously been tolerated, but also generated growing resentment on the part of basic grade officers. The new prison professionals enjoyed better pay and conditions of service by virtue of their qualifications than ordinary prison officers, but were considered to be usurping a role to which prison officers also aspired, however unsuited to it they might be by temperament, training or ideology. Growing tension between the various categories of prison workers was reflected in the findings of a survey into the attitudes of Scottish prison officers towards those with whom they worked. Many more of them expressed concern about relations with social workers, psychologists and psychiatrists in particular (28 per cent, 27 per cent and 43 per cent respectively) than they did about relations with prisoners (8 per cent) (Wozniak and McAllister, 1991). The survey also showed a high level of concern about relations with prison governors, who were blamed, among other things, for giving in to prisoners and failing to offer staff sufficient support.

Much of the resentment expressed by prison officers stems from a feeling that they are undervalued for the necessary, and increasingly dangerous, work they are expected to do. Moreover, as Fitzgerald and Sim point out (1982: 123), they are also concerned that their job itself is under attack. In addition to the vociferous (and increasingly violent) protests of prisoners, and the alleged insensitivity on the part of the authorities towards their own concerns, must now be added the threat of privatization. This has already resulted in the loss of certain former functions, such as court escort duties, which used to provide welcome relief to an otherwise tedious routine, and is increasingly seen as a threat to the jobs and livelihood of many prison officers. Another major source of prison staff resentment is over the issue of prisoners' rights and conditions, efforts to improve which are likely to be equated with attempts to subvert their own legitimate authority. Such attitudes are linked to the widely shared perception that society cares more about prisoners than about prison staff; in a 1983 attitude survey 84 per cent of staff expressed such a view (Home Office, 1985: 57). The Woolf Report also referred to the deep sense of frustration on the part of prison officers that their efforts were not appreciated (Woolf and Tumim, 1991: para. 12.1). Faced with this threat to their jobs, pay and conditions, and frustrated by a management in which – often for understandable reasons – they have no confidence, prison officers have tended to look to their trade union – the Prison Officers' Association – for support. This in turn has fuelled the ongoing industrial relations crisis we discussed earlier, and for which senior politicians, Prison Service management and prison staff trade unions are equally culpable. Or, as a senior businessman who was asked to look into the management of the Prison Service concluded: '[d]ifficult unions fill the vacuum left by ineffective management and all managements are ineffective if they are not allowed to manage' (Lygo, 1991: 6; as quoted by Coyle, 2005: 88).

Woolf acknowledged that any substantial change in the way prisoners are treated would require a major contribution from prison officers and considered that the best way of ensuring this, given the poor state of Prison Service morale, would be through improved in-service training. Among the benefits that he antic-ipated were improvements in staff self-esteem, reductions in racial discrimination and improved relations with inmates as increased skills enabled staff to offer train-ing and advice. While such recommendations represented a step in the right direc-tion, Woolf had surprisingly little to say about the basic role, attitudes and cultural values of the prison staff themselves, despite the critical importance of these to the nature of prison regimes. All too often in the past attempts by governors and oth-ers to liberalize the prison system have been obstructed and frustrated by the actions and prejudices of basic grade officers fearful of losing their authority and control.

The clearest assessment of the need for a fundamental cultural change on the part of all staff working in the prison system came from Martin Narey when Director General of the Prison Service. In his 1999 speech which marked the commencement of the decency agenda (see section 6.4 above), he complained of a 'litany of failure and moral neglect', of the 'very immorality of our treatment of some prisoners and the degradation of some establishments'. It is hard to imagine a clearer indication of the scale of the crisis of authority facing the Prison Service than for its own Director General to feel compelled to publicly challenge the stubbornly recalcitrant elements within that service and to threaten to resign unless his reforms were supported.

Privatization has done little to resolve the crises of control and authority. While private prison staff seem fairly consistently to score more highly than their public sector counterparts with regard to their attitudes and behaviour towards inmates, being much more likely to treat them with fairness and respect (Bottomley et al., 1996; Liebling and Arnold, 2002; National Audit Office, 2003; Liebling and Arnold, 2004; Prison Reform Trust, 2005), it is also true that private prisons have a fairly dismal track record in maintaining control, securing compliance and chal-lenging inappropriate behaviour including bullying and aggression towards staff and other inmates (James et al., 1997; James and Bottomley, 1998; National Audit Office, 2003; Prison Reform Trust, 2005). Virtually all privately managed prisons have experienced serious control problems, at least during the initial period after opening. Such failings are attributable, to a considerable degree, to understaffing and high staff turnover, aggravated by inexperience and inadequate training on the part of private sector staff and management. These are the predictable consequences of commercial undertakings seeking to reduce costs by minimizing staff numbers, wages and ancillary costs without sufficient regard to the probable consequences within a coercive and potentially unstable prison setting.

The Crisis of Accountability

Accountability is the term used to describe the various mechanisms for ensuring that those who wield power or take decisions that affect the lives of others can be made answerable for them (Mulgan, 2000). We have already described one such device – the doctrine of ministerial responsibility – and noted that it constitutes a deeply flawed mechanism for securing the *political* accountability of those senior policy-makers up to and including the Justice Secretary who have the power to determine how the prison system will operate. Fortunately, other forms of accountability exist, and some modest gains have been achieved by a variety of agencies in ensuring a degree of answerability for its conduct and decisions on the part of the Prison Service. However, it would be fair to say that their cumulative effect has been merely to ameliorate rather than resolve the ongoing crisis of accountability from which the Prison Service continues to suffer. In this section we will focus mainly on various forms of *administrative* and *judicial* accountability mechanisms.

For most of the twentieth century, the world of the prisons was a closed one whose secrecy was such that critics talked of a crisis of visibility (see Chapter 1, section 1.3). Prisons were screened from public view under a cloak of protective legislation that was originally designed to safeguard national security. One symptom of this equation between prison security and national security can be seen in the scope of the Official Secrets Act, whose inhibiting effects on those working within the prison system were tellingly (and, naturally enough, anonymously) described in 1975 by two assistant governors in the following terms:

> This all-pervasive Act not only inhibits disclosures of injustices which inevitably occur in any system but also prevents open dialogue between those within and outside the Prison Service wishing to improve the quality of training in our prisons and borstals. The ruling that prison officers should not express a view publicly leads to frustration, sterility and inertia. (cited in Briggs, 1975: 22)

Operating alongside this cloak of secrecy was a legal and regulatory framework whose main aim was not to set out the rights and entitlements of prisoners but rather to serve the administrative convenience of the prison authorities. It did so by conferring on them wide discretionary power that was for the most part impervious to scrutiny and challenge. The main piece of primary legislation – the Prison Act 1952 – was conceived of as an enabling Act, and was intended to confer as much discretion as possible on the Secretary of State (Livingstone and Owen, 1999: 5). The 1952 Act has been repeatedly condemned as anachronistic by penal reform groups (see, for example, Prison Reform Trust, 1996). As it was a consolidation measure, many of its main sections date back almost unaltered to the nineteenth century. It thus takes no account of important subsequent national developments such as the introduction of the Prisons Ombudsman and the adoption of agency status. Nor of equally important international developments such as the European Prison Rules, to say nothing of the incorporation of the European Convention on Human Rights in the Human Rights Act 1998. Much of the regulatory framework governing prison life is contained not in primary legislation but in the Prison Rules, which take the form of delegated legislation drawn up and amended by the Secretary of State. Even these Prison Rules provide only an outline framework and, like the Prison Act itself, are designed to maximize the discretion conferred on the prison authorities. The Rules are, in turn, supplemented by Standing Orders (which cover all aspects of prison life) and Prison Service Orders and Instructions, none of which have the force of law (Creighton and King, 2000: 13–14). In short, a wholesale revision of existing prison law is long overdue. This does not mean that it is likely to happen, however, because – cynical but true – governments are aware that such reforms win few votes.

Despite its air of permanence, the prison system's façade of inscrutability is a relatively recent accretion. During the early part of the nineteenth century, at a time when prisons were locally managed, the government introduced a system of inspectors in 1835, to monitor them, report on what they found and make recommendations for what needed to be done to put things right (Coyle, 2005: 55). Once central government assumed control over the entire prison system in 1877, this embryonic monitoring system became moribund as inspectors' reports were no longer published separately and lost their critical edge.

It was not until 1979, during an era of growing unease about recurrent allegations of prison disturbances and their brutal suppression, that an official committee of inquiry (May, 1979) called for the resurrection of an independent prison inspectorate. Despite strong opposition from the Home Office, this recommendation was accepted and the first Chief Inspector of Prisons was appointed in 1981. Since then (and especially since the appointment of Judge Stephen Tumim as Chief Inspector in 1987) the reports published by the prisons inspectorate – often expressed in trenchant terms – have shed valuable light on the workings of the Prison Service as well as the conditions to be found in individual prisons. In dispelling the air of secrecy and puncturing the aura of complacency that surrounded the Prison Service for so long they have acquired a well-deserved reputation around the world as a model to be emulated (although for a more critical assessment, see Morgan, 1985 and Laming, 2000). As a watchdog and whistle-blower the prisons inspectorate has undoubtedly performed an exemplary service. As an accountability mechanism, however, the inspectorate lacks teeth since neither the Prison Service nor ministers are in any meaningful sense answerable to it. The familiar response of prison governors to a critical report on their prison is to delay its publication and then proclaim, however implausibly, that all has been put in order since the last inspection. The problem at ministerial level is that almost invariably there is no response at all, even to the Chief Inspector's annual reports, causing one former incumbent of the office to doubt whether they had even been read by the various Secretaries of State to whom they were addressed (Ramsbotham, 2005: 214).

One obvious reform would be to require the responsible minister to produce a written annual response to the Chief Inspector's reports, commenting on its findings and outlining the government's reactions to each of the main recommendations, as currently happens in Western Australia (Ramsbotham, 2005: 247). Instead, the government announced in November 2005 that it was planning to merge the five separate criminal justice inspectorates – for prisons, probation, courts, crown prosecutors and police – into a single super inspectorate. This proposal understandably raised concerns among penal reform groups that the government's hidden agenda was to muzzle one of its sharpest and most authoritative critics by blurring its commendably single-minded focus on the most crucial and controversial agency of them all. The proposal was subsequently dropped after the Bill containing it was defeated in the **House of Lords** in October 2006.

The prisons inspectorate is by no means the only body to exercise a watchdog role with regard to the Prison Service. Another monitoring body was established in 1878 when central government assumed responsibility for prisons and established visiting committees of local magistrates for each prison to ensure that they were being properly managed (Coyle, 2005: 56). These became known as Boards of Visitors in 1898, when their composition was also broadened to include local community volunteers as well as magistrates. In 2003 they were renamed Independent Monitoring Boards. Compared with the prisons inspectorate, however, they lack the resources, status and perceived independence that are required to adequately discharge such a demanding role.

If the effectiveness of an accountability mechanism is measured in terms of its ability to render those who wield power answerable to an independent body, then mention should also be made of the European Committee for the Prevention of Torture and Inhuman or Degrading Treatment or Punishment. Like the domestic prisons inspectorate it, too, has the right of access to any place where people can be deprived of their liberty together with the power to inspect documents and conduct private interviews with inmates. This committee has produced a number of well-publicized reports that have been highly critical of aspects of the English prison system. Moreover, unlike the national prisons inspectorate, the government is expected to respond to the criticisms directed against it, though convention requires that the two documents are published simultaneously, which provides an opportunity to show that action has been taken. Valuable though the CPT monitoring regime undoubtedly is, its reports are less systematic, intensive and frequent than those of the domestic inspectorate, which has also developed a reputation for producing extremely thorough thematic reports. If the prison inspectorate were to be emasculated, however, as once seemed probable, then the role of the CPT would assume still greater importance.

Another important aspect of accountability is that abuses of power should be rectified, legitimate grievances remedied and improper decisions set aside. Before 1990 there was a complex and cumbersome internal grievance procedure through which prisoners with grievances were expected to make their complaints. Like the prison disciplinary procedure, however, this evoked precious little confidence among those it was intended to assist, largely because it lacked any provision for independent review, and reserved the sole power to remedy grievances for the governors and the Home Secretary. Moreover, some of the Prison Rules seemed to have been designed to intimidate and deter prisoners who might have a legitimate grievance from pursuing it. For example, before 1989 it was an offence against the Prison Rules to make a 'false and malicious' allegation against a prison officer, which meant that complainants ran the risk of being found guilty of a disciplinary offence unless they could be certain of proving the allegation.

Following widespread concern over the perceived inadequacies of the grievance procedure, the system was reviewed by the Chief Inspector of Prisons (HM Chief Inspector of Prisons, 1987), leading to a reform of the system in September 1990. However, the new procedure was only marginally less cumbersome than the old (Woolf and Tumim, 1991: paras 14.321–325) and still lacked an independent element. Prisoners had a number of avenues of complaint including the prison governor, the Board of Visitors, the Prison Service area manager, a Member of Parliament, the Home Secretary and also the courts, via an action for judicial review. However, none of these could be said to be effective in protecting prisoners from injustice and ill-treatment. Those procedures which were internal to the Prison Service were perceived by prisoners as unfair and ineffective, while those which involved recourse to outside bodies such as the courts were expensive, time-consuming and severely limited in their scope.

Woolf recommended that, as a matter of good practice, reasons should be given to prisoners for any decisions that might adversely affect them to any material extent. He anticipated that this might forestall a number of complaints under the grievance procedure by reducing the sense of injustice to which such decisions often give rise; and that it might also improve the quality of decision-making by deterring arbitrary decisions. Woolf also agreed that an independent element in the complaints procedure was not just an optional extra. Accordingly, he recommended the appointment of what he called an independent Complaints Adjudicator who would both act as the final avenue of appeal in disciplinary matters, and also 'recommend, advise and conciliate' at the final stage of the grievance procedure (para. 14.349).

The government accepted the broad thrust of the Woolf proposals on this issue, and the first Prisons Ombudsman was appointed in October 1994. (The current Ombudsman is Nigel Newcomen CBE, who was appointed in 2011.) The early years of the Prisons Ombudsman were marred by a series of serious and damaging disputes over his initial appointment and terms of reference that cast doubt on the government's commitment to the principle of an independent Ombudsman. Since 1997, however, these concerns have subsided and indeed the Ombudsman's remit has been considerably extended. The main responsibility is to investigate complaints about prisoners' treatment in both public and privately run prisons, including disciplinary decisions, but excluding complaints about convictions, sentence lengths and release dates. In September 2001, the Ombudsman's remit (and title) was extended to embrace the probation service as well following the creation of the National Probation Service. Since April 2004, the Prisons and Probation Ombudsman has been responsible for investigating all fatalities in prison. In addition, the Ombudsman has also been asked to conduct a number of special investigations including one into allegations of racism at an immigration reception centre at Oakhampton. Another special investigation examined the handling of a case by the National Probation Service involving a serious sex offender who committed further very serious offences while under supervision on licence following a lengthy sentence of imprisonment.

All internal procedures have to be exhausted before a complaint can be made to the Ombudsman, whose powers are in any event limited to making recommendations and do not extend to the award of compensation, although he may recommend an *ex gratia* payment. In 2011–12 the Ombudsman received almost 5,300 complaints of which nine out of ten related to the Prison Service. The largest single category of complaints related to the handling of prisoners' property and money, making up around 17 per cent overall. About half of all complaints are ineligible for investigation, usually because the internal complaints procedures have not been completed before coming to the Ombudsman. And it is unclear what proportion of recommendations are accepted by NOMS, which is a cause for concern (Prisons and Probation Ombudsman, 2012).

The advent of the Prisons Ombudsman did at least address one outstanding defect that was long associated with the prison system's complaints procedures: the absence of any independent oversight. However, the system still suffers from a number of weaknesses that could serve to increase rather than alleviate prisoners' feelings of injustice. One relates to the legal status of the post of Ombudsman, which lacks any statutory backing – an issue that the Ombudsman is fully aware of and that the Justice Select Committee has recommended should be rectified. However, legislation has not yet been brought forward (Prisons and Probation Ombudsman, 2012: 11). A second weakness relates to the stipulation that all internal complaints procedures have to be satisfied before a complaint becomes eligible, which is still a matter of concern with regard to both the Prison Service and the Probation Service. A third, related problem is that of delay in dealing with the complaints internally, which means that many complaints relate to events that are more than a year old. A fourth problem is that some prisons have been suspected of placing barriers in the way of prisoners who wish to make a complaint. A fifth and final weakness relates to the adequacy of staffing levels within the Ombudsman's office itself – despite a five-fold increase since 2002 – particularly in view of the recent substantial increases in its remit, the growth of the prison population and increasing demands for its services. Currently, cuts in resources of around 21 per cent are planned for the Ombudsman's office between 2010–11 and 2014–15.

There are also some more general factors which may limit the effectiveness of grievance procedures such as the Ombudsman, however formally fair. One is the closed nature of prisons. If an action that is complained of is invisible, taking place behind closed doors, it may be impossible for a prisoner to establish that it has in fact occurred. Second, a successful complaint is only likely if it can be shown that a rule has been broken or that specific entitlements have been denied. In other words, grievance procedures are of limited value where the rules themselves are defective or lack the full force of the law: hence the importance of properly enforceable minimum standards and safeguards covering all aspects of prison life. A third and final limitation with grievance procedures generally is their relatively narrow focus (Vagg, 1991: 152ff), since they are primarily intended to deal with individual complaints rather than collective issues affecting groups of prisoners or even the inmate population as a whole.[11] And yet many of the issues about which prisoners feel most aggrieved (for example, regarding prison conditions and facilities, or the attitude or behaviour of members of staff) affect them collectively and not just as individuals.

In addition to these administrative remedies, prison inmates also retain their rights to seek judicial redress either in the domestic courts, for example, by seeking judicial review, or by applying to the European Court of Human Rights in Strasbourg. The record of the courts in holding the authorities legally accountable for mistaken, arbitrary or oppressive use of their powers has also been variable, however. For many years the English courts appeared reluctant to challenge the authority of the executive which, as we have seen, was generally buttressed by exceedingly wide-ranging discretionary powers, though they have become far less deferential in recent years (see Lennon, 2003: 449; Livingstone et al., 2003: 76). The European Court of Human Rights adopted a more vigorous approach from the outset, and was the setting for a number of famous victories including prisoners' entitlement to correspond with their lawyers without interference from prison authorities and their entitlement to legal representation in connection with disciplinary proceedings.[12] Since 1998, the Human Rights Act has incorporated the European Convention on Human Rights (ECHR) into UK law, which means that English judges also have to apply its provisions in reaching their decisions. This is unlikely to render the European Court of Human Rights redundant, however, and it has continued to uphold challenges brought by prison inmates against the British government on a number of occasions since 1998. One notable example was a case brought by the parents of a mentally ill pre-trial inmate who had been kicked to death by his schizophrenic cellmate in Chelmsford prison in 1994. Eight years later, the European Court finally affirmed that the British government had violated their son's right to life under Article 2 of the Convention.[13]

---

[11]There is no intrinsic reason why this should be the case. Other jurisdictions, notably that of the United States, have developed procedures such as the class action which enables similar cases to be dealt with as a single action with implications for all the members of the class in question. Courts in the United States have also been prepared to adopt a more activist approach in relation to complaints about prison life, in which they are prepared to consider complaints about, for example, prison conditions and their effects in the aggregate, and not just the impact of a grievance on an individual (Vagg, 1991: 153).

[12]*Golder* v. *UK* (1975) 1EHRR 524; *Silver* v. *UK* [1983] 5 EHRR 347; *Campbell and Fell* v. *UK* (1985) 15 EHRR 137.

[13]*Paul and Audrey Edwards* v. *UK* [2002] ECtHR, App No. 46477/99.

However, even a successful legal challenge does not necessarily guarantee that the authorities will be held accountable for their failure to uphold prisoners' rights. One notable example relates to the indiscriminate ban on the entitlement of all convicted inmates to vote in elections. This was successfully challenged in Strasbourg on the ground that it violates Article 3 of the ECHR.[14] Nevertheless, the government responded to the European Court's judgment by making it clear it had no intention of lifting the ban. So although there have been some improvements in the procedures for making prison authorities accountable in recent years, there is still a long way to go before they can be considered fully accountable.

The advent of private prisons raises a number of accountability issues that do not apply to public sector prisons. Private corporations are accountable in the first instance to their shareholders (although also to government funders and inmates to a certain extent), and this creates tensions. Because of their overriding commercial interests, there is a constant danger that the profit motive will take precedence over any commitment that the private prison operators may have to the public interest. For example, it is in the commercial interests of private prisons to prolong rather than curtail the length of time inmates remain in custody (since the private firms are paid per prisoner accommodated). Although the Criminal Justice Act 1991 provided for a controller to be appointed by the Secretary of State for each private prison, these individuals run the risk of being co-opted onto the private prison team when they are based on-site. There is little evidence to suggest that political, administrative or judicial accountability are better served in private prisons (Cavadino and Dignan, 2007: 276–7). Indeed, the evidence suggests the opposite.

The Crisis of Legitimacy and How to Tackle It

The English prison system continues to suffer from a long-running, chronic, crisis of legitimacy that seems as far as ever from being resolved. This final crisis has four main aspects: the prison system is generally viewed by its several audiences – the general public, politicians and the media, penal staff and prison inmates themselves – as being simultaneously ineffective in controlling crime, inefficient in its use of resources, insensitive in dealing with prison staff at all levels and, all too often, downright inhumane in its treatment of offenders. We have already fully discussed most of these failings, and will be relatively brief here.

The prison system's failure to provide an effective means of controlling crime is reflected in the chronically poor reconviction rates we examined at the start of this chapter. The fact that sections of the general public – supported and encouraged by parts of the media and by many politicians – believe that we need to have even greater recourse to this failed institution and to intensify its harshness underscores the intractability of this particular aspect of the crisis. The Prison Service's crisis of legitimacy with regard to prison staff is closely bound up with the chronic state of industrial relations and the broader managerial crisis that we discussed earlier in

---

[14]*Hirst v. United Kingdom (No. 2)* (2004) 38 EHRR 40.

this section. But as we shall see in this final part, senior prison staff have also on occasion been treated by their superiors with extraordinary insensitivity.

As for the Prison Service's crisis of legitimacy with regard to the inmates in its charge, we have already commented on the disturbingly high suicide rate in England's prisons, the litany of well-documented instances of cruel or brutal treatment and the disturbing official reports by inspectors on prison conditions. Concern over the treatment of prison inmates is not confined to prisoners themselves, but also horrifies many criminal justice practitioners, informed observers (see, for example, Department for Christian Responsibility and Citizenship, 2004) and ordinary members of the public. Another aspect of the crisis of legitimacy that we have not yet touched on relates to corruption on the part of prison staff, a long-standing problem to which blind eyes must often have been turned. However, in August 2006, a leaked report suggested that at least 1,000 prison officers are involved in smuggling contraband items such as drugs or mobile phones into prisons or accepting bribes in order to facilitate transfers to less secure institutions (*Guardian*, 1 August 2006).

How to Tackle the Crisis of Legitimacy

The scale, depth and multi-faceted nature of the prison system's crisis of legitimacy are all too apparent and yet at the same time all too intractable. One response would be to follow the agenda of prison abolitionists (for example, de Haan, 1990; Hulsman, 1991; Sim, 1992, 1994; Bianchi, 1994; Wilson, 2006) and get rid of the institution altogether. But of course – however tellingly the rational case for **abolitionism** may be presented – this hardly seems politically plausible at the present time, especially since many politicians and ordinary members of the public appear to be in denial that some important aspects of the legitimacy crisis (notably justice and humanity for prisoners) even pose a problem. The fact that the crisis is multi-faceted suggests that it can only be tackled by dealing with its different dimensions and addressing their respective audiences.

Many of the legitimacy problems of prisons stem indirectly from the numbers crisis, which exacerbates poor conditions and regimes and is likely to thwart any efforts to make prisons better managed, more decent and less hopelessly ineffective at turning offenders away from crime. In view of the generally unsympathetic attitudes towards prison inmates on the part of many politicians and members of the public, the prison system's most vulnerable aspect is almost certainly its lack of effectiveness. This can be easily demonstrated, and one might think that a rational government following an evidence-led approach would be persuaded to take steps to consign fewer people to an institution which 'can be an expensive way of making bad people worse' (Home Office, 1990a: para. 2.7). But government is proving largely impervious to such rational arguments. One reason for this may be that imprisonment also serves a number of symbolic functions (see section 6.2 above), even though many of its instrumental functions could be discharged equally effectively by community penalties (Cavadino et al., 1999: 120). Another is that governments appear to have calculated that there are more votes to be gained in pursuing a tough punitive policy however ineffective it might be, provided it is popular with the electorate. This only makes sense as a political strategy, however, on the assumption that the electorate is homogeneous and united in its attitudes towards offenders, which is far from being the case. Public opinion surveys, for example, regularly show that attitudes towards offenders are far less punitive than they are portrayed by the media (see Chapter 10, section 10.3). Demonstrating that the electorate is both less blinkered and more rationally sophisticated than politicians often assume may therefore offer the most hopeful long-term strategy for weaning politicians off their fixation with custodial forms of punishment.

Turning now to the prisons' crisis of legitimacy with their own inmates, there is mounting evidence, both anecdotal and empirical, that the best way to create legitimacy with inmates is to treat prisoners justly, respecting their dignity and their rights, just as the Woolf Report urged. Fairer and better regimes are not only more popular with prisoners, they also encourage them to behave better (Cooke, 1989; Bottoms et al., 1990: 91; Cooke, 1991; Sparks and Bottoms, 1995; Liebling and Arnold, 2004). However, this is by no means simply a question of giving prisoners *formal* rights and *formally* fair procedures, important though these are, for there is always likely to be a significant gap between the provision of formal justice 'in the books' and substantive justice in practice. Moreover, this gap will almost inevitably be increased in an institution like the prison which lacks visibility and legitimacy, where prisoners are relatively powerless and where relationships between different groups of inhabitants are in a poor state. Lip-service justice, however formally impressive on paper, will never deliver legitimacy. We need to create an atmosphere and ethos in which prisoners' rights are genuinely and effectively respected, and where they in return afford legitimacy to the institution and behave accordingly.

How is this to be achieved? In our view the conventional approach to regulating life within prisons suffers from many of the same defects as the approach that is typically adopted outside the prison walls: namely, that the prevailing carrot and stick approach discussed earlier places a disproportionate emphasis on *material* rewards and punishments. Liebling (2001: 159) has astutely pointed out that this rational choice model – which is based on a rather crude form of instrumental reasoning – is singularly inappropriate for a group of emotionally unstable and often brutalized individuals. Many prison inmates who pose the greatest control problems have very little control over their own behaviour and most are probably habituated to high levels of material deprivation. Very many inmates suffer from chronic under-socialization, and exceptionally low levels of self-esteem. And yet almost all prisoners have a highly developed sense of fair and unfair treatment and, whatever their perceptions of their own esteem, are acutely aware when they are not accorded the respect to which they feel they are entitled. Not surprisingly, these often highly charged perceptions on the part of prisoners are shaped above all by their personal dealings and relationships with prison staff. When staff act unfairly or unnecessarily punitively, this is likely to reinforce inmates' intuitive perception that they themselves are the unjustly wronged victims of a cruel and vindictive system.

Counter-intuitive as it might seem, appealing to prisoners' ability for *moral reasoning* – by means of an approach whereby prison staff not only treat inmates fairly and with respect but also seek constantly to engage and interact with them as fellow human beings – is likely to be more successful than the failed instrumentalist (or carrot and stick) approaches of the past (see, for example, Liebling, 2001 and Liebling and Arnold, 2004). The approach we favour is best described as a relational one in the sense that the fostering of constructive and respectful social relationships between staff and inmates should be accorded the highest priority. (This is similar to the restorative justice approach (see Dignan, 2005a) and to social crime prevention techniques developed for use in schools (see Hope, 1995; Tonry and Farrington, 1995; Tremblay and Craig, 1995). Efforts have been made to implement such an approach both in this country and abroad: see Aertsen and Peters, 1998; Stern, 2005.) For relationships not only provide the context in which prisoners' perceptions of the way they are being treated are fostered, but also afford the only context in which any kind of constructive dialogue, emotional engagement and behavioural or attitudinal change is likely to be possible. This kind of approach is all too rare within the English prison system. Moreover, as we have seen, most recent attempts at reform have also sadly neglected the state of relations between staff and inmates. Nevertheless, the very few successful initiatives that have been developed in British prisons in recent years have all been founded on a relational approach of the kind we have just outlined.

The best known of these was the pioneering regime that evolved at the Special Unit which was set up in Barlinnie Prison in 1973 to house some of Scotland's most violent and disruptive prisoners. The regime that evolved at Barlinnie afforded considerable scope for prisoners to plan their own daily routines, and also to participate with others in the day-to-day running of the community (Whatmore, 1987). It had a relatively high staff–prisoner ratio and an ethos encouraging much less authoritarian relationships between staff and inmates. Although not entirely problem-free (there were a number of political difficulties fuelled by resentment towards the unit from other parts of the Scottish prison system), the unit appears to have been unusually successful in reducing the overall level of assaultive and disruptive behaviour on the part of inmates (Cooke, 1989: 133ff). Its most famous achievement was the remarkable rehabilitation of Glasgow gangster Jimmy Boyle (see Boyle, 1977). However, in spite of its international acclaim as one of the very few success stories within the British prison system, the Barlinnie Special Unit closed in March 1995 (Bowden, 1995). The ending of this liberal Scottish experiment (a similar unit in Shotts Prison also in Scotland ended in April 2000 when it was merged with the rest of the prison) marked a partial return to the failed policies of the past, and a revival of more austere isolation and control units including the recommissioning of the notorious cage cells at Inverness for prisoners who are considered to be particularly recalcitrant.

Exceptional though it was, the Barlinnie unit was not a unique outpost of enlightenment in Britain. In England, Grendon Underwood Prison is also run on the lines of a therapeutic community or TC (or, more precisely, five separate therapeutic communities within the prison) for prisoners with personality disorders, many of whom are among the most difficult and dangerous in the prison system. Selection for Grendon is unique since prisoners must first have been recommended by a medical officer and are then interviewed by Grendon staff to see if they will fit in (Leech and Cheney, 1999: 298). No one is compelled to go there, and inmates are free to return to the general prison system at any time, or they may be returned without consent if they fail to comply with the exacting requirements that are expected of them. While at Grendon, prisoners are expected to take part in a group therapy process, which teaches them about responsibility and the effect their actions have on other people. They are called to account for their behaviour (by fellow inmates rather than staff), and have to explain their conduct to the community as a whole. Like Barlinnie, Grendon has achieved some notable success stories. They include a prisoner who, having spent time in the strip cells of Dartmoor, graduated from Grendon with 'a different (and far more successful) outlook on life', and ultimately went on to produce the highly acclaimed *Prisons Handbook* (Leech and Cheney, 1999: 102). Nor was Mark Leech's experience unique. A seven year reconviction study showed significant reductions in levels of re-imprisonment and violent offences for those who stayed at Grendon for more than 18 months after controlling for risk and mode of leaving Grendon (Taylor, 2000; see also Marshall, 1997; Genders and Player, 1995). In spite (or possibly because) of its unique nature within the prison system as a whole, Grendon Prison was for a long time engaged in a battle for survival, in which it was denied both adequate resources and appropriate support from Prison Service Headquarters (HM Chief Inspector of Prisons, 1998). This pariah status is now at an end, however, following the opening of another special therapeutic unit at Dovegate in Staffordshire, which is a new (private) prison for Category B and C prisoners. It must be acknowledged that the Dovegate unit has also had its difficulties. An inspection of the therapeutic unit in 2008 found that around 40 per cent of the prisoners in the unit were not in therapy, which was undermining the progress of those prisoners who were; this problem was exacerbated by staffing and contractual issues, all of which 'seriously undermined the TC' (HM Chief Inspector of Prisons, 2008: 5).

A third 'beacon of enlightenment' within the British penal system in recent years, at least until May 2000, was Blantyre House, a Category C prison that provided a resettlement function for longer-term prisoners within a relatively open regime. The prison was almost unique in that for 13 years it had enabled prisoners to develop and pursue 'personal career plans', which were negotiated with management (Leech and Cheney, 1999: 40). Prisoners were encouraged to grow in self-reliance and self-respect, chiefly through their relations with staff, with each other and with people from the outside community. Indeed, they were expected to work in the community rather than in the prison workshops. Security systems had a very low profile, but escapes were almost unknown; violence, alcohol and drugs were not acceptable and resulted in instant transfer. The reconviction rate of those released from Blantyre was just 8 per cent after two years, compared with a rate of 57 per cent for those who left all other prisons in 1996 (Cullen and Minchin, 2000). Even allowing for the fact that Blantyre inmates were carefully selected and may thus have presented a lower risk of reoffending, these are impressive results, and a succession of official inspections by the prisons inspectorate and also the Home Affairs Select Committee attested to its achievements (Ramsbotham, 2005: ch. 9).

Not everyone was impressed by Blantyre House's performance, however, and the therapeutic unit was closed down following a raid by prison officers that claimed to uncover a considerable amount of contraband material. The truth was rather more prosaic (no charges were ever brought) but the damage had been done and the Blantyre House fiasco serves as another unwelcome reminder of the Prison Service's enduring capacity to snatch failure from the jaws of success, and its chronic inability to learn even from its own all-too-rare successes, let alone its much more numerous failures (for more details of the Blantyre House case see the previous edition of this book, Cavadino and Dignan, 2007: 241). Equally importantly, it also underlines the scale of the managerial crisis within the Prison Service which we discussed earlier. Defects in the governance of prisons resulted in the cynical and bullying behaviour of an area manager being condoned by the head of the Prison Service and senior politicians alike while a successful and respected prison governor's career was effectively destroyed. The Blantyre House saga is by no means unique (Ramsbotham, 2005 describes an episode involving the same area manager and Ford open prison which also took place in 2000) but epitomizes much that is wrong with the way the Prison Service is managed. Unless and until senior managers and the politicians to whom they are accountable can act with more wisdom – one could even say integrity – than was shown on this occasion the prospects for resolving this aspect of the crisis of legitimacy seem as distant as ever.

While debate will continue about the merits of using public or private sector agencies to deliver punishment, we would argue that prison privatization does raise a number of special legitimation problems of its own that are not easily dismissed. First is the possibility that private rather than public interests will be pursued, with the first of these being profit and the extension of corporate hegemony, although the promotion of personal self-interest and even the pursuit of private vendettas are also possible. There are numerous examples of politicians and civil servants joining private prison firms shortly after being involved in policy-making or the awarding of contracts (Nathan, 1994; 1995a; 1999). Private prison staff have been involved in several cases which have put the rights and safety of inmates at risk (Nathan, 1995b; Prison Reform Trust, 1998a). Prison privatization, therefore, offers no panacea for the crisis of legitimacy – indeed, it may be exacerbating the crisis.

In conclusion, if we are to create legitimacy within prisons we need to alter regime methods, atmospheres, attitudes and relationships as well as the formal entitlements of prisoners. And one additional, inescapable issue is that of resources. For example, one vital factor in the success of the Barlinnie Special Unit was its high staff–inmate ratio, which facilitated positive relationships while also maintaining necessary levels of security and control. More generally, it will be impossible to give prisoners effective entitlements to decent conditions without the material resources required. Consequently there can be little chance of successfully implementing reforms in anything more than small pockets within the prison system while an acute crisis of penal resources prevails. At present this crisis is set to worsen further as the prison population continues to soar. This trend needs to be forcibly reversed if we are ever to progress towards the goal of just and legitimate confinement, rather than continuing to travel at an ever quickening pace (in Judge Tumim's words) along the road to the concentration camp.

7

Early Release: The Penal System's Safety Valve

Early Release: Useful, Controversial, Troublesome

7.1 We saw in Chapter 4 that sentencing can be seen as the crux of the crisis. Changing metaphors, it is sentencing practice that stokes up both the prison population and much of the overall penal crisis. Given that there has been little success to date in turning down the heat and restraining sentencing, whether by governmental encouragement, legislation, initiatives by the senior judiciary or the use of sentencing guidelines (see Chapter 4, section 4.3), a perennially attractive alternative tactic has been to provide a safety valve to prevent the prisons from boiling over or even exploding. That safety valve has taken the form of the early release of prisoners before the end of their sentences. And indeed it has long been the case that the vast majority of offenders who are sentenced to imprisonment do not stay in prison for their entire sentence, but are released early at some point. For example, an offender who receives a sentence of imprisonment for four years will normally be released after two years, or even earlier. (This is despite the fact that a sentence such as four years' imprisonment is somewhat misleadingly known as a fixed-term sentence, which means only that the absolute maximum period which can be spent in prison under the sentence is fixed, in contrast to the indeterminate sentence of life imprisonment.)

From the government's point of view, one great advantage of early release as a mechanism for limiting the numbers of people in prison is that unlike sentencing it can be operated *administratively* rather than judicially – decisions to release early can be made by members of the executive arm of the state in a pragmatic fashion rather than being made by judges on the basis of legal rules or the judges' own discretion – and can thus promise to be more effective in serving the government's managerial ends. But there are severe disadvantages to early release, and these concern the legitimacy of the system. One major problem with early release is that the more extensively it is used, the more tenuous becomes the relationship between the original sentence of the court and the time actually served in prison. A second, rather different threat to legitimacy is that – precisely because early release schemes tend to be administrative rather than judicial – it may be felt that vital decisions concerning the liberty of the individual and the protection of the public are not being taken in a fair and proper way. As a result, the system of early release has always been vulnerable to criticism from commentators, penal reformers and sentencers alike, and has also contributed to cynicism and bitterness on the part of many prisoners, as well as being a potential source of outrage when released prisoners reoffend.

Indeed, the whole concept of early release is difficult to justify from a variety of value positions, and in principle many would prefer a system where 'what you get is what you serve' – in other words, the sentence pronounced by the judge specifies the exact length of time to be spent in prison. (This is variously known as 'real time sentencing', 'honesty in sentencing' and 'truth in sentencing'.)

Those who favour a punitive Strategy A approach to criminal justice tend to dislike early release because it lets prisoners off with a lesser punishment than the law and order mentality deems to be appropriate, and which (it is argued) leaves the public dangerously vulnerable to crimes committed by offenders released early. The traditional, classicist legal view which informs the justice model (see Chapter 2) has a different objection. It holds that early release offends against due process and the rule of law, because it means that the amount of punishment undergone for the crime is not determined by a judge following a hearing in open court. A judicial procedure would ensure that offenders had the full rights of natural justice, rights to hear all the evidence, present evidence, argue their case, be legally represented, have the decision justified by reasons and have rights of appeal; but instead the length of their punishment is determined by a discretionary administrative process which may be both secretive and unaccountable. It may also lead to unfair disproportionality, with offences of similar seriousness ultimately being punished by very different penalties (or vice versa).

Arguments of this kind tend to appeal to judges, whose power to control the punishments offenders actually receive is infringed by early release schemes. Consequently judges have often opposed and obstructed proposals to extend such schemes. Objections founded on natural justice grounds resonate with prisoners, who may feel that the vital question of when they will be released is governed by a cruelly opaque and arbitrary process. Most supporters of the human rights-oriented Strategy C are also repelled by the defects in due process and proportionality that are typically associated with early release procedures. On the other hand, they also believe that prison terms should be humanely short, at least for inmates who pose no serious threat to the safety of the public. Consequently, they may well favour early release but insist that it should as far as possible be automatic. Where it is discretionary, the discretion should be exercised according to procedures which maximize due process and natural justice. Ideally, decisions to grant or withhold parole should be made by a court, or at least by a process which mimics court procedures as far as possible, with judicial-style hearings, reasons for decisions, rights to legal representation and appeal, and so on. As we shall see, such arguments have borne fruit over the years, and two important long-term trends in early release have been, first, towards making early release automatic (especially for shorter term prisoners), and second towards the judicialization of discretionary parole decisions. (The latter development has been greatly assisted by a long series of court cases under both the English common law and European human rights law challenging existing discretionary arrangements.)

On the other hand, support for a highly discretionary early release system comes from two quarters. The first of these is the positivistic individualized treatment model (see Chapter 2, section 2.5), according to which it is only right that experts should make administrative decisions about when release occurs, since they are in the best position to judge when the offender is fit to be released. However, even though modern-day advocates of rehabilitation for offenders may still favour retaining early release, they tend to agree with other proponents of Strategy C that discretion should be limited by considerations of due process and fairness. The strongest support for discretionary early release comes from Strategy B – such a system seems well designed for the practical, managerial task of regulating the size of the prison population both flexibly and cheaply. (Even here, however, a managerial approach might also see virtue in much early release being automatic, which economizes on the time, cost and effort of making thousands of individualized decisions, which has often placed great stress on the Parole Board.) But a strategy of using discretionary early release to reduce the prison population runs into the highly practical problem of legitimacy, since principled opposition to the system makes it difficult to implement with long-term political success. An equally serious weakness of a penal management strategy based on early release is its failure to address the main root cause of prison overcrowding, namely the sentencing practices of the courts – the real crux of the crisis. As the Carlisle Committee's influential report on the parole system pointedly said in 1988: 'Expediting the release of prisoners while doing nothing to stem the flow of admissions is like bailing water from a boat without repairing the gaping hole in its bottom' (1988: para. 236). Consequently, as experience has repeatedly shown, expanding early release can only ever manage to contain the crisis in prison numbers temporarily.

As we shall see, early release can take different forms, the most important being *automatic* early release, traditionally known as **remission**, and *discretionary* early release, traditionally known as *parole*. Since 1999 these have been augmented by the *home detention curfew*, a scheme which allows short-term prisoners to be released early subject to a home curfew enforced by electronic monitoring. We will next provide brief historical accounts of the development of remission and parole, and then proceed to consider the system of early release now in place.

History of Early Release

From Remission to Automatic Early Release

7.2 The practice of releasing prisoners early by remitting the rest of the sentence has a long history, dating back to the eighteenth century when offenders were transported to the colonies. Since the end of the nineteenth century, prisoners in England could achieve early release if they earned sufficient marks which were awarded for industry and good conduct. Over time, however, remission became increasingly used to control the size of the prison population rather than to encourage prisoners' industry and good conduct, and release after a set fraction of the prison sentence became in practice automatic unless the prisoner positively lost some remission for breaches of prison rules or discipline. The proportion of the sentence that could be remitted also increased, from a sixth to a third in 1940 and in 1987 to one half for sentences of 12 months or less.

This system of remission (and the word itself) was abolished by the Criminal Justice Act 1991. But as we shall see, most prisoners are still normally released automatically before the end of their nominal sentence if they have not already received discretionary early release. This *automatic early release*, unlike the old remission system, now comes augmented for many with a licence to which conditions including compulsory supervision are attached, and prisoners can be recalled to custody during the period of their licence or made to serve the rest of their sentences if they reoffend. Prisoners' release dates can still be delayed if they misbehave in prison, as up to 42 *additional days* (as loss of remission is now called) may be imposed for offences against prison discipline. Until 2002 these additional days could be imposed by a prison governor presiding over internal disciplinary hearings. However, this system was changed following a ruling of the European Court of Human Rights, with the result that release dates can now only be postponed by independent adjudicators (see section 7.3 below).

Parole (Discretionary Early Release)

Whereas remission over the years became more or less automatic unless forfeited for bad behaviour (which now needs to be formally and fairly proven), parole developed as a mechanism for release – at an earlier stage in the sentence – which was granted at the discretion of the administrative authorities, and revocable at any time. Thus, parole is traditionally regarded as a privilege rather than an entitlement. Release on parole has always been on licence: parolees are subject to compulsory supervision by a probation officer, and other conditions can be inserted into the parole licence.

Parole was first introduced to England and Wales (imported from other jurisdictions such as the USA) by the Criminal Justice Act 1967, which allowed prisoners to be paroled once they had served one third of their sentences and at least 12 months. When it was first introduced, the parole system was highly influenced and shaped by the ideology of positivism. As we saw in Chapter 2, the positivistic treatment model favours the kind of indeterminacy and discretion which parole gives to punishment: offenders are treated in custody until they are sufficiently reformed, at which point (whenever that is) they are released, with further treatment being provided after release in the form of compulsory supervision. Until the experts deem the prisoner to be sufficiently reformed, however, he or she remains in prison in order to protect the public and facilitate further treatment. So the introduction of parole was by no means entirely driven by a pragmatic desire to use it as a safety valve to limit the size of the prison population. Indeed, at first, the parole system was not well designed for this practical task. Prisoners had first to be approved for release by a Local Review Committee (LRC) at their own prison. The LRC could then recommend prisoners for consideration by the Parole Board, an independent national body. If the Board then recommended parole, the case passed to the Home Secretary, who took the final decision. So three different decision-makers had to agree before a prisoner could be freed. Combined with an understandable desire on all parts to play safe in the early days of the scheme, this made for a very modest parole rate at first.

The early 1970s saw the collapse of rehabilitative optimism (see Chapters 1 and 2, sections 1.3 and 2.5), which seriously undermined parole's original positivistic rationale. But parole survived – indeed, the numbers of prisoners paroled expanded dramatically – because it was seen as too useful a safety valve for the practical purpose of reducing the numbers of people in prison. As a result, the development of the parole system over the next two decades was shaped much more by pragmatic considerations than by rehabilitative ideology. Home Secretaries gained the power to release some categories of prisoners without reference to the Parole Board, and explicitly encouraged the granting of parole much more readily, especially to relatively minor property offenders. As a result, by 1981 parole was being granted at double the rate it had been a decade earlier – in 55 per cent of cases considered compared with 27 per cent in 1969. But even this was not sufficient to abate the prison numbers crisis. A more radical proposal in 1981 to release short-term prisoners *automatically* after one third of their sentences was dropped, partly as a result of strong opposition from the judiciary and partly due to the hostile reception given to Home Secretary William Whitelaw at the Conservative Party Conference for law and order policies which were perceived as being too soft. Following this setback the government adopted an alternative approach: *bifurcation* (see Chapter 1, section 1.4). In 1983 parole was made available to more shorter-term prisoners while being simultaneously restricted for some more serious offenders. In this way the government hoped to relieve the problem of prison overcrowding while appeasing those who demanded tough law and order policies. The new twin-track policy did have the desired effect of increasing the overall rate of early release. But the changes also contributed to a growing sense of unease about the way the entire parole process was operating.

After two decades of almost continuous modification, the scope and importance of the parole system had changed beyond recognition. Between 1969 and 1989, the number of parole applications granted went up more than sevenfold (from 1,833 to 13,751). Equally noteworthy, however, was a marked *decline* in the parole rate for long-term prisoners, virtually cancelling out the reduction in prison numbers secured by extending parole to short-term prisoners. Short-term prisoners were much more likely to be granted parole than those serving longer sentences, and parole was thus serving to *increase the differentials* in the time served by the two groups of offenders – classic bifurcation – which served to exacerbate the sense of injustice felt by many long-term prisoners. According to some, it removed any incentive for many long-termers to behave well in prison because their chances of early release were now so slim in any event.

Another fiercely criticized aspect of the parole system – which had caused widespread resentment among prisoners from the very beginning – concerned the decision-making process itself, and its failure to comply with even the most elementary requirements of natural justice and due process. Not only was the procedure highly discretionary, it was also highly secretive. There was no hearing as such: prisoners were excluded from the deliberations of the Local Review Committee and the Parole Board, nor were they represented at them. Consequently, there was no way of challenging any of the evidence on which the parole decision was based, even though much of it was said to be subjective and anecdotal (Cohen and Taylor, 1978: 90). No reasons were given where parole was not granted, and there was no right of appeal against a refusal of parole, nor any effective way to review or question the decision-making process. This lack of fairness and natural justice was all of a piece with the generally pragmatic nature of parole policies over the years – political and administrative expediency ruled at the expense of principle and justice. There was also the issue of the veto which the Home Secretary could and in practice still often did wield over the release of prisoners: technically Parole Board decisions were still merely recommendations to the Home Secretary, meaning that the ultimate decision over the prisoner's freedom could rest, not with the quasi-judicial and independent Board but with an elected politician. This arrangement was to prove increasingly vulnerable to legal challenges on human rights grounds, and ultimately would be abolished.

Further problems included the sheer volume of cases to be dealt with. For long-term inmates this led to serious delays in the processing of applications for parole – it was even happening that prisoners' dates for release on parole were passing before they were informed of the decision. Shorter-sentenced prisoners on the other hand were being hurriedly granted parole on the basis of minimal scrutiny, thereby fuelling criticism that in effect they were being given automatic early release. All things considered, parole was seen as being in urgent need of review, which the government commissioned in the form of Lord Carlisle's report on parole published in 1988. Carlisle favoured two key principles: first, the idea of *parsimony* in the use of custody, and second, the notion of *real time* custodial sentencing (i.e. 'truth in sentencing'). Unfortunately, however, without a reduction in the sentences passed by judges, these two principles inevitably clashed with each other, leading to a slightly uneasy compromise which came into being with the passing of the Criminal Justice Act 1991. It has been estimated that – contrary to Carlisle's desire for parsimony in punishment – the 1991 reforms overall actually added about 1,000 prisoners to the total prison population (Hood and Shute, 1996: 86).

One major change in the 1991 Act was the replacement of one third remission by *automatic early release* – bringing the system of early release much closer to present day arrangements. Those sentenced to imprisonment for less than four years were automatically released after serving half of their sentence (subject to delays for misbehaviour in prison). Offenders sentenced to four years or more (but not life imprisonment) were released automatically after serving two thirds of the sentence. Following automatic release the remaining portion of the sentence which the prisoner had not served was held in suspense following release and could be reactivated following a reconviction or recall to prison, whereas under the old system time remitted would never be served. Discretionary release via parole lived on for those serving life imprisonment and those sentenced to four years or more: the latter could apply to the Parole Board for discretionary conditional release after serving half of their sentence. (Previously the minimum eligibility had been one third, so this represented a move towards real time sentencing.)

Reforms around this time also introduced some important changes in the *procedures* for deciding on discretionary early release. Local Review Committees were abolished by the 1991 Act, and the Home Secretary's veto on Parole Board decisions to release was restricted to long-term prisoners. Further procedural changes introduced in 1992 represented a move towards a less administrative and more judicialized system. All applicants for parole were now interviewed by a member of the Parole Board and were allowed to see the dossier of reports on which the Parole Board's decision was made. The Parole Board now had to give reasons for its decisions, but still sat in private to decide whether to grant parole. There was still no right to an oral hearing, and no right of appeal from the Parole Board's decision, but it was clearly becoming a more judicial and less administrative body.

For a short time in the 1990s, the whole system of early release came under the threat of near-abolition. This was during the period 1993–97 when the Conservative government and its Home Secretary Michael Howard wholeheartedly adopted Strategy A between 1993 and 1997. As we saw previously, the Strategy A, law and order mindset regards almost any early release as abhorrent because it lets criminals off too lightly, and sure enough provisions in the Crime (Sentences) Act 1997, passed shortly before the 1997 general election, provided that in future no prisoner could be released before having served at least five-sixths of the sentence originally passed. It was calculated (Penal Affairs Consortium, 1995a) that this extra massive shift in the direction of real time sentencing would have increased the prison population by 24,000. But these drastic proposals were never implemented. Although the Act was passed – shortly before the 1997 general election which removed the Conservatives from office – the relevant sections were never brought into force, and were eventually repealed in 1998.

The incoming New Labour government took the system of early release in rather different directions. One was the introduction in 1999 of the home detention curfew (HDC) scheme (explained in more detail in section 7.3 below), allowing many prisoners to be released even before their normal automatic release at the halfway point of the sentence – originally up to 60 days early but now for up to 135 days – subject to a home curfew enforced by electronic monitoring. This scheme – a classic safety valve measure – marked a reversal of the general trend towards real time sentencing and also a step away from judicialization, since the decision to release prisoners on HDC is (as we shall see in section 7.3) a highly discretionary one.

Further reforms were introduced by the Criminal Justice Act 2003. This Act continued the previous trend that early release (with the notable but time-limited exception of releases under home detention curfew) was increasingly to be either automatic or else decided upon by the Parole Board acting in an ever more judicial manner. Henceforth all normal fixed-term prisoners would be released automatically at the halfway point in their sentences (if not previously granted HDC). The Parole Board was now only to deal with the cases of offenders who received life sentences or other sentences designed for offenders deemed to pose special risks to the public (extended sentences and the now abolished imprisonment for public protection). The 2003 Act also – anticipating the day when a human rights court case would make this inevitable – finally removed the power of the Home Secretary to veto the release of prisoners by the Parole Board. (However, as we shall see, the Justice Secretary can still veto the release of prisoners under home detention curfew, set the conditions upon which prisoners are released on licence and recall released inmates to prison.) Further procedural changes in the Parole Rules 2004 – see section 7.3 below – also represented moves towards judicialization.

New Labour's changes to early release thus embodied some aspects of Strategy B (the pragmatic, managerial introduction of a new safety valve in the form of HDC) and of the justice model strand of Strategy C (further judicialization). Strategy A was not to be left out, however. Licences were henceforth to last until the very end of the original sentence; there was a new indeterminate sentence in the form of imprisonment for public protection, and provisions to be discussed in section 7.3 below ensured that many murderers would spend longer in prison. Towards the end of New Labour's term in office, however, there was another injection of Strategy B and another safety valve opened. This was known as **end of custody licence**, a scheme which ran between June 2007 and April 2010 whereby existing Prison Rules were used to release prisoners up to 18 days early, reducing the prison population by around 1,000 and earning the prison system a period of respite while awaiting the new prison capacity to come onstream.

The effects on early release of the Conservative–Liberal Democrat coalition which came to power in 2010 have been limited so far. When in opposition the Conservatives had consistently criticized the Labour government's early release policies and practices, in particular the home detention curfew and end of custody licence. They had promised to introduce a more honest system whereby the sentencing court would pass prison terms with specified minimum and maximum terms and early release would not be automatic but earned by good behaviour in prison. However the Coalition's actual reforms in the Legal Aid, Sentencing and Punishment of Offenders Act 2012 merely restricted early release in a couple of aspects, tightening the rules on the granting of a home detention curfew and increasing the minimum time to be served by prisoners on extended sentences.

Early Release Today

7.3 Various mechanisms exist which allow the early release of prisoners. For example, the Justice Secretary has discretionary powers to release a prisoner on licence on compassionate grounds in exceptional circumstances. (These powers are used to release prisoners in the last stages of terminal illness; for example, to release the gangster Reggie Kray a few weeks before his death from cancer in 2000.) Again, Prison Rule 9 allows for prisoners to be released on licence temporarily for various purposes. (It was this rule which was used to operate the end of custody licence scheme from 2007 to 2010: see section 7.2 above.) What follows chiefly concerns arrangements for *automatic early release, discretionary early release (parole)* and extra-early release on the *home detention curfew.*

Provisions and arrangements for early release differ according to the custodial sentence passed, with different rules applying to normal *fixed-term* sentences, such as a sentence of six months' or five years' imprisonment; to *extended* sentences passed on sexual and violent offenders who are deemed to pose special risks; and to sentences of *life imprisonment* and *imprisonment for public protection* passed on those found guilty of murder and other serious offences.

Fixed-term (Determinate) Sentences

Fixed-term (or determinate) sentences are those which are expressed as being for a definite length of time, such as imprisonment for six months or five years. (The phrase 'fixed-term sentence' is actually somewhat misleading, as the period of time the prisoner spends in custody is not of course entirely fixed given the possibility of early release. With fixed-term sentences the absolute *maximum* period which can be spent in prison under the sentence is fixed, in contrast to indeterminate sentences such as life imprisonment.)

Offenders serving prison sentences of *less than 12 months* are normally released automatically after serving half of their sentences. By 'normally' we mean that they can be released later should additional days be imposed on them for misbehaviour while in prison, and they can be released earlier on home detention curfew. Release for these prisoners is unconditional, which means they are *not on licence* and are thus not subject to licence conditions such as supervision. However, the unexpired portion of the sentence is held in suspense (like a suspended sentence), so that ex-prisoners who reoffend before the very end of their sentences can be made to serve the rest of it as well as any penalty imposed for the new offence.

Those sentenced to fixed-term prison sentences of *12 months or more* (but not to life imprisonment or extended sentences, which we discuss later) are normally released automatically halfway through their sentences (Criminal Justice Act 2003, s. 244) – again, with possibilities of home detention curfew and additional days. These ex-prisoners are released *on licence*, which lasts for all the rest of their sentences (Criminal Justice Act 2003, ss. 249–250). The licence contains conditions which the offender must abide by. A set of standard conditions, including good behaviour and keeping in touch with a supervising officer as instructed, is laid down by the Justice Secretary and extra conditions can be included in the licence by the prison governor. It is also possible for the court which originally sentenced the offender to recommend particular conditions for inclusion in the licence (Criminal Justice Act 2003, s. 238).

Fixed-term prisoners can be released on licence before the halfway point under the HDC scheme first introduced by the New Labour government in 1999 (now governed by section 246 of the Criminal Justice Act 2003). Release on HDC is subject to a home curfew enforced by electronic monitoring (or tagging), as described more fully in Chapter 5. Prisoners can be released on HDC up to 135 days before the date on which they would normally have been released on licence (but not before serving at least four weeks, and at least a quarter of the full sentence in prison). Thus, an offender sentenced to 12 months' imprisonment will normally be automatically released on licence after six months, but will be eligible for HDC after three months (a quarter of the sentence), while a prisoner serving a four-year sentence may be eligible for HDC after one year and 230 days. The conditions of HDC licences include a home curfew for at least nine hours per day, enforced by electronic monitoring (or tagging), as described more fully in Chapter 5 (section 5.3).

The decision to release prisoners on HDC is a highly discretionary one: this is not a scheme designed to maximize natural justice, but a flexible administrative arrangement intended to achieve the (Strategy B) practical, managerial goals of reducing prison numbers and hopefully achieving a smooth and safe transition from custody to freedom for many prisoners. The discretion to decide who gets HDC and when rests formally with the Justice Secretary but in practice normally with the prison governor, not with any judicial or quasi-judicial body such as the Parole Board. The governor's decision is taken on the basis of a risk assessment carried out by prison and probation staff. Prisoners should be given reasons for refusal of HDC, and appeals are possible. A governor's decision to release can be overridden: this occurred in 2004 in the high-profile case of Maxine Carr, the ex-girlfriend of the Soham child murderer Ian Huntley, who was imprisoned for conspiring to pervert the course of justice. Carr's release was blocked by Commissioner for Correctional Services Martin Narey, partly on the grounds that her release could undermine public confidence in the HDC scheme.

When the HDC scheme was first introduced in January 1999 prisoners could be released on HDC up to 60 days early. The scheme initially succeeded in bringing about a slight decrease in the prison population in 1999–2000, but only about half the amount expected. As prison numbers began to climb again thereafter, the period of early HDC release was increased to 90 days in 2002 and to 135 days (four and a half months) in 2003. In 2002, presumptive HDC was introduced for short-term prisoners: prison governors were instructed that HDC should normally be granted to prisoners serving less than 12 months (except for violent, sexual and serious drug offenders) unless there were compelling reasons not to. Conversely, various other categories of prisoner are ineligible for HDC or are presumed unsuitable unless there are exceptional circumstances.

The Conservative Party when in opposition repeatedly criticized Labour's introduction of new early release schemes including HDC, which it pledged to abolish when and if they regained power. But the Conservative–Liberal Democrat coalition government which came to power in 2010 backed away from abolishing HDC, now accepting that 'it can enable effective resettlement and public protection' (Ministry of Justice, 2011a: 53). However, the Legal Aid, Sentencing and Punishment of Offenders Act 2012 (s. 112) removed eligibility for HDC from prisoners serving four years or more (who were already in the category presumed unsuitable for HDC), and also from prisoners who had already been released early and recalled for breaching licence conditions or for committing further offences.

Home detention curfew's proponents can argue that it reduces the prison population (by about 3,000 currently), that it makes for a successful supervised transition from prison to liberty, and that only a tiny percentage of those released are convicted of further offences or recalled to prison while on HDC (Dodgson et al., 2001). However, since many thousands of prisoners are released on HDC the figures can be (and have been) presented in a more alarming manner. Much publicity was given in October 2006 to figures showing that 1,021 serious offences had been committed by offenders on HDC. Although it is doubtful just how serious many of these crimes were (over half seemed to be minor assaults: House of Commons Public Accounts Committee, 2006), they did include four cases of manslaughter and one high-profile murder. HDC is also seen by some as eroding public confidence in the criminal justice system, because it breaches the 'what you get is what you serve' principle and can be perceived as undermining the sentence of the court and reducing public safety.

The various times at which prisoners may be released early, whether automatically or under the discretionary HDC scheme, can be delayed if *additional days* are awarded against the prisoner for breaches of prison discipline (Criminal Justice Act 2003, s. 257). Since a ruling of the European Court of Human Rights in 2002[1] these additional days are no longer imposed by a prison governor in internal disciplinary hearings. Governors now have to refer more serious disciplinary cases to hearings held before independent adjudicators (district judges, who also sit in magistrates' courts: see the Introduction) at which prisoners may be legally represented. The independent adjudicator can postpone a prisoner's release date by imposing a maximum of 42 additional days for each disciplinary offence.

Prisoners on licence (including HDC) are under a legal duty to abide by their licence conditions. They can be recalled to prison by the Justice Secretary at any time (Criminal Justice Act 2003, s. 254), and this power is not restricted to cases where the offender has breached the terms of the licence or reoffended. Thus released prisoners can be recalled, for example, simply because it is feared that they may be about to reoffend. The number of prisoners recalled from early release has increased drastically in recent years, from 1,272 in 1999–2000 to 15,631 in 2010–11, reflecting tougher enforcement practices by the probation

---

[1]*Ezeh and Connors* v. *United Kingdom* (2002) 35 EHRR 28 and (2004) 39 EHRR 1.

service.[2] All this naturally adds to the inflationary pressure on prison numbers. It also threatens the running of the system in other ways. Recalled prisoners must be informed of the reasons for their recall. Prior to the Criminal Justice and Immigration Act 2008, the cases of all recalled prisoners (other than those on HDC) were then considered by the Parole Board, which could order their immediate re-release. The dramatic rise in the number of recalls meant that this was adding hugely to the Parole Board's administrative burden. Consequently, the 2008 Act attempted to ease this burden by providing that recalled offenders who were not considered dangerous should instead be released again automatically after 28 days.

Other than this role in considering the cases of prisoners recalled from licence, the Parole Board is no longer involved in release decisions for prisoners serving most ordinary sentences of imprisonment passed after 2005 (when the sentencing provisions of the Criminal Justice Act 2003 came into force). The Board's role under the current sentencing framework is limited to prisoners serving certain special types of sentence: *extended sentences* and sentences of *life imprisonment*. (It also still deals with long-term sentences passed before 2005, and for some time will be encumbered with the legacy of imprisonment for public protection, the sentence introduced by the Criminal Justice Act 2003 but abolished by the Legal Aid, Sentencing and Punishment of Offenders Act 2012: see section 4.4 of Chapter 4 and later in this section.)

Extended Sentences (Extended Determinate Sentences)

Extended sentences of imprisonment, designed to incapacitate either particularly persistent offenders or those considered to be particularly dangerous for a limited period of time rather than indefinitely, have a long and arguably consistently unsuccessful history. Specially extended sentences have been repeatedly introduced in different forms and then been unused, overused and/or misused, tinkered with and abolished, leading to no obvious benefits in terms of crime control but extremely obvious breaches of principles such as proportionality of punishment (see, for example, Ashworth, 2005: 182–4). The current version of the extended sentence – now also known as the 'extended determinate sentence' – is aimed at offenders who are thought to pose special risks of committing sexual or violent offences. It was introduced by the Criminal Justice Act 2003 (s. 227) and has been altered twice since.

Originally the extended sentence was mandatory for offenders who had committed certain specified violent or sexual offences whenever the court considered that there was a significant risk to the public of serious harm because they were likely to commit similar offences again, but they did not qualify for sentences of life

---

[2]Statistics from *Offender Management Statistics Quarterly*, available online at: www.justice. gov.uk/statistics/prisons-and-probation/oms-quarterly (accessed 18 December 2012).

imprisonment or imprisonment for public protection. However, since the Criminal Justice and Immigration Act 2008 extended sentences are no longer mandatory, and may only be passed if there is a previous conviction for a particularly serious offence, or the normal term of imprisonment for the offence would be at least four years. The court specifies an 'appropriate custodial term' equivalent to what would be a normal overall sentence for the offence *plus* an extended period to be served on licence thereafter, 'of such length as the court considers necessary' to protect the public, up to a maximum of five years for a violent offence and eight years for a sexual offence. Extended sentence prisoners are not eligible for release under home detention curfew, and are not automatically released after half their appropriate custodial term as are other fixed term prisoners. Following the Legal Aid, Sentencing and Punishment of Offenders Act 2012, extended sentence prisoners who have neither been sentenced to a custodial term of at least ten years nor convicted of particular specified serious offences are released on licence after *two thirds* of the custodial term. More serious offenders are referred to the Parole Board who may release if satisfied that continued imprisonment is no longer necessary for the protection of the public. If the Board decides not to release, these prisoners can remain in custody until the very end of their appropriate custodial term. On release, all extended sentence prisoners are then subject to the extra-long licence period specified by the court which passed the original sentence.

Life Imprisonment and Imprisonment for Public Protection

'Life' sometimes does mean life in prison – as we shall see – but most offenders sentenced to life imprisonment are released at some stage. Nevertheless, life imprisonment is a fully *indeterminate* sentence, meaning that people who receive such sentences can be kept in prison for the rest of their lives, and if they are ever released this will be the result of a discretionary decision. When they are released, this is on a life licence which continues until death.

Until 2005 life imprisonment was the only fully indeterminate sentence in the English system (although in a sense every sentence with possibilities of early release could be said to be partially indeterminate). However, the Criminal Justice Act 2003 (s. 225) introduced a new indeterminate sentence, imprisonment for public protection, for offenders who were considered to be dangerous but did not necessarily qualify for a life sentence. This highly controversial sentence – whose effect in terms of the prisoner's eligibility for release was almost identical to a life sentence – was abolished by the Coalition government's Legal Aid, Sentencing and Punishment of Offenders Act 2012, but not before thousands of offenders had received one. Many of these are likely to remain in prison for quite some time yet. In March 2012 there were 13,836 prisoners serving indeterminate sentences in England and Wales (16 per cent of the prison population): 7,819 on life sentences and 6,017 on IPP (Ministry of Justice, 2012b). These numbers have grown rapidly over the years, from 3,000 in 1992, 1,535 in 1980, 730 in 1970 (2 per cent of the prison population) and only 140 in 1957 (Penal Affairs Consortium, 1994: 2; Ministry of Justice, 2012b).

Even before the advent of the IPP this country had a very large number of prisoners serving indeterminate sentences by international standards. There are as many inmates serving sentences of imprisonment for life in England and Wales as there are in all the rest of the European Union put together. (Now added to these numbers are IPP prisoners: no other European country has anything resembling IPP in scale.)[3] One reason why England has so many lifers is that life imprisonment is the *maximum* sentence for a remarkably large number of offences in English law (about 70), for which judges can pass a *discretionary* life sentence. (Discretionary life sentences are passed for these offences when the court believes the offender poses a significant risk of causing serious harm to members of the public *and* the seriousness of the offence is such as to justify a life sentence – Criminal Justice Act 2003, s. 225). Another is that this is one of the few countries with a *mandatory* sentence of life imprisonment for all those convicted of murder. The judiciary and the overwhelming majority of commentators over the years (see for example Blom-Cooper and Morris, 2004) have called for the abolition of the mandatory life sentence, on the grounds that there are many different kinds of murder ranging from mercy killings to terrorist bombings. As a wide range of degrees of blameworthiness attaches to those responsible, the judge should – as with other crimes – decide (assisted by guidelines) what sentence is just and proportionate in each individual case. However, successive governments have taken the position that murder is a uniquely serious offence which needs to be marked with the mandatory imposition of the most severe sentence and special arrangements to guard against premature release from prison. As we shall see below, far from removing the mandatory element from the life sentence, the current Coalition government in 2012 introduced a new mandatory life sentence for those convicted for a second time of certain serious crimes other than murder.

All offenders sentenced to life imprisonment (or to imprisonment for public protection) have a *tariff* period set for them. This tariff is the *minimum* amount of time they must spend in prison, and is based on the seriousness of the offence. Once this tariff period has expired, the prisoner is eligible for parole. If paroled, the prisoner will be on a licence which will never come to an end. If not paroled, the lifer will stay in prison indefinitely. Over the years there was a long drawn-out process of successive alterations to the way in which tariff periods are set and the way in which it is decided whether a lifer whose tariff has expired should be released. To cut a long story short (for fuller details of this history see Shute, 2004), originally the decision to release lifers on licence was entirely at the discretion of the Home Secretary. In 1983 the tariff system was introduced, but again the final decision on what each lifer's tariff should be was taken by the Home Secretary (although the judiciary were consulted). Thus – in breach of such principles as the separation of powers and the right to a fair trial before an independent tribunal enshrined in

---

[3]In 2010 there were 7,475 lifers in England and Wales; within the EU Germany came second with 2,048 (Council of Europe Annual Penal Statistics 2010, Table 8).

Article 6 of the European Convention on Human Rights – a politician (the Home Secretary, or often in practice a junior Home Office minister) could and often did overrule the judiciary about how long a lifer had to stay in prison. These powers of the Home Secretary were gradually whittled away by a long series of court challenges over the years, both in the English courts and in the European Court of Human Rights in Strasbourg.[4] Finally the New Labour government (in the shape of Home Secretary David Blunkett) grudgingly accepted that henceforth it would have to be judges rather than politicians who set the minimum tariff terms, and the Parole Board rather than the Home Secretary who then made the final decision on release. And this is what the Criminal Justice Act 2003 provides.

When someone is convicted of murder, the sentence must still be imprisonment for life. But both in these mandatory cases and in cases where the judge passes a discretionary life sentence, the trial judge must then proceed to impose a 'minimum term order' (the statutory term for a tariff) which seems appropriate taking into account the seriousness of the particular crime. After the tariff has elapsed the Parole Board alone is responsible for deciding whether or not the prisoner is released on licence, based on the perceived risk to the public. However, in the case of murderers the politicians were not prepared to let matters rest wholly in the hands of judges and the Parole Board. The Criminal Justice Act 2003 (Schedule 21) contains *statutory guidelines* for the setting of tariffs for murderers. For certain particularly serious types of murder (including terrorist murders), the starting point provided in the guidelines is a *whole life order*, meaning that the lifer can never be considered for release (cases where life means life). (Whole life tariffs were first introduced by Home Secretary Douglas Hurd in 1988. Currently around 40 lifers are subject to such tariffs and as a result have no hope of ever being released. The best known prisoner of this kind was the Moors murderer Myra Hindley, who waged a long campaign to be freed but died in prison in November 2002 after serving 36 years.) The guidelines also provide starting points for murders falling into other categories, which can be adjusted upwards or downwards depending on the aggravating and mitigating circumstances of the individual case. Thus, for example, the starting point for murders of police officers is a tariff of 30 years, and for normal murders by adults 15 years. These guidelines in the 2003 Act were in many respects substantially more severe than previous guidance, and are helping to contribute to the continued pile-up of indeterminate prisoners in the English prison system. This has come on top of previous increases, for already lifers in general had been spending much longer in prison than they used to. The average time spent in prison by a mandatory lifer released in 2009 was 17 years (Ministry of Justice, 2010c: 143) compared with 14 years in 2005 and around nine years in 1965.

Imprisonment for public protection was introduced by section 225 of the Criminal Justice Act 2003 at a time when New Labour, along with the governments of many other countries, was placing strong emphasis on public protection

---

[4]The process was all but completed by two cases in 2002, *Dennis Stafford* v. *United Kingdom* (2002) 35 EHRR 32 and *R. (on the application of Anderson)* v. *Secretary of State for the Home Department* [2002] UKHL 46; [2003] 1 AC 837.

from dangers including terrorism and violent crime (see, for example, Seddon, 2008). Originally this was a mandatory sentence for offenders who were convicted of specified serious offences provided that the court believed there was a significant risk to the public of serious harm from the offender committing further crimes – even if the crimes already committed were not punishable by life imprisonment, and whether or not the seriousness of the offence justified such a sentence. Objections to the introduction of such a sentence were both principled and pragmatic. The principled objection is that such sentences mean that offenders are being imprisoned and kept in prison on the basis of what it is (speculatively) feared they might do in the future rather than what they have been proved to have done in the past, thus profoundly violating the principles of proportionality and just deserts (see section 2.3 of Chapter 2). Moreover it is well established that techniques for assessing dangerousness are inherently (indeed, inevitably) inaccurate, and in particular that future violent behaviour always tends to be over-predicted (see e.g. Bottoms, 1977; Monahan, 1981). So in practice the use of such measures is always likely to mean that many safe individuals are detained for everyone who would pose a genuine danger.

The practical (or Strategy B) objection to such a sentence was that this inevitable over-use would lead to an intolerable increase in the prison population, and also in the workload of the Parole Board (who have the task of deciding exactly when each and every IPP prisoner is safe to release) and the probation service (who supervise them indefinitely following release). These predictions duly came true. Despite receiving fair warning from a number of quarters – including senior judges, who expressed grave concern – the government was taken by surprise by the number of IPP sentences which were passed. By the end of February 2008 there were 4,000 prisoners serving IPP sentences, with numbers projected to rise to 12,000 by 2012. This build-up of IPP prisoners in prison and needing to be considered for release by the Parole Board led to a situation in which the courts held that their legal rights were being infringed. The courts upheld the complaints of two IPP prisoners whose tariff periods had expired but who could not demonstrate to the Parole Board that they were safe to release. This was because to do so they needed to undertake rehabilitation courses, which were not available because of shortages of resources.[5]

A review of the IPP sentence (HM Chief Inspector of Prisons and HM Chief Inspector of Probation, 2008: see also Jacobson and Hough, 2010) found that the situation was not sustainable in terms of penal resources. The government responded by introducing measures in the Criminal Justice and Immigration Act 2008 which made the sentence discretionary instead of being mandatory in specified circumstances, and also prevented IPP sentences except in cases where a tariff of at least two years was thought appropriate. This resulted in a decrease in the use of the IPP sentence by about a half. Even so, by the end of 2011 over 7,000 IPP sentences had been passed and only 502 IPP prisoners had ever been released. In

---

[5]*R. (on the application of Walker)* v. *Secretary of State for the Home Department* [2008] EWCA Civ 30; *Secretary of State for Justice* v. *James* [2009] UKHL 22.

March 2012 there were 6,017 prisoners serving IPPs of whom 3,506 were being held after their tariffs had expired.[6]

The Conservative–Liberal Democrat coalition government (after toying with the idea of retaining the IPP but restricting it to the most serious cases) eventually decided to abolish the IPP altogether by section 123 of the Legal Aid, Sentencing and Punishment of Offenders Act 2012. However, this was far from the end of indeterminate sentences which lead to offenders serving much longer than their offences might be felt to deserve. The life imprisonment sentence is of course still with us, and is mandatory for murderers even if their particular crime might not be felt to deserve such a punishment. Section 122 of the Legal Aid, Sentencing and Punishment of Offenders Act 2012 also introduced a new 'two strikes and you're out' mandatory life imprisonment sentence to replace the IPP. The sentence is mandatory for adult offenders convicted for a second time of one of a list of 45 offences. This is subject to (a) the previous offences having attracted a custodial sentence of at least ten years; and (b) the normal sentence for the second offence (one commensurate with its seriousness) being at least ten years' imprisonment. The court need not pass a life sentence if there are particular circumstances which would make this unjust in all the circumstances, but remarkably there is no requirement that the court should actually regard the offender as likely to commit serious offences in future, so if anything it is even less well designed than the IPP to protect the public from genuinely dangerous offenders. It remains to be seen what effect it may have on the crisis of penal resources.

The Parole Board

The Parole Board's members include judges, psychiatrists, psychologists, probation officers, criminologists and laypeople. The Board dealt with the cases of 26,414 prisoners in 2010–11, of which the majority (14,977) involved prisoners recalled to prison from licence (see above) (Parole Board for England and Wales, 2012). The rest of its caseload is now dominated by prisoners serving indeterminate sentences (life imprisonment and imprisonment for public protection), although it also deals with extended sentence prisoners and a decreasing number of fixed-term prisoners sentenced before 2005 whose release is still at the Parole Board's discretion. Fixed-term prisoners sentenced thereafter do not come before the Parole Board (unless on extended sentences or recalled from licence), as they are now normally released automatically after half their sentence. The Board does not decide on whether prisoners should be released on home detention curfew, as this is at the discretion of the prison authorities.

Some Parole Board hearings are not actually oral hearings with the prisoner present. 'Paper panels' consisting of one, two or three Board members deal with

---

[6]Statistics from *Offender Management Statistics Quarterly*, available online at: www.justice.gov.uk/statistics/prisons-and-probation/oms-quarterly (accessed 18 December 2012) and *Sentencing Tables* available online at: www.justice.gov.uk/statistics/criminal-justice/criminal-justice-statistics (accessed 18 December 2012).

most cases where a (pre-2005) fixed-term prisoner is applying for parole, or a fixed-term prisoner is recalled to prison from licence. However, in respect of life sentence and other indeterminate prisoners, the Board's procedure has changed radically in recent years. As we saw in section 7.2, the Board's procedures were originally highly secretive and open to objection on grounds of natural justice, but over the years its procedures have become increasingly judicialized. The Parole Board Rules 2004 provided for a full procedure which is now used for the majority of indeterminate sentence prisoners. Under this system, prisoners are entitled to a full oral hearing with many natural justice features. Oral hearings are held in private by a panel of three Parole Board members chaired by a judge or lawyer. Prisoners are entitled to attend the hearing, may be represented by a lawyer or other person, and can give evidence to the hearing, call and question witnesses and argue for their release. Also present may be a 'public protection advocate', and it is even possible for the victim of the crime to attend and present a 'victim personal statement' explaining how the offence has affected them. The Board must give written reasons for all decisions.

However, even in this greatly judicialized process there is still no right of appeal from the Board's refusal to grant parole; nor is there always an absolute right to know all the information which the Board uses to make its decisions. Normally the prisoner can hear and see all the evidence (including reports on the prisoner made within the prison system and by probation officers etc.). But the 2004 Rules allow the Justice Secretary to withhold certain information from both prisoners and their representatives and divulge it only to the Parole Board on the grounds that disclosing it 'would adversely affect national security, the prevention of disorder or crime or the health or welfare of the prisoner'. In 2005[7] the courts held that it was lawful for information to be withheld from the prisoner in this way and disclosed only to a special advocate who was appointed to make representations on the prisoner's behalf concerning the secret information, but was also bound not to communicate the information to the prisoner or his or her representative.

When making its decisions, the Parole Board is bound to apply set criteria known as 'release directions',[8] issued by the Home Secretary in 2004 and now the responsibility of the Justice Secretary. The Board's task is not to resentence offenders, or to reward or punish them for their behaviour in prison, or (despite the positivistic origins of the parole system) to make decisions designed to ensure that prisoners are most effectively rehabilitated. They are required to focus on whether the release of the prisoner poses an unacceptable risk to the public.

The release directions state that the Board should focus primarily on the risk of future reoffending by the prisoner if released, balanced against the benefits of

---

[7]*Roberts* v. *Parole Board and the Secretary of State for the Home Department* [2005] UKHL 45; [2005] 2 AC 738. The case concerned the application for parole of Harry Roberts, who was serving life sentences for the murders of three policemen in 1966.

[8]The Secretary of State's directions are available online at: www.justice.gov.uk/offenders/parole-board/sos-directions (accessed 18 December 2012).

supervised early release to both the offender and the community. However, the criteria are framed in such a way as to make any possible risk bear almost paramount importance: in the case of **determinate sentence** prisoners the Board is directed to 'take into account that safeguarding the public may often outweigh the benefits to the offender of early release'. In the case of lifers, the Board must not grant parole if 'the lifer's level of risk to the life and limb of others is considered to be more than minimal'. Following the introduction of these criteria there was a steep decline in the rate of parole. We have already seen that lifers are spending longer in prison than previously. The parole rate for determinate sentence prisoners considered for parole in 1996–97 was 36 per cent compared with 53 per cent in 1991 (and 62 per cent in 1984). In 2011–12 the parole rate in these cases was just 22 per cent, although it needs to be borne in mind that the remaining cases in this category are the most serious cases of long-term fixed sentences dating from before 2005, so release rates are not properly comparable to those for previous years.

There are concerns about some of the other (formal and informal) criteria used by the Parole Board when assessing applications for release. The formal release directions include whether prisoners have shown willingness to address their offending behaviour and have made a 'positive effort and progress in doing so'. Such a criterion is both vague and subjective, leaving the prisoner's liberty largely at the mercy of the possibly arbitrary assessments and reports of Prison Service staff and the interpretations put on them by Parole Board panel members. Recently (as we have seen) there have been particular difficulties since rehabilitation courses have often not been available due to a lack of resources and the growing number of IPP prisoners, so many prisoners have not even received the opportunity to show willingness and progress in this respect. There is also a further particular problem concerning those prisoners who continue to deny that they were ever guilty of the offence for which they were convicted. Although there is no blanket Parole Board policy against granting parole to 'offence deniers' (which would be unlawful), denial is often a potent factor working against a prisoner since it is seen as an indication of a poor attitude and unwillingness to address one's offending behaviour. Lifers who are in denial of murder seem to have particular difficulty in obtaining release: it is believed that only one person to date has been released on licence despite proclaiming her innocence of the murder for which she was convicted. This, of course, places genuinely innocent prisoners in a cruel Catch-22 dilemma – should they continue to honestly deny the offence and jeopardize their parole chances, or lie and admit the offence, crushing their chances of ever having their miscarriage of justice righted? Given the number of such miscarriages which have come to light in recent years and the likelihood that many more have not, there is no saying how many people, wrongly in prison to start with, have been kept in because they honestly assert their innocence.

The Parole Board currently faces severe problems concerning not merely its resources and procedures but also its legitimacy and even legality. On the resources front, the Board's workload is higher than it has ever been, thanks to factors such as the massive surge in the number of prisoners serving indeterminate sentences, the increase in recalls to prison from licence and the continuing pressure to provide a more judicialized (and hence more time- and resource-consuming) system of decision-making. In April 2010 there was a peak backlog of 2,600 cases awaiting an oral hearing; in April 2012 the figure still stood at 1,600, at a time when government austerity measures mean that funding is effectively frozen (Parole Board for England and Wales, 2012).

Perhaps more serious in the long run are the threats to the Board's legitimacy and legality. In 2008 the Court of Appeal held in the case of *Brooke*[9] that the Parole Board was insufficiently independent of the government, meaning that it was legally deficient not only under the European Convention on Human Rights but also under English common law. It is generally recognized that the problems stem from the evolution of the Board over the years. Originally the Parole Board was merely a body which advised the Home Secretary, making recommendations as to which prisoners should be released. Now, however, its role is legally more akin to that of a court or tribunal which itself makes decisions about the liberty of the individual (hence its judicialization over the years). According to legal and constitutional principles, therefore, it needs to be properly independent of the government (and hence should be incapable of acting as an agent of government policy). Yet its historical development has left this process incomplete and the Board is stranded in no man's land.

Parole Board and government literature proclaims that the Parole Board is an independent body. Technically it is an 'executive non-departmental public body' which is not part of the Ministry of Justice (previously the Home Office), but is sponsored and funded by it. Its members are appointed (in a formal sense at least) by the Secretary of State for Justice. As we have seen, the Justice Secretary issues directions to the Board laying down the criteria they should use in making release decisions. In the *Brooke* case the Court of Appeal decided that under these arrangements the Board could not be said to be properly independent of the government, since they placed the Justice Secretary in an inappropriate position of apparent influence over the Board's exercise of its duties. Moreover, Secretaries of State had in the past overtly sought to influence the way in which the Board does its job: the court referred, for instance, to a lecture given to the Board by then Home Secretary John Reid in 2006 in which he stressed that prisoners serving indeterminate sentences should be released only if the Board was 'absolutely satisfied' that it was safe to do so. Reid further announced that he was about to appoint new members of the Board who were either victims of crime or involved with supporting victims, in order to 're-balance the whole system in favour of victims'. Another incidence of government interference came in 2004 when the government sought successfully to prevent panel members granting interviews to prisoners in cases without an oral hearing by reducing the Board's budget accordingly.

The *Brooke* case prompted a review and consultation by the government on *The Future of the Parole Board* (Ministry of Justice, 2009b). This consultation discussed the options of turning the Parole Board into a full-blown court or tribunal (which

---

[9] *R (on the application of Brooke)* v. *Parole Board* [2008] EWCA Civ 29.

would be the most logical and principled step), but – although there has been no full official government response to the consultation as yet – the government has made clear that the Board will remain as a body sponsored by the Ministry of Justice for the time being, although it could become a tribunal in future (Parole Board for England and Wales, 2012: 9). The issue of Parole Board independence seems unlikely to disappear, and further challenges to its legality seem likely unless and until full judicialization is ever achieved.

Conclusion: Early Release Evaluated

7.4
Should we release prisoners early at all? Or is real time sentencing preferable, safer and fairer?

There is certainly a case against early release. Any such system is likely to lead to a variety of unfairnesses and discontents which will reduce the legitimacy of the system. On the one hand, discretionary procedures can lead to a sense of injustice on the part of those denied release; on the other hand, judges and members of the public can be dismayed to find that the sentence served sometimes bears a fairly tenuous relationship to the one passed in court. Sentencing courts are now directed (by section 174 of the Criminal Justice Act 2003) not only to pronounce the headline term of the prison sentences they pass (for example, four years' imprisonment), but also to explain in ordinary language the effect of the sentence, including when early release may occur. However, this attempt at making sentences transparent has its limitations, especially given the complicated nature of early release arrangements and the uncertainty generated by their discretionary elements. Again, increasing media attention on the *minimum* terms to be spent in custody rather than the headline terms ('X could be freed in as little as Y years') may well have had the effect of undermining the legitimacy of sentences. It also seems likely that the development of early release provisions (and indeed this transparency) has had the undesirable effect of encouraging courts to pass longer overall sentences to compensate, deciding first how long the offender should stay in prison and then calculating what overall sentence will achieve this (Coulsfield, 2004: 29). If so, early release will not actually be succeeding in reducing the prison population, merely ensuring that offenders are subject to onerous licence conditions on release and the threat of recall on top of serving time in prison.

What is to be said on the other side? Broadly speaking, three arguments are put forward for releasing prisoners early, and in our opinion they do provide valid reasons for retaining an early release system of some kind. First, early release is a way of mitigating the effects of the over-use of custody by sentencers and the excessive length of many custodial sentences which creates the prison numbers crisis. Ideally, this over-use should be tackled at source, at the sentencing stage; nevertheless it would probably be politically impractical in the foreseeable future to engineer the massive reduction in overall sentence lengths which would be required to compensate for a complete abolition of early release. So even if progressive moves in the direction of real time sentencing might be generally desirable in the long run, there is a strong case for retaining some kind of early release in the interests of humanity and of limiting prison numbers in a manner which is both practical and acceptable to the public.

A second argument for early release stems from the remarkable fact that parole is one of the relatively few penal measures which has actually been shown to work to a modest but significant extent in the sense of reducing reoffending rates for those who receive it. Research has shown that reconviction rates are significantly lower for those who are released on parole than for those who have been refused it. For example, one study found that parolees were 12 per cent less likely to commit a violent offence than might have been predicted from their histories of offending (Ellis and Marshall, 1998); another found that 8 per cent of paroled prisoners were reconvicted within six months of release compared with 29 per cent of non-parolees (Nuttall et al., 1977). It is true that 'better risk' offenders do tend to be selected for discretionary parole to start with; but even taking account of risk factors, parolees still seem to do better (Hann et al., 1991: 68–73). It seems that the combination of supervision and the threat of being returned to prison does serve to reduce the rate of reoffending after release. And it seems at least intuitively likely that a degree of support and supervision in the months following release from prison could well be of genuine assistance to many prisoners who would otherwise be left completely to their own devices as soon as they find themselves outside the prison walls. If this is the case, it argues for a system of *automatic* early release (with compulsory supervision) so that as many prisoners as possible receive its benefits, rather than a discretionary system, especially one which denies potential parolees many of the rights of natural justice.

A third argument – and one that, conversely, argues for *discretionary* early release, at least in certain cases – is that a parole system enables the length of a prison sentence to be modified in the light of developments after the time it is passed. Perhaps most importantly, parole allows an offender to be released when (and not until) the degree of risk to the public is thought to have diminished to an acceptable level. And indeed, even the most radical penal reformers (such as abolitionists – see Sim, 1992: 296) envisage some continuing need for at least a few exceptionally dangerous offenders to be detained on an indeterminate basis for purposes of incapacitation. (This is also true of our own vision for the future of the penal system which we outline in Chapter 10, section 10.3.) So long as this is the case, there will obviously have to be some means for determining when they are sufficiently safe to be released. However, the systems of highly discretionary early release which have predominated in the past represent a poor method of doing this. The oral hearings which now deal with lifers are a distinct improvement in terms of procedure, but still do not provide a fully fair system. There should be a full judicial hearing with a right to publicly funded legal representation and an unrestricted right of appeal, and certainly no political veto on releases and no political direction or influence over decision-making. In principle, the Parole Board should either become or be replaced by a fully-fledged court or tribunal. Bearing in mind all the difficulties associated with the assessment of dangerousness and the well-established tendency for dangerousness to be officially over-predicted (Bottoms, 1977; Monahan, 1981; Cavadino, 1989: 99–100), decisions should as far as possible not be based on the impressions, guesses and hunches even of experienced experts, since these are known to be unreliable and to give rise to the risk of unconscious prejudices swaying release decisions. They ought instead to be based on precise criteria which have an established and valid bearing on the genuine likelihood of the prisoner posing a serious risk if released. Nor should release criteria be framed (as they currently are) to encourage excessive caution in releasing.

So in our opinion, a morally defensible penal system would include provision for early release, although under a system different from the existing one. And this would need to form part of a more comprehensive reform package containing measures to reduce levels of custodial sentencing, which remains the crux of the crisis. The Carlisle Committee (1988: para. 236) was quite right to say that bailing out water from the boat is futile without repairing the hole in its bottom. On the other hand, to abolish or restrict early release without at the same time effectively tackling sentencing practice would be courting disaster.

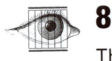

8

The Youth Justice System

There is a curious ambivalence in what Durkheim (see Chapter 3, section 3.3) would have called our 'collective sentiments' about young offenders. On the one hand, the image of the young thug is a perennial focus for fear, hatred and periodic moral panics (Cohen, 1980; Pearson, 1983), and this sometimes leads to particularly repressive measures being devised for young offenders. On the other hand, our attitudes towards children in trouble can also be infected with the sentimentality evoked by children more generally in our culture, particularly where they are mistreated, and this can lead to less harsh measures being countenanced for them. (For more on public attitudes towards young offenders, see Hough and Roberts, 2005: ch. 6.) Perhaps because of this ambivalence, the history of the penal treatment of young offenders has been especially chequered and contradictory.

Experience in England and Wales in the last few decades shows this particularly well. An Act of Parliament (the Children and Young Persons Act 1969) which was intended to create a radically new and more lenient system for dealing with juvenile offenders led paradoxically to a massive increase in the incarceration of young people in the 1970s. In the 1980s, despite an apparently discouraging political climate, developments in juvenile justice were hailed as highly successful in reducing the custody rate for young people and as showing the way forward for a more general reform of the criminal justice system. But these approaches to youthful offending were in turn to fall out of favour with the government in the 1990s as the pendulum swung against the young offender once more. We are still treating young offenders more harshly than we did (and than other countries do), but at the same time there are some current developments pointing in a more humane direction – although perhaps the most significant issue at present is the overriding need to reduce expenditure on keeping young offenders in custody.

Young People, Crime and the Penal Crisis

8.1 There hardly seems to have been a time, at least since the early nineteenth century, when the criminal activity of young people has not been a cause of major public concern. We seem to be repeatedly told, not least by the media, that crime among young people is a serious and ever-worsening problem, often in contrast to a previous golden age – perhaps about 50 years ago – when youth posed no great threat to public order and safety. If we check the historical record, however, we find that at the time of the supposed golden age people were saying exactly the same things (Pearson, 1983).

It is true that adolescents do appear to commit a disproportionate number of crimes compared with their elders (although it is also worth noting that children and young people are more than twice as likely as any other age group to be victims of crime: Wood, 2003; Evans, 2005); and in 2012–13 almost one-quarter of those found guilty of indictable offences were under 21. The rate of known offending for males between the ages of 15 and 20 is around five times the rate of known offending for adult males and the peak age for committing a detected offence is 17 for boys and 15 for girls. But little of this is serious crime, especially for offenders under 18. The vast majority of really serious crime is committed by adults.

As the above figures suggest, offending by young people is in the great majority of cases a transient phenomenon of adolescence. Research studies (see for, example, Belson, 1975; West, 1982; Graham and Bowling, 1995) suggest that most young people commit at least some minor offences, which in the main go undetected, while even the ones who are repeatedly caught offending in their teens typically grow out of crime as they progress to adulthood (Osborn and West, 1980; Rutherford, 1992: ch. 2; Flood-Page et al., 2000: 18–19). To complete this comparatively unthreatening picture of young people's crime, the official statistics suggest that – far from a youth crime wave being upon us – offending by young people has been *decreasing* in recent years. In 2001–2 a total of 83.7 thousand defendants aged 10–17 were proceeded against in the youth courts for indictable offences, while the figure for 2012–13 was 45.7 thousand – a decrease of almost 50 per cent. And the number of young people under the age of 18 held in custody has been dropping since 2008.

Yet young people continue to contribute to the numbers crisis in the custodial system. In June 2012 offenders under the age of 21 accounted for around 10 per cent of the prison population (which includes custodial institutions for young offenders). Hardly any other Western European countries lock up as many young people proportionately (NACRO, 2003; see also Cavadino and Dignan, 2006: 300–1), despite research results suggesting that young English people commit fewer offences than their counterparts in other Western European countries (see Junger-Tas et al., 1994).

The way we deal with young offenders also affects the penal system's crisis of legitimacy. The most commonly voiced concerns – apart, of course, from the usual perennial complaints about alleged softness – relate to the conditions and regimes of the custodial institutions which contain so many young people, many of whom are officially classified as 'vulnerable' (see Howard League for Penal Reform, 2006). Custodial institutions for young offenders – and certain ones in particular – have repeatedly been the focus of serious concern. In 1999 the Chief Inspector of Prisons described conditions at Feltham Young Offender

Institution as 'unacceptable in a civilised country'. In March 2000 he was similarly scathing about Portland Young Offender Institution, describing conditions there as a 'moral outrage' (HM Chief Inspector of Prisons, 1999d and 2000b); there have also been serious allegations about brutal staff behaviour in Portland over many years, culminating in the dismissal of two members of staff in 2002. Reports by the Chief Inspector of Prisons voicing concerns about bullying, staff intimidation and the use of inappropriate control and restraint techniques at a number of other YOIs including Stoke Heath, Brinsford and Onley suggest that these are far from being isolated incidents (see also Amnesty International, 2002). Following the death in 2004 of 15-year-old Gareth Myatt at Rainsbrook Secure Training Centre while being restrained by staff, the Howard League for Penal Reform commissioned an independent inquiry into the restraint, strip searching and seclusion of children in STCs and secure children's homes. Lord Carlile (2006), who conducted the inquiry, found that children were being subjected to painful restraint methods and forcible strip searching, while hundreds were being held in solitary confinement, often for weeks at a time. Another concern is that young people who are sentenced to custody are often housed many miles from home, which makes it extremely difficult for them maintain contact with their families.

Perhaps the most disturbing single recent incident concerning young offenders was the brutal murder of 19-year-old Zahid Mubarek at Feltham in 2000. Mubarek, serving a short sentence for minor property offences, was battered to death by his cellmate, a known violent racist. A public inquiry (Keith, 2006) found that 186 separate individual and systemic failures had led to the murder, and that prison staff possibly did at times (as had been alleged) deliberately put unsuitable inmates together in cells (although not on this occasion). The young offender institution had been overstretched, under-resourced and blighted by racism, both institutional and at times overt.

Not surprisingly, perhaps, there is a disturbingly high level of suicide and self-harm within custodial institutions for young offenders: no fewer than 29 young people under the age of 17 are known to have committed suicide between 1990 and 2005 (see also Goldson and Coles, 2005). In August 2004, 14-year-old Adam Rickwood became the youngest person to commit suicide in a British penal institution when he took his own life in Hassockfield Secure Training Centre. Finally, even the government-appointed **Youth Justice Board** (YJB) – whose job it is to manage custody for young offenders – has called into question the effectiveness of locking up young people as we do, noting that 'reoffending rates remain high and there are still young people sentenced to custody for whom a community sentence would be more appropriate' (Youth Justice Board, 2011: 2).

Young offenders represent a crucial facet of the penal crisis. For while, on the one hand, concern about young offenders has helped to fuel the ideology of law and order, thereby worsening the crisis, the youth justice system has also provided examples of successful ways of dealing with young offenders that suggest ways of defusing the crisis if the right lessons could be learned and applied.

Responding to Youth Crime: Models of Youth Justice

8.2 The history of the English youth justice (or juvenile justice) system[1] has been turbulent, complex and frequently paradoxical. In particular, the pace and scale of the changes that have been made since 1998 are so great that the current system is now often referred to as 'the New Youth Justice' (e.g. Goldson, 2000). We will present a detailed account of the current youth justice system later in the chapter. Before doing so, however, we provide an overview of five distinct approaches that have influenced youth justice policy-making over the years (see further Cavadino and Dignan, 2006: ch. 12): the *welfare*, *justice*, *minimum intervention*, *restorative justice* and *neo-correctionalist* approaches. They are in approximate chronological order in the sense that the successive models have enjoyed their greatest popularity with British governments roughly in the order in which we discuss them, but none of these approaches has ever been pursued to the total exclusion of all the others. In practice policy is always a mixture of models, which can often give rise to tensions and contradictions. The models we discuss here have some obvious connections with the three Strategies we set out in the Introduction, although they do not map perfectly on to each other. In essence, the welfare, minimum intervention and restorative justice models all represent different versions of the humanitarian Strategy C. Justice model thinking can be aligned with either Strategy C or the more punitive Strategy A. Neo-correctionalism – the dominant strand in recent years – combines elements of Strategy A and the managerial Strategy B along with some traces of Strategy C.

The Welfare Model

The emergence in the nineteenth century of a juvenile justice system that was distinct from its adult counterpart owed much to the influence of the **welfare model**. This approach incorporates the positivistic assumption (see Chapter 2, section 2.5) that juvenile wrongdoing is the product of social or environmental factors over which the young person has little or no control, and maintains that young offenders should, accordingly, be helped rather than punished. The influence of the welfare model on the English youth justice system has in general been much less pervasive than in many other countries (see Cavadino and Dignan, 2006: chs 12–15 for details). Nevertheless, it is reflected in a long-standing statutory duty requiring all courts to 'have regard to the welfare of the child' in making its decisions and to ensure that 'proper provision is made for his education and training' (Children and Young Persons Act, 1933 s. 44(1)). Although still in force, the impact of this stipulation has been greatly diminished by the fact that it has

---

[1]The former term is now used more generally following the establishment of the 'youth court' in place of the 'juvenile court' by the Criminal Justice Act 1991. However, the term 'juvenile' is still useful to refer (since 1992) to the age range 10 to 17 inclusive.

not been consistently reflected in subsequent youth justice policy and legislation. A very radical attempt to reform the juvenile justice system in line with the welfare model *was* introduced in 1969 with the passing of the Children and Young Persons Act (CYPA) by the Labour government of the day. This did aim to promote a much more positivistic approach in which the young person's welfare would be the prime consideration and the intention was that almost all children who offended under the age of 14 would be dealt with by means of civil care proceedings rather than prosecution. The Act also intended to phase out criminal proceedings for all but the most serious juvenile offenders over the age of 14 and to ensure that even those who were convicted would be placed in care rather than punitive custody.

This radical reform agenda never came to pass, however, for a change of government in 1970 meant that the CYPA was only partially implemented and, as a result, the traditional function and custodial sentencing powers of the juvenile court remained largely unscathed (an equally radical reform of the Scottish juvenile justice system was implemented at around the same time by the Social Work (Scotland) Act 1968 and this largely continues today: see Martin and Murray, 1982; Pratt, 1986; Bottoms and Dignan, 2004). Although the intention of the CYPA was that juveniles who offended should be helped rather than punished and that they should be dealt with in the community rather than sent to custody, the actual result was, spectacularly, the reverse. There was a distinct decline in the use of community-based disposals for juvenile offenders coupled with a massive rise in the use of custody, from 3,000 custodial sentences in 1970 to over 7,000 in 1978. The most telling figures are for males between the ages of 14 and 16 inclusive. Only 6 per cent of sentenced offenders in this category were sent to custodial institutions in 1970 (the last year before the CYPA came into force). By 1978 the proportion had doubled to 12 per cent (Home Office, 1981: Table 7.7).

The Justice Model

In contrast to the positivism of the welfare model, the justice model (see Chapter 2, section 2.5) espouses a more classicist punishment-oriented approach, which treats young offenders as reasoning agents who are responsible for their actions. Accordingly, it places more emphasis on the deeds and deserts of the child rather than their welfare needs. It also seeks to reduce official discretion in the system; to ensure that like cases are treated alike according to the offenders' just deserts; and to ensure that suspects' rights of due process are upheld (Taylor et al., 1979; Morris et al., 1980). The strong influence of justice model thinking is reflected in the fact that the English youth court has essentially remained a 'junior criminal court' with only minor modifications from its adult counterpart as opposed to the welfare tribunal that has become established in a number of other jurisdictions such as Scotland and the Scandinavian countries (see Cavadino and Dignan, 2006: Chapter 15). It was also reflected in the replacement, in 1983, of a semi-indeterminate treatment-oriented form of custody known as 'borstal training' with a determinate, more explicitly punitive, custodial sentence known as 'youth custody' (now detention and training orders). A variety of procedural reforms during the final quarter of the twentieth century – including the growth of state-aided legal representation for defendants and advance disclosure of the prosecution case – were likewise consistent with a justice model approach. However, these reforms also resulted in increased delay and expenditure, which fuelled concerns about the efficiency and effectiveness of the youth justice system. These were to come to a head in the 1990s with a hard-hitting review by the politically independent Audit Commission (1996: 26–9). It complained that a preoccupation with procedural reforms had slowed down procedures, increased the number of court appearances before a young defendant was finally dealt with and added greatly to the expense of the system.

Justice model thinking also strongly influenced a fundamental change in the orientation and structure of the English youth justice system that came into force in 1991. Hitherto, the English juvenile court had incorporated two distinct jurisdictional strands, for it was responsible for dealing both with young offenders and also with vulnerable young people who were considered to be in need of care and protection. These two strands were disaggregated, however, by the Children Act 1989. Since then, responsibility for children who are in need of care and protection has been vested in a separate care jurisdiction that is administered by lower civil courts known as 'family proceedings courts'. Here, the welfare of the child continues to be the paramount consideration save in exceptional circumstances (s. 1(1) Children Act 1989). This left the juvenile court – renamed the **youth court** by the Criminal Justice Act 1991 – to deal exclusively with criminal cases. This reform was politically uncontentious at the time, having been the subject of extensive consultation. Indeed, it was welcomed by many leading child law experts for removing civil care cases from 'the criminal overtones associated with the juvenile court' (Bainham, 1990: 181–2). Subsequently, this rigid institutional separation between the civil care jurisdiction and the criminal jurisdiction has been retained throughout the many turbulent changes that have since been visited upon the youth justice system. One very important consequence, however, has been to further dilute the influence of welfare considerations when the youth court is dealing with young offenders even though the court is still bound to 'have regard to the welfare of the child'. This can cause particular problems for those young people with acute welfare needs who also break the law, since they now find themselves subject to two separate sets of agencies, courts and operational philosophies. Many commentators see it as a matter for growing concern that such troubled young people, when they are prosecuted in the youth court with its unambiguous criminal orientation, may be dealt with without a proper regard for their welfare needs (see, for example, Ball, 2004: 37; Bottoms and Dignan, 2004: 124–7).

Minimum Intervention and Systems Management

A third approach that exerted a considerable influence over youth justice policy-making and (more particularly) youth justice practice during the 1980s and early 1990s is characterized by a philosophy of minimum intervention. One of its conceptual roots derived from Rutherford's influential thesis that – as we noted earlier – the great majority of young offenders simply grow out of crime (Rutherford, 1986). A second root – strongly influenced by criminological 'labelling theory' (see Chapter 2, section 2.2) and Schur's (1973) theory of 'radical non-intervention' – derives from the belief that formally processing offenders by catching and punishing them is harmful and can make matters worse by increasing the likelihood of reoffending. The minimum intervention strategy is linked with a number of specific policies with regard to young offenders:

- Decriminalization, whereby certain offences – particularly so-called 'status offences' that involve wayward or dissolute behaviour on the part of young people, such as truancy, under-age drinking and illicit sexual behaviour – no longer carry the threat of prosecution and punishment.

- Diversion from prosecution by cautioning or warning young offenders instead.

- Avoiding 'net widening' (see Chapter 5, section 5.5) by trying to ensure that alternatives to prosecution such as cautioning are only used for those who would otherwise have been prosecuted.

- Diversion from custody by encouraging sentencers to make use wherever possible of community-based alternatives.

- Depenalization: removing some or all young offenders from the criminal jurisdiction entirely and dealing with them instead by means of civil proceedings involving the use of child sensitive institutions or tribunals.

This minimum intervention philosophy was enthusiastically embraced by a remarkably influential coalition of academics (all of whom were experienced former juvenile justice workers) and practitioners who collectively became known as the 'juvenile justice movement' (and later, the 'youth justice movement'). The movement was led by the Lancaster Group – so-called because of its association with Lancaster University's Centre of Youth, Crime and Community – which not only engaged in research and published influential writings (most notably *Out of Care* by Thorpe et al., 1980) but also pioneered a highly effective strategy for promoting and implementing a minimum intervention approach. The strategy was based on the development and systematic application of a new approach to youth justice known as *systems management*, which seeks to harness *managerialist* techniques associated with a Strategy B approach to criminal justice, though with the ultimate aim in this instance of achieving *humanitarian* (Strategy C) goals.

The systems management approach starts with systems *analysis*: a rigorous attempt to elucidate how the criminal or youth justice systems and their constituent parts interact and interconnect, why they function in the way that they do, and what this means for suspects and defendants as they pass through the system. Armed with this knowledge, it may then be possible to devise and facilitate systems *interventions* in order to modify the process to achieve specific desired outcomes, such as a decrease in the numbers of young people being prosecuted or ending up in custody. Various techniques were developed in order to pursue minimum interventionist policies such as decarceration, diversion from prosecution and custody and the avoidance of net-widening. These techniques included the *targeting* of offenders known to be at risk of formal processing, developing **gatekeeping** mechanisms to divert young suspects and offenders away from prosecution and custody (see previous editions of this book for details of these various techniques and mechanisms), fostering **inter-agency** co-operation and monitoring to ensure that the interventions were having the desired effect.

In terms of its impact on the youth justice system, this kind of *systems management* could claim a substantial degree of success during the 1980s and early 1990s, including dramatic reductions in the rates of prosecution and custody. For example, by 1992, 82 per cent of known indictable offenders under the age of 17 were being cautioned, compared with just 49 per cent in 1980 (Home Office, 1990b and 1993); and with regard to diversion from custody, the proportion of custodial sentences imposed on prosecuted male offenders aged between 14 and 16 declined from a peak of 12 per cent in the years 1979 to 1985 to 7 per cent in 1990 (although it did rise to 9 per cent in 1992). One of the factors contributing to this success was that – at least for a time and albeit for largely pragmatic reasons – it gained the interest and active support of the Conservative government of the day. Despite that government's enthusiastic espousal of law and order rhetoric generally, it encouraged the use of police cautioning as an alternative to prosecution and invested heavily in diversionary alternatives to custody. Ultimately, however, this uneasy alliance between ideological opponents foundered during the early 1990s when John Major's Conservative government responded to a growing moral panic over youth crime by reverting to a more characteristic law and order approach that castigated any attempts to limit punishment.

The Restorative Justice Model

A fourth approach which, as we shall see, is becoming increasingly influential in the youth justice sphere is the restorative justice approach. This advocates a more participatory decision-making process in which those with an interest in a particular offence – offenders, victims and other interested parties – have the opportunity to deliberate together and seek agreement on the most appropriate way of responding to it (see also Chapters 2, 5 and 10). In terms of youth justice policies and processes, the restorative justice model shares the minimum intervention model's preference for diverting many, if not most, offenders from prosecution since the conventional criminal trial process is seen as an inappropriate forum for collective decision-making. Strategies aimed at decarceration are likewise favoured for most offenders who continue to be tried and sentenced in the conventional manner, on the grounds that custodial penalties often make it very difficult to secure restorative outcomes. Penalties which contain elements of reparation (such as compensation orders, reparation orders and community service) are preferred where possible. Many restorative justice advocates also share the minimum intervention model's view that formal responses to offending are potentially harmful, though not simply because of their stigmatizing effect on offenders. An additional weakness in their view is that they are typically insensitive to the needs of victims and deaf to the concerns of the wider community. Other restorative justice advocates are more optimistic about the compatibility of restorative justice and criminal justice values and processes and view the former as a valuable means of reforming and ameliorating the latter. Restorative justice advocates do not favour a minimum intervention approach, however, since this does nothing to address the needs and concerns of any of the key protagonists. It fails to provide help, where needed, for offenders – or hold them accountable for their actions – does nothing to facilitate reparation and support for victims and fails to provide a forum in which the views and concerns of the relevant 'community of interest' might be addressed.

The adoption of a full-blown restorative justice model would restrict the role of the youth court to determining issues of guilt and innocence in contested cases and providing a back-up in cases for which a restorative justice approach would be unsuitable. No jurisdiction has gone quite this far (although the New Zealand youth justice system has gone further than most, see Morris, 2004), and the English youth justice system is a long way from it. Indeed, before 1997 there was no specific legal basis or framework within which restorative justice initiatives might operate and, consequently, these were confined for the most part to small-scale, local, *ad hoc* experimental projects. Most of these were not in any way integrated within the mainstream criminal justice system, but co-existed, often rather precariously, on its margins, though some did enjoy short-term Home Office funding linked to an evaluation study (Marshall and Merry, 1990). Most projects operating during this period were either based on the process of victim–offender mediation (see Chapters 2 and 5, sections 2.4 and 5. 3) or relied on indirect mediation to negotiate reparation agreements between victims and offenders. Many were also linked to diversionary initiatives that were inspired by the systems management approach and, perhaps as a result, several were criticized for being more concerned with avoiding prosecution or custody for offenders than with meeting the needs of victims (see Davis et al., 1988; 1989).

Since 1997, as we shall see, certain aspects of a restorative justice approach have been incorporated as part of the regular mainstream response to youth offending in England and Wales, though this has been done on a rather piecemeal basis that supplements rather than supplants the existing youth justice system. Consequently, the strength and direction of this particular current within the overall post-1997 reform programme remain rather weak and uncertain, largely due to the overwhelming influence exerted by a hybrid approach that might be termed neo-correctionalist.

Neo-correctionalism

The neo-correctionalist approach has much in common with the punishment-oriented Strategy A law and order ideology (see the Introduction) which flourished most notably in the period of the Conservatives' law and order counter-reformation between 1992 and 1997. But it is much more than this and in certain respects it has more in common with some of the other approaches we have been examining.

We can see precursors of neo-correctionalism in the 'short sharp shock' detention centres of the early 1980s (Cavadino and Dignan, 2002: 291), the backlash against the minimum intervention approach of the 1980s reflected in the withdrawal of the presumption in favour of cautioning juvenile offenders following the James Bulger murder in Liverpool in February 1993, and in the interest in **boot camps** imported from America in the early 1990s.

The main aim of the neo-correctionalist approach is the prevention of offending and reoffending rather than imposing punishment for its own sake, and all other aims are subordinated to this overriding objective. However, the type of behaviour that a neo-correctionalist approach aims to prevent is not confined to purely criminal behaviour but extends also to acts of 'pre-delinquency', including truancy and other forms of rowdy or anti-social behaviour, which is reminiscent of early welfare approaches. This much broader focus reflects a far more ambitious agenda for the entire criminal justice system, which is no longer restricted to responding to crime *per se*, but is also concerned about the preservation of community safety and public order in general. Moreover, the techniques that are used to combat such behaviour likewise draw on a wider armoury of measures comprising diversionary, civil and quasi-criminal interventions as well as more traditional criminal penalties.

Within a more traditional youth justice context, neo-correctionalism explicitly rejects the 'don't make matters worse' philosophy of the minimum intervention approach in favour of a policy of *zero tolerance* (see Cavadino et al., 1999: 28–30). This requires offending behaviour to be nipped in the bud even if it is petty or first time offending. With regard to more serious or persistent young offenders the neo-correctionalist approach seeks to intervene progressively – with increasing intensiveness with each successive offence – rather than making the severity of the punishment fit the seriousness of the offence as the justice model demands. As for the nature of the intervention, the neo-correctionalist approach is interested in measures that are considered likely – in the light of known evidence – to succeed in preventing a recurrence of the problem rather than simply imposing punishment for its own sake. But in contrast with the welfare model, with its holistic emphasis on the personal rehabilitation of convicted offenders, the neo-correctionalist approach seeks to address a relatively limited range of risk factors – for example, truancy, poor parenting or dysfunctional peer relationships – that are known to be predictive of offending behaviour.

This ostensibly evidence-led approach underscores another important aim of the neo-correctionalist model: to improve the effectiveness and efficiency of the youth justice system by co-ordinating the activities of the relevant agencies, targeting interventions according to the perceived degree of risk and by speeding up youth justice processes. In this respect the neo-correctionalist approach shares with the minimum intervention model an enthusiasm for applying systems management techniques, though in this case the main goal is the reduction of crime rather than the diversion of young offenders from court and custody. Thus, as in other spheres of penal policy-making, the neo-correctionalist agenda has likewise been strongly influenced by the managerialism that is associated with a Strategy B approach to criminal justice (see Chapter 1, section 1.4).

Although the origins of the neo-correctionalist approach can be traced back to the 1990s and beyond, as we shall see in the next section, it came to epitomize the youth justice policies of the New Labour government (1997–2010) and has more or less continued under the Coalition government that took office in 2010.

Neo-Correctional Youth Justice from 1997

8.3 When the New Labour government of Tony Blair was elected in 1997 after a period of 18 years in opposition, the influence of three major youth justice approaches – welfare, justice and minimum intervention – had already been eclipsed by its Conservative predecessor's adoption of a more strident law and order approach (for details see earlier editions of this book). Further radical reform of the English youth justice system had been signalled as a major priority by the new administration in a series of policy documents, the earliest of which pre-dated the general election (Straw and Michael, 1996; Home Office, 1997a). Two major pieces of legislation – the Crime and Disorder Act 1998 and the Youth Justice and Criminal Evidence Act 1999 – were implemented during the government's first term in office. The new youth justice system that they ushered in was indelibly stamped with neo-correctionalist hallmarks, though it also incorporated important elements of restorative justice thinking and a systems management approach. These influences were reflected in five key principles that guided the government's youth justice reform programme.

1 *The primacy of offending prevention.* The Crime and Disorder Act 1998 adopted as the principal aim of the youth justice system 'to prevent offending by children and young persons' (s. 37). Although the Act did not repeal the various earlier provisions imposing different obligations, such as the duty of the youth court to have regard for the welfare of children and young people, it did nevertheless represent an important symbolic change of emphasis away from the principles of the welfare, justice and minimum intervention models. As we shall see, this change of direction was reflected in the introduction of a range of new and often controversial preventive measures for dealing with pre-delinquent offenders, including some who are under the age of criminal responsibility (currently ten).

2 *Responsibilization.* This rather inelegant neologism was appropriated by Muncie (1999: 169)[2] in order to draw attention to another important feature of the new youth justice system: its insistence on making people accountable for their actions (or, in some instances, for their omissions). **Responsibilization** means, first, that young

---

[2]The term has also been used in a very different sense by Garland (1996: 452), to mean the increasing tendency by the modern state to devolve responsibility for crime prevention and other responses to crime onto other agencies, private organizations and individuals.

offenders are expected to accept responsibility for their own actions instead of being absolved on account of their age or a belief that they will grow out of crime. One early manifestation of this principle was New Labour's abolition of the traditional legal doctrine of **doli incapax** whereby children aged 10 to 13 were presumed to be incapable of committing a crime unless they could be shown to appreciate the difference between right and wrong (see below). Second, responsibilization also means that *parents* may be held responsible for the offending behaviour of their children, and the Crime and Disorder Act 1998 introduced parenting orders which permit courts to require parents of misbehaving children to attend counselling and guidance sessions and comply with other conditions.

3 *Reparation.* In addition to – but explicitly subordinate to – the new primary aim of preventing offending, the new youth justice system also encouraged the principle of reparation. Reparation was made to serve a double purpose in the new youth justice. First, it was proclaimed as a tangible manifestation of an offender's willingness to take responsibility for an offence, so it was seen as a suitable response for relatively minor offenders who might in the past have been let off with a caution. In addition, the introduction of a range of penalties including the reparation order (see below, section 8.4) that require offenders to make amends for the harm they have caused to victims or the community also served to demonstrate the government's oft-voiced commitment to prioritize the needs of victims. Another innovation to be explained in section 8.4 below – the referral order for young offenders who are being prosecuted for the first time – was intended to have reparation at its core. Reparation constitutes one element of the wider restorative justice approach, but as we shall see shortly these new measures in practice only embody restorative justice in a very partial and watered-down way.

4 *Early, effective and progressive intervention.* In pursuit of its overriding aim of preventing offending – and in line with the notion of zero tolerance – New Labour's youth justice strategy was based on the principle of early intervention with first time offenders in order to nip offending in the bud (Straw and Michael, 1996: 18) instead of diverting them or making excuses for them. This shift marked a decisive break with the minimum intervention philosophy of the youth justice movement, and was reflected in the adoption of a new statutory pre-trial diversion process that was set up in place of the old system of juvenile cautioning with which that movement was inextricably associated. As we shall see, this procedure entailed a *graduated* response in which young offenders who carry on offending can expect to receive progressively more intensive and intrusive interventions, the aim of which is to confront them with their behaviour, investigate its causes and take action to address it. The same approach also underpinned the introduction from 2001 of community-based Intensive Supervision and Surveillance Programmes (ISSPs), which were intended for persistent young offenders either as an alternative to custody or as part of the post-release supervisory arrangements for those given detention and training orders.

5 *Efficiency.* Shortly before the 1997 election, the old youth justice system was lambasted by the politically independent Audit Commission (1996) for being expensive, inefficient, inconsistent and ineffective and for devoting too much time, effort and resources to processing young offenders rather than taking effective remedial action with them. This conclusion chimed well with the Labour Party's own analysis and New Labour sought to improve the efficiency of the system through a combination of measures intended to speed up the processing of youth justice cases (the Party's manifesto pledge to halve the average time taken to bring persistent young offenders to court from 142 to 71 days was achieved by August 2001; see Audit Commission, 2004) and a radical programme of institutional reform.

In order to pursue its reform agenda, one of New Labour's first priorities was to reconfigure the organizational framework that had developed in the era of minimum interventionism, while relying on similar managerialist techniques involving inter-agency work and system monitoring. Most of New Labour's reforms in this area remain in existence, although there have been a few changes under the Coalition. Responsibility for policy-making for youth justice had been located in the Home Office, while care policy for children was the responsibility of the Department for Education and Skills. Subsequent changes in the organisation and structure of ministries, the creation of the Ministry of Justice in 2007 and the arrival of the Coalition government in 2010 have led to new arrangements. Today, youth justice policy is in the hands of the Ministry of Justice while care and welfare issues policy lies with the Department for Education.

Responsibility for overseeing the strategic development, direction, implementation and monitoring of youth justice policy is vested in a separate national body known as the Youth Justice Board set up by the Crime and Disorder Act 1998. This is a non-departmental public body (or quango) whose members are appointed by the Justice Secretary. Its responsibilities include advising the Justice Secretary on how the principal aim of the youth justice system (preventing offending) might most effectively be pursued, setting national standards, promoting good practice, overseeing the provision of youth justice services and monitoring the operation of the system. It is also responsible for commissioning and managing the juvenile secure estate, i.e. all custodial and other secure facilities for young people under the age of 18. (Originally, the Coalition government had planned to scrap the YJB as part of a bonfire of the quangos and move its responsibilities to the Ministry of Justice, but following a defeat in the House of Lords in 2011 this plan was reversed and the YJB retains its responsibilities.)

Local authorities also now have significant responsibilities relating to crime prevention and for formulating (in consultation with other agencies) annual youth justice plans to ensure the delivery of comprehensive youth justice services within their localities. However, the primary operational responsibility for delivering those local services has been assigned to multi-agency youth offending teams (or YOTs, as they have become colloquially known), which local authorities have also been required to establish (see Holdaway et al., 2001 for an evaluation of YOTs). The composition of each YOT is partially prescribed by statute: it must include representatives from the police, probation service, local education and health services and local authority social service departments, though it can also include other occupational groups.

In addition to their general task of preventing juvenile offending, YOTs spend much of their time preparing reports for and generally servicing the youth court (see section 8.4 below).

The establishment of YOTs and the wider institutional changes with which they are associated were a good example of New Labour's much-vaunted commitment to a more co-ordinated and integrated – or 'joined up' in the approved jargon – approach to policy-making and service delivery (an approach which is still being followed by the Coalition government). Radical though this reform programme was in many respects, however, it did nothing to disturb the marked institutional separation between the criminal jurisdiction dealing with the criminal needs of young offenders and the care jurisdiction dealing with the welfare needs of vulnerable young people.

Turning more briefly now to the care jurisdiction, this has also experienced upheavals. A major catalyst for change was a succession of damning reports following inquiries that had been set up to investigate the deaths of vulnerable children who had been let down by the care and protection authorities (e.g. Laming, 2003). The Children Act 2004 set out a comprehensive programme of local and national action designed to bring about a transformation of children's services and the way they are delivered. Responsibility for policy-making with regard to the care jurisdiction is now vested in the Department for Education. There is no overarching agency equivalent to the Youth Justice Board that is responsible for the strategic implementation of the programme. Children's Trusts were established in 2003 in order to pioneer and develop the Labour government's preferred model for achieving the closer integration and co-ordination of children's services within each local area. The Trusts were intended to operate on a **multi-agency** basis, co-ordinating the activities of local education authorities, children's social services departments and also community and acute health services. They were expected to operate on the basis of multi-disciplinary teams, joint training arrangements, better information-sharing procedures and a common assessment framework across all services. The Apprenticeship, Skills, Children and Learning Act 2009 brought schools, colleges and Jobcentre Plus under the duty to co-operate through Children's Trusts, and required all local areas to have a Children's Trust Board which was to prepare a Children and Young People's Plan by April 2011. The Coalition government, however, now plans to remove the duty on schools to co-operate, the requirement for local areas to have a Children's Trust Board, and the requirement to publish a Children and Young People's Plan. Naturally, it claims this development is a positive move designed to free up areas to address local issues more effectively, but just how far this happens in practice will be interesting to monitor. Judicial responsibility for the conduct of 'care and protection' litigation is unchanged and remains in the hands of the lower civil courts known as 'family proceedings courts'.

Whatever impact these changes may have on the level of co-ordination between children's service agencies, a sharp divide remains between their activities and those of the YOTs. For the foreseeable future, therefore, young people who offend will continue to be dealt with in criminal courts principally on the basis of their offending behaviour and largely irrespective of any welfare needs they might have. There is little sign of anything being done to promote *horizontal* co-ordination *across* the two jurisdictions. This would require a more holistic approach to be taken, in which account is taken of the welfare needs of young offenders as well as any criminal deeds that they may have committed. Things could be managed differently. Scotland's unique system of children's hearings deals with both offence and care and protection cases within a civil procedure that combines a welfare approach with a strong diversionary commitment, and offers one accessible model of how such a system might operate (see Bottoms and Dignan, 2004 for details).

New Labour sought to pursue its aim of preventing juvenile offending by means of four key strategies:

- reducing restrictions on prosecuting offenders under 14;

- extending the range of pre-emptive interventions;

- strengthening the array of reactive measures for dealing with young offenders; and

- broadening the category of unacceptable and punishable behaviour.

The **age of criminal responsibility** in England and Wales is ten, which is one of the lowest in Western Europe. In Scotland it was – until recently – eight and in 2005 the European Social Rights Committee declared the UK to be in breach of Article 17 of the European Social Charter because the age of criminal responsibility was 'manifestly too low' (Children's Rights Alliance, 2005). In 2011 the age of criminal prosecution was raised from 8 to 12 in Scotland by the Criminal Justice and Licensing (Scotland) Act 2012, although the age of criminal responsibility remains at eight. Before 1998, the effect of this low threshold was mitigated to some extent by the doctrine of *doli incapax*, whereby children between the ages of 10 and 13 could only be convicted of an offence if the prosecution could establish that they knew the difference between right and wrong. However, this doctrine was abolished by section 34 of the Crime and Disorder Act 1998, as a result of which all children of ten or over are now liable to prosecution. Moreover, even children below this age are increasingly exposed to the risk of formal intervention by a range of criminal justice and other agencies, as we shall see shortly.

In pursuit of its preventive agenda, the New Labour government introduced a variety of purely *pre-emptive initiatives* directed at pre-delinquent young people: those who are considered likely to engage in criminal, disruptive or anti-social behaviour. Their aim was to divert them in other directions and to encourage their social inclusion into the law-abiding community. They included play schemes known as Splash (subsequently renamed as Positive Activities for Young People) which seek to engage 13 to 17 year olds living in deprived areas who are considered to be at risk of offending by providing them with a range of purposeful activities during school holidays. Youth Inclusion Programmes (YIPs) are somewhat similar but operate throughout the year in some of the most deprived neighbourhoods in

England and Wales (in 2011 there were 110 YIPs), where they seek to engage and work with those most at risk of offending, including those who fail to attend school regularly. A further variation on a broadly similar theme involves the establishment of multi-agency teams known as Youth Inclusion and Support Panels (YISPs) in areas with high levels of street crime. Their task is to identify and offer support to young children aged between 8 and 13 (and also their parents) whose anti-social or problematic behaviour is considered to put them at high risk of offending. Ninety-two local authorities had set up YISPs by the end of 2004, and the government pledged to increase the number by 50 per cent by 2008 (Home Office, 2004b). In 2011 there were 220 YISPs. Given the pressure to cut public expenditure, it is unlikely that there will be any significant expansion of YIPs or YISPS – indeed their numbers may fall.

In addition to these schemes, some of which seek to provide positive alternatives to criminal activity as carrots to discourage misbehaviour, the government also created a number of new sticks – sanctions and coercive measures intended to nip in the bud incipient criminality in a zero tolerance fashion. The Crime and Disorder Act 1998 and later legislation empowered local authorities to introduce local *child curfews* banning children under the age of 10 – later raised to 16 – from streets and other public places at night unless supervised by a responsible adult, although no such scheme had been set up under these powers by 2011. Powers were also introduced, under the Anti-Social Behaviour Act 2003, enabling police officers to issue *dispersal orders* against groups of two or more young people under the age of 16 in designated areas, requiring them to disperse and, if after 9 p.m., to return home.

As well as these preventive initiatives, the Labour government also introduced an extensive array of *reactive* measures, several of which have proved highly controversial. One such measure involves a quasi-criminal procedure known as a *child safety order*. This is imposed by a civil court (the magistrates' family proceedings court) on the application of a local authority social services department. Child safety orders may be imposed on children under the age of ten who have committed (or are thought to be at risk of committing) an act for which they could have been prosecuted if over the age of ten, or who have behaved in an anti-social manner. The effect of a child safety order is to place the child under the supervision of a social worker or youth justice worker subject to whatever specific requirements may be imposed by the court. For example, the court may seek to ensure that the child receives appropriate care, protection and support and is subject to proper control; or to prevent any repetition of the behaviour that gave rise to the order. Very little use has been made of this power, however: only 12 such orders were imposed in the 21-month period following their introduction in April 2000.

The most contentious of the reactive measures is another quasi-criminal intervention known as the *anti-social behaviour order* (ASBO; in operation since 1999).[3]

---

[3]The measure was originally introduced under the Crime and Disorder Act 1998 s. 1; the powers it conferred were considerably strengthened by the Anti-Social Behaviour Act 2003. The ASBO went on to form the cornerstone of the Respect Agenda, a centrepiece of New Labour's third term programme (2005 onwards; see especially Home Office, 2006a).

ASBOs are technically civil orders, but they can have severe consequences in the event of non-compliance. The orders may be issued against any person aged ten or over who has acted 'in an anti-social manner', defined as behaviour 'that caused or was likely to cause harassment, alarm or distress to one or more persons not of the same household'. Although it was originally expected that ASBOs would chiefly be used against adults (Home Office, 1998a), they have often been imposed on those aged 10 to 17. Of all ASBOs issued to the end of June 2005, 43 per cent were imposed on young people, and in 2010 the figure was 32 per cent (although of a much-reduced total of 536 ASBOs: Home Office, 2011a: Table 1). In response to pressure from the Youth Justice Board, young people who are subject to an ASBO may now also be assigned to a YOT-based 'responsible officer' with the power to issue directions to them for a period of six months (an Individual Support Order).

ASBOs may be made in civil proceedings by a magistrates' court following an application by the local council, chief police officer or a registered social landlord including Housing Action Trusts; or they may be made by a criminal court following a conviction. If the proceedings are civil, the rules of evidence are less rigorous, although proof beyond reasonable doubt is still required to impose an ASBO.[4]

Critics have expressed alarm at the vagueness of the term 'anti-social behaviour' and the fact that only 1 per cent of applications were refused in the first five years in which they were available. All ASBO applications in civil proceedings are heard in the adult magistrates' court, regardless of the age of the person against whom it is sought. This has also proved to be a contentious issue, not least because the reporting restrictions that normally apply in the youth court do not routinely operate in a magistrates' court. As a result, ASBO proceedings are often reported in the press with the youngsters involved being named, although this would not be possible if they were convicted of an actual crime in the youth court.

The order itself may contain any kind of prohibition which the court feels is necessary to prevent further anti-social behaviour from the recipient of the order. Failure to comply with an ASBO is an offence. For juveniles aged 10 to 17 the maximum sentence is a 24-month detention and training order (see section 8.4 below). Just under half (47 per cent) of ASBOs issued to persons aged 10 to 17 during the period 1 June 2000 to 31 December 2003 were breached (House of Commons Written Answer, 24 January 2006), and a YJB study showed that 43 per cent of young people under the age of 18 who breached them received an immediate custodial term (Brogan, 2005: 18). This fuelled concerns that ASBOs were increasingly accelerating young people into custody, thereby escalating the juvenile prison population and adding to the accommodation pressures experienced by the juvenile secure estate. The use of ASBOs on young people has been strongly criticized (by, for example, Martin Narey, former head of the prison and correctional services, and Rod Morgan, former Director of the Youth Justice Board), and doubts about their effectiveness in curbing anti-social behaviour have been buttressed by research suggesting that they are regarded by many offending teenagers and their parents as badges of honour (Youth Justice Board, 2006).

---

[4]*McCann* [2003] 1 A.C. 787.

Prior to 1998, criminal justice commentators (for example, Moynihan, 1992; Garland, 1996) had spoken of a tendency for criminal justice agencies to moderate their ambitions by 'defining deviance down' and only invoking formal interventions in respect of the more serious forms of criminal wrongdoing. As the title of the 1998 Crime and Disorder Act suggested, however, this process has been dramatically reversed and *the category of unacceptable and punishable behaviour has been broadened*. It is no longer restricted to actual crime, but also encompasses a wide and ill-defined range of disorderly and anti-social conduct.

It is likely that the ASBO's days are numbered – at least under that name. The number of orders imposed has dropped sharply since 2005. Coalition Home Secretary Theresa May has described them as 'bureaucratic, slow and expensive' (Home Office, 2011b: 5), noting that the breach rate had increased to 59 per cent by the end of 2009 from 40 per cent in 2003, and that ASBOs represent a centrally driven approach which is not favoured by the Coalition government. In its place, a toolkit of five orders is proposed: a criminal behaviour order, a crime prevention injunction, a community protection order (with two levels), and a police direction power. The aim is to support 'the move towards local accountability, with practitioners able to deal effectively with issues that matter to local people' (Home Office, 2011b: 11). However, the proposed new 'criminal behaviour orders' and 'crime prevention injunctions' bear an uncanny resemblance to ASBOs in both their requirements and their legal effects.

The approach of both the Labour and the Coalition governments to anti-social behaviour betrays an increasingly authoritarian attitude towards young people whose behaviour may be deemed unacceptable even though it falls a long way short of what would have been considered criminal in the past. As for those who do go on to offend, or reoffend, the prevailing principle that underpins the operation of the new youth justice system itself is one of progressive interventionism, whereby increasingly intrusive measures are taken with each successive transgression (although, perhaps for financial reasons, the Coalition government has been placing less emphasis on this more recently).

Responding to Youth Crime: The Youth Justice System in Operation

8.4 The youth justice system, which deals with young offenders between their tenth and eighteenth birthdays, is summarized diagrammatically in Figure 8.1 and differs in certain respects from the equivalent scheme for adults shown in Figure 1.1 in the Introduction. The police and Crown Prosecution Service have a number of diversionary options available to them when dealing with young offenders, which provide an alternative to prosecution. Where the offence is very trivial or there is insufficient evidence linking it to a suspected offender the police may decide to take no further action (NFA), which effectively means that the case is dropped. Alternatively, they may decide to issue an informal warning, which means that no formal record is made and the incident cannot be

Pre-Court	Youth Rehabilitation Order	Custodial Sentences
Reprimand*	Activity Requirement	Detention & Training Order
Final Warning*	Supervision Requirement	s. 91 – serious offence
Youth Conditional Condition	Curfew Requirement	s.228 – extended sentence/ public protection
	Programme Requirement	s. 226 – indeterminate/ public protection
First Tier Court Disposals	Residence requirement (16–17 year olds only)	s. 90 – mandatory life/ murder
Absolute Discharge	Mental Health Treatment Requirement	
Conditional Discharge	Attendance Centre Requirement	
Compensation Order	Exclusion Requirement	
Fine	Education Requirement	
Referral Order	Prohibited Activity Requirement	
Reparation Order	Electronic Monitoring Requirement	
Deferred Sentence	Drug Testing Requirement	
	Drug Treatment Requirement	
	L.A. Residence Requirement	
	Unpaid Work Requirement (16–17 year olds only)	
	Intoxicating Substance Requirement	
	Intensive Supervision & Surveillance Requirement**	
	Intensive Fostering Requirement**	

*To be replaced by Youth Cautions

**These two requirements should only be used where the offence is so serious that a custodial sentence would normally be appropriate

FIGURE 8.1   Disposals for Young Offenders

mentioned in court in the event of future proceedings. Since 1998, however, this practice has been discouraged by the Home Office, which has been keen to hold offenders accountable for any wrongdoing. Consequently, the approach that is now favoured relies on a graded system of formal warnings leading up to a prosecution in the event of reoffending.

Under the statutory regime that was introduced by the Crime and Disorder Act 1998 the appropriate response for a young offender committing a minor offence for the first time is for the police to issue a *reprimand*, which is a formal warning that is recorded (equivalent to a police caution for an adult offender). If a further minor offence is committed this is liable to be dealt with by means of a *final warning* (the statutory name for which is simply 'warning') which is intended as a last chance measure after which any further offending is almost certain to result in prosecution. When a young person is issued with a final warning the police are also required to refer the case to the local youth offending team, which should then undertake an assessment to identify the factors that may have been responsible for the offending behaviour. If some form of intervention is thought appropriate in order to address such problems, the young person will be required to participate in a 'change programme'(the statutory name for which is a 'rehabilitation programme'), and the Home Office has made it clear that it expects this to be the norm. Such programmes may include measures intended to achieve reparation and restoration as well as rehabilitation. The system of reprimands and final warnings is thus intended to operate on a progressive 'three strikes and you're out' basis, culminating almost inevitably in a prosecution if there is a third minor offence. However, if any of the previous offences are felt to be sufficiently serious the police and Crown Prosecution Service are expected to move straight to a prosecution rather than proceeding down the diversionary route.

Current government plans are to change this system in spring 2013, when a system of youth cautions and youth conditional cautions will replace reprimands and warnings. Youth cautions are introduced by the Legal Aid, Sentencing and Punishment of Offenders Act 2012 and are similar to reprimands. Youth conditional cautions were created by the Criminal Justice and Immigration Act 2008 and have already been introduced on a pilot basis in five police force areas in January 2010. YCCs can currently be used as a last step after a final warning and the CPS has to decide that it is in the public interest to issue one. The conditions that can be attached to a YCC can include provisions that aim to rehabilitate, to provide reparation or to punish. The pilot scheme only covered 16–17 year olds, and between January 2010 and March 2012 a total of 173 YCCs were issued in three of the five areas (figures were not available for two areas),[5] which suggests that the YCC may not be especially popular.

Decisions on whether suspected offenders should be charged and prosecuted (or offered a YCC) are now normally taken by the Crown Prosecution Service rather than the police. The CPS can also decide to discontinue prosecution proceedings at a later stage. Discontinuation may occur because the CPS considers either that the available evidence is insufficiently strong or that it is not in the public interest to prosecute.

When young offenders under the age of 18 are prosecuted, their cases are normally dealt with by the youth court, though exceptionally in more serious cases they may be tried and sentenced instead by the adult Crown Court. The youth court is a specialized version of the magistrates' court where offenders under 18 are prosecuted and, if convicted, sentenced. (Until 1992, this court was known as the juvenile court, and dealt only with offenders who had not reached the age of 17.) Youth court magistrates are drawn from a special panel of local magistrates who have particular experience of or interest in work with young people. Unlike adult magistrates' proceedings, youth courts are not open to the public, though in most other respects their procedures are broadly similar to those of their adult counterparts. Steps have been taken, however, to open up the youth court by encouraging greater communication between youth court magistrates and young offenders and their families and making them more accessible to victims also (Allen et al., 2000;

---

[5]www.cypnow.co.uk (accessed 16 August 2012).

Home Office and Lord Chancellor's Department, 2001). The sentencing powers of the youth court have always included punitive measures (detailed below), notwithstanding the continuing statutory duty to 'have regard to the welfare of the child'. Nevertheless, youthfulness is still seen as a mitigating factor in sentencing, and research shows that young offenders are generally sentenced less harshly than adults who have committed similar offences (see, for example, Flood-Page and Mackie, 1998: 123–4).

Where a young offender pleads guilty the youth court may pass a sentence known as a referral order (a procedure first introduced in 2002 by the Youth Justice and Criminal Evidence Act 1999), and if the offender is being prosecuted for the first time the court is normally required to make such an order. A referral order requires the young offender to attend a meeting of the **youth offender panel** (YOP).

The YOP is convened by the local youth offending team, which also provides one member of the three-person YOP panel, the other two being lay members drawn from an approved list of volunteers. The YOP procedure was inspired in part by restorative justice thinking (see above, section 8.2) and consequently the victim of an offence may also be invited to attend, in addition to the young offender and his or her parents. The purpose of the panel meeting is to provide a forum in which the offence can be discussed with the victim, if present, and to devise an appropriate 'youth offender contract' containing one or more elements that are intended to prevent further offending (with reparation also featuring prominently). The duration of the order (between 3 and 12 months) is determined by the youth court on the basis of the seriousness of the offence, though the terms of the contract are a matter for negotiation within the panel. If no agreement can be reached, however, or the offender fails to comply with the agreement, the young offender will be returned to the court to be sentenced for the original offence. In 2010–11 a total of 24,709 young people were sentenced to a referral order – one third of all those sentenced by the courts – but the number of referral orders has been dropping steadily since a peak of 31,597 in 2007–8 (Ministry of Justice, 2012d).

For offenders who are prosecuted and sentenced in the normal way, a wide range of disposals is available. Leaving aside ASBOs (discussed in section 8.3 above), these can be divided into three main categories: custodial penalties; the **youth rehabilitation order** (YRO); and first tier sentences (by which we mean disposals such as fines and discharges which rank below the YRO in the tariff of juvenile sentences).

Prior to 1998, the commonest first tier disposal for young offenders appearing in the youth court for the first time for less serious offences was the conditional discharge (see Chapter 5, section 5.2). However, statute now discourages its use for most such offenders,[6] and it has declined sharply; in 2010–11 only 9,849 absolute or conditional discharges were given to young people, a decrease of 10,000 over the previous ten years (Ministry of Justice, 2012d). Other first tier disposals

---

[6]Under s. 66 of the Crime and Disorder Act 1998 the conditional discharge is not available when a young offender has received a final warning within the previous two years unless there are exceptional circumstances relating either to the offender or the offence.

include fines and compensation orders, both of which may be imposed either on young offenders themselves or on their parents.

Another first tier disposal for young offenders (available since 1998) is the reparation order. Such orders require the offender to make reparation either to the victim of the offence (provided the victim consents to this) or to the community at large (for example, by doing unpaid work). Although the court is supposed to specify the nature of the reparation that is to be undertaken, in practice the YOT has an important part to play in assessing and advising what may be appropriate, and also in facilitating and monitoring it. The reparation that is imposed must be proportionate to the seriousness of the offence, and may not exceed 24 hours in total, while the reparation order itself lasts for a maximum of three months. Although the courts are required to give reasons for not imposing such an order where they have the power to do so, in practice its usage appears to have been largely eclipsed by the introduction of the referral order. In 2010–11, 2,000 reparation orders were made, more than 1,200 fewer than the previous year (Ministry of Justice, 2012d).

On 30 November 2009 the Youth Rehabilitation Order (YRO) was introduced (by the Criminal Justice and Immigration Act 2008), replacing older sentences such as the **action plan order**, the supervision order, the attendance centre order and various others. The YRO is similar to the community order for adults (see Chapter 5, section 5.2) in that it can contain one requirement or a combination of a number of requirements, in this case 18 (see Figure 8.1). Two particular intensive requirements – the intensive supervision and surveillance requirement and the intensive fostering requirement can be used only if the offence is imprisonable and so serious that a custodial sentence would have been used were these intensive requirements not available. In 2010–11, the first full year of the YRO, a total of 18,204 orders were made, one-quarter of all sentences passed on young people; 70 per cent of YROs have one or two requirements, the most commonly used requirement being supervision (50 per cent), followed by an activity requirement and a curfew (both at 15 per cent) (Ministry of Justice, 2012d).

The intensive supervision and surveillance requirement is based on Intensive Supervision and Surveillance Programmes which were introduced in 2001 and could be attached to supervision orders, community orders or bail supervision packages. (ISSPs – and now the intensive supervision and surveillance requirement – can also form part of the post-custodial supervision arrangements for those given detention and training orders.) ISSPs were originally intended to be targeted on persistent offenders who had been charged or warned at least four times within a 12-month period, and who had previously been subject to a custodial sentence or community service order. The criteria were later extended to include offenders who were less persistent but had committed more serious offences, or had a history of repeat offending while on bail. ISSPs involved intensive monitoring of the young offender's movements and whereabouts by means such as electronic monitoring and telephone monitoring using voice verification technology. They also included highly structured individually tailored packages of measures that were intended to address the young person's offending behaviour (for example, training and education programmes lasting up to five hours per day) and also encourage the performance of reparation. A study of the original pilot trial, when ISSPs were introduced in selected areas only, found that just under half the ISSPs were completed successfully, with 31 per cent of those who breached the requirements being sent to custody; 91 per cent of youngsters given ISSPs were reconvicted at least once in the following two years, but this was hardly surprising since they had committed an average of 11.6 offences in the previous two years. In fact, both the frequency and seriousness of offending were reduced, as was the use of custody for young offenders in the ISSP areas. However, these changes were probably not attributable to the ISSPs themselves, since similar results were also reported from comparison areas without ISSPs (Gray et al., 2005).

So far the sentences that we have mentioned are imposed on the young offenders themselves (although parents can be ordered to pay their fines and compensation orders). However, there are also various orders which can be imposed on the parents of young offenders, some of which have been around for a considerable time. One such measure is the parental bind-over, a common law power that enables the court to require any person to 'be of good behaviour and keep the peace' on forfeit of a specified sum of money. Since 1998 the courts can also issue a **parenting order** against the parents or guardians of young offenders or those who are guilty of anti-social behaviour (Crime and Disorder Act 1998, s. 8). The parenting order consists of two main elements. The first requires parents to attend counselling or guidance sessions, which can last for up to three months and which are intended to improve their parenting skills. The second may require parents to exercise a measure of control over their child (for example, by ensuring that they attend school, or avoid certain people or places) for a period of up to 12 months. Failure to comply with the order (which is supervised by YOT workers) constitutes a criminal offence punishable with a fine of up to £1,000.

With regard to custodial options, young offenders between the ages of 12 and 17 inclusive may be given a detention and training order (introduced by the Crime and Disorder Act 1998) for a period of between 4 and 24 months if certain criteria are satisfied (mainly that the offence is so serious that a lesser sentence cannot be justified, and for offenders under the age of 15 that the court believes they are persistent). The first half of a DTO is served in custody, while the second half is served under supervision in the community. In 2011, a total of 3,712 young people received a DTO, which represented almost nine out of ten immediate custodial sentences for this age group (Ministry of Justice, 2012d). Offenders aged 18 to 20 can receive a sentence of detention in a young offender institution. Finally, with regard to those young offenders who are, exceptionally, dealt with by the Crown Court, additional custodial options are also available. If the offence is murder, the penalty will be a mandatory indeterminate sentence of long-term detention known as 'detention at Her Majesty's pleasure'. For other serious offences, a specified period of long-term detention may be imposed. This long-term detention is subject to the same maximum lengths as in the case of adult offenders. (Another indeterminate sentence known as 'detention for public protection' – the equivalent of imprisonment for public protection for adult offenders – was introduced by the Criminal Justice Act 2003 but later abolished along with its adult counterpart by the Legal Aid, Sentencing and Punishment of Offenders Act 2012.)

Young offenders who are sentenced to custody may be held in one of three main types of facilities, which together comprise the juvenile secure estate. Younger children (up to the age of 16) may be kept in **secure children's homes** run by local authorities (with 300 places in March 2012); privately run secure training centres (STCs) house boys and girls between 12 and 17 (301 places); while young offender institutions (YOIs) account for the great majority (2,500 places) of the estate. These young offender institutions, which are run by the prison service, cater for offenders aged 15 to 20. Even though they are physically separate from adult prisons, the facilities and regimes in young offender institutions are not that different from those catering for adult inmates.

So far the Coalition government has done little to change youth justice, although it did set out its plans in the Green Paper *Breaking the Cycle* (Ministry of Justice, 2010a). But whatever its plans, the government's thinking will be constrained at every level by the need to save money wherever possible and to cut expenditure as far as possible. The rhetoric of the Green Paper is no different from that used by New Labour with its emphasis on cutting offending by young people and dealing with them effectively. It proposes to give more discretion to police and prosecutors to deal with youth crime before it reaches court, and to encourage the use of restorative justice. 'Compliance panels' are proposed to ensure that court orders are enforced more consistently. Some changes are proposed to the laws on remanding young offenders in custody and secure accommodation prior to trial. Currently 17 year olds are treated as adults for the purposes of remand; the government proposes to create a single and separate 'youth remand order' which – unlike the present system – would comply with the United Nations Convention on the Rights of the Child. Perhaps most significant, however, are the proposals to organize a payment by results approach to YOTs – indeed, to all work on juvenile reoffending – in line with government policy for offenders of all ages (see Chapter 2, section 2.2): 'We will no longer provide rehabilitation services directly without testing where the private, voluntary or community sectors can provide them more effectively and efficiently' (Ministry of Justice, 2011a: 7). Just how this will work in practice and how much impact it will have on youth justice remains to be seen.

Concluding Assessment: No More Excuses?

8.5 Since New Labour arrived in power in 1997 there has been no one clear direction in youth justice, although the neo-correctionalist model is probably the one that fits New Labour best. How far can this also be said of Coalition policy? On the one hand, this kind of punitive approach would seem to fit well with the general ideology of the Conservatives (although not perhaps with that of the Liberal Democrats). On the other hand, some aspects of Coalition policy do not fit with this approach: their interest in expanding restorative justice, for example, and their stated desire to free up agencies from central control (which goes against the centralizing, co-ordinating thrust of neo-correctionalism). Coalition rhetoric about trying to encourage more informal interventions for young people to avoid them being drawn into the criminal justice system and to increase the use of restorative justice may bode well, although one could question how far such ideas are driven by the need to cut expenditure rather than a real desire to be less punitive towards young people.

It is certainly true that the number of young people entering the criminal justice system for the first time has been dropping in the last few years, as recent Youth Justice Board Annual Reports have been keen to point out (see, for example, Youth Justice Board, 2012: 2). In 2000–1 a total of 144,638 young people were proceeded against in the youth court; in 2011–12 the figure was 77,700, a decrease of more than 65,000 over the decade. The average custodial population of those under 18 has also decreased from over 3,000 in 2008 to 1,643 in August 2012 (Ministry of Justice, 2012d). But this is not to suggest that all is well in youth justice.

In the first place, this must be seen in the context of a country which has been imprisoning its children at a rate almost unknown in any comparable country. And in the recent past young people have been increasingly criminalized in England and Wales for minor youthful misbehaviour which would previously have been dealt with informally. This change in practice was driven by a government target set in 2002 to increase the proportion of offences brought to justice (NACRO, 2008). According to Rod Morgan, former chair of the Youth Justice Board (*Guardian*, 19 February 2007), 'to meet crime targets, the police are picking low-hanging fruit' including minor misbehaviour by young people. (See also Morgan, 2008; Allen, 2011.) The offences brought to justice target was then revised, and (almost certainly not coincidentally) figures for young people formally entering the criminal justice system fell thereafter. At the same time, in a development redolent of the minimum intervention and systems management approaches (discussed in section 8.2 above), agencies and practitioners – including local authorities, youth offending teams, police and courts – have been working together to ensure that custody is used as a last resort, including the development of new informal measures to divert young offenders out of the formal criminal justice system (Allen, 2011).

However, given the punitive bent of Conservative ideology it is by no means certain that such gains will continue. Second, the pressing need to cut expenditure could well impact negatively upon the gains we have seen. Third, the riots of August 2011 – in which many young people were involved – and the high unemployment rates for young people generally, could lead to a more punitive turn towards young offenders. Fourth, the fragmentation of youth justice which looks likely to occur due to part-privatization and payment by results (similar to the fragmentation of the probation service discussed in Chapter 5) is not likely in the short term to lead to a better service for young offenders. For all these reasons, the present decreases in the criminalization and incarceration of young people may well prove to be fragile.

And despite the recent decreases in the use of custody for young offenders, we continue to incarcerate large numbers of young people, despite the abiding truism that 'prison doesn't work' to reform young offenders. Certain kinds of intervention – such as cognitive behavioural training to try to alter attitudes towards crime (see Chapter 2, section 2.2) – may well help to reduce offending. This is more likely to happen, however, where the young person is not locked up in custody (Andrews et al., 1990: 382; Lipsey, 1992: 138; McGuire, 1995; Vennard et al., 1997). Yet the government remains reluctant to take effective steps to substantially reduce the use of custody for young people and keep it to a minimum. We think this is a mistake. Essentially there are two opposing views about young offenders: the zero tolerance view (Strategy A) and the Strategy C approach which combines an inclination to minimum intervention with a preference for restorative and rehabilitative measures where intervention is warranted. Governments seem unwilling to accept the view that young offenders simply grow out of crime – although in general it seems that they do (Cavadino et al., 1999: 182–4; Flood-Page et al., 2000: 18–19) – and believe that tough early intervention is needed to nip offending in the bud. Even if some of this tough early intervention takes positive forms such as reparation or programmes to confront offending behaviour, getting tough earlier simply increases the likelihood that young offenders will suffer the adverse effects of stigmatizing labelling. These effects include accelerating young people 'up the tariff' into overcrowded and damaging custodial institutions before they have a chance to grow out of crime. The new youth conditional cautions may be aimed at keeping young people out of the courts, but there is always the danger that by widening the net (see Chapter 5, section 5.5) they will end up having the reverse effect.

The Coalition government seems to be bent on fragmenting youth justice services by maximizing private-sector involvement – in other words another policy turn which involves dismantling the joined-up approach created by New Labour. Although Labour's approach failed to devise a truly effective strategy for dealing with young offenders this was more to do with failures of practice than failures of theory. YOTs would seem, by any measure, to have been a success, yet the Coalition's plans throw their future into doubt.

Ideally, any government's youth justice strategy ought to be realistic, and accept that – whatever exactly it does with young offenders – the potential of the criminal justice system to prevent juvenile offending is strictly limited. There are no quick fixes to juvenile crime and persistently tinkering with the youth justice system is not likely to help matters. Accepting this, it would make sense for the government to borrow more from the systems management approach (see section 8.2 above), adopting its humanitarian (Strategy C) goals and its minimum-intervention bias as well as its managerial (Strategy B) techniques while simultaneously increasing the emphasis on restorative justice and other constructive approaches. Such techniques may or may not have a serious impact on the level of juvenile crime, but at least they could help us to avoid damaging young lives – in particular by the excessive use of penal custody – to the extent we currently do.

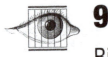

9

Bias in the Criminal Justice System

Introductory

9.1 In Chapter 2 (section 2.3), we referred to the fundamental principle of justice which states that *like cases should be treated alike*. If two people have committed crimes of similar gravity, then justice demands that they should normally be equally liable to punishment, unless there is some important *relevant* difference between the two cases or some other strong justification for departing from equal treatment. We have already seen in Chapter 4 how the arrangements for sentencing in England and Wales fail to ensure even rough equality of treatment for similar offenders – on the contrary, the wide discretion granted to sentencers ensures that there are enormous disparities, geographical and otherwise. Such disparities can, and doubtless often do, operate in a more or less arbitrary manner, so that the punishment an offender suffers bears little relation either to the offence or to the characteristics of the offender, being more a result of factors such as the local sentencing culture or the whims of the particular sentencers. In this chapter, however, we concentrate on *biases* within the criminal justice system – injustices which are related to certain characteristics of the offender. We consider three such characteristics: social class, race and gender.

As we shall see, these biases do not only – or indeed, primarily – occur at the sentencing stage, or even within the *penal* system, as opposed to the wider *criminal justice* system. Bias can operate at any or every stage of the criminal process, stages which include investigation and charge by the police, prosecution decisions by the Crown Prosecution Service, bail decisions, court verdicts and sentencing decisions (see Figure I.1 in the Introduction). Further possibilities for bias arise after sentence, in official decisions concerning *inter alia* allocation to different prisons and early release. The penal system cannot be viewed in isolation when considering the issue of bias. Suppose, for example, that the sentencing practices of the courts were unbiased, but the prior actions of the police ensured that members of an oppressed group were prosecuted to an unfair extent. In that case the sentencing system viewed on its own would seem fair, but would have the effect of reproducing the bias created in a previous stage of the process. Consequently, this chapter deals with the entire criminal justice system.

At any stage, bias can occur for a variety of reasons. It often results, not from deliberate discrimination (though this may also happen), but from unconscious prejudices and stereotypes (fixed preconceptions that some kinds of people are more criminal than others) and even as an unintended consequence of *prima facie* reasonable attitudes, practices and decisions. But whatever the causes, such biases add weight to radical critiques which claim that the penal system functions to reinforce the position of powerful sections of society over the less powerful (see Chapter 3, section 3.2). They also – yet again – suggest that the penal system's crisis of legitimacy may be largely self-inflicted: the system is perceived as unjust because it really is unjust.

Legislation prohibiting discrimination on grounds such as race, gender, religion, disability and sexual orientation (such as the Equality Act 2010) has expanded in scope over the years (although a notable exception is any general legal requirement to avoid discrimination on the basis of social class). The issue of possible bias in the criminal justice system received particular official recognition in section 95 of the Criminal Justice Act 1991. This requires the government to publish information regularly 'for the purpose of … facilitating the performance by [persons engaged in the administration of criminal justice] of their duty to avoid discriminating against any persons on the ground of race or sex or any other improper ground'. This provision has prompted the issuing of a regular series of publications (for the most recent examples, see Ministry of Justice, 2010b; 2011c) containing the results of research and monitoring. To some extent this has helped in the identification of possible biases within the system. But so far there is little sign that it has brought about any diminution in the actual occurrence of bias.

Class

9.2 Although the regular official series of criminal and penal statistics do not provide data on social class or occupation, it is clear that the penal system's subjects are overwhelmingly working class, and that unskilled and unemployed people are particularly over-represented in the penal population. The 1991 National Prison Survey found that 6 per cent of prisoners aged 17 or over had never had a job. Of the rest, 82 per cent had had manual occupations (compared with 56 per cent of the general population), and 41 per cent were unskilled (compared with 19 per cent generally) (Walmsley et al., 1992: 10–11, 21). Just prior to imprisonment, two thirds of prisoners were unemployed (Social Exclusion Unit, 2002: 20). Similarly, Harris and Webb (1987: 115–16) found that almost all of a sample of 971 boys on supervision orders were working class, and fewer than 8 per cent had a parent in a white-collar job. Surveys of defendants in criminal courts have yielded similar results. Bottoms and McClean (1976: 75), for example, found that only 5 per cent of defendants in Sheffield in 1971 and 1972 (excluding motoring cases) were from social classes I and II, compared with 35 per cent of the general population. (In similar vein, a study of four magistrates' courts in the North of England in 1993 found that between 75 and 91 per cent of defendants sampled were unemployed: Crow et al., 1995: 46).

This does not in itself demonstrate that there is a class bias operating in the criminal justice system to produce these results, for they could occur without bias if a similar proportion of *crimes* were committed by members of the working class. But self-report research studies (in which respondents are asked in confidence what offences they have committed) suggest that this is not the case. It seems that there is *some* greater tendency for people from lower socio-economic groups to commit offences, or at least the kind of offences which tend to be dealt with by means of the normal criminal justice system. (This is not perhaps surprising when – just to mention the most obvious line of explanation – the vast majority of recorded crime is against property, which is exactly what poorer people lack.) But the class differential in commission of crimes as measured by self-report studies is much smaller than the class differential in officially processed offenders (see, for example, Rutter and Giller, 1983: 132–7). Gold's (1966: 44) American findings were fairly typical: 'About five times more lowest than highest status boys appear in the official records; if records were complete and unselective we estimate that the ratio should be closer to 1.5:1.' Somehow, between the commission of offences and the official responses of prosecution and punishment, the difference between the classes gets vastly magnified.

Such magnification could occur for a variety of reasons, not all of them necessarily connected with bias. Perhaps some misdeeds of middle-class offenders are relatively invisible and hence unlikely to come to official notice. This is probably true of embezzlement and tax evasion compared to burglary and robbery, for example. But there could also be biases operating at the various stages of the criminal process which ensure that middle-class offenders are dealt with more leniently. At many of these stages, there is little research evidence to confirm or deny the existence of class bias in the system. But there are some straws in the wind.

A classic study in the United States in the 1960s by Piliavin and Briar (1964) indicates one way in which unintended class bias could occur at the police stage. The authors found that police officers who came across juveniles committing offences were expected to exercise discretion as to whether to arrest or reprimand the juvenile. The result was that, for nearly all minor violators and for some serious delinquents, it was the police's *assessment of the youth's character* which was the prime determinant of the officers' decisions. Officers decided whether the young person was basically law-abiding and 'salvageable', or an incorrigible 'punk', and made their decisions accordingly. This assessment of character was, however, based on the very limited information available to the officers, notably cues such as the youths' race, dress and – most importantly – their *demeanour*. Those who failed to show the police what was considered to be sufficient respect received negative character assessments and harsher treatment. Since attitudes towards the police vary across socio-economic groups (see, for example, Skogan, 1990; 1995), such a criterion is extremely likely to result in effective class discrimination. It could also be that a 'rougher' demeanour not intended to convey disrespect could be misinterpreted, again to the disadvantage of the suspect from the lower socio-economic group.

Such a bias could occur at a very early stage in the criminal process, before the police have even discovered or decided that an offence has been committed. When police officers encounter members of the public they often have to decide – perhaps instantly – whether this person is a potential criminal or not. There is usually little to go on in making this decision except by using stereotypical cues which mark people as either 'rough' or 'respectable', yet a snap decision of this kind may condition the entire ensuing interaction (Cain, 1971: 81–4). This suggests that the police may be much less likely to suspect or investigate middle-class people – or, probably equally importantly, people who give the impression of belonging to the stably employed respectable working class. And indeed studies have found that unemployed people are significantly more likely to be stopped by the police than those who have a job (Clancy et al., 2001: 56, 65). As a result, the police will be likely to detect or recognize a higher proportion of offences committed by those in lower socio-economic groups.

Subsequent to detection of a possible offence comes the decision whether or not to prosecute or caution. In England, Bennett (1979) found that middle-class juvenile offenders in London were more likely than their working-class counterparts to be cautioned instead of being prosecuted for minor offences. There could be several factors influencing the police decision which have the effect of creating a class bias. Farrington and Bennett (1981) demonstrated that a juvenile's perceived bad attitude is a potent determining factor of the police decisions in London as well as in the USA; other studies have found that the offenders' *parents'* perceived attitudes are influential (Gold, 1966; Bennett, 1979; Fisher and Mawby, 1982). And Landau and Nathan (1983), again in London, found that the police were more inclined to prosecute latch-key children, a practice likely to work against low-income families.

It is also the case that, at the investigation and prosecution stages, typically middle-class offences can be dealt with in a radically different manner from ordinary crime, often by agencies other than the police. For example, HM Revenue and Customs very rarely prosecutes tax fraud offenders, but prosecution is much more likely for people from lower socio-economic groups who defraud the benefits system, typically of much smaller amounts[1] (NACRO, 1986a: ch. 10; Cook, 1989: ch. 7). Again, breaches of factory health and safety regulations, including those which threaten or cause serious accidents, are policed by an agency (the Health and Safety Executive) which prefers to warn rather than prosecute. Carson (1971) found that in the 1960s the HSE's predecessor, the Inspectorate of Factories, prosecuted a mere 1.5 per cent of detected offences. However, when a firm was detected offending three or more times the rate of prosecution increased – to 3.5 per cent! Even disregarding cases where the Inspectorate took no formal action at all, this made an overall cautioning rate of 98 per cent. This rate has since declined, standing at a mere 87 per cent in 2008–9, but it still puts the police's cautioning rate of 33 per cent in the shade (see further Sanders, 1985; Sanders et al., 2010: 410–15). This is indeed if the offences come to light at all. A recent study of deaths and injuries at work found that they are far more prevalent than official

---

[1]It has been estimated that the public purse loses about £900 million per year because of benefit fraud compared with between £97 and £150 *billion* to tax evasion (*Guardian*, 10 January 2007).

figures suggest, but safety crimes are decriminalised: undetected, not labelled as crime, and rarely prosecuted (Tombs and Whyte, 2008). Recently the law has been changed as regards accidents causing death to make it easier to convict *companies* of manslaughter (Corporate Manslaughter and Corporate Homicide Act 2007), but this does not affect the criminal liability of the *individual* managers who might be at fault. In several high-profile cases in recent years, including major fatal rail crashes, no individuals have been convicted of crimes, although some have been prosecuted and acquitted.

There is a distinct lack of studies at the sentencing stage which directly compare the sentences received by working-class and middle-class offenders *for the same offences*, although it is (for example) highly plausible that sentencers might perceive a middle-class offender as less incorrigible and therefore deserving of a lesser sentence. Again, sentencers (themselves overwhelmingly middle class) might well feel that a middle-class offender has already suffered enough through the disgrace of conviction, and sentence leniently as a result. Or richer defendants may be able to afford better lawyers who are more adept at representing their clients' circumstances as mitigating their culpability. There is plenty of anecdotal evidence of apparent leniency towards middle-class offenders, especially those convicted of typical white-collar offences. Examples include the £3 million fraudsters in the 1960s whose prison sentences were a fraction of those imposed on the £2 million Great Train Robbers (Morris, 1980: 92); the non-custodial sentences passed on insider dealer Geoffrey Collier in 1987 and fraudulent trader Roger Levitt in 1993; and the halving of 'Guinness trial' defendant Ernest Saunders' sentence to two and a half years by the Court of Appeal in 1991 following evidence that he was suffering from pre-senile dementia (which, remarkably, went into remission after his release).

Research does seem to have confirmed that the courts are often much more punitive towards the relatively poor people who fraudulently draw more benefits than they are entitled to than towards the relatively well-off people who defraud the Revenue of what may be much greater sums (Cook, 1989: 160–5). Again, this is presumably not the result of intentional class bias, but the effect of the prevailing (Marxists might say bourgeois) ideology which holds that the latter method of defrauding the public purse is less reprehensible than the former.

Unemployed people can again get a particularly raw deal at the sentencing stage. Traditionally, the fact that an offender has a job and a steady work record has been regarded as counting in his or her favour, whereas unemployment has been seen as reflecting negatively on the offender's character. Again, sentencers may sometimes decide to pass non-custodial sentences on employed offenders so that they do not lose their jobs although they would imprison a similar but unemployed offender. (An analogous effect can occur when the court decides whether to grant bail or remand in custody.) Finally, unemployment can restrict the sentencing options the court perceives itself as having. In particular, the court may be reluctant to impose a fine or other financial penalty on an unemployed offender. This might be because the sum imposed would seem (to the relatively affluent sentencer) ridiculously small if related to the offender's means, or because it is felt that the offender cannot or will not pay up. Research studies have confirmed that unemployed offenders are significantly less likely to be fined than those who are employed (Softley, 1978; Crow et al., 1989; Flood-Page and Mackie, 1998: 144 and 165; Halliday, 2001: 82). Although some of the unemployed who might otherwise have been fined are given discharges or probation orders, others receive custodial sentences.

Following a sentence of imprisonment, white-collar offenders are much more likely to be allocated to open prisons, where the conditions and regime may be distinctly preferable (Jones et al., 1977: especially 66–70). This fact was highlighted in August 1990 when three businessmen found guilty of dishonesty offences involving millions of pounds in the 'Guinness affair' were transferred instantly from the slum conditions of Brixton Prison to the relatively salubrious Ford Open Prison. It is also possible that white-collar offenders get parole more easily (Levi, 1989: 102–5). Certainly this was suggested by the experience of jockey Lester Piggott, who in 1988 was paroled at the earliest opportunity from his (relatively speaking, hardly draconian) three-year prison sentence imposed for evading over £3 million in taxes.

None of this will come as any surprise to Marxists, who as we saw in Chapter 3 (section 3.2) view the penal system as an instrument of class power. The particular injustices suffered by the unemployed can be explained by a sophisticated Marxism which sees the role of the criminal justice system (and especially the historic role of the police) as imposing order on the rough rather than respectable sections of the working class (for example, Cohen, 1981). (It can also be maintained that the roles of criminal justice agencies have recently been shifting towards a greater emphasis on controlling an emerging underclass of the impoverished and permanently unemployed – a perception by no means confined to Marxists.) However, traditional Marxism has more difficulty in providing explanations for the injustices we now proceed to investigate, concerning race and gender.

Race

9.3 According to 2011 census figures (Office for National Statistics, 2012b), around 14 per cent of the population of England and Wales is now of non-white ethnic origin (referred to as BME, or black and minority ethnic). Yet in 2010, 26 per cent of prisoners were non-white (Ministry of Justice, 2011c). These figures are partly due to the large number of foreign inmates in English prisons (in 2010, 16 per cent of all prisoners, and 32 per cent of ethnic minority prisoners, were not of UK nationality).[2] But only partly. When non-UK nationals are excluded from the figures, 20 per cent of prisoners are of ethnic minority origin.

---

[2]Drug couriers – who tend to receive harsh sentences as a supposed deterrent – account for some of this disparity, especially among females. New sentencing guidelines in force from 2012 may reduce the sentences received by some of these offenders.

The overall racial disparity in these figures is smaller than appeared to be the case in previous years (partly due to recent estimates suggesting increases in the proportion of the general population which is of ethnic minority origin). However, the most dramatic racial disparity in these prison figures, and the one we will be concentrating on in this section, concerns black people (mostly of African-Caribbean or African ethnic origin) who account for only around 2 per cent of the England and Wales population but comprise 14 per cent of the prison population (11 per cent if foreign nationals are excluded). It has been estimated that at this rate nearly one in ten young black men will have received a custodial sentence before their twenty-first birthdays, double the proportion of their white peers (*New Law Journal*, 30 March 1990; *Guardian*, 27 February 1989). Already it is reported that four in ten male inmates in young offender institutions are from ethnic minorities (Summerfield, 2011). Why do such disproportionately large numbers of black people find their way into custody?

One obvious hypothesis would be that black people are more likely to commit offences than white people. Since racial discrimination (conscious and unconscious, direct and indirect) results in black people being disproportionately materially deprived in the realms of employment, housing and education, it might not be surprising if this led to higher levels of offending. However, there is little evidence that this is the case. When it has been claimed – notoriously, by the Metropolitan Police in 1982 and 1995 – that black people are disproportionately involved in crime, the statistics produced to back up these claims have been rightly criticized as unreliable and misleading (Smith, 1982; Crow, 1987: 305). The 2000 British Crime Survey found that, for crimes where the victim could identify the race of the offender, 5 per cent of offenders were black; but we need to take into account that most offenders are under 30 and that ethnic minority populations are significantly younger than the population as a whole (Clancy et al., 2001: 15–7). Home Office research has found that *young* black people have very similar rates of offending to white youths (Graham and Bowling, 1995; Flood-Page et al., 2000: 20; Sharp and Budd, 2003).

However, it is clear from a plethora of research studies over the years that Afro-Caribbean people are disproportionately the object of police attention and suspicion. The manifestation of this which has attracted most attention is the use of police powers to *stop and search* people on the street. Overall, black people are, according to official figures, seven times more likely to be stopped and searched by the police on the streets than white people. Asian people are also now disproportionately likely to be stopped and searched (currently twice as often as white people) (Ministry of Justice, 2011c: 34–9). These figures may not be quite as bad as they seem when different social, demographic and lifestyle characteristics of different ethnic groups are taken into account. For example, ethnic minorities are generally younger than the white population and more concentrated in the inner cities, so the average black person may well be more likely to be found on the city streets than the average white person, and hence more available to be stopped and searched. Nevertheless it seems unlikely that the massive disproportionality in the use of stop and search can be satisfactorily explained away by such factors (see Bowling and Phillips, 2007; Sanders et al., 2010: 97–100).

These results could well be related to what the Policy Studies Institute found when they researched the work of the Metropolitan police in the early 1980s: that 'racialist language and racial prejudice were prominent and pervasive and that many individual officers and also whole groups were preoccupied with ethnic differences'. (Only 5 per cent of police officers are currently from ethnic minorities.) Although this racism did not usually manifest itself on the street, the Policy Studies Institute specifically noted that 'one criterion that police officers use for stopping people (especially in areas of *low* ethnic concentration) is that they are black' (Smith and Gray, 1983: 109–10). It seems that many police officers hold inaccurate, stereotyped views of black people, automatically placing them in the rough (potentially criminal) category, especially when they are seen in areas where they don't belong. Research has found instances of police officers acting on the basis of stereotypes such as 'the assumption that West Indians running or carrying a bag are up to no good' (Southgate and Ekblom, 1986: 11). Demeanour could also be important here. Either stereotyping by the police, or the fact that black people tend to be more critical of the police than whites (see, for example, Clancy et al., 2001: ch. 6), or both, could lead to the police perceiving black people as having a bad attitude towards them and discriminating against them as a result.

Black and Asian people have in recent years been particularly likely to be stopped and searched under two special powers which (unlike normal searches to look for drugs or stolen property, for example) do not legally require the searching officers to have a reasonable suspicion that they will find something illicit on the person searched. One of these powers concerned terrorism-related searches (Terrorism Act 2000, s. 44), which – especially following the London bombings of July 2005 – have been disproportionately imposed not only on Asians but also (for some reason even more so) on black people. In 2005 both senior police officers and government ministers were publicly quoted as explicitly accepting that Asians would inevitably be disproportionately stopped and searched in the post-9/11 climate. However, following a European Court of Human Rights case in 2010 – in which the likelihood of such powers being used in a discriminatory manner was a key issue – the availability of this power was drastically reduced.[3] Another similar power – temporary and limited to particular areas, but easy for the police to invoke – concerns searches for guns, knives and other weapons (s. 60 of the Criminal Justice and Public Order Act 1994), most used in London. An Asian in England and Wales is three times as likely to be searched under this power as a white person, and a black person 12 times (according to figures in Ministry of Justice, 2011c).

The issue of police racism, and of their use of stop and search powers in particular, came to the fore long ago in Lord Scarman's inquiry into the Brixton riots of 1981 (Scarman, 1986) and again on the publication of the Policy Studies Institute

---

[3] *Gillan and Quinton* v. *United Kingdom* [2010] ECHR 28. Following this case the section 44 powers were replaced by a more limited power under section 47A of the Terrorism Act 2000.

research on the Metropolitan Police in 1983. But little seemed to have changed by the time the Macpherson Report was published in 1999. This was the report of an official inquiry into the case of Stephen Lawrence, a black student who was murdered by a gang of white youths at a South East London bus stop in 1993. Macpherson concluded that the bungled police investigation into the murder, as a result of which none of the murderers was brought to justice until 2012, was affected by the *institutional racism* evident in the Metropolitan Police. This institutional racism, Macpherson thought, was for the most part unintentional and unconscious, but the police were nevertheless infected by 'processes, attitudes and behaviour which amount to discrimination through unwitting prejudice, ignorance, thoughtlessness, and racist stereotyping which disadvantage minority ethnic people' (Macpherson, 1999: 6.34). Macpherson identified stop and search practices as a particular cause of ill-feeling between the police and the black community, and declared: 'we are clear that the perception and experience of the minority communities that discrimination is a major element in the stop and search problem is correct' (para. 45.8).

Although police practices may have improved in some respects since the Macpherson Report (Foster et al., 2005), there is no evidence that much has changed for the better in relation to the use of stop and search powers on members of ethnic minorities. There is now official ethnic monitoring of searches (following a Macpherson recommendation), and police codes of practice were altered in 2003 and 2005 to require stops and searches (and the reasons for them) to be recorded, and copies of the records to be immediately handed to the person stopped. There have been claims that police use of stop and search is now more targeted and intelligence-led (for example, O'Connor, 2000), but there are suspicions that this often amounts to the controversial practice of racial profiling: targeting of searches on people who fit profiles of likely criminals which include racial characteristics. Arguably this is just a new and officially endorsed form of stereotyping which is bound to encourage further discrimination.

Black people are *arrested* more often than their numbers in the general population would lead one to expect – over three times as often as white people in 2009–10 (Ministry of Justice, 2011c: 47). Some of this difference may be explained by the fact that many arrests result from stop/searches, which as we have just seen happen more often to black people. It is also the case that black people are arrested particularly often for offences 'in which there is considerable scope for selective perception of potential or actual offenders' (Stevens and Willis, 1979: 41). Phillips and Brown (1998: 44–5) found that the evidence against arrested black and Asian suspects was less often sufficient to charge them than in cases with white suspects.

There is also evidence that race can make a difference to the decision whether to *caution* offenders or proceed to prosecution. In 2009, 14 per cent of arrested black suspects were cautioned, compared with 21 per cent of white and 17 per cent of Asian suspects (Ministry of Justice Statistics on Race and the Criminal Justice System 2010, Table S4.02). Landau and Nathan (1983) found in London that white juveniles were significantly more likely to be cautioned than their black counterparts, and a white juvenile with previous convictions was over four times more likely to be cautioned than a similar black youth. Some other studies have found that black defendants are more likely to have been brought to court for offences which caused no loss, damage or injury (Stevens and Willis, 1979: 37; Crow and Cove, 1984), raising the possibility that similar white offenders might not have been prosecuted. This could, however, be partly due to the actions of victims rather than the police and CPS: perhaps similar offences by white people might have gone unreported to the police in the first place (see Shah and Pease, 1992).

Interestingly, research has found that ethnic minority defendants (both black and Asian) are more likely to have the prosecutions against them dropped after being charged, that black defendants are more likely to plead not guilty, and that black and Asian defendants who plead not guilty are more likely to be acquitted in court (Phillips and Brown, 1998). This suggests that ethnic minority suspects may often be charged on the basis of a lesser amount of solid evidence than might be required in the case of a white suspect – indeed, may be more often charged and prosecuted when they are in fact innocent. There is comparatively little evidence about whether there is racial disparity in decisions by the Crown Prosecution Service to bring or drop charges. The Denman Report of 2001, which found the CPS guilty of institutional racism, focused on the CPS's employment practices and how it treated its own ethnic minority staff, but also suggested that it was failing to correct for institutional racism at the police stage of the process by allowing a disproportionate number of weak cases against ethnic minority defendants to go forward to trial.

Ethnic minority defendants are more likely than whites to be *committed for Crown Court trial*, according to a number of studies (e.g. Fitzgerald, 1993) – and, as we saw in Chapter 4, defendants who are tried in the Crown Court are likely to receive harsher sentences than those tried by magistrates. The higher committal rate seems to be partly the result of ethnic minority defendants more often electing to be tried at the Crown Court, but it is at least as often due to magistrates declining jurisdiction. Moreover, black Crown Court defendants are *remanded in custody*, instead of being granted bail, more often than whites: one study found 26 per cent of sentenced black defendants had been remanded in custody compared with 20 per cent of whites and 18 per cent of Asians (Hood, 1992: 146–7). The fact that black defendants who are remanded in custody are much more likely than their white counterparts to be acquitted or not proceeded against (Fitzgerald, 1993: 22) suggests that they may often be wrongly denied bail.

There is good evidence that race can also play an important part in *sentencing*. Several studies in the United States indicate that black defendants tend to receive more severe sentences (including more custodial sentences and more death sentences; see, for example, Spohn et al., 1981–82; Baldus et al., 1989; Lambie, 2002; see also Cavadino and Dignan, 2006: 59), but the evidence from the USA is not entirely consistent (Pruitt and Wilson, 1983). Nor is it consistent in England, where several studies (for example, Crow and Cove, 1984; Moxon, 1988: 59) have found no evidence of racial bias in sentencing, but a variety of others (see, for example, NACRO, 1986b: ch. 3; Hudson, 1989) have found that black defendants are more likely to receive custodial sentences than are comparable white defendants. Overall in 2010, 27 per cent of black defendants and 29 per cent of Asians convicted of indictable offences were sentenced to immediate custody compared with 23 per cent of whites, and average sentence lengths were also higher for black and Asian defendants (Ministry of Justice, 2011c: 52). However, these raw statistics do not control for factors which may differ between ethnic groups (such as types of offence and whether the defendant pleads guilty or not guilty) and will make a difference to sentences.

The largest and most rigorous study of this question – Roger Hood's *Race and Sentencing* (1992) – provides the best evidence to date of a race effect in sentencing in England. Hood carefully examined sentencing at five Crown Courts in the West Midlands in 1989, and found that 57 per cent of black male defendants were sentenced to custody compared with 48 per cent of the white men; for women the figures were 29 per cent and 23 per cent. Taking into account all other relevant variables such as the offence charged, plea and the offender's previous record, black men were 5 per cent more likely than white men to be sent to prison (Hood, 1992: 75–9; 163). At one court (Dudley Crown Court), black defendants were 23 per cent more likely to receive custody. Adult black and Asian males also received longer average sentences of imprisonment, and were particularly likely to receive sentences of over three years. Recent Ministry of Justice figures also show ethnic minority defendants receiving harsher sentences in a wide variety of offence categories, with, for example, black offenders being 44 per cent more likely than whites to be sentenced to imprisonment for driving offences and Asians being 41 per cent more likely to be imprisoned for drug offences (Ball et al., 2011). Again, however, these calculations do not correct for at least some important differences between the racial groups – notably the fact that ethnic minority defendants are significantly more likely to plead not guilty, which is likely to make any subsequent sentence substantially harsher.

Several studies have found that, although black offenders are to be found disproportionately in prisons, they are *under*-represented in other sectors of the penal system. Notably, black offenders have been found to receive proportionately fewer probation orders; and there have also been claims that young black offenders have been under-represented on non-custodial programmes (NACRO, 1986b: ch. 4; Moxon, 1988). These phenomena could well be related: for some reason black offenders are deemed unsuitable for non-custodial supervisory sentences and as a result find their way into custody relatively quickly. This raises questions not only about sentencers, but also about the provision of suitable non-custodial programmes for ethnic minority offenders (see Kemshall et al., 2004), and about the role of the probation officers and youth justice workers who assess offenders' suitability for these disposals and relay their assessments to the courts in pre-sentence reports (PSRs).

Some studies have indeed suggested that PSRs serve to disadvantage black defendants. For example, de la Motta (1984) found that reports on young black defendants in Nottingham were three times as likely as those on whites to make no recommendation as to sentence – usually interpreted by the sentencing court to amount to a veiled recommendation for custody. It has been suggested that 'probation officers may well make fewer recommendations for supervision in the community because they lack the confidence to carry this out successfully' (NACRO, 1986b: 16). However, other studies have found no such differences between recommendations in reports on black and white defendants (Mair, 1986; Moxon, 1988; Hood, 1992: 150–60) – but still fewer black defendants received probation orders than whites. One factor seems to be that PSRs are prepared less often on black defendants (for example, Hood, 1992: 150–1; Flood-Page and Mackie, 1998: 117), which is partly (but only partly) because reports are usually prepared in advance only on defendants pleading guilty, and black defendants are more likely to plead not guilty. Concerns remain about not only sentencing but also the quality of treatment ethnic minority offenders receive from the probation service. HM Inspectorate of Probation (2000) found that the quality of pre-sentence reports on white offenders was significantly higher than those prepared for offenders from ethnic minorities. The quality of supervision given to African and Afro-Caribbean probationers also raised significant concerns with regard to risk assessments, the level of contact received and enforcement practice.

Bias against black people in the criminal justice system does not by any means cease at the point of sentence. Black prisoners are less likely than whites to be allocated to open prisons (NACRO, 1986b: 20). Elaine Genders and Elaine Player (1989) provided substantial evidence of racial discrimination within prisons, finding, for example, that the best jobs were regularly allocated to white prisoners. Again, inaccurate racial stereotypes (this time held by prison officers) had a lot to answer for. Prison officers (only 2.5 per cent of whom are black: Ministry of Justice, 2011c) believed that Afro-Caribbean prisoners were arrogant, lazy and anti-authority, had chips on their shoulders and tended to stick together. Although these stereotypes were demonstrably false, they led prison staff to perceive black prisoners as unsuitable for the most desirable jobs.

Genders and Player's findings were perfectly exemplified by the case of John Alexander. The courts found in 1987 that the Home Office had unlawfully discriminated against Mr Alexander, a black prisoner whose application to work in the kitchen at Parkhurst was refused on the basis of an assessment report which stated that 'he displays the usual traits associated with his ethnic background, being arrogant, suspicious of staff, anti-authority, devious and possessing a very large chip on his shoulder'. The Prison Service has had a formal race relations policy since 1983 and has made repeated statements in recent years opposing any discrimination or display of prejudice by prison staff or by prisoners against each other, but racism is of course not so easily eradicated. This was reflected in the findings of the 1991 National Prison Survey (Walmsley et al., 1992: 38) that only 29 per cent of black Caribbean prisoners felt that prison officers treated them well, compared with 43 per cent of white prisoners. Another study (Burnett and Farrell, 1994) found that nearly half of black prisoners reported having been racially victimized by prison staff and over half thought they had been discriminated against over access to facilities and activities. In 2001, Prison Service Director General Martin Narey reported receiving hate mail following his own admissions that institutional racism and indeed 'pockets of malicious racism' exist within the Prison Service (*Guardian*, 14 February 2001).

Even more disturbing was the murder of Zahid Mubarek in March 2000 by his rabidly racist cellmate in Feltham Young Offender Institution. Inquiries into this incident discovered that ethnic minority staff and inmates at Feltham were subjected to both overt racist abuse and less explicit discrimination from prison officers. A judicial inquiry into the Mubarek case by Mr Justice Keith (2006) took it to be an established and uncontested fact that both Feltham and the Prison Service generally suffered from institutional racism (and also proposed the adoption of a parallel concept of 'institutional religious intolerance'). The Mubarek murder also led to an investigation into the Prison Service by the Commission for Racial Equality (2003), which found 14 areas of failure and made 17 findings of unlawful discrimination against the service. A survey by HM Inspectorate of Prisons (2005a) again found that ethnic minority prisoners were significantly more likely to feel that they were treated badly, felt they were treated with less respect and felt less safe than white prisoners, with 30 per cent saying that they had been victimized by members of staff (see also Edgar and Martin, 2004).

The Prison Service responded by working in partnership with the Commission for Racial Equality on a five-year action plan, including carrying out race equality reviews in all establishments, and in 2008 announced that significant progress had been made, especially in reducing the most blatant and explicit manifestations of racism in prisons (NOMS, 2008). It did not, however, try to claim that all was now well, noting, for example, that black prisoners were consistently more likely than whites to be placed in segregation units and have force used against them by staff. Further discouraging news came with figures disclosed in 2010 which showed that there had been a 25 per cent rise in complaints about racism by staff and prisoners in English and Welsh prisons (*Guardian*, 7 February 2010), and with the agreement by the Prison Service to pay compensation to prisoners who claimed they had been beaten and suffered racial discrimination at Leeds Prison (*Guardian*, 25 April 2008). Racism and racial discrimination remain a potent and undeniable reality in English prisons.

There is little evidence, however, of any relationship between race and the *parole* decision. One Home Office study (Moorthy et al., 2004) found that the release rates for ethnic minority prisoners were actually higher than for white prisoners; these variations could be explained by other factors which influenced the parole decision (such as type of offence and length of sentence).

To sum up: it may not be true to say that there is bias working consistently against black people throughout the entire criminal justice system. Nevertheless, it seems that a black person who comes into contact with the criminal justice system has a good chance of being seriously disadvantaged compared with a white person, and may be particularly likely to end up in prison. There may be some cause for hope, if not necessarily optimism, in the fact that the race issue has become recognized as one of the most pressing issues in criminal justice, especially since the Macpherson Report of 1999. Steps have been taken, for example, to ensure that sentencers receive racial awareness training and that ethnic monitoring is introduced and improved throughout the criminal justice system. Race is clearly now seen as a potential source of serious illegitimacy – and rightly, since studies have repeatedly shown not only that black people have considerably less confidence in criminal justice than white people (see, for example, Skogan, 1990: 55; Dholakia and Sumner, 1993: 34–5), but also that large proportions of white as well as black people believe that justice is biased against black people (for example, Smellie and Crow, 1991: 20; Flood-Page et al., 2000: 54). Hopeful signs are detectable in a more recent study in magistrates' and Crown Courts (Shute et al., 2005), which found fewer ethnic minority defendants feeling that they had been unfairly treated because of their race. Some things may be changing, and there is no reason to doubt the genuine concern of many people within the criminal justice system about the issue of racial discrimination. But – especially with regard to the police and the Prison Service – there is clearly still a long way to go.

Gender

9.4 Within the criminal justice system, the dimension of gender differs in one crucial respect from those of class and race: in this case, members of the oppressed group (women) are distinctly *under*-represented in the criminal statistics. Women and girls accounted for a mere 5 per cent of the prison population in July 2012 despite comprising just over half of the general population. (Nevertheless, there are currently more women prisoners than in previous times, their numbers having nearly trebled between 1993 and 2003.) Women are also under-represented at previous stages of the criminal justice system, though to lesser extents. In 2009, 23 per cent of those sentenced for indictable offences were female (this proportion has risen in recent years), as were 26 per cent of those cautioned and only 17 per cent of those arrested (figures taken or calculated from Ministry of Justice, 2010b).

Again the question arises as to whether this difference is due to a real difference in offending behaviour between the two sections of the population (in this case, males and females). With very rare exceptions, commentators agree that females do, in fact, commit significantly fewer offences than do males. (The very rare and misguided exceptions include a notoriously sexist book by Otto Pollak (1961), who claimed that women are responsible for vast amounts of crime which go undetected because of women's more deceitful nature and because chivalrous men do not want to see women prosecuted or punished.) However, the difference in offending between the genders may be much smaller than the official figures suggest. For example, a self-report study in the late 1990s found that males aged 12 to 30 were two and a half times more likely than females to admit (in confidence, to researchers) having committed a crime in the last year (26 per cent compared with 11 per cent: see Home Office, 2004a: 3); this would mean that 30 per cent of all offenders were female. As well as committing fewer crimes female offenders generally commit less serious offences than their male counterparts, and have committed fewer offences previously: the typical detected female offender is 'a young girl, a first offender charged with shoplifting' (Heidensohn, 1985: 11). Explanations for this state of affairs vary. Positivistic explanations exist which claim that differing male and female biologies are the cause: girls may not literally be made out of sugar and spice and all things nice, but their hormones lead them to be more law-abiding. More plausible in our opinion are theories which emphasize the different social experiences of males and females. Girls have traditionally been socialized to be more passive and conformist than boys, and throughout their lives girls and women may find themselves subject to greater informal social controls; they may also have less opportunity to commit certain types of crime (see, for example, Heidensohn, 1985: ch. 9).

Whatever the explanation, if we accept that women and girls do in fact commit fewer (and generally less serious) offences than men and boys, then the bare statistics say nothing about whether there is any bias operating in the criminal justice system either in favour of women or against them. Perhaps there would be even fewer women in prison if they were treated the same as comparable male offenders; or perhaps there would be more. There have traditionally been two rival schools of thought on this issue, one holding that female offenders are dealt with more leniently than males and one asserting the reverse.

The first view – the **'chivalry' theory** – claims that chivalry leads male police officers and sentencers to afford women less harsh treatment. It is easy to point to incidents which appear to bear this out. Our personal favourite is a case reported in the *Daily Mirror* in 1978: '*Judge frees "inhuman" mum*. A mother who flogged her eight-year-old son with a belt, gave him cold baths and forced him to stand naked for hours at night … was saved from prison *because she has another child to care for*' (cited by Heidensohn, 1985: 51; our italics). Were the chivalry theory to be correct, this would not of course mean that there is no sexist bias in the criminal justice system, but that the sexism takes the form of a patronizing 'chivalry' which may benefit some female offenders but is hardly likely to advance the general cause of female social equality. (It is, however, the kind of view often propounded by anti-feminists of the 'women should stop moaning because they get the better deal as things are' ilk.)

The opposing view, put forward in particular by feminist commentators, has been termed the **'evil woman' theory** (Nagel and Hagan, 1983). It asserts that women who offend will receive *harsher* treatment from the criminal justice system. This is because women who commit crimes are seen as doubly deviant: they have offended not only against the law, but also against deeply ingrained social norms about how women should be, so they are perceived as being particularly depraved. Rebellious, anti-social behaviour on the part of a young man may be reprehensible, but it is less disturbing because such behaviour is after all masculine – 'boys will be boys'. Similar conduct on the part of a young woman is far more unsettling because it is unfeminine. Moreover, there is a tendency for female criminality to be sexualized in a way that male offending is not. Female offenders are assumed to be sexually deviant, or their sexuality is regarded as associated with their offending, assumptions which are not generally made with male offenders. The result is that women's crime evokes an especially punitive response. This punitiveness may be overt, or it may be disguised as paternalistic concern for the woman's welfare. The woman's disturbing deviance may be rationalized away as sickness, leading to a positivistic treatment measure which could be more intrusive than the sentence a male offender would receive for a similar offence (see generally Heidensohn, 1985: ch. 3).

These theories can be tested against the evidence that exists concerning the different stages of the criminal process. At the first stages of initial contact between the police and possible female suspects, one clearly established fact is that the police stop and search males much more often than females. A national survey of boys and girls aged 14 and 15, carried out by Home Office researchers in 1983 (Riley and Shaw, 1985; Riley, 1986) casts some light on the phenomenon. Boys were more than twice as likely to have been stopped by the police than girls of the same age (29 per cent compared with 13 per cent in the preceding 12 months). Boys were more likely to be stopped if they and their friends were delinquent, but this was not true for girls. Girls were more likely to be stopped if their lifestyles were 'unfeminine' – if they went around in mixed-sex groups, were relatively more involved with drugs and alcohol, spent more time with their friends and were subject to less parental supervision. These findings do not show that the police treat girls worse than boys, but they do lend some support to the feminist claim that females are dealt with by criminal justice agencies according to different criteria from those applied to males, criteria related to traditional female gender roles, with the result that their femininity is being policed as much as their offending. This is a theme which will recur as we progress through the criminal process.

Moving on to the decision whether to *arrest* a suspect, while there is little directly relevant British research evidence, a study of drug arrests in Chicago between 1942 and 1970 (De Fleur, 1975: 101) found 'a tendency not to arrest females as often as males if they behaved in expected, stereotypic ways. During drugs raids females often cried, claimed to have been led astray by men, or expressed concern about the fate of their children. These behaviors usually were successful.' However, females who were more aggressive and hostile were arrested more often than those who behaved in more traditionally feminine ways.

There is no doubt that detected female offenders are *cautioned* much more often than males. In 2009, 48 per cent of females found guilty of or cautioned for an indictable offence received a caution, compared with 29 per cent of males (calculated from figures in Ministry of Justice, 2010d). To try to determine whether this shows any chivalry operating in women's favour, or indeed any bias in the opposite direction, it is of course necessary to take into account the type of offences involved and the offenders' previous records. Ideally, one should also allow for other variables which may affect the decision whether to caution or prosecute, such as social class and race. Landau and Nathan's (1983) study of juvenile cautioning in London found that, when such other variables were controlled for, the sex of the offender made no significant difference to the decision of the police (see also Landau, 1981; cf. Home Office, 2004a: 9). (However, Gelsthorpe (1989: 106) found evidence that girls were more likely than boys to be cautioned for offences of similar seriousness.) Again, although girls are not overall dealt with more harshly than boys, it may be that they are judged by different, gender role related criteria. It has been suggested that police again act more leniently towards female offenders who act in stereotypically feminine ways, such as showing remorse by crying or apologizing – although it also seems that boys who show remorse (which they do less often) are also more likely to be cautioned (Gelsthorpe, 1985: 3; 1989: 105).

Women are *remanded in custody* less often than men, apparently because they commit less serious offences, have fewer previous convictions and are less likely to have breached bail in the past or to be of no fixed abode (Flood-Page and Mackie, 1998: 121; Ministry of Justice, 2010b: 36). When women are remanded in custody, they are less likely than remanded males to be subsequently sentenced to custody by the court (66 per cent of female and 75 per cent of male remandees in 2009 – Ministry of Justice, 2010b: 36). This could mean that some women are being remanded in custody when comparable male offenders are not; certainly it means that many women offenders are being sent to prison before trial although their actual offence is subsequently not deemed serious enough to warrant deprivation of liberty.

The 'chivalry' and 'evil woman' theories have both been put forward in respect of *sentencing*. The bare statistics show, as one would expect, that women and girls sentenced for indictable offences on the whole receive less severe sentences than males. In 2009, 14 per cent of females' sentences were custodial compared with 26.5 per cent of males' (Ministry of Justice, 2010b: 37). Sentencing patterns differ in some other respects as well: women are more likely than males to receive supervisory court orders and discharges, and less likely to be fined. Do these figures indicate bias – and if so, in what direction?

Pat Carlen (1983) argues that sexist bias enters into the sentencing decision to the disadvantage of women who offend against the norms of traditional femininity. From her interviews with sheriffs (Scottish judges) she concludes that when sentencers are 'faced with a sentencing dilemma in a case where the offender is female, they mainly decide their sentence on the basis of their assessment of the woman as mother' (Carlen, 1983: 63). All the sheriffs she interviewed said (chivalrously) that they particularly hated sending women to prison. Nevertheless, they admitted that they sometimes imprisoned women in circumstances when they would have fined a man, because women were normally financially dependent on their husbands and often could not afford to pay a fine appropriate to the offence. They would be particularly inclined to send a woman to prison if her children were in care. Carlen quotes sheriffs as commenting: 'If she's a good mother we don't want to take her away. If she's not a good mother it doesn't really matter', and 'One often finds out, when inquiries are made, that the women have left their husbands and their children are already in care. In those cases it may seem a very good idea to send them to prison for three months to sort themselves out' (Carlen, 1983: 67).

Carlen's claim that sentencers make their decisions in this manner receives some support from surveys of women in prison, a disproportionate number of whom seem to have unconventional family backgrounds. Of Carlen's own sample of 20

Scottish women prisoners only one was currently married and living with her husband (Carlen, 1983: 38). In another Scottish sample, 65 per cent of the women prisoners had children under 18, but only half of these had been looking after them immediately prior to being imprisoned (Dobash et al., 1986: 193). In England, Genders and Player found that half of their sample of women prisoners over the age of 30 had a non-conventional background; fewer than half of those with dependent children lived within a 'traditional nuclear family setting' (in which they included living with a long-term cohabitee) (Genders and Player, 1986: 360). The findings of the 1991 National Prison Survey (Walmsley et al., 1992: 17) differed only slightly from this: 49 per cent of female prisoners of 18 or over had been living with a spouse or partner prior to their imprisonment, and nearly a half of those with dependent children were unmarried. Further support for Carlen's thesis comes from a study of magistrates' sentencing in Cambridge by Farrington and Morris. They found that women who were divorced or separated or had a 'deviant family background' were more likely to receive a relatively severe sentence, but these factors made no difference to the kind of sentences which male offenders received (Farrington and Morris, 1983: 244–5). (In the United States, Nagel (1981) made similar findings.)

Overall, Farrington and Morris found that the sentences received by female defendants at the Cambridge City Magistrates' Court were not significantly heavier or lighter than those passed on men when the relevant factors of offence type and offender's previous record were controlled for. In combination with their findings about the effects of deviant family backgrounds, this suggests the possibility that there could be sexist biases in sentencing operating *in both directions* (and, in this study, cancelling each other out). Women who are married and looking after their children may be the beneficiaries of chivalry and receive a lighter sentence than a man, but women who are less acceptably feminine – who are perceived as 'evil women' because they are not good wives and mothers – may be treated more harshly. The case of Susan Jones[4] is interesting in this context. Her four-year prison sentence for robbing seven building societies was quashed by the Court of Appeal in 1991 and a probation order with a condition of psychiatric treatment was substituted. The trial judge had referred to her 'wicked crimes', but the Court of Appeal judges stated that she was *'not a wicked woman'* and had only robbed because she had become desperate about her family's debts and was concerned about her twin children but 'did not want to worry her husband'.

However, the same cancelling out of biases was not apparent in two studies of Crown Court sentencing practice (Moxon, 1988; Hood, 1992: ch. 11); chivalry seemed to predominate. (This has also been found to be true in the USA – Nagel, 1981.) After allowing for factors such as offence and criminal record, women were significantly less likely than men to receive a custodial sentence. For example, Moxon (1988: 54) found that male first offenders charged with theft or fraud were almost twice as likely to receive unsuspended custody as were comparable women.

---

[4](1992) 13 Cr. App. R. (S.) 275.

Similarly, Hedderman and Hough (1994) found that in 1992 female first offenders were only half as likely to receive a sentence of immediate imprisonment than were male first offenders, and the pattern was similar for specific offences such as theft and for offenders with one, two or three previous convictions. Flood-Page and Mackie (1998: 121–3) found much the same picture emerging in the mid-1990s. Dowds and Hedderman (1997) found a more mixed picture when they examined a large sample of male and female adult offenders sentenced in 1991 for shoplifting, violence and drugs offences. Taking other factors into account, female shoplifters were less likely than comparable males to receive a prison sentence. Men and women were equally likely to be imprisoned for their first conviction for violence or a repeat drug offence – but women were less likely to receive custody for a *first* drug conviction or *repeated* violent offence. Thus the general picture is that results often show women receiving lighter sentences than comparable males, but never show them being sentenced more harshly.

It is often claimed (for example, Mawby, 1977) that women must be sentenced more harshly because a greater proportion of women who receive prison sentences have no previous convictions compared with imprisoned men: this was true of 26 per cent of women serving prison sentences in 2012 but only 12 per cent of male prisoners (Prison Reform Trust, 2012: 31). (Similarly, a much smaller proportion of female than male prisoners have been found guilty of a violent offence – Ministry of Justice, 2010b: 50–2.) This argument looks convincing at first sight, but it is fallacious. For these kinds of percentages are just what we should expect to find given that the great majority of female offenders have no or few previous convictions, and the figures are perfectly compatible with women receiving sentences which are similar to or more lenient than those passed on comparable male offenders (Walker, 1981). The correct comparison – of how female and male offenders with similar records are actually dealt with at the sentencing stage – was made in the studies we mentioned in the previous two paragraphs.

There seems to be a certain reluctance on the part of sentencing courts to impose *fines* on women. This could be partly – though probably not entirely – due to sentencers taking into account the fact that women are less likely to have their own income and more likely to have childcare responsibilities (Dowds and Hedderman, 1997; Gelsthorpe and Loucks, 1997). The result of this seems to be that (like unemployed offenders, whom courts are also reluctant to fine: see section 9.2 above) a woman may end up receiving a less severe sentence than a male offender (such as a discharge rather than a fine) but may also sometimes receive a more intrusive sentence such as a community order with probation supervision.

However, the preponderance of research evidence reviewed above suggests that women who offend are not on the whole sentenced more severely than comparable males, and that they sometimes receive more lenient sentences, including escaping custody where a male would not. But is this actually due to chivalry? What we do not know is to what extent the differences in sentencing may be accounted for by relevant differences in the situations of male and female offenders. One such obvious difference in many cases concerns childcare responsibilities, which of course fall disproportionately on women, including women offenders.

Even if a woman with a young child to look after does not herself deserve to escape imprisonment any more than an otherwise comparable male offender without such a responsibility, does the child deserve to lose its mother? It seems very likely that such considerations concerning not the offender's deserts but the interests of the child account for the differences between men and women as regards whether they receive custodial sentences. (Note that the same considerations have been held by the courts to apply in the less common case where a male offender has sole child care responsibilities: *R. v. Franklyn* (1981) 3 Cr. App. R. (S.) 65.)

Although the general picture is not one of sentencing bias against women, the possibility nevertheless remains that some women – perhaps those who are perceived as especially deviant because of their lifestyles or their particular crimes – could come off worse than comparable male offenders because of their gender, and certainly worse than other women who come across as more acceptably feminine. As Chris Tchaikovsky of the organization Women in Prison once aptly put it: 'Judges tell me all the time that they never send women to prison. The truth is that the woman in the neat white blouse who is sorry and depressed is acceptable, but the girl in the leather jacket with the Mohican haircut and the drug problem is treated very badly' (*Guardian*, 9 February 1994).

If courts are sometimes relatively lenient with female offenders, especially as regards custody, this could be a leniency bought by exploiting stereotyped notions about women and their crimes, at the price of reinforcing these stereotypes. Defence lawyers' pleas in mitigation and pre-sentence reports might encourage leniency by playing on the positivistic idea that women who offend are sick, or 'mad rather than bad', or by portraying the woman as weak, and led astray by a dominant man. In thus arguing that the women cannot help their actions, lawyers and probation officers could be helping to perpetuate the sexist ideology which holds that women are in general weaker, less rational than men and more driven by their emotions. Mary Eaton (1986) makes the wider claim that mitigation pleas and pre-sentence reports reinforce prevailing ideologies about women's rightful roles within the family by stressing either the normality of the woman's domestic behaviour (and therefore her essential goodness) or else its abnormality (as either a cause or a symptom of the pathology that has led her to offend).

This stereotyped perception that women who offend are 'mad rather than bad' and in need of help (perhaps combined in some cases with reluctance to impose a fine) is doubtless a factor in the tendency we mentioned previously for female offenders to receive more supervisory orders than males. Such paternalism could sometimes have the effect of moving some female offenders with comparatively trivial offending records 'up the tariff' (if, for example, the woman is given a community order rather than a fine or discharge), leading to an increased danger of a more severe sentence if they reoffend subsequently.

When women are sentenced to custody, how does their treatment compare to that of men? At first sight it might seem that they are treated better, since penal establishments for females are on the whole (superficially at least, and with some notable exceptions) physically less unpleasant places than those for males. But in some respects women prisoners are worse off. For example, because women comprise such a small percentage of the prison population, currently only 13 out of the 131 prisons in England and Wales accommodate females (none of them in Wales); this means that women are often held at enormous distances from their homes (the current average is 55 miles), in remote locations, making visiting a particular problem. Again, it is probably the case that, for a variety of social and psychological reasons, women find the experience of imprisonment much more traumatic than men do (Heidensohn, 1985: 75–9), leading to a higher incidence of flare-ups and self-mutilation in women's prisons.

It can be argued that women prisoners *should* be treated differently from men rather than following a gender-neutral approach. For one thing, women generally pose less risk to the public than do men, and are less likely to abscond (di Lustro, 2004: 6). And many commentators (for example, Hale, 2006) have argued cogently that the principle of equal treatment should not lead to identical treatment of men and women, because the circumstances and experiences of male and female offenders are typically so different that this would not be fair. Most female prisoners have children under 16, of whom only a quarter are being cared for by the child's father or a spouse or partner.[5] Many women prisoners are vulnerable, in a wide variety of ways, including poor physical health. Female inmates are more likely to be dependent on opiate drugs. Over half report having been physically and/or sexually abused as a child. Over one third have attempted suicide at some time. Women account for nearly half of the incidents of self-harm within prison despite making up only 5 per cent of the prison population. (For a round-up of research evidence, see Prison Reform Trust, 2012: 32–3.) So are women prisoners indeed 'mad rather than bad'? If by 'mad' we mean suffering from psychoses such as schizophrenia, then this is far from the case for the vast majority of prisoners, male or female. A large-scale survey (Singleton et al., 1998) rated 14 per cent of female prisoners as 'probably having a psychotic disorder' compared with 10 per cent of male remandees and 7 per cent of male sentenced prisoners. But they also assessed two thirds of women prisoners as suffering from less extreme neurotic disorders, notably depression and anxiety. Clearly women prisoners suffer greatly from mental distress and disturbance, exacerbated by the stresses of being imprisoned.

And indeed women prisoners *are* treated differently from men, although how far these differences are appropriate to their needs is another question. Traditionally, the training of female prisoners is directed towards equipping them to perform the work they are thought most likely to do when they are released, namely housework. The general picture has not changed much: the work that women do in prison is still dominated by domestic-type tasks such as cleaning, sewing and cooking, which also figure prominently in the training provided for female prisoners, along with training for traditionally female jobs such as typing, catering and

---

[5]There are currently seven mother and baby units within women's prisons with places for over 77 women and their babies, who can stay with their mothers up to the age of 18 months. It is a controversial question whether this is the right approach to the needs of mothers and their children, as opposed to ensuring that as few mothers as possible are in prison in the first place.

hairdressing (Hamlyn and Lewis, 2000: chs 4 and 5). Genders and Player, who studied female youth custody centres (now called young offender institutions), found this stereotyping of women's work to be combined with psychological rehabilitation theory:

> an important part of the treatment and training of young women serving youth custody relates to the building of self-confidence and self-esteem, the lack of which is deemed responsible for much of the attention- and approval-seeking which causes many girls to come into conflict with the law. The skills which are taught in youth custody centres, however, continue to permit success mainly within the boundaries of stereotypical female roles. The concentration upon personal hygiene and appearance, through training in beauty care and hairdressing, and the development of domestic skills, such as cleaning, cooking and household budgeting, makes clear those areas in which delinquent young women are expected to develop feelings of self-worth. (Genders and Player, 1986: 368)

The positivistic stereotype which sees female offenders (but not males) as invariably being 'mad not bad' has had a particular historical influence on prison regimes for women. An official Home Office publication of 1977 stated that 'most of the women in prison wish to conform with society but for various reasons are unable to do so. For example, many are in need of medical or psychiatric treatment' (Home Office, 1977: 101). In 1968 – roughly at the zenith of the rehabilitative ideal – it was announced that Holloway (by far the largest women's penal establishment in England) was to be redesigned and rebuilt as, in essence, a secure psychiatric hospital. The new design turned out to be disastrous, and in 1981 the prison was given a modified brief by the Home Office, abandoning the notion that all its inmates should be treated according to a medical model. This did not prevent the rebuilt Holloway from suffering severe problems, including overcrowding and low staff morale, compounded by a public scandal which blew up in 1984 about the prisoners' living conditions, especially (and ironically) in the psychiatric unit. The scandal resulted in a Home Office inquiry, following which the prison improved significantly (HM Chief Inspector of Prisons, 1992). Subsequently, however, conditions deteriorated again, provoking an unprecedented walkout by the Chief Inspector of Prisons in 1995 after inspectors had reportedly found squalid conditions and a heavy-handed, over-zealous security regime in place at Holloway (see Ramsbotham, 2005: chs 1 and 11). This was again followed by an apparent improvement in conditions, but Holloway's problems seem to recur on a regular basis, with a 2005 inspection finding squalid conditions (including mice-infested cells), and high levels of bullying and self-harm among inmates (HM Inspectorate of Prisons, 2005b). The most recent inspection (HM Chief Inspector of Prisons, 2010) found some things to approve but continuing problems, not least the chronically poor design which contributed to prisoners feeling less safe than in other women's establishments.

Female prisoners seem to suffer at least as much as male inmates from concerns about prison security, despite the fact that women generally pose much less of a threat to security. For example, in 1995 (in the 'security first' atmosphere engendered following escapes of some high security male prisoners – see Chapters 1 and 6, sections 1.2

and 6.4) a policy was introduced that women prisoners (including those in advanced stages of pregnancy) should be handcuffed or chained when being treated in hospitals outside prisons. The outcry which followed a TV news report of a prisoner chained to a prison officer shortly before and after giving birth led to a modification of the policy in 1996, but only to exempt women arriving at hospital to give birth (and most of those attending ante-natal checks) from being cuffed or chained while in the hospital.

Overall, though, female offenders do not in general seem to receive harsher treatment than their opposite numbers of the opposite sex; and sometimes they may receive more lenient treatment, perhaps especially as regards the decision to impose custodial sentences. However, it also seems very likely that *some* women are effectively punished for deviating from conventional feminine norms, and that the system tends to react to female offenders in a manner which is, one way or another, imbued with sexism. To use Althusser's terminology, the penal system can be seen both as part of the 'Repressive State Apparatus' visiting deviant women with punitive sanctions and as an 'Ideological State Apparatus' communicating and reproducing the sexist ideology which structures patriarchal society (Eaton, 1986: 88–9; above, Chapter 3, section 3.4). Or, as a Durkheimian might put it (section 3.3), our social culture is still permeated with sexism, which is bound to find expression in our punitive practices.

Although we accept the possibility that women offenders sometimes escape custody where men would not, this is not an argument for sending more women to prison. On the contrary, since women in prison are predominantly relatively petty, non-violent offenders with few previous convictions (and indeed are mostly serving sentences of six months or less), a large proportion of them could probably be decarcerated or diverted from custody with comparatively little difficulty, if there were the will to do so. As long ago as 1986 (when there were far fewer women in prison) Nancy Seear and Elaine Player (1986: 12) were surprised to find near-unanimous agreement from prison governors, prison officers, educationalists and ex-offenders that very many women in prison should not be there at all, and proposed a plausible programme for reducing the female prison population to tiny proportions (see also Carlen, 1990). In a penal system which was generally fair and did not exercise the massive 'overkill' of punishment we exposed in Chapter 2, this could be achieved without any need to exercise chivalry, although account should certainly be taken of women's different needs and circumstances.

In the decade prior to 2003, however, the trend was very much in the opposite direction, as women offenders were being punished increasingly harshly for their deviance. Indeed, at that time the female prison population was increasing much more rapidly than the numbers of male prisoners. Between 1993 and 2003 the male prison population increased by a massive 59 per cent, but the numbers of female prisoners nearly *trebled*, from 1,560 to 4,595. This disproportionate rise was not because women were now being sentenced more harshly than men, nor did it seem to result from any increase in the seriousness of female offending (Home Office, 2004a: 21). Rather, it seemed to be because the increase in sentence severity since 1993 had in particular meant that a great many more relatively petty offenders were being sent to prison, or sent there for longer. And since as we have seen most female offenders are relatively petty criminals, this shift affected women disproportionately (see also Hedderman, 2002).

However – unusually in the context of this book, and perhaps encouragingly – in the last decade there have been attempts to address this situation which have shown some signs of having an effect. One initiative came from the judiciary in the shape of Lord Chief Justice Lord Woolf in the 2002 Court of Appeal case of *R. v. Mills*.[6] In this case Lord Woolf referred to what he described as the recent remarkable and undesirable rise in the female prison population, and stated that courts should avoid imprisoning women who were the sole carers for young children, especially in cases which did not involve violence and where the woman was of previous good character. Governments (both New Labour and Coalition) have also sought to encourage the use of non-custodial penalties for female offenders. A strategy for women offenders was first published in 2000, and in 2004 the Women's Offending Reduction Programme was launched, aimed at improving community-based provision for women offenders, tailoring it to meet their needs (with particular emphasis on mental health and substance abuse), in the hope that courts would be encouraged to make greater use of these improved community disposals as a result.

In 2007 a government-commissioned review by Baroness Corston (2007) put forward radical proposals for reducing and reforming custody for women by means of a holistic and woman-centred approach. Her most radical proposal was that all existing women's prisons should be closed within ten years and replaced with local secure units. Although this particular goal never seemed likely to come to pass, government has been genuinely responsive to a number of Corston's ideas, notably the need for a joined-up approach transcending the boundaries of different government and state agencies and the importance of tailoring penal provisions to the actual, gender-specific needs of female offenders (especially in the provision of non-custodial facilities) (see Ministry of Justice, 2007; 2008b). (For an explanation of the woman-centred approach to community facilities for offenders and some pioneering examples, see Heidensohn and Silvestri, 2012: 357–8.) Thus, for example, the government set up a cross-departmental Criminal Justice Women's Unit and committed extra resources to the development of community alternatives to divert female offenders from custodial sentences and remands. In November 2011 the Coalition government Prisons Minister Crispin Blunt even said that he aspired to having no women in prison at all.

Such an outcome would be a staggering achievement (and we are not holding our breath for it to occur). Nevertheless, the message is currently being heard to the extent that the numbers of female prisoners have decreased by 9 per cent from their 2003 peak of 4,595, to 4,167 on 27 July 2012, at a time when the male prison population has still been rising. Progress, but still much more than double the figure in 1993 (up by 167 per cent). We are still dealing with female offenders much more punitively than we used to.

---

[6][2002] EWCA Crim 26; (2002) 2 Cr App R (S) 52.

10

Solving the Crisis?

A Grim Fairy Tale _____

10.1 There was once a land where all the people firmly believed that sacrificing animals to the gods was certain to bring prosperity and good fortune to the nation. Whenever there was bad weather, or a poor harvest, or a military setback, the people would all go clamouring to the emperor, demanding that even more animals should be sacrificed. As we now know, all this achieved was an ever-increasing amount of pointless suffering.

One day an enlightened emperor declared that animal sacrifice was wrong, and banned the practice. He was immediately torn to pieces by an angry mob, and replaced by a more popular ruler who promised to double the numbers of animals sacrificed. Over time, more and more of the country's resources were devoted to devising new and increasingly cruel methods of sacrifice. Eventually the whole civilisation (if such it could be called) died out when there were no animals left to provide milk and eggs, no horses to pull the carts and no oxen to draw the ploughs.

Fortunately, no modern society would ever be so foolish and primitive. Would it?

Throughout this book we have seen how wide, deep and persistent the penal crisis is. It pervades every area and aspect of the penal system, manifesting itself in both a running malaise and periodic dramatic eruptions. In this final chapter we trace the recent history of strategies to solve the penal crisis and assess the likely (and in our view grim) future for the penal system if current policies are continued. We go on to expound our own ideas of the kind of short-, medium- and long-term measures and programmes which should be adopted to tackle the crisis, and discuss the prospects of this type of approach being adopted.

Responses to the Crisis, 1970–2012 _____

From Positivism to Law and Order
with Bifurcation: 1970–1987 _____

10.2 In the heyday of the rehabilitative ideal in the 1960s, penal strategies on the whole moved fairly straightforwardly in a single, seemingly progressive direction. New penal measures (such as parole) were introduced for avowedly rehabilitative purposes, with the double advantage that they were not only ideologically attractive but also promised to reduce the prison population and hence ease the penal system's resource problems. In the 1970s, however, the penal system's ideological and resource difficulties both worsened as the legitimating ideology of the rehabilitative ideal collapsed and the penal population threatened to spiral out of control.

The response to this by both Conservative and Labour governments in the 1970s was predominantly pragmatic. Efforts were made to restrain the prison population by exhorting sentencers to use custody less extensively and for shorter periods, while providing them with a greater variety of non-custodial penalties to use as alternatives (the *strategy of encouragement*: see Chapter 4, section 4.4). At the same time, an increasing number of prisoners were released before the ends of their sentences (see Chapter 7, section 7.2). The discrediting of rehabilitation led to a shift towards 'law and order ideology' (Hall, 1979), and Tony Bottoms made his first perceptive sighting of the trend towards *bifurcation* in penal policy (Bottoms, 1977; see Chapter 1, section 1.4) as measures to increase the punishment inflicted on more serious criminals were combined with attempts to deal more leniently with some lesser offenders. The overall strategy for the prison population was to attempt to achieve a *standstill*, keeping the lid on prison numbers but not trying to reduce them substantially. But by the end of the 1970s this strategy was clearly failing.

It was at this stage – in 1979 – that the Conservative government of Margaret Thatcher came to power. The Conservative Party has usually portrayed itself as being tougher on crime than its Labour opponents, and has more often than not been rewarded by general public approval for this stance. However, law and order had never been such a prominent election campaign theme as it was in 1979, when the Conservatives committed themselves to increase the resources of the criminal justice system (especially the police), to introduce a 'short sharp shock' regime into detention centres for young offenders and to increase the sentencing powers of the courts. Although Home Secretary William Whitelaw tried to inject an element of liberal pragmatism by introducing earlier automatic release for short-term prisoners, this proposal was defeated by the combined opposition of the judges and the Conservative Party Conference. In 1982, Whitelaw effectively announced the end of the standstill policy by telling Parliament: 'We are determined to ensure that there will be room in the prison system for every person whom the judges and magistrates decide should go there, and we will continue to do whatever is necessary for that purpose' (HC Deb., 25 March 1982). This heralded the most extensive programme of prison building of the twentieth century up to that point.

This did not, however, mean that the Thatcher government's penal policies in the early 1980s were entirely determined by law and order ideology. Pragmatic considerations still led to some attempts to *limit the rise* in the prison population, and the government continued to encourage a diversion from court and custody and shorter sentences for many run-of-the-mill offenders. Thus, for example, the same White Paper that introduced the 'short sharp shock' detention centre for young offenders (see Cavadino and Dignan, 2002: 291) also approved the practice of cautioning juveniles, an approval later extended to older less serious offenders. The government also lent support to the use of alternatives to custody such as community service orders, and supported attempts by the Lord Chief Justice to reduce the lengths of custodial sentences for non-violent petty offenders. But these measures were to apply only to supposedly less serious offenders. Bifurcation was alive and well, with less harsh measures still being advocated for petty offenders while the full force of law and order rhetoric and treatment was focused on the more serious 'violent criminals and thugs' (as the 1979 Conservative Manifesto called them).

Overall, it could hardly be claimed that the penal strategy of the early 1980s had proved an outstanding success. The prison population continued to rise throughout the 1980s, while outbreaks of riots and disorder within prisons were a regular occurrence. The 'short sharp shock' proved a disappointment, recorded crime rose almost every year, and Britain's inner cities were hit by serious rioting in the summers of 1981 and 1985. The magazine *Punch* once memorably observed that Mrs Thatcher's bark might be dogmatic but her bite was pragmatic, and so it proved now. In the second half of the 1980s, the Conservative government altered course.

Just Deserts and Punishment in the Community: 1987–1992

A profound change in the government's approach to criminal justice took place from 1987 onwards, with the shift first occurring under Douglas Hurd (Home Secretary from 1985 to 1989). One symbolic moment was a meeting of Home Office ministers and civil servants at Leeds Castle in Kent in September 1987, two months after the prison population had reached a then record high of 50,979. When presented with statistical projections of an increase in the prison population to over 60,000 in the foreseeable future, possibly reaching 70,000 by the year 2000, ministers resolved that this should not be allowed to happen (Windlesham, 1993: 237–9).

The resulting new 'Hurd approach' (as we like to call it) represented a shift towards eclectic pragmatism. In terms of the typology of penal strategies we sketched out in the Introduction, it was a predominantly managerial, Strategy B approach, although it also contained some elements of the humanitarian Strategy C, and retained echoes of the harshly punitive Strategy A. The volume of law and order rhetoric emanating from government was significantly toned down, and was combined with other themes and approaches to crime and punishment such as privatization and crime prevention. Prominent in this new pragmatic mix was *managerialism* (see Chapter 1), with the government continuing to favour the systems management approach to criminal justice (see Chapter 8, section 8.2), and in particular the expanded use of cautioning for adult offenders as well as juveniles. Above all, there was the 'just deserts' package of reforms contained in the Criminal Justice Act of 1991.

These reforms were based on the notion that 'imprisonment is not the most effective punishment for most crime', and indeed (in a famous phrase) 'can be an expensive way of making bad people worse'. Consequently, 'custody should be reserved for very serious offences, especially when the offender is violent and a continuing risk to the public' (Home Office, 1988a: para. 1.8; 1990a: para. 2.7), with many more offenders than hitherto being dealt with by means of community penalties instead. Philosophically, this package of reforms was heavily influenced by the justice model (see Chapter 2, section 2.5). The legislative framework for sentencing contained in the 1991 Act was based on the just deserts notion of proportionality between the seriousness of the current offence and the severity of the sentence. But this was heavily qualified by exceptions for violent and sexual offenders, who were liable to get *more* than their just deserts if this was thought necessary to protect the public.

The Act again embodied the *bifurcation* approach, for although less serious offenders were to be diverted from custody, at the same time violent and sexual offenders were to be treated more harshly. Moreover, it was what we call *punitive bifurcation* – meaning that it was punitive not only towards the more serious offenders, but also towards the less serious. True, the intention was to deal with them in the community rather than in custody; but the influence of law and order ideology lingered on in the insistence that the non-custodial measures were to be tough and punitive in nature rather than being primarily intended to rehabilitate offenders or to make them perform reparation for victims. Punishment in the community, with the emphasis on both 'punishment' and 'community'. Nevertheless, this was a serious attempt to tackle not only the material crisis of resources (by reducing the prison population) but also the general ideological crisis of legitimacy by putting forward just deserts as a legitimating ideology for punishment.

Another strand of the government's strategy around this time was its response to the Woolf Report on the 1990 disturbances in Strangeways and other prisons (Woolf and Tumim, 1991). As we saw in Chapters 1 and 6, Woolf implicitly diagnosed the major cause of prison disorder as being a lack of justice in prisons leading to a crisis of legitimacy, and produced a set of recommendations aimed at improving conditions and regimes within prisons and alleviating prisoners' sense of injustice, with particular emphasis on improving grievance and disciplinary procedures. The government accepted the main thrust of the Woolf Report and implemented a number of its recommendations (see Chapter 6), including a programme to abolish 'slopping out', relaxations of restrictions on prisoners' contact with their families and the outside world, and the creation of the Prisons Ombudsman. Until the autumn of 1992, the government held to this strategy based upon the Criminal Justice Act 1991, acceptance of the Woolf Report and a generally managerial approach to criminal justice. This more liberal and pragmatic strategy for criminal justice started showing some signs of success. In the first months following the implementation of the Criminal Justice Act 1991 in October 1992, sentencing became less harsh, and the prison population fell from 45,835 in September to 40,606 in December 1992. But it was not to last.

Law and Order Reinvigorated: 1993–1997

The extraordinary U-turn of John Major's Conservative government on criminal justice policy – the 'law and order counter-reformation' – is difficult to explain without reference to the general political situation and party political electoral calculations. The government, in deep trouble with desperately low opinion poll ratings, made what looked like a deliberate strategic decision to try to regain popularity by playing the law and order card. This strategy, which had served them well in the past, was to be further encouraged by events such as the murder of two-year-old James Bulger by two ten year olds in February 1993. October 1992 saw the implementation of the Criminal Justice Act 1991, followed rapidly by a backlash from sections of the media and the judiciary against its perceived softness. Instead of defending their Act, the government assumed the remarkable role of criticizing and reversing its own policies and legislation. Key components of its Hurd era strategy – the attempt to reduce the prison population by means of the 1991 legislation, the positive response to the Woolf Report, and the encouragement of systems management – were all abandoned. In May 1993 Home Secretary Kenneth Clarke announced the swift repeal of two significant provisions of the Criminal Justice Act 1991: the unit fines system (see Chapter 5, section 5.3) and a section which had restricted the ability of courts to take previous convictions into account when sentencing offenders.

In May 1993 the office of Home Secretary passed to Michael Howard, a right winger with a profound attachment to the rhetoric and ideology of law and order, who was put in charge of implementing the government's 'crusade against crime'. At the Conservative Party conference of October 1993, he famously proclaimed that 'prison works' and said of his proposals to toughen up the criminal justice system: 'This may mean that more people will go to prison. I do not flinch from that. We shall no longer judge the success of our system of justice by a fall in the prison population.' A retreat from Woolf's strategy for prisons was also evident, with Mr Howard proclaiming that conditions in prisons should be 'decent but austere', a remark given substance by moves to increase disciplinary powers for prison governors and reduce home leave for prisoners. Subsequently, the government moved even further in the direction of Strategy A, introducing legislation to provide for mandatory 'two- or three strikes and you're out' sentences for certain categories of repeat offenders (see Chapter 4, sections 4.3–4.4) and proposing massive cutbacks to the system of early release (see Chapter 7, section 7.2). The effects of this atmosphere of law and order were predictable. Sentencers responded to the encouragement to make more punitive decisions, and the prison population rose immediately from its low point of 40,600 in December 1992. By 1997 the daily average prison population was 61,114 – a spectacular 51 per cent above the December 1992 figure. The pursuit of Strategy A was now at its zenith, but the 'ratcheting up' of sentencing (see Chapter 4, section 4.1) was only just under way, and the prison population was destined to hit even greater heights in succeeding years.

However, the Conservatives failed to reap the reward in terms of their popularity with the electorate which they must have hoped for. Although opinion polls had always favoured the Conservatives as having the best policies on crime, the Labour

Party took a lead on this issue from 1993 onwards. This shift was facilitated by the efforts of Tony Blair (Labour leader from 1994 to 2007), whose much-reiterated slogan – 'tough on crime and tough on the causes of crime' – did much to shed Labour's public image of being soft on crime. The phrase 'tough on the causes of crime' evoked the Labour Party's more traditional concerns with what it saw as the social roots of crime such as unemployment. However, the slogan as a whole (and Labour's general rhetoric) was calculated to appeal to populist sentiments by fostering the impression that Labour wanted to deal severely with offenders. By the time of the 1997 general election the two main parties were bidding against each other for who could sound the toughest on law and order.

'Tough on Crime, Tough on the Causes of Crime': New Labour, 1997–2010

The 1997 general election resulted in a landslide victory for Tony Blair's New Labour party. For all their recurrent use of the word 'tough', it would have been difficult for Labour to incline more towards Strategy A than Michael Howard had. And indeed Labour's approach proved to be a mixture of Strategies A, B and C, well summed up by the term 'neo-correctionalism' (see Chapter 8, section 8.2). Soon after taking office, Home Secretary Jack Straw declared that he had 'no interest in chanting a simplistic mantra that prison works'. Yet Strategy A rhetoric lived on in talk of toughness and zero tolerance: the title of Mr Straw's 1997 White Paper on young offenders, *No More Excuses* (Home Office, 1997a), was typical.

Overtly, the New Labour strategy was one of rational, *evidence-based* crime control: finding out what works to combat crime and then firmly implementing effective policies: a managerial, Strategy B approach. (One prominent strand in this was an increasing emphasis on the use of *risk assessment* techniques and procedures in order to apply the appropriate management to offenders according to the level and nature of the risk they pose – see for example Robinson, 1999; 2002.) But the clear subtext was always a determination not to give the Conservatives political ammunition on law and order issues by appearing to be soft on crime. Elements of Strategy C – such as restorative justice measures like reparation orders for young offenders – found their place in the overall approach, but it was a very limited one.

There were some pragmatic attempts to limit prison numbers, notably the introduction of the home detention curfew in 1999 (see Chapter 7, sections 7.2–7.3) and a further temporary early release scheme known as the end of custody licence which ran between 2007 and 2010 (see section 7.2). There were also fairly half-hearted attempts to encourage the use of tough and rigorous non-custodial alternatives to short prison sentences for less serious offenders, in a manner reminiscent of Hurd era 'punitive bifurcation'. But there was no sustained or concerted attempt to limit the numbers going to prison or the lengths of their sentences. Indeed, measures such as the implementation of 'three strikes and you're out' and other minimum sentences, and tougher enforcement of community penalties were deliberately aimed at putting more people into prison. Similarly, the introduction of new mandatory and indeterminate sentences and of statutory guidelines designed to ensure longer minimum periods of imprisonment for those convicted of murder (see Chapter 7, section 7.3) were designed to keep some offenders in for longer. The government's Respect Agenda aimed at reducing anti-social behaviour, with its centrepiece provision the ASBO (see Chapter 8 section 8.3), had the effect of increasing the number of people sent to custody as a result of breaches of the orders imposed for relatively petty misbehaviour.

There were moments in the history of the New Labour government when it seemed possible that there might be a determined shift towards a less punitive policy and a serious attempt to reduce the prison population. But they all proved to be false dawns, inexorably followed by a reversion to a harsher stance. One such moment was in 1998, when Home Secretary Jack Straw gave an enthusiastic welcome to a major Home Office research report which expressed scepticism about the effectiveness of punitive measures such as custody in controlling crime while pointing out that targeted anti-burglary crime prevention methods were likely to be ten times more cost-effective than locking up burglars (Goldblatt and Lewis, 1998: 98, 135). But although in succeeding years the government did expand crime prevention initiatives it did not follow the parallel logic and reduce the rate of imprisonment. On the contrary, numbers of prisoners were still rising. Michael Howard had bequeathed Labour a daily average prison population of 61,114 in 1997; in 1998 it was 65,298. Following a slight and temporary dip in 1999–2000 (brought about by the introduction of the home detention curfew) the numbers rose again, to new all-time records actually exceeding the prison system's 'bust limit' (see Chapter 1, section 1.2 and Chapter 6, section 6.5) for a while in April 2004.

In 2004 Home Secretary David Blunkett's acceptance of the Carter Report again seemed a potential harbinger of a positive change in direction (Carter, 2003; Blunkett, 2004). Carter to his credit had recognized and stressed that sentencing had become noticeably harsher in recent years, and to no good purpose, and suggested a strategy to ratchet sentencing levels back down and to prevent the prison population rising above 80,000 by ensuring that guidelines were designed to target the right level of sentence on offenders. But in 2005 Blunkett's successor Charles Clarke dropped this aspiration to hold the line at 80,000, which was giving unwanted ammunition to political opponents and was in any event unlikely to be achieved. By the end of October 2006 prison numbers had exceeded Carter's ceiling of 80,000, and the bust limit was just a few hundred inmates away.

However, Clarke's own plans again contained elements of a positive strategy to contain prison numbers. A 'Five Year Strategy' published in February 2006 stated that 'overall ... prison should be used for the most dangerous, violent and seriously persistent offenders, and that others are usually best punished in the community' (Home Office, 2006b, para. 3.26). Central to Clarke's plan was community service (or 'unpaid work'), which was rebranded as Community Payback (see Chapter 5, section 5.3). The intention was to double the hours of unpaid work performed as punishment, diverting (it was hoped) many offenders from short prison sentences to community orders. At the same time, prison sentences of less than 12 months were (under provisions in the Criminal Justice Act 2003) to be replaced by a new sentence called 'custody plus', which would have meant a shorter taste of prison followed by a period in the community subject to requirements which would again include unpaid work. Whether this would have worked to control the prison population we will never know. Following a fiasco surrounding the failure of foreign prisoners to be considered for deportation, Charles Clarke lost his job in May 2006.

His replacement as Home Secretary was John Reid, a man with a tough image and corresponding rhetoric (who famously declared on taking over that the Home Office was 'not fit for purpose'). The planned introduction of custody plus sentences was shelved (and never came into being, the provisions for it being eventually repealed by the Legal Aid, Sentencing and Punishment of Offenders Act 2012). It was replaced by a set of harsher proposals including the creation of 8,000 more prison places. However, the target date for providing these 8,000 places was 2012, and the crunch point was to arrive in the autumn of 2006. The government was forced to revive the practice (not regularly employed since 1995) of housing prisoners in cells in police stations, an emergency measure which continued until October 2008; and a scheme known as 'end of custody licence' giving many prisoners extra early release was in operation between 2007 and 2010. This did not stop the bust limit from again being exceeded in February 2008. By the time the Labour government lost the 2010 general election it had taken the prison population over 85,000 for the first time.

Coalition False Dawn: 2010 Onwards

Following the general election of May 2010 a Conservative–Liberal Democrat coalition came to power with David Cameron as Prime Minister. Prior to the election, the Conservatives had promised a more restrictive approach to the early release of prisoners, increased sentencing powers for magistrates, mandatory custodial sentences for carrying knives and a further expansion in prison capacity. They also planned a 'rehabilitation revolution', to be brought about by a system of payment by results so that agencies with responsibility for offenders would be paid more for producing lower reoffending rates (Conservative Party, 2008; 2010), with a much greater role being envisaged for private and voluntary agencies (see further Chapter 2, section 2.2, and Chapter 5, section 5.4). The Liberal Democrats on the other hand had proposed introducing a presumption against short-term sentences of less than six months, moving drug addicts and mentally ill offenders into alternative secure accommodation, championing restorative justice schemes and cancelling the Labour government's prison building programme. Overall it could be said that the Conservatives' approach was the most punitive of the three main parties and the Liberal Democrats' the least so.

The Coalition agreement of May 2010 included the Conservatives' 'rehabilitation revolution' and a promise to explore alternatives to imprisonment for mentally ill and drug offenders. Early indications were that the new government would seek to pursue a less punitive approach than their New Labour predecessors and make a serious attempt to reduce the prison population (thus among other things making financial savings in their bid to reduce the national budget deficit following the credit crunch of 2008 and subsequent economic recession). New Justice Secretary Kenneth Clarke said that his search for cuts in the Ministry of Justice's budget would include asking 'why is the prison population twice what it was when I was the Home Secretary not so very long ago [1992–93]?' (*Guardian*, 14 June 2010). Opposition to Clarke's approach came from voices on the Conservative right wing, and reservations about the possibility of restrictions on short-term sentences were voiced by the Magistrates' Association. And it was not long before there were signs of potential reforms being stymied by populist law and order ideology. Junior Justice Minister Crispin Blunt announced the rescinding of an order on allowing parties in prison, an announcement immediately followed by a *Daily Mail* headline 'Now You Pay for Prison Parties' (23 July 2010) and then by the news that Prime Minister David Cameron had overturned the decision.

A Green Paper published in December 2010, *Breaking the Cycle* (Ministry of Justice, 2010a; see also Ministry of Justice, 2011a) contained proposals which aimed to reduce the demand for prison places by 6,450. About half of this reduction was expected as a result of a single proposal, to increase the maximum 'discount' from sentences given to defendants who plead guilty from one third to 50 per cent. The government also proposed to seek greater use of financial penalties and community sentences, with an emphasis on 'strenuous unpaid work'. But the idea (favoured by Clarke and the Liberal Democrats) of introducing statutory restrictions on the powers of courts to pass short prison sentences had already been dropped, having encountered strong opposition from (among others) magistrates, whose sentencing discretion might in theory have been severely restricted as a result. This diluted package, and especially the central proposal to increase sentencing discounts, ran into further serious difficulties. In May 2011 the media and the Labour Opposition targeted the discount proposal emphasizing the crime of rape ('Soft Justice for Rapists: Rapists will have their jail terms halved if they admit guilt' – *Daily Mail*, 18 May 2011), and Kenneth Clarke in defending the proposal made unfortunate remarks in a radio interview which seemed to suggest that not all rapes were serious. Clarke was forced (according to some reports, by Prime Minister David Cameron personally) to drop the sentence discount proposal.

The ensuing Legal Aid, Sentencing and Punishment of Offenders Act 2012 contained a miscellany of provisions which had survived from the Green Paper, of which the only one likely to reduce the prison population to any noticeable extent was a restriction on courts' powers to remand unconvicted defendants in custody if they are unlikely to receive a custodial sentence. The imprisonment for public protection sentence (see Chapters 4 and 7, sections 4.4 and 7.3) was abolished, but it was replaced by a new 'two strikes and you're out' mandatory life sentence for those committing a second serious offence (see Chapter 7, section 7.3). The 'rehabilitation revolution' survived, as did plans to divert some mentally disordered offenders from prison and the criminal justice system and foster greater use of restorative justice. However, overall this revised package seemed likely to ensure that the prison population would not be reduced, but continue to rise. Indeed, by March 2012 Kenneth Clarke was overtly promoting tougher community sentences for their own sake, abandoning even any vain hope that they might be used as alternatives to custodial sentences (Ministry of Justice, 2012c: Foreword). In September 2012 Clarke was moved from his post as Justice Secretary in a reshuffle and replaced by Chris Grayling, a right winger who lost no time in asserting that he had no intention of reducing the numbers of people in prison while simultaneously ensuring that almost all community orders would contain a punitive element (although he did also announce his support for Clarke's 'rehabilitation revolution') (*Guardian*, 20 September 2012).

Thus the story so far of the Coalition's penal policy is largely one of well-intentioned proposals for reform (notably by Kenneth Clarke) being stymied by political forces (including the Prime Minister), the media and law and order ideology. Clarke's attempts to bring about a limited reduction in the prison population had already seemed doomed when in the autumn of 2011 (following the urban riots of that summer) it reached more all-time records, now exceeding 88,000. It had been another false dawn.

The Labour Opposition had played a part in this. Following the departure from top-level politics of such icons of penal harshness as Michael Howard and New Labour's architects Tony Blair and Gordon Brown there were some brief signs that the penal policy 'arms race' – whereby each major party accuses the other of being soft on crime resulting in an ever-escalating harshness of punishment – might be coming to an end. On being elected as Labour leader in September 2010, Ed Miliband declared: 'when Ken Clarke says we need to look at short sentences in prison because of high re-offending rates, I'm not going to say he's soft on crime', and his Shadow Justice Secretary Sadiq Khan similarly declared: 'As Ed Miliband has said, we won't accuse the government of being soft on crime just for the sake of it' (*Guardian*, 7 March 2011). Yet Labour – and Miliband and Khan – were prominent in the torpedoing of Mr Clarke's proposal to increase sentence discounts, while Labour also opposed votes for prisoners (see Chapter 6, section 6.5) and the plans to limit custodial remands and abolish IPP sentences.

It seems fair to say – with perhaps a measure of understatement – that the penal crisis has not yet been solved. And if the immediate future for the penal system looks none too healthy, the long-term prospects could be even worse. Unless, that is, a new and different approach is taken to the penal system and the penal crisis.

How to Solve the Crisis

Approaches to the Penal Crisis

10.3

In the Introduction, we briefly set out three broad strategies for criminal justice: the highly punitive Strategy A (allied to the new punitiveness discussed in Chapter 3, section 3.6), the managerial Strategy B (associated with the new penology, for which also see Chapter 3) and the humanitarian, rights-based Strategy C. Government penal strategies in recent years have combined elements of all three approaches, but it is fair to say that the first two have tended to dominate. Strategy A rhetoric and ideology reached its zenith under Michael Howard between 1993 and 1997; as we have seen, New Labour's approach was more mixed but had much more of Strategies A and B than C in the mixture. The Coalition government to date has flirted with elements of Strategy C (in its 'rehabilitation revolution' and nods towards restorative justice) and began by expressing a Strategy B-ish wish to make the prison population more manageable and less expensive, but still seems largely mired in Strategy A.

Strategies A and B have both failed to solve the penal crisis to date, and indeed the enduring effects of Strategy A have exacerbated the crisis to an unprecedented degree. As we have argued more fully elsewhere (Cavadino et al., 1999: ch. 2), Strategy A is both ineffective and inefficient in controlling crime, while its immorality (in inflicting excessive punishment) inevitably creates crises of legitimacy. Strategy B, on the other hand, is morally empty and hence equally incapable of providing legitimacy to punishment, unless its managerial techniques are wedded to – and placed in the service of – a valid moral ideology based on human rights. So, although the difficulties involved are immense, we are firmly of the opinion that only an approach based on Strategy C has any chance of providing a real, long-term solution to the crisis. For only a systematic strategy of affording a consistent respect for human rights can effectively create the legitimacy whose lack is the key to the crisis. And on a more practical note, only a principled drive to avoid unnecessary human suffering by restricting incarceration to cases where it is genuinely necessary is likely to limit the numbers in prison to suitably manageable and affordable levels. We proceed to discuss what such a strategy would entail, and what chance it might have of being deployed in the foreseeable future.

Measures to Solve the Crisis

The penal crisis is a pressing political and moral problem, which requires drastic action. It cannot await a detailed blueprint for radical reform. On the other hand, it is also a deep-seated, long-running problem which requires the wholesale reform of the system along principled lines. If the crisis is to be solved, we need an evolutionary approach, combining short-term measures and medium- and long-term reform in the context of a coherent overall strategy.

Any such strategy needs to commence from the recognition of the unpopular truth that *the penal system can do very little to control crime*. As we saw in Chapter 2 (section 2.2), alleged reductive mechanisms such as deterrence, incapacitation, denunciation and reform can at best only have very limited effects in reducing the amount of crime. No doubt the ways in which we treat offenders could be made more effective than they currently are, and we certainly favour attempts to pursue rehabilitation and investigate what works to reform offenders. But even if such efforts were highly successful, they could still have little effect on overall crime rates given the fact that only about two offences in every hundred committed result in a conviction, with another one in a hundred attracting a police caution. Consequently it is foolish, as well as inhumane, to look to punitive policies to solve the problems of crime. Crime levels have much more to do with social factors (such as the fragmentation of communities and the lack of legitimate opportunities for young people) and economic trends (see, for example, Field, 1990) than with punishment. Consequently, they would be better tackled by concentrating on the social causes of crime and on crime prevention strategies than by looking to punishment for a solution.

The only really plausible theory put forward in recent years linking national crime rates with punishment methods – John Braithwaite's theory of *reintegrative shaming* (see Chapter 2, section 2.4) – provides a prescription not for greater punitiveness but for much *less* harsh levels of punishment than we currently indulge in, together with a shift towards a different approach. Such an approach fits well with our preference for a much greater employment of reparation and other restorative justice measures among our responses to crime (Dignan, 1994). (We shall expand on our own vision for a much more restorative approach to crime later in this chapter.) If we are right about this, then it follows that the interests of victims and potential victims of crime do not demand harsh punishment for offenders. (Hence it is wrong to talk glibly, as governments often have recently, of 'rebalancing criminal justice in favour of victims' by making it harsher for offenders and suspects.) On the contrary, a less punitive strategy could not only be more beneficial to the public generally (and considerably less expensive), but could also be more victim friendly, while running little risk of creating more victims. Indeed, the strategy we advocate could well be said to fit the old New Labour motto of being 'tough on crime and tough on the causes of crime'. It is tough in the sense of being hard-headed about implementing an effective (and cost-effective) system of responding to *crime*. Being excessively tough *on criminals* may be hard-*hearted* (which holds attraction for some people), but in terms of effectiveness and cost it is actually soft-*headed* (see further Cavadino et al., 1999: 53–5).

The most urgent priority in tackling the penal crisis is the pressing need to tackle the crisis of resources by reducing prison numbers as quickly as possible. In the short term, there is much to be said for implementing emergency measures to relieve the pressure on the prison system. This could be achieved relatively easily simply by using the Justice Secretary's existing powers (under section 32 of the Criminal Justice Act 1982) to order that whole categories of prisoners should be released a few months early. (Such amnesties are common in other countries such as France.) In the slightly longer term, it would be perfectly possible to instruct prison governors to use their powers of temporary release and home leave as soon as a prison became full to ensure that no prison exceeded its Certified Normal Accommodation, or even to place non-violent offenders on a waiting list to enter prison, as used to occur in the Netherlands. Above all, perhaps, government could assist the numbers crisis by ceasing to encourage harsher court decisions with law and order rhetoric.

However, numbers and material resources are only part of the problem. If we are right in identifying the crisis of legitimacy as the key to the crisis, and in our further claim that the widespread sense of injustice surrounding the penal system is mainly due to the fact that it really is deeply unjust, then the inference is clear.

It is as true as ever that more than anything, as the Woolf Report suggested in 1991, the penal system needs a massive injection of genuine justice. We would go further and submit that in the long term – but as soon as is humanly possible – *the penal system needs to be reconstructed around the principle of respect for human rights*. We are fortified in this (Strategy C) conclusion by the evidence we cited in Chapter 6 (section 6.5) demonstrating that, while it may not be easy to create genuine improvements in justice, there are nevertheless hopeful signs that when these are achieved they do indeed foster legitimacy.

Adopting a human rights approach in the present penal situation means recognizing that it is morally and practically imperative both to *provide* those resources which will improve conditions for penal subjects from their present state and increasingly to *deny* those resources (notably places within prisons) which worsen them. This kind of approach also requires a consistent and principled approach to the question of *prisoners' rights*. If human beings have fundamental rights (such as the equal right to maximum positive freedom we proposed in Chapter 2, section 2.7), then it follows that prisoners have a great many more specific rights – that is, strong moral entitlements which should be guaranteed by law and which they do not automatically lose by virtue of having transgressed the law. These include rights to certain decent minimum standards of living conditions, the right to fair and independent channels for pursuing grievances against others who infringe their rights, the right to an equally fair disciplinary procedure before their liberties are further infringed, and so on. A minimum code of standards for prison conditions should become legally enforceable as soon as possible and prisoners should be able to feel that they can get a genuinely fair hearing in disciplinary and grievance procedures.

Vital as they undoubtedly are, however, neither better physical conditions nor improved grievance and discipline procedures are sufficient in themselves. One of the most important rights that prisoners should have is the preservation of as much autonomy and personal responsibility as is compatible with their inevitable loss of liberty. (And yes, this should include prisoners having the right to vote.) This is of central importance both in providing constructive and successful prison regimes, and in securing legitimacy for the prison system as a whole by those who are most directly and immediately affected by it. If we are to make a reality of this right to inmate autonomy, there are important implications for prison regimes and, crucially, for the relationship between staff and inmates. As we saw in Chapter 6 (section 6.5), staff–prisoner relationships within the English penal system generally leave much to be desired, although a great deal could still be learned from positive examples such as Grendon Underwood, Blantyre House and the erstwhile Barlinnie Special Unit in Scotland.

Of equal importance to the rights of those who are imprisoned is the justice of imprisonment itself, which leads to the issue of *the justice of sentencing* (and indeed, the justice of other decisions made within the criminal justice system, such as remand and parole decisions). This can be divided into two further questions, the first relating to consistency (or fairness between different offenders), and the second relating to the general severity of punishment and in particular the extent to which it takes the form of incarceration. We saw in Chapter 4 (section 4.1) that there is much inconsistency in sentencing, and in Chapter 9 that some sections of the population can rightly claim that they are the subject of bias at various stages of the criminal and penal process. We also noted in Chapter 2 that it is a principle of justice that like cases should be treated alike, and that there is something to be said for trying to achieve at least a rough proportionality between severity of punishment and gravity of offence (sections 2.3 and 2.7). These considerations lead us to support the guidelines approach to sentencing (see Chapter 4, section 4.3), with guidelines being issued to courts to bring about both a greater measure of consistency and a more suitable degree of proportionality in sentencing.

However, inconsistency is not the worst possible evil of a penal system. There would be little to recommend a system which was perfectly consistent but appallingly vicious, and indeed it could be said from past experience in the United States that over-emphasizing consistency (especially in an ideological climate of 'law and order') can have just this kind of result (Hudson, 1987; but see von Hirsch, 1993: ch. 10). From a human rights point of view, the worst fault of our penal system is not inconsistency but excess of punishment: every single day that an individual is imprisoned unnecessarily represents not only a shamefully extravagant waste of resources but, more importantly, a grave infringement of human rights. For this reason, sentencing guidelines need to be explicitly and strongly geared towards reducing general levels of punishment as well as to pursuing consistency.

A similar approach, involving guidelines aimed not only at consistency but also at the reduction of punishment by the encouragement of cautions and other methods of diversion should also be applied to the decision of whether to prosecute alleged offenders. The role of the Crown Prosecution Service could well prove to be just as crucial as that of the courts if a substantial reduction of the prison population were to be secured and sustained. This has certainly been the experience elsewhere in Europe, for example in the Netherlands and West Germany at different times (Cavadino and Dignan, 2006: chs 7 and 8).

In the short-to-medium term, therefore, we would advocate the following specific measures – many of them explained and canvassed in the preceding chapters – for tackling the penal crisis. We favour:

- Emergency steps to reduce the prison population by means of executive powers;

- Restrictions on the use of custodial remands;

- Abandonment of such misguided initiatives as mandatory and minimum sentences, including mandatory life imprisonment sentences;

- A return to a just deserts sentencing framework such as that contained in the Criminal Justice Act 1991, with only a small degree of increased harshness in sentencing for more persistent offenders;

- Giving the Sentencing Council an explicit remit to produce comprehensive guidelines for all offences aimed at achieving a significant reduction in the use of custody as well as consistency and proportionality in sentencing;

- Revival of the custody plus sentence (see section 10.2 above), using guidelines and monitoring to ensure that it produces a reduction in custody;

- Reintroducing unit fines (or day fines) on a statutory basis;

- Allocation of more resources for the treatment of drug offenders in the community, linked to the introduction of drug courts with a rehabilitative and restorative ethos;

- Ensuring the continued existence of a probation service with its own identity and national presence, without the threat of partial abolition via privatization;

- Guidelines for probation officers to promote the use of positive methods to encourage compliance with community orders and licences and to ensure that offenders are not recalled to prison for mere technical breaches of their licences;

- Transfer of prisoners who are profoundly mentally ill to appropriate hospitals, and increased diversion of less serious offenders with mental illnesses from the criminal justice system to appropriate community treatment;

- Enforceable ceilings on the numbers in individual prisons;

- Implementation of Woolf's scheme for community prisons;

- A legally enforceable code of minimum standards for prison conditions together with a short and rigid timetable for implementation and the allocation of sufficient resources to make this possible;

- Implementation within prisons of the humanistic approach which proved so successful at the Barlinnie Special Unit and at Blantyre House;

- An expansion of home leave and visiting rights for prisoners;

- Extension of the remit and resources of the Prisons Ombudsman to enable prisoners to take their grievances directly to it;

- An end to further privatization in the prison system with the ultimate aim of abandoning the policy altogether;

- Reform of discretionary early release to make the procedures fairer;

- Encouragement and application of systems management techniques to the criminal justice system, including:
  - New guidelines to encourage higher rates of cautioning; and
  - The expansion of schemes aimed at diverting offenders from prosecution and from custody.

Another proposed measure which has been much touted recently – including finding favour with the Liberal Democrats and, temporarily, with Kenneth Clarke – is the introduction of statutory restrictions on the passing of short custodial sentences by the courts. This might, for example, take a form similar to that of section 17 of the Criminal Justice and Licensing (Scotland) Act 2010 which introduces a presumption against passing prison sentences of three months or less. It is argued (see, for example, National Association of Probation Officers, 2010) that short prison sentences provide no opportunity for rehabilitative work, that there is no compulsory post-release supervision, and that (perhaps partly as a result) the reconviction rates following release are particularly high for such offenders (around 75 per cent within two years). The administration costs of allocating, admitting and discharging such prisoners are also seen as excessive for a stay in prison averaging less than two months. And since offenders who receive such sentences are hardly likely to be regarded as posing a serious danger to the public, there is no reason why they should not be dealt with by means of non-custodial penalties such as community orders. Were such a rule to be introduced and made effective, it could affect a great many people, as sentences of less than six months represent the majority of custodial sentences passed. However, because by definition short-term prisoners only stay in prison for a short time, they only occupy a relatively small proportion of the total prison population at any one time (about 8 per cent). Hence, to engineer a more significant drop in the prison population it would also be necessary to reduce the lengths of longer sentences.

Other questions can also be raised about the proposal for a legal restriction on short sentences. It would inevitably contain some form of get-out clause such as that contained in the 2010 Scottish legislation (which forbids a short prison sentence 'unless the court considers that no other method of dealing with the person is appropriate'). In how many cases would courts in practice invoke such get-out clauses, and might the provision prove largely ineffective as a result? Another possibility is that courts might *increase* sentences from what they would have passed up to the legal minimum of six months (or whatever), leading to at least some offenders going to prison for longer. On balance we would favour such legislation while also recognizing its limitations. Its chances of having a favourable impact would be improved if combined with legislation to make a range of more minor offences entirely non-imprisonable, and with something like the now-defunct custody plus scheme which would ensure that short-term prisoners served the great majority of their time in the community.

These are all measures that could be introduced in the short- to medium-term. Our longer-term vision of a human rights-based penal system would require a radical reframing of the objectives of punishment. As we explained in Chapter 2 (section 2.7), a human rights approach does not deny that punishment to a large extent exists in order to deter crime, that some offenders need to be confined for the protection of the public, or that principles of just deserts have an important role in deciding how much punishment it is legitimate to inflict on offenders. We also envisage an enduring role for measures aimed at the reform and rehabilitation of offenders. However, we particularly favour the *restorative justice* approach, whereby offenders perform *reparation* for victims and the community and attempts are made to bring about the *reintegrative shaming* of the offender. This is an *inclusive* approach (see Chapter 2, section 2.6) which aims to keep offenders within the mainstream community (or bring them back in) rather than *excluding* them by punitive measures such as custody or other types of stigmatizing punishment. We explained in Chapter 2 why we think the restorative approach is particularly appropriate within a system based upon human rights (and see also Cavadino and Dignan, 1997; Dignan, 2003). Indeed, as we have outlined elsewhere (Dignan, 1994; Dignan and Cavadino, 1996; Cavadino and Dignan, 1997) they could point the way forward – in the long term – to a radically different and radically more just penal system in which reparative and restorative measures constituted the normal response to offending, with punitive measures being very much the exception.

It is possible to envisage a perfectly workable future criminal justice system which made minimal use of imprisonment. (Such a vision has affinities with the position of abolitionists such as Joe Sim (1992; 1994), who does not in fact call for the total abolition of confinement but merely of the institution of prison as we know it.) Most offences could be dealt with by a local community justice service (or youth offending team for juvenile offenders; YOTs already do some work similar to this). A suitable restorative package could be agreed between the offender and any victim who is willing to participate, and arranged by the local community justice service, with the Crown Prosecution Service certifying that the overall package was an appropriate resolution of the case bearing in mind the public interest and maintaining at least a rough proportionality between the seriousness of the offence and the severity of the sanction. However, a more serious case could still go to court if no suitable agreement was reached, if mediation was inappropriate, if either party refused mediation or if the alleged offender denied guilt.

The most serious crimes would normally still go to court in any event. But even in cases which reached court, the usual outcome would be that the offender would be ordered to make reparation either to the victim or to the community generally, perhaps combined with some measures aimed at the reformation of the offender. Many existing forms of non-custodial punishment (for example, the fine, unpaid work and even probation supervision) could readily be reformulated to serve restorative justice rather than purely retributive or reformative ends (see Cavadino et al., 1999; Dignan, 2003). Thus, even in cases for which informal diversionary restorative justice processes are inappropriate, inapplicable or inadequate by themselves, it is possible to envisage a range of court-imposed punishments that could be adapted to promote restorative justice outcomes. There is potential, in other words, for restorative justice to change the terms of reference within which we discuss and think about punishment (to provide a 'replacement discourse': Ashworth, 1997: 14–15) so that in future we concentrate on seeking the reintegration and inclusion of offenders rather than automatically thinking in terms of their punitive exclusion by way of imprisonment. Custody would only be used where this was necessary to incapacitate genuinely dangerous offenders from committing serious offences (or perhaps, very exceptionally, as a genuine last resort sanction for failure to comply with court orders when all other sanctions had failed). Even then, the custodial regime should be geared towards respecting the prisoner's rights, encouraging reparative work, facilitating the voluntary rehabilitation of the offender, and securing the earliest possible release from custody. In this way, society and its criminal justice system could finally end their 'love affair with custody' (Travis, 2003).

The Prospects

This kind of model for a penal system seems a long way from where we are now, and it will probably strike many readers as incredible that it could ever be implemented successfully, or that public opinion would ever allow it to be. For it is usually assumed that public opinion is irredeemably wedded to the punitive attitude of 'law and order' and will not tolerate much of a shift in the direction of leniency. However – while accepting that public opinion would hardly take kindly to the immediate introduction of a model such as the one we have sketched – it is also the case that governments can often succeed with measures which go against the current state of public opinion. A classic example is the abolition of capital punishment in 1965: even today opinion polls in this country regularly demonstrate that most of the public would like to see capital punishment restored, yet this is perhaps the least of the penal system's legitimacy problems. Progressive measures can be acceptable in the sense that the public will accept them even if they are not what the public will tell opinion pollsters they want. We are not naive enough to believe that the utopia of a just and minimalist penal system can be rapidly achieved, but there is no reason why moves in that direction could not be pursued and given every encouragement by an enlightened government. In the longer term, however, it will be necessary to involve the public and assemble public support for a different kind of punishment if it is ever to become a reality.

Fortunately, there is a great deal of evidence that the public, although apparently at present more punitive in Britain than in most other countries (see, for example, Mayhew and van Kesteren, 2002: 87–9), is by no means as closed-minded as is often supposed. It seems, for example, that although most people when asked say they think sentences should be tougher than they are, this is because they underestimate the harshness of the sentences that courts typically pass at present (Hough and Roberts, 1998; Mattinson and Mirrlees-Black, 2000; Roberts and Hough, 2005: ch. 4). Compensation, community service and restorative justice find great favour with the public (see, for example, Hough and Mayhew, 1985: ch. 6; van Dijk and Mayhew, 1992: 46; Roberts and Hough, 2005: ch. 7), including many victims of crime (see, for example, Mattinson and Mirrlees-Black, 2000: ch. 6). Only 18 per cent of people agree that it is right to 'build more prisons and pay for them by raising taxes or cutting spending in other areas' (Hough and Roberts, 1998: 35). These findings suggest that what the public really wants to see is an *adequate* response to crime, but they do not necessarily demand a punitive one, let alone an inhumane one. Nor do they wish vast quantities of public money to be spent on keeping offenders locked up. Another encouraging finding is that the more informed members of the public become about criminal justice, the less punitive they typically become (Roberts and Hough, 2005: 153–60), suggesting that those who seek progressive penal reform should favour involving the public in informed debate rather than trying to exclude them (see also Cavadino and Dignan, 2006: 341–2).

Apart from public opinion, another obstacle to progressive reforms could well be the opposition of certain occupational groups within the criminal justice system with vested interests in retaining the *status quo*, perhaps most notably prison officers and the judiciary. Most criminal justice agencies contain only a small minority of individuals who already espouse a human rights approach: Rutherford (1993: 7) found that such people constituted 'a rather small and distinct minority' among the upper echelons of the criminal justice system. Joanna Shapland (1988) has perceptively suggested that one of the reasons for this kind of resistance stems from the tendency towards stasis that results from the existence of a largely decentralized collection of relatively autonomous agencies, which she likens to feudal 'fiefdoms', each jealously guarding its own independence and methods of working. In such circumstances she suggests that change is difficult, since the fiefs are hard either to persuade or coerce successfully. However, a strategy for change is possible if it combines a measure of both coercion (*via* legislation imposing some legally enforceable duties on the fiefs) and persuasion following a 'Round Table' consultation and negotiation with the fiefdoms.

Nor is it necessarily the case that the interests of the fiefdoms invariably lead them to favour illiberal policies. For example, judicial criticisms of government penal policy have in the past gone in both directions. The judiciary tend to favour arrangements which maximize their own power and oppose those which *confine* (limit) their discretion or negate their decisions: hence, for example, their hostility towards mandatory and minimum sentences as well as restrictions on their powers to send offenders to custody. On the other hand, they are less concerned about the *structuring* (guidance) of their discretion by means of guidelines, and some senior members of the judiciary – most notably Lord Woolf, who was Lord Chief Justice from 2000 to 2005 and who reportedly clashed with Home Secretaries on several occasions – have strongly favoured a reduction in prison numbers. In the circumstances, the chances would be good for a Round Table agreement between government, judiciary and the Sentencing Council for a guideline system aimed at reducing the use of custody from its present level. Whether this would lead to more junior, frontline sentencers genuinely using prison as a last resort and keeping sentence lengths to a minimum is less certain. But currently it looks to be the government, not the judges, that poses the greater barrier to such a development.

Similarly, it should be borne in mind that prison officers actively support some progressive reforms, such as the introduction of minimum standards for physical conditions within prisons, for the very good reason that they perceive such measures to be in their own best interests as well as the prisoners'. They tend, however, to oppose measures which would improve standards of justice for prisoners in potential disputes with prison officers, such as giving prisoners the right to legal representation in disciplinary hearings (see Wozniak and McAllister, 1991). But – given that governments have in recent years had little compunction about confronting prison officers over pay, conditions, trade union rights and privatization – it is hard to see why they could not be brought onside by a committed government using a shrewd combination of reason and power. Persuasive techniques could include, for example, the provision of appropriate financial and career incentives for co-operation with the government's strategy.

There is also the possibility – to return to the feudal metaphor – of change being forced by a revolt among the peasants. So far peasants' revolts – in the shape of prison riots – have been contained, albeit sometimes with difficulty. But they would potentially strengthen the hand of a government which had the will to use its power to bring about change from above. Is any of this likely to happen?

The immediate political situation is clearly not encouraging for the kind of penal programme we should wish to see. We would like to see a concerted drive to reduce the prison population; the government is unwilling to pursue this, and this failure combined with politicians' obsession with appearing tough on crime seems likely to bring about further increases. We want a major reorientation of penality towards restorative justice; there have merely been some tentative steps in this direction, mainly for young offenders (see Chapters 5 and 8, sections 5.3 and 8.2). Above all we wish to see a demotion of toughness towards criminals as the benchmark of policy and the hallmark of political rhetoric, while politicians still seem wedded to both.

Nevertheless, it could be argued that the prospects for penal improvement are not all hopeless. It has usually proved to be the case in Britain that law and order ideology only prevails in penal policy for a limited time before its effects in exacerbating the crisis bring government into a rude collision with very concrete material realities. In a highly competitive political situation, long-term penal and financial consequences can be ignored by political parties for the sake of a hoped-for electoral advantage. And individual politicians with instincts which lead them to favour tough rhetoric and policies can also play their part. But will such a situation endure forever? We have seen occasions (such as at Leeds Castle in 1987) when fiscal and other pragmatic considerations have overridden powerful ideological pressures to pursue punitive policies. Perhaps the best hope for the penal system is that this will happen again.

There have been occasional suggestions that hyperincarceration, even on the American scale, could actually be functional to the economy, at least in the short term, by providing jobs and at the same time disguising the true rate of unemployment (Downes, 1997; Western and Beckett, 1999; Downes, 2001; and see Cavadino and Dignan, 2006: 58). But such a strategy could be unsustainable over a longer time frame. The longer we go on consigning more and more offenders to prison for longer and longer periods, the more the expense soars. The rapidly escalating cost is just taxpayers' money down the drain. For every pound that is spent on keeping inmates wastefully and counterproductively under lock and key is a pound that is not available for other pressing needs such as investing in education, health care or tackling poverty or climate change – or even to be left in citizens' pockets to spend on themselves. Such a waste of the nation's economic resources should hardly be a recipe for political success. Nor should presiding over a system whose crisis of resources leaves it constantly just a step away from critical overload.

It has to be admitted that recent years have not added weight to this less pessimistic view about the prospects for progress. Even in the depths of the worst recession for many decades, and as the Coalition government engages in its frenzied cutting of most areas of state expenditure, there has been insufficient motivation to carry through measures designed to cut costs by cutting the use of custody. And although there have been periodic attempts by governments or individual ministers (such as Kenneth Clarke) to scale back on imprisonment, these have all proved to be false dawns. We are left at present with just a few rays of hope. Despite the general picture and the overall upward trajectory of the prison population, the last few years have seen progress in a few areas. Determined efforts have resulted in some reductions in the custodial numbers of women (see Chapter 9, section 9.4) and of young people (Chapter 8, section 8.5). And the government has at least shown some interest in rehabilitation and restorative justice as well as more punitive options.

There is a Chinese word for crisis which literally translates into English as 'danger-opportunity'. The penal crisis is still with us and could escalate at any time. This is a situation of great danger, but if the danger is recognized it could provide the opportunity and incentive for making bold and far-sighted moves in a progressive direction. In the long run, we still have to make a choice between a morally and financially bankrupt, permanently crisis-ridden and inexorably deteriorating penal system and one worthy of a modern and civilized society. We said at the end of Chapter 1 that we need to change people's minds about punishment. There is a long way to go, and the way looks much longer than it did 20 years ago, but the task is not impossible. We saw in Chapter 2 (section 2.5) that ideas about punishment have changed radically in the past when the times and conditions were right. Perhaps – just perhaps – the time for another such change is not quite as far off as it now seems.

Glossary of Key Terms

Terms explained in this glossary are in **bold type** when they first appear in the main text of the book.

Words and phrases in *italics* have their own entry in this glossary.

Abolitionism A penal reform movement that seeks to abolish all or part of the *penal system*, particularly its most coercive practices such as the use of capital punishment and *imprisonment*.

Action Plan Order A *community sentence* for young offenders (aged 10–17) consisting of a short (three months) intensive intervention programme that sought to address their offending behaviour. Abolished by the Criminal Justice and Immigration Act 2008.

Agency Status A term used to describe the relationship between the Prison Service and senior policy-makers, whereby responsibility for operational matters is vested in the former while responsibility for strategic policy-making is vested in the latter.

Age of Criminal Responsibility The age at which it becomes possible to *prosecute* an offender (ten in *England* and Wales).

Anti-social Behaviour Order (ASBO) A court order that prohibits behaviour deemed to be anti-social. Breach of an ASBO is a criminal offence punishable by a fine or (in the case of adult offenders) up to five years in prison.

ASBO See *anti-social behaviour order*.

Attorney General The government law officer responsible for the *Crown Prosecution Service*.

Bail Conditional freedom granted to a suspect, normally during police investigations or pending trial.

Bifurcation A dual-edged (or twin-track) approach to punishment which distinguishes between 'ordinary' offenders with whom less severe measures can be taken and serious or dangerous offenders who are subjected to much tougher measures.

Bifurcation, Punitive A term we use to describe the policy underlying the Criminal Justice Act 1991, which combined *bifurcation* with a concern to make *non-custodial penalties* more *punitive*. See also *punishment in the community*.

Bind-overs Akin to a suspended *fine*. A sum of money is forfeited unless the person bound over complies with an undertaking to be of good behaviour and keep the peace.

Boot Camps *Custodial* institutions for young offenders with a military-style training regime. See also *'short sharp shock'*.

Breach Failure to comply with the terms of a court order. The term is also used to refer to the proceedings whereby an offender who has not complied with an order is returned to court to be sanctioned for the breach.

Bust Limit An informal term for the total 'useable operational capacity' of the prison system, or the total number of prisoners that the system can safely hold.

Caution A formal disposal of a criminal case, consisting of a warning administered to an offender by a police officer. The measure is an alternative to *prosecution* and therefore does not involve either *prosecution* or the courts. In 1998 cautions for offenders under the age of 18 were replaced by *reprimands* and (final) *warnings,* but these were subsequently replaced in their turn by *youth cautions* and *youth conditional cautions*. See also *conditional caution.*

Certified Normal Accommodation (CNA) The officially prescribed capacity of a prison indicating the number of inmates for whom it has adequate space.

Charge The first step in the *prosecution* process. Normally the police charge a suspect on the advice of the *Crown Prosecution Service*.

Chief Inspector of Prisons A government-appointed official who heads an independent inspectorate responsible for monitoring and reporting on conditions in prisons.

Chivalry Theory The theory that female offenders are treated more leniently than males due to the 'chivalry' of criminal justice practitioners.

Classicism The school of penal thought that holds that offenders should be held responsible for their actions and punished in proportion to their wrongdoing. See also *just deserts/justice model; proportionality, principle of.*

CNA See *Certified Normal Accommodation*.

Cognitive Behavioural Treatment A form of treatment focusing on the way offenders think about themselves, their offending behaviour and its consequences.

Combination Order A *community sentence* combining *community service* with *probation* supervision. Known between 2001 and 2005 as the 'community punishment and rehabilitation order'. Superseded by the *community order.*

Community Order A court order, introduced by the Criminal Justice Act 2003, which may contain one or more of a number of different requirements, including *unpaid work, probation supervision* or a *curfew* enforced by *electronic monitoring*.

Community Prison A multi-purpose prison housing different kinds of prisoners close to their homes.

Community Payback The name given by the government to *community service* when rebranding the scheme in 2006.

Community Punishment Order The official name for a *community service* order between 2001 and 2005.

Community Rehabilitation Order The official name for a *probation order* between 2001 and 2005.

Community Sentence A category of sentences which include the *community order* and also various measures for *young offenders.*

Community Service Work for the benefit of the community carried out by offenders as a requirement of their *punishment*. This may be under an *unpaid work* requirement in a *community order*, or under some other court order. See also *community payback, community punishment order.*

Comparative Penology The study of penal systems and penal policies in different countries, their similarities and differences and the factors that may account for them.

Compensation Financial redress provided for *victims* of crime. A court sentencing an offender can pass a compensation order requiring the offender to pay compensation to the *victim*.

Conditional Caution A *caution* combined with additional conditions.

Containment, Crisis of See *crisis of containment*.

Contestability The principle that private organizations (see *privatization*) should compete to run public services, including the provision of penal facilities.

Control, Crisis of See *crisis of control*.

Corporatism (or **Conservative Corporatism**) A term used to describe countries such as Germany, where important national interest groups are integrated with the national state and are expected to act in accordance with the national interest.

CPS See *Crown Prosecution Service*.

Criminal Justice System A collective term encompassing the various agencies responsible for enforcing the criminal law and administering criminal justice, including the police, the *prosecuting* authorities, the criminal courts and the prison and *probation* services.

Crisis of Containment An aspect of the wider *penal crisis* that relates to concerns over prison escapes and *security* matters in general.

Crisis of Control An aspect of the wider *penal crisis* that relates to the problem of maintaining order within prisons.

Crisis of Legitimacy An aspect of the *penal crisis* consisting of the *penal system*'s lack of *legitimacy* with, among others, (a) the general public; (b) 'penal subjects' such as prisoners; and (c) practitioners working within the *penal system*.

Crisis of Resources An aspect of the wider *penal crisis* that relates to the scarcity of material resources – including staff, money, buildings and equipment – needed for punishing offenders, whether in prison or in the community.

Crisis of Visibility An aspect of the *penal crisis* that relates to the existence, and dispelling, of secrecy surrounding what happens within prisons.

Crown Court The court that tries the more important criminal cases in *England* and Wales, hearing both *indictable* and *triable either way* cases.

Crown Prosecution Service (CPS) The state agency with responsibility for conducting the great majority of *prosecutions* in *England* and Wales.

Culture The collective beliefs, norms, feelings and practices of a society.

Curfew A form of punishment in which restrictions are imposed on the hours during which an offender is free to leave home, usually enforced by *electronic monitoring*. *Community orders* may include curfew requirements.

Custody Confinement in a prison or similar institution.

Custody Plus A penalty which was intended to replace sentences of imprisonment of up to 12 months, consisting of a short period in *custody* followed by a longer period during which an offender is punished in the community. The Criminal Justice Act 2003 made provision for this sentence, but it was never implemented and the provisions were repealed by the Legal Aid, Sentencing and Punishment of Offenders Act 2012.

Day Fine A system of relating fines to the means of the offender, similar to the *unit fine* system. The day fine system exists in some other countries, and its introduction in *England and Wales* was recommended by the Carter Report in 2003.

DCMF Contracts A form of prison privatization in which a private sector operator is contracted to design, construct, manage and finance a prison in return for daily payments per prisoner from the government once the prison begins to admit prisoners. The normal duration of such contracts is 25 years.

Decarceration A policy of attempting to reduce or abolish the use of *custodial* and other institutional methods of dealing with offenders and other *deviants*. Can also mean the widespread closure of *custodial* and other institutions housing *deviants*.

Denunciation The theory that *punishment* is justified because it expresses the community's condemnation of the crime.

Detention Centre *Custodial* institution for *juvenile* and *young adult* offenders, abolished in 1988.

Detention and Training Order (DTO) A *custodial penalty* for young offenders (aged 12 to 18), part of which is served in custody and part under supervision in the community.

Determinate Sentence A *sentence* with a fixed end point, such as a specific number of years' imprisonment. Also known as *fixed-term sentence*.

Determinism See *positivism*.

Deterrence The prevention of crime by inducing potential offenders to fear that they will be punished.

Deviants A term encompassing offenders and others who deviate from the norms of society.

Discharge The most lenient penalty available to the court. An absolute discharge requires nothing from an offender and imposes no obligations on future conduct. A conditional discharge requires an offender not to commit a further offence during a specified period on pain of being further punished for the original offence.

Discipline A term used by Foucault (1977) to refer to a technique of social control that involves the use of constant surveillance and the imposition of a highly regulated physical routine often involving repetitive forced labour.

Dispersal Prison See *high security prison*.

Diversion Dealing with offenders by means other than either *prosecution* or *custody*.

Doli Incapax A legal doctrine whereby it was presumed that children aged 10 to 13 were incapable of committing a crime unless they could be shown to appreciate the difference between right and wrong. Abolished by the Crime and Disorder Act 1998.

DTO See *detention and training order*.

Due Process A system of legal safeguards designed to prevent the conviction of the innocent or other wrongful *punishment*. Due process safeguards include the right to a fair trial and the presumption of innocence.

Early Release The release of a prisoner before the end of the *sentence*, whether automatically or by a discretionary process. See also *parole* and *remission*.

Economic Determinism The idea (associated with some forms of Marxism) that economics determines everything, that the superstructure of law, politics and ideology merely reflects the state of the economic base.

Either Way Offence An offence which can be tried in either the *Crown Court* or the *magistrates' court*.

Electronic Monitoring (Or *tagging*) The use of electronic surveillance techniques (such as a tag fastened around the wrist or ankle) to monitor an offender's compliance with the terms of a court order or *licence*.

End of Custody Licence A scheme whereby certain prisoners were released up to 18 days early, which operated between June 2007 and April 2010.

England In this book we normally use the words England and English to refer to the legal and penal systems of England and Wales.

Evil Woman Theory The theory that female offenders are treated more harshly than males due to being seen as doubly *deviant* because they flout the social norms of femininity as well as breaking the law.

Exclusionary Approach An approach to dealing with offenders or other *deviants* by excluding them from the life of mainstream society, for example by imprisonment. See also *inclusive approach*.

Exclusion Requirement A restriction that may be imposed as part of a *community order*, which prohibits the offender from entering a specified place.

Extended Sentence Specially extended sentence of imprisonment for offenders convicted of certain specified offences who are thought to pose significant risks. Such prisoners cannot be granted early release until they have served two thirds of their sentences, and are subject to extended licence periods following release.

Fiefdoms Fiefdoms were semi-autonomous realms within feudal society. Shapland (1988) likened both non-state groups and state agencies within the *criminal justice system* (such as the police and the courts) to fiefdoms.

Final Warning See *caution*.

Fine A *punishment* which consists of the offender being required to pay a sum of money to the state.

Fixed Penalty Notice (or spot fine) A financial *penalty* which can be imposed by police officers and other specified officials for a variety of minor offences.

Fixed-term Sentence A *sentence* with a fixed end point, such as a specific number of years' imprisonment. Also known as *determinate sentence*.

Freedom See *positive freedom*.

Gatekeeping A term which refers to the power of agencies such as the police or *Crown Prosecution Service* to determine who is admitted to the formal *criminal justice system* by being *prosecuted* and who is *diverted* from it.

'Great Transformation' A major shift in the nature of punishment from corporal to carceral, which took place during the late eighteenth and early nineteenth centuries.

Green Paper A term sometimes used for a government discussion or consultation document. See also *White Paper*.

Guidelines See *sentencing guidelines*.

HDC See *home detention curfew*.

High Security Prison Maximum-security prisons capable of housing high-risk inmates whose escape would be dangerous. Formerly known as dispersal prisons.

Home Detention Curfew (HDC) A type of *early release* which includes a *curfew* enforced by *electronic monitoring*.

Home Office The government department responsible until May 2007 for prisons, *probation* and the formulation of *criminal justice policy*. Still responsible for the police, crime, anti-social behaviour, drugs policy, anti-terrorism and immigration.

Home Secretary The Secretary of State (i.e. the senior minister) in charge of the *Home Office*.

Honesty in Sentencing See *truth in sentencing*.

House of Lords (1) The Upper House of Parliament, forming (with the House of Commons) the supreme legislature of the United Kingdom. (2) The highest court in the United Kingdom; replaced by the Supreme Court in 2009.

Human Rights See *Human Rights Act 1998; rights theory*.

Human Rights Act 1998 The Act by which the European Convention on Human Rights was incorporated into English law.

Hurd Era The period between 1987 and 1992 when a reform agenda influenced by *just deserts* culminated in the 1991 Criminal Justice Act. Douglas Hurd was Home Secretary for part of this period (1985–89).

Ideology We use this word to refer to the entire realm of ideas, including philosophies, which may affect people's attitudes and practices. (This is wider than the classic Marxist concept, which sees ideologies as ideas that function in the interests of particular social classes.)

Imprisonment for Public Protection An *indeterminate* sentence introduced by the Criminal Justice Act 2003 and imposed on offenders who had committed a serious violent or sexual offence and were considered dangerous, but who did not qualify for a *life imprisonment sentence*. Abolished by the Legal Aid, Sentencing and Punishment of Offenders Act 2012.

Imprisonment Rate A measure of *punitiveness* based on the number of prisoners in a country expressed as a proportion of its total population (usually per 100,000).

Incapacitation The prevention of crime by making it impossible for a person to offend, for example by means of execution, imprisonment or disqualification.

Inclusive Approach An approach to dealing with offenders or other *deviants* by seeking to keep them included in the life of mainstream society, or by reintegrating them into society. See also *exclusionary approach, Strategy C*.

Indeterminate Sentence A *sentence* with no fixed end point, such as *life imprisonment*.

Indictable Offence An Offence that can be tried in the *Crown Court*. Statistics presented in this book typically refer to indictable offences meaning both indictable only offences (triable only in the *Crown Court*) and offences *triable either way* (i.e. in either the *Crown* or *magistrates' courts*).

Intensive Supervision and Surveillance Programmes (ISSPs) Community programmes for serious and persistent *young offenders* which may be attached to *community orders, supervision orders, licences* or *bail* supervision. They involve intensive monitoring of the young offender's movements (including *electronic monitoring*) and training and education programmes lasting up to five hours per day.

Inter-agency Approach See *multi-agency approach*

Intermittent Custody A *sentence* of imprisonment which may be served at intervals, for example at weekends. Introduced on an experimental basis by the Criminal Justice Act 2003, but subsequently abandoned and abolished by the Legal Aid, Sentencing and Punishment of Offenders Act 2012.

ISSP See *Intensive Supervision and Surveillance Programmes*.

Judicial Independence, Doctrine of A constitutional doctrine which holds that the executive (i.e. government) should not interfere with the decisions of courts.

Judicialization A process whereby decision-making procedures (such as those for *early release*) become progressively more like court procedures, in particular incorporating *due process* safeguards.

Just Deserts A doctrine and movement which advocates that the amount of *punishment* imposed on an offender should be proportionate to the seriousness of the offence that has been committed. Allied to the *retributivist* theory of punishment. See also *proportionality, principle of.*

Justice Model See *just deserts*.

Justice Secretary The *Secretary of State for Justice,* the senior government minister who has responsibility for the *Ministry of Justice* and is also the *Lord Chancellor.*

Juvenile Justice See *youth justice.*

Key Performance Indicators (KPI) A *managerialist* technique involving the setting of targets for an organization and regular monitoring of its performance.

KPI See *key performance indicators*.

Labelling Theory The idea that catching and punishing offenders labels and stigmatizes them as criminals, which makes it harder for them to lead a law-abiding life in future. See also *minimum intervention.*

Law and Order Counter-Reformation A term we use to refer to the abandonment of the sentencing reform strategy pursued during the *Hurd era* and the adoption of harsh *Strategy A* inspired policies during the period 1993–97.

Law and Order Ideology A set of attitudes including the belief that people must be strictly disciplined by restrictive rules, and that they should be harshly punished if they break the rules. See also *Strategy A, populist punitiveness.*

Legitimacy The perception that power (as exercised by, for example, government or the *penal system*) is morally acceptable.

Licence Conditional freedom at the end of a *custodial sentence* as part of *early release.* Licences may contain requirements regarding, for example, residence or supervision.

Life Imprisonment An *indeterminate* prison *sentence* that is potentially lifelong, from which an offender will only be released when the *Parole Board* is satisfied that there is no longer an unacceptable risk of serious reoffending.

Local Prison A prison used mainly for housing lower security inmates on *remand* and serving short prison *sentences*.

Lord Chancellor The senior government minister who has responsibility for the administration of justice and is also the *Secretary of State for Justice* (or *Justice Secretary*). See *Ministry of Justice.*

Lord Chief Justice The head of the judiciary in *England* and Wales, and also of the Court of Appeal (Criminal Division).

Magistrates' Court The court in which around 95 per cent of criminal cases are tried in *England* and Wales, presided over by lay magistrates and district judges, and hearing both *summary* and *triable either way* cases.

Managerialism (Managerialist Approach) An approach based on the notion that modern managerial techniques can be successfully applied to the problems of crime and punishment, both to control crime and to deploy penal resources effectively and efficiently. It is the basis of the *Strategy B* approach to criminal justice.

Mediation An informal dispute resolution process involving the parties who are directly involved and an independent mediator who facilitates the process. See also *restorative justice.*

Minimum Intervention The belief that formal responses to crime involving prosecution and punishment can increase the likelihood of reoffending and that the best approach is one based on *diversion* from *prosecution* and *custody*. See also *labelling theory*, and contrast *zero tolerance*.

Ministry of Justice Ministry created in May 2007, replacing the Department for Constitutional Affairs and assuming responsibility for *NOMS*, criminal justice policy and *youth justice* (formerly the responsibility of the *Home Office*). Also responsible for courts, civil law and legal aid. The *Lord Chancellor*, who is also the *Secretary of State for Justice* (or *Justice Secretary)* has responsibility for the Ministry

Mode of Trial Whether a criminal case is tried in the *Crown Court* or *magistrates' court.*

Multi-agency (or Inter-agency) Approach The policy of promoting closer collaboration between *criminal justice* agencies in pursuit of a common set of objectives. See also *youth offending teams.*

National Offender Management Service (NOMS) An organization set up in 2004 combining the prison and *probation* services.

Neo-classicism A school of *penal* thought associated with Jeremy Bentham among others, sharing some characteristics of the *classicist* approach but also concerned to achieve the *reform* of offenders.

Neo-correctionalism An approach associated with the *New Labour* government that combines the *punitiveness* of *Strategy A* with an illiberal approach towards those who behave in an anti-social manner, a willingness to adopt pre-emptive strategies for pre-delinquent young people and a measure of *managerialism*. See also *zero tolerance.*

Neo-liberalism Free-market capitalism, as exemplified by the United States.

Net-widening The process whereby *diversionary* measures result in those who might otherwise have been dealt with informally end up receiving a more formal intervention, thus widening the net of the *criminal justice system.*

New Labour The Labour Party as led by Tony Blair (and later Gordon Brown) from 1994 to 2010.

New Penology A *managerial* approach which is 'concerned with techniques to identify, classify, and manage groupings sorted by dangerousness' (Feeley and Simon, 1992), including risk assessments of offenders.

New Punitiveness An international trend, on the rise since the 1970s, for increased harshness of *punishment* associated with *Strategy A* policies and *law and order ideology*.

NOMS See *National Offender Management Service*.

Non-custodial Penalty Any *punishment* that does not involve *custody*.

Normalization A term associated with Foucault (1977), referring to a process whereby offenders are schooled into conformity (for example, by *discipline*). The term is also used to refer to attempts to approximate prison life more closely to life on the outside.

'Nothing Works' The idea, associated with Martinson (1974), that no method of treating offenders will make any difference to their propensity to reoffend.

Numbers Crisis An aspect of the wider *penal crisis* that relates specifically to the fact that the number of prisoners exceeds the amount of suitable accommodation that is available.

Open Prisons Prisons designed for relatively low-risk inmates who can safely be housed in less secure establishments.

Orthodox Account (of the *penal crisis*) An account which explains the *penal crisis* as the natural outcome of a combination of factors including the *numbers crisis*, prison over-crowding and poor conditions, staff unrest, poor *security* and a *toxic mix* of prisoners.

Panopticon A prison designed by Jeremy Bentham (but never built) in which inmates were to be kept under constant surveillance by warders in a central observation tower.

Parenting Orders Court orders that require parents of misbehaving children to attend counselling and guidance sessions and comply with other conditions.

Parole *Early release* granted at the discretion of the *Parole Board*.

Parole Board An independent body which decides on the granting of *parole*.

Parsimony, Principle of The principle that punishments, and especially imprisonment, should be used as sparingly as possible.

Penal Crisis The parlous state of affairs affecting the *penal system*.

Penality This word includes ideas about *punishment* as well as concrete penal practices (cf. Garland and Young, 1983a; Garland, 1990b.)

Penal System The system that exists to *punish* and otherwise deal with those who have been convicted of criminal offences.

Penalty Any *punishment* or *sentence* imposed for an offence.

Penology The study of *punishment*.

PFI See *private finance initiative*.

Pluralism The sociological theory which holds that power in society is distributed between a number of competing interest groups. See also *radical pluralism*.

POA See *Prison Officers' Association*.

Populism (Penal) Defined by Roberts et al. (2003: 5) as 'allowing the electoral advantage of a policy to take precedence over its penal effectiveness'. See also *populist punitiveness*.

Populist Punitiveness A near-synonym for *law and order ideology* coined by Bottoms (1995a). See also *populism, penal*.

Positive Freedom Freedom defined as the ability of people to make effective choices about their lives. (As opposed to negative freedom, defined as the absence of constraint and coercion imposed by other people.)

Positivism The theory that crime, together with all other natural and social phenomena, is caused by factors and processes that can be discovered by scientific investigation. It is a *deterministic* approach, i.e. one which denies that human actions such as crime are the result of an exercise of free will, and hence also denies that offenders are responsible for their crimes. Associated with the *treatment model, welfare model* and *rehabilitative ideal.*

Post-Marxism Theories which continue the Marxist tradition but depart from Marxism in certain fundamental respects, for example by abandoning a belief in an economic base ultimately determining all social phenomena (see *economic determinism*).

Post-modernism A range of theories which depart from modernism by abandoning the search for general (totalizing) theories and (in some cases) rejecting any notion of universal reason.

Post-structuralism A school of social theory which continues the tradition of *structuralism*, but sees the structures of society and thought as constantly changing.

Pragmatism, Penological The tendency of governments to respond to penal developments and attempt to manage the *crisis of resources* 'with no clear or coherent philosophical or other theoretical basis' (Bottoms, 1980: 4).

Pre-sentence Report (PSR) A report compiled by a *probation* officer or *youth offending team* officer that provides sentencers with information about an offender and usually includes a proposal for how the offender might be *sentenced*.

Prison Officers' Association (POA) A trade union representing the interests of prison officers.

Prisons Ombudsman An independent official who is responsible for investigating complaints about the way prisoners have been treated, including disciplinary decisions, but excluding complaints about convictions, *sentence* lengths and release dates. Their remit now also includes the *probation* service and deaths in prison.

Private Finance Initiative (PFI) A self-imposed Treasury rule forbidding any public expenditure on new projects unless the use of private finance has first been considered.

Privatization A policy of promoting greater private sector involvement in the operation of the prison system (including the construction and management of prisons) and also in the delivery of *non-custodial penalties*.

Probation The name given to the penal supervision of offenders. For many years this was undertaken almost exclusively by members of the probation service.

Probation Order A court order requiring the offender to be supervised by a *probation* officer. Known as a *community rehabilitation order* between 2001 and 2005; replaced by supervision requirements in *community orders* since the Criminal Justice Act 2003.

Proportionality, Principle of The principle that the severity of an offender's *punishment* should be proportionate to the seriousness of the offence. See also *just deserts, retributivism*.

Prosecution The process whereby a suspected offender is taken to court and tried for the alleged offence.

PSR See *pre-sentence report*.

Punishment We use this term to refer to any measure that is imposed on an offender in response to an offence, regardless of whether it is *punitive*.

Punishment in the Community The name given to *non-custodial penalties* that impose restrictions on the liberty of an offender. Also refers to a policy (associated with the *Hurd era*) of making *non-custodial penalties* more *punitive* in the hope of encouraging sentencers to use them more often in preference to imprisonment. See also *strategy of encouragement*.

Punitive We use this word to refer to *punishments* which are intended to make the offender suffer, for purposes such as *retribution* or *deterrence*. Also refers to the mindset we call *law and order ideology*.

Punitive Bifurcation See *bifurcation, punitive*.

Radical Pluralism A theory which represents a compromise between *pluralism* and Marxism.

Recidivism The repetition of criminal behaviour by an offender.

Reconviction Rate One (imperfect) measure of *recidivism*, based on how many offenders subject to a *penalty* receive another conviction within a certain length of time (typically one or two years).

Reductivism The theory that *punishment* can be justified by its effects in controlling crime, by means such as *deterrence, incapacitation* and *reform*.

Referral Order An order imposed by a court on a young offender (aged 10 to 17) who pleads guilty and is convicted for the first time. The order consists of a referral to a *Youth Offender Panel*.

Reform/Rehabilitation The prevention of crime by improving an offender's character or behaviour.

'Rehabilitation Revolution' The policy pursued by the Coalition government (2010 onwards) whereby the providers of penal services are 'paid by results' according to rates of reoffending.

Rehabilitative Ideal The notion that the aim of all *punishment* should be *rehabilitation*. See also *positivism, treatment model, welfare model*.

Reintegrative Shaming A term coined by John Braithwaite (1989) and used to describe a process whereby an offender is shamed in the company of *victims* and significant others for what they have done, while treating the offender with concern and respect, the aim being to strengthen the moral bonds between the offender, the offender's family and the wider community.

Remand A court order specifying what is to happen to a defendant or convicted offender pending trial or *sentence*, which may be remand on *bail* or in *custody*.

Remand Centres/Remand Prisons *Custodial* institutions housing prisoners on *remand*.

Remission Automatic *early release*, forfeited only if the prisoner is judged to have misbehaved while in prison.

Reparation Any action that is undertaken by an offender to help put right or repair the wrong they have done, thereby acknowledging the wrongfulness of their actions. Reparation is an important component of *restorative justice*.

Reparation Order A sentence which requires a young offender to perform *reparation* to the *victim* or to the community.

Reprimand See *caution*.

Resources, Crisis of See *crisis of resources*.

Responsibilization The policy of requiring people (especially young offenders) to be accountable for their actions; or holding parents responsible for the actions of their children.

Restorative Justice A term used to refer to a wide range of informal processes that seek to resolve offences by involving offenders, *victims* and others affected by the offence, with an emphasis on *reparation*. These processes include *mediation*.

Retribution Punishing offenders because they are thought to deserve *punishment*.

Retributivism The theory that wrongdoers may and should be *punished* because (and as much as) they deserve to be. See also *just deserts, proportionality, principle of*.

Rights Theory (or **Human Rights Theory**) The theory that individuals possess certain fundamental moral entitlements.

SAP See *Sentencing Advisory Panel*.

Secretary of State for Justice (or Justice Secretary) The senior government minister who has responsibility for the *Ministry of Justice* and is also the *Lord Chancellor*.

Secure Children's Homes Secure accommodation for younger children (up to the age of 16) run by local authorities.

Secure Training Centre (STC) Privately run secure accommodation for *young offenders* (boys aged 12 to 15 and girls between 12 and 17) who are serving *custodial sentences*.

Security A term variously used to mean (1) keeping prisoners *contained* within prisons (i.e. preventing escapes); (2) exercising appropriate *control* over prisoners; (3) keeping prisoners and staff safe while within the prison.

Sentence A court order specifying the *punishment* to be imposed on a person who has been convicted of an offence.

Sentence Management This is now the generic term for dealing with offenders who have received a community order, suspended sentence order or custodial sentence. Essentially, it is what the National Offender Management Service does with offenders.

Sentencing Advisory Panel (SAP) An official body which advised the *Sentencing Guidelines Council*. In 2010, both these bodies were abolished and their functions combined in the *Sentencing Council*.

Sentencing Council An official body which issues *sentencing guidelines* to the courts. It replaced the *Sentencing Council* and *Sentencing Advisory Panel* as from April 2010.

Sentencing Guidelines Relatively imprecise rules which guide courts in making their *sentencing* decisions.

Sentencing Guidelines Council (SGC) An official body chaired by the *Lord Chief Justice* which issued *sentencing guidelines* to the courts. Replaced by the *Sentencing Council* in 2010.

SGC See *Sentencing Guidelines Council.*

'Short Sharp Shock' A brisk militaristic regime that operated in certain *detention centres* in the 1980s, historical precursor to *boot camps.*

'Slopping Out' The former daily prison routine of emptying chamber pots when most prison cells lacked integral sanitation.

Social Control A term which encompasses all the methods whereby society keeps its members obedient to its rules.

Social Democracy A political system (whose prime example is Sweden) which shares the consensual approach of conservative *corporatism*, but with a more generous and egalitarian welfare system.

SSO See *suspended sentence.*

Statute An Act of Parliament.

STC See *secure training centre.*

Strategy A A highly *punitive* approach to crime and *punishment*, embodying *law and order ideology* and an *exclusionary approach* to offenders.

Strategy B A *managerialist approach* to crime and *punishment* which seeks to apply administrative and bureaucratic mechanisms to criminal justice in an attempt to make the system as smooth-running and cost-effective as possible.

Strategy C An *inclusive approach* to crime and *punishment* which seeks to protect and uphold the human *rights* of offenders and *victims* of crime, to minimize punishment and to ensure fairness and humane treatment within the *criminal justice system.*

Strategy of Encouragement A policy of encouraging, but not requiring, courts to make greater use of *non-custodial penalties* in preference to imprisonment. See also *punishment in the community.*

Structuralism A type of social theory which regards the structure of the social system as central to the understanding of society.

Summary Offences Offences which can only be tried in the *magistrates' court.*

Supervision Order A penalty for young offenders (under the age of 18) equivalent to the former *probation* order for adult offenders.

Suspended Sentence/Suspended Sentence Order (SSO) A sentence of imprisonment that is held in suspense for a specified period and not activated provided that no further offence is committed during this time. Under the Criminal Justice Act 2003 suspended sentences were replaced by the suspended sentence order, which enables a court to add one or more additional requirements (similar to those in *community orders*).

Systems Management An approach to criminal justice, especially influential in *juvenile justice* in the 1980s, which seeks to apply *managerialist* techniques to achieve goals such as a decrease in the use of *custody*. Systems management techniques include *decarceration, diversion* and *inter-agency* co-operation.

Tagging See *curfews, electronic monitoring, exclusion orders, home detention curfew.*

Tariff A set of punishments of varying severity which are matched to crimes of differing seriousness ('offence-based tariff') or to offenders with different criminal records ('offender-based tariff'). Also denotes the minimum period which must be served in prison under an *indeterminate sentence*.

'Three Strikes and You're Out' Laws which prescribe mandatory or minimum prison *sentences* for a third offence.

'Tough on Crime and Tough on the Causes of Crime' A slogan associated with *New Labour*, and in particular with Tony Blair, first used in 1992.

'Toxic Mix' A combination of different types of difficult prisoners within a single institution, said by the *orthodox account* of the *penal crisis* to be an important factor in riots and disorder within prisons.

Treatment Model The notion that offenders should be treated (as if they were ill) to *reform* them rather than dealing with them in a *punitive* manner. See also *positivism, rehabilitative ideal, welfare model*.

Triable Either Way See *either way offences*.

'Truth in Sentencing' (also known as *honesty in sentencing*) The notion that the *sentence* pronounced by the judge in court should denote the exact length of time the offender spends in prison, i.e. that there should be no *early release*.

Twin-Track Strategy See *bifurcation*.

Unit Fines A system introduced into magistrates' courts by the Criminal Justice Act 1991 designed to relate *fines* to the offenders' means. Abolished by the Criminal Justice Act 1993. See also *day fines*.

Unpaid Work See *community service, community payback, community order*.

Utilitarianism The theory that moral actions are those which promote the 'greatest happiness of the greatest number' (Jeremy Bentham). Associated with *reductivism*.

Victim Someone who is harmed by a criminal act.

Visibility, Crisis of See *crisis of visibility*.

Warning See *caution*.

Welfare Model The notion that criminal justice (and especially *youth justice*) should aim to promote the welfare of the offender above all. Associated with *positivism*. See also *rehabilitative ideal, treatment model*.

White Paper An official document setting out the government's plans for new legislation or policy.

YCC See *youth conditional caution*.

YJB See *Youth Justice Board*.

YOI See *young offender institution*.

YOP See *youth offender panel*.

YOT See *youth offending team*.

Young Adult Offenders Offenders aged between 18 and 20 inclusive.

Young Offenders Usually means offenders under the age of 18; sometimes includes *young adult offenders* aged 18 to 20.

Young Offender Institution (YOI) Secure institution run by the Prison Service for *young offenders* serving custodial sentences.

Youth Caution The juvenile equivalent of an adult *caution.*

Youth Conditional Caution (YCC) The juvenile equivalent of an adult *conditional caution.*

Youth Court The court which tries *young offenders* under the age of 18.

Youth Justice The *criminal justice system* as it applies to *young offenders* under the age of 18.

Youth Justice Board (YJB) A public body with strategic responsibility for the *youth justice* system as a whole, including the provision of *custodial* institutions for those aged under 18.

Youth Offender Panel (YOP) A forum to which *young offenders* who receive a *referral order* are sent by the court. The panel meets the offender and seeks to agree a contract aimed at *reparation* and tackling the causes of the young person's offending behaviour.

Youth Offending Team (YOT) *Multi-agency* team (including representatives of the police, social services, *probation* service, local education and health authorities) that is responsible for delivering community-based interventions and supervision for *young offenders*.

Youth Rehabilitation Order (YRO) The juvenile equivalent of the adult *community order.*

YRO See *youth rehabilitation order*.

Zero Tolerance The notion that there should always be a firm response to even minor offending and other anti-social behaviour. Contrast with *minimum intervention.*

References

NB: Official documents and publications produced by the government (e.g. the Ministry of Justice) and organizations (e.g. the Prison Reform Trust) can often be found on the appropriate website. For the addresses of these sites, see the Weblinks section of the Companion Website for this book.)

Abt Associates (1998) *Private Prisons in the United States: An Assessment of Current Practice*. Cambridge, MA: Abt Associates Inc.

Adam Smith Institute (1984) *Justice Policy*. London: ASI Research.

Adams, R. (1994) *Prison Riots in Britain and the USA.* Basingstoke: Macmillan.

Advisory Council on the Penal System (1968) (chaired by Sir Leon Radzinowicz) *The Regime for Long-term Prisoners in Conditions of Maximum Security*. London: HMSO.

Aertsen I. and Peters T. (1998) 'Mediation and Restorative Justice in Belgium', *European Journal on Criminal Policy and Research*, 6: 507–25.

Allen, C., Crow, I. and Cavadino, M. (2000) *Evaluation of the Youth Court Demonstration Project*, Home Office Research Study No. 214. London: Home Office.

Allen, R. (2011) *Last Resort: Explaining the Reduction in Child Imprisonment 2008–11*. London: Prison Reform Trust.

Althusser, L. (1969) *For Marx*. London: Allen Lane.

Althusser, L. (1971) *Lenin and Philosophy and Other Essays*. New York and London: Monthly Review Press.

American Friends Service Committee (1971) *Struggle for Justice*. New York: Hill and Wang.

Amnesty International (1997) *Special Security Units: Cruel, Inhuman or Degrading Treatment*. London: Amnesty International.

Amnesty International (2002) *United Kingdom: Failing Children and Young People in Detention – Concerns Regarding Young Offender Institutions*. London: Amnesty International.

Andrews, C. (2000) *Contracted and Publicly Managed Prisons: Cost and Staffing Comparisons 1997–8*. London: HM Prison Service.

Andrews, D. A. (2001) 'Principles of Effective Correctional Programming', in L. Motiuk and R. Serin (eds), *Compendium 2000 on Effective Correctional Programming*. Ottawa: Correctional Service of Canada, pp. 9–17.

Andrews, D. A., Zinger, I., Hodge, R. D., Bonta, J., Gendreau, P. and Cullen, F. T. (1990) 'Does Correctional Treatment Work? A Clinically Relevant and Psychologically Informed Meta-Analysis', *Criminology*, 28: 369–429.

Ashworth, A. (1983) *Sentencing and Penal Policy*. London: Weidenfeld & Nicolson.

Ashworth, A. (1997) 'Sentenced by the Media', *Criminal Justice Matters*, 29: 14–15.

Ashworth, A. (2005) *Sentencing and Criminal Justice* (4th edn). Cambridge: Cambridge University Press.

Ashworth, A. (2010) 'Coroners and Justice Act 2009: Sentencing Guidelines and the Sentencing Council', *Criminal Law Review*: 389–401.

Attorney General (2009) *Attorney General's Guidelines on the Acceptance of Pleas and the Prosecutor's Role in the Sentencing Exercise.* London: Attorney General's Office

Audit Commission (1996) *Misspent Youth: Young People and Crime.* London: Audit Commission.

Audit Commission (2004) *Youth Justice 2004: A Review of the Reformed Youth Justice System.* London: Audit Commission.

Austin, J. and Coventry, G. (2001) *Emerging Issues on Privatized Prisons.* National Council on Crime and Delinquency Bureau of Justice Assistance Monograph.

Bach, S.D. (2002) 'Public Sector Employment Relations Under Labour: Muddling Through on Modernization', *British Journal of Industrial Relations*, 40 (2): 319–39.

Bainham, A. (1990) *Children – The New Law: The Children Act 1989.* Bristol: Jordan and Sons.

Baldus, D. C., Woodworth, G. W. and Pulaski, C. A. Jr (1989) *Equal Justice and the Death Penalty: A Legal and Empirical Analysis.* Dartmouth, NH: Northeastern University Press.

Ball, C. (2004) 'Youth Justice? Half a Century of Responses to Youth Offending', *Criminal Law Review*, 28–41.

Ball, J., Bowcott, O. and Rogers, S. (2011) 'Race Variation in Jail Sentences, Study Suggests', *Guardian*, 26 November.

Barak-Glantz, I. L. (1981) 'Towards a Conceptual Schema of Prison Management Styles', *The Prison Journal*, 61 (2): 42–60.

Barclay, G. C. and Tavares, C. (2000) *International Comparisons of Criminal Justice Statistics 1998*, Home Office Statistical Bulletin 04/00. London: Home Office.

Barclay, G. C., Tavares, C. and Prout, A. (eds) (1995) *Digest 3: Information on the Criminal Justice System in England and Wales.* London: Home Office Research and Statistics Department.

Baxter, R. and Nuttall, C. (1975) 'Severe Sentences: No Deterrent to Crime?', *New Society*, 2 January: 11–13.

Beccaria, C. (1963) *On Crimes and Punishments.* Indianapolis: Bobbs-Merrill.

Belson, W. A. (1975) *Juvenile Theft: The Causal Factors.* London: Harper & Row.

Bennett, T. (1979) 'The Social Distribution of Criminal Labels', *British Journal of Criminology*, 19: 134–45.

Bennett, T. and Wright, R. (1984) *Burglars on Burglary.* Aldershot: Gower.

Bentham, J. (1970) *An Introduction to the Principles of Morals and Legislation.* London: Methuen.

Bergman, D. (1991) *Deaths at Work: Accidents or Corporate Crime?* London: Workers' Educational Association.

Beyleveld, D. (1980) *A Bibliography on General Deterrence Research.* Westmead: Saxon House.

Bianchi, H. (1994) *Justice as Sanctuary: Towards a New System of Social Control,* Bloomington, IN: Indiana University Press.

Blom-Cooper, L. (1988) *The Penalty of Imprisonment.* London: Prison Reform Trust.

Blom-Cooper, Sir L. and Morris, T. (2004) *With Malice Aforethought: A Study of the Crime and Punishment for Homicide.* Oxford: Hart Publishing.

Blunkett, D. (2004) *Reducing Crime, Changing Lives.* London: Home Office.

Boag, D. (1988) 'The Special Unit at Lincoln Prison: Descriptive Account of the First Six Months', unpublished report to the Home Office.

Boag, D. (1989) 'The Lincoln Special Unit: 30 November 1987 to 25 July 1988: The Second Descriptive Account', unpublished report to the Home Office.

Bottomley, A. K. (1980) 'The "Justice Model" in America and Britain: Development and Analysis', in Bottoms and Preston (1980) pp. 25–52.

Bottomley, A. K. (1990) 'Lincoln Special Unit', unpublished report to the Home Office.

Bottomley, A. K. and Hay, W. (eds) (1991) *Special Units for Difficult Prisoners.* Hull: University of Hull.

Bottomley, A. K., James, A., Clare, E. and Liebling, A. (1996) *Wolds Remand Prison: An Evaluation*, Home Office Research Findings No. 32. London: HMSO.

Bottoms, A. E. (1977) 'Reflections on the Renaissance of Dangerousness', *Howard Journal of Criminal Justice*, 16: 70–96.

Bottoms, A. E. (1980) 'An Introduction to "The Coming Crisis"', in Bottoms and Preston (1980) pp. 1–24.

Bottoms, A. E. (1981) 'The Suspended Sentence', *British Journal of Criminology*, 21: 1–26.

Bottoms, A. E. (1983) 'Neglected Features of Contemporary Penal Systems', in Garland and Young (1983a) pp. 166–202.

Bottoms, A. E. (1987) 'Limiting Prison Use: Experience in England and Wales', *Howard Journal of Criminal Justice*, 26: 177–202.

Bottoms, A. E. (1995a) 'The Philosophy and Politics of Punishment and Sentencing', in C. Clarkson and R. Morgan (eds), *The Politics of Sentencing Reform*. Oxford: Clarendon Press, pp. 17–49.

Bottoms, A. E. (1995b) *Intensive Community Supervision for Young Offenders: Outcomes, Process and Cost*. Cambridge: Institute Of Criminology.

Bottoms, A. E. (2000) Oral contribution in the course of a conference on 'Restorative Justice: Exploring the Aims and Determining the Limits', Institute of Criminology, Cambridge, 6–8 October 2000.

Bottoms, A. E. (2004) 'Empirical Research Relevant to Sentencing Frameworks', in Bottoms et al. (2004) pp. 59–82.

Bottoms, A. E. and Brownsword, R. (1983) 'Dangerousness and Rights', in J. W. Hinton (ed.), *Dangerousness: Problems of Assessment and Prediction*. London: George Allen and Unwin, pp. 9–24.

Bottoms, A. E. and Dignan, J. (2004) 'Youth Justice in Great Britain', in M. Tonry and A. N. Doob (eds), *Crime and Justice: A Review of Research*, Vol. 31. Chicago: University of Chicago Press. pp. 21–183.

Bottoms, A. E., Hay, W. and Sparks, J. R. (1990) 'Situational and Social Approaches to the Prevention of Disorder in Long-term Prisons', *The Prison Journal* (Journal of the Pennsylvania Prison Society), 70: 83–95.

Bottoms, A. E. and McClean, J. D. (1976) *Defendants in the Criminal Process*. London: Routledge and Kegan Paul.

Bottoms, A. E. and Preston, R. H. (eds) (1980) *The Coming Penal Crisis: A Criminological and Theological Exploration*. Edinburgh: Scottish Academic Press.

Bottoms, A., Rex, S. and Robinson, G. (eds) (2004) *Alternatives to Prison: Options for an Insecure Society*. Cullompton: Willan Publishing.

Bottoms, A. E. and Stevenson, S. (1992) '"What Went Wrong?": Criminal Justice Policy in England and Wales, 1945–70', in D. Downes (ed.), *Unravelling Criminal Justice*. Basingstoke: Macmillan Press, pp. 1–45.

Bowden, J. (1995) 'Barlinnie Special Unit: The End of an Experiment', *Prison Report*, 30: 24–5.

Bowling, B. and Philliips, C. (2007) 'Disproportionate and Discriminatory: Reviewing the Evidence on Police Stop and Search', *Modern Law Review*, 70: 936.

Boyle, J. (1977) *A Sense of Freedom*. London: Pan Books.

Braggins, J. and Talbot, J. (2003) *Time to Learn: Prisoners' Views on Prison Education*. London: Prison Reform Trust.

Braithwaite, J. (1989) *Crime, Shame and Reintegration*. Cambridge: Cambridge University Press.

Briggs, D. (1975) *In Place of Prison*. London: Temple Smith.

Brody, S. R. (1976) *The Effectiveness of Sentencing*, Home Office Research Study No. 35. London: HMSO.

Brody, S. R. and Tarling, R. (1980) *Taking Offenders out of Circulation*, Home Office Research Study No. 64. London: HMSO.

Brogan, D. (2005) *Anti-social Behaviour: An Assessment of Current Management of Information Systems and the Scale of Anti-Social Behaviour Order Breaking Resulting in Custody*. London: Youth Justice Board.

Burke, R. H. (2009) *An Introduction to Criminological Theory* (3rd edn). Cullompton: Willan Publishing.

Burnett, R. and Farrell, G. (1994) *Reported and Unreported Racial Incidents in Prison*, University of Oxford Centre for Criminological Research Occasional Paper No. 14.

Burton, M. (1983) 'Understanding Mental Health Services: Theory and Practice', *Critical Social Policy*, 3: 54–74.

Cabinet Office (2008) *Engaging Communities in Fighting Crime: A Review by Louise Casey*. London: Cabinet Office.

Cain, M. (1971) 'On the Beat: Interactions and Relations in Rural and Urban Police Forces', in S. Cohen (ed.), *Images of Deviance*. Harmondsworth: Penguin, pp. 62–97.

Carlen, P. (1983) *Women's Imprisonment: A Study in Social Control*. London: Routledge and Kegan Paul.

Carlen, P. (1990) *Alternatives to Women's Imprisonment.* Milton Keynes: Open University Press.

Carlen, P. (2006) 'The Nonsense of the Therapunitive Prison for Women and Men', *Howard League Magazine*, 24 (3): 6.

Carlile, A. (2006) *The Carlile Inquiry*. London: Howard League for Penal Reform.

Carlisle, M. (1988) *The Parole System in England and Wales: Report of the Review Committee*, Cm 532. London: HMSO.

Carlsson, K. (2003) 'Intensive Supervision with Electronic Monitoring in Sweden', in M. Mayer, R. Haverkamp and R. Levy (eds), *Will Electronic Monitoring Have a Future in Europe?* Freiburg: Max Planck Institute, pp. 69–76

Carson, W. G. (1971) 'White Collar Crime and the Enforcement of Factory Legislation', in W. G. Carson and P. Wiles (eds), *Crime and Delinquency in Britain*. London: Martin Robertson, pp. 192–206.

Carter, P. (2003) *Managing Offenders, Reducing Crime*. London: Home Office.

Carter, P. (2007) *Securing the Future: Proposals for the Efficient and Sustainable Use of Custody in England and Wales*. London: Ministry of Justice.

Cavadino, M. (1989) *Mental Health Law in Context: Doctors' orders?* Aldershot: Dartmouth.

Cavadino, M. (1992) 'Theorising the Penal Crisis', in K. Bottomley, D. Farrington, T. Fowles, R. Reiner and S. Walklate (eds), *Criminal Justice: Theory and Practice*. London: British Society of Criminology, pp. 1–22.

Cavadino, M. (1997a) 'A Vindication of the Rights of Psychiatric Patients', *Journal of Law and Society*, 24: 235–51.

Cavadino, M. (1997b) *The Law of Gravity: Offence Seriousness and Criminal Justice*. Sheffield: Joint Unit for Social Services Research.

Cavadino, M., Crow, I. and Dignan, J. (1999) *Criminal Justice 2000.* Winchester: Waterside Press.

Cavadino, M. and Dignan, J. (1992) *The Penal System: An Introduction*. London: Sage Publications.

Cavadino, M. and Dignan, J. (1997) 'Reparation, Retribution and Rights', *International Review of Victimology*, 4: 233–53.

Cavadino, M. and Dignan, J. (2002) *The Penal System: An Introduction* (3rd edn). London: Sage Publications.

Cavadino, M. and Dignan, J. (with others) (2006) *Penal Systems: A Comparative Approach*. London: Sage Publications.

Cavadino, M. and Dignan, J. (2007) *The Penal System: An Introduction* (4th edn). London: Sage Publications.

Cavadino, M. and Dignan, J. (2010) 'Penal Comparisons: Puzzling Relations', in A. Crawford (ed.), *International and Comparative Criminal Justice and Urban Governance:*

Convergence and Divergence in Global, National and Local Settings. Cambridge: Cambridge University Press, pp. 193–213.

Central Statistical Office (1991) *The CSO Blue Book*, UK National Accounts, ed. D. Ruffles. London: HMSO.

Centre for Public Services (2002) *Privatizing Justice: The Impact of the Private Finance Initiative in the Criminal Justice System*. Sheffield: Centre for Public Services.

Chaplin, C., Flatley, J. and Smith, K. (2011) *Crime in England and Wales 2010/11*, Home Office Statistical Bulletin10/11. London: Home Office.

Chapman, L. (1978) *Your Disobedient Servant*. London: Chatto and Windus.

Charles, N., Whittaker, C. and Ball, C. (1997) *Sentencing without a Pre-Sentence Report*, Home Office Research Findings No. 47. London: Home Office Research and Statistics Directorate.

Charman, E., Gibson, B., Honess, T. and Morgan, R (1996). *Fine Impositions and Enforcement Following the Criminal Justice Act 1993*, Home Office Research Findings 36. London: Home Office.

Children's Rights Alliance (2005) *State of Children's Rights 2005*. London: Children's Rights Alliance.

Christiansen, K. O. (1975) 'On General Prevention from an Empirical Viewpoint', in National Swedish Council for Crime Prevention, *General Deterrence: A Conference on Current Research and Standpoints, June 2–4, 1975*. Stockholm: National Swedish Council for Crime Prevention, pp. 60–74.

Christie, N. (1978) 'Conflicts as Property', *British Journal of Criminology*, 17: 1–15.

Christie, N. (1981) *Limits to Pain*. London: Routledge.

Clancy, A., Hough, M., Aust, R. and Kershaw, C. (2001) *Crime, Policing and Justice: The Experience of Ethnic Minorities*, Home Office Research Study No. 223. London: Home Office.

Clare, E. and Bottomley, K. (eds) (2001) *Evaluation of Close Supervision Centres*, Home Office Research Study No. 136. London: Home Office Research, Development and Statistics Directorate.

Clarke, K. (2010) 'The Government's Vision for Criminal Justice Reform', speech delivered at the Centre for Crime and Justice Studies, 30 June.

Codd, H. (2008) *In the Shadow of Prison: Families, Imprisonment and Criminal Justice*. Cullompton: Willan.

Coggan, G. and Walker, M. (1982) *Frightened for My Life*. London: Fontana.

Cohen, P. (1981) 'Policing the Working Class City', in M. Fitzgerald, G. McLennan and J. Pawson (eds), *Crime and Society: Readings in History and Theory*. London: Routledge and Kegan Paul, pp. 116–33.

Cohen, S. (1979) 'The Punitive City: Notes on the Dispersal of Social Control', *Contemporary Crises*, 3: 339–63.

Cohen, S. (1980) *Folk Devils and Moral Panics: The Creation of the Mods and Rockers*. Oxford: Martin Robertson.

Cohen, S. (1985) *Visions of Social Control*. Cambridge: Polity Press.

Cohen, S. and Taylor, L. (1978) *Prison Secrets*. London: National Council for Civil Liberties/ Radical Alternatives to Prison.

Commission for Racial Equality (2003) *Race Equality in Prisons*. London: Commission for Racial Equality.

Confederation of British Industry (2003) *Competition: A Catalyst for Change in the Prison Service*. London: Confederation of British Industry.

Conservative Party (2008) *Prisons with a Purpose*. London: Conservative Party.

Conservative Party (2010) *Conservative Manifesto 2010*. London: Conservative Party.

Cook, D. (1989) *Rich Law, Poor Law: Differential Response to Tax and Supplementary Benefit Fraud*. Milton Keynes: Open University Press.

Cooke, D. J. (1989) 'Containing Violent Prisoners: An Analysis of the Barlinnie Special Unit', *British Journal of Criminology*, 29: 129–43.

Cooke, D. J. (1991) 'Violence in Prisons: The Influence of Regime Factors', *Howard Journal of Criminal Justice*, 30: 95–109.

Corston, J. (2007) *A Report by Baroness Jean Corston of a Review of Women with Particular Vulnerabilities in the Criminal Justice System*. London: Home Office, March.

Coulsfield, L. (2004) *Crime, Courts and Confidence: Report of an Inquiry into Alternatives to Prison*. London: The Stationery Office.

Coyle, A. (2005) *Understanding Prisons: Key Issues in Policy and Practice*. Cullompton: Willan Publishing.

CPT (European Committee for the Prevention of Torture and Inhuman and Degrading Treatment) (1991) *Report to the United Kingdom Government on the Visit to United Kingdom Carried Out by the CPT from 29 July 1990 to 10 August 1990*, CPT/Inf (91) 15. CPT: Strasbourg. Available at: www.cpt.coe.int/documents/gbr/1991-15-inf-eng.pdf (last accessed 18 December 2012).

CPT (European Committee for the Prevention of Torture and Inhuman and Degrading Treatment) (2005) *Report to the Government of the United Kingdom on the visit to the United Kingdom and the Isle of Man Carried Out by the European Committee for the Prevention of Torture and Inhuman or Degrading Treatment or Punishment (CPT) from 12 to 23 May 2003*, CPT/Inf (1). CPT: Strasbourg. Available at: www.cpt.coe.int/documents/gbr/2005-01-inf-eng.pdf (last accessed 18 December 2012).

CPT (European Committee for the Prevention of Torture and Inhuman and Degrading Treatment) (2006) *Report to the United Kingdom Government on the Visit to the United Kingdom Carried Out by the European Committee for the Prevention of Torture and Inhuman or Degrading Treatment or Punishment (CPT) from 20 to 25 November 2005*, CPT/Inf (28). CPT: Strasbourg. Available at: www.cpt.coe.int/documents/gbr/2006-28-inf-eng.pdf (last accessed 18 December 2012).

Creighton, S. and King, V. (2000) *Prisoners and the Law* (2nd edn). London: Butterworths.

Crighton, D. and Towl, G. (1997) 'Self-inflicted Deaths in England and Wales: An Analysis of the Data for 1988–90 and 1994–5', in Suicide and Self-Injury in Prisons, *Issues in Criminological and Legal Psychology*, 28.

Criminal Justice Joint Inspectorates (2008) *A Complicated Business: A Joint Inspection of Electronically Monitored Curfew Requirements, Orders and Licences*. London: CJJI.

Crow, I. (1987) 'Black People and Criminal Justice in the UK', *Howard Journal of Criminal Justice*, 26: 303–14.

Crow, I., Cavadino, M., Dignan, J., Johnston, V. and Walker, M. (1995) *The Impact of the Criminal Justice Act 1991 in Four Areas in the North of England*. University of Sheffield.

Crow, I. and Cove, J. (1984) 'Ethnic Minorities and the Courts', *Criminal Law Review*, 413–17.

Crow, I., Richardson, P., Riddington, C. and Simon, F. (1989) *Unemployment, Crime and Offenders*. London: Routledge.

Cullen, C. and Minchin, M. (2000) *The Prison Population in 1999: A Statistical Review*, Home Office Research Findings No. 118. London: Home Office Research and Statistics Directorate.

Dahl, R. A. (1961) *Who Governs?*. New Haven: Yale University Press.

Dahl, R. A. (1985) *A Preface to Economic Democracy*. Cambridge: Polity Press.

Davis, G., Boucherat, J. and Watson, D. (1988) 'Reparation in the Service of Diversion: The Subordination of a Good Idea', *Howard Journal of Criminal Justice*, 27: 127–262.

Davis, G., Boucherat, J. and Watson, D. (1989) 'Pre-court Decision-making in Juvenile Justice', *British Journal of Criminology*, 29: 219–35.

Davis, K. C. (1969) *Discretionary Justice: A Preliminary Inquiry*. London: University of Illinois Press.

De Fleur, L. B. (1975) 'Bias Influences on Drug Arrest Records: Implications for Deviance Research', *American Sociological Review*, 40: 88–103.

de Haan, W. (1990) *The Politics of Redress: Crime, Abolition and Penal Abolition*. London: Unwin Hyman.

de la Motta, K. (1984) 'Blacks in the Criminal Justice System', unpublished MSc thesis, Aston University.

Debidin, M. and Lovbakke, J. (2005) 'Offending Behaviour Programmes in Prison and Probation', in G. Harper and C. Chitty (eds), *The Impact of Corrections on Re-offending: A Review of 'What Works'* (3rd edn), Home Office Research Study 291. London: Home Office Research, Development and Statistics Directorate.

Denman, S. (2001) *Race Discrimination in the Crown Prosecution Service – Final Report*. London: Crown Prosecution Service.

Department for Christian Responsibility and Citizenship (2004) *A Place Of Redemption: A Christian Approach to Punishment and Prison*, Catholic Bishops' Conference of England and Wales. London: Burns and Oates.

Dholakia, N. and Sumner, M. (1993) 'Research, Policy and Racial Justice', in D. Cook and B. Hudson (eds), *Racism and Criminology*. London: Sage, pp. 28–44.

di Lustro, M. (2004) 'Containment at the Expense of Care?' *Howard League Magazine*, 22 (4): 6.

Dignan, J. (1991) *Repairing the Damage: An Evaluation of an Experimental Adult Reparation Scheme in Kettering, Northamptonshire*. Sheffield: University of Sheffield, Centre for Criminological and Legal Research.

Dignan, J. (1992) 'Repairing the Damage: Can Reparation be Made to Work in the Service of Diversion?', *British Journal of Criminology*, 32: 453–72.

Dignan, J. (1994) 'Reintegration through Reparation: A Way Forward for Restorative Justice?', in A. Duff, S. Marshall, R. E. Dobash and R. P. Dobash (eds), *Penal Theory and Penal Practice: Tradition and Innovation in Criminal Justice*. Manchester: Manchester University Press, pp. 231–44.

Dignan, J. (1999) 'The Crime and Disorder Act and the Prospects for Restorative Justice', *Criminal Law Review*, 48–60.

Dignan, J. (2002) 'Restorative Justice and the Law: The Case for an Integrated, Systemic Approach', in L. Walgrave (ed.), *Restorative Justice and the Law*. Cullompton: Willan Publishing, pp. 168–90.

Dignan, J. (2003) 'Towards a Systemic Model of Restorative Justice' in A. von Hirsch, J. Roberts, A. E. Bottoms, K. Roach and M. Schiff (eds), *Restorative Justice and Criminal Justice: Competing or Reconcilable Paradigms?* Oxford: Hart Publishing, pp. 135–56.

Dignan, J. (2005a) *Understanding Victims and Restorative Justice*. Maidenhead: Open University Press.

Dignan, J. (2005b) 'Alternatives to the Prosecution of Unruly Children and Young Persons: The Position in England and Wales', in T. Wing Lo, D. Wong and G. Maxwell (eds), *Alternatives to Prosecution: Rehabilitative and Restorative Models of Youth Justice*. Singapore: Marshall Cavendish Academic, pp. 46–93.

Dignan, J. and Cavadino, M. (1996) 'Towards a Framework for Conceptualising and Evaluating Models of Criminal Justice from a Victim's Perspective', *International Review of Victimology*, 4: 153–82.

Dignan, J. and Wynne, A. (1997) 'A Microcosm of the Local Community?' *British Journal of Criminology*, 37: 184–97.

Ditchfield, J. (1990) *Control in Prisons: A Review of the Literature*. Home Office Research Study No. 118. London: HMSO.

DLA MCG Consulting (2003) *Privately Managed Custodial Services*. Liverpool: DLA MCG Consulting.

DLA MCG Consulting (2005) *Privately Managed Custodial Services*. Liverpool: DLA MCG Consulting.

Dobash, R. P., Dobash, R. E. and Gutteridge, S. (1986) *The Imprisonment of Women*. Oxford: Basil Blackwell.

Dodgson, K., Goodwin, P., Howard, P., Llewellyn-Thomas, S., Mortimer, E., Russell, N. and Weiner, M. (2001) *Electronic Monitoring of Prisoners: An Evaluation of the Home Detention Curfew Scheme*. Home Office Research Study No. 222. London: Home Office Research, Development and Statistics Directorate.

Dowds, L. and Hedderman, C. (1997) 'The Sentencing of Men and Women', in Hedderman and Gelsthorpe (1997) pp. 9–22.

Downes, D. (1988) *Contrasts in Tolerance: Post-War Penal Policy in The Netherlands and England and Wales*. Oxford: Oxford University Press.

Downes, D. (1997) 'Prison Does Wonders for the Jobless Figures', *The Guardian*, 25 November.

Downes, D. (2001) 'The *Macho* Penal Economy: Mass Incarceration in the United States – A European Perspective', *Punishment & Society*, 3: 61–80.

Duff, A., Marshall, S., Dobash, R. E. and Dobash, R. P. (eds) (1994) *Penal Theory and Penal Practice: Tradition and Innovation in Criminal Justice*. Manchester: Manchester University Press.

Duff, R. A. (1986) *Trials and Punishments*. Cambridge: Cambridge University Press.

Duff, R. A. (2001) *Punishment, Communication and Community*. Oxford; Oxford University Press.

Durkheim, E. (1960) *The Division of Labor in Society*. Glencoe: Free Press.

Durkheim, E. (1973) 'Two Laws of Penal Evolution', *Economy and Society*, 2: 285–308.

Dworkin, R. (1978) *Taking Rights Seriously* (new impression). London: Gerald Duckworth.

Eaton, M. (1986) *Justice for Women? Family, Court and Social Control*. Milton Keynes: Open University Press.

Edgar, K. and Martin, C. (2004) *Perceptions of Race and Conflict: Perspectives of Minority Ethnic Prisoners and of Prison Officers*. Home Office Online Report, 11/04. London: Home Office.

Edgar, K., O'Donnell, I. and Martin, C. (2003) *Prison Violence: The Dynamics of Conflict, Fear and Power*. Cullompton: Willan Publishing.

Edwards, I. (2002) 'The Place of Victims' Preferences in the Sentencing of "Their" Offenders', *Criminal Law Review*, 689–702.

Eley, S., Malloch, M., McIvor, G., Yates, R. and Brown, A. (2002) *Glasgow's Pilot Drug Court in Action: The First Six Months*. Edinburgh: Scottish Executive Social Research.

Ellis, T., Hedderman, C. and Mortimer, E. (1996) *Enforcing Community Sentences*, Home Office Research Study 158. London: Home Office.

Ellis, T. and Marshall, P. (1998) 'Does Parole Work?', *Home Office Research Bulletin*, 39: 43–50.

Esping-Andersen, G. (1990) *The Three Worlds of Welfare Capitalism*. Cambridge: Polity Press.

Evans, K. (2005) 'Young People in the Media: A Dangerous and Anti-Social Obsession', *Criminal Justice Matters*, 60 (Spring): 14–15.

Fabelo, T. (2000) '"Technocorrections": The Promises, the Uncertain Threats'. Available at: www.ncjrs.gov/pdffiles1/nij/181411.pdf (last accessed 18 December 2012).

Fagan, J. (2005) *Deterrence and the Death Penalty: A Critical Review of New Evidence*. Testimony to the New York State Assembly Standing Committee on Codes, Assembly Standing Committee on Judiciary and Assembly Standing Committee on Correction Hearings on the Future of Capital Punishment in the State of New York.

Farrall, S. and Calverley, A. (2006) *Understanding Desistance from Crime: Theoretical Directions in Resettlement and Rehabilitation*. Maidenhead: Open University Press.

Farrington, D. P. and Bennett, T. (1981) 'Police Cautioning of Juveniles in London', *British Journal of Criminology*, 21: 123–35.

Farrington, D. P. and Morris, A. M. (1983) 'Sex, Sentencing and Reconviction', *British Journal of Criminology*, 23: 229–48.

Faulkner, D. (2005) 'Parties, Politics and Punishment', *Criminal Justice Matters*, 60: 6–7 and 39.

Fazel, S., Benning, R. and Danesh, J. (2005) 'Suicides in Male Prisoners in England and Wales, 1978–2003', *The Lancet*, 36: 1242–4.

Feeley, M. and Simon, J. (1992) 'The New Penology', *Criminology*, 39: 449–74.

Field, S. (1990) *Trends in Crime and their Interpretation: A Study of Recorded Crime in Post War England and Wales*, Home Office Research Study No. 119. London: HMSO.

Fisher, C. J. and Mawby, R. L. (1982) 'Juvenile Delinquency and Police Discretion in an Inner City Area', *British Journal of Criminology*, 22: 63–75.

Fitzgerald, M. (1993) *Ethnic Minorities and the Criminal Justice System*, The Royal Commission on Criminal Justice, Research Study No. 20. London: HMSO.

Fitzgerald, M. and Sim, J. (1980) 'Legitimating the Prison Crisis: A Critical Review of the May Report', *Howard Journal of Criminal Justice*, 19: 73–84.

Fitzgerald, M. and Sim, J. (1982) *British Prisons* (2nd edn). Oxford: Basil Blackwell.

Flood-Page, C., Campbell, S., Harrington, V. and Miller, J. (2000) *Youth Crime: Findings from the 1998/99 Youth Lifestyles Survey*, Home Office Research Study No. 209. London: Home Office.

Flood-Page, C. and Mackie, A. (1998) *Sentencing Practice: An Examination of Decisions in Magistrates' Courts and the Crown Court in the Mid-1990s*, Home Office Research Study No. 180. London: Home Office.

Foster, J., Newburn, T. and Souhami, A. (2005) *Assessing the Impact of the Stephen Lawrence Inquiry*, Home Office Research Study No. 294. London: Home Office.

Foucault, M. (1967) *Madness and Civilization*. London: Tavistock.

Foucault, M. (1977) *Discipline and Punish: The Birth of the Prison*. London: Allen Lane.

Foucault, M. (1980) 'Prison Talk', in C. Gordon (ed.), *Michel Foucault: Power/ Knowledge, Selected Interviews and Other Writings 1972–1977*. Brighton: Harvester Press, pp. 37–54.

Fox, C. and Albertson, K. (2011) 'Payment by Results and Social Impact Bonds in the Criminal Justice System: New Challenges for the Concept of Evidence-based Policy?', *Criminology and Criminal Justice*, 11 (5): 395–413.

Fox, L. W. (1934) *The Modern English Prison*. London: Routledge and Kegan Paul

Franko Aas, L. (2005) *Sentencing in the Age of Information: From Faust to Macintosh*. London: Glasshouse Press.

Garland, D. (1985) *Punishment and Welfare: A History of Penal Strategies*. Aldershot: Gower.

Garland, D. (1990a) *Punishment and Modern Society: A Study in Social Theory*. Oxford: Clarendon Press.

Garland, D. (1990b) 'Frameworks of Inquiry in the Sociology of Punishment', *British Journal of Sociology*, 41: 1–15.

Garland, D. (1995a) 'Penal Modernism and Postmodernism', in T. Blomberg and S. Cohen (eds), *Punishment and Social Control: Essays in Honour of Sheldon Messinger*. New York: Aldine De Gruyter, pp. 181–209.

Garland, D. (1995b) 'Panopticon Days: Surveillance and Society', *Criminal Justice Matters*, 20: 3–4.

Garland, D. (1996) 'The Limits of the Sovereign State: Strategies of Crime Control in Contemporary Society', *British Journal of Criminology*, 36: 445–71.

Garland, D. (2001) *The Culture of Control: Crime and Social Order in Contemporary Society*. Oxford: Oxford University Press.

Garland, D. and Young, P. (eds) (1983a) *The Power to Punish: Contemporary Penality and Social Analysis*. London: Heinemann.

Garland, D. and Young, P. (1983b) 'Towards a Social Analysis of Penality', in Garland and Young (1983a) pp. 1–36.

Garside, R. (2004) *Crime, Persistent Offenders and the Justice Gap*. London: Crime and Society Foundation.

Geis, G. (1987) 'The Privatization of Prisons: Panacea or Placebo?', in B. J. Carroll, R. W. Conant and T. A. Easton (eds), *Private Means, Public Ends: Private Business in Social Service Delivery*. New York: Praeger, pp. 76–97.

Gelsthorpe, L. (1985) 'Girls and Juvenile Justice', *Youth and Policy*, 11: 1–5.

Gelsthorpe, L. (1989) *Sexism and the Female Offender: An Organizational Analysis*. Aldershot: Gower.

Gelsthorpe, L. and Loucks, N. (1997) 'Magistrates' Explanations of Sentencing Decisions', in Hedderman and Gelsthorpe (1997) pp. 23–53.

Genders, E. and Player, E. (1986) 'Women's Imprisonment: The Effects of Youth Custody', *British Journal of Criminology*, 26: 357–71.

Genders, E. and Player, E. (1989) *Race Relations in Prisons*. Oxford: Clarendon Press.

Genders, E. and Player, E. (1995) *Grendon: A Study of a Therapeutic Prison*. London: Clarendon Press.

Gewirth, A. (1978) *Reason and Morality*. Chicago: University of Chicago Press.

Gill, M. (2000) *Commercial Robbery*. London: Blackstone Press.

Gold, M. (1966) 'Undetected Delinquent Activity', *Journal of Research in Crime and Delinquency*, 3: 27–46.

Goldblatt, P. and Lewis, C. (eds) (1998) *Reducing Offending: An Assessment of Research Evidence on Ways of Dealing with Offending Behaviour*, Home Office Research Study No. 187. London: HMSO.

Goldson, B. (2000) *The New Youth Justice*. Lyme Regis, Dorset: Russell.

Goldson, B. and Coles, D. (2005) *In the Care of the State: Child Deaths in Penal Custody in England and Wales*. London: Inquest.

Gowers, E. (1953) *Report of the Royal Commission on Capital Punishment*, Cmd 8932. London: HMSO.

Graham, J. and Bowling, B. (1995) *Young People and Crime*, Home Office Research Study No. 145. London: HMSO.

Gramsci, A. (1971) *Selections from the Prison Notebooks of Antonio Gramsci*, ed. Q. Hoare and G. Nowell-Smith. London: Lawrence and Wishart.

Gray, E., Taylor, E. Merrington, S. and Roberts, C. (2005) *ISSP: The Final Report*. Oxford Centre for Criminology/Youth Justice Board.

Green, D. G., Grove, E. and Martin, N. (2005) *Crime and Civil Society: Can We Become a More Law Abiding People?* London: Civitas.

Greenberg, D. (1999) 'Punishment, Division of Labor, and Social Solidarity', in W. S. Laufer and F. Adler (eds), *The Criminology of Criminal Law*, Advances in Criminological Theory Vol. 8. New Brunswick: Transaction Books, pp. 283–361.

Griffith, J. A. G. (1997) *The Politics of the Judiciary* (5th edn). London: Fontana.

Gunn, J., Maden, T. and Swinton, M. (1991) *Mentally Disordered Prisoners*. London: Home Office.

Haggerty, K. D. (2004) 'Displaced Expertise: Three Constraints on the Policy Relevance of Criminological Thought', *Theoretical Criminology*, 8: 211–31.

Haggerty, K. D. and Ericson, R. V. (2000) 'The Surveillant Assemblage', *British Journal of Sociology*, 51 (4): 605–22.

Hale, B. (2006) *The Sinners and the Sinned Against: Women in the Criminal Justice System*, 4th Longford Lecture. Available at: www.longfordtrust.org/lecture_details.php?id=10 (last accessed 18 December 2012).

Hall, S. (1979) 'The Great Moving Right Show', *Marxism Today*, 23: 14–20.

Hall, S. (1980) *Drifting into a Law and Order Society*. London: Cobden Trust.

Hall, S., Clarke, J., Critcher, C., Jefferson, T. and Roberts, B. (1978) *Policing the Crisis*. London: Macmillan.

Halliday, J. (2001) *Making Punishments Work: Report of a Review of the Sentencing Framework for England and Wales*. London: Home Office Communication Directorate.

Hamlyn, B. and Lewis, D. (2000) *Women Prisoners: A Survey of Their Work and Training Experiences in Custody and on Release*, Home Office Research Study No. 208. London: Home Office.

Hann, R., Harman, R. and Pease, K. (1991) 'Does Parole Reduce the Risk of Reconviction?', *Howard Journal of Criminal Justice*, 30: 66–75.

Hansbury, S. (ed.) (2011) *Evaluation of the Intensive Alternatives to Custody Pilots*, Research Summary 3/11. London: Ministry of Justice.

Harris, R. and Webb, D. (1987) *Welfare, Power and Juvenile Justice*. London: Tavistock.

Hart, H. L. A. (1968) *Punishment and Responsibility*. Oxford: Oxford University Press.

Hearnden, I. and Millie, A. (2003) *Investigation Links between Probation Enforcement and Reconviction*, Home Office Online Report 41/03. London: Home Office.

Hedderman, C. (2002) 'Going Up', *Prison Report*, 59: 23.

Hedderman, C. (2003) 'Enforcing Supervision and Encouraging Compliance', in W.-H. Chui and M. Nellis (eds), *Moving Probation Forward: Evidence, Arguments and Practice*. Harlow: Longman, pp. 181–94.

Hedderman, C. and Gelsthorpe, L. (eds) (1997), *Understanding the Sentencing of Women*, Home Office Research Study No. 170. London: Home Office.

Hedderman, C. and Hough, M. (1994) *Does the Criminal Justice System Treat Men and Women Differently?* Home Office Research and Statistics Department Research Findings No. 10. London: Home Office.

Hedderman, C. and Hough, M. (2004) 'Getting Tough or Being Effective; What Matters?' in G. Mair (ed.), *What Matters in Probation.* Cullompton: Willan Publishing, pp. 146–69.

Hedderman, C. and Moxon, D. (1992) *Magistrates' Court or Crown Court? Mode of Trial Decisions and Sentencing*, Home Office Research Study No. 125. London: HMSO.

Heidensohn, F. (1985) *Women and Crime*. Basingstoke: Macmillan.

Heidensohn, F. and Silvestri, M. (2012) 'Gender and Crime', in Maguire et al. (2012) pp. 336–69.

Hennessy, J. (1987) *Report of an Inquiry by Her Majesty's Chief Inspector of Prisons for England and Wales into the Disturbances in Prison Service Establishments in England between 29 April–2 May 1986*. London: HMSO.

HM Chief Inspector of Prisons (1987) *A Review of Prisoners' Complaints*. London: HMSO.

HM Chief Inspector of Prisons (1990a) *Report of a Review by Her Majesty's Chief Inspector of Prisons for England and Wales of Suicide and Self-harm in Prison Service Establishments in England and Wales.* London: HMSO.

HM Chief Inspector of Prisons (1990b) *Report of HM Chief Inspector of Prisons, 1989*, HC 598. London: HMSO.

HM Chief Inspector of Prisons (1992) *HMP Holloway: Report by HM Chief Inspector of Prisons*. London: Home Office.

HM Chief Inspector of Prisons (1995) *HM Prison, Blakenhurst: A Report by HM Chief Inspector of Prisons.* London: Home Office.

HM Chief Inspector of Prisons (1998) *Report on HM Prisons Grendon and Springhill, February 1998.* London: Home Office.

HM Chief Inspector of Prisons (1999a) *Report of an Unannounced Inspection of HM Prison Wormwood Scrubs, 8–12 March, 1999.* London: Home Office.

HM Chief Inspector of Prisons (1999b) *Suicide Is Everyone's Concern: A Thematic Review by Her Majesty's Chief Inspector of Prisons.* London: The Stationary Office

HM Chief Inspector of Prisons (1999c) *1998–9 Annual Report of Chief Inspector of Prisons*. London: Home Office.

HM Chief Inspector of Prisons (1999d) *HMYOI and Remand Centre Feltham, Report of an Unannounced Full Inspection 30 November–4 December 1998*. London: Home Office.

HM Chief Inspector of Prisons (1999e) *Inspection of Close Supervision Centres: A Thematic Inspection by Her Majesty's Chief Inspector of Prisons*. London: Home Office.

HM Chief Inspector of Prisons (2000a) *Unjust Deserts: A Thematic Review by Her Majesty's Chief Inspector of Prisons of the Treatment and Conditions of Unsentenced Prisoners in England and Wales*. London: Home Office. Available at: www.justice.gov.uk/downloads/publications/inspectorate-reports/hmipris/thematic-reports-and-research-publications/unjust-rps.pdf (last accessed 18 December 2012).

HM Chief Inspector of Prisons (2000b) *Inspection Report on a Full Announced Inspection of HMYOI Portland 24 October–3 November 1999*. London: Home Office.

HM Chief Inspector of Prisons (2003) *Report on a Full Announced Inspection of HMP Wealstun, 27–31 October 2003*. London: Home Office.

HM Chief Inspector of Prisons (2004) *Report of an Unannounced Inspection of HMYOI Portland, 12–16 July 2004*. London: Home Office.

HM Chief Inspector of Prisons (2005a) *Report on an Unannounced Inspection of HMP Rye Hill, 11–15 April 2005*. London: Home Office.

HM Chief Inspector of Prisons (2005b) *Report on an Unannounced Full Follow-up Inspection of HMP Leeds, 22–26 August 2005*. London: Home Office.

HM Chief Inspector of Prisons (2005c) *Report on an Announced Inspection of HMP Kirkham, 5–10 December 2004*. London: HM Inspectorate of Prisons.

HM Chief Inspector of Prisons (2006), *Report on an Unannounced Full Follow-up Inspection of HMP Pentonville, 7–16 June 2006*.

HM Chief Inspector of Prisons (2008) *Report on an Announced Inspection of HMP Dovegate Therapeutic Unit, 16–20 June 2008*. London: HM Inspectorate of Prisons.

HM Chief Inspector of Prisons (2010), *Report on a Full Unannounced Inspection of HMP Holloway 15–23 April 2010*. London: HM Inspectorate of Prisons.

HM Chief Inspector of Prisons and HM Chief Inspector of Probation (2008) *The Indeterminate Sentence for Public Protection: A Thematic Review*. London: HM Inspectorate of Prisons.

HM Inspectorate of Prisons (2005a) *Parallel Worlds: A Thematic Review of Race Relations in Prisons*. London: HM Inspectorate of Prisons.

HM Inspectorate of Prisons (2005b) *Report on a Full Unannounced Inspection of HM Prison/Young Offenders Institution Holloway October 2004*. London: HM Inspectorate of Prisons.

HM Inspectorate of Prisons (2008) *Time Out of Cell: A Short Thematic Review*. London: HM Inspectorate of Prisons.

HM Inspectorate of Probation (2000) *Towards Race Equality*, Thematic Inspection Report. London: Home Office. Available at: www.justice.gov.uk/downloads/publications/inspectorate-reports/hmiprobation/joint-thematic/hmiprobthematicracefulldoc-rps.pdf (last accessed 18 December 2012).

HM Inspectorate of Probation (2006) *Working to Make Amends: An Inspection of Enhanced Community Punishment and Unpaid Work by the National Probation Service*. London: HM Inspectorate of Probation.

HM Prison Service (1999) *Framework Document*. London: The Stationery Office.

HM Prison Service (2006) *Business Plan 2006–2007*. London: National Offender Management Service.

Hogg, R. (1979) 'Imprisonment and Society under Early British Capitalism', in T. Platt and P. Takagi (eds), *Punishment and Penal Discipline: Essays on the Prison and the Prisoners' Movement*. Berkeley, CA: Crime and Social Justice Associates.

Holdaway, S., Davidson, N., Dignan, J., Hammersley, R., Hine, J. and Marsh, P. (2001) *New Strategies to Address Youth Offending: The National Evaluation of Pilot Youth Offending Teams*, RDS Occasional Paper No. 69. London: Home Office Research, Development and Statistics Directorate.

Home Office (1964) *The Sentence of the Court.* London: HMSO.

Home Office (1966) *Report of the Inquiry into Prison Escapes and Security by Admiral of the Fleet, the Earl Mountbatten of Burma*, Cmnd 3175. London: HMSO.

Home Office (1977) *Prisons and the Prisoner: The Work of the Prison Service in England and Wales*. London: HMSO.

Home Office (1981) *Criminal Statistics, England and Wales, 1980*, Cmnd 8668. London: HMSO.

Home Office (1984a) *Managing the Long Term Prison System: The Report of the Control Review Committee*. London: HMSO.

Home Office (1984b) *Statement of National Objectives and Priorities for the Probation Service*. London: Home Office.

Home Office (1985) *Staff Attitudes in the Prison Service*. London: HMSO.

Home Office (1988a) *Punishment, Custody and the Community*, Cm 424. London: HMSO.

Home Office (1988b) *Private Sector Involvement in the Remand System*, Cm 434. London: HMSO.

Home Office (1990a) *Crime, Justice and Protecting the Public: The Government's Proposals for Legislation*, Cm 965. London: HMSO.

Home Office (1990b) *Criminal Statistics, England and Wales 1989*, Cm 1322. London: HMSO.

Home Office (1991) *Custody, Care and Justice: The Way Ahead for the Prison Service in England and Wales*, Cm 1647. London: HMSO.

Home Office (1993) *Criminal Statistics, England and Wales 1992*, Cm 2410. London: HMSO.

Home Office (1994) *Monitoring of the Criminal Justice Acts 1991 and 1993 – Results from a Special Data Collection Exercise*, Home Office Statistical Bulletin 20/94. London: Home Office.

Home Office (1997a) *No More Excuses: A New Approach to Tackling Youth Crime in England and Wales*, Cm. 3809. London: Stationery Office.

Home Office (1997b) *Tackling Delays in the Youth Justice System: A Consultation Paper.* London: Home Office.

Home Office (1998a) *Crime and Disorder Act 1998: Introductory Guide.* London: Home Office Communication Directorate.

Home Office (1998b) *Joining Forces to Protect the Public.* London: HMSO.

Home Office (1999) *Reconviction of Offenders Sentenced or Discharged from Prison in 1994, England and Wales*. London: Home Office Research and Statistics Department.

Home Office (2002) *National Standards for the Supervision of Offenders in the* Community. London, Home Office.

Home Office (2003a) *Prison Statistics 2002*, Cm 5996. London: The Stationery Office.

Home Office (2003b) *Restorative Justice: The Government's Strategy*. London: Home Office.

Home Office (2003c) *Youth Justice: The Next Steps.* London: Home Office.

Home Office (2003d) 'Bind Overs – A Power for the 21st Century', archived consultation paper, May. London: Home Office.

Home Office (2004a) *Statistics on Women and the Criminal Justice System – 2003*. London: Home Office.

Home Office (2004b) *Confident Communities in a Secure Britain: The Home Office Strategic Plan 2004–2008*. London: Home Office.

Home Office (2004c) *Reducing Crime – Changing Lives: the Government's Plans for Transforming the Management of Offenders.* London: Home Office.

Home Office (2005) *Restructuring Probation to Reduce Re-offending*. London: NOMS.

Home Office (2006a) *Respect Action Plan.* London: Home Office

Home Office (2006b) *A Five Year Strategy for Protecting the Public and Reducing Re-offending* (February), Cm 6717. London: The Stationery Office.

Home Office (2006c) *Rebalancing the Criminal Justice System in Favour of the Law-Abiding Majority: Cutting Crime, Reducing Reoffending and Protecting the Public.* London: Home Office.

Home Office (2011a) *Anti-Social Behaviour Order Statistics England and Wales 2010.* London: Home Office.

Home Office (2011b) *More Effective Responses to Anti-Social Behaviour*. London: Home Office.

Home Office (2012) *More Effective Responses to Anti-Social Behaviour*. London: Home Office.

Home Office and Lord Chancellor's Department (2001) *The Youth Court 2001: The Changing Culture of the Youth Court – Good Practice Guide.* London: Home Office.

Home Office, Department of Health and Welsh Office (2000) *National Standards for the Supervision of Offenders in the Community*. London: Home Office.

Honderich, T. (1984) *Punishment: The Supposed Justifications* (new edn). Harmondsworth: Penguin.

Hood, C. (1991) 'A Public Management for all Seasons', *Public Administration*, 69: 3–19.

Hood, R. (1962) *Sentencing in Magistrates' Courts*. London: Stevens.

Hood, R. (1972) *Sentencing the Motoring Offender*. London: Heinemann.

Hood, R. (1992) *Race and Sentencing: A Study in the Crown Court* (in collaboration with G. Cordovil). Oxford: Clarendon Press.

Hood, R. and Shute, S. (1996) 'Parole Criteria, Parole Decisions and the Prison Population: Evaluating the Impact of the Criminal Justice Act 1991', *Criminal Law Review*, 77–87.

Hope, T. (1995) 'Community Crime Prevention', in M. Tonry and D. P. Farrington (eds), *Building a Safer Society: Strategic Approaches to Crime Prevention*. Chicago: University of Chicago Press.

Hough, M. (2006) 'Introduction', in Hough et al. (2006) ch. 1.

Hough, M., Allen, R. and Padel, U. (eds) (2006) *Reshaping Probation and Prisons: The New Offender Management Framework*. Bristol: The Policy Press.

Hough, M., Jacobson, J. and Millie, A. (2003) *The Decision to Imprison: Sentencing and the Prison Population*. London: Prison Reform Trust.

Hough, M. and Mayhew, P. (1985) *Taking Account of Crime: Key Findings from the 1984 British Crime Survey*, Home Office Research Study No. 85. London: HMSO.

Hough, M. and Roberts, J. (1998) *Attitudes to Punishment: Findings from the British Crime Survey*, Home Office Research Study No. 179. London: Home Office.

Hough, M. and Roberts, J. (2005) *Understanding Public Attitudes to Crime and Justice*. Maidenhead: Open University Press.

House of Commons Education and Skills Committee (2005) *Prison Education.* Seventh Report of Session 2004–2005. London: HMSO.

House of Commons Home Affairs Committee (1997) *The Management of the Prison Service (Public and Private) Volume 1, 19 March 1997* (Second Report, Session 1996–97, HC 57–1). London: HMSO.

House of Commons Home Affairs Committee (1998) *Third Report. Alternatives To Prison Sentences*, Vol. 1. London: HMSO.

House of Commons Home Affairs Committee (2005) *First Report. Session 2004–05*. London: The Stationery Office.

House of Commons Justice Committee (2011) *The Role of the Probation Service*. London: The Stationery Office.

House of Commons Public Accounts Committee (2006) *Sixty-Second Report*.

Howard League for Penal Reform (2002) *Suicide and Self-Harm Prevention Following Release from Prison*. London: Howard League.

Howard League for Penal Reform (2005) 'Shocking New Suicide Figures Expose the Prison Death Toll', press release, 5 July.

Howard League for Penal Reform (2006) 'Howard League for Penal Reform Fears over Enforced Cell-sharing for Children in Prison', press release, 15 August.

Hudson, B. (1984) 'The Rising Use of Imprisonment: The Impact of "Decarceration" Policies', *Critical Social Policy*, 11: 46–59.

Hudson, B. (1987) *Justice Through Punishment: A Critique of the 'Justice Model' of Corrections*. London: Macmillan Education.

Hudson, B. (1989) 'Discrimination and Disparity: The Influence of Race on Sentencing', *New Community*, 16: 23–34.

Hulsman, L. H. C. (1991) 'The Abolitionist Case: Alternative Crime Policies', *Israel Law Review*, 25 (3–4): 681–709.

Humphry, D. and May, D. (1977) 'Why the Prisons Could Explode', *Sunday Times*, 23 January.

Hutto, T. D. (1990) 'The Privatization of Prisons' in J. W. Murphy and J. E. Dison (eds), *Are Prisons any Better? Twenty Years of Correctional Reform*, Newbury Park, CA: Sage Publications, pp. 111–27.

Ignatieff, M. (1978) *A Just Measure of Pain: The Penitentiary in the Industrial Revolution 1750–1850*. New York: Columbia University Press.

Ignatieff, M. (1981) 'State, Civil Society, and Total Institution: A Critique of Recent Social Histories of Punishment', in M. Tonry and N. Morris (eds), *Crime and Justice*, vol. 3. Chicago: University of Chicago Press, pp. 153–92.

International Bar Association (1990) 'Sentencing Questionnaire' (2nd edn), unpublished. Presented at the 23rd biennial conference of the International Bar Association, 19–23 September.

Jacobson, J. and Hough, M. (2010) *Unjust Deserts: Imprisonment for Public Protection*. London: Prison Reform Trust.

James, A. and Bottomley, K. (1998) 'Prison Privatisation and the Remand Population: Principle versus Pragmatism?', *Howard Journal of Criminal Justice*, 37: 223–33.

James, A. L., Bottomley, A. K., Liebling, A. and Clare, E. (1997) *Privatizing Prisons: Rhetoric and Reality.* London: Sage.

Jenkins, S. (1995) 'Another Fine Mess of Porage', *The Times*, 18 October.

Jewkes, Y. (2004/5) 'High-Tech Solutions to Low-Tech Crimes? Crime and Terror in the Surveillance Assemblage', *Criminal Justice Matters*, 58: 6–7.

Jones, H., Cornes, P. and Stackford, R. (1977) *Open Prisons*. London: Routledge and Kegan Paul.

Jones, Sir Digby (2005) 'Offender Rehabilitation: Business as a Deliverer of Criminal Justice', PBA Annual Lecture. London: Probation Boards' Association.

Junger-Tas, J., Terlouw, G.-J. and Klein, M. W. (1994) *Delinquent Behaviour Among Young People in the Western World: First Results of the International Self-Report Delinquency Study.* Amsterdam: Kugler.

Kamenka, E. and Tay, A. E.-S. (1975) 'Beyond Bourgeois Individualism: The Contemporary Crisis in Law and Legal Ideology', in E. Kamenka and R. S. Neale (eds), *Feudalism, Capitalism and Beyond*. London: Edward Arnold, pp. 126–44.

Kamerman, S. B. and Kahn, A. J. (eds) (1989) *Privatization and the Welfare State*. Princeton, NJ: Princeton University Press.

Keith, B. (2006) *Report of the Zahid Mubarek Inquiry*, HC 1082. London: The Stationery Office.

Kellner, P. and Crowther-Hunt, N. (1980) *The Civil Servants: An Inquiry into Britain's Ruling Class*. London: Macdonald Futura.

Kemshall, H., Canton, R. and Bailey, R. (2004) 'Dimensions of Difference', in Bottoms et al. (2004) pp. 341–65.

Kershaw, C. (1999) *Reconviction of Offenders Sentenced or Discharged from Prison in 1994*, Home Office Statistical Bulletin 5/99. London: Home Office.

Kershaw, C., Goodman, J. and White, S. (1999) *Reconvictions of Offenders Sentenced or Discharged from Prison in 1995, England and Wales*, Home Office Statistical Bulletin 19/99. London: Home Office.

Killias, M., Aebi, M. and Ribeaud, D. (2000) 'Does Community Service Rehabilitate Better than Short-Term Imprisonment? Results of a Controlled Experiment', *Howard Journal of Criminal Justice*, 39 (1): 40–57.

King, R. D. (1985) 'Control in Prison', in Maguire, Vagg and Morgan (1985), pp. 187–203.

King, R. D. and Elliott, K. W. (1977) *Albany: Birth of a Prison – End of an Era*. London: Routledge & Kegan Paul.

King, R. D. and McDermott, K. (1989) 'British Prisons 1970–1987: The Ever-Deepening Crisis', *British Journal of Criminology*, 29: 107–28.

King, R. D. and Morgan, R. (1980) *The Future of the Prison System*. Farnborough, Hants: Gower.

Kochan, N. (2002) 'Is the PFI About to Hit the Buffers?', *The Banker*, 2 August.

Kuhn, T. S. (1962) *The Structure of Scientific Revolutions*. Chicago: University of Chicago Press.

Labour Party (1997) *New Labour: Because Britain Deserves Better* (General Election Manifesto). London: Labour Party.

Lambie, A. (2002) 'When Colour Is an Issue', *Howard League Magazine*, 20 (1): 14.

Laming of Tewin, Lord (2000) *Modernising the Management of the Prison Service: An Independent Report by the Targeted Performance Initiative Working Group*. London: HM Prison Service.

Laming of Tewin, Lord (2003) *The Victoria Climbie Inquiry*. Available at: www.dh.gov.uk/ prod_consum_dh/groups/dh_digitalassets/documents/digitalasset/dh_110711.pdf (last accessed 18 December 2012).

Landau, S. F. (1981) 'Juveniles and the Police: Who Is Charged Immediately and Who Is Referred to the Juvenile Bureau?', *British Journal of Criminology*, 21: 27–46.

Landau, S. F. and Nathan, G. (1983) 'Selecting Delinquents for Cautioning in the London Metropolitan Area', *British Journal of Criminology*, 23: 128–49.

Lane, Lord (1993) *Report of the Committee on the Penalty for Homicide*. London: Prison Reform Trust.

Lash, S. and Urry, J. (1987) *The End of Organised Capitalism*. Cambridge: Polity.

Lash, S. and Urry. J. (1994) *Economies of Signs and Space*. London: Sage.

Law Commission (1994) *Binding Over*, Cm 2439. London: HMSO.

Learmont, J. (1995) *Review of Prison Service Security in England and Wales and the Escape from Parkhurst Prison on Tuesday 3rd January 1995*, Cm 3020. London: HMSO.

Leech, M. (1995) *The Prisoners' Handbook*. Oxford: Oxford University Press.

Leech, M. and Cheney, D. (1999) *The Prisons Handbook 2000* (4th edn). Winchester: Waterside Press.

Lennon, J. (2003) 'Penal Case Law', in M. Leech and J. Shepherd (eds), *Prisons Handbook 2003–4*. Manchester: MLA Press.

Levi, M. (1989) 'Fraudulent Justice? Sentencing the Business Criminal', in P. Carlen and D. Cook (eds), *Paying for Crime*. Milton Keynes: Open University Press, pp. 86–108.

Lewis, D. (1996) 'Prisons: The Case for Constitutional Reform', *Prison Report*, 35: 10–11.

Lewis, D. (1997) *Hidden Agendas: Politics, Law and Disorder*. London and New York: Hamish Hamilton/Penguin Books.

Liebling, A. (1992) *Suicides in Prison*. London: Routledge.

Liebling, A. (1997) 'Risk and Prison Suicide', in H. Kemshall and J. Pritchard (eds), *Good Practice in Risk Assessment and Risk Management.* London: Jessica Kingsley, pp. 188–205.

Liebling, A. (2001) 'Policy and Practice in the Management of Disruptive Prisoners: Incentives and Earned Privileges, the Spurr Report and Close Supervision Centres', in E. Clare and K. Bottomley (eds), *Evaluation of Close Supervision Centres*, Home Office Research Study No. 136. London: Home Office Research, Development and Statistics Directorate.

Liebling, A. (2006) 'Lessons from Prison Privatisation for Probation', in Hough et al. (2006) ch. 6.

Liebling, A. and Arnold, H. (2002) *Measuring the Quality of Prison Life*, Home Office Research Findings No. 174. London: Home Office.

Liebling, A. and Arnold, H. (2004) *Prisons and their Moral Performance: A Study of the Values, Quality and Prison Life.* Oxford: Oxford University Press.

Liebling, A. and Krarup, H. (1993) *Suicide Attempts and Self-Injury in Male Prisons.* Cambridge: Institute of Criminology.

Liebling, A. and Maruna, S. (eds) (2005) *The Effects of Imprisonment.* Cullompton: Willan Publishing.

Liebling, A., Muir, G., Rose, G. and Bottoms, A. (1999) *Incentives and Earned Privileges for Prisoners – An Evaluation*, Home Office Research Findings No. 87. London: Home Office Research and Statistics Directorate.

Lilly, J. R. and Knepper, P. (1990) 'The Corrections-Industrial Complex', *Prison Service Journal*, 87: 43–52.

Lilly, J. R. and Knepper, P. (1992) 'An International Perspective on the Privatization of Corrections', *Howard Journal of Criminal Justice*, 31: 174–91.

Lipsey, M. W. (1992) 'The Effect of Treatment on Juvenile Delinquents: Results from Meta-Analysis', in Friedrich Lösel, Doris Bender and Thomas Bliesener (eds), *Psychology and Law: International Perspectives.* Berlin: Walter de Gruyter, pp. 131–43.

Lipsey, M. W. (1995) 'What Do We Learn from 400 Research Studies on the Effectiveness of Treatment with Juvenile Delinquents?', in McGuire (1995) pp. 63–78.

Lipton, D., Martinson, R. and Wilks, J. (1975) *Effectiveness of Treatment Evaluation Studies.* New York: Praeger.

Livingstone, S. and Owen, T. (1993) *Prison Law.* Oxford: Oxford University Press.

Livingstone, S. and Owen, T. (1999) *Prison Law.* Oxford: Oxford University Press.

Livingstone, S., Owen, T. and Macdonald, A. (2003) *Prison Law* (3rd edn). Oxford: Oxford University Press.

Lloyd, C., Mair, G. and Hough, M. (1994) *Explaining Reconviction Rates: A Critical Analysis*, Home Office Research Study No. 136. London: HMSO.

Lloyd, C., Mair, G. and Hough, M. (1995) *Exploring Reconviction Rates: A Critical Analysis*, Home Office Research Study 136. London: Home Office.

Lodge, G. and Rogers, B. (2006) *Whitehall's Black Box: Accountability and Performance in the Senior Civil Service.* London: The Institute for Public Policy Reform.

Logan, C. (1990) *Private Prisons: Cons and Pros.* Oxford: Oxford University Press.

Lombroso, C. (1876) *L'Uomo Delinquente.* Milan: Hoepli.

Lukes, S. (1975) *Émile Durkheim: His Life and Work.* Harmondsworth: Penguin.

Lygo, R. (1991) *Management of the Prison Service: A Report.* London: Home Office.

McConville, S. (1981) *A History of English Prison Administration Volume 1, 1760–1877.* London: Routledge and Kegan Paul.

McDonald, D. C. (1994) 'Public Imprisonment by Private Means: The Re-emergence of Private Prisons in the United States, the United Kingdom and Australia', *British Journal of Criminology*, 34: 29–48.

McElrea, F. W. (1994) 'Justice in the Community: The New Zealand Experience', in J. Burnside and N. Baker (eds), *Relational Justice: Repairing the Breach*. Winchester: Waterside Press, ch. 7.

McEvoy, K. (2001) *Paramilitary Imprisonment in Northern Ireland: Resistance, Management and Release*. Oxford: Oxford University Press.

McGuire, J. (ed.) (1995) *What Works: Reducing Re-offending – Guidelines from Research and Practice*. London: Wiley.

McGuire, J. and Priestley, P. (1995) 'Reviewing 'What Works': Past, Present and Future', in McGuire (1995) pp. 3–34.

McIvor, G. (1992) *Sentenced to Serve*. Aldershot: Avebury.

McIvor, G. (1998) 'Pro-social Modeling and Legitimacy: Lessons from a Study of Community Service', in *Pro-social Modeling and Legitimacy: The Clarke Hall Day Conference*, University of Cambridge; cited in G. McIvor (2004), p. 176.

McIvor, G. (2004) 'Reparative and Restorative Approaches', in Bottoms et al. (2004), pp. 162–94.

McIvor, G. (2009) 'Therapeutic Jurisprudence and Procedural Justice in Scottish Drug Courts', *Criminology and Criminal Justice*, 9 (1): 29–49.

McKnight, J. (2009) 'Speaking Up for Probation', *Howard Journal*, 48 (4): 327–43.

McLaughlin, E., Muncie, J. and Hughes, G. (2001) 'The Permanent Revolution: New Labour, New Public Management and the Modernization of Criminal Justice', *Criminal Justice*, 1: 301–18.

McLennan, G. (1989) *Marxism, Pluralism and Beyond*. Cambridge: Polity Press.

McMahon, M. W. (1992) *The Persistent Prison? Rethinking Decarceration and Penal Reform*. Toronto: University of Toronto Press.

McNeill, F. (2006) 'A Desistance Paradigm for Offender Management', *Criminology and Criminal Justice*, 6 (1): 39–62.

Macpherson, W. (1999) *The Stephen Lawrence Inquiry: Report of an Inquiry by Sir William Macpherson*, Cm 4262-I. London: The Stationery Office.

MacRae, D. G. (1974) *Weber*. Glasgow: Fontana/Collins.

McSweeney, T., Stevens, A., Hunt, N. and Turnbull, P. J. (2008) 'Drug Testing and Court Review Hearings: Uses and Limitations', *Probation Journal*, 55 (1): 39–53.

McGuire, J. (2002) 'Criminal Sanctions Versus Psychologically-based Interventions with Offenders: A Comparative Empirical Analysis', *Psychology, Crime and Law*, 8: 183–208.

Maguire, M., Morgan, R. and Reiner, R. (eds) (2012) *The Oxford Handbook of Criminology* (5th edn). Oxford: Oxford University Press.

Maguire, M. and Pointing, J. (eds) (1988) *Victims of Crime: A New Deal*. Milton Keynes and Philadelphia: Open University Press.

Maguire, M., Vagg J. and Morgan R. (eds) (1985) *Accountability and Prisons: Opening Up a Closed World*. London: Tavistock.

Mair, G. (1986) 'Ethnic Minorities, Probation and the Magistrates' Courts', *British Journal of Criminology*, 26: 147–55.

Mair, G. (2004a) 'Diversionary and Non-supervisory Approaches to Dealing with Offenders', in A. Bottoms, S. Rex and G. Robinson (eds), *Alternatives to Prison: Options for an Insecure Society*. Cullompton: Willan Publishing, pp. 135–61.

Mair, G. (ed.) (2004b) *What Matters in Probation*. Cullompton: Willan.

Mair, G. (2005) 'Electronic Monitoring in England and Wales: Evidence-based or Not ?', *Criminology and Criminal Justice*, 5 (3): 257–77.

Mair, G. (2011) 'The Community Order in England and Wales: Policy and Practice', *Probation Journal*, 58 (3): 215–32.

Mair, G. and Burke, L. (2012) *Redemption, Rehabilitation and Risk Management: A History of Probation*. London: Routledge.

Mair, G., Cross, N. and Taylor, S. (2007) *The Use and Impact of the Community Order and the Suspended Sentence Order*. London: Centre for Crime and Justice Studies.

Mair, G., Cross, N. and Taylor, S. (2008) *The Community Order and the Suspended Sentence Order: The Views and Attitudes of Sentencers*. London: Centre for Crime and Justice Studies.

Mair, G. and Millings, M. (2011) *Doing Justice Locally: The North Liverpool Community Justice Centre*. London: Centre for Crime and Justice Studies.

Mair, G. and Mills, H. (2009) *The Community Order and the Suspended Sentence Order Three Years On: The Views and Experiences of Probation Officers and Offenders*. London: Centre for Crime and Justice Studies.

Maltz, M. (1984) *Recidivism*. London: Academic Press.

Marshall, S. (1997) *Control in Category C Prisons*, Home Office Research Findings No. 54. London: Home Office Research and Statistics Directorate.

Marshall, T. F. and Merry, S. (1990) *Crime and Accountability: Victim/Offender Mediation in Practice*. London: HMSO.

Martin, F. M. and Murray, K. (eds) (1982) *The Scottish Juvenile Justice System*. Edinburgh: Scottish Academic Press.

Martin, J. P. (1991) 'Parkhurst Special Unit: Some Aspects of Management', in R. Walmsley (ed.), *Managing Difficult Prisoners: the Parkhurst Special Unit*, Home Office Research Study No. 122. London: HMSO.

Martinson, R. (1974) 'What Works? – Questions and Answers about Prison Reform', *The Public Interest*, 35, Spring: 22–54.

Marx, K. (1977) *Selected Writings*, ed. D. McLellan. Oxford: Oxford University Press.

Mathiesen, T. (1974) *The Politics of Abolition: Essays in Political Action Theory*. Oxford: Martin Robertson.

Mathiesen, T. (1983) 'The Future of Control Systems – the Case of Norway', in D. Garland and P. Young (1983a), pp. 130–45 (first published in 1980 in *International Journal of the Sociology of Law*, 8: 149–64).

Mathiesen, T. (1990) *Prison on Trial*. London: Sage.

Mathiesen, T. (2000) *Prison on Trial*. Winchester: Waterside Press.

Matthews, R. (1979) 'Decarceration and the Fiscal Crisis', in B. Fine et al., *Capitalism and the Rule of Law: From Deviancy Theory to Marxism*. London: Hutchinson, pp. 100–17.

Matthews, R. (ed.) (1989) *Privatizing Criminal Justice*. London: Sage Publications.

Matthews, R. (1999) *Doing Time: An Introduction to the Sociology of Imprisonment*. Basingstoke: Macmillan.

Mattinson, J. and Mirrlees-Black, C. (2000) *Attitudes to Crime and Criminal Justice: Findings from the 1998 British Crime Survey*, Home Office Research Study No. 200. London: Home Office.

Mawby, R. (1977) 'Sexual Discrimination and the Law', *Probation Journal*, 24: 38–43.

May, C. (1999) *Exploring Reconviction Following Community Sentences: The Role of Social Factors*, Home Office Research Study 192. London: Home Office.

May, C. and Wadwell, J. (2001) *Enforcing Community Penalties: The Relationship Between Enforcement and Reconviction*, Home Office Research Findings 155. London: Home Office.

May, J. (1979) *Committee of Inquiry into the United Kingdom Prison Services: Report*, Cmnd 7673. London: HMSO.

Mayhew, P. (1994) *Findings from the International Crime Survey*, Home Office Research Findings No. 8. London: Home Office.

Mayhew, P. and van Kesteren, J. (2002) 'Cross-National Attitudes to Punishment', in J. V. Roberts and M. Hough (eds), *Changing Attitudes to Punishment: Public Opinion, Crime and Justice*. Cullompton: Willan, pp. 63–92.

Merton, R. K. (1968) *Social Theory and Social Structure* (enlarged edn). New York: Free Press.

Mills, H., Silvestri, A. and Grimshaw, R. with Silberhorn-Armantrading, F. (2010) *Prison and Probation Expenditure, 1999–2009*. London: Centre for Crime and Justice Studies.

Ministry of Justice (2007) *The Government's Response to the Report by Baroness Corston of a Review of Women with Particular Vulnerabilities in the Criminal Justice System*, Cm 7261. London: The Stationery Office.

Ministry of Justice (2008a) *Sentencing Statistics, 2007 England and Wales*. London: Ministry of Justice.

Ministry of Justice (2008b) *Delivering the Government Response to the Corston Report: A Progress Report on Meeting the Needs of Women with Particular Vulnerabilities in the Criminal Justice System*. London: Ministry of Justice.

Ministry of Justice (2009a) *Engaging Communities in Criminal Justice*. London: The Stationery Office.

Ministry of Justice (2009b) *The Future of the Parole Board*. London: Ministry of Justice.

Ministry of Justice (2010a) *Breaking the Cycle: Effective Punishment, Rehabilitation and Sentencing of Offenders*, Cm 7972. London: The Stationery Office.

Ministry of Justice (2010b) *Statistics on Women and the Criminal Justice System*. London: Ministry of Justice.

Ministry of Justice (2010c) *Offender Management Caseload Statistics 2009*. London: Ministry of Justice.

Ministry of Justice (2010d) *Criminal Statistics: England and Wales 2009.* London: Ministry of Justice.

Ministry of Justice (2011a) *Breaking the Cycle: Government Response*, Cm 8070. London: The Stationery Office.

Ministry of Justice (2011b) *2011 Compendium of Re-offending Statistics and Analysis*. London: Ministry of Justice.

Ministry of Justice (2011c) *Statistics on Race and the Criminal Justice System 2010*. London: Ministry of Justice.

Ministry of Justice (2011d) *Prison Population Projections 2011–2017 England and Wales*. London: Ministry of Justice.

Ministry of Justice (2011e) *Costs per Place and Costs per Prisoner by Individual Prison; National Offender Management Service Annual Report and Accounts 2010–11: Management Information Addendum*. London: Ministry of Justice.

Ministry of Justice (2012a) *Getting it Right for Victims and Witnesses*. London: The Stationery Office.

Ministry of Justice (2012b) *Offender Management Statistics Quarterly – October–December 2011*. London: Ministry of Justice.

Ministry of Justice (2012c) *Punishment and Reform: Effective Community Sentences*. Consultation Paper CP8/2012. London: The Stationery Office.

Ministry of Justice (2012d) *Youth Justice Statistics 2010/11 England and Wales*. London: Ministry of Justice.

Ministry of Justice (2012e) *Proven Re-offending Quarterly – October 2009 to September 2010*. London: Ministry of Justice.

Ministry of Justice (2012f) *Punishment and Reform: Effective Probation Services*. Consultation Paper CP7/2012. London: The Stationery Office.

Ministry of Justice (2012g) *Statistical Notice: Prisoners Working in Custody: Public Sector Prisons 2010/11–2011/12*. London: Ministry of Justice.

Ministry of Justice (2012h) *Offender Management Statistics Quarterly – January–March 2012*. London: Ministry of Justice.

Ministry of Justice (2012i) *National Offender Management Service Annual Report and Accounts 2011–12*. London: The Stationery Office.

Monahan, J. (1981) *Predicting Violent Behavior: An Assessment of Clinical Techniques*. London: Sage Publication.

Monbiot, G. (2002) 'Public Fraud Initiative', *Guardian*, 18 June.

Moore, L., Phillips, A. and Kostadintcheva, K. (2010) *Community Payback and Local Criminal Justice Engagement Initiatives: Public Perceptions and Awareness*, Research Summary 3/10. London: Ministry of Justice.

Moorthy, U., Cahalin, K. and Howard, P. (2004) *Ethnicity and Parole*, Home Office Research Findings No. 222. London: Home Office.

Morgan, R. (1985) 'Her Majesty's Inspectorate of Prisons', in Maguire, Vagg and Morgan (1985) pp. 106–23.

Morgan, R. (2003) 'Thinking about the Demand for Probation Services', *Probation Journal*, 50: 7.

Morgan, R. (2008) *Summary Justice: Fast but Fair?* London: Centre for Crime and Justice Studies.

MORI (2003) *Magistrates' Perceptions of the Probation Service*. London: MORI.

Morris, A. (2004) 'Youth Justice in New Zealand', in M. Tonry and A. N. Doob (eds), *Crime and Justice: A Review of Research*, Vol. 31. Chicago. University of Chicago Press, pp. 243–92.

Morris, A., Giller, H., Szwed, E. and Geach, H. (1980) *Justice for Children*. London: Macmillan.

Morris, A., Maxwell, G. M. and Robertson, J. P. (1993) 'Giving Victims a Voice: A New Zealand Experiment', *Howard Journal of Criminal Justice*, 32: 304–21.

Morris, N. (1974) *The Future of Imprisonment*. London: University of Chicago Press.

Morris, T. (1980) 'Penology and the Crimes of the Powerful', in Bottoms and Preston (1980) pp. 84–108.

Morris, T. (1989) *Crime and Criminal Justice Since 1945*. Oxford: Basil Blackwell.

Moxon, D. (1988) *Sentencing Practice in the Crown Court*, Home Office Research Study No. 103. London: HMSO.

Moynihan, D. P. (1992) 'Defining Deviance Down', *The American Scholar*, 62: 17–30.

Mulgan, R. (2000) '"Accountability": An Ever-Expanding Concept?', *Public Administration*, 78 (3): 555–73.

Muncie J. (1999) 'Institutionalized Intolerance: Youth Justice and the 1998 Crime and Disorder Act', *Critical Social Policy*, 19: 147–75.

Murphy, J. (1979) *Retribution, Justice and Therapy: Essays in the Philosophy of Law*. London: D. Reidel Publishing.

Murphy, J. (1992) *Retribution Reconsidered*. Dordrecht: Kluwer Academic Publishers.

NACRO (1986a) *Enforcement of the Law Relating to Social Security: Report of a NACRO Working Party*. London: NACRO.

NACRO (1986b) *Black People and the Criminal Justice System*. London: NACRO.

NACRO (1998) *Contrasting Judgements: Report on Two International Sentencing Seminars*. London: NACRO.

NACRO (2003) *A Failure of Justice: Reducing Child Imprisonment*. London: NACRO.

NACRO (2008) *Some Facts about Children and Young People Who Offend*. London: NACRO.

Nagel, I. (1981) 'Sex Differences in the Processing of Criminal Defendants', in A. Morris and L. Gelsthorpe (eds), *Women and Crime*. Cambridge: Institute of Criminology, pp. 104–24.

Nagel, I. H. and Hagan, J. (1983) 'Gender and Crime: Offence Patterns and Criminal Court Sanctions', in M. Tonry and N. Morris (eds), *Crime and Justice*, Vol. 4. Chicago: University of Chicago Press, pp. 91–144.

Narey, M. (1999) Speech to the Prison Service Conference at Harrogate, February.

Narey, M. (2001) Speech to the Prison Service Conference at Nottingham, February.

Nathan, S. (1994) 'Privatisation Factfile 7', *Prison Report*, 28: 11–18.

Nathan, S. (1995a) 'Privatisation Factfile 9', *Prison Report*, 30: 13–20.

Nathan, S. (1995b) 'Privatisation Factfile 10', *Prison Report*, 31: 13–20.

Nathan, S. (1999) 'Privatisation Factfile 28', *Prison Report*, 44: 13–16.

National Association of Probation Officers (2005) *Electronically Monitored Curfew Orders: Time for a Review*. London: NAPO.

National Association of Probation Officers (2010) *Short-term Jail Sentences – An Effective Alternative*. Available at: www.napo.org.uk/publications/Briefings.cfm (last accessed 18 December 2012).

National Audit Office (2003) *The Operational Performance of PFI Prisons: Report by the Comptroller and Auditor General*, HC Session 2002–3, 18 June. London: HMSO.

National Audit Office (2006) *The Electronic Monitoring of Adult Offenders*. London: The Stationery Office.

National Audit Office (2008) *National Probation Service: The Supervision of Community Orders in England and Wales*. London: The Stationery Office.

National Probation Service (2001) *A New Choreography: An Integrated Strategy for the National Probation Service*. London: Home Office.

Nellis, M. (2003) 'Electronic Monitoring and the Future of Probation', in W.-H. Chui and M. Nellis (eds), *Moving Probation Forward: Evidence, Arguments and Practice*. Harlow: Longman, pp. 245–58.

Nellis, M. (2004) 'Electronic Monitoring and the Community Supervision of Offenders', in Bottoms et al. (2004) pp. 224–47.

Nellis, M. (2005) 'Out of this World: The Advent of Satellite Tracking of Offenders in England and Wales', *Howard Journal of Criminal Justice*, 44 (2): 125–50.

Nellis, M. (2006) 'NOMS, Contestability and the Process of Technocratic Innovation', in Hough et al. (2006) pp. 49–68.

Nellis, M. (2007) 'Humanising Justice: The English Probation Service up to 1972', in L. Gelsthorpe and R. Morgan (eds), *Handbook of Probation*. Cullompton: Willan, pp. 25–58.

Nicholas, S., Povey, D., Walker, A. and Kershaw, C. (2005) *Crime In England and Wales 2004/2005*, Home Office Statistical Bulletin 11/05. London: Home Office.

NOMS (2006) *Population in Custody: Monthly Tables*, September, England and Wales. London: National Offender Management Service.

NOMS (2008) *Race Review 2008: Implementing Race Equality in Prisons – Five Years On*. London: National Offender Management Service.

Norris, C. (1995) 'Video Charts: Algorithmic Surveillance', *Criminal Justice Matters*, 20: 7–8.

Norris, C. (2003) 'From Personal to Digital: CCTV: The Panopticon and the Technological Mediation of Suspicion and Social Control', in D. Lyon (ed.), *Surveillance as Social Sorting: Privacy, Risk and Digital Discrimination*. London: Routledge, pp. 249–81.

Nuttall, C. P. with Barnard, E. E., Fowles, A. J., Frost, A., Hammond, W. H., Mayhew, P., Pease, K., Tarling, R. and Weatheritt, M. J. (1977), *Parole in England and Wales*, Home Office Research Study No. 38. London: HMSO.

O'Connor, D. (2000) 'Stop and Think', *Guardian Society*, 19 January.

O'Donnell, I. and Edgar, K. (1996) *Victimisation in Prisons*, Home Office Research Findings No. 37. London: Home Office Research and Statistics Directorate.

O'Donnell, I. and Edgar, K. (1998) 'Routine Victimisation in Prisons', *Howard Journal*, 37: 266–79.

Office for National Statistics (2012a) *Crime in England and Wales, Quarterly First Release to March 2012*. London: ONS. Available at: www.ons.gov.uk/ons/rel/crime-stats/crime-statistics/period-ending-march-2012/stb-crime-stats-end-march-2012.html (last accessed 18 December 2012).

Office for National Statistics (2012b) *Ethnicity and National Identity in England and Wales 2011.* London: ONS. Available at: www.ons.gov.uk/ons/rel/census/2011-census/key-statistics-for-local-authorities-in-england-and-wales/rpt-ethnicity.html (last accessed 18 December 2012).

Olkiewicz, E. (2003) 'The Evaluation of a Three Year Project on Electronic Monitoring in Sweden', in M. Mayer, R. Haverkamp and R. Levy (eds), *Will Electronic Monitoring Have a Future in Europe?* Freiburg: Max Planck Institute, pp. 77–80.

Osborn, S. G. and West, D. J. (1980) 'Do Young Delinquents Really Reform?', *Journal of Adolescence*, 3: 99–114.

Palmer, T. (1975) 'Martinson Revisited', *Journal of Research in Crime and Delinquency*, 12: 133–52.

Palumbo, D. J. (1986) 'Privatization and Corrections Policy', *Policy Studies Review*, 5: 598–605.

Park, I. (2000) *Review of Comparative Costs and Performance of Privately and Publicly Operated Prisons, 1998–9*, Home Office Statistical Bulletin, 6/00. London: Home Office.

Parker, H., Sumner, M. and Jarvis, G. (1989) *Unmasking the Magistrates: The 'Custody or Not' Decision in Sentencing Young Offenders.* Milton Keynes: Open University Press.

Parole Board for England and Wales (2012) *Annual Report and Accounts, 2011/12*, HC 401. London: The Stationery Office.

Parsons, T. (1937) *The Structure of Social Action.* New York: McGraw-Hill.

Parsons, T. (1951) *The Social System.* New York: Free Press.

Paternoster, R., Saltzman, L. E., Waldo, G. P. and Chiricos, T. G. (1983) 'Perceived Risk and Social Control: Do Sanctions Really Deter?', *Law and Society Review*, 17: 457–79.

Pearson, G. (1983) *Hooligan: A History of Respectable Fears.* London: Macmillan.

Pease, K. (1985) 'Community Service Orders', in N. Morris and M. Tonry (eds), *Criminal Justice: An Annual Review of Research*, Vol. 6. Chicago: University of Chicago Press, pp. 51–94.

Pease, K. (1992) 'Punitiveness and Prison Populations: An International Comparison', *Justice of the Peace*, 156: 405–8.

Pease, K. (1994) 'Cross-national Imprisonment Rates: Limitations of Method and Possible Conclusions', *British Journal of Criminology*, 34, Special Issue: 116–30.

Pease, K. and Wasik, M. (1987) *Sentencing Reform: Guidance or Guidelines?* Manchester: Manchester University Press.

Penal Affairs Consortium (1994) *The Mandatory Life Sentence.* London: Penal Affairs Consortium.

Penal Affairs Consortium (1995a) *Sentencing and Early Release: The Home Secretary's Proposals.* London: Penal Affairs Consortium.

Penal Affairs Consortium (1995b) *The 'Supermax' Option.* London: Penal Affairs Consortium.

Phillips, C. and Brown, D. (1998) *Entry into the Criminal Justice System: A Survey of Police Arrests and Their Outcomes*, Home Office Research Study No. 185. London: Home Office.

Piliavin, I. and Briar, S. (1964) 'Police Encounters with Juveniles', *American Journal of Sociology*, 70: 206–14.

Pitts, J. (1988) *The Politics of Juvenile Crime.* London: Sage.

Policy Exchange (2011) *Inside Job: Creating a Market for Real Work in Prison.* London: Policy Exchange.

Policy Exchange (2012) *Proceed with Caution: Use of Out-of-court Disposals in England and Wales.* London: Policy Exchange.

Pollak, O. (1961) *The Criminality of Women.* New York: A. S. Barnes.

Pratt, J. (1986) 'A Comparative Analysis of Two Different Systems of Juvenile Justice: Some Implications for England and Wales', *Howard Journal of Criminal Justice*, 25: 33–51.

Pratt, J. (2000) 'The Return of the Wheelbarrow Men: Or, The Arrival of Postmodern Penality', *British Journal of Criminology*, 40: 127–45.

Pratt, J., Brown, D., Hallsworth, S., Brown, M. and Morrison, W. (eds) (2005) *The New Punitiveness: Trends, Theories, Perspectives.* Cullompton: Willan.

Pratt, T. C. and Maahs, J. (1999) 'Are Private Prisons More Cost Effective than Public Prisons? A Meta Analysis of Evaluation Research Studies', *Crime and Delinquency*, 45 (3): 358–71.

Prior, P. J. (1985) *Report of the Committee on the Prison Disciplinary System*, Cmnd 9641-I. London: HMSO.

Prison Industries Review Team (2003) *Prison Industries: An Internal Review of the Strategic Oversight and Management of Public Sector Prison Industries in England and Wales*, report by the Prison Industries Review Team.

Prison Reform Trust (1991) *Management and Structure of the Prison Service: Woolf Briefing Paper No. 2.* London: Prison Reform Trust.

Prison Reform Trust (1996) 'Act of Immunity', *Prison Report*, 36: 3.

Prison Reform Trust (1997) *The Rising Toll of Prison Suicides.* London: Prison Reform Trust.

Prison Reform Trust (1998a) 'Boards of Visitors: Whistle-blowers or Governors' Patsies?', *Prison Report*, 44: 6–7.

Prison Reform Trust (1998b) *Prison Privatization Report International*, Volume 21. London: Prison Reform Trust.

Prison Reform Trust (1999) *Prison Privatization Report International*, Volume 27. London: Prison Reform Trust.

Prison Reform Trust (2005) *Private Punishment: Who Profits?* London: Prison Reform Trust.

Prison Reform Trust (2006a) 'Prisons Face Renewed Crowding Crisis', Prison Facts briefing 4.

Prison Reform Trust (2006b) *Bromley Briefings, Prison Factfile*, November. London: Prison Reform Trust.

Prison Reform Trust (2011) *Bromley Briefings Prison Factfile*, December. London: Prison Reform Trust.

Prison Reform Trust (2012) *Bromley Briefings Prison Factfile*, June. London: Prison Reform Trust.

Prisons and Probation Ombudsman (2012) *Annual Report 2011–2012.* London: Prisons and Probation Ombudsman.

Pruitt, C. R. and Wilson, J. Q. (1983) 'A Longitudinal Study of the Effect of Race on Sentencing', *Law and Society Review*, 17: 613–35.

Pugh, R. B. (1968) *Imprisonment in Medieval England.* Cambridge: Cambridge University Press.

Raher, S. (2002) 'Private Prisons and Public Money: Hidden Costs borne by Colorado's Taxpayers'. Available at: www.ccjrc.org/pdf/CostDataReport2002.pdf (last accessed 18 December 2012).

Ramsbotham, D. (2005) *Prisongate: The Shocking State of Britain's Prisons and the Need for Visionary Change.* London: The Free Press.

Raynor, P. and Vanstone, M. (2007) 'Towards a Correctional Service', in L. Gelsthorpe and R. Morgan (eds), *Handbook of Probation.* Cullompton: Willan, pp. 59–89.

Reed, J. and Lyne, M. (2000) 'Inpatient Care of Mentally Ill Prisoners: Results of a Year's Programme of Semistructured Inspections', *British Medical Journal*, 320: 1031–4.

Richardson, G. (1985) 'The Case for Prisoners' Rights', in Maguire, Vagg and Morgan (1985) pp. 19–28.

Riley, D. (1986) 'Sex Differences in Teenage Crime: The Role of Lifestyle', *Home Office Research Bulletin*, 20: 34–8.

Riley, D. and Shaw, M. (1985) *Parental Supervision and Juvenile Delinquency*, Home Office Research Study No. 83. London: HMSO.

Roberts, J. (2003) 'Evaluating the Pluses and Minuses of Custody: Sentencing Reform in England and Wales', *Howard Journal of Criminal Justice*, 42: 229–47.

Roberts, J. V. and Hough, M. (2005) *Understanding Public Attitudes to Criminal Justice*. Maidenhead: Open University Press.

Robinson, G. (1999) 'Risk-management and Rehabilitation in the Probation Service: Collision and Collusion', *Howard Journal of Criminal Justice*, 38 (4): 421–33.

Robinson, G. (2002) 'Exploring Risk Management in Probation Practice: Contemporary Developments in England and Wales', *Punishment & Society*, 4: 5–25.

Robinson, G. and Dignan, J. (2004) 'Sentence Management', in Bottoms et al. (2004) pp. 313–40.

Rothman, D. J. (1971) *The Discovery of the Asylum*. Boston and Toronto: Little, Brown.

Rottman, D. and Casey, P. (1999) 'Therapeutic Jurisprudence and the Emergence of Problem-Solving Courts', *National Institution of Justice Journal*, 240: 12–19.

Ruggles-Brise, E. (1921) *The English Prison System*. London: Macmillan.

Rusche, G. and Kirchheimer, O. (1939) *Punishment and Social Structure*. New York: Columbia University Press.

Rutherford, A. (1985) 'The New Generation of Prisons', *New Society*, 20 September, 73: 408–10.

Rutherford, A. (1986a) *Growing Out of Crime*. Harmondsworth: Penguin.

Rutherford, A. (1986b) *Prisons and the Process of Justice*. Oxford: Oxford University Press.

Rutherford, A. (1992) *Growing out of Crime: The New Era*. Winchester: Waterside Press.

Rutherford, A. (1993) *Criminal Justice and the Pursuit of Decency*. Oxford: Oxford University Press.

Rutter, M. and Giller, H. (1983) *Juvenile Delinquency: Trends and Perspectives*. Harmondsworth: Penguin.

Ryan, M. (1978) *The Acceptable Pressure Group*. Farnborough: Saxon House.

Sachdev, S. (2004) *Paying the Cost? Public Private Partnerships and the Public Sector Workforce*, A Catalyst Working Paper. London: Catalyst.

Sanders, A. (1985) 'Class Bias in Prosecutions', *Howard Journal of Criminal Justice*, 24: 176–97.

Sanders, A., Young, R. and Burton, M. (2010) *Criminal Justice* (4th edn). Oxford: Oxford University Press.

Scarman, L. (1986) *The Scarman Report*. Harmondsworth: Penguin.

Schur, E. M. (1973) *Radical Nonintervention: Rethinking the Delinquency Problem*. Englewood Cliffs, NJ: Prentice-Hall.

Scott, D. and Codd, H. (2010) *Controversial Issues in Prisons*. Maidenhead: Open University Press.

Scraton, P., Sim, J. and Skidmore, P. (1991) *Prisons Under Protest*. Milton Keynes: Open University Press.

Scull, A. (1977) *Decarceration: Community Treatment and the Deviant – A Radical View*. Englewood Cliffs, NJ: Prentice-Hall.

Scull, A. (1983) 'Community Corrections: Panacea, Progress or Pretence?' in Garland and Young (1983a) pp. 146–65.

Scull, A. (1984) *Decarceration: Community Treatment and the Deviant – A Radical View* (2nd edn). Cambridge: Polity Press.

Seddon, T. (2008) 'Dangerous Liaisons: Personality Disorder and the Politics of Risk', *Punishment & Society*, 10; 301–17.

Seear, N. and Player, E. (1986) *Women in the Penal System*. London: Howard League for Penal Reform.

Sennett, R. (1998) *The Corrosion of Character: The Personal Consequences of Work in the New Capitalism*. New York: W. W. Norton.

Sentencing Commission Working Group (2008) *Sentencing Guidelines in England and Wales: An Evolutionary Approach*. London: Ministry of Justice.

Sentencing Council (2010) *Consultation Stage Resource Assessment*. Available at: http://sentencingcouncil.judiciary.gov.uk/docs/Assault_Guideline_Resource_Assessment.pdf (last accessed 18 December 2012).

Sentencing Guidelines Council (2004a) *New Sentences, Criminal Justice Act 2003*. London: Sentencing Guidelines Council.

Sentencing Guidelines Council (2004b) *Overarching Principles: Seriousness*. London: Sentencing Guidelines Council.

Sentencing Guidelines Council (2008) *Magistrates Court Sentencing Guidelines: Definitive Guideline*. London: Sentencing Guidelines Council.

Sentencing Guidelines Council and Sentencing Advisory Panel (2006) *Annual Report 2005/06*. London: Sentencing Guidelines Council.

Shah, R. and Pease, K. (1992) 'Crime, Race and Reporting to the Police', *Howard Journal of Criminal Justice*, 31: 192–9.

Shapland, J. (1984) 'The Victim, the Criminal Justice System and Compensation', *British Journal of Criminology*, 24: 131–49.

Shapland, J. (1988) 'Fiefs and Peasants: Accomplishing Change for Victims in the Criminal Justice System', in Maguire and Pointing (1988) pp. 187–94.

Shapland, J., Atkinson, A., Atkinson, H., Chapman, B., Colledge, E., Dignan, J., Howes, M., Johnstone, J., Robinson, G. and Sorsby, A. (2006) *Restorative Justice in Practice: The Second Report from the Evaluation of Three Schemes*. Sheffield: Centre for Criminological Research.

Shapland, J., Atkinson, A., Atkinson, H., Chapman, B., Dignan, J., Howes, M., Johnstone, J., Robinson, G. and Sorsby, A. (2007) *Restorative Justice: The Views of Victims and Offenders*, Ministry of Justice Research Series 3/07. London: Ministry of Justice.

Shapland, J., Atkinson, A., Atkinson, H., Dignan, J., Edwards, J., Hibbert, J., Howes, M., Johnstone, J., Robinson, G. and Sorsby, A. (2008) *Does Restorative Justice Affect Reconviction? The Fourth Report from the Evaluation of Three Schemes*, Ministry of Justice Research Series 10.08. London: Ministry of Justice.

Shapland, J., Atkinson, A., Colledge, E., Dignan, J., Howes, M., Johnstone, J., Pennant, R., Robinson, G. and Sorsby, A. (2004) *Implementing Restorative Justice Schemes (Crime Reduction Programme). A Report on the First Year*, Home Office Online Report 32/04. London: Home Office.

Shapland, J., Willmore, J. and Duff, P. (1985) *Victims in the Criminal Justice System*. Aldershot: Gower.

Sharp, C. and Budd, T. (2003) *Minority Ethnic Groups and Crime: Findings from the Offending, Crime and Justice Survey 2003* (2nd edn). Home Office Online Report 33/05. London: Home Office.

Shaw, S. (1992a) 'Prisons', in E. Stockdale and S. Casale (eds), *Criminal Justice under Stress*. London: Blackstone, pp. 160–78.

Shaw, S. (1992b) 'The Short History of Prison Privatization', *Prison Service Journal*, 87: 30–2.

Sheridan, A. (1980) *Michel Foucault: The Will to Truth*. London: Tavistock.

Shichor, D (1995) *Prisons for Profit: Private Prisons/Public Concerns*. Thousand Oaks: Sage.

Shute, S. (2004) '50th Anniversary Article: Punishing Murderers: Release Procedures and the "Tariff" 1952–2004', *Criminal Law Review*, 873–95.

Shute, S. (2007) *Satellite Tracking of Offenders: A Study of the Pilots in England and Wales*, Research Summary 4. London: Ministry of Justice.

Shute, S., Hood, R. and Seemungal, F. (2005) *A Fair Hearing? Ethnic Minorities in the Criminal Courts*. Devon: Willan.

Silvestri, A. (2009) *Partners or Prisoners? Voluntary Sector Independence in the World of Commissioning and Contestability*. London: Centre for Crime and Justice Studies.

Sim, J. (1992) '"When You Ain't Got Nothing You Got Nothing to Lose": The Peterhead Rebellion, the State and the Case for Prison Abolition', in K. Bottomley, T. Fowles and R. Reiner (eds), *Criminal Justice: Theory and Practice*. London: British Society of Criminology, pp. 273–300.

Sim, J. (1994) 'The Abolitionist Approach: A British Perspective', in Duff et al. (1994) pp. 263–84.

Simon, J. (1993) *Poor Discipline: Parole and the Social Control of the Underclass, 1890–1990*. Chicago: University of Chicago Press.

Singleton, N., Meltzer, H. and Gatward, R. with Coid, J. and Deasy, D. (1998) *Psychiatric Morbidity Among Prisoners in England and Wales*. London: The Stationery Office.

Skogan, W. G. (1990) *The Police and Public in England and Wales: A British Crime Survey Report*, Home Office Research Study No. 117. London: HMSO.

Skogan, W. G. (1995) *Policing and the Public in England and Wales: Findings from the 1994 British Crime Survey*, Home Office Research Findings No. 28. London: Home Office.

Smellie, E. and Crow, I. (1991) *Black People's Experience of Criminal Justice*. London: NACRO.

Smith, D. J. and Gray, J. (1983) *Police and People in London. IV: The Police in Action*. London: Policy Studies Institute.

Smith, S. (1982) *Race and Crime Statistics*. London: Board for Social Responsibility, Church of England.

Social Exclusion Unit (2002) *Reducing Re-offending by Ex-prisoners*. London: Social Exclusion Unit.

Softley, P. (1978) *Fines in Magistrates' Courts*, Home Office Research Study No. 46. London: HMSO.

Southgate, P. and Ekblom, P. (1986) *Police–Public Encounters*, Home Office Research Study No. 90. London: HMSO.

Sparks, J. R. and Bottoms, A. E. B. (1995) 'Legitimacy and Order in Prisons', *British Journal of Sociology*, 46: 45–62.

Sparks, J. R., Bottoms, A. E. B. and Hay, W. (1996) *Prisons and the Problem of Order*. Oxford: Clarendon Press.

Spohn, C., Gruhl, J. and Welch, S. (1981–82) 'The Effect of Race on Sentencing: A Re-examination of an Unsettled Question', *Law and Society Review*, 16: 71–88.

Stern, V. (2005) *Prisons and Their Communities: Testing a New Approach: An Account of the Restorative Prison Project 2000–2004*. London: International Centre for Prison Studies.

Stevens, P. and Willis, C. F. (1979) *Race, Crime and Arrests*, Home Office Research Study No. 58. London: HMSO.

Stolzenberg, L. and D'Alessio, S. J. (1997) '"Three Strikes and You're Out": The Impact of California's New Mandatory Sentencing Law on Serious Crime Rates', *Crime & Delinquency*, 43: 457–69.

Straw, J. and Michael, A. (1996) *Tackling Youth Crime, Reforming Youth Justice: A Consultation Paper on an Agenda for Change*. London: Labour Party.

Summerfield, A. (2011) *Children and Young People in Custody 2010–11: An Analysis of the Experiences of 15–18-year-olds in Prison*. London: HM Inspectorate of Prisons and Youth Justice Board.

Sutherland, E. H. (1956) 'Crime of Corporations', in A. Cohen, A. Lindesmith and K. Schuessler (eds), *The Sutherland Papers*. Bloomington IN: Indiana University Press, pp. 78–96.

Tarling, R. (1993) *Analysing Offending: Data, Models and Interpretations*. London: HMSO.

Tarling, R., Moxon, D. and Jones, P. (1985) 'Sentencing of Adults and Juveniles in Magistrates' Courts', in D. Moxon (ed.), *Managing Criminal Justice*. London: HMSO, pp. 159–74.

Taylor, I., Walton, P. and Young, J. (1973) *The New Criminology: For a Social Theory of Deviance*. London: Routledge and Kegan Paul.

Taylor, L., Lacey, R. and Bracken, D. (1979) *In Whose Best Interests? The Unjust Treatment of Children in Courts and Institutions*. London: Cobden Trust/MIND.

Taylor, R. (2000) *A Seven-Year Reconviction Study of HMP Grendon Therapeutic Community*, Home Office Research Findings No. 115. London: Home Office Research and Statistics Directorate.

Thomas, J. E. (1972) *The English Prison Officer Since 1850*. London: Routledge and Kegan Paul.

Thomas, J. E. and Pooley, R. (1980) *The Exploding Prison: Prison Riots and the Case of Hull*. London: Junction Books.

Thompson, E. P. (1977) *Whigs and Hunters: The Origin of the Black Act*. Harmondsworth: Penguin.

Thompson, E. P. (1978) *The Poverty of Theory and Other Essays*. London: Merlin Press.

Thorpe, D. H., Smith, D., Green, C. J. and Paley, J. G. (1980) *Out of Care: The Community Support of Juvenile Offenders*. London: George Allen and Unwin.

Tombs, S. and Whyte, D. (2008) *A Crisis of Enforcement*. London: Centre for Crime and Justice Studies, King's College.

Tonry, M. and Farrington, D. P. (eds) (1995) *Building a Safer Society: Strategic Approaches to Crime Prevention*. Chicago: University of Chicago Press.

Törnudd, P. (1993) *Fifteen Years of Decreasing Prisoner Rates in Finland*. Helsinki: National Research Institute of Legal Policy.

Travis, A. (1993) 'Ministers' Tough Rhetoric to Blame for Overcrowding, Say Prison Reformers', *Guardian*, 8 September.

Travis, A. (2003) 'Courts Send Record Numbers to Prison', *Guardian*, 29 December.

Tremblay, R. E. and Craig, W. M. (1995) 'Developmental Crime Prevention', in Tonry and Farrington (1995) pp. 151–234.

Tyler, T. R. (1990) *Why People Obey the Law*. New Haven: Yale University Press.

Underdown, A. (2001) 'Making "What Works" Work: Challenges in the Delivery of Community Penalties', in A. E. Bottoms, L. Gelsthorpe and S. Rex (eds), *Community Penalties: Change and Challenges*. Cullompton: Willan Publishing, pp. 117–25.

United States General Accounting Office (1991) *Private Prisons*. Washington DC: US Government Printing Office.

United States General Accounting Office (1996) *Private and Public Prisons: Studies Comparing Operational Costs and/or Quality of Service*. Reference Number GAO/GGD-96–198. Gaithersburg MD: US General Accounting Office.

Vagg, J. (1991) 'Correcting Manifest Wrongs: Prison Grievance and Inspection Procedures in England and Wales, France, Germany and the Netherlands' in J. Muncie and R. Sparks (eds), *Imprisonment: European Perspectives*. Hemel Hempstead: Harvester Wheatsheaf, pp. 146–65.

van Dijk, J. J. M. and Mayhew, P. (1992) *Criminal Victimization in the Industrialized World: Key Findings of the 1989 and 1992 International Crime Surveys*. The Hague: Directorate for Crime Prevention, Ministry of Justice.

van Kesteren, J., Mayhew, P. and Nieuwbeerta, P. (2001) *Criminal Victimisation in Seventeen Industrialised Countries: Key Findings from the 2000 International Crime Victims Survey*. The Hague: WODC.

Vanstone, M. (2004) *Supervising Offenders in the Community: A History of Probation Theory and Practice*. Aldershot: Ashgate.

Vennard, J., Sugg, D. and Hedderman, C. (1997) *Changing Offenders' Attitudes and Behaviour: What Works?* Home Office Research Study No. 171. London: Home Office.

von Hirsch, A. (1976) *Doing Justice: The Choice of Punishments*, Report of the Committee for the Study of Incarceration. New York: Hill and Wang.

von Hirsch, A. (1986) *Past or Future Crimes: Deservedness and Dangerousness in the Sentencing of Criminals*. Manchester: Manchester University Press.

von Hirsch, A. (1993) *Censure and Sanctions*. Oxford: Clarendon Press.

von Hirsch, A., Bottoms, A. E., Burney, E. and Wikström, P.-O. (1999) *Criminal Deterrence and Sentence Severity: An Analysis of Recent Research*. Oxford: Hart Publishing.

Wacquant, L. (2009) *Punishing the Poor: The Neoliberal Government of Social Insecurity*. London: Duke University Press.

Walgrave, L. (1999) 'Community Service as a Cornerstone of a Systemic Restorative Response to (Juvenile) Crime', in G. Bazemore and L. Walgrave (eds), *Restorative Juvenile Justice: Repairing the Harm of Youth Crime*. Monsey, NY: Criminal Justice Press, pp. 129–54.

Walker, N. (1972) *Sentencing in a Rational Society*. Harmondsworth: Penguin.

Walker, N. (1981) 'Feminists' Extravaganzas', *Criminal Law Review*, 379–86.

Walker, N. and Marsh, C. (1984) 'Do Sentences Affect Public Disapproval?', *British Journal of Criminology*, 24: 27–48.

Walmsley, R. (2005) *World Prison Population List* (6th edn). London: International Centre for Prison Studies, King's College.

Walmsley, R., Howard, L. and White, S. (1992) *The National Prison Survey 1991: Main Findings*, Home Office Research Study No. 128. London: HMSO.

Walters, I. (2002) *Evaluation of the National Roll-Out of Curfew Orders*. Home Office Online Report 15/02. London: Home Office.

Ward, T. and Maruna, S. (2007) *Rehabilitation: Beyond the Risk Paradigm*. London: Routledge.

Wasik, M. (2004a) 'What Guides Sentencing Decisions?', in Bottoms et al. (2004) pp. 290–312.

Wasik, M. (2004b) 'Sentencing Guidelines: Past, Present and Future', in M. Freeman (ed.), *Current Legal Problems 2003*. Oxford: Oxford University Press, pp. 239–64.

Watson, D., Boucherat, J. and Davis, G. (1989) 'Reparation for Retributivists', in M. Wright and B. Galaway (eds), *Mediation and Criminal Justice: Victims, Offenders an Community*. London: Sage, pp. 212–28.

Weber, M. (1930) *The Protestant Ethic and the Spirit of Capitalism*. London: George Allen and Unwin.

Weber, M. (1968) *Economy and Society*. New York: Bedminster Press.

West, D. J. (1982) *Delinquency: Its Roots, Careers and Prospects*. London: Heinemann.

Western, B. and Beckett, K. (1999) 'How Unregulated is the US Labor Market? The Penal System as Labor Market Institution', *American Journal of Sociology*, 104: 1030–60.

Whatmore, P.B. (1987) 'Barlinnie Special Unit: An Insider's View', in A. E. Bottoms and R. Light (eds), *Problems of Long-Term Imprisonment*. Aldershot: Gower, pp. 249–60.

Whitehead, P. and Statham, R. (2006) *The History of Probation: Politics, Power and Cultural Change 1876–2005*. Crayford: Shaw and Sons.

Willcock, H. D. and Stokes, J. (1968) *Deterrents and Incentives to Crime among Boys and Young Men Aged 15–21 Years*. London: HMSO.

Wilson, D. (2006) 'The Case for Penal Abolition in England and Wales', lecture delivered to the Public Management and Policy Association, 17 February.

Windlesham, D. (1993) *Responses to Crime, Volume 2: Penal Policy in the Making*. Oxford: Clarendon Press.

Wood, M. (2003) *Victimisation of Young People: Findings from Crime and Justice Survey 2003*, Home Office Research Findings No. 246. London: Home Office.

Woodbridge, J. (1999) *Review of Comparative Costs and Performance of Privately and Publicly Operated Prisons, 1997–8*, Home Office Statistical Bulletin, 13/99. London: Home Office.

Woodcock, J. (1994) *The Escape from Whitemoor Prison on Friday 9th September 1994 (The Woodcock Enquiry)*, Cm 2741. London: HMSO.

Woolf, H. and Tumim, S. (1991) *Prison Disturbances April 1990*, Cm 1456. London: HMSO.

Wozniak, E. and McAllister, D. (1991) 'Facilities, Standards and Change in the Scottish Prison Service: The Prison Survey 1990/91', paper presented at the British Criminology Conference, University of York, July.

Wynne, J. (1996) 'Leeds Mediation and Reparation Service: Ten Years' Experience with Victim–Offender Mediation', in B. Galaway and J. Hudson (eds), *Restorative Justice: International Perspectives*. Monsey, NY: Criminal Justice Press and Amsterdam: Kugler Publications, pp. 445–62.

Young, P. (1987) *The Prison Cell*. London: Adam Smith Institute.

Youth Justice Board (2006) *Anti-Social Behaviour Orders.* London: Youth Justice Board.

Youth Justice Board (2011) *Annual Report and Accounts 2010/11*. London: Youth Justice Board.

Youth Justice Board (2012) *Annual Report and Accounts 2011/12*. London: Youth Justice Board.

Zehr, H. (1985) *Retributive Justice, Restorative Justice*. Elkhart, IN: Mennonite Central Committee, US Office of Criminal Justice.

Zimring, F. E., Hawkins, G. and Kamin, S. (2001) *Punishment and Democracy: Three Strikes and You're Out in California.* Oxford: Oxford University Press.

Index

Glossary entries explaining a term are marked with an asterisk.
Significant information included in the notes is indexed in the form 258 (nn40, 41), ie notes 40 and 41 on page 258.

Custody, Care and Justice (White Paper) 197–8
'custody plus' 120, 142, 189, 312–3, 320–1, 329*

dangerous offenders 27, 38, 59, 79, 172–3, 189, 196,
    230, 244–5, 248–9, 254–5, 312, 322
  see also serious offences and offenders; violence
Darwin, Charles 52
day fines *see* fines
decarceration 152–5, 162–4, 166, 263, 330*
  Canada 154, 164
  England and Wales 154–5, 164
  Netherlands 154, 164
  thesis 152–3
decriminalization 262
de la Motta, K. 292–3
Denman Report (2001) 291
Denning, Lord 44–5
denunciation 33, 41, 44–6, 54, 56–8, 90, 101, 113,
    122, 165, 316, 330*
  expressive 45, 58
  instrumental 44, 58
depenalization 262
detention and training orders (DTOs) 4, 260, 267,
    272, 277–8, 330*
detention centres (young offenders) 34, 265, 307, 330*
detention in a young offender institution 4, 278
determinism 52, 67
  see also economic determinism; free will; positivism
deterrence 7, 33–7, 38, 42, 44, 49–50, 52, 54–8,
    60, 90, 101, 113, 121–2, 147, 159, 165, 169,
    316, 330*
  general 34–6, 44, 58
  individual 34
discharges 4–5, 91, 113–4, 120–1, 128,
    138, 156, 165, 274, 276, 287, 298,
    300, 301, 330*
  absolute 4, 113–4, 120–1, 274, 330*
  conditional 4–5, 113–4, 120–1, 128,
    156, 165, 274, 276, 330*
disciplinary procedures in prisons *see* prisons,
    disciplinary procedures
discipline 25, 52, 68–9, 130, 156–63, 330*
  concept of 68, 330*
  dispersal thesis *see* dispersal of discipline thesis
  see also prison discipline
discourse 39, 68, 79, 86, 155, 163–4,
    166–7, 322
  replacement 163–4, 166–7, 322
discretion in the criminal justice system viii, 8, 49, 51,
    53–4, 90, 92–101, 102–11, 119, 126, 143, 145,
    151, 163, 220–1, 225, 233–43, 245–9, 253–4,
    260, 279, 282–4, 314, 320, 324
  in sentencing *see* sentencing, judicial discretion
dispersal of discipline thesis 156–63
dispersal orders 271
dispersal prisons *see* prisons,
    dispersal prisons
disqualification from driving 36–7, 93,
    115, 165
distribution of punishment, principles of
    33, 45, 58–9
district judges 4, 88, 243
diversion 126–7, 164, 262–7, 270, 273, 275, 307,
    319–20, 322, 330*
doli incapax 267, 270, 330*
Doncaster Prison 41, 181, 190, 203
Dovegate Prison 201, 230

Dowds, Lisanne 300
drug abuse, drug offences 3, 19, 37, 38, 93, 101, 104,
    175, 186, 193, 201, 211, 227, 230, 242, 287, 289,
    292, 297, 300, 302, 313, 320
drug courts 118, 147, 320
drug rehabilitation requirements 114, 116, 118, 147
drug treatment and testing orders 121
due process 49, 51–5, 124, 234–5, 238, 260, 330*
Duff, Antony 45, 47, 135, 166
Durham Prison 215
Durkheim, Émile 44, 61, 71–4, 75, 77, 83, 172,
    256, 304
Dworkin, Ronald 57
  early release 5, 6, 19, 23, 49, 86, 102, 233–55, 282,
    310–1, 313, 320, 330*administrative benefits
    233, 235
    automatic 234–6, 238, 240–5, 249, 254, 307
    see also remission discretionary 235–43,
      245–55, 320
      see also home detention curfew; parole
    effect on crisis of penal resources 249
    effect on prison numbers 248–9
    end of custody licence 240–1, 311, 313, 331*
    extended sentences 244–5
    fixed-term sentences 241–4
    legitimacy defects 233–5, 237, 248, 253
    licence conditions 241, 243, 253
    life imprisonment and imprisonment for public
      protection 245–9
      recall to prison 86, 132, 137, 145, 236, 239–40,
        243–4, 249–53, 320 *see also* home detention
        curfew; parole; remission

Eaton, Mary 301
economic determinism 63–8, 153–4, 331*
economics 26, 29–31, 36, 61–83, 107, 132, 149,
    152–5, 177–85, 314, 317, 325
  see also economic determinism; political economy
Edwards, Christopher 200, 225
'either way' offences 3–4, 85, 331*
electronic monitoring ('tagging') 5, 118–9, 130, 136–9,
    151, 156, 158, 160, 163, 165–6, 235, 239, 242,
    274, 277, 331*
  involvement of private security firms
    137–8, 151
  satellite tracking 158
  Sweden 138, 163
  usage 138
  young offenders 274, 277
  see also home detention curfew
end of custody licence 240–1, 311, 313, 331*
Engels, Friedrich 65, 76
Enlightenment 50, 62
Equality Act 2010 283
escapes from prison *see* prisons, escapes from
Europe 9, 14–5, 36, 49, 62, 80, 86, 89, 171, 181, 184,
    234, 246, 257, 270, 319
  prison populations 14–5, 36, 80, 86, 246, 257
  sentencing 80, 86, 257
European Committee for the Prevention of Torture
    and Inhuman or Degrading Treatment (CPT)
    199, 202, 204, 205, 222
European Convention on Human Rights 5, 204, 208,
    214, 221, 225, 246–7, 252
  prison conditions 204, 214
  right to a fair trial 246–7
  right to life 225

reform (of offenders) *cont.*
   see also rehabilitation, rehabilitative ideal;
      transformation of offenders; treatment model
reform (of penal system, penal reformers) xii, 10, 30,
      49–50, 103–4, 108–9, 111–2, 122, 125–6, 135,
      149–50, 162, 165, 178, 186, 188, 192–3, 198,
      211, 219, 221–3, 229, 233–4, 238–40, 254–6,
      260–1, 264, 266, 268–9, 305, 308–9, 314–6,
      320, 322–4
rehabilitation 6, 23, 28, 33, 38–40, 45, 79, 90, 101,
      114, 116–8, 121, 130–1, 133–4, 147, 150, 154,
      166, 177, 190, 218, 229, 235, 248, 251, 265, 275,
      279, 303, 307, 316, 321–2, 326, 337*
   see also community rehabilitation orders, reform (of
      offenders), youth rehabilitation orders
'rehabilitation revolution' 40–1, 55–6, 106, 133, 144,
      149, 189–90, 313–6, 337*
rehabilitation programmes, young offenders 275
rehabilitative ideal 38–9, 52–3, 70, 163–4, 303,
      306, 337*
   collapse of 23, 25, 29–31, 39, 53, 129, 165,
      170, 307
rehabilitative optimism *see* rehabilitative ideal
Reid, John 123, 142, 189, 252, 313
reintegration, reintegrative shaming 6, 46, 48, 57, 125,
      135, 148, 166, 189, 208, 317, 321–2, 337*
relative autonomy 66, 77
remand centres *see* prisons, remand centres
remand decisions 13, 85, 106, 279, 286, 305, 314–5,
      318–9, 337*
remand prisoners 1, 3, 15, 85, 173, 175–6, 196, 199,
      202, 205, 291, 298
   contribution to the penal crisis 13, 15, 20, 85,
      175–6, 199, 205, 291, 298, 318
   harmful consequences of imprisonment 85, 175,
      205, 302
   overcrowding 13, 15, 20, 85, 175–6, 205
   prison conditions 85, 175, 205
   and privatization 175–6
   suicides 85, 199
   remission 235–6, 238, 338*
   see also early release, automatic
reoffending 5, 28, 36–7, 39–41, 48, 100, 108, 130,
      133, 138, 144, 149, 168, 170, 174–5, 188, 192–3,
      203, 231, 250, 254, 258, 262, 265, 274, 279, 313
   Blantyre House 231
   community penalties 133, 144, 149
   community service 135
   fine 122
   Grendon Underwood 230
   imprisonment 168, 170, 174–5, 188
   rates 39, 41, 108, 133, 254, 258, 313
   young offenders 258, 262, 265, 274, 279
   see also persistent offenders, rehabilitation
      revolution
reparation 6, 8, 32–3, 47–8, 56–7, 59, 71, 90, 101,
      114, 124–8, 134–5, 148, 159, 161, 164, 166,
      263–4, 267, 175–8, 281, 309, 311, 317,
      321–2, 338*
   see also reparation orders, young offenders;
      reparative penalties; restorative justice
reparation orders, young offenders 263–4, 267, 274,
      277, 338*
reparative penalties 48, 117, 122, 126–8,
      134–5, 322
Repressive State Apparatus (RSAs) 67, 70, 304
reprimands, young offenders 3, 274–5, 284, 338*

requalification 161
resources *see* penal resources; crisis, penal, crisis of
      (penal) resources
Respect Agenda 271, 312
responsibilization 266–7, 338*
restorative justice 6, 28, 46–9, 55–7, 59, 117, 126–8,
      134–5, 148, 166, 180, 229, 259, 263–4, 266–7,
      276, 279–81, 311, 313–4, 316–7, 321–3,
      325–6, 338*
   as a 'new paradigm' 46–7, 125, 127, 264, 322, 325
   forms of 47, 126, 135, 148, 166, 276
   young offenders 47, 128, 259, 263–4, 266–7, 276,
      279–81
   see also conferencing; reparation; reparative
      penalties; victim offender mediation and
      reparation schemes
retribution *see* retributivism
retribution in distribution 58
retributivism 33, 38, 41–5, 50–2, 55–9, 79, 101, 110, 338*
   limiting 43–4, 59, 107
   modern 43
Rickwood, Adam 258
rights *see* human rights
riots *see* prisons, riots
risk assessment 79, 242, 293, 311
risk management 132
Roberts, Harry 250.
Royal Commission on Capital Punishment (1953) 44
Rusche, Georg 63–4
Rutherford, Andrew 6, 217, 261–2, 324
Rye Hill Prison 201

Salford Prison (officially known as 'HMP Forest
      Bank') 176
sanctions, external and internal 166
Sarjeant, Marcus 44
Saunders, Ernest 286
Scarman, Lord 21, 289–90
Scotland 1, 14, 108, 147–8, 204, 215, 229,
      260, 270, 318, 320–1
   age of criminal responsibility 270
   children's hearings system 270
   juvenile justice system 260
   prison population 14
   prisons 204, 215, 229, 318
Scull, Andrew 64, 152–6, 162
secrecy *see* crisis, penal, crisis of visibility; prisons,
      secrecy
Secretary of State for Justice 5, 7, 12–3, 56, 84, 100,
      106, 109, 128, 133, 147, 162, 189–90, 192, 220,
      240–3, 250, 252, 268, 314–5, 317, 333*
secure children's homes 173, 258, 279, 338*
secure training centres 173, 258, 338*
Securicor Ltd 175
security *see* prisons, escapes from, security; crisis, penal,
      crisis of containment
security classification *see* Categories A to D
Seear, Nancy 304
semi-custodial sentences (and quasi-custodial
      sentences) 112, 119–20, 142
semi-mandatory sentences 4, 93–4, 104, 108
sentence management 112, 140, 146–7, 338*
sentencers 4, 13, 78, 86–99, 101, 103, 107–11, 113,
      117, 122–3, 125, 129, 131–4, 140, 143, 145–7,
      163–4, 234, 253, 262, 282, 286, 292, 294, 296,
      298, 300, 307, 310, 324
   see also judges; magistrates

sentences 4–5, 12–3, 15, 18–20, 33, 37–8, 43, 49,
    53–4, 59, 84–7, 89, 91–8, 100–9, 113–4, 116,
    119–22, 128, 131–3, 135, 139, 142, 144–5,
    147–8, 161–3, 173, 195–6, 199, 213, 233,
    236–41, 244–6, 248–53, 260, 263, 274, 276–8,
    276, 286–7, 291–2, 298–301, 304–5, 307–8,
    310–5, 319–21, 323–4, 338*
    see also custodial sentences; extended sentences;
        fixed-term sentences, imprisonment;
        indeterminate sentences; mandatory sentences;
        maximum sentences; non-custodial penalties;
        seamless sentences; semi-custodial sentences;
        semi-mandatory sentences; sentencing;
        suspended sentences; targeting; 'three strikes
        and you're out' sentences
sentencing 4–6, 12, 29, 35–6, 43, 47, 51, 54, 59, 75,
    84–111, 113–9, 121–5, 128, 134, 141–3, 145,
    147, 151, 163, 174, 233–5, 238–40, 244, 253–5,
    260, 276–9, 282, 286–7, 291–3, 298–301, 307,
    309–10, 312–4, 318–9, 324
    aims of 47, 54, 90, 96–7, 101, 103–4, 113, 122,
        124, 265
    see also philosophy of punishment
    class bias 282–3, 286–7
    culture 88–9, 108, 111, 146, 282
    discount 106, 314
    framework 90, 99, 101–5, 110, 112–4, 116, 121,
        143, 244, 309, 319
    gender bias 282–3, 296, 298–302
    geographical variation 87, 282
    guidelines 75, 87–8, 90, 92, 94–102, 105–6, 108–11,
        117, 123–4, 141, 145, 233, 246–7, 287, 311–2,
        319–20, 324, 338*
    see also Minnesota Sentencing Guidelines Grid
    inconsistency 43, 87–8, 99, 108, 110, 318–9
    judicial discretion 8, 49, 51, 90, 92–6, 98, 101–2,
        104–5, 108–11, 119, 143, 163, 233, 282,
        314, 324
    see also sentencing, guidelines
    philosophy 122
    policy 102, 106
    purposes, *see* sentencing, aims of racial bias 282–3,
        291–5 'ratcheting up' 84, 91, 108–9, 123–4.
        131, 133, 162, 310, 312
    rational approach 107–11
    system 92, 101, 282
    young offenders 260, 276–9
    see also sentences; targeting
Sentencing Advisory Panel (SAP) 98–9, 105, 338*
Sentencing Commission 99
Sentencing Council 99–101, 105, 109–11, 124, 319,
    324, 338*
Sentencing Guidelines Council (SGC) 98–9, 102, 105,
    110, 145, 339*
Serco 41, 177, 190
serious offences and offenders 3, 27, 41, 73–4, 94, 103,
    105, 107, 124, 128, 138, 142–3, 148, 224, 237,
    241, 243, 245–6, 248–9, 274, 276–8, 309,
    314, 322
    see also dangerous offenders; violence
seriousness of offences 3, 6–7, 37, 41, 44, 72, 84, 92,
    96, 98–103, 110, 114–5, 117, 122, 148, 161, 210,
    234, 246–9, 265, 276–8, 297, 304, 309, 322
    see also just deserts
sex offenders 102–4, 117, 148, 214, 224, 241–2,
    244–5, 309
Shapland, Joanna 76, 127, 149, 324

Shaw, Stephen 176
Sheridan, Alan 68
'short, sharp shock' 34, 265, 307–8, 339*
Shotts Prison 229
Shrewsbury Prison 15
Sim, Joe, 21–2, 30, 75, 218, 254, 322
Singleton, Nicola 302
social contract 43, 50–1
social control 72–3, 113, 136–7, 151–64, 339*
    theories of 151–62
    see also sanctions, external and internal
social democracy 80–2, 339*
sociology of punishment (penal sociology)
    1, 6, 61–83
'something works' 39
'spot fines' *see* fixed penalty notices
state 2, 27, 62, 65, 67, 69, 73, 76–7, 80, 112, 115, 125,
    128, 152–4, 156, 176–9, 184–5, 196, 233, 266,
    305, 326
    see also welfare state
Statement of National Objectives and Priorities
    (SNOP), probation service 129
Stoke Heath Young Offender Institution 258
stop and search 284–5, 288–90, 297
    class bias 284–5
    gender bias 297
    racial bias 288–90
Strangeways Prison 9–10, 19–20, 169, 177, 186, 191,
    203, 214, 309
    see also Manchester Prison
strategies for criminal justice 6–7, 25–8, 54–7, 113,
    121, 259, 306–15
Strategy A 6–7, 25–8, 42, 54–7, 59, 79, 104–5, 234,
    239–40, 259, 264, 281, 308, 310–1, 315–6, 339*
    see also law and order ideology
Strategy B 6–7, 25, 28, 39, 55–7, 59, 75, 79, 104, 235,
    240, 242, 248, 259, 262, 265, 281, 308, 311,
    315–6, 339*
    see also managerialism
Strategy C 6–7, 25, 28, 55–7, 59–60, 234–5, 240, 259,
    262, 281, 308, 311, 315–6, 318, 339*
    see also human rights
strategy of encouragement 102–3, 107, 143, 162–3,
    307, 339*
Straw, Jack 177, 311–2
structuralism 66, 69–70, 339*
Styal Prison 212
suicides, *see* prisoners, suicides
summary offences 3–4, 98, 131, 141, 339*
summary trial *see* magistrates' courts
supervision 9, 21, 102, 108, 112, 114, 116–8, 129–30,
    132, 134, 136–40, 144, 151, 153, 160–1, 163,
    224, 236, 241, 254, 267, 271, 274, 277–8, 283,
    293, 300, 321–2
    see also probation
supervision orders, young offenders 267, 277, 283, 339*
supervisory penalties 120, 129–36
surveillance 51, 68–9, 79, 112, 136–8, 144, 157–61,
    180, 197, 217, 267, 274, 277
    in the community 112, 136–8, 144, 267, 274, 277
    in prisons 51, 69, 180, 197, 217
suspended sentences, suspended sentence orders 5, 92,
    101, 103, 113–4, 116–7, 119–20, 128, 139–44,
    147, 160–2, 165, 241, 339*
    Canada 141
    usage 120–1, 139–41
Sweden 14, 81–2, 122, 138, 163

Woolf Report (1991)
    prisoner grievances 21, 24, 197, 203, 211, 216, 223,
      228, 309
    security, control and justice 24–5, 197
Wormwood Scrubs Prison
    assaults by officers 187, 212–3
    riots 212
Wymott Prison 20

Yarl's Wood asylum and immigration centre 185
Yes, Minister 76
young adult offenders (18–20) 4, 173, 340*
    crimes by 257
    custodial sentences 4
young offender institutions (YOIs) 4, 200, 258, 279,
      288, 303, 341*
    see also detention in a young offender institution
young offenders 4, 126–7, 129, 256, 260, 265, 270,
      272, 284–5, 290, 308, 322, 341*
    and the penal crisis 257–8
    cautions 3, 262–3, 265, 267, 274–5, 285, 290–1,
      297–8, 307–8
conditional discharges 274, 276
    crimes by 256–7
custodial sentences 278–9
    see also detention and training orders; detention in a
      young
      offender institution; secure training centres
    custody rate 256–7
    custodial institutions for young offenders
      260, 278–9
    diversion of 126, 262–4, 265, 267, 270, 273,
      275, 307–8
    penalties 273–9
    persistent 265, 267–8, 277–8
    preventing reoffending 34, 101, 229, 265–73,
      276, 281
    restorative justice 28, 126–8, 259, 263–4, 266–7,
      276, 279–81, 325
    restraint techniques 258

custodial sentences *cont.*
    reoffending rates 258
    sentencing of 271–2, 274–9
    suicide and self harm 258
    and youth courts 257, 259–61, 264, 266, 269, 272,
      275–6, 280, 341*
    see also youth justice
youth cautions and youth conditional cautions
    275, 341*
youth court 257, 259–61, 264, 266, 269, 272, 275–6,
    280, 341*
youth custody 260, 303
Youth Inclusion Programmes 270–1
youth justice 5–6, 256–81, 341*
    age of criminal responsibility in England and
      Wales 270
    and civil care jurisdiction 260–1, 268–9, 270
    and penal strategies (A, B and C) 259, 265,
      281, 311
    history of 259–66
    justice model 259–61, 265
    minimum interventionism 121, 259, 261–8, 280–1
    models of 259–66
    neo-correctionalism 259, 264–6, 280, 334*
    restorative justice model 259, 263–4
    system 256–81
    systems management 28, 163, 261–5, 280–1,
      308, 339*
    welfare model 259–60, 265, 340*
    see also young offenders
Youth Justice and Criminal Evidence Act 1999
    266, 276
Youth Justice Board 258, 268–9, 272, 280, 341*
youth offender panels 276, 341*
youth offending teams (YOTs) 4, 91, 268, 274, 276,
    280, 322, 341*
Youth Rehabilitation Order (YRO) 274, 277, 341*

Zeitgeist, penal 83
zero tolerance 79, 265, 267, 271, 281, 311, 341*